INGLÊS e ESPANHOL PARA CONCURSOS

Edição 2013

WANDER GARCIA
Coordenador

INGLÊS e ESPANHOL PARA CONCURSOS

Edição 2013

800 QUESTÕES COMENTADAS

FCC
CESPE
CESGRANRIO
ESAF
VUNESP
e outras examinadoras

2013 © Wander Garcia

Coordenador: Renan Flumian
Autores: Anthony Rosenberg, Mark Hughes e Rodrigo Goyena Soares
Editor: Márcio Dompieri
Capa: Wilton Garcia - WCG Propaganda e R2 Editorial
Projeto gráfico e diagramação: R2 Editorial
Impressão e acabamento: RR Donnelley

**Ficha Catalográfica elaborada pelo
Sistema de Bibliotecas da UNICAMP / Diretoria de Tratamento da Informação**
Bibliotecário: Helena Joana Flipsen – CRB-8ª / 5283

G165c   Garcia, Wander.
         Como Gabaritar – Inglês e Espanhol para Concursos /
         Wander Garcia. – Campinas, SP : Foco Jurídico, 2013.
         216 p.

         1. Direito. 2. Exames - Questões. I. Título.

                                              CDD - 340
                                                - 371.261

ISBN 978-85-8242-048-5

Índices para Catálogo Sistemático:
1. Direito   340
2. Exames - Questões   371.261

Direitos Autorais: as questões de concursos públicos, por serem atos oficiais, não são protegidas como direitos autorais, na forma do art. 8º, IV, da Lei 9.610/98. Porém, os comentários e a organização das questões são protegidos na forma da lei citada, ficando proibido o seu aproveitamento ou a reprodução total ou parcial dos textos. Os infratores serão processados na forma da lei."

Atualizações e erratas: a presente obra é vendida como está, sem garantia de atualização futura. Porém, atualizações voluntárias e erratas são disponibilizadas no site www.editorafoco.com.br, na seção *Atualizações*. Esforçamo-nos ao máximo para entregar ao leitor uma obra com a melhor qualidade possível e sem erros técnicos ou de conteúdo. No entanto, nem sempre isso ocorre, seja por motivo de alteração de software, interpretação ou falhas de diagramação e revisão. Sendo assim, disponibilizamos em nosso site a seção mencionada (*Atualizações*), na qual relataremos, com a devida correção, os erros encontrados na obra. Solicitamos, outrossim, que o leitor faça a gentileza de colaborar com a perfeição da obra, comunicando eventual erro encontrado por meio de mensagem para contato@editorafoco.com.br.

Edição – 2013
Proibida a reprodução total ou parcial.
Os infratores serão processados na forma da lei.
Todos os direitos reservados à Editora Foco Ltda.
Rua Alberto Santos Dumont, 1697 – sala 07 – Cidade Nova
CEP 13334-150 – Indaiatuba – SP
E-mail: contato@editorafoco.com.br

www.editorafoco.com.br

APRESENTAÇÃO

Se você realmente quer ser aprovado num concurso público, saiba que não basta estudar milhares de horas a fio.

O fator decisivo não é o número de horas de estudo, mas a qualidade deste.

E um estudo de alto rendimento requer que você siga à risca as técnicas da neurociência.

De acordo com esta, o estudo perfeito passa por quatro etapas: 1) CONTATO; 2) COMPREENSÃO; 3) PRÁTICA; 4) NOVO CONTATO.

O CONTATO consiste em estudar pra valer, dedicando efetivamente tempo e disposição pra esse desafio.

A COMPREENSÃO consiste em estudar de modo concentrado e com postura proativa.

A PRÁTICA consiste em resolver o maior número de questões possível, de preferência questões comentadas, pra que haja reforço e feed back.

Por fim, o NOVO CONTATO consiste na revisão constante da matéria.

Este livro oferece a oportunidade de você seguir os quatro passos do aprendizado perfeito.

Com ele você garantirá o CONTATO com a matéria, pois é muito mais gostoso e atrativo estudar por questões comentadas e você vai querer estudar o tempo todo.

Com ele você garantirá a COMPREENSÃO da matéria, pois é muito mais fácil prestar atenção e entender a matéria resolvendo questões, do que lendo textos puramente teóricos.

Com ele você garantirá a PRÁTICA, pois vai treinar como nunca, garantindo o elemento que é considerando o mais importante, segundo a neurociência, para o efetivo aprendizado.

Com ele você garantirá o NOVO CONTATO, pois o extraordinário número de questões do livro possibilitará que você resolva várias vezes questões diferentes, mas que tratam das matérias recorrentes, num processo de revisão com alto grau de retenção.

Bom, agora é com você. Aproveite a oportunidade de estudar certo, pois agora você já sabe COMO GABARITAR em concursos públicos!

SUMÁRIO

1. LÍNGUA INGLESA 9

2. LÍNGUA ESPANHOLA 175

1. Língua Inglesa

Mark Hughes e Anthony Rosenberg

From Science Fiction to Reality: Personal Robots

Emerge at Work, Home and School

It's 6 a.m., and the Clarks awake to fresh coffee served to them by Millie, one of the family's personal robots. As they get ready for work, Millie makes the bed, and their robotic dog Mickey gently reminds Mr. Clark to
5 take his medicine.
This scenario is not a page from a lost "Jetsons" script. It's likely to be a normal day in the life of a family in as few as 20 years from now, according to robotics experts at the Georgia Institute of Technology. Already, the global
10 market for personal robots is growing 400 percent a year, says Professor Henrik Christensen, director of the newly formed Robotics and Intelligent Machines Center in the Georgia Tech College of Computing. "Personal robots are becoming more popular as people want to do more and
15 more with their lives," Christensen says. "Technology is making it possible...We live stressful lives now, and we can use technology to take away the boring tasks of everyday life."
Robots are not novel technology in industry, the
20 military and even space exploration. However, a new generation of intelligent machines called personal robots — ones that work with and directly for humans, especially in the home, workplace and school — have begun to emerge only recently. A confluence of smart materials,
25 low-cost, high-speed computing power, better batteries and knowledge of how humans interact with machines is creating an explosion in the market for personal robots, researchers say. "To get a personal robot to do things you need, you have to have onboard processing,
30 perception, motion and power," says roboticist Tucker Balch, an associate professor in the College of Computing.
"Until two or three years ago, you couldn't put all of that on one small, light platform. Motors and computers take a lot of energy, and the batteries we had couldn't do the
35 job. Now, demand for better cell phone and laptop batteries is driving improvements," Balch adds. "Therefore, we have all the technologies which can support a consumer robot that is not too expensive." Balch predicts that truly useful, multi-function personal robots will cost between $1,000
40 and $1,500. Single-purpose robots, such as the Roomba vacuum cleaner already on the market, cost between $150 and $300.
While some personal robots are already available, important research is under way to address the remaining
45 technical and societal challenges. Georgia Tech researchers in computer science, engineering, psychology and the liberal arts are collaborating under the umbrella of the new Robotics and Intelligent Machines Center that Christensen directs. That cooperation is vital to creating
50 the best-designed personal robots. "If you just have computer scientists designing them, you're not going to build a robot that's as good as one that could be built by computer scientists and mechanical engineers working together," Christensen says. "We are leveraging Georgia
55 Tech's world-class expertise in all of these domains and want to make something that no one else in the United States is doing today."

Research Horizons Magazine - June 8, 2007
(slightly adapted) http://gtresearchnews.gatech.edu/
newsrelease/personal_robotics.htm

(ADVOGADO – PETROBRÁS – 2008 – CESGRANRIO) Based on Professor Henrik Christensen's words in Paragraph 2, it is possible to affirm that

(A) people consider robots unexciting and disturbing.
(B) people do not expect robots to perform daily boring activities.
(C) intelligent robots are making modern life stressful.
(D) technology will never improve people's quality of life.
(E) new technological inventions can make people's lives easier.

(Interpretation) A: Incorrect – Robots are said to help performing boring tasks, B: Incorrect – This is one of the main functions of robots, C: Incorrect – It is suggested they can help deal with the stress of modern life, D: Incorrect – This is contrary to the entire message of the text, E: Correct – "We live stressful lives now, and we can use technology to take away the boring tasks of everyday life". Gabarito "E".

(ADVOGADO – PETROBRÁS – 2008 – CESGRANRIO) According to Paragraph 3, one of the aspects that has contributed to the expansion of the personal robot market is the

(A) very high price of speedy computing power.
(B) smaller and less efficient computer batteries.
(C) better knowledge of human-machine interaction.
(D) sudden popularity of American robotics experts.
(E) high consumption of energy by the new machines.

(Interpretation) A: Incorrect – This was a limiting factor not a contributing factor, B: Incorrect – Less efficient batteries are becoming more efficient, C: Correct – Lines 26-27, D: Incorrect – This is not stated, E: Incorrect – The contrary is true. Gabarito "C".

(ADVOGADO – PETROBRÁS – 2008 – CESGRANRIO) Roboticist Tucker Balch, mentioned in Paragraph 3, believes that

(A) the reasonable cost for the multi-function robots is in the $150-$300 price range.
(B) most personal robots that can handle a variety of tasks will be sold for a minimum of a thousand dollars.
(C) in three years, scientists will start developing the batteries needed to power single-purpose personal robots.
(D) the latest developments in laptops and cell phones have taken the scientists' attention away from personal robots.
(E) no robots will ever perform multi-functions because it is impossible to combine processing, perception, motion and power in one platform.

(Interpretation) A: Incorrect – This is the cost for single-function robots, B: Correct – They will be sold for between $1,000 and $1,500, C: Incorrect – The necessary batteries already exist, D: Incorrect – They have helped improving the technology needed for robots, E: Incorrect – 'Until two or three years ago', this means that it is now possible to combine them into one platform.
Gabarito "B".

(ADVOGADO – PETROBRÁS – 2008 – CESGRANRIO) Which option expresses an accurate relationship between the items?

(A) "take away" (line 17) and remove are synonymous.
(B) "novel" (line 19) is the opposite of new.
(C) "emerge" (line 24) means the same as disappear.
(D) "improvements" (line 36) and advances reflect contradictory ideas.
(E) "useful" (line 38) can not be replaced by helpful.

(Vocabulary) A: Correct - These are synonyms, B: Incorrect – Novel means new, C: Incorrect – These are opposing ideas, D: Incorrect – They represent similar ideas, E: Incorrect – It can be substituted by it, as it is a synonym.
Gabarito "A".

(ADVOGADO – PETROBRÁS – 2008 – CESGRANRIO) In terms of reference, the only item that DOES NOT refer to "robot(s)" is

(A) "one" (line 2).
(B) "their" (line 15).
(C) "ones" (line 22).
(D) "that" (line 38).
(E) "them" (line 51).

(Grammar) B: Correct – This refers to people's lives.
Gabarito "B".

(ADVOGADO – PETROBRÁS – 2008 – CESGRANRIO) The boldfaced item introduces a conclusion in

(A) "**As** they get ready for work, Millie makes the bed," (line 3)
(B) "**However**, a new generation of intelligent machines called personal robots" (lines 20-21)
(C) "**Therefore**, we have all the technologies which can support a consumer robot..." (lines 36-37).
(D) "**While** some personal robots are already available, important research is under way..." (lines 43-44)
(E) "**If** you just have computer scientists designing them, you're not going to build a robot that's ...". (lines 50-52)

(Grammar) A: Incorrect - As (conjunction) to indicate one thing happening at the same time as another, B: Incorrect – However (adverb) used for contract or contradiction, C: Correct – Therefore (adverb) means 'for that reason' or 'consequently', D: Incorrect – While (conjunction) meaning 'although', E: Incorrect – If (conjunction) means 'granting that'.
Gabarito "C".

(ADVOGADO – PETROBRÁS – 2008 – CESGRANRIO) From the sentence "That cooperation is vital to creating the best-designed personal robots." (lines 49-50) it is possible to infer that the

(A) expertise of Georgia Tech's computer science researchers alone will help develop the best personal robots in the United States.
(B) joint effort of computer scientists and mechanical engineers is not likely to improve robot design.
(C) alliance between computer scientists, designers and psychologists can be harmful to the future of robotics.
(D) collaboration of researchers from different areas of knowledge will be extremely beneficial to the future of robotics.
(E) collaboration between Georgia Tech researchers and the Robotics and Intelligent Machines Center is inefficient.

(Interpretation) A: Incorrect – Not just the help of computer science researchers is needed, B: Incorrect – Joint effort means cooperation. Cooperation will improve robot design, C: Incorrect – Harmful means damaging – Alliance will help the future of robotics, D: Correct – Collaboration is synonymous with cooperation, E: Incorrect – Georgia Tech researchers are part of Intelligent Machines Center and there is no mention of inefficiency.
Gabarito "D".

(ADVOGADO – PETROBRÁS – 2008 – CESGRANRIO) Where in the text does the author refer to possible tasks to be performed by personal robots in the near future?

(A) Paragraphs 1 and 2 (lines 1-5 ; 6-18).
(B) Paragraph 2, only (lines 6-18).
(C) Paragraph 3, only (lines 19-42).
(D) Paragraph 4, only (lines 43-57).
(E) Paragraphs 3 and 4 (lines 19-42 ; 43-57).

(Vocabulary) A: Correct - Making coffee, making the bed, reminders to take medicine, performing boring tasks and helping with stressful lives.
Gabarito "A".

(ADVOGADO – PETROBRÁS – 2008 – CESGRANRIO) "These domains" (line 55) include all the areas below, EXCEPT one. Mark it.

(A) Psychology
(B) Liberal arts
(C) Engineering
(D) Physiology
(E) Computer Science

(Grammar) D: Correct – Physiology is part of life sciences.
Gabarito "D".

(ADVOGADO – PETROBRÁS – 2008 – CESGRANRIO) The verb form in italics transmits an idea of probability in

(A) "you *have to* have onboard processing, perception, motion and power," (lines 29-30)
(B) "we have all the technologies which *can* support a consumer robot…" (lines 36-37)
(C) "multi-function personal robots *will* cost between $1,000 and $1,500." (lines 39-40)
(D) "That cooperation *is* vital to creating the best-designed personal robots." (lines 49-50)
(E) "you're not going to build a robot that's as good as one that *could* be built by computer scientists and mechanical engineers working together," (lines 51-54)

(Grammar) A: Incorrect – 'have to' refers to obligation, B: Incorrect – 'can' refers to ability. C: Incorrect – 'will' indicates certainty or likelihood. D: Incorrect – 'is' refers to a fact or permanent characteristic, E: Correct – 'could' refers to probability or possibility.
Gabarito "E".

Texto

At the same time that President Bush is urging America to free itself from its addiction to oil from unstable parts of the world, European leaders are calling for a more self-sufficient energy policy that relies less on oil and
5 natural gas.
"Europe is becoming ever more dependent on oil and gas imports from geopolitically uncertain regions," European Commission President Jose Manuel Barroso alerted last month in a speech. "We have to do something
10 about this, and we have to do it now."
British Prime Minister Tony Blair and German Chancellor Angela Merkel said after a meeting in Berlin that Europe must develop an energy policy for the next 15 years that includes more renewable sources of energy.
15 The new emphasis on energy security is a result of soaring energy prices and signs that supplies may not always be available. Oil prices tripled in the last three years, from about $20 a barrel to $60. And Russia, which has become a major supplier of oil and gas to Europe,
20 raised concerns when it cut off natural gas to Ukraine last month during a dispute over prices.
These developments have motivated a new debate on the continent about nuclear energy and brought about ambitious biofuels programs.
25 • Nuclear power, which with the exception of France, was disappearing in Western Europe, has re-emerged as a clean and reliable source of energy. Germany is reconsidering its plan to phase out nuclear power generation by 2020. So, too, is Britain. With the
30 exception of France, which gets more than 70% of its power from nuclear sources, Europe has rejected nuclear generation as too costly or unsafe since the Chernobyl accident in Ukraine nearly 20 years ago.
• Sweden has just announced that it wants to be
35 the first nation in the world to eliminate oil as an energy source in the next 15 years. It would use ethanol for its cars, and geothermal heat and burning everything from agricultural byproducts to trash would replace heating oil.
"Our dependency on oil should be broken by 2020," said
40 Mona Sahlin, Sweden's minister of Sustainable Development.
• The European Commission adopted in February 2006 an ambitious biofuels program to set off the production of ethanol and gas from crops and organic
45 waste. The goal: to more than double production — from a 1.4% share of the European fuel supply in 2005 to 5.75% in 2010.

Although Europe relies less on oil than the USA, the tripling of oil prices over the last three years has been
50 felt. Oil provides 40% of the USA's energy supply and about 36% of Europe's.
Europe is the largest producer of wind and solar power. Also, biofuels can help give this continent a more diverse supply of energy. But it is unlikely that Europe
55 can replace fossil fuel entirely, as Sweden plans.
"It's not a crisis," says Claude Mandil, executive director of the International Energy Agency in Paris, of Europe and the USA's energy situation. But, he remarks, "Everybody is understanding that capacities are limited
60 ... and the problem will not be solved overnight."

By Jeffrey Stinson, USA Today, Feb. 20, 2006

(ADVOGADO – PETROBRÁS – 2006 – CESGRANRIO) The main purpose of the text is to:

(A) criticize the re-emergence of nuclear power as a major source of energy.
(B) blame President Bush for America's dependency on oil from hostile countries.
(C) complain angrily about sharp increases in oil and gas prices in the last three years.
(D) describe in detail Sweden's efforts to promote the use of energy sources other than oil.
(E) present Europe's actions to depend less on energy imported from unstable world regions.

(Interpretation) A: Incorrect – Nuclear energy's re-emergence is not criticized, B: Incorrect – President Bush is not blamed, he is urging for change, C: Incorrect – The focus of the text is not mainly on complaining about price increases, D: Incorrect – Sweden is mentioned but it is neither detailed nor the main purpose of the text, E: Correct – This embodies the overall purpose of the text.
Gabarito "E".

(ADVOGADO – PETROBRÁS – 2006 – CESGRANRIO) European Commission President Jose Manuel Barroso's statement in Paragraph 2 sounds like a/an:

(A) warning.
(B) complaint.
(C) accusation.
(D) apology.
(E) excuse.

(Interpretation) A: Correct – Use of the word 'alerted' means to warn of approaching danger.
Gabarito "A".

(ADVOGADO – PETROBRÁS – 2006 – CESGRANRIO) According to the fourth paragraph, there was reason to worry when:

(A) Ukraine raised oil prices from $20 a barrel to $60 in the last three years.
(B) Ukraine refused to buy natural gas from Russia because of high prices.
(C) Russia became a major supplier of oil and gas to the whole continent.
(D) Russia stopped supplying natural gas to Ukraine in January 2006.
(E) Europe asked Russia to cut natural gas supplies to Ukraine.

(Interpretation) D: Correct – Use of Russia 'raised concerns' gave cause to worry, whereas 'cut off' supplies to Ukrania means they stopped supplying.
Gabarito "D".

(ADVOGADO – PETROBRÁS – 2006 – CESGRANRIO) Mark the correct statement about nuclear power according to the information found in lines 28-33.

(A) Germany and Britain are planning to start using nuclear power in 2020.
(B) Less than half of France's energy comes exclusively from nuclear sources.
(C) France is the only country in Western Europe that now relies heavily on nuclear power.
(D) All European countries stopped using nuclear power after the Chernobyl accident.
(E) Nuclear power has always been considered as a clean but costly source of energy.

(Interpretation) A: Incorrect – Both countries already use nuclear power, B: Incorrect – 'more than 70% comes from nuclear sources', C: Correct – 'with the exception of France' means France is the only European country to rely on nuclear power, D: Incorrect – European countries didn't stop but reconsidered its use and safety. E: Incorrect – Not after the Chernobyl accident.
Gabarito "C".

(ADVOGADO – PETROBRÁS – 2006 – CESGRANRIO) In "Sweden has just announced that it wants to be the first nation in the world…"(lines 34-35), the pronoun *it* refers to "Sweden". Check the other pronoun that also refers to the name of a country.

(A) this (line 10).
(B) it (line 10).
(C) which (line 25).
(D) its (line 30)
(E) it (line 54).

(Grammar) A: Incorrect – Refers to oil dependency, B: Incorrect – Refers to action needed to reduce oil dependency, C: Incorrect – Refers to nuclear power, D: Correct – Refers to France, E: Incorrect – Refers to the fact that Europe can replace fossil fuel entirely.
Gabarito "D".

(ADVOGADO – PETROBRÁS – 2006 – CESGRANRIO) Check the item in which *should* is used in the same sense as in "Our dependency on oil should be broken by 2020," (line 39).

(A) America should reduce both petroleum fuel use and emissions of greenhouse gases.
(B) European governments should focus their efforts on large-scale fuel-saving projects.
(C) Developing countries should work to establish policies to coordinate energy planning.
(D) The European Commission should encourage all countries to adopt a biofuels program.
(E) The results of this research on biofuels should be available to the public in a few months.

(Grammar) A: Incorrect –Refers to obligation, B: Incorrect –Refers to obligation, C: Incorrect – Refers to obligation, D: Incorrect – Refers to obligation, E: Correct – Refers to future expectation.
Gabarito "E".

(ADVOGADO – PETROBRÁS – 2006 – CESGRANRIO) In (line 48), "Although Europe relies less on oil than the USA," could be paraphrased as:

(A) Despite the fact that the USA is a major oil supplier.
(B) As Europe is less dependent on oil than the United States.
(C) Even though Europe consumes less oil than the United States.
(D) Because Europe is not so dependent on oil as the United States.
(E) Europe's dependency on oil, however, is greater than that of the USA.

(Grammar) C: Correct – 'Although', in this case, works as a synonym of 'even though'.
Gabarito "C".

(ADVOGADO – PETROBRÁS – 2006 – CESGRANRIO) In "…it is unlikely that Europe can replace fossil fuel entirely," (lines 54-55), unlikely can be replaced by:

(A) illogical.
(B) improbable.
(C) unexpected.
(D) unacceptable.
(E) unpredictable.

(Vocabulary) B: Correct – Improbable means unlikely.
Gabarito "B".

(ADVOGADO – PETROBRÁS – 2006 – CESGRANRIO) When Claude Mandil said that "…the problem will not be solved overnight." (line 60) He meant that:

(A) such problematic situation will never be resolved.
(B) there is no easy or quick solution for the problem.
(C) this difficult state of affairs emerged quite suddenly.
(D) the solution for this puzzle will be rather unexpected.
(E) it may take some time before the problem becomes critical.

(Vocabulary) B: Correct – This idiomatic expression means there is no easy or quick solution but it does not exclude the probability of there being a solution.
Gabarito "B".

(ADVOGADO – PETROBRÁS – 2006 – CESGRANRIO) Check the only item in which the phrasal verb in bold type has the same meaning as the verb in italics.

(A) "European leaders are **calling for** a more self-sufficient energy policy …" (lines 3-4) – *demanding*.
(B) "raised concerns when it **cut off** natural gas to Ukraine last month…" (lines 20-21) – *delivered*.
(C) "These developments have (…) and **brought about** ambitious biofuels programs." (lines 22-24) – *discontinued*.
(D) "Germany is reconsidering its plan to **phase out** nuclear power generation by 2020." (lines 28-29) – *encourage*.
(E) "The European Commission adopted (…) an ambitious biofuels program to **set off** the production of ethanol and gas …" (lines 42-44) – *discuss*.

(Vocabulary) A: Correct – To call for means to demand, B: Incorrect – To cut off means to sever or discontinue, C: Incorrect – To bring about means to cause to happen, D: To phase out means to bring to an end in stages, E: Incorrect – To set off means to start or initiate.
Gabarito "A".

Money Doesn't Grow on Trees, But Gasoline Might

Researchers make breakthrough in creating gasoline from plant matter, with almost no carbon footprint

April 7, 2008
National Science Foundation

Researchers have made a breakthrough in the development of "green gasoline," a liquid identical to standard gasoline yet created from sustainable biomass sources like switchgrass and poplar trees. Reporting
5 in the cover article of the April 7, 2008 issue of Chemistry & Sustainability, Energy & Materials, chemical engineer and National Science Foundation (NSF) researcher George Huber of the University of Massachusetts-Amherst and his graduate students
10 announced the first direct conversion of plant cellulose into gasoline components.

Even though it may be 5 to 10 years before green gasoline arrives at the pump or finds its way into a jet airplane, these breakthroughs have bypassed
15 significant difficulties to bringing green gasoline biofuels to market. "It is likely that the future consumer will not even know that they are putting biofuels into their car," said Huber.

"Biofuels in the future will most likely be similar in
20 chemical composition to gasoline and diesel fuel used today. The challenge for chemical engineers is to efficiently produce liquid fuels from biomass while fitting into the existing infrastructure today."

For their new approach, the UMass researchers
25 rapidly heated cellulose in the presence of solid catalysts, materials that speed up reactions without sacrificing themselves in the process. They then rapidly cooled the products to create a liquid that contains many of the compounds found in gasoline. The entire process
30 was completed in less than two minutes using relatively moderate amounts of heat.

"Green gasoline is an attractive alternative to bioethanol since it can be used in existing engines and does not incur the 30 percent gas mileage penalty of
35 ethanol-based flex fuel," said John Regalbuto, who directs the Catalysis and Biocatalysis Program at NSF and supported this research.

"In theory it requires much less energy to make than ethanol, giving it a smaller carbon footprint and
40 making it cheaper to produce," Regalbuto said. "Making it from cellulose sources such as switchgrass or poplar trees grown as energy crops, or forest or agricultural residues such as wood chips or corn stover, solves the lifecycle greenhouse gas problem that has recently
45 surfaced with corn ethanol and soy biodiesel."

Beyond academic laboratories, both small businesses and petroleum refiners are pursuing green gasoline. Companies are designing ways to hybridize their existing refineries to enable petroleum products
50 including fuels, textiles, and plastics to be made from either crude oil or biomass and the military community has shown strong interest in making jet fuel and diesel from the same sources.

"Huber's new process for the direct conversion of
55 cellulose to gasoline aromatics is at the leading edge of the new 'Green Gasoline' alternate energy paradigm that NSF, along with other federal agencies, is helping to promote," states Regalbuto.

http://www.nsf.gov/news/news_summ.jsp?cntn_id=111392

(ADVOGADO – PETROBRÁS DISTRIB. – 2008 – CESGRANRIO)
The main purpose of this text is to

(A) report on a new kind of fuel that might harm the environment.
(B) advertise the recent findings of chemical engineers concerning gasoline components.
(C) criticize the latest research on biofuels that could not find a relevant alternative to oil.
(D) justify why corn ethanol and soy biodiesel are the best alternatives to standard gasoline.
(E) announce a significant advance in the development of an eco friendly fuel that may impact the market.

(Interpretation) A: Incorrect – The opposite is true, the new fuel should benefit the environment, B: Incorrect – The text is to inform not to advertise which would imply a direct commercial link, C: Incorrect – No idea of criticism is related to the research, D: Incorrect – It does not justify them and questions the environmental impact of corn and soy biodiesel, E: Correct – This covers the broad nature of The text most accurately.
Gabarito "E".

(ADVOGADO – PETROBRÁS DISTRIB. – 2008 – CESGRANRIO)
According to the text, it is NOT correct to affirm that green gasoline

(A) is cheaper to produce than ethanol.
(B) derives from vegetables and plants.
(C) can already be used in jet airplanes.
(D) requires much less energy to make than ethanol.
(E) results in smaller amounts of carbon emissions than ethanol.

(Interpretation) C: Correct – Line 11 – It may be 5-10 years before this fuel finds its way into a jet airplane.
Gabarito "C".

(ADVOGADO – PETROBRÁS DISTRIB. – 2008 – CESGRANRIO) In the sentence "It is likely that the future consumer will not even know that they are putting biofuels into their car," (lines 16-17), "It is likely that" could be substituted by

(A) Surely.
(B) Certainly.
(C) Probably.
(D) Obviously.
(E) Undoubtedly.

(Vocabulary) A: Incorrect - Strong assertion that something will happen, B: Incorrect – Strong assertion that something will happen, C: Correct – Likely has the idea of probability, D: Incorrect – Implies that the fact is guaranteed, E: Incorrect – Implies that the fact is beyond doubt.
Gabarito "C".

(ADVOGADO – PETROBRÁS DISTRIB. – 2008 – CESGRANRIO)
The item "themselves" (line 27) refers to

(A) "researchers" (line 24).
(B) "materials" (line 26).
(C) "reactions" (line 26).
(D) "compounds" (line 29).
(E) "amounts" (line 31).

(Grammar) B: Correct: 'materials that speed up reaction without sacrificing themselves'.
Gabarito "B".

(ADVOGADO – PETROBRÁS DISTRIB. – 2008 – CESGRANRIO)
Which alternative contains a correct correspondence of meaning?

(A) "speed up" (line 26) means accelerate.
(B) "rapidly" (line 27) is the opposite of quickly.

(C) "entire" (line 29) could not be replaced by whole.
(D) "residues" (line 43) and leftovers are antonyms.
(E) "surfaced" (line 45) and emerged are not synonyms.

(Vocabulary) A: Correct – Speed up is a synonym for accelerate, B: Incorrect - Rapidly means quickly, C: Incorrect – Entire and whole can be synonyms. D: Incorrect - Residues and leftovers are synonyms, E- Incorrect – Surfaced and emerged are synonyms.
Gabarito "C".

(ADVOGADO – PETROBRÁS DISTRIB. – 2008 – CESGRANRIO)
Mark the sentence in which the idea introduced by the word in bold type is correctly described.

(A) "Even though it may be 5 to 10 years before green gasoline arrives at the pump or finds its way into a jet airplane," (lines 12-14) – comparison
(B) "…while fitting into the existing infrastructure today." (lines 22-23) – consequence
(C) "…then rapidly cooled the products to create a liquid that contains many of the compounds found in gasoline." (lines 27-29) – contrast
(D) "'Green gasoline is an attractive alternative to bio-ethanol since it can be used in existing engines…'" (lines 32-33) – reason
(E) "'Making it from cellulose sources such as switchgrass or poplar trees grown as energy crops," (lines 40-42) – addition

(Grammar) A: Incorrect – 'even though' refers to an existing condition or fact, B: Incorrect – 'while' refers to one action occurring at the same time as another, C: Incorrect – 'then' refers to a process. D: Correct – 'since' indicates a reason, E: Incorrect – 'such as' is used to give an example
Gabarito "C".

(ADVOGADO – PETROBRÁS DISTRIB. – 2008 – CESGRANRIO)
Paragraph 4 (lines 24-31) informs that UMass researchers produce green gasoline by

(A) creating a hot liquid from standard gasoline adding catalysts.
(B) using cellulose with liquids that catalyze gasoline in less than two minutes.
(C) applying moderate heat to compounds found in gasoline to produce a solid catalyst.
(D) slowly cooling the product of solid catalytic reactions which will produce cellulose.
(E) heating cellulose with specific catalysts and then cooling the product so it transforms into a liquid.

(Interpretation) E: Correct – "For their new approach, the UMass researchers rapidly heated cellulose in the presence of solid catalysts, materials that speed up reactions without sacrificing themselves in the process. They then rapidly cooled the products to create a liquid that contains many of the compounds found in gasoline. The entire process was completed in less than two minutes using relatively moderate amounts of heat."
Gabarito "E".

(ADVOGADO – PETROBRÁS DISTRIB. – 2008 – CESGRANRIO)
According to this text, it might be said that corn ethanol and soy biodiesel have

(A) contributed to the greenhouse gas problem.
(B) increased consumption in cars by 30 percent.
(C) produced residues such as wood chips or corn stover.
(D) caused the extinction of sustainable biomass sources.
(E) generated a smaller carbon footprint than green gasoline.

(Interpretation) A: Correct – "solves the lifecycle greenhouse gas problem that has recently surfaced with corn ethanol and soy biodiesel." (lines 43-45) Recently surfaced means recently appeared.
Gabarito "A".

(ADVOGADO – PETROBRÁS DISTRIB. – 2008 – CESGRANRIO)
The text says that research on green gasoline has

(A) had no printed space in scientific journals.
(B) not received support from scientific foundations.
(C) found no interest among the military and the businessmen.
(D) been neglected by academic laboratories and graduate research programs.
(E) had to overcome problems to discover an efficient means of producing and marketing this fuel.

(Interpretation) E: Correct – To bypass significant difficulties (line 14) means to overcome problems.
Gabarito "E".

(ADVOGADO – PETROBRÁS DISTRIB. – 2008 – CESGRANRIO)
The title of the text, "Money Doesn't Grow on Trees, But Gasoline Might", refers to the

(A) planting of trees near oil wells that produce gasoline.
(B) exciting possibility of developing an effective green fuel.
(C) amazing solution of diluting gasoline with forest and agricultural residues.
(D) incredible discovery of trees that produce more when irrigated with a mixture of gasoline.
(E) sensational invention of new green fuel that will cost three million dollars in reforestation.

(Interpretation) B: Correct – This is correct due to the elimination of all the other options as being neither mentioned in the text or extrapolations from the text. It uses a common idiomatic expression (money doesn't grow on trees) in an ironic way.
Gabarito "B".

Texto

The oil and natural gas industry has developed and applied an impressive array of innovative technologies to improve productivity and efficiency, while yielding environmental benefits. According to the U.S. Department
5 of Energy, "the petroleum business has transformed itself into a high-technology industry."
State-of-the-art technology allows the industry to produce more oil and natural gas from more remote places – some previously unreachable – with significantly
10 less adverse effect on the environment. Among the benefits: increased supply to meet the world's growing energy demand, reduced energy consumption at oil and natural gas facilities and refineries, reduced noise from operations, decreased size of facilities, reduced
15 emissions of pollutants, better protection of water resources, and preservation of habitats and wildlife.
With advanced exploration and production technologies, the oil and gas industry can pinpoint resources more accurately, extract them more efficiently
20 and with less surface disturbance, minimize associated wastes, and, ultimately, restore sites to original or better condition.

Exploration and production advances include advanced directional drilling, slimhole drilling, and 3-D
25 seismic technology. Other segments of the industry have benefited from technological advances as well. Refineries are becoming highly automated with integrated process and energy system controls; this results in improved operational and environmental performance and enables
30 refineries to run harder and produce more products safer than ever before. Also, new process equipment and catalyst technology advances have been made very recently to meet new fuel regulations requiring very low levels of sulfur in gasoline and diesel.
35 Technology advances such as these are making it possible for the oil and natural gas industry to grow in tandem with the nation's energy needs while maintaining a cleaner environment. The industry is committed to investing in advanced technologies that will continue to
40 provide affordable and reliable energy to support our current quality of life, and expand our economic horizons. For example, we are researching fuel cells that may power the vehicles of tomorrow with greater efficiency and less environmental impact. We are investigating ways
45 to tap the huge natural gas resources locked in gas hydrates. Gas hydrates are common in sediments in the ocean's deep waters where cold temperatures and high pressures cause natural gas and water to freeze together, forming solid gas hydrates. Gas hydrates could
50 be an important future source of natural gas for our nation. Some of our companies are also investigating renewable energy resources such as solar, wind, biomass and geothermal energy. By conducting research into overcoming the many technological hurdles that limit
55 these energy resources, they hope to make them more reliable, affordable and convenient for future use. Although the potential for these energy resources is great, scientists do not expect them to be a significant part of the nation's energy mix for many decades. For this
60 reason, the industry must continue to invest in conventional resources such as oil and natural gas. We will need to rely on these important energy resources for many decades to come.

In: http://api-ec.api.org/focus/index

(ADVOGADO – PETROBRÁS TRANSP. – 2006 – CESGRANRIO)
The fragment "…an impressive array of innovative technologies…" (line 2) could best be replaced by a/an:

(A) careful selection of up-to-date technologies.
(B) remarkable number of well-known technologies.
(C) unsatisfactory arrangement of brand-new technologies.
(D) extraordinary collection of creative technologies.
(E) immense display of useful technologies.

(Interpretation) D: Correct – 'an impressive array' is a positive statement meaning an impressive range or collection. 'Innovative technologies' refers to being new technologies.
Gabarito "D".

(ADVOGADO – PETROBRÁS TRANSP. – 2006 – CESGRANRIO)
According to the second paragraph, state-of-the-art technology brings many benefits, EXCEPT:

(A) protecting habitats and wildlife.
(B) using larger facilities.
(C) decreasing emissions of pollutants.
(D) running less noisy operations.
(E) preserving water resources.

(Interpretation) B: Correct – Line 14 'decreased size of facilities'. Therefore, this statement is false.
Gabarito "B".

(ADVOGADO – PETROBRÁS TRANSP. – 2006 – CESGRANRIO)
The function of the fourth paragraph is to:

(A) describe in detail the automation process in oil refineries.
(B) list some technological advances that are benefiting the oil industry.
(C) criticize the new regulations that have reduced sulfur levels in fuels.
(D) demand that refineries become more automated to improve performance.
(E) explain how 3-D seismic technology can help oil production.

(Interpretation) B: Correct – Paragraph four is essentially a list of advances that benefit the sector.
Gabarito "B".

(ADVOGADO – PETROBRÁS TRANSP. – 2006 – CESGRANRIO)
According to lines 44-50, gas hydrates:

(A) can be found in deep-water sediments.
(B) are contained in natural gas resources.
(C) have been used as a source of natural gas.
(D) may cause water to freeze under the ocean.
(E) form sediments under low temperatures and pressures.

(Interpretation) A: Correct – Lines 46-47 'Gas hydrates are common in sediments in the ocean's deep waters', None of the other options are stated or correct.
Gabarito "A".

(ADVOGADO – PETROBRÁS TRANSP. – 2006 – CESGRANRIO) In "…the industry must continue to invest in conventional resources such as oil and natural gas." (lines 60-61), the word that could replace "must" without changing the meaning of the sentence is:

(A) ought to.
(B) could.
(C) has to.
(D) may.
(E) will.

(Grammar) A: Incorrect – 'ought to' is a polite suggestion, B: Incorrect – 'could' means possibility, C: Correct – 'has to' means strong obligation similar to 'must'. D: Incorrect – 'may' means possibility, E: Incorrect – 'will' implies a strong obligation or certainty.
Gabarito "A".

(ADVOGADO – PETROBRÁS TRANSP. – 2006 – CESGRANRIO)
According to the last paragraph:

(A) people will be able to count on renewable fuels in the near future.
(B) scientists do not believe that alternative energy resources are useful.
(C) societies will depend on traditional energy resources for still many years.
(D) the limitations of renewable energy resources have finally been conquered.
(E) oil companies do not intend to make energy resources cheaper in the future.

(Interpretation) C: Correct – 'We will need to rely on these important energy sources for many decades to come' – 'we', meaning all societies will depend on traditional energy resources for still many years.
Gabarito "C".

Reducing the dependence on oil

Ildo Sauer,
Gas and Energy Director, Petrobras

Brazil's energy sector is following the worldwide tendency towards greater diversification of primary energy sources and the increased use of natural gas and biofuels. There are several reasons for this change. The
5 most important are the environmental restrictions that are gradually being adopted in the world's principal energy-consuming markets and the need to reduce the dependence on oil, set against a scenario of accelerated depletion in oil reserves and escalating prices.
10 The share of gas in Brazilian primary energy consumption has more than doubled in a short period, increasing from 4.1% in 1999 to 8.9% in 2004, and this share is forecast to rise to 12% by 2010.
Over the past two decades, the world gas industry
15 has experienced a structural and regulatory transformation. These changes have altered the strategic behavior of gas firms, with an intensification of competition, the search for diversification (especially in the case of power generation) and the internationalization
20 of industry activities. Together, these changes have radically changed the economic environment and the level of competition in the industry.
Brazil's gas industry is characterized by its late development, although in recent years, internal supply
25 imports and demand have grown significantly — the growth trajectory of recent years exceeds that of countries with more mature markets, such as Spain, Argentina, the UK and the US. And the outlook is positive for continued growth over the next few years, particularly
30 when set against the investment plans already announced in Brazil.
The country has a small transportation network concentrated near the coast. The distribution network is concentrated in the major consumption centres.
35 Domestic gas sources are largely offshore in the Campos basin and Bolivia provides imports. Given the degree of gas penetration in the country's primary energy consumption, the industry is poorly developed when compared with other countries. The industry requires
40 heavy investment in expanding the transport and distribution (T&D) networks, as well as in diversifying and increasing its supplies. Such investments are necessary for realizing the industry's enormous potential.
Another key industry highlight is the changing profile
45 of gas supply. A large part of the gas produced domestically to date has been associated with oil production. The latter diluting or even totally absorbing the costs of exploiting the gas. In most cases, gas production was feasible only in conjunction with oil
50 production activities. However, the country's latest gas finds are non-associated. Thus, an exclusively dedicated structure must be developed to produce this gas — translating into a significant rise in production costs. This is more significant when analyzed against the high costs
55 associated with the market for exploration and production (E&P) sector equipment. In recent years, the leasing costs of drilling rigs and E&P equipment have been climbing in parallel with escalating oil prices. This directly affects end consumer prices.
60 In a world of primary energy consumption diversification, of greater environmental restrictions and the reduced dependence on oil, Brazil has been seeking to develop alternative energy sources – principally natural gas and biofuels. The gas industry holds enormous
65 potential for Brazil, although there is still a long way to go before it reaches maturity and major investment is required.

World Energy in 2006. copyright © 2006, World Energy Council. p.29-31 (adapted)

(ADVOGADO – PETROBRÁS TRANSP. – 2006 – CESGRANRIO)
The only correct statement concerning reference is:
(A) "itself" (line 5) refers to "U.S. Department of Energy".
(B) "some" (line 9) refers to "oil and natural gas".
(C) "them" (line 19) refers to "exploration and production technologies".
(D) "it" (line 35) refers to "new fuel regulations".
(E) "they" (line 55) refers to "some of our companies".

(Grammar) A: Incorrect – 'itself' refers to the petroleum business, B: Incorrect - 'some' refers to remote places, C: Incorrect – 'them' refers to resources, D: Incorrect – 'it' refers to possibility, E: Correct – 'they' refers to 'some of our companies'.
Gabarito "E".

(ADVOGADO – PETROBRÁS TRANSP. – 2006 – CESGRANRIO)
The only pair of antonyms is:
(A) "unreachable" (line 9) – inaccessible.
(B) "to meet" (line 11) – to reduce.
(C) "accurately" (line 19) – incorrectly.
(D) "recently" (line 33) – lately.
(E) "reliable" (line 40) – dependable.

(Vocabulary) A: Incorrect – Unreachable means inaccessible, B: Incorrect – To meet means to match, C: Correct – Accurately means the opposite of incorrectly, D: Incorrect – Recently means the same as lately, E: Incorrect – Reliable means dependable.
Gabarito "C".

(ADVOGADO – PETROBRÁS TRANSP. – 2006 – CESGRANRIO)
Check the item in which there is a verb in the passive voice.
(A) "The oil and natural gas industry has developed and applied…" (lines 1 - 2)
(B) "Other segments of the industry have benefited from technological advances as well." (lines 25-26)
(C) "Also, new process equipment and catalyst technology advances have been made very recently…" (lines 31-33)
(D) "The industry is committed to investing in advanced technologies…" (lines 38-39)
(E) "Gas hydrates could be an important future source of natural gas…" (lines 49-50)

(Grammar) C: Correct – 'have been made' is the verb 'to make' in the passive voice structure and in the present perfect verb tense.
Gabarito "C".

(ADVOGADO – PETROBRÁS TRANSP. – 2006 – CESGRANRIO)
Mark the title that best expresses the main idea of the text.
(A) Fuel cell research and the latest automobile developments.
(B) How to reduce energy consumption in the U.S.
(C) The role of technology in generating environmental benefits.
(D) The impact of advanced technology on the oil and natural gas industry.
(E) Automating oil refineries to improve operational and environmental performance.

(Interpretation) D: Correct – This is the only option that is broad enough to cover the main idea and not specific parts of the text.
Gabarito "D".

(ADVOGADO – EPE – 2007 – CESGRANRIO) The main purpose of the text is to:

(A) criticize the significant rise in production costs of gas in Brazil.
(B) list the advantages and disadvantages of the changing profile of gas supply.
(C) discuss relevant issues in the use of gas as a primary energy resource in Brazil.
(D) recommend the need for intensification of competition and greater diversification of primary energy sources.
(E) evaluate all the current environmental restrictions adopted in the world's principal energy-consuming markets.

(Interpretation) C: Correct – The only option that captures the broad nature of the text. Paragraph 1 (introduction) and the conclusion show the broad subject to be dealt within the text.
Gabarito "C".

(ADVOGADO – EPE – 2007 – CESGRANRIO) According to the author, the world gas industry, since the late 80s, has:

(A) maintained a local focus and faced huge losses.
(B) felt the need to resort to traditional power generation mechanisms.
(C) become a less competitive market due to the rising competition of biofuels.
(D) suffered changes in both the structure of the industry and the norms that regulate it.
(E) banned the internationalization of its activities in search for higher national economic advantages.

(Interpretation) D: Correct – Line 14 - 'Over the past two decades' i.e. since the late 80s. 'Transformation' refers to suffering changes.
Gabarito "D".

(ADVOGADO – EPE – 2007 – CESGRANRIO) In Brazil, the gas industry can currently be considered:

(A) a segment growing at a slow rate, despite the forecast of a few prospective investments in the area.
(B) a promising economic segment that has recently exceeded results of more traditional markets.
(C) more mature than the Argentinian gas industry, yet not as profitable.
(D) feasible, as it requires no investment in transport and distribution.
(E) potentially weak in terms of national demands for its growth.

(Interpretation) B: Correct – Line 64 – The gas industry 'holds enormous potential'. Line 25 - The markets "growth trajectory exceeds that of countries with more mature markets".
Gabarito "B".

(ADVOGADO – EPE – 2007 – CESGRANRIO) Mark the only correct statement.

(A) "this change" (line 4) refers to "reasons" (line 4).
(B) "that of" (line 26) refers to "years" (line 26).
(C) "its" (line 42) refers to "industry" (line 39).
(D) "The latter" (line 47) refers to "gas produced domestically" (lines 45-46).
(E) "This" (line 53) refers to "(E&P) sector equipment" (line 56).

(Grammar) A: Incorrect - 'this change' refers to greater diversification, B: Incorrect –'that of' refers to growth trajectory, C: Correct – 'its' refers to industry, D: Incorrect – 'The latter' refers to oil production, E: Incorrect – 'This' refers to a rise in production costs.
Gabarito "C".

(ADVOGADO – EPE – 2007 – CESGRANRIO) According to the text, which of the following is NOT going to be a problem for the future of the gas industry in Brazil?

(A) The need for Bolivian imports and the domestic offshore gas sources.
(B) The need for intense capital investments to expand the distribution networks.
(C) The restricted transportation network and its concentration along the Brazilian coastline.
(D) The increased competition in the world market, which can easily stifle the sector in Brazil.
(E) The interest of Brazilian authorities in developing alternative energy sources including biofuels and natural gas.

(Interpretation) E: Correct – Line 30 – 'the outlook is positive for continued growth over the next few years, particularly when set against the investment plans already announced in Brazil'.
Gabarito "B".

(ADVOGADO – EPE – 2007 – CESGRANRIO) Choose the only alternative that corresponds in meaning to the following sentence in Paragraph 5 "Given the degree of gas penetration in the country's primary energy consumption, the industry is poorly developed when compared with other countries."(lines 36 - 39).

(A) The Brazilian gas industry is less developed in relation to that of other countries if one considers the share of gas in Brazilian primary energy consumption.
(B) The Brazilian government gives large incentives for an increased penetration of primary energy sources in the market.
(C) The degree of industrial development in Brazil is poor and requires alternative primary energy sources from other countries.
(D) The poor development of the gas industry in other countries results in a lower share in primary energy consumption.
(E) The gas penetration in Brazilian primary energy consumption reveals a poorly developed country.

(Interpretation) A: Correct – Lines 36-39 – "Given the degree of gas penetration in the country's primary energy consumption, the industry is poorly developed when compared with other countries".
Gabarito "A".

(ADVOGADO – EPE – 2007 – CESGRANRIO) Check the only correct option.

(A) "depletion" (line 9) means the same as abundance.
(B) "forecast" (line 13) and backcast are perfect antonyms.
(C) "set against" (line 30) and set forth have equivalent meanings.
(D) "to date" (line 46) and until now have the same meanings.
(E) "feasible" (line 49) means unlikely.

(Vocabulary) A: Incorrect – 'depletion' means the use of a resource faster than it is replenished, B: Incorrect – 'forecast' means to predict, 'backcast' means to have failure or to reverse, C: Incorrect – 'set against' means compared with, and 'set forth' means to begin a journey or to present for consideration, D: Correct – 'to date' means until, E: Incorrect – 'feasible' – viable or likely.
Gabarito "D".

(ADVOGADO – EPE – 2007 – CESGRANRIO) According to Paragraph 6 (lines 44 - 59), it is correct to state that:
(A) production costs will not affect end-consumer prices in the gas industry.
(B) the need for drilling rigs and other equipment for exploring gas are not major concerns for the Brazilian gas industry.
(C) the most recently found sources of gas have the advantage of being associated with oil exploration and production.
(D) the production of gas in Brazil has, until recently, been separated from the production of oil and has thus been economically advantageous.
(E) heavy investment in a gas-dedicated structure will be the major drawback for the exploration and production of the recently found gas supplies.

(Interpretation) A: Incorrect – Production costs will affect end-consumer prices, B: Incorrect – They are major concerns as their costs have been rising sharply, C: Incorrect – The most recent findings are non-associated to oil exploration and require independent infrastructure, D: Incorrect – Until recently, gas production had in large taken place alongside oil production, E: Correct – The infrastructure needed is growing in cost. Drawback refers to a disadvantage. In this case, the disadvantage is the increasing costs of exploration and production of gas supplies.
Gabarito "E".

(ADVOGADO – EPE – 2007 – CESGRANRIO) Check the item in which there is an INCORRECT correspondence between the idea expressed by the words in bold type and the idea in italics.

(A)	"— the growth trajectory of recent years exceeds that of countries with more mature markets, **such as** Spain, Argentina, the UK and the US." (lines 25-28)	Such as → *example*
(B)	"The industry requires heavy investment in expanding the transport and distribution (T&D) networks, **as well** as in diversifying and increasing its supplies." (lines 39-42)	As well as → *addition*
(C)	"**However**, the country's latest gas finds are non-associated." (lines 50-51)	However → *contrast*
(D)	"**Thus**, an exclusively dedicated structure…" (lines 51-52)	Thus → *result*
(E)	"The gas industry holds enormous potential for Brazil, **although** there is still a long way to go…" (lines 64-65)	Although → *consequence*

(Grammar) E: Correct – 'Although' is used similarly to 'even though', 'despite the fact that' and 'whilst'. It is not used as a consequence.
Gabarito "E".

"Natural gas is fast becoming the economic and environmental fuel of choice. The last 30 years have seen the global industry almost triple in size and similar growth can be expected in the next 30, as national governments and global industry look to gas to ensure the stability and diversity of their energy supplies."

(ADVOGADO – EPE – 2007 – CESGRANRIO) This comment by Linda Cook, Executive Director of a British Gas and Power Company, reproduces a similar idea to that in the following segment from Ildo Sauer's text:
(A) "Brazil's energy sector is following the worldwide tendency towards greater diversification of primary energy sources and the increased use of natural gas and biofuels." (lines 1-4)
(B) "Over the past two decades, the world gas industry has experienced a structural and regulatory transformation." (lines 14-16)
(C) "The distribution network is concentrated in the major consumption centres." (lines 33-34)
(D) "The industry requires heavy investment in expanding the transport and distribution (T&D) networks," (lines 39-41)
(E) "In most cases, gas production was feasible only in conjunction with oil production activities." (lines 48-50)

(Interpretation) A: Correct – References to a global industry and worldwide tendency echo each other. Both excerpts mention the theme of diversity. The other options are too narrow to be correct.

REPORT: BIOFUELS POISED TO DISPLACE OIL

Biofuels such as ethanol and biodiesel can significantly reduce global dependence on oil, according to a new report by the Worldwatch Institute.
Last year, world biofuel production surpassed 670,000 barrels per day, the equivalent of about 1 percent of the global transport fuel market. Although oil still accounts for more than 96 percent of transport fuel use, biofuel production has doubled since 2001 and is poised for even stronger growth as the industry responds to higher fuel prices and supportive government policies. "Coordinated action to expand biofuel markets and advance new technologies could relieve pressure on oil prices while strengthening agricultural economies and reducing climate-altering emissions," says Worldwatch Institute President Christopher Flavin.
Brazil is the world's biofuel leader, with half of its sugar cane crop providing more than 40 percent of its non-diesel transport fuel. In the United States, where 15 percent of the corn crop provides about 2 percent of the non-diesel transport fuel, ethanol production is growing even more rapidly. This surging growth may allow the U.S. to overtake Brazil as the world's biofuel leader this year. Both countries are now estimated to be producing ethanol at less than the current cost of gasoline.
Figures cited in the report reveal that biofuels could provide 37 percent of U.S. transport fuel within the next 25 years, and up to 75 percent if automobile fuel economy doubles. Biofuels could replace 20–30 percent of the oil used in European Union countries during the same time frame.
As the first-ever global assessment of the potential social and environmental impacts of biofuels, **Biofuels for Transportation** warns that the large-scale use of biofuels carries significant agricultural and ecological risks. "It is

35 essential that government incentives be used to minimize competition between food and fuel crops and to discourage expansion onto ecologically valuable lands," says Worldwatch Biofuels Project Manager Suzanne Hunt. However, the report also finds that biofuels have the potential
40 to increase energy security, create new economic opportunities in rural areas, and reduce local pollution and emissions of greenhouse gases.
The long-term potential of biofuels is in the use of non-food feedstock that include agricultural, municipal, and
45 forestry wastes as well as fast-growing, cellulose-rich energy crops such as switchgrass. It is expected that the combination of cellulosic biomass resources and "next - generation" biofuel conversion technologies will compete with conventional gasoline and diesel fuel without subsidies
50 in the medium term.
The report recommends policies to accelerate the development of biofuels, while maximizing the benefits and minimizing the risks. Recommendations include: **strengthening the market** (i.e. focusing on market
55 development, infrastructure development, and the building of transportation fleets that are able to use the new fuels), **speeding the transition to next-generation technologies** allowing for dramatically increased production at lower cost, and **facilitating sustainable**
60 **international biofuel trade**, developing a true international market unimpeded by the trade restrictions in place today.

Worldwatch Institute - June 7, 2006. Adapted from: http://www.worldwatch.org/node/4079

(ADVOGADO – REPAF – 2007 – CESGRANRIO) The main purpose of the text is to:

(A) criticize the release of the report Biofuels for Transportation.
(B) highlight the potential of biofuels as substitutes for conventional fuels.
(C) expose the several risks associated with the use of biofuels in transportation.
(D) suggest the elimination of oil as transport fuel to reduce pollution and emissions of greenhouse gases.
(E) warn against the agricultural and ecological damages associated with the production of biofuels.

(Interpretation) B: Correct – The overall theme of the text is to inform. The main part of the text discusses the potential for biofuels.
„Gabarito „B".

(ADVOGADO – REFAP – 2007 – CESGRANRIO) Based on what Christopher Flavin, President of the Worldwatch Institute, has said, it is possible to state that:

(A) reducing climate-altering emissions ought to relieve pressure on oil prices.
(B) strengthening agricultural economies will naturally increase the environmental impact of oil production.
(C) creating new technologies is an alternative to expanding biofuel markets in an effort to reduce oil prices.
(D) extending the market for biofuels will ultimately reduce the price of oil and improve agricultural economies.
(E) in fighting against higher fuel prices and supportive government polices, the Worldwatch Institute will support the growth of oil production.

(Interpretation) D: Correct – "Coordinated action to expand biofuel markets and advance new technologies could relieve pressure on oil prices while strengthening agricultural economies and reducing climate altering emissions," says Worldwatch Institute President" – Line 10.
„Gabarito „D".

(ADVOGADO – REFAP – 2007 – CESGRANRIO) According to the text, Brazil:

(A) actually grows 40% of the sugar cane crop in the world.
(B) currently produces biofuel that costs far more than gasoline.
(C) will eventually lead the world market of non-diesel transport fuel.
(D) competes with the United States for the 2% of non-diesel transport fuel.
(E) will possibly be surpassed by the United States in terms of biofuel production.

(Interpretation) E: Correct – surpassed means overtaken. "This surging growth may allow the U.S. to overtake Brazil as the world's biofuel leader this year. Both countries are now estimated to be producing ethanol at less than the current cost of gasoline".
„Gabarito „E".

(ADVOGADO – REFAP – 2007 – CESGRANRIO) "This surging growth..." (line 21) refers to:

(A) ethanol production.
(B) sugar cane crop.
(C) corn crop.
(D) gasoline.
(E) diesel.

(Grammar) A: Correct – The surging growth refers to ethanol production.
„Gabarito „A".

(ADVOGADO – REFAP – 2007 – CESGRANRIO) Some of the benefits of the increase in biofuel production listed by the author are:

(A) increase the profits achieved in agriculture and maximize ecological risks.
(B) boost energy security and hinder next-generation biofuel conversion techniques.
(C) improve the economic potential of rural areas and reduce global dependence on oil.
(D) reduce pollution in rural areas and minimize competition between food and fuel crops.
(E) control emission of greenhouse gases and discourage expansion onto ecologically valuable lands.

(Interpretation) C: Correct – Line 35 - "The report also finds that biofuels have the potential to increase energy security, create new economic opportunities in rural areas and reduce local pollution and emissions of green house gases."
„Gabarito „C".

(ADVOGADO – REFAP – 2007 – CESGRANRIO) Check the item in which there is an INCORRECT correspondence between the idea expressed by the words in bold type and the idea in italics.

(A)	"**Although** oil still accounts for more than 96 percent of transport fuel use, biofuel production has doubled …" (lines 6-8)	Although → *consequence*
(B)	"**However**, the report also finds that biofuels have the potential to …" (lines 39-40)	However → *contrast*
(C)	"…forestry wastes **as well as** fastgrowing, cellulose-rich energy crops …" (lines 45-46)	as well as → *addition*
(D)	"cellulose-rich energy crops **such as** switchgrass." (lines 45-46)	such as → *example*
(E)	"…policies to accelerate the development of biofuels, **while** maximizing the benefits…" (lines 51-52)	while → *simultaneity*

(Grammar) A: Correct – 'Although' is used similarly to: 'even though', 'despite the fact that' and 'whilst'. It is not used as a consequence.
Gabarito "A".

What are the best jobs of 2008?

If you're job hunting in the professional or service oriented fields, we have good news. Of the ten categories into which the Bureau of Labor Statistics (BLS) divides
5 jobs, the "professional" and "service" categories — already the two largest in the economy — will boast the most job openings in 2008. In the next decade, 17 percent more employees will be employed in these two categories than are today, nearly double the expansion of other categories. With an increase in demand, professional and service
10 jobs, which include professions like educator, scientist, health care worker and artist in the "professional" category, and police officer, child caretaker and cosmetologist in the "service" category, will also add roughly a million new jobs to the economy. By comparison, other categories
15 such as construction, sales and administration, are predicted to grow by only 10 percent; all eight other occupational groups combined will add only about half a million jobs to the economy in 2008.
But wait a second: Aren't we heading for recession?
20 Where are all these open jobs coming from? While new jobs are being created, they don't represent the majority of the open positions workers will see this year. Career switching and baby-boomer retirement will create a higher turnover than ever, which will continue to increase the
25 supply of jobs available. The Bureau of Labor Statistics notes that while a slightly expanding economy is spurring job growth in a majority of fields, "the need to replace workers who leave a field permanently is expected to create more openings than growth will."
30 According to Chris Higgins, Senior Associate Director of Career Management at the University of Pennsylvania's Wharton School, the retirement boom has increased students' interest in general management rotation programs, introduced by many companies to prevent the
35 loss of a record number of retirees. He notes that companies are using these rotation programs as a way of "fast-tracking" replacements in management, and students are using them as a way of getting a taste for different departments and niches within a company. "It turns out to
40 benefit the employers as well as the employees," observes Higgins.
If you're job searching in certain occupational groups — namely farming, production, or transportation — you're looking at slow or negative growth and poor job availability.
45 Peer occupational groups, however, are hiring at a brisker pace: construction, administration, and maintenance and repair are all groups that are experiencing healthy growth or job availability. On the other hand, if you're looking in the white-collar realm, you're better set for 2008; both
50 growth and availability are predicted to be healthy for the foreseeable future.
Within the "professional" rubric, three particular sectors are displaying the most aggressive growth rates: computer/ mathematical, community/social service, and health
55 practices jobs are each projected to grow by more than 20 percent in the next decade, with education/library jobs following at 14 percent. That means that if you're an aspiring teacher or health worker, you won't be looking for jobs — the jobs will be looking for you.
60 While computer and mathematical science jobs are projected to grow at nearly double the rate of other types of jobs, growth in this demographic has actually slowed in the last decade "as the software industry matures and as routine work is increasingly outsourced abroad," says
65 the BLS. There's still healthy hiring here, however, and some experts are saying computer science jobs will be in increasing demand. "Tech firms are picking up hiring again," Higgins notes, "in a way they haven't in nearly a decade." Companies like Google are hiring online sales,
70 operations, and Internet services employees in droves. In short, computer and mathematical experts continue to be a sought-after demographic. They may not see the same demand that educators and health professionals are enjoying anytime soon, but it may not be long before
75 the tech industry reaches 90s-level hiring and growth once again.

By Chris Dannen. Portfolio.com updated
5:22 p.m. ET Feb. 22, 2008.

(ADVOGADO – BNDES – 2008 – CESGRANRIO) The main purpose of this text is to

(A) point out the most promising careers in the near future.
(B) discuss the growth of the economy in the technical sector only.
(C) advise companies to implement rotation programs for students.
(D) criticize new college programs that train professionals for the new markets.
(E) warn against the negative health effects of early retirement for baby-boomers.

(Interpretation) A: Correct – This choice reflects the title of the article and the content of the opening and closing paragraphs.
Gabarito "A".

(ADVOGADO – BNDES – 2008 – CESGRANRIO) The fragment "But wait a second: Aren't we heading for recession?" (line 19) reveals an attitude of

(A) anger and shock.
(B) surprise and irony.
(C) resignation and hope.
(D) refusal and complaint.
(E) indifference and submission.

(Interpretation) B: Correct – The fragment is ironic in that it questions what is being said in the text. The suprising and ironic factor is that the jobs market is expanding when a recession is expected. The ironic and surprising statement is used to draw the reader's attention to the information, which is contrary to the perceived wisdom.
Gabarito "B".

(ADVOGADO – BNDES – 2008 – CESGRANRIO) In lines 20-29, Chris Dannen, the author of the text, states that the new job openings available are a result of

I. people moving into other careers or occupations;
II. the implementation of new professional positions;
III. women who leave their jobs to take care of their babies;
IV. the retirement of the workers who have reached their 60s.

The ONLY correct statement(s) is(are)

(A) III.
(B) I and III.
(C) III and IV.
(D) I, II and IV.
(E) II, III and IV.

(Interpretation) D: Correct – Line 21 – "Career switch and baby-boomer retirement will create a higher turnover than ever, which will continue to increase the supply of jobs available". This covers points I and IV. Lines 10-15 – both discussing the upcoming of new professional positions to the job market.
Gabarito "D".

(ADVOGADO – BNDES – 2008 – CESGRANRIO) According to Paragraph 4 (lines 30-41), why are rotation programs beneficial to the companies that implement them?

(A) Such programs help managers learn more about the companies before they retire.
(B) Employees are switching to and from different departments in order to find the one that pays best.
(C) Most retirees are interested in going back to work in their companies to prevent financial losses.
(D) The companies need to increase the supply of jobs available and, therefore, implement rotating shifts for employees.
(E) It is a way to train college students in different areas in the company and train professionals who will be able to replace the retiring managers.

(Interpretation) E: Correct – Students are using these programs to get a taste of different areas of the company and existing employees can be fast-tracked into replacing managers.
Gabarito "E".

(ADVOGADO – BNDES – 2008 – CESGRANRIO) Which of the following occupations are NOT seen as promising?

(A) Teaching, child caretaker and police officer.
(B) Health care jobs and community social service.
(C) Cosmetologist, computer science specialist and librarian.
(D) Farming, positions in the transport or production industry.
(E) Business administration, technical maintenance or repair.

(Interpretation) D: Correct – Line 42 - "If you're job searching in certain occupational groups – namely farming, production or transport – you're looking at slow or negative growth and poor job availability"
Gabarito "D".

(ADVOGADO – BNDES – 2008 – CESGRANRIO) Check the option that contains a correct correspondence of meaning.

(A) "roughly" (line 13) and approximately are antonyms.
(B) "spurring" (line 26) and preventing are synonyms.
(C) "replacements" (line 37) and substitutions have the same meaning.
(D) "brisker" (line 45) could not be substituted by quicker.
(E) "displaying" (line 53) and showing express contrasting ideas.

(Vocabulary) A: Incorrect – 'roughly' and 'approximately' are synonyms, B: Incorrect – 'spurring' means encouraging the opposite of preventing, C: Correct – 'replacements' and 'substitutions' have the same meaning, D: Incorrect – 'brisker' means 'at a faster pace or rate', E: Incorrect – 'displaying' means in this context 'showing' and has no connotation of contrast.
Gabarito "C".

(ADVOGADO – BNDES – 2008 – CESGRANRIO) "…if you're an aspiring teacher or health worker, you won't be looking for jobs – the jobs will be looking for you." (lines 57-59) implies that

(A) employers will be seeking for teachers to work in health related jobs.
(B) employers are expected to hire fewer teachers and health workers than they do nowadays.
(C) there will be plenty of job positions available for teachers and health workers.
(D) it will not be easy to find a position as a teacher or health worker in the near future.
(E) only teachers and health workers will need to find new jobs in other fields.

(Interpretation) C: Correct – There will be more jobs available than workers available to do them. As demand is greater than supply, there will be lots of positions for teachers and health workers.
Gabarito "C".

(ADVOGADO – BNDES – 2008 – CESGRANRIO) In terms of reference, it is correct to affirm that

(A) "17 percent more employees…" (lines 6-7) refers to employees in the construction, sales and administration categories.
(B) "nearly double the expansion…" (line 8) refers to the expansion of the professional and service categories.
(C) "are predicted to grow by only 10 percent;" (lines 15-16) refers to the growth of jobs in all eight other occupational groups.
(D) "…14 percent." (line 57) refers to estimated increase of community and social service jobs.
(E) "…nearly double the rate of other types of jobs," (lines 61-62) refers to the predicted growth of educational and library jobs.

(Interpretation) A: Incorrect – This refers to professional and service categories, B: Correct – Refers to the expansion of the professional and service categories, C: Incorrect – Refers to construction, sales and administration, D: Incorrect – Refers to education and library jobs, E: Incorrect – Refers to computer and mathematical science jobs.
Gabarito "B".

(ADVOGADO – BNDES – 2008 – CESGRANRIO) Check the item where there is a correct correspondence between the boldfaced word(s) and the idea in italics.

(A) "If you're job hunting in the professional or service-oriented fields, we have good news." (lines 1-2) – consequence.

(B) "While new jobs are being created, they don't represent the majority of the open positions workers will see this year." (lines 20-22) - exemplification.
(C) "Peer occupational groups, however, are hiring at a brisker pace:" (lines 45-46) – addition.
(D) "On the other hand, if you're looking in the white-collar realm, you're better set for 2008;" (lines 48-49) – condition
(E) "In short, computer and mathematical experts continue to be a sought-after demographic." (lines 70-72) - concluding summary.

(Grammar) A: Incorrect – 'If' is used to show condition, B: Incorrect – 'While' is used to show something happening at the same time, i.e. 'although' or 'whereas', C: Incorrect – 'however' is used to show contrast or contradiction, D: Incorrect - 'On the other hand' is used to show contrast, E: Correct – 'In short' means 'in summary' or 'to conclude'.
Gabarito "E".

(ADVOGADO – BNDES – 2008 – CESGRANRIO) According to the last paragraph in the text, which statement is true about the IT (Information Technology) job market?

(A) Computer science jobs will only be available for healthy professionals.
(B) Tech firms are on their way to show the same employment rates of the 90s.
(C) Companies such as Google are significantly cutting down their regular labor force in different areas.
(D) The BLS states that the software industry has eliminated job reduction in the previous decade because of the tendency to outsource abroad.
(E) The IT industry has matured and suffered a slower growth rate in hiring during the last decade and this is not expected to change in 2008.

(Interpretation) B: Correct – Line 74 - 'it may not be long before the tech industry reaches 90's level hiring and growth once again'. None of the other options are true.
Gabarito "B".

INTERNATIONAL WOMEN'S DAY

Some 40 women entrepreneurs from the Middle East and North Africa told a World Bank-sponsored roundtable that education and wealth were usually not enough to overcome barriers to business in their countries.
5 The women made it clear they still faced barriers men might not.
For example, a Harvard-educated woman had to establish a medical waste management company under her brother's name, because women were not allowed to
10 be issued licenses in her country. Another woman building the first private petrochemical terminal in the Persian Gulf could not take her two foreign business partners to lunch because she had to sit in the women's section of the restaurant.
15 The examples show that women make up an increasing number of small, medium and large-scale producers, investors, and entrepreneurs in the Middle East and North Africa region, and they are creating significant number of jobs in the process. But as the world marks
20 International Women's Day today, the examples also show there are many, usually gender-based, obstacles in their way – including obstructed access to decision makers, inaccessibility of finance, unequal treatment under the law, and resistant social norms.
25 The women who took part in the World Bank's recent roundtable were among those who made it despite the hurdles – successful owners or founders of businesses in a wide variety of sectors from Algeria, Morocco, Tunisia, Libya, Egypt, WBG, Lebanon, Iraq, Iran, Jordan, Kuwait,
30 Saudi Arabia, Bahrain, Qatar, Yemen, Syria and the United Arab Emirates. But as statistics and anecdotal evidence show many other women are held back, costing the Middle East and North African countries millions of jobs; the region has the world's lowest rate — 32 percent — of female
35 workforce participation.
"The World Bank's goal is to increase women's entrepreneurship to strengthen the private sector, create jobs, and advance women's empowerment through economic opportunities," says Nadereh Chamlou, Senior
40 Advisor and Gender Coordinator in the Office of the Chief Economist for the Bank's Middle East and North Africa (MENA) region. The Middle East and North Africa region needs to create some 90 million jobs over the next 20 years — "twice as fast as in the past," says Mustapha
45 Nabli, Chief MENA Economist at the World Bank. "These jobs can only be created by a competitive and diversified private sector, since the public sector and oil-driven models of the past have failed to create the needed jobs." [...]
Women in the Middle East and North Africa have
50 considerable financial resources, sometimes through inheritance. A study in one country found $26.6 billion in women's bank accounts sitting idle because of laws and regulations, which prevented women from opening businesses. Other obstacles were more cultural than
55 structural, such as the negative perception often attached to working women in the Middle East and North Africa.
[...]
In the United States, women-owned business is the fastest growing segment of the private sector – which
60 has an impact on the productivity and competitiveness of the economy. With the investments that the Middle East and North Africa has made to advance women's education, identifying and removing barriers that women face to start up their businesses can spur growth, according to the
65 Bank.

News and Broadcast, March 8, 2006

(ADVOGADO – BNDES – 2006 – CESGRANRIO) The main purpose of the text is to:

(A) reveal that, in some parts of the world, women entrepreneurs come up against gender-based discrimination.
(B) report that female workforce participation is very low in the Middle East and in North African countries.
(C) discuss the impact that the recent growth of businesses run by women has on the economy of the U.S.
(D) criticize the public sector in several world regions for not being able to create the needed jobs.
(E) list a few countries in which women overcame barriers to become successful business owners.

(Interpretation) A: Correct – The overall theme of the text is to discuss obstacles women entrepreneurs face. The phrasal verb 'come up against' means to encounter or face an obstacle.
Gabarito "A".

(ADVOGADO – BNDES – 2006 – CESGRANRIO) Where in the passage are there examples of obstacles some women have to face in the business world?

(A) Paragraphs 1, 2 and 3.
(B) Paragraphs 2, 3 and 4.

(C) Paragraphs 2, 3 and 5.
(D) Paragraphs 2, 3 and 6.
(E) Paragraphs 3, 4 and 5.

(Interpretation) D: Correct – Paragraph 2 – Licenses, women's separate section in restaurants, Paragraph 3 – the law, social norms, restrictions on finance and unequal access to decision makers, Paragraph 6 – Negative perceptions of women who work.
Gabarito "D".

(ADVOGADO – BNDES – 2006 – CESGRANRIO) According to the text, one of the obstacles faced by women in the Middle East and North Africa is:

(A) easy access to people who decide.
(B) high status of working women.
(C) availability of financing.
(D) flexible social norms.
(E) unfair legal treatment.

(Interpretation) E: Correct – Line 23 – 'unequal treatment under the law'.
Gabarito "E".

(ADVOGADO – BNDES – 2006 – CESGRANRIO) In "The women who took part in ... were among those who made it despite the hurdles–" (lines 25-27), "those who made it" refers to women who:

(A) achieved success.
(B) anticipated hurdles.
(C) created obstacles.
(D) fought and failed.
(E) gave it all up.

(Vocabulary) A: Correct – 'To make it' means to achieve a goal or achieve success.
Gabarito "A".

(ADVOGADO – BNDES – 2006 – CESGRANRIO) The statement "A study in one country found $26.6 billion in women's bank accounts sitting idle…" (lines 51-52), means that this large amount of money:

(A) will be invested in a study.
(B) is not being used at the moment.
(C) cannot be taken out of the country.
(D) has been confiscated by the bank.
(E) has been inherited by women.

(Vocabulary) B: Correct – 'To be idle' means not being used or operative. In this case, money is sitting in a bank account not being used for investment.
Gabarito "B".

(ADVOGADO – BNDES – 2006 – CESGRANRIO) The words "establish" (line 8) and "prevented" (line 53) could be replaced in text with, respectively:

(A) purchase – avoided.
(B) certify – refrained.
(C) set up – stopped.
(D) register – escape.
(E) create – disturbed.

(Vocabulary) C: Correct – 'To set up' means 'to establish and' 'to prevent' means 'to stop'.
Gabarito "C".

(ADVOGADO – BNDES – 2006 – CESGRANRIO) Mark the option in which there is a correct correspondence between pronoun and referent.

(A) "it" (line 5) – "business" (line 4).
(B) "her" (line 9) – "a Harvard-educated woman" (line 7).
(C) "they" (line 18) – "examples" (line 15).
(D) "which" (line 59) – "the private sector" (line 59).
(E) "their" (line 64) – "barriers" (line 63).

(Grammar) A: Incorrect – 'it' refers to making something clear, B: Correct – 'her' refers to a Harvard-educated woman, C: Incorrect – 'they' refers to producers, investors and entrepreneurs, D: Incorrect – 'which' refers to women owned business, E: Incorrect – 'their' refers to women.
Gabarito "B".

(ADVOGADO – BNDES – 2006 – CESGRANRIO) Check the item in which "make up" is used in the same sense as in the sentence "The examples show that women make up an increasing number of small, medium and large-scale producers," (lines 15-17).

(A) Some non-governmental organizations are making up parcels of old clothes to donate to the Red Cross.
(B) North African entrepreneurs must make up what they owe before the end of the month.
(C) Most workers in that company had to make up all the work they missed when they were ill.
(D) The World Bank made up the money to the amount the committee needed.
(E) Female representatives from all Middle East countries make up the business committee.

(Vocabulary) A: Incorrect – This means to put together or construct, B: Incorrect – This means to compensate for a deficit, C: Incorrect – This means to compensate for time missed, D: Incorrect – This means to compensate for a deficit, E: Correct – This means they constitute the business committee.
Gabarito "E".

(ADVOGADO – BNDES – 2006 – CESGRANRIO) Check the item in which the word(s) in boldtype can be replaced in the sentence by the one(s) in italics.

(A) "because women were not allowed to be issued licenses in her country." (lines 9-10) – thus.
(B) "The women who … were among those who made it despite the hurdles–" (lines 25-27) – in spite of.
(C) "But as statistics and anecdotal evidence show many other women are held back," (lines 31-32) – moreover.
(D) "…since the public sector and oil-driven models of the past have failed to create the needed jobs." (lines 47-48) – therefore.
(E) "such as the negative perception often attached to working women in the Middle East and North Africa." (lines 55-56) – once.

(Grammar) B: Correct – 'despite' and 'in spite of' are both subordinating conjunctions of contrast, and, in this case, they are interchangeable.
Gabarito "B".

(ADVOGADO – BNDES – 2006 – CESGRANRIO) Mark the only correct statement according to the last paragraph of the text.

(A) Most private-owned businesses in the United States belong to prosperous and successful women.
(B) North American female entrepreneurs are more productive and competitive than their male counterparts.
(C) Middle Eastern and North African countries have invested large sums of money to improve local economy.
(D) The World Bank believes that enabling women in the Middle East and North Africa to open businesses can stimulate economic development.
(E) The removal of all economic and social barriers to businesses owned by women worldwide is of vital importance to global economy.

(Interpretation) D: Correct – 'to spur growth' means in this context 'to stimulate economic development'.
Gabarito "D".

A FADED GREEN

Shades of peach adorn America's recently redesigned $20 note, but currency traders care little for pretty colours. The dollar has steadily been losing value in the foreign-exchange markets. This week it reached its
5   low against the euro since the single European currency was launched in 1999, breaking through $1.20. The dollar has fallen by 31% against the euro from its peak in July 2001. Recently it has also hit a three-year low against the yen and a five-year low against sterling.
10 It may seem curious that the dollar is falling when America is enjoying a remarkable burst of growth and Europe looks far less lively. America's GDP grew at an annual rate of 8.2% in the third quarter. The Institute of Supply Management's widely watched index of
15 manufacturing activity hit a 20-year high in November. Meanwhile, the euro area's economies are on the mend, but are expected to grow by only 0.5% this year and 1.8% next, according to the Economist's monthly poll of economic forecasters.
20 However, currencies are not economic virility symbols, but assets on which investors expect a return. The dollar used to be buoyant because investors expected to make more from dollar assets than from those denominated in other currencies. Now they are not so
25 sure. Their worries over America's twin deficits, on the current-account and the federal budget, loom large. With a current-account deficit of 5% of GDP, America must borrow $2 billion each business day. Tax cuts, spending on the war in Iraq and a new scheme to provide prescription
30 drugs to the old are dragging the government's books into disarray.
How much further might the dollar fall? Predicting the future price of a currency is useless. But there are good reasons to believe that over the medium term the
35 dollar could drop a lot lower, especially against the euro. Whether that will have the desired effects, in reducing America's imbalances, or in causing the expected chaos in Europe's economies, is a different question.
A stronger euro should be bad news for European
40 firms, even if it means cheaper Florida holidays for their employees. A rise in the euro against the dollar causes exports from European firms to become more expensive relative to American ones, cutting into Europe's sales. Similarly, American firms' products become relatively
45 cheaper, both for Americans and for foreign buyers. By creating more exports and curbing imports, a weaker dollar should thus help to cut America's huge current-account deficit.
Or so the textbooks have it. In the past, a falling
50 dollar has indeed reduced America's imports. In the 1980s, the last time America had such a large current-account deficit relative to GDP, an agreement to let the dollar depreciate helped to reduce America's consumption of Japanese cars and Swiss watches.
55 But there is reason to think that these days currency movements are not as effective as they once were in bringing economies into balance. A recent report of an investment bank doubts that a sliding dollar will do much to eliminate America's trade and current-account
60 imbalances.
In an increasingly integrated global economy, companies' pricing power has been eroded around the world. In addition, low inflation has made price increases more obvious. So it is more difficult for a European car
65 company, say, to raise its prices in America in response to a stronger euro. According to a study cited in the report, the ability to pass on the effects of a stronger currency has been waning in recent years.

The Economist, Dec. 6, 2003 http://www.tradewithvision.com/kbase/pdf/fadedGreen.pdf

(ADVOGADO – BNDES – 2004 – CESGRANRIO) In the sentence "Shades of peach adorn America's recently redesigned $20 note, but currency traders care little for pretty colours." (lines 1-3), the author means that:

(A) currency traders are not really concerned about aesthetic changes in dollar notes.
(B) currency traders are very worried about the recent changes in some dollar bills.
(C) currency traders prefer the traditional green dollar notes to the newly designed ones.
(D) the exchange market is totally against the use of pretty colours in currency notes.
(E) the attractive new colours in most dollar notes are totally unimportant in the trade market.

(Interpretation) A: Correct – The text explicitly says, "currency traders care little for pretty colours", meaning they are more interested in values than aesthetics.
Gabarito "A".

(ADVOGADO – BNDES – 2004 – CESGRANRIO) And (line 9) introduces an idea of addition. Check the option in which the idea introduced by the word in the first column is correctly stated.

(A) Since (line 5) – cause.
(B) But (line 17) – condition.
(C) Even (line 40) – conclusion.
(D) Thus (line 47) – consequence.
(E) So (line 64) – opposition.

(Grammar) A: Incorrect – 'since' in this sentence refers to a point in time (since the single European currency was launched in 1999), B: Incorrect – 'but' in this sentence shows a contrast (on one hand "the euro area's economies are on the mend (getting better), but are expected to grow by only 0.5% this year (only a little bit better)); C: Incorrect – 'even (if)' in this sentence refers to a condition ("even if it means cheaper Florida holidays for their employees" means it doesn't matter if this is good, the other part is bad - "A stronger euro should be bad news for European firms"), D: Correct – 'thus' in this sentence means 'consequently', E: Incorrect – 'so' in this sentence means 'consequently'.
Gabarito "A".

(ADVOGADO – BNDES – 2004 – CESGRANRIO) According to line 16, "the euro area's economies are on the mend," which means that they are:

(A) improving.
(B) stagnant.
(C) perfectly healthy.
(D) getting worse.
(E) in trouble.

(Vocabulary) A: Correct – 'on the mend' means 'recovering' or 'improving' (from what they were); B: Incorrect – 'stagnant' means 'inert' or 'dormant'; C: Incorrect – 'perfectly healthy' means they can not be any better; D: Incorrect – 'getting worse' is the opposite of 'on the mend'; E: Incorrect – 'in trouble' means 'in difficulty' or "struggling'.
Gabarito "A".

(ADVOGADO – BNDES – 2004 – CESGRANRIO) The fragment "Tax cuts, spending on the war in Iraq and (...) are dragging the government's books into disarray." (lines 28-31) suggests that such books will soon be:

(A) under control.
(B) under severe investigation.
(C) fully inaccurate.
(D) absolutely useless.
(E) in a state of disorder.

(Vocabulary) A: Incorrect – 'drag something into disarray' means 'to put something into a state of disorder' or 'make something a mess'; 'under control' means the opposite; B: Incorrect – 'under severe investigation' means 'being heavily investigated'; 'drag something into disarray' means 'to put something into a state of disorder' or 'make something a mess'; C: Incorrect – 'fully inaccurate' means 'completely wrong'; 'drag something into disarray' means 'put something into a state of disorder' or 'make something a mess'; D: Incorrect – 'absolutely useless' means 'completely ineffective'; E: Correct - 'drag something into disarray' means 'put something into a state of disorder' or 'make something a mess'.
Gabarito "E".

(ADVOGADO – BNDES – 2004 – CESGRANRIO) In the 1980s, according to lines 50-54, a weaker dollar:

(A) forced American consumers to stop buying foreign cars and watches.
(B) made the United States discontinue imports from Japan and Switzerland.
(C) contributed to the decrease of sales of Japanese cars and Swiss watches in the U.S.
(D) caused a rise in prices of cars and watches in Japan and in Switzerland, respectively.
(E) was the result of an agreement between car makers and the U.S. government.

(Interpretation) A: Incorrect – The text explicitly says, "an agreement to let the dollar depreciate helped to reduce America's consumption of Japanese cars and Swiss watches", meaning that the depreciating dollar was one of the factors that reduced such sales, but it did not 'force' consumers to stop making these purchases; B: Incorrect – The text explicitly says, "an agreement to let the dollar depreciate helped to reduce America's consumption of Japanese cars and Swiss watches", meaning that imports dropped, but did not stop altogether; C: Correct – see A; D: Incorrect – While a rise in prices on imported goods could be inferred from the falling dollar, The text does not explicitly say this; E: Incorrect - The text explicitly says there was "an agreement to let the dollar depreciate", not who made the agreement.
Gabarito "C".

(ADVOGADO – BNDES – 2004 – CESGRANRIO) Mark the only true statement concerning the ideas presented in paragraphs 4 to 7.

(A) Although it is difficult to guess the future price of a currency, it can be safely predicted that the dollar will soon drop slightly against other currencies.
(B) European firms may benefit from a stronger euro, since their exports will cost more than those from America.
(C) The employees of European companies cannot spend their holidays in Florida because the whole trip is too expensive for them.
(D) The present current-account deficit relative to the GDP is the first the United States has since the eighties.
(E) The report mentioned in the text insists that a devaluation of the dollar will bring U.S. economy into balance.

(Interpretation) A: Incorrect – The text explicitly says, "Predicting the future price of a currency is useless. But there are good reasons to believe that over the medium term the dollar could drop a lot lower, especially against the euro", meaning that there is a lot of speculation as to whether the dollar will actually drop. To say that it "will drop" is too strong for the information in the text; B: Incorrect – The text explicitly says, "A rise in the euro against the dollar causes exports from European firms to become more expensive relative to American ones, cutting into Europe's sales", meaning European firms will not benefit; C: Incorrect – The text explicitly says, "A stronger euro should be bad news for European firms, even if it means cheaper Florida holidays for their employees", meaning that if the dollar drops, they can spend their holidays in Florida; D: Correct – The text explicitly says, "In the 1980s, the last time America had such a large current-account deficit relative to GDP", meaning that this current-account deficit is the first since the 1980s; E: Incorrect – The text explicitly says, "A recent report of an investment bank doubts that a sliding dollar will do much to eliminate America's trade and current-account imbalances", meaning the report believes a depreciated dollar would NOT bring the US economy into balance.
Gabarito "D".

(ADVOGADO – BNDES – 2004 – CESGRANRIO) Mark the option that best reflects the rhetorical structure of the last paragraph of the text.

(A) Problem-solution.
(B) Time sequence.
(C) Definition and exemplification.
(D) Listing and classification.
(E) Cause and effect.

(Interpretation) A: Incorrect – The last paragraph presents the causes of problems (companies' pricing power has been eroded, low inflation has made price increases more obvious), but no solution is offered, only the effects of these problems; B: Incorrect – the only time reference in this paragraph is "in recent years", which does not show a sequence; C: Incorrect – while there are some examples offered in this paragraph, no definitions are presented; D: Incorrect – no listings or classifications are offered in this paragraph; E: Correct - The last paragraph presents the causes of problems (companies' pricing power has been eroded, low inflation has made price increases more obvious), and the consequences of said problems (So it is more difficult for a European car company, say, to raise its prices in America in response to a stronger euro).
Gabarito "E".

(ADVOGADO – BNDES – 2004 – CESGRANRIO) Check the correct statement about vocabulary.

(A) Remarkable (line 11) and uncommon are synonymous.
(B) Lively (line 12) is the opposite of deadly.
(C) Quarter (line 13) refers to a period of four months.
(D) Curbing (line 46) could be replaced by encouraging.
(E) These days (line 55) means actually.

(Vocabulary) A: Correct – in the context of the text, 'remarkable', here, means 'uncommon' in that it is not expected; B: Incorrect – 'lively', in the context of the text, means 'active'; the opposite would be 'inactive', not deadly, which means 'fatal' or 'lethal'; C: Incorrect – 'quarter' refers to a period of three months. In English economics, the fiscal year is split into 4 quarters, with each quarter consisting of three months; D: Incorrect – 'curbing' means to control with the intention of reducing; E: Incorrect – 'actually' is a false cognate in English. It means 'in reality' or 'in fact'. It is not necessarily related to time.
Gabarito "A".

(ADVOGADO – BNDES – 2004 – CESGRANRIO) Mark the correct statement concerning reference.

(A) Its (line 7) refers to euro.
(B) Those (line 23) refers to investors.
(C) Their (line 25) refers to investors.
(D) Ones (line 43) refers to European firms.
(E) It (line 64) refers to European car company.

(Grammar) A: Incorrect – The text explicitly says, "The dollar has fallen by 31% against the euro from its peak in July 2001", meaning that the dollar was at a peak in July and has fallen when compared to the euro; B: Incorrect – The text explicitly says, "The dollar used to be buoyant because investors expected to make more from dollar assets than from those denominated in other currencies", meaning that investors will make more from those [assets] denominated in other currencies than the dollar assets; C: Correct - the word "their" refers back to the word "they" in the previous sentence, "Now they are not so sure. Their worries over America's twin deficits…", which in turn refers back to investors in the previous sentence, "The dollar used to be buoyant because investors expected…". It is the investors that are not so sure and worried; D: Incorrect – The text explicitly says, "A rise in the euro against the dollar causes exports from European firms to become more expensive relative to American ones", meaning that American exports are cheaper than European exports; E: Incorrect – The word 'it' on line 64 it being used as what is known as the "dummy 'it'"; that is, it is used to create a style of sentence known as a 'cleft sentence', which emphasizes certain elements. In this sentence (So it is more difficult for a European car company, say, to raise its prices in America), 'it' refers to the situation, not the car company (The situation is more difficult for the car company).
Gabarito "C".

(ADVOGADO – BNDES – 2004 – CESGRANRIO) Mark the sentence that could also be completed with ON, as in "to pass on the effects" (line 67).

(A) The board meeting may be put _____ until next week.
(B) African nations always depended heavily _____ food imports.
(C) Because of the elections on Thursday, classes will be called _____ .
(D) The Minister's assistants have to carry _____ many administrative duties.
(E) You should be concerned if your application for a credit card has been turned _____ .

(Vocabulary) A: Incorrect – The context of this sentence requires the phrasal verb 'put back', which means 'delayed' or 'postponed'. This is due to the conjunction 'until' which means up to a specific moment in time; the phrasal verb 'put on', in this context, means 'hold', which is unsuitable here; B: Correct – The verb 'depend' requires the preposition 'on' in most cases; C: Incorrect – The context of this sentence requires the phrasal verb 'call off', which means 'canceled'. The elections would mean that classes would be cancelled; the phrasal verb 'call on' is unsuitable for this context; D: Incorrect – The context of this sentence requires the phrasal verb 'carry out', meaning 'perform'; the phrasal verb 'carry on' means 'continue', which is unsuitable for this context; E: Incorrect – The context of this sentence requires the phrasal verb 'turned down', meaning 'rejected'; the phrasal verb 'turned on' means 'started' or 'excited', both of which are unsuitable for this context.
Gabarito "B".

(ADVOGADO – BNDES – 2004 – CESGRANRIO) Current-account deficit" (line 27) means a deficit in the current account. Check the option in which the phrase is INCORRECTLY explained.

(A) A risk-taking, hard-working financial advisor = a financial advisor who takes risks and works hard.
(B) A four-million-dollar twelve-storey building = a building with twelve stories that is worth four million dollars.
(C) A three-hundred-page, double-spaced report = a report that has three hundred pages and is written with double space.
(D) Twenty green-colored ten-dollar bills = twenty bills of ten dollars, in the color green.
(E) Three financially-troubled government-owned companies = three financial companies that have caused troubles to the government.

(Vocabulary) A: Incorrect – The definition is correct: risk-taking = someone who takes risks / hard-working = someone who works hard; B: Incorrect – The definition is correct: four-million-dollar = a building worth four million dollars / twelve-storey = a building with twelve stories (floors); C: Incorrect - The definition is correct: three-hundred-page = a report with three hundred pages / double-spaced = written with double spaces; D: Incorrect - The definition is correct: ten-dollar = bills worth ten dollars each / green-colored = in the color green; E: Correct - The definition is incorrect: financially-troubled = companies with financial troubles, but not necessarily from the financial area / government-owned = the government owns the companies; they did not cause troubles to the government.

Note: This question refers to compound adjectives, which usually requires the use of hyphens. This phenomenon in English merely carries the two senses of the adjective (e.g. government-owned = owned by the government) to qualify the following noun (government-owned companies = companies owned by the government).
Gabarito "E".

(ADVOGADO – BNDES – 2004 – CESGRANRIO) Check the only item that DOES NOT contain an adjective used in the comparative form.

(A) "It may seem curious that the dollar is falling when America is enjoying a remarkable burst of growth and Europe looks far less lively." (lines 10-12)
(B) The dollar used to be buoyant because investors expected to make more from dollar assets than from those denominated in other currencies." (lines 22-24)

(C) "A rise in the euro against the dollar causes exports from European firms to become more expensive relative to American ones," (lines 41-43)
(D) "Similarly, American firms' products become relatively cheaper, both for Americans and for foreign buyers." (lines 44-45)
(E) "But there is reason to think that these days currency movements are not as effective as they once were in bringing economies into balance." (lines 55-57)

(Grammar) A: Incorrect – The word 'lively' is an adjective that means 'energetic' or 'dynamic'; Europe's 'lively' quality, or lack thereof, is compared with 'America's growth'; B: Correct – The comparison in this sentence compares noun ideas (make more [money]) and NOT adjective ideas; C: Incorrect – The word 'expensive' is an adjective, which is used to compare the prices of exports; D: Incorrect – The word 'cheaper' is the comparative form of the adjective 'cheap', which is being used to compare the prices of product; E: Incorrect – the word 'effective' is an adjective that is being used to compare the currency movements.
Gabarito "B".

(ADVOGADO – BNDES – 2004 – CESGRANRIO) Check the item in which the detached verb expresses a necessity.

(A) "It may seem curious that the dollar is falling…" (line 10)
(B) "…America must borrow $2 billion each business day." (lines 27-28)
(C) "How much further might the dollar fall?" (line 32)
(D) "… the dollar could drop a lot lower," (lines 34-35)
(E) "…a weaker dollar should thus help to cut America's (…) deficit." (lines 46-48)

(Grammar) A: Incorrect – The modal verb 'may' is used to show probability not necessity (It probably seems curious…); B: Correct – The modal verb 'must', in this context, is used to show necessity (America needs to borrow money); C: Incorrect – The modal verb 'might' is used to show probability not necessity (How much further will the dollar probably fall?); D: Incorrect – The modal verb 'could' is used to show possibility not necessity (it is possible that the dollar will drop a lot lower); E: Incorrect – The modal verb 'should' is used to show expectation not necessity (a cheaper dollar is expected to help…).
Gabarito "B".

(ADVOGADO – BNDES – 2004 – CESGRANRIO) Complete the text below so that it could be a possible and meaningful paragraph to continue the article you have read.

"Other factors also weaken the power of currency movements. Rather than _____ prices when their 'home' currency strengthens, foreign firms may hold prices and accept _____ margins, especially if they think the currency will weaken again or if they are determined to _____ the market share."

The appropriate words are:

(A) push up – higher – increase
(B) maintain – reduced – preserve
(C) reduce – unchanged – lose
(D) increase – affordable – reduce
(E) raise – lower – maintain

(Vocabulary) A: Incorrect – The part 'foreign firms may hold prices and accept _____ margins' would be contradictory if the word 'higher' were used. By holding prices, margins would not be higher; B: Incorrect – The word 'preserve' does not goes along 'market share'; C: Incorrect – It would seem odd to affirm that a foreign firm is 'determined to lose market share'. Foreign firms want to increase or maintain market share. D: Incorrect - It would seem odd to affirm that a foreign firm is 'determined to reduce market share'. Foreign firms want to increase or maintain market share; E: Correct – The part 'Rather than raise prices… foreign firms may hold or lower margins' is coherent grammatically and logically. Foreign firms are usually determined to increase or 'maintain market share'.
Gabarito "E".

(ADVOGADO – BNDES – 2004 – CESGRANRIO) Check the option which DOES NOT have a verb in the passive voice.

(A) "… the single European currency was launched in 1999," (lines 5-6)
(B) "…but are expected to grow by only 0.5% this year…" (line 17)
(C) "The dollar used to be buoyant because investors expected to make more from dollar assets…" (lines 2223)
(D) "… companies' pricing power has been eroded around the world." (lines 62-63)
(E) "According to a study cited in the report," (line 66)

(Grammar) A: Incorrect – The verb phrase 'was launched' is the passive voice (to be launched); B: Incorrect – The verb phrase 'are expected' is the passive voice (to be expected); C: Correct - There is no passive voice structure in this example. The verb phrase 'used to be buoyant' lacks a past participle, while all other verbs are in the active voice; D: Incorrect – The verb phrase 'has been eroded' is the passive voice (to be eroded) in the present perfect tense; E: Incorrect – The reduced verb phrase 'cited' is the passive voice (to be cited – which was cited). This could be misleading due to the reduced structure.
Gabarito "C".

GLOBAL PETROLEUM

The outlook for oil supply and demand fundamentals over the next two years points to an easing of the oil market balance in 2009. Higher non-OPEC production and planned additions to OPEC
5   capacity should more than offset expected moderate world oil demand growth, and relieve some of the tightness in the market. As a result, surplus production capacity could grow from its current level of under 2 million to over 4 million barrels per day by the end of
10 2009. This balance suggests some price softening, although delays or downward revisions in capacity additions in both OPEC and non-OPEC nations could alter the outlook, as could OPEC production decisions.
World oil consumption is expected to rise by
15 1.6 million barrels per day in both 2008 and 2009 compared with the estimated 1 million barrels per day increase recorded last year. The larger volume gains expected in 2008 and 2009 compared with 2007 mainly reflect higher consumption expected in the
20 Organization for Economic Cooperation and Development (OECD), particularly Europe, where weather factors constrained oil consumption last year. Projections of continued strong world economic growth will spur oil consumption gains in a number of non-
25 OECD markets, including China, non-OECD Asia, and the Middle East countries, over the next 2 years.

OPEC members' production decisions and the pace and timing of capacity additions in a number of countries will play a key role in determining oil market trends over the next 2 years. The Energy Information Administration projects that OPEC crude oil production will average about 32.6 million barrels per day in 2008 and 31.8 million barrels per day in 2009 compared with the 31.7 million barrels per day seen during the fourth quarter of 2007. Increased production from Angola, Saudi Arabia, Kuwait, and Iraq boosted OPEC's crude output during the fourth quarter 2007.

Non-OPEC production is expected to rise by about 0.9 million barrels per day in 2008 and by 1.6 million barrels per day in 2009. This compares with a gain of 0.6 million barrels per day recorded last year. Azerbaijan, Russia, Canada, Brazil, the United States, China, Sudan, and Kazakhstan account for a large share of the gain in non-OPEC production growth in 2008 and 2009. Increases in these nations will more than offset expected declines in production in a number of countries including Mexico, the United Kingdom, and Norway.

EIA – Energy Information Administration Short-Term Energy Outlook, January 8, 2008

(ADVOGADO – ANP – 2008 – CESGRANRIO) The purpose of the first paragraph is to

(A) announce that world oil production capacity will soon increase to 4 million barrels per day.
(B) criticize both OPEC and non-OPEC countries for causing unexpected delays in production.
(C) discuss the prospects for global oil supply and demand until the end of the year 2009.
(D) predict increasing losses in the oil markets if the surplus production capacity remains unaltered.
(E) report what will certainly happen in the international oil market over the next two years.

(Interpretation) A: Incorrect – The text explicitly says, "As a result, surplus production capacity could grow from its current level of under 2 million to over 4 million barrels per day by the end of 2009", meaning that the capacity will grow, not the production itself; B: Incorrect – The text explicitly says, "although delays or downward revisions in capacity additions in both OPEC and non-OPEC nations could alter the outlook", meaning that the delays are not in production, but rather in capacity additions; C: Correct – The text explicitly says, "The outlook for oil supply and demand fundamentals over the next two years points to an easing of the oil market balance in 2009"; D: Incorrect – The first paragraph of the text does not focus on losses. It mentions price softening, but these are not properly losses; E: Incorrect – The text explicitly says, "This balance suggests some price softening, although delays or downward revisions in capacity additions in both OPEC and non-OPEC nations could alter the outlook, as could OPEC production decisions", meaning that nothing is certain.
Gabarito "C".

(ADVOGADO – ANP – 2008 – CESGRANRIO) According to Paragraph 2, oil consumption

(A) achieved a record-breaking increase in the world last year.
(B) fell sharply in Europe in 2007 due to weather factors.
(C) is likely to speed economic growth in a number of markets.
(D) may increase in 2008-2009 at a higher rate than in 2007.
(E) will certainly grow in OECD countries for the next 2 years.

(Interpretation) A: Incorrect – The text explicitly says, "World oil consumption is expected to rise by 1.6 million barrels per day in both 2008 and 2009 compared with the estimated 1 million barrels per day increase recorded last year", meaning that in 2007, records (registered data) showed 1 million barrels per day. The text does not claim this is a record (highest ever achieved); B: Incorrect – The text explicitly says, "particularly Europe, where weather factors constrained oil consumption last year", meaning oil consumption was low, but this does not suggest that it fell sharply; C: Incorrect – The text explicitly says, "Projections of continued strong world economic growth will spur oil consumption gains in a number of non-OECD markets", meaning the economic growth will speed oil consumption, not the other way round; D: Correct – The text explicitly says, "The larger volume gains expected in 2008 and 2009 compared with 2007"; E: Incorrect – The text explicitly says, "economic growth will spur oil consumption gains in a number of non-OECD markets, including China, non-OECD Asia, and the Middle East countries".
Gabarito "D".

(ADVOGADO – ANP – 2008 – CESGRANRIO) Concerning the oil production of both OPEC and non-OPEC members the text informs that

(A) OPEC crude oil production is expected to grow steadily over the next two years.
(B) the oil output of Mexico and Norway, among other countries, decreased last year.
(C) non-OPEC countries' daily production averaged six hundred thousand barrels of oil in 2007.
(D) an upward trend in oil production of non-OPEC nations is expected in 2008-2009.
(E) Angola, Saudi Arabia, Kuwait and Iraq could not pump any oil in the first three quarters of 2007.

(Interpretation) A: Incorrect – The text explicitly says, "OPEC crude oil production will average about 32.6 million barrels per day in 2008 and 31.8 million barrels per day in 2009 compared with the 31.7 million barrels per day seen during the fourth quarter of 2007", meaning that OPEC crude oil production will not grow steadily, but rather remain stable; B: Incorrect – The text explicitly says, "Increases in these nations will more than offset expected declines in production in a number of countries including Mexico, the United Kingdom, and Norway", meaning that future production is expected to decline, not that of last year; C: Incorrect – The text explicitly says, "Non-OPEC production is expected to rise by about 0.9 million barrels per day in 2008 and by 1.6 million barrels per day in 2009. This compares with a gain of 0.6 million barrels per day recorded last year", meaning that the increase in production in 2007 was 600,000 barrels. This was not the daily production, but rather the increase; D: Correct – The text explicitly says, "Non-OPEC production is expected to rise by about 0.9 million barrels per day in 2008 and by 1.6 million barrels per day in 2009"; E: Incorrect – The text explicitly says, "Increased production from Angola, Saudi Arabia, Kuwait, and Iraq boosted OPEC's crude output during the fourth quarter 2007".
Gabarito "D".

(ADVOGADO – ANP – 2008 – CESGRANRIO) The sentence in which "should" is used in the same sense as in "… planned additions to OPEC capacity should more than offset…" (lines 4-5) is:

(A) I should say that the salaries make up very nearly two thirds of the budget
(B) If you should be fired, your health benefits will not be automatically cut off.
(C) In such cases the officer should first give notice to those in the house.

(D) Should he go back to the office and wait for you to telephone?
(E) This year's treasury deficit should be six billion dollars or more.

(Grammar) A: Incorrect – The modal verb 'should' in this context is used as a more formal and polite form of 'would'; B: Incorrect – The modal verb 'should' in this sentence is used in a subjunctive (conditional) tense. This is possible in zero and first conditional structures to give a more formal and polite tone; C: Incorrect – The modal verb 'should' in this sentence is used to establish rules or suggestions; D: Incorrect – The modal verb 'should' in this sentence is used to ask for a suggestion; E: Correct – The modal verb 'should' is used to show expectation, as in the verb 'should' in "...planned additions to OPEC capacity should more than offset..." (planned additions to OPEC are expected to more than offset...).
Gabarito "E".

(ADVOGADO – ANP – 2008 – CESGRANRIO) The statement which describes accurately the meaning relationship between the pair of words is

(A) "offset" (line 5) means compensate for.
(B) "softening" (line 10) is the opposite of reduction.
(C) "constrained" (line 22) and restrained are antonyms.
(D) "spur" (line 24) could be replaced by discourage.
(E) "boosted" (line 36) and hindered are synonyms.

(Vocabulary) A: Correct – 'offset' carries the sense of 'compensate for' something; B: Incorrect – 'softening' is not the opposite of reduction, but rather a synonym; C: Incorrect – 'constrained' is a synonym of 'restrained'; D: Incorrect – 'spur' means 'encourage', thus it cannot be replaced by 'discourage'; D: Incorrect – 'boosted' means 'increased'; 'hindered' means 'delayed' or 'obstructed'; they are antonyms, not synonyms.
Gabarito "A".

Free enterprise principle nowadays is subject to certain regulations imposed by States. This is reflected in the guidelines of the state economic policy applicable to specific areas of the market economy, such as hydrocarbon operations. Brazilian 1988 Constitution, in its first article, when dealing with the fundamental principles of the Brazilian Federative Republic, sets up the social value of the free initiative. This free initiative required by the Brazilian Constitution is not new to the Brazilian Constitutional Law. All previous Brazilian constitutions, except the Republican Constitution of 1891, have always considered the free initiative a reflection of human freedom, sometimes a way to build a more just and fraternal society. In Brazil, free competition and free enterprise have given rise to a constitutional principle, according to which the establishment of a monopoly in the free market is prohibited, as provided by article 5 of Law 4.137 about the repression of the economic power abuse, dated October 9, 1962. This prohibition is directly applied to economic monopoly while a legalized monopoly established exclusively in favor of the State is allowed in certain fields. Among these fields, we can mention the right to engage in prospecting and exploration for production, import, export and transportation of oil and natural gas as well as refining of national or foreign oil. Brazilian oil and gas regulation rests upon the concept that deposits are real property, distinct from the soil, to the effect of exploration and benefit. This is determined by the Federal Constitution of Brazil, being, nevertheless, granted the product of the mining to concessionaires.

Internet: <http://www.bomchilgroup.org/brasep97.html> (with adaptations).

(ADVOGADO – PETROBRÁS – 2003 – CESPE) According to the text above, judge the following items.

(1) Free enterprises do not have to follow regulations.
(2) State economic policy can only deal with hydrocarbon operations.
(3) Brazil has some particular guidelines for certain areas of its market economy.
(4) Free initiative principles can be found in the Brazilian latest constitution.
(5) The Republican Constitution dated 1891 was the first one to account for the fundamental principles of the free initiative in Brazil.

(Interpretation) 1: Incorrect – The text explicitly says, "Free enterprise principle nowadays is subject to certain regulations imposed by States"; 2: Incorrect – The text explicitly says, "state economic policy applicable to specific areas of the market economy, such as hydrocarbon operations", meaning that this is an example of one of the specific areas, but not the only one; 3: Correct – The text explicitly says, "the guidelines of the state economic policy applicable to specific areas of the market economy"; 4: Correct – The text explicitly says, "Brazilian 1988 Constitution, in its first article, when dealing with the fundamental principles of the Brazilian Federative Republic, sets up the social value of the free initiative"; 5: Incorrect – The text explicitly says, "All previous Brazilian constitutions, except the Republican Constitution of 1891, have always considered the free initiative a reflection of human freedom", meaning the Republican Constitution did NOT account for the fundamental principles of the free initiative in Brazil;
Gabarito 1E, 2E, 3C, 4C, 5E

(ADVOGADO – PETROBRÁS – 2003 – CESPE) Judge the following items.

(1) Free initiative is always a way to promote social solidarity.
(2) In accordance with article 5, Law 4.137, monopolies are forbidden, in Brazil.
(3) In Brazil, the state monopoly is allowed for some specific areas.
(4) Brazilian oil and gas deposits are state-owned.
(5) In Brazil, under no circumstances can concessions be granted to private enterprises regarding the exploration of mineral deposits.

(Interpretation) 1: Incorrect – The text explicitly says, "the free initiative a reflection of human freedom, sometimes a way to build a more just and fraternal society", not always; 2: Correct – The text explicitly says, "the establishment of a monopoly in the free market is prohibited, as provided by article 5 of Law 4.137"; 3: Correct – The text explicitly says, "a legalized monopoly established exclusively in favor of the State is allowed in certain fields"; 4: Correct – The text says, "Brazilian oil and gas regulation rests upon the concept that deposits are real property, distinct from the soil, to the effect of exploration and benefit", meaning that the State can explore and benefit from its own oil and gas deposits; 5: Incorrect – The text explicitly says, "This is determined by the Federal Constitution of Brazil, being, nevertheless, granted the product of the mining to concessionaires".
Gabarito 1E, 2C, 3C, 4C, 5E

Text LI-I

PETROBRAS became the latest oil group to benefit from last year's surge in oil prices when the Brazilian company reported that net profits in 2000 had more than quadrupled to R$ 9.94 bn (US$ 4.97 bn) — the highest figure ever recorded by a Brazilian company.

The rise in net profits was the result of increases in production and the company's efforts to scale up bureaucracy.

Under the leadership of Henri Philippe Reichstul, who took over as president in 1999, PETROBRAS has embarked on a US$ 33 bn investment plan over five years to virtually double oil and gas production, clean up the company's financial affairs and expand abroad.

In August last year, PETROBRAS boosted its profile in the international investment community with a successful US$ 4 bn share offering, the largest made by a Brazilian company.

However, the group's efforts to modernize its image suffered a setback in December when the government forced it to abandon a plan to change its name to "PETROBRAX" which was designed to reflect its increasing international presence.

Internet: <http://news.ft.com/news/worldnews/americas> (with adaptations).

(ADVOGADO – PETROBRÁS – 2001 – CESPE) From text LI-I, it can be gathered that

(1) it took some time for PETROBRAS to benefit from 2000's increase in oil prices.
(2) in 2000, the relation between dollars and reais was, at least once, one to two, respectively.
(3) US$ 4.97 bn means four billion and ninety-seven dollars.
(4) never before last year, had any Brazilian company had the same financial performance as PETROBRAS did.
(5) PETROBRAS net profit added up to R$ 39.76 bn in 2000.

(Interpretation) 1: Gabarito: Correct / Nosso Gabarito: Incorrect – The text uses the word 'latest' to refer to Petrobras' benefits from the increase in oil prices. This term does not necessarily mean that the firm took a long time to benefit from the increase in prices, but rather that it was the most recent to record such benefits. It suggests that other benefited before Petrobras, but there is nothing explicit in the text that refers to the amount of time Petrobras took to feel such benefits; 2: Correct – The references to the amounts in both dollar and real account for a one to two exchange rate (R$ 9.94 bn (US$ 4.97 bn)); 3: Incorrect – US$ 4.97 means four billion and 970 million dollars; 4: Correct – The text explicitly says, "the highest figure ever recorded by a Brazilian company", meaning that no other company had recorded such a figure; 5: Incorrect – The text explicitly says, "net profits in 2000 had more than quadrupled to R$ 9.94 bn", meaning that the end result was R$ 9.94 bn.

Gabarito 1C, 2C, 3E, 4C, 5E

(ADVOGADO – PETROBRÁS – 2001 – CESPE) Based on text LI-I, it can be concluded that

(1) at least three factors contributed to the rise in PETROBRAS's net profits.
(2) Henri Philippe Reichstul became PETROBRAS's president the year before last.
(3) three goals were settled when Henri Philippe Reichstul took over PETROBRAS's presidency.
(4) PETROBRAS's name should be kept as it is according to a special group created to modernize its image.
(5) PETROBRAS not only got the highest profit ever recorded by a Brazilian company, but it was also the one to offer the largest share in Brazil.

(Interpretation) 1: Incorrect – The text explicitly says, "The rise in net profits was the result of increases in production and the company's efforts to scale up bureaucracy", which presents two factors, not three; 2: Correct – The text explicitly says, "Under the leadership of Henri Philippe Reichstul, who took over as president in 1999"; 3: Correct – The text explicitly says, "plan over five years to virtually double oil and gas production, clean up the company's financial affairs and expand abroad", which totals three goals; 4: Incorrect - The text explicitly says, "the group's efforts to modernize its image suffered a setback in December when the government forced it to abandon a plan to change its name to "PETROBRAX", meaning the special group suggested the name change; 5: Correct – The text explicitly says, "the Brazilian company reported that net profits in 2000 had more than quadrupled to R$ 9.94 bn (US$ 4.97 bn) — the highest figure ever recorded by a Brazilian company" and "In August last year, PETROBRAS boosted its profile in the international investment community with a successful US$ 4 bn share offering, the largest made by a Brazilian company".

Gabarito 1E, 2C, 3C, 4E, 5C

Text LI-II

1 In 1995, the stated-owned PETROBRAS lost the oil monopoly it enjoyed since 1953 and is now starting to face competition. It still dominates almost every segment of the
4 country's upstream and downstream oil industry. But the company is now changing at a fast pace. The new management is grafting modern structures onto the company
7 by dividing it into business units, creating profit centers and introducing benchmarking* for all activities. Though, by law, the government must hold a controlling majority in the
10 company, it plans to sell excess stock, raising a minimum of about US$ 2 billion.

*benchmarking – standard example or point of reference for making comparisons.

Internet: <http://www.buybrazil.org/econ.html> (with adaptations).

(ADVOGADO – PETROBRÁS – 2001 – CESPE) From text LI-II, it can be deduced that

(1) PETROBRAS lost the oil monopoly 48 years ago.
(2) PETROBRAS controls every segment of Brazil's up and downstream oil industry.
(3) PETROBRAS has always been facing competition.
(4) the new management is introducing slow changes in the company.
(5) the modern structures are based on decentralization of PETROBRAS's activities.

(Interpretation) 1: Incorrect – The text explicitly says, "In 1995, the stated-owned PETROBRAS lost the oil monopoly it enjoyed since 1953 and is now starting to face competition", meaning the loss was 42 years ago, not 48; 2: Incorrect – The text explicitly says, "It still dominates almost every segment of the country's upstream and downstream oil industry", which is not every segment; 3: Incorrect – The text explicitly says, "PETROBRAS lost the oil monopoly it enjoyed since 1953 and is now starting to face competition", meaning that the company didn't always face competition; 4: Incorrect – The text explicitly says, "But the company is now changing at a fast pace. The new management is grafting modern structures onto the company"; 5: Correct - The text explicitly says, "The new management is grafting modern structures onto the company by dividing it into business units", which means it is decentralizing its activities.

Gabarito 1E, 2E, 3E, 4E, 5C

(ADVOGADO – PETROBRÁS – 2001 – CESPE) In text LI-II,

(1) "stated-owned" ($\ell.1$) means owned by the state.
(2) "all activities" ($\ell.8$) is the same as every activity.
(3) "Though" ($\ell.8$) can be correctly replaced by Although.
(4) "must" ($\ell.9$) is synonymous with can.
(5) "it" ($\ell.10$) refers to PETROBRAS.

(Grammar) 1: Correct – The compound adjective has this meaning; 2: Correct – 'all' is used for the plural form of the noun, while 'every' is used for the singular form; however, both refer to the group or plural idea; 3: Correct – 'though' is synonymous with 'although'; however, it is more informal; 4: Incorrect – The modal verb 'must', in the text, refers to obligation (the government must hold a controlling majority in the company); the modal verb 'can' is used to refer to ability or permission; 5: Incorrect – The text explicitly says, "Though, by law, the government must hold a controlling majority in the company, it plans to sell excess stock', in which it refers back to the subject used in the first clause (the government).

Gabarito 1C, 2C, 3C, 4E, 5E

1 Because we live next door to the United States of America and share some of their programming and commercials, most moviegoers in Ontario are probably more
4 familiar with the American system than our home-grown one. However, our systems are very different.
Films and trailers are classified in the United States
7 of America by the Rating Board of the Motion Picture Association of America (MPAA), located in Los Angeles. This industry-sponsored Rating Board consists of 13.
10 members who serve for varying periods of time. There are no special qualifications for Board membership except for having a shared parenthood experience, an intelligent
13 maturity, and an ability to put themselves in the role of most American parents. The Board is funded through fees charged to producers and distributors for the ratings of their
16 films.
The MPAA Rating Board members, like those of the Ontario Film Review Board (OFRB), do not classify movies
19 on personal judgements of quality. Their judgements are based on specific guidelines in areas including theme, violence, language, nudity, sexuality, drug use, and others.
22 Like the OFRB, they consider the film in its entirety, and take context into account in classification decisions.
The first main area of difference between the Ontario
25 classification system and the American one is that the OFRB is a government body established by statute that requires distributors to submit their films for classification. In the United States of America, the rating system is a voluntary one that is administered by the movie industry through the MPAA.

Internet: <http://www.ofrb.gov.on.ca/english/page14.htm> (with adaptations).

(ADVOGADO – ANCINE – 2005 – CESPE) Based in the text above, judge the following items.

(1) Ontarians and Americans are always watching the same programming and commercials.
(2) Possibly the majority of Ontarians moviegoers know more about the American System of Films and Trailers Classification than about their own.
(3) "However" ($\ell.5$) means Nevertheless.
(4) American and Ontarian systems are entirely alike.
(5) No qualifications whatsoever are required to become a member of the MPAA.
(6) "Board" ($\ell.14$) refers to "MPAA" ($\ell.8$).
(7) Both MPAA and OFRB members classify movies according to their personal judgements of quality and some specific guidelines.

(Interpretation) 1: Incorrect – The text explicitly says, "Because we live next door to the United States of America and share some of their programming and commercials, most moviegoers in Ontario", The text doesn't state that all Ontarians always follow American programming; 2: Correct – The text explicitly says, "most moviegoers in Ontario are probably more familiar with the American system than our home-grown one"; 3: Correct – 'however' and 'nevertheless' are conjuncts that both refer to contrast (a meaning similar to the coordinating conjunction 'but'); 4: Incorrect – The text explicitly says, "our systems are very different"; 5: Incorrect – The text explicitly says, "There are no special qualifications for Board membership except for having a shared parenthood experience, an intelligent maturity, and an ability to put themselves in the role of most American parents", meaning there is no requirement for special qualification, but there are others; 6: Incorrect – The text explicitly says, "the Rating Board of the Motion Picture Association of America (MPAA)", meaning that the 'Board' is part of the MPAA, but not the entire Association per se; 7: Incorrect – The text explicitly says, "The MPAA Rating Board members, like those of the Ontario Film Review Board (OFRB), do not classify movies on personal judgements of quality";

Gabarito 1E, 2C, 3C, 4E, 5E, 6E, 7E

(ADVOGADO – ANCINE – 2005 – CESPE) Judge the following items.

(1) Whereas the OFRB is a public institution, the American Rating System is private.
(2) "one" ($\ell.29$) refers to "rating system" ($\ell.28$).

(Interpretation) 1: Correct – The text explicitly says, "the OFRB is a government body" and "In the United States of America, the rating system is a voluntary one that is administered by the movie industry through the MPAA", meaning the former is a public institution (government) and the latter private (movie industry); 2: Correct – The word 'one' represents the previous noun (rating system) so as not to repeat it in the same sentence.

Gabarito 1C, 2C

Food control systems: integrated farm-to-table concept

1 The objective of reduced risk can be achieved most effectively by the principle of prevention throughout the production, processing and marketing chain. To achieve
4 maximum consumer protection, it is essential that safety and quality be built into food products from production through to consumption. This calls for a comprehensive and
7 integrated farm-to-table approach in which the producer, processor, transporter, vendor, and consumer all play a vital role in ensuring food safety and quality.
10 It is impossible to provide adequate protection to the consumer by merely sampling and analyzing the final product. The introduction of preventive measures at all

13 stages of the food production and distribution chain, rather than only inspection and rejection at the final stage, makes better economic sense, because unsuitable products can be
16 identified earlier along the chain. The more economic and effective strategy is to entrust food producers and operators with primary responsibility for food safety and quality.
19 Government regulators are then responsible for auditing performance of the food system through monitoring and surveillance activities and for enforcing legal and regulatory
22 requirements.
    Food hazards and quality loss may occur at a variety of points in the food chain, and it is difficult and
25 expensive to test for their presence. A well-structured, preventive approach that controls processes is the preferred method for improving food safety and quality. Many but not
28 all potential food hazards can be controlled along the food chain through the application of good practices agricultural, manufacturing and hygienic.

Internet: <http://www.fao.org> (with adaptations).

(ADVOGADO – ANVISA – 2004 – CESPE) According to the text above, judge the following items.

(1) To improve food quality, it is really crucial that safety measures be implemented at the processing stage.
(2) In the farm-to-table approach, products are sold directly by farmers to consumers.
(3) Transporters and vendors won't play any significant role along the food production and distribution chain.
(4) Primary responsibility for food safety and quality should rest with producers and operators.
(5) Prevention eliminates all potential food hazards.

(Interpretation) 1: Correct – The text explicitly says, "To achieve maximum consumer protection, it is essential that safety and quality be built into food products from production through to consumption", which includes all stages between production and consumption, that is, processing, too; 2: Incorrect – The text explicitly says, "This calls for a comprehensive and integrated farm-to-table approach in which the producer, processor, transporter, vendor, and consumer all play a vital role in ensuring food safety and quality", meaning that safety should be a recurring topic in every step of food processing. It does not mean that products are sold directly to consumers; 3: Incorrect - The text explicitly says, "This calls for a comprehensive and integrated farm-to-table approach in which the producer, processor, transporter, vendor, and consumer all play a vital role in ensuring food safety and quality"; 4: Correct – The text explicitly says, "The more economic and effective strategy is to entrust food producers and operators with primary responsibility for food safety and quality"; 5: Incorrect – The text explicitly says, "Many but not all potential food hazards can be controlled along the food chain through the application of good practices", meaning that prevention does NOT eliminate ALL hazards.
Gabarito 1C, 2E, 3E, 4C, 5E.

(ADVOGADO – ANVISA – 2004 – CESPE) Judge the following items, related to the text above.

(1) The sentence "it is essential that safety and quality be built into food products" (ℓ.4-5) follows the same structure as it's vital that he go straight to the house.
(2) "their presence" (ℓ.25) refers to food hazards and quality loss.

(Grammar) 1: Correct – The structure is known as a cleft sentence, which is used to emphasize the adjective (essential / vital). The structure requires the use of a subjunctive verb structure (be built into / go). Both sentences contain this format; 2: Correct – The text says, "Food hazards and quality loss may occur at a variety of points in the food chain, and it is difficult and expensive to test for their presence" (to test for the presence of food hazards and quality loss).
Gabarito 1C, 2C.

(ADVOGADO – ANVISA – 2004 – CESPE) In the text above,

(1) "achieve" (ℓ.3) is to accomplish as "hazards" (ℓ.23) is to security.
(2) "calls for" (ℓ.6) means requires.
(3) "rather than" (ℓ.13-14) could be correctly replaced by instead of with no change in meaning.

(Vocabulary) 1: Incorrect – 'achieve' is a synonym for 'accomplish', while 'hazard' means 'danger' or 'risk', and 'security' means 'safety'; 2: Correct – The phrasal verb 'call for' means require; 3: Correct – 'rather than' and 'instead of' are synonymous and interchangeable in this sentence.

TEXT I

Africa's Oil

The world is looking to West Africa for its next big energy bet. But oil can be a curse as much as a blessing. This time, which will it be?

(TIME, June 11, 2007)

(ADVOGADO – ELETROBRÁS – 2006 – NCE/UFRJ) This text is about oil that Africa may:

(A) import;
(B) burn;
(C) have;
(D) control;
(E) donate.

(Interpretation) A: Incorrect – The text explicitly says, "The world is looking to West Africa for its next big energy bet', meaning that the world believes that Africa has oil"; B: Incorrect – The text focuses on the possibility that Africa may have oil, not on its consumption; C: Correct - The text explicitly says, "The world is looking to West Africa for its next big energy bet', meaning that the world believes that Africa has oil"; D: Incorrect – The text explicitly says, "The world is looking to West Africa for its next big energy bet', suggesting that control may go to other countries in the world, not to Africa; E: Incorrect – The text does not cogitate how the negotiations of the oil in question will be handled (donated? Imported?).
Gabarito "C".

(ADVOGADO – ELETROBRÁS – 2006 – NCE/UFRJ) The final sentence introduces a:

(A) certainty;
(B) solution;
(C) warning;
(D) surprise;
(E) doubt.

(Grammar) A: Incorrect – The final sentence is a question that raises doubt, not certainty; B: Incorrect – The final sentence is a question that raises doubt; it does not offer a solution; C: Incorrect - The final sentence is a question that raises doubt; it does not issue a warning; D: Incorrect - The final sentence is a question that raises doubt; it does not present a surprise; E: Correct - The final sentence is a question that raises doubt.
Gabarito "E".

(ADVOGADO – ELETROBRÁS – 2006 – NCE/UFRJ) next in "its next big energy bet" indicates:

(A) space;
(B) time;
(C) size;
(D) length;
(E) weight.

(Vocabulary) A: Incorrect – 'space' refers to 'place' or 'area', while 'next' refers to 'time' or 'order'; B: Correct – 'next' refers to 'time' or 'order'; C: Incorrect – 'size' refers to 'dimension', while 'next' refers to 'time' or 'order'; D: Incorrect – 'length' refers to 'physical size' or 'duration', while 'next' refers to 'time' or 'order'; E: Incorrect – 'weight' refers to 'mass' or 'heaviness', while 'next' refers to 'time' or 'order'.
Gabarito "B".

Note: 'next' refers to 'order' in the sense that there was a former energy bet, and West Africa is the next in the order of bets.

(ADVOGADO – ELETROBRÁS – 2006 – NCE/UFRJ) The underlined word in "oil can be a curse" implies:

(A) permission;
(B) prohibition;
(C) consent;
(D) certainty;
(E) possibility.

(Grammar) E: Correct - 'can', in this sentence, refers to possibilities, not to permission, prohibition, consent or certainty. (It is possible that oil is a curse).
Gabarito "E".

(ADVOGADO – ELETROBRÁS – 2006 – NCE/UFRJ) as much as in "a curse as much as a blessing" signals a:

(A) contrast;
(B) conclusion;
(C) condition;
(D) comparison;
(E) consequence.

(Grammar) D: Correct – 'as much as' is a comparative structure, and not one used for contrast, conclusion, condition or consequence. (In a comparison, oil is both a curse and a blessing).
Gabarito "D".

TEXT II

RECYCLE CITY: The Road to Curitiba
By ARTHUR LUBOW

On Saturday mornings, children gather to paint and draw in the main downtown shopping street of Curitiba, in southern Brazil. More than just a charming tradition, the child's play commemorates a key victory in a hard-fought, ongoing war.
5   Back in 1972, the new mayor of the city, an architect and urban planner named Jaime Lerner, ordered a lightning transformation of six blocks of the street into a pedestrian zone. The change was recommended in a master plan for the city that was approved six years earlier, but fierce objections
10 from the downtown merchants blocked its implementation. Lerner instructed his secretary of public works to institute the change quickly and asked how long it would take. "He said he needed four months," Lerner recalled recently. "I said, 'Forty-eight hours.' He said, 'You're crazy.' I said, 'Yes, I'm crazy, but do it in 48 hours.'"

(from http:// www.nytimes.com on July 19th, 2007)

(ADVOGADO – ELETROBRÁS – 2006 – NCE/UFRJ) The plan described was to create a:

(A) parking lot;
(B) traffic-free area;
(C) shopping mall;
(D) protected playground;
(E) bus terminal.

(Interpretation) A: Incorrect – The text explicitly says, "a lightning transformation of six blocks of the street into a pedestrian zone", meaning that the area would be for pedestrians, not vehicles; B: Correct – The text explicitly says, "a lightning transformation of six blocks of the street into a pedestrian zone", meaning that the area would have no vehicles; C: Incorrect – The text explicitly says, "children gather to paint and draw in the main downtown shopping street of Curitiba", meaning that the street has lots of shops, not that it is a closed, privately-owned building with shops in it (a mall); D: Incorrect – The text reveals that children use the space to paint on Saturday mornings, but this does not constitute a playground; E: Incorrect – There is no mention of a 'bus terminal' in the text.
Gabarito "B".

(ADVOGADO – ELETROBRÁS – 2006 – NCE/UFRJ) The text implies that the project, when started, was implemented:

(A) rapidly;
(B) slowly;
(C) cautiously;
(D) gradually;
(E) carefully.

(Vocabulary) A: Correct – The text explicitly says, "a lightning transformation of six blocks of the street into a pedestrian zone", meaning that the implementation of the project was carried out 'rapidly', and not slowly, cautiously, gradually or carefully.
Gabarito "A".

(ADVOGADO – ELETROBRÁS – 2006 – NCE/UFRJ) The celebration mentioned occurs:

(A) on weekends;
(B) on Mondays;
(C) in the afternoon;
(D) once a month;
(E) in 48 hours.

(Interpretation) A: Correct – The text explicitly says, "On Saturday mornings, children gather to paint and draw in the main downtown shopping street of Curitiba, in southern Brazil".
Gabarito "A".

(ADVOGADO – ELETROBRÁS – 2006 – NCE/UFRJ) The text refers to a project created:

(A) one year before;
(B) last weekend;
(C) on a Thursday night;
(D) years ago;
(E) three days earlier.

(Interpretation) D: Correct – The text explicitly says, "The change was recommended in a master plan for the city that was approved six years earlier". "six years earlier = years ago".
Gabarito "D".

(ADVOGADO – ELETROBRÁS – 2006 – NCE/UFRJ) The city merchants were:

(A) hostile;
(B) supportive;

(C) happy;
(D) pleased;
(E) indifferent.

(Vocabulary) A: Correct – The text explicitly says, "but fierce objections from the downtown merchants blocked its implementation", meaning they were unreceptive and angry.
Gabarito "A".

(ADVOGADO – ELETROBRÁS – 2006 – NCE/UFRJ) The war mentioned (ℓ.4) was:

(A) deadly;
(B) short;
(C) difficult;
(D) glorious;
(E) light.

(Vocabulary) C: Correct – The war is described as being "a hard-fought" and "ongoing", meaning difficult and long.
Gabarito "C".

(ADVOGADO – ELETROBRÁS – 2006 – NCE/UFRJ) The underlined word in "children gather to paint and draw" (ℓ.1) can be replaced by:

(A) try;
(B) prepare;
(C) meet;
(D) dress;
(E) study.

(Vocabulary) C: Correct – 'gather' means 'come together' or 'meet'.
Gabarito "C".

(ADVOGADO – ELETROBRÁS – 2006 – NCE/UFRJ) main in "the main downtown shopping street" (ℓ.2) means:

(A) messy;
(B) narrow;
(C) peripheral;
(D) principal;
(E) side.

(Vocabulary) A: Incorrect – 'messy' means 'disorganized'; B: Incorrect – 'narrow' is the opposite of 'wide'; C: Incorrect – 'peripheral' means 'secondary'; D: Correct – 'main' is a synonym for 'principal'; E: Incorrect – 'side' means 'lateral part'.
Gabarito "D".

(ADVOGADO – ELETROBRÁS – 2006 – NCE/UFRJ) "a key victory" (ℓ.4) means that the victory is:

(A) irrelevant;
(B) important;
(C) irresponsible;
(D) interesting;
(E) illegal.

(Vocabulary) A: Incorrect – 'irrelevant' means 'unrelated'; B: Correct – 'important' is a synonym for 'key' or 'vital'; C: Incorrect – 'irresponsible' means 'negligent'; D: Incorrect - 'interesting' means 'appealing' or 'fascinating'; E: Incorrect – 'illegal' means 'unlawful' or 'illicit'.
Gabarito "B".

(ADVOGADO – ELETROBRÁS – 2006 – NCE/UFRJ) When we say that a war is "ongoing" (ℓ.4), we mean it is:

(A) atypical;
(B) unique;
(C) intermittent;
(D) conventional;
(E) uninterrupted.

(Vocabulary) A: Incorrect – 'atypical' means 'unusual'; B: Incorrect – 'unique' means 'singular' or 'distinctive'; C: Incorrect – 'intermittent' means 'irregular' or 'sporadic'; D: Incorrect – 'conventional' means 'conformist' or 'predictable'; E: Correct – 'uninterrupted' is a synonym for 'ongoing' or 'continuous'.
Gabarito "E".

Read the text below, entitled "2005 – First Nine Months Results", in order to answer questions:

2005 – First Nine Months Results
Source: www.iii.org
Dec 27th, 2005 (Adapted)

The property/casualty insurance industry reported a statutory rate of return on average surplus of 9.5 percent through the first nine months of 2005. The results were released by the Insurance Services Office (ISO) and the Property Casualty Insurers Association of America (PCI). The financial performance of the industry during the period featured a surprisingly low combined ratio of 100, a figure that provided stunning proof of the resilience of the property/casualty insurance industry in the face of record catastrophe losses approaching $50 billion.

Insurers also benefited from rising interest rates and modest stock market gains to generate $40.7 billion on their investment portfolio. Policyholder surplus also climbed by $20.4 or 5.2 percent, through the first nine months, again a surprise. Profitability in the industry is still disappointingly low, however, coming in well below the expected 14 percent return for the benchmark Fortune 500 group of companies this year. Prior to Hurricane Katrina the industry was on a trajectory to record its highest level of profitability since 1987.

(ADVOGADO – IRB – 2006 – ESAF) In paragraph 1, the author refers to the resilience of the property/casualty insurance industry. In other words, its

(A) ability to recover.
(B) current financial losses.
(C) inability to predict trends.
(D) undeniable prosperity.
(E) delayed recovery.

(Interpretation) A: Correct – 'resilience' means it is strong and capable of recovering; B: Incorrect – 'financial losses' refer to unearned or misused money; C: Incorrect – 'inability to predict trends' refers to an 'incapacity to foresee the future'; D: Incorrect – 'undeniable prosperity' means 'unquestionable wealth'; E: Incorrect – 'delayed recovery' means 'late recuperation'.
Gabarito "A".

(ADVOGADO – IRB – 2006 – ESAF) The text

(A) focuses on the effort by insurers to reassess risk.
(B) predicts the losses to be faced by insurance companies.
(C) states that reinsurance prices will rise in 2006.
(D) foresees a sluggish growth for the sector in 2006.
(E) also recalls a period of financial growth.

(Interpretation) A: Incorrect – The text focuses on financial returns, financial performance, interest rates, gains and profitability. There is no mention of efforts to assess risk; B: Incorrect – The text mentions that "Profitability in the industry is still disappointingly low", but makes no prediction as to the losses; C: Incorrect – The only rise mentioned in the text is that of interest rates and some modest stock market gains, not prices; D: Incorrect – The text says, "Profitability in the industry is still disappointingly low, however, coming in well below the expected 14 percent return for the benchmark Fortune 500 group of companies this year", meaning that profitability is lower than expected, but this is not a clear projection of sluggish growth for the coming year; E: Correct – The text explicitly says, "Prior to Hurricane Katrina the industry was on a trajectory to record its highest level of profitability since 1987".
Gabarito "E".

(ADVOGADO – IRB – 2006 – ESAF) In paragraph 2, the author refers to the insurers' investment portfolio which

(A) is about to be created.
(B) has brought significant gains.
(C) produced fairly small gains.
(D) was beyond their expectations.
(E) has been impressively expanded.

(Grammar) A: Incorrect – The text explicitly says, "Insurers also benefited from rising interest rates and modest stock market gains to generate $40.7 billion on their investment portfolio", meaning that the portfolio already exists and is generating gains; B: Incorrect – The text explicitly says, "Insurers also benefited from rising interest rates and modest stock market gains to generate $40.7 billion on their investment portfolio", not significant gains; C: Correct – 'modest gains' is synonymous with 'very small gains'; D: Incorrect – Insurers benefited, but 'modest gains' are not beyond expectations; E: Incorrect – The text refers to the values and financial gains of the portfolio, not the reach or size of it.
Gabarito "C".

Read the text below, which is entitled "Avian Influenza (Bird Flu)" in order to answer questions:

Avian Influenza (Bird Flu)
Source: www.iii.org
Dec 2005 (Adapted)

A current influenza outbreak, formally called H5N1 after two distinctive proteins on the flu virus, (but commonly referred to as bird or avian flu), has so far mainly affected birds. However, four countries – Thailand, Vietnam, Indonesia and Cambodia – have reported a total of 120 human cases of the H5N1 flu since 1997. These people are thought to have caught the disease by their contact with infected poultry. There has been no known human-to-human transmission of the virus.

Even if the H5N1 strain does not mutate to infect humans, the economic costs associated with avian flu strains could easily be in the billions if other countries, such as Mexico, impose bans on imported U.S. poultry and U.S. consumers avoid buying domestic poultry. Still, the economic costs are very different from the insurance costs. The following is an overview of two potential types of insurance coverages involved:

Workers Compensation: Workers involved in the handling of poultry could be at risk. Because such an exposure is work-related, workers compensation coverage would apply.

Tort-Related Exposures: If the infected poultry were found to have gotten into the food supply and people become ill as a result, litigation could ensue.

(ADVOGADO – IRB – 2006 – ESAF) According to the author, insurance costs related to the avian flu

(A) could reach billions of dollars in Mexico.
(B) have been estimated by four specific countries.
(C) equal to the economic costs recently estimated.
(D) may include at least two possibilities.
(E) exclude workers compensation in the USA.

(Interpretation) A: Incorrect – The text explicitly says, "the economic costs associated with avian flu strains could easily be in the billions if other countries, such as Mexico, impose bans on imported U.S. poultry", meaning that the costs could be high in the US if Mexico prohibits the imports of US chicken; B: Incorrect – The text explicitly says, "However, four countries – Thailand, Vietnam, Indonesia and Cambodia – have reported a total of 120 human cases of the H5N1 flu since 1997", meaning four countries has several cases of the flu, but not that costs have been estimated in all four; C: Incorrect – There is no comparison in The text to other estimates. D: Correct – The text explicitly says, "The following is an overview of two potential types of insurance coverages involved", referring to the two possible costs related to the flu; E: Incorrect – The text explicitly says, "The following is an overview of two potential types of insurance coverages involved: Workers Compensation", meaning that costs actually cover (include) Worker's Compensation.
Gabarito "D".

(ADVOGADO – IRB – 2006 – ESAF) In paragraph 2, the author

(A) resorts to scientific data to explain the virus mutation.
(B) points out the economic interdependence between two countries.
(C) provides exact figures related to the economic and social losses.
(D) explains why workers compensation might cause liquidity problems.
(E) defines the duration of the outbreak and/or quarantine.

(Interpretation) A: Incorrect – The first paragraph, not the second, uses scientific data to explain virus mutation; B: Correct – The second paragraph show the economic interdependence between Mexico and the US; C: Incorrect – No figures are mentioned in the second paragraph; D: Incorrect – The second paragraph explains that workers may be exposed to the virus and, therefore, coverage may apply, but it does not explain liquidity problems; E: Incorrect – The second paragraph makes no mention to the duration of the virus outbreak.
Gabarito "B".

Thinking Without Limits: Qualifications of the 21st Century CEO
By Stephen A. Unger
Possess Cultural Fluency

To succeed in the global environment, the 21st century CEO must possess a high degree of cultural fluency. As organizations expand globally and compete internationally, their CEOs must understand the challenges specific to each regional market. Each region has its own regulatory environment and style of doing business. Successful CEOs understand the need to adjust their communication style and timeline to the culture in which they are conducting business.

http://www.careerpath.com/ows-bin/editorial.cgi/special/wolimits.htm

(ADVOGADO – BNDES – 2002 – VUNESP) According to the text, cultural fluency

(A) is a concept that depends on regional markets.
(B) is essential for specific business events in the area of communication and media.
(C) promotes a high degree of foreign language fluency.
(D) may be developed through technological evolution.
(E) is very important for successful CEOs.

(Interpretation) A: Incorrect – The text says 'cultural fluency' is important to 'understand the challenges specific to each regional market', but it is not dependent on them; B: Incorrect – The text says, "Successful CEOs understand the need to adjust their communication style", but 'cultural fluency' is not essential for events in communication. Media is not mentioned in the text; C: Incorrect – 'foreign language fluency' is not mentioned in the text; D: Incorrect – 'technological evolution' is not mentioned in the text; E: Correct – The text explicitly says, "To succeed in the global environment, the 21st century CEO must possess a high degree of cultural fluency". Gabarito "E".

(ADVOGADO – BNDES – 2002 – VUNESP) Successful CEOs should

(A) expand globally, that is, both regionally and nationally.
(B) avoid and control challenges because they generate communication conflicts.
(C) develop their personal communication style and stick to it.
(D) adapt their communication style to the environment they are working in.
(E) establish strict timelines and ensure they are fulfilled.

(Interpretation) A: Incorrect – The text explicitly says, "As organizations expand globally and compete internationally", meaning that companies or organizations expand, not the CEOs; B: Incorrect – 'communication conflicts' are not mentioned in the text; C: Incorrect – The text explicitly says, "Successful CEOs understand the need to adjust their communication style"; D: Correct – The text explicitly says, "Successful CEOs understand the need to adjust their communication style and timeline to the culture in which they are conducting business"; E: Incorrect - The text explicitly says, "Successful CEOs understand the need to adjust their communication style and timeline to the culture in which they are conducting business", meaning they need to be flexible with timelines. Gabarito "D".

(ADVOGADO – BNDES – 2002 – VUNESP) The word "To" in the passage from the text "To succeed in the global environment…" can, without changing its meaning, be replaced for

(A) In order to.
(B) Because of.
(C) So.
(D) As.
(E) Such as.

(Grammar) A: Correct – 'To succeed' is an abbreviated form of 'In order to succeed', which is used to show purpose; B: Incorrect – 'because of' is a conjunction used to show cause or reason; C: Incorrect: 'so' is a conjunction used to show consequence; D: Incorrect – 'as' is a conjunction used to show cause or time; E: Incorrect – 'such as' is a determiner used to introduce examples. Gabarito "A".

(ADVOGADO – BNDES – 2002 – VUNESP) The word "they" in the passage from the text "…the culture in which they are conducting business" refers to

(A) the culture.
(B) business.
(C) successful CEOs.
(D) communication style and timeline.
(E) organizations.

(Grammar) A: Incorrect – The word 'they' in the sentence "Successful CEOs understand the need to adjust their communication style and timeline to the culture in which they are conducting business" refers back to the nearest plural noun. 'The culture' is a singular noun; B: Incorrect – The word 'they' in the sentence "Successful CEOs understand the need to adjust their communication style and timeline to the culture in which they are conducting business" refers back to the nearest plural noun. 'Business' is a singular noun; C: Correct - The word 'they' in the sentence "Successful CEOs understand the need to adjust their communication style and timeline to the culture in which they are conducting business" refers back to the nearest plural noun, which, in this case, is successful CEOs; D: Incorrect - The word 'they' in the sentence "Successful CEOs understand the need to adjust their communication style and timeline to the culture in which they are conducting business" refers back to the agent 'conducting business' (who is conducting business?). 'Communication style and timeline' are not conducting business; E: Incorrect - The word 'they' in the sentence "Successful CEOs understand the need to adjust their communication style and timeline to the culture in which they are conducting business" refers back to the nearest plural noun. 'Organizations' is plural, but it is not the nearest plural noun. Gabarito "C".

(ADVOGADO – BNDES – 2002 – VUNESP) The word "must" in the expressions from the text "must possess" and "must understand" expresses the meaning of

(A) request.
(B) requirement.
(C) possibility.
(D) certainty.
(E) permission.

(Grammar) A: Incorrect – 'must' never expresses an idea of 'request'; B: Correct – 'must' often expresses an idea of 'requirement'; C: Incorrect - 'must' never expresses an idea of 'possibility'; D: Incorrect - 'must' never expresses an idea of 'certainty'; E: Incorrect - 'must' never expresses an idea of 'permission'. Gabarito "B".

Poor change their habits

Brazilian entrepreneurs are taking note of the fact that although buying power has declined in recent years, people with low incomes do everything to maintain the habits acquired previously, especially after having entered the consumer market after the currency stabilization plan initiated with the Real Plan.

Economists' suspicions about this fact were confirmed by data disclosed by AC Nielsen. Traditional items from the basket of basic food staples are losing space in the supermarkets. Between 2000 and 2001, rice, a staple in Brazilian meals, fell almost 1% in sales volume and sugar dropped 3.1%. But sales of bakery cakes rose 19%. Manufacturers of cookies and refrigerated products also have no reason to complain. Other items incorporated into consumer habits of the low middle class are the mobile phone, computer, motorcycle, 21-inch TV and airline ticket. AC Nielsen shows that even with the declining buying power of the average salary in recent years, the share in consumption of socio-economic classes C and D increased. From 1997 to 1999, the portion of economically active population rose from 46.8% to 48.2%, with the incorporation of portions of class E that gained and of B that lost income.

The sales growth in basic products has been stable in recent years, says Renata Aisen Wolf, a consultant in market development with Integration Consultoria Empresarial. Soft drinks, disposable diapers and household cleaning products, even with new product launches and innovations, have not persuaded the consumer to buy more than is necessary. But products for entertainment or individual and family enjoyment, like mobile phone, CD and DVD players and personal computer keep rolling out.

GAZETA MERCANTIL International Weekly Edition, March 4 to 10, 2002

(ADVOGADO – BNDES – 2002 – VUNESP) After the Real Plan,

(A) buying power stabilized and only recently increased.
(B) Brazilian entrepreneurs noticed that industry promoted new habits.
(C) foreign currencies defined the fluctuation rate of the Brazilian currency.
(D) low income people entered the consumer market.
(E) poor people maintained the consuming habits they had before the Real Plan.

(Interpretation) A: Incorrect – The text explicitly says, "Brazilian entrepreneurs are taking note of the fact that although buying power has declined in recent years", meaning that buying power did not stabilize nor did it increase; B: Incorrect – The text says that the Brazilian entrepreneurs noted that changes in buying power promoted new habits. Industry was not considered the reason for these new habits: C: Incorrect – 'foreign currencies' are not mentioned in the text; D: Correct – The text explicitly says, "people with low incomes do everything to maintain the habits acquired previously, especially after having entered the consumer market after the currency stabilization plan initiated with the Real Plan"; E: Incorrect – The text explicitly says, "people with low incomes do everything to maintain the habits acquired previously, especially after having entered the consumer market after the currency stabilization plan initiated with the Real Plan", meaning that the new consumer habits only began after the Real Plan was implemented, not before.
Gabarito "D".

(ADVOGADO – BNDES – 2002 – VUNESP) The sales volume of the following product increased:

(A) cookies.
(B) refrigerators.
(C) rice.
(D) sugar.
(E) meals.

(Interpretation) A: Correct – The text explicitly says, "But sales of bakery cakes rose 19%. Manufacturers of cookies and refrigerated products also have no reason to complain", meaning that cookie producers are as happy as those that manufacture bakery cakes because sales of both items increased; B: Incorrect – 'refrigerators' are not mentioned in the text; C: Incorrect – The text explicitly says, "Between 2000 and 2001, rice, a staple in Brazilian meals, fell almost 1% in sales volume"; D: Incorrect - The text explicitly says, "sugar dropped 3.1%"; E: Incorrect – 'meals' are not mentioned in the text.
Gabarito "A".

(ADVOGADO – BNDES – 2002 – VUNESP) According to the second paragraph of The text,

(A) the average salary of the lower-middle class increased.
(B) class E started to consume computers and mobile phones.
(C) the economically active population was larger in 1997.
(D) all economic classes now equally consume items like 21-inch TVs and airline tickets.
(E) the income of the socio-economic class B decreased.

(Interpretation) A: Correct – The text says, "AC Nielsen shows that even with the declining buying power of the average salary in recent years, the share in consumption of socio-economic classes C and D increased", which means that spending and consumption increased, not the salaries; B: Incorrect – The text says, "Other items incorporated into consumer habits of the low middle class are the mobile phone, computer, motorcycle, 21-inch TV and airline ticket", but 'class E' is not the 'low middle class'; C: Incorrect – The text explicitly says, "From 1997 to 1999, the portion of economically active population rose from 46.8% to 48.2%", meaning that in 1997 the percentage of the economically active population was lower; D: Incorrect - The text says, "Other items incorporated into consumer habits of the low middle class are the mobile phone, computer, motorcycle, 21-inch TV and airline ticket", which still excludes the low-income earners; E: Correct - The text explicitly says, "with the incorporation of portions of class E that gained and of B that lost income", meaning that class E gained income, but class B's income decreased.
Gabarito "A".

(ADVOGADO – BNDES – 2002 – VUNESP) According to the last paragraph of The text,

(A) as a general rule, people don't buy more than necessary.
(B) the increase in certain electrical appliances sales shows that people care about entertainment or individual and family enjoyment.
(C) new products and innovations boosted sales.
(D) low-income people are drinking more soft drinks.
(E) women are consuming more disposable diapers because their income is higher now.

(Interpretation) A: Incorrect – The text says, "Soft drinks, disposable diapers and household cleaning products, even with new product launches and innovations, have not persuaded the consumer to buy more than is necessary", which could suggest that people normally do not buy more than they need. However, the following sentence says, "But products for entertainment or individual and family enjoyment, like mobile phone, CD and DVD players and personal computer keep rolling out", meaning that somebody is buying these luxury items. Therefore, people do buy more than what is necessary; B: Correct – The text explicitly says, "But products for entertainment or individual and family enjoyment, like mobile phone, CD and DVD players and personal computer keep rolling out", meaning that people are spending their money on these items, which can be translated as they care about these issues; C: Incorrect – The text explicitly says, "even with new product launches and innovations, have not persuaded the consumer to buy more than is necessary", meaning that these issues are NOT responsible for boosting sales; D: Incorrect – The text explicitly says, "Soft drinks, disposable diapers and household cleaning products, even with new product launches and innovations, have not persuaded the consumer to buy more than is necessary", meaning that people are not drinking more soft drink than they normally would; E: Incorrect - The text explicitly says, "Soft drinks, disposable diapers and household cleaning products, even with new product launches and innovations, have not persuaded the consumer to buy more than is necessary", meaning that women are not anymore consumer of this item.
Gabarito "B".

(ADVOGADO – BNDES – 2002 – VUNESP) AC Nielsen

(A) proved that the Real plan was a good solution.
(B) took note of the entrepreneurs' analysis.
(C) confirmed the economists' suspicions.
(D) is specialized in low-income population behavior.
(E) identified that family entertainment is gaining importance.

(Interpretation) A: Incorrect – In the text, AC Nielsen neither confirms that the Real Plan was good or bad; B: Incorrect – The text explicitly says, "Economists' suspicions about this fact were confirmed by data disclosed by AC Nielsen". AC Nielsen is not attributed with having even considered the entrepreneurs' analysis; C: Correct – The text explicitly says, "Economists' suspicions about this fact were confirmed by data disclosed by AC Nielsen"; D: Incorrect – AC Nielsen's specialization is not mentioned in the text; E: Incorrect – AC Nielsen is not attributed with this identification. The text 'suggests' that 'Renata Aisen Wolf, a consultant in market development with Integration Consultoria Empresarial' poses that 'family entertainment is gaining importance'.
Gabarito "C".

IFC may give Brazil more

The World Bank arm could step up loans by "neutralizing" foreign exchange risk

The International Finance Corporation (IFC), an arm of the World Bank which finances projects in the private sector, may soon step up loans to Brazil. "I am happy because the IFC has some hundreds of thousands of dollars available [for Brazil]," Bernard Pasquier, IFC's soon-to-be director for Latin America and Caribbean, told Gazeta Mercantil in an interview. "Brazil will now need the IFC more than it did in the last two years," he added. Pasquier is due to take office in September.

More financing to Brazil, IFC's second biggest beneficiary after Argentina, will be made possible after the international organ develops financial products to neutralize foreign exchange risk.

The IFC has outstanding loans to Brazil of some $1.217 billion by June 2000, or an amount that had reached IFC's limit for Brazil exposure. In the last fiscal year which ended in June, IFC took part in ten smaller-scale projects worth a total $182.7 million.

The IFC acknowledges that a slower US economy and reduced liquidity in international markets are the main factors putting the brakes on investments in developing countries. However, Pasquier says the IFC could step up financing in times like this. "The IFC is known to react the opposite way normal investors do," he said. "When most people leave the market, that's when our appetite grows. Brazil will continue to be one of our priorities." He added that IFC loans were longer in term compared to those by private banks, and for that reason, "difficult times could be good for the IFC."

Source: IFC

Loans to Brazil	
(of a total $1.217 b by June 2000)	
Sector	(in%)
Food and Agribusiness	20
Infrastructure	14
Chemical and Petrochemical products	14
Industry	9
Wood, paper and pulp	7
Services	6
Vehicles and autoparts	6
Mining	6
Cement and construction material	6
Others	12

(GAZETA MERCANTIL International Weekly Edition Sept. 3 to 9, 2001)

(ADVOGADO – BNDES – 2001 – VUNESP) The International Finance Corporation

(A) is located in Latin America and Caribbean.
(B) works exclusively with Argentina and Brazil.
(C) controls the World Bank activities.
(D) finances projects in the private sector.
(E) will step up foreign currency loans to private banks.

(Interpretation) A: Incorrect – The text does not identify the location of the IFC. It suggests that there is a division within the IFC that is dedicated to Latin America and the Caribbean, but the location is not mentioned; B: Incorrect – The name of the IFC stands for 'International Finance Corporation', which suggests it works with countries other than Argentina and Brazil; C: Incorrect - The text explicitly says, "The International Finance Corporation (IFC), an arm of the World Bank", meaning that it is part of the World Bank, not that it controls it; D: Correct – The text explicitly says, "The International Finance Corporation (IFC), an arm of the World Bank which finances projects in the private sector"; E: Incorrect – The text explicitly says, "The International Finance Corporation (…) may soon step up loans to Brazil", meaning the loans would be to the government and not to private banks.
Gabarito "D".

(ADVOGADO – BNDES – 2001 – VUNESP) Bernard Pasquier

(A) directs the World Bank.
(B) will be IFC's CFO (Chief Financial Officer).
(C) will take office in Brazil and Argentina next September.
(D) is happy to live in Brazil.
(E) is the future IFC's director for Latin America and Caribbean.

(Interpretation) A: Incorrect – The text explicitly says, "Bernard Pasquier, IFC's soon-to-be director for Latin America and Caribbean"; however, his current position is not revealed; B: Incorrect – The text explicitly says, "Bernard Pasquier, IFC's soon-to-be director for Latin America and Caribbean". The text does not specify what type of director; C: Incorrect - The text explicitly says, "Bernard Pasquier, IFC's soon-to-be director for Latin America and Caribbean". The text does not reveal where he will be based; D: Incorrect - The text explicitly says, "Bernard Pasquier, IFC's soon-to-be director for Latin America and Caribbean". The text does not reveal where he will be based; E: Correct – The text explicitly says, "Bernard Pasquier, IFC's soon-to-be director for Latin America and Caribbean", meaning he will take this position in the future (soon). This is reinforced by the sentence, "Pasquier is due to take office in September", which means he will only take the position in September.
Gabarito "E".

(ADVOGADO – BNDES – 2001 – VUNESP) IFC's first beneficiary is

(A) Brazil.
(B) Argentina.
(C) Caribbean.
(D) USA.
(E) Latin America.

(Interpretation) A: Incorrect – The text explicitly says, "More financing to Brazil, IFC's second biggest beneficiary after Argentina", meaning that Argentina is the IFC's first or largest beneficiary, and Brazil is the second; B: Correct – The text explicitly says, "More financing to Brazil, IFC's second biggest beneficiary after Argentina", meaning that Argentina is the IFC's first or largest beneficiary, and Brazil is the second; C: Incorrect - The text explicitly says, "More financing to Brazil, IFC's second biggest beneficiary after Argentina", meaning that Argentina is the IFC's first or largest beneficiary. The ranking for the Caribbean is not mentioned; D: Incorrect - The text explicitly says, "More financing to Brazil, IFC's second biggest beneficiary after Argentina", meaning that Argentina is the IFC's first or largest beneficiary; E: Incorrect - The text explicitly says, "More financing to Brazil, IFC's second biggest beneficiary after Argentina", meaning that Argentina is the IFC's first or largest beneficiary.
Gabarito "B".

(ADVOGADO – BNDES – 2001 – VUNESP) Read the following passage from the paragraph 4 in the text: "When most people leave the market, that's when our appetite grows. Brazil will continue to be one of our priorities." The word "our" refers to

(A) IFC.
(B) Pasquier.
(C) priorities.
(D) Brazil.
(E) appetite.

(Interpretation) A: Correct – Considering the sentence preceding that mentioned in the question ("The IFC is known to react the opposite way normal investors do," he said. "When most people leave the market, that's when our appetite grows"), it is possible to see that this is a quote from Bernard Pasquier, who is speaking on behalf of the IFC. He uses the plural possessive 'our' to refer to the organization rather than himself. 'Our appetite', then, refers to the IFC's appetite.
Gabarito "A".

(ADVOGADO – BNDES – 2001 – VUNESP) By June 2000 IFC's loans to Brazil

(A) had a total of $182.7 million.
(B) concentrated in private banking.
(C) had an unpaid total of $1.217 billion.
(D) had already neutralized foreign exchange risk.
(E) were less competitive than in private banks.

(Interpretation) A: Incorrect – The text explicitly says, "IFC took part in ten smaller-scale projects worth a total $182.7 million", meaning that the projects were worth that amount. This does not means the loans were of that value; B: Incorrect – The text explicitly says, "The International Finance Corporation (IFC), an arm of the World Bank which finances projects in the private sector, may soon step up loans to Brazil", meaning that the projects are in the private sector, but the loans are not for private banks; C: Correct – The text explicitly says, "The IFC has outstanding loans to Brazil of some $1.217 billion by June 2000". The word 'outstanding', in this context, means unpaid or overdue; D: Incorrect – The text explicitly says, "More financing to Brazil, IFC's second biggest beneficiary after Argentina, will be made possible after the international organ develops financial products to neutralize foreign exchange risk", meaning that it has NOT YET neutralized the foreign exchange risk; E: Incorrect – The text explicitly says, "IFC loans were longer in term compared to those by private banks, and for that reason, "difficult times could be good for the IFC", meaning that terms for repayment were better (longer) than those offered by private banks; hence, they are more competitive.
Gabarito "C".

(ADVOGADO – BNDES – 2001 – VUNESP) The IFC

(A) has already diminished foreign exchange risk.
(B) has longer loan terms than the private banks.
(C) confirms that reduced liquidity is good for developing countries.
(D) usually reacts according to their normal investors.
(E) needs Brazil more now than two years ago.

(Interpretation) A: Incorrect – The text explicitly says, "More financing to Brazil, IFC's second biggest beneficiary after Argentina, will be made possible after the international organ develops financial products to neutralize foreign exchange risk", meaning that it has NOT YET neutralized the foreign exchange risk; B: Correct – The text explicitly says, "IFC loans were longer in term compared to those by private banks", meaning that terms for repayment were longer than those offered by private banks; C: Incorrect – The text explicitly says, "The IFC acknowledges that a slower US economy and reduced liquidity in international markets are the main factors putting the brakes on investments in developing countries", meaning that reduced liquidity slows (puts the brakes on) investment, which, in economic terms, is not good; D: Incorrect - The text explicitly says, "The IFC is known to react the opposite way normal investors do"; E: Incorrect - The text explicitly says, "Brazil will now need the IFC more than it did in the last two years".
Gabarito "B".

(ADVOGADO – BNDES – 2001 – VUNESP) According to the Chart "Loans to Brazil", choose the correct assertion.

(A) Food and agribusiness got the least.
(B) Chemical and petrochemical products got less than the mining sector.

(C) Cement and construction material got the same as vehicles and autoparts.
(D) Infrastructure got twice as much as the chemical and petrochemical sector.
(E) Wood, paper and pulp got half the amount food and agribusiness did.

(Interpretation) A: Incorrect – The chart explicitly shows, "Food and agribusiness" got 20%, while the least (6%) was given to "Wood, paper and pulp; Services; Vehicles and autoparts; Mining; Cement and construction material"; B: Incorrect – The chart explicitly shows, "Chemical and Petrochemical products" got 14%, while "Mining" got 6%; therefore, "Chemical and Petrochemical products" got more, not less; C: Correct – The chart explicitly shows, "Vehicles and autoparts" with 6% and "Cement and construction material" with 6%; D: Incorrect – The chart explicitly shows, both "Infrastructure" and "Chemical and Petrochemical products got 14% - exactly the same amount; E: Incorrect – The chart explicitly shows, "Wood, paper and pulp" got 7%, while "Food and agribusiness" got 20; therefore it got less than half.
Gabarito "C".

(ADVOGADO – BNDES – 2001 – VUNESP) "IFC may soon step up loans in Brazil" means that IFC
(A) can increase loans in Brazil.
(B) reduced investments in Brazil.
(C) surely will give advancement to Brazil.
(D) will keep the loans in Brazil at the same level.
(E) will keep track of the loans in Brazil.

(Vocabulary) A: Correct – 'step up loans' means to 'increase loans'; B: Incorrect – 'soon' suggest an action in the future; 'reduced' is in the past; C: Incorrect – 'step up loans' does not guarantee advancement, only that the money will be made available; D: Incorrect – 'step up loans' means 'increase loans', not to keep them the same; E: Incorrect – 'keep track of' means 'monitor'.
Gabarito "A".

(ADVOGADO – BNDES – 2001 – VUNESP) The word "However" in "However, Pasquier says the IFC could step up financing in times like this" (paragraph 4) can, without changing its meaning, be substituted for
(A) Therefore.
(B) Because.
(C) For example.
(D) Moreover.
(E) In spite of this.

(Grammar) A: Incorrect – 'therefore' is a conjunct that means 'in conclusion' or 'as a consequence'; B: Incorrect – 'because' is a conjunction that means 'for that reason'; C: Incorrect – 'for example' is a determiner that means 'for instance' or 'such as'. It is used to introduce an example; D: Incorrect – 'moreover' is a conjunct that means 'in addition to' or 'besides'; E: Correct – 'in spite of [this]' is a conjunction that means 'nevertheless' or 'however'. It is used to show contrast.
Gabarito "E".

(ADVOGADO – BNDES – 2001 – VUNESP) According to the text, one of the two main factors that diminished investments in developing countries is
(A) the foreign exchange risk.
(B) the limit for Brazilian exposure.
(C) that most people are leaving the market.
(D) the reduced liquidity in international markets.
(E) that private banks ceased investments.

(Interpretation) D: Correct - The text explicitly says, "The IFC acknowledges that a slower US economy and reduced liquidity in international markets are the main factors putting the brakes on investments in developing countries", meaning that reduced liquidity diminishes (puts the brakes on) investment.
Gabarito "D".

Gadget Designers Push the Limits of Size, Safety

By Brian X. Chen, August 28, 2008

Just as small, fast-moving mammals replaced lumbering dinosaurs, pocketable gadgets are evolving to fill niches that larger, deskbound computers can't reach. But as they shrink, these gadgets are faced with problems mammals face, too, such as efficiently dissipating heat.

The recent example of Apple's first-generation iPod nanos causing fires in Japan raises the question of whether increasingly innovative product designs are impinging on safety. The nano incident illustrates how risk can increase as devices decrease in size, says Roger Kay, an analyst at Endpoint Technologies.

"As [gadgets] get smaller, the tradeoffs become more difficult, the balance becomes more critical and there's less room for error," Kay said. "I'm not surprised it's happening to the nano because that's the small one. You're asking it to do a lot in a very, very small package and that's pushing the envelope."

There's no question that industrial designers' jobs have become much more difficult as the industry demands ever more powerful and smaller gadgets. With paper-thin subnotebooks, ultrasmall MP3 players, and pinkie fingersized Bluetooth headsets becoming increasingly popular, it's questionable where exactly designers draw the line between innovation and safety.

(ADVOGADO – DATAPREV – 2009 – UFF) In the sentence: "But as they shrink, these gadgets are faced with problems mammals face, too, such as efficiently dissipating heat." First paragraph, the author of the text believes that…

(A) like the early mammals, gadgets will have to be able to maintain heat;
(B) like early mammals, nano technology will have to develop better condition of safety to survive;
(C) pocketable gadgets are evolving to overtake deskbound computers positions;
(D) people are in danger when they use their newest gadgets;
(E) gadgets may be compared to lumbering dinosaurs and have no survival chance in the future.

A: Incorrect – The text explicitly says, "these gadgets are faced with problems mammals face, too, as efficiently dissipating heat". The word 'dissipating' means 'disperse' or 'expel', quite the opposite of to 'maintain'; B: Correct – Considering the previous sentence ("Just as small, fast-moving mammals replaced lumbering dinosaurs, pocketable gadgets are evolving to fill niches that larger, deskbound

computers can't reach. But as they shrink, these gadgets are faced with problems mammals face, too, such as efficiently dissipating heat"), it is possible to see the comparison between early mammals and nano technology, especially referring to the problems and the adaptations they will have to make; C: Incorrect – The text explicitly says, "pocketable gadgets are evolving to fill niches that larger, deskbound computers can't reach", meaning the pocketable gadgets are not evolving to take the positions of deskbound computers, but to take others that are too small for these large table-top computers. The name 'pocketable' suggests they would be carried around in pockets rather than used on the desks; D: Incorrect – The first paragraph does not mention 'danger'; E: Incorrect – The author compares 'small, fast-moving mammals' to pocketable gadgets. 'Larger, deskbound computers' are compared with 'lumbering dinosaurs'.
Gabarito "B".

(ADVOGADO – DATAPREV – 2009 – UFF) The title of the text lets us know that there must be a close relation between...

(A) design and safety;
(B) technology and safety;
(C) nano technology and design;
(D) nano technology and safety;
(E) design and technology.

(Interpretation) A: Incorrect – The title affirms that designers need to consider two aspects: 'Size' and 'Safety'. The title does not connect technology design to safety, but rather 'size' and 'safety'; B: Incorrect – The title affirms that designers need to consider two aspects: 'Size' and 'Safety'. The title does not connect technology itself to safety, but rather 'size' and 'safety'; C: Incorrect - The title affirms that designers need to consider two aspects: 'Size' and 'Safety'. The title does not connect nano technology to design, but rather 'size' and 'safety'; D: Correct – The title affirms a close relation between these ideas with the words 'size' (nano technology) and 'safety'; E: Incorrect - The title affirms that designers need to consider two aspects: 'Size' and 'Safety'. The title does not connect design to technology, but rather 'size' and 'safety'.
Gabarito "D".

(ADVOGADO – DATAPREV – 2009 – UFF) The reason given in the third paragraph of the text for the problem with smaller gadgets is that...

(A) it gets hard to deal with anything in a tiny space;
(B) gadgets designer will never know how to deal with nano technology;
(C) gadgets designer are not able to deal with high technology;
(D) science hasn't reach the necessary safety;
(E) it is very difficult to work with high technology at any rate.

(Interpretation) A: Correct – The text explicitly says, "there's less room for error" and "You're asking it to do a lot in a very, very small package and that's pushing the envelope", meaning that it is becoming hard (pushing the envelope) to deal with things in such small gadgets; B: Incorrect – The paragraph in question only focuses on the problems, not the impossibility of knowing how to deal with the technology; C: Incorrect - The paragraph in question only focuses on the problems, not the inability of dealing with the technology; D: Incorrect – 'safety' is not mentioned in the third paragraph; E: Incorrect - The paragraph in question only focuses on the problems for nano technology; it does not include high technology of all sizes. 'At any rate' means 'in any way', which would include, for example, large-scale technology.
Gabarito "A".

(ADVOGADO – DATAPREV – 2009 – UFF) According to the text industrial designers' jobs have become more difficult because they...

(A) require more responsibility;
(B) require a production of smaller and safer gadgets;
(C) require more skills;
(D) demand a whole lot of patience;
(E) demand too much time of research and of tests.

(Interpretation) A: Incorrect – The text says, "The nano incident illustrates how risk can increase as devices decrease in size", which talks about risk; however, responsibility is not mentioned in the text; B: Correct – The text explicitly says, "There's no question that industrial designers' jobs have become much more difficult as the industry demands ever more powerful and smaller gadgets. With paper-thin subnotebooks, ultrasmall MP3 players, and pinkie fingersized Bluetooth headsets becoming increasingly popular, it's questionable where exactly designers draw the line between innovation and safety", meaning that the difficulty in their work lies in how to design smaller and safer gadgets; C: Incorrect – The text does not focus on the amount of skills that designers have, but rather on the complexity of their work; D: Incorrect – The text does not mention the level of patience required by designers; E: Incorrect – Research and tests are not mentioned in the text.
Gabarito "B".

(ADVOGADO – DATAPREV – 2009 – UFF) The expression such as in the last line of the first paragraph could be changed by _____ and its meaning would not altered.

(A) by;
(B) like;
(C) although;
(D) but;
(E) because.

(Grammar) But as they shrink, these gadgets are faced with problems mammals face, too, such as efficiently dissipating heat.
A: Incorrect – 'by' is used to show how something is done. If you replaced 'such as' with 'by' in the sentence, the meaning would change. The sense would be that mammals would face problems because they would be dissipating heat; B: Correct – 'like' is an informal synonym for 'such as', and both are used to introduce examples; C: Incorrect – 'although' is used to show a contrast. If you replaced 'such as' with 'although' in the sentence, the meaning would change. The sense would be that mammals efficiently dissipate heat, even though they face problems; D: 'but' is a coordinating conjunction used to show a contrast. Grammatically, it would be incorrect to use a reduced clause (gerund) after 'but' (dissipating); E: Incorrect – 'because' is a conjunction used to show cause. If you replaced 'such as' with 'because' in the sentence, the meaning would change. The sense would be that mammals efficiently dissipate heat, even though they face problems. Grammatically, it would be incorrect to use a reduced clause (gerund) after 'because' (dissipating).
Gabarito "B".

Choose the best option.

(ADVOGADO – DATAPREV – 2009 – UFF) Dumping your entire music collection _____ your iPod is a simple, one click process. But what about getting your music _____ your iPod?

(A) in / out;
(B) in / off;

(C) on / off;
(D) onto / off;
(E) into / out.

(Grammar) A: Incorrect – 'dump music in' is not plausible because the preposition needs to convey an idea of transference or movement, which 'in' does not; 'get music out' an iPod is not plausible. The phrasal verb 'get out' is intransitive and means 'leave' or 'depart'; B: Incorrect – 'dump music in' is not plausible because the preposition needs to convey an idea of transference or movement, which 'in' does not; 'get music off' an iPod is plausible; C: Incorrect – 'dump music on' has a physical sense; 'get music off' an iPod is plausible; D: Correct - 'dump music onto' is plausible because the iPod carries the idea of a virtual vessel, hence 'on' (on a computer, on a television etc), and the transfer carries the idea of movement, hence 'to' (on + to); 'get music off' an iPod is plausible; E: Incorrect – 'dump music into' is not plausible because the preposition 'in' is not used for virtual vessels (on computers, on iPods, on televisions); 'get music out' an iPod is not plausible. The phrasal verb 'get out' is intransitive and means 'leave' or 'depart'.

Gabarito "D".

(ADVOGADO – DATAPREV – 2009 – UFF) Boeing _____ this week that it _____ successfully _____ a manned airplane powered _____ hydrogen fuel cells.

(A) announced / has / flown / on;
(B) has announced / had / flown / by;
(C) announced / has / flown / by;
(D) have announced / has / flown / on;
(E) announced / had / flown / on.

(Grammar) A: Incorrect – 'powered' requires 'by' because it is a (reduced) passive voice structure. The passive agent for the passive voice is usually 'by'; B: Incorrect – 'had' is not possible because the past perfect tense (had flown) is used to show a sequence of events all of which happened in the past. There is not time reference concerning when this flight happened. 'This week' refers to when Boeing made the announcement; C: Correct – 'has flown' is the correct verb tense because there is no time reference, even though the action happened sometime in the past. 'By' is the correct word for the passive voice structure (powered by something); D: Incorrect – 'have announced' requires a plural subject and Boeing is a singular noun. 'Powered' requires 'by' because it is a (reduced) passive voice structure. The passive agent for the passive voice is usually 'by'; E: Incorrect - had' is not possible because the past perfect tense (had flown) is used to show a sequence of events all of which happened in the past. There is not time reference concerning when this flight happened. 'This week' refers to when Boeing made the announcement.

Gabarito "C".

(ADVOGADO – DATAPREV – 2009 – UFF) Robots _____ have the brains to "intelligently and autonomously search _____ objects" _____ their own.

(A) didn't / for / in;
(B) don't / of / in;
(C) haven't / for / on;
(D) don't / for / on;
(E) doesn't / for / on.

(Grammar) A: Incorrect – 'didn't' is an auxiliary verb in the simple past tense; however, there is no time reference to the past; 'search for' is the correct verb-preposition agreement; 'in their own' is not the correct collocation (see D); B: Incorrect – 'don't' is a plural auxiliary verb that concords with 'robots' the plural subject, and the verb tense is adequate do to the generic sense of the sentence with no specified time reference; 'search of' is the incorrect verb-preposition agreement; 'in their own' is not the correct collocation (see D); C: Incorrect – 'haven't' is the auxiliary verb in the present perfect tense, but the main verb 'have' does not concord with this verb tense ('haven't have' is not possible); 'search for' is the correct verb-preposition agreement; 'on their own' is the correct collocation that means 'by themselves'; D: Correct – 'don't' is a plural auxiliary verb that concords with 'robots' the plural subject, and the verb tense is adequate to the generic sense of the sentence with no specified time reference; 'search for' is the correct verb-preposition agreement; 'on their own' is the correct collocation that means 'by themselves'; E: Incorrect – 'doesn't' is the auxiliary verb in the singular, which does not concord with the plural subject 'robots'; 'search for' is the correct verb-preposition agreement; 'on their own' is the correct collocation that means 'by themselves'.

Gabarito "D".

(ADVOGADO – DATAPREV – 2009 – UFF) If this scientific breakthrough is reliable, after years testing it, it _____ lead to the cure of this type of cancer in the future.

(A) must;
(B) should;
(C) might;
(D) ought to;
(E) could.

(Grammar) A: Incorrect – 'must' is a modal verb used to show an idea of obligation, deduction, or requirement. In the sentence, the conditional structure suggests an idea of possibility; B: Incorrect – 'should' is a modal verb used to show an idea of expectation. In the sentence, the conditional suggests an idea of possibility; C: Correct – 'might' is a modal verb used to show an idea of possibility; D: Incorrect – 'ought to' is a quasi-modal structure used to show an idea of duty or expectation. In the sentence, the conditional structure suggests an idea of possibility; E: Incorrect – 'could' is the past for of the modal verb 'can'. In this sense, it would be grammatically incorrect to mix a past form with a simple present (...is reliable).

NOTE: There are three possible answers to this question; 'Should, might and could' are all acceptable forms for this sentence. 'Should' is possible because the sentence can convey an idea of expectation, especially because it talks about a cure for cancer; 'Might' is possible because it to shows an idea of possibility; and 'Could' is possible because there is a polite use of this modal verb which does not necessarily refer to the past, and it conveys an idea of possibility.

Gabarito "C".

(ADVOGADO – DATAPREV – 2009 – UFF) He was very precise about the proper procedure and the material to be used, he said he didn't want anything especial, only the regular, _____ one.

(A) unique;
(B) ordinary;
(C) rare;
(D) exquisite;
(E) unknown.

(Vocabulary) B: Correct – The text emphasizes the fact that the procedure and material should NOT be special. The only word in the list of possible answers that conveys an idea of NOT being special is 'ordinary'. 'Unique' means 'singular' or 'special'; 'rare' means 'unusual' or 'atypical'; 'exquisite' means 'superb' or 'outstanding'; 'unknown' means 'mysterious' or 'undefined'.

Gabarito "B".

This text refers to the following three questions.

Godzilla's grandchildren

1 In Japan there is no kudos in going to jail for your art. Bending the rules, let alone breaking them, is largely taboo. That was one reason Toshinori Mizuno was terrified as he
4 worked undercover at the Fukushima Dai-ichi nuclear-power plant, trying to get the shot that shows him in front of the mangled third reactor holding up a referee's red card. He was
7 also terrified of the radiation, which registered its highest reading where he took the photograph. The only reason he did not arouse suspicion, he says, is because he was in regulation
10 radiation kit. And in Japan people rarely challenge a man in uniform.
   Mr. Mizuno is part of ChimPom, a six-person
13 collective of largely unschooled artists who have spent a lot of time getting into tight spots since the disaster, and are engagingly thoughtful about the results.
16 It is easy to dismiss ChimPom's work as a publicity stunt. But the artists' actions speak at least as loudly as their images. There is a logic to their seven years of guerrilla art that
19 has become clearer since the nuclear disaster of March 11th 2011. In fact, Noi Sawaragi, a prominent art critic, says they may be hinting at a new direction in Japanese contemporary
22 art.
   Radiation and nuclear annihilation have suffused Japan's subculture since the film *Gojira* (the Japanese
25 Godzilla) in 1954. The two themes crop up repeatedly in manga and anime cartoons.
   Other young artists are ploughing similar ground.
28 Kota Takeuchi, for instance, secretly took a job at Fukushima Dai-ichi and is recorded pointing an angry finger at the camera that streams live images of the site. Later he used public news
31 conferences to pressure Tepco, operator of the plant, about the conditions of its workers inside. His work, like ChimPom's, blurs the distinction between art and activism.
34 Japanese political art is unusual and the new subversiveness could be a breath of fresh air; if only anyone noticed. The ChimPom artists have received scant coverage in
37 the stuffy arts pages of the national newspapers. The group held just one show of Mr. Mizuno's reactor photographs in Japan. He says: "The timing has not been right. The media will
40 just want to make the work look like a crime."

Internet: <www.economist.com> (adapted).

(Diplomacia – 2012 – CESPE) According to the text, judge if the following items are right (C) or wrong (E).

(1) Toshinori Mizuno was more concerned with the radiation he was exposed to while he was at the nuclear-power plant than with the fact that his art challenged the Japanese established rules.

(2) Some Fukushima Dai-ichi employers have turned into political activists after the accident of 2011.

(3) The Japanese in general are enthusiastic about artists who get in trouble for breaking the traditional dogmas prevalent in the artistic milieu.

(4) Mr. Mizuno believes the radiation kit protected him from more than the radiation in the area.

(Interpretation) 1: Incorrect – It cannot be asserted that he was more afraid of the radiation. He was equally 'terrified' of both being caught and of the radiation (lines 3 and 7); 2: Incorrect – The artists deliberately took jobs in order to gain access to the plant. They were not employees of the company before the accident; 3: Incorrect – (Line 1) There is no kudos/acclaim/praise in Japan for going to jail for your art; 4: Correct – (Line 10) He believes it also protected him from being challenged and from arousing suspicion due to Japanese deference to people in official uniforms.

Gabarito 1E, 2E, 3E, 4C

(Diplomacia – 2012 – CESPE) The words "mangled" ($\ell.6$) and "suffused" ($\ell.23$) mean respectively

(A) ruined and permeated.
(B) mutilated and obscured.
(C) subdued and covered.
(D) humongous and imbued.
(E) torn and zeroed in on.

(Vocabulary) A: Correct – Mangled means mutilated or ruined. Suffused means pervaded or permeated; B: Incorrect – Mutilated means mangled. Obscured means concealed or hidden; C: Incorrect – Subdued means calm or conquered. Covered is too physical to mean suffused; D: Incorrect – Humongous means enormous. Imbued means permeated; E: Incorrect – Torn is the past participle of tear – this could work as a synonym for mangled but not quite as strong. Zeroed in on means to target or to focus on.

Gabarito "A".

(Diplomacia – 2012 – CESPE) Based on the text, it is correct to say that ChimPom

(A) adopts some artistic-political stance which is being largely ignored by the Japanese media nationwide.
(B) produces art which is dissonant with its members' attitudes.
(C) is unique in mixing art with political protest.
(D) is a large group of untrained artists whose work blend art and political activism.
(E) creates art which is avant-garde, and is setting the path of modern art in Japan.

(Interpretation) A: Correct – The group adopts a combination of art and politics, but it receives scant/little attention (line 36) from the stuffy/formal arts pages of national newspapers; B: Incorrect – Dissonant means unharmonious/disagreeing – as the members are so committed, this is a strange assertion to make; C: Incorrect – (Line 28) Kota Takeuchi is also an artist/activist and is not a member of ChimPom; D: Incorrect – Largely means mainly and does not refer to how many people are in the group; E: Incorrect – It is only stated that the group may be hinting at a new direction in Japanese contemporary art. Hinting at - to give a slight indication – setting the path then is too strong an assertion to agree with.

Gabarito "A".

This text refers to the following three questions.

Can a planet survive the death of its sun? Scientists find two that did.

1 Natalie Batalha has had plenty of experience fielding questions from both layfolk and other scientists over the past couple of years — and with good reason. Batalha is the deputy
4 principal investigator for the spectacularly successful Kepler space telescope, which has found evidence of more than 2,000 planets orbiting distant stars so far — including, just last week,
7 a world almost exactly the size of Earth.
   But Kepler is giving astronomers all sorts of new information about stars as well, and that's what an European
10 TV correspondent wanted to know about during an interview last year. Was it true, she asked, that stars like the sun will eventually swell up and destroy their planets? It's a common
13 question, and Batalha recited the familiar answer, one that's been in astronomy textbooks for at least half a century: Yes, it's true. Five or six billion years from now, Earth will be burnt
16 to a cinder. This old news was apparently quite new to the European correspondent, because when she reported her terrifying scoop, she added a soupçon of conspiracy theory to
19 it: NASA, she suggested, was trying to downplay the story.

It was not a proud moment for science journalism, but unexpectedly, at about the same time the European correspondent was reporting her nonbulletin, Kepler scientists did discover a whole new wrinkle to the planet-eating-star scenario: it's apparently possible for planets to be swallowed up by their suns and live to tell the tale. According to a paper just published in Nature, the Kepler probe has taken a closer look at a star called KOI 55 and identified it as a "B subdwarf", the red-hot corpse of a sunlike star, one that already went through its deadly expansion. Around it are two planets, both a bit smaller than Earth — and both so close to their home star that even the tiniest solar expansion ought to have consumed them whole. And yet they seem, writes astronomer Eliza Kempton in a Nature commentary, "to be alive and well. Which begs the question, how did they survive?"

How indeed? A star like the sun takes about 10 billion years to use up the hydrogen supply. Once the hydrogen is gone, the star cools from white hot to red hot and swells dramatically: in the case of our solar system, the sun's outer layers will reach all the way to Earth. Eventually, those outer layers will waft away to form what's called a planetary nebula while the core shrinks back into an object just like KOI 55.

If a planet like Earth spent a billion years simmering in the outer layers of a star it would, says astronomer Betsy Green, "just evaporate. Only planets with masses very much larger than the Earth, like Jupiter or Saturn, could possibly survive."

And yet these two worlds, known as KOI 55.01 and KOI 55.02, lived through the ordeal anyway. The key to this seeming impossibility, suggest the astronomers, is that the planets may have begun life as gas giants like Jupiter or Saturn, with rocky cores surrounded by vast, crushing atmospheres. As the star expanded, the gas giants would have spiraled inward until they dipped into the stellar surface itself. The plunge would have been enough to strip off their atmospheres, but their rocky interiors could have survived — leaving, eventually, the bleak tableau of the naked cores of two planets orbiting the naked core of an elderly star.

Internet: <www.time.com> (adapted).

(Diplomacia – 2012 – CESPE) Based on the text, judge if the following items are right (C) or wrong (E).

(1) The recent discovery of a planet with some features very similar to those of the Earth is one of the interesting finds of the Kepler space telescope.
(2) The European TV correspondent reported a scientific find that had been long known as if it were a recent breakthrough.
(3) The researchers seem baffled by the recent find of the probe, since they did not expect planets to survive their sun's expansion and subsequent shrinkage.
(4) The article mocks the European TV correspondent's disinformation about astronomy.

(Interpretation) 1: Incorrect – The discovery was of 2,000 planets and their stars. The world similar in size to Earth was no more interesting than any other discovery made by Kepler. (lines 6-7) This could be just as easily argued to be correct – a tricky question and perhaps worth missing out; 2: Correct – (Lines 13-16) It was old news, the scientist gave a familiar answer, it has been in astronomy books for at least half a century; 3: Correct – Baffled/bewildered/confused – (line 22) to add a new wrinkle – to add a new unknown element. (Line 34) – Which begs the question – which poses the question – this would mean the scientists were confused or baffled; 4: Incorrect – The article does mock the correspondent, i.e. to ridicule her. However, disinformation relates to deliberately giving out false information usually by governments or intelligence services. In this case it was not disinformation. It could be construed as poor use of information, but not disinformation.

Gabarito 1E, 2C, 3C, 4E

(Diplomacia – 2012 – CESPE) According to the text, judge if the items below about Natalie Batalha are right (C) or wrong (E).

(1) She is the chief researcher of the space project that involves the Kepler telescope.
(2) She was taken aback by the European TV correspondent's ignorance about the natural process of a star's living cycle.
(3) Natalie Batalha demonstrated how planets can survive the death of the star they orbit.
(4) Natalie Batalha is used to talking about her research to specialists and non-specialists alike.

(Interpretation) 1: Incorrect – She is the deputy principal investigator (line 4), therefore, she is not the chief. Deputy – an assistant to another; 2: Incorrect – Taken aback means surprised/confused. No evidence to suggest how she reacted to the correspondent's ignorance; 3: Incorrect – Astronomer Betsy Green (line 43) demonstrated this, not Natallie Batalha; 4: Correct – (Lines 2-3) plenty of experience fielding questions/dealing with questions form scientists (specialists) and layfolk (non-specialists).

Gabarito 1E, 2E, 3E, 4C

(Diplomacia – 2012 – CESPE) Each of the options below presents a sentence of the text and a version of this sentence. Choose which one has retained most of the original meaning found in the text.

(A) "A star like the sun takes about 10 billion years to use up the hydrogen supply" (ℓ.35-36) / **It would take a sunlike star around 10 billion years to supply the necessary hydrogen.**
(B) "Eventually, those outer layers will waft away to form what's called a planetary nebula while the core shrinks back into an object just like KOI 55" (ℓ.39-41) / **Eventually, those outer layers will spew away to shape what's called a planetary nebula while the core shrinks back into an object just like KOI 55**.
(C) "Natalie Batalha has had plenty of experience fielding questions from both layfolk and other scientists over the past couple of years — and with good reason" (ℓ.1-3) / **Natalie Batalha was quite adept at discerning which questions were made by layfolk or by other scientists over the past couple of years — and with good reason**.
(D) "at about the same time the European correspondent was reporting her nonbulletin, Kepler scientists did discover a whole new wrinkle to the planet-eating-star scenario" (ℓ.21-24) / **at about the same time the European correspondent was reporting her nonbulletin, Kepler scientists did stumble upon a whole new crease to the planet-eating-star scene**.
(E) "This old news was apparently quite new to the European correspondent, because when she reported her terrifying scoop, she added a soupçon of conspiracy theory to it" (ℓ.16-19) / **This old news was apparently quite new to the European correspondent, because when she reported her terrifying scoop, she added a dab of conspiracy theory to it**.

(Interpretation) A: **Incorrect** – To 'use up' means consume completely; it is the opposite idea of to supply; B: Incorrect – 'Waft away' means to go away gently. In contrast, 'spew away' means to violently/with great force go away; C: Incorrect - Adept would mean skillful. It isn't clear if she was good at it or not, just that she had lots of experience. There is no evidence that she had to discern/distinguish which questions came from scientists or layfolk; D: Incorrect – Crease and wrinkle are synonyms in terms of clothes which are creased or wrinkled – crumbled. In this context, wrinkle means a problem. Stumble upon means to find by accident; E: **Correct – Soupçoun is a synonym of dab/a small amount.**
Gabarito "E".

This text refers to the following three questions.

1   While on their way, the slaves selected to go to the great House farm would make the dense old woods, for miles around, reverberate with their wild songs, revealing at once the
4   highest joy and the deepest sadness. (...) They would sing, as a chorus, to words which to many would seem unmeaning jargon, but which, nevertheless, were full of meaning to
7   themselves. I have sometimes thought that the mere hearing of those songs would do more to impress some minds with the horrible character of slavery, than the reading of whole
10 volumes of philosophy on the subject could do.
    I did not, when a slave, understand the deep meaning of those rude and apparently incoherent songs. I was myself
13 within the circle; so that I neither saw nor heard as those without might see and hear. They told a tale of woe which was then altogether beyond my feeble comprehension; they were
16 tones loud, long, and deep; they breathed the prayer and complaint of souls boiling over with the bitterest anguish.
    Every tone was a testimony against slavery, and a prayer to
19 God for deliverance from chains. The hearing of those wild notes always depressed my spirit, and filled me with ineffable sadness. I have frequently found myself in tears while hearing
22 them. The mere recurrence to those songs, even now, afflicts me; and while I am writing these lines, an expression of feeling has already found its way down my cheek. To those songs I
25 trace my first glimmering conception of the dehumanizing character of slavery. I can never get rid of that conception. Those songs still follow me, to deepen my hatred of slavery,
28 and quicken my sympathies for my brethren in bonds. If any one wishes to be impressed with the soul-killing effects of slavery, let him go to Colonel Lloyd's plantation, and, on
31 allowance-day, place himself in the deep pine woods, and there let him, in silence, analyze the sounds that shall pass through the chambers of his soul, and if he is not thus impressed, it will
34 only be because "there is no flesh in his obdurate heart."

Frederick Douglass. **Narrative of the life of Frederick Douglass, an American slave**. Charleston (SC): Forgotten Books, 2008, p. 26-7 (adapted).

(Diplomacia – 2012 – CESPE) To state that the songs "told a tale of woe" ($l.14$) means that the songs

(A) were accounts of intertribal warfare.
(B) were hymns praising God.
(C) were delusions of grandeur of an African idyllic time.
(D) had to do with grief and sorrow.
(E) had the purpose of keeping slaves' minds away from their hard work.

(Vocabulary) A: Incorrect – There is no mention of warfare in this text; B: Incorrect – Not all hymns tell a tale of "woe", that is sadness and grief; C: Incorrect – "Woe" makes no reference to grandeur; D: **Correct** – "Woe" refers to deep distress, grief or sorrow; E: Incorrect – There is no reference as to the purpose of these songs.
Gabarito "D".

(Diplomacia – 2012 – CESPE) Based on the text, judge if the following items are right (C) or wrong (E).

(1) The music produced by the slaves had the power to incite them to rebel against their appalling condition.

(2) The author of the text ascribes his nascent political awareness regarding slavery to the tunes he heard the slaves sing.

(3) The narrator believes that his fellow slaves managed to translate their dire predicament into moving tunes.

(4) To outsiders, the music sung by the slaves would probably sound like babbling.

(Interpretation) 1: Incorrect – There is no mention of a connection between rebellion and the slave music; 2: Correct – (Line 25) the author traces a first glimmering conception of how dehumanizing slavery was; 3: Correct – They were fellow slaves as he describes them as brethren (line 28) and as being part of their circle (line 13). Dire means desperate/terrible. The author describes in lines 16-19 how the songs were a cry of anguish against their condition as slaves; 4: Correct – Babbling means to make confusing or meaningless sounds. The author states in lines 6-7 the sound of the singing would be like unmeaning jargon.
Gabarito 1E, 2C, 3C, 4C

(Diplomacia – 2012 – CESPE) Regarding the text, judge if the items below are right (C) or wrong (E).

(1) The fragment "quicken my sympathies for my brethren in bonds" ($l.28$) means that the narrator is fast when it comes to forging emotional and spiritual bonds with his own real family through music.

(2) In "than the reading of whole volumes" ($l.9$-10), the omission of the definite article would not interfere with the grammar correction of the sentence.

(3) The relationship the word "within" ($l.13$) bears with "without" ($l.14$) is one of opposition.

(4) Although the slaves' songs touched the narrator's heart, the uncultured quality of their music sometimes annoyed him, as shown in the fragment "The hearing of those wild notes always depressed my spirit" ($l.19$-20).

(Interpretation) 1: Incorrect – The idea is not one of speed but one of intensity or awakening. That is, to make the author more deeply sympathetic or to revive the author's sympathies; 2: Incorrect – If the definite article was omitted, the sentence would have to be changed to – than reading whole volumes – i.e. the preposition 'of' would also have to be omitted. Employing the preposition "of" after a noun (postmodification) usually requires the use of an article before said noun; 3: Correct – In this context, it refers to a circle to be within/part of or to be without – not part of/outside the circle. It does not refer to without in terms of not possessing, i.e. to be without money; 4: Incorrect – The songs did not annoy him, but stirred him. The wild notes were a representation of the slaves' sadness and the depression came from the salves' predicament, not the quality of their singing.
Gabarito 1E, 2E, 3C, 4E

This text refers to the following three questions.

Darkness and light

1   Caravaggio's art is made from darkness and light. His pictures present spotlit moments of extreme and often agonized human experience. A man is decapitated in his bedchamber,
4   blood spurting from a deep gash in his neck. A woman is shot in the stomach with a bow and arrow at point-blank range. Caravaggio's images freeze time but also seem to hover on the
7   brink of their own disappearance. Faces are brightly illuminated. Details emerge from darkness with such uncanny clarity that they might be hallucinations. Yet always the
10 shadows encroach, the pools of blackness that threaten to obliterate all. Looking at his pictures is like looking at the world of flashes of lightning.
13 Caravaggio's life is like his art, a series of lightning flashes in the darkness of nights. He is a man who can never be known in full because almost all that he did, said and thought
16 is lost in the irrecoverable past. He was one of the most electrifying original artists ever to have lived, yet we have only one solitary sentence from him on the subject of painting —
19 the sincerity of which is, in any case, questionable, since it was elicited from him when he was under interrogation for the capital crime of libel.
22 When Caravaggio emerges from the obscurity of the past he does so, like the characters in his own paintings, as a man in extremis. He lived much of his life as a fugitive, and
25 that is how he is preserved in history — a man on the run, heading for the hills, keeping to the shadows. But he is caught, now and again, by the sweeping beam of a searchlight. Each
28 glimpse is different. He appears in many guises and moods. Caravaggio throws stones at the house of his landlady and sings ribald songs outside her window. He has a fight with a
31 waiter about the dressing on a plate of artichokes. His life is a series of intriguing and vivid tableaux — scenes that abruptly switch from low farce to high drama.

Andrew Graham-Dixon. **Caravaggio: a life sacred and profane**. New York – London: W. W. Norton & Company, 2010 (adapted).

(Diplomacia – 2012 – CESPE) Based on the text, judge if the following items are right (C) or wrong (E).

(1) In the second paragraph, the author suggests that information collected under duress is not reliable.

(2) The text is built on images associated with darkness, which suggests that Caravaggio's life, as well as the quality of his art, was shadowy and shady.

(3) The author provides the opening paragraph with a cinematic quality for he attempts to create dynamic scenes.

(4) From the passage "He is a man who can never be known in full because almost all that he did, said and thought is lost in the irrecoverable past." (*l*.14-16) it can be correctly inferred that the author is of the opinion that the study of history is a futile attempt to reconstruct events from the past.

(Interpretation) 1: Correct – The information was elicited/brought about under interrogation. If interrogated, it is feasible to say the information was elicited under duress/under threat or coercion; 2: Incorrect – This is a question with many possible interpretations. Shadowy can mean lacking substance or full of dark shadows. Shady can mean full of shade or being of dubious quality. If we accept the second definition in both cases, the question is clearly incorrect as Caravaggio's art is not of dubious quality. Perhaps it is too much to infer from the information in the text about his life or that darkness in the text represented him, his life and his work. A difficult question requiring a deep understanding of the vocabulary used in the text and question; 3: Correct – It is possible to say that in lines 3-7 the author provides a dynamic, open scene, similar to that of a film; 4: Incorrect – This is too strong an assertion to agree with. We only have information about Caravaggio and not about history and its study on the whole.

Gabarito 1C, 2E, 3C, 4E

(Diplomacia – 2012 – CESPE) In line 5, "at point-blank range" means

(A) in a cold-blooded manner.
(B) summarily.
(C) without intention.
(D) fatally.
(E) within a short distance.

(Vocabulary) A: Incorrect – This means without pity/ruthlessly; B: Incorrect – This means quickly and without ceremony; C: Incorrect – This means by accident; D: Incorrect – This means causing death; E: Correct – To shoot someone at point-blank range means at a short distance.

Gabarito "E".

(Diplomacia – 2012 – CESPE) In the last paragraph of the text, the cause for Caravaggio's disagreement with the waiter was

(A) the sauce served with the artichokes.
(B) the inartistic appearance of the food.
(C) the unaffordable price of the plate.
(D) the frugality of the dish.
(E) the lack of freshness of the artichokes.

(Vocabulary) A: Correct – Dressing (noun) refers to a sauce usually for salads; B: Incorrect – No evidence; C: Incorrect – No evidence; D: Incorrect – Frugality refers to meanness/small portion; E: Incorrect – No evidence.

Gabarito "A".

This text refers to the next three questions.

1   Nobel was an ardent advocate of arbitration, though not of disarmament, which he thought a foolish demand for the present. He urged establishment of a tribunal and agreement
4   among nations for a one-year period of compulsory truce in any dispute. He turned up in person, though incognito, at a Peace Congress in Bern in 1892 and told Bertha von Suttner
7   that if she could "inform me, convince me, I will do something great for the cause". The spark of friendship between them had been kept alive in correspondence and an occasional visit over
10 the years and he now wrote her that a new era of violence seemed to be working itself up: "one hears in the distance its hollow rumble already." Two months later he wrote again,
13 "I should like to dispose of my fortune to found a prize to be awarded every five years" to the person who had contributed most effectively to the peace of Europe. He thought that it
16 should terminate after six awards, "for if in thirty years society cannot be reformed we shall inevitably lapse into barbarism". Nobel brooded over the plan, embodied it in a will drawn in
19 1895 which allowed man a little longer deadline, and died the following year.

Barbara Tuchman. **The proud power**. MacMillan Company, 1966, p. 233 (adapted).

(Diplomacia 2011) Based on the text, judge if the following items are right (C) or wrong (E).

(1) It can be inferred from the text that Nobel did a dramatic volte-face concerning his stance on peace or disarmament.

(2) Nobel predicted that peace would only last thirty years, because violence in Europe was increasing.

(3) Nobel suggested that ominous signs of impending violence could be discerned in the offing
(4) The author puts forward a tentative suggestion that Nobel's continued commitment to the cause of arbitration rendered him impervious to the idea of disarmament.

(Interpretation) 1: Correct – On lines 1 to 3, Nobel is described as a man who was not an advocate of disarmament, meaning he believed in people bearing arms. On lines 12 to 15, Nobel changes his mind, offering his fortune, in the form of a prize, to anyone who had contributed to peace. The fact that two months after meeting Bertha von Suttner he should suddenly wish for peace, instead of arbitration (line 1), proves his volte-face (180° change of mind); **2:** Incorrect – Nobel did not predict peace would last 30 years, but rather that peace should be established in this period. He originally wanted to cancel the prize if peace had not been established within 30 years. He believed that after 30 years, if there were no peace, society would have already collapsed into barbarianism; **3:** Correct – On lines 10 to 12, Nobel wrote a letter to Bertha von Suttner in which he mentions a new era of violence. "In the offing" (imminent, looming) is equivalent, in this case, to "in the distance". The "hollow rumble of violence" suggests it is "ominous"; **4:** Incorrect – The author makes no such correlation of cause and effect concerning arbitration and disarmament. On lines 1 and 2, the author identifies these traits, but does not suggest any cause or effect between them.

Gabarito 1C, 2E, 3C 4E

(Diplomacia 2011) In the text,

(1) "brooded over" and "will", both on line 18, mean respectively pondered and **an official statement disposing of a person's property after his or her death.**
(2) the pronoun "it" (ℓ.15) refers to Nobel's fortune.
(3) the word 'for' (ℓ.16) can be replaced by since with no change in the original meaning of the sentence.
(4) the term "spark" (ℓ.8) is used in its connotative meaning.

(Vocabulary) 1: Correct – "Brood" means "dwell on", "ponder", "contemplate". "Will" and "testimony" are words used to talk about the official document concerning one's estate after decease; **2:** Incorrect – The word "it" refers to the "prize" on line 13 (which should terminate after 6 editions, or 30 years); **3:** Correct – "For" and "since" can both be conjunctions used in adverbial structures of cause/reason. "For" tends to be used more in literary texts; **4:** Correct – The connotative meaning of a word is that which is figurative or symbolic. The denotative meaning is literal. As there is no real fire involved in this question, the connotative meaning of "spark", in this case, "sparkle", "ignite", and "flicker", is more fitting.

Gabarito 1C, 2E, 3C 4C

(Diplomacia 2011) Which of the following statements about the verbs in the text is correct?

(A) The forms "brooded" (ℓ.18), "embodied" (ℓ.18) and "died" (ℓ.19) can be replaced, respectively, by has brooded, has embodied and has died without effecting a significant change in the original meaning of the text.
(B) In "The spark of friendship between them had been kept alive" (ℓ.8-9), the use of the form "had been" implies the connection between von Suttner and Nobel took place after the Peace Congress.
(C) The verbal form 'should' (ℓ.13) could be replaced by would without effecting a significant change in the meaning of the text.
(D) The use of the form 'to be awarded' (ℓ.13-14) directs the focus of the sentence to those who award the prize.
(E) In 'I will do something great' (ℓ.7-8), the use of 'will' conveys the idea of imposition.

(Grammar) A: Incorrect – Due to the fact that Nobel is dead, none of his actions can be referred to in the present perfect. All must necessarily be in the past; **B:** Incorrect - The use of the perfect structure here does not suggest that the "spark/connection" took place after the Peace Congress, but rather it took place AT the Peace Congress and continued on "after" it; **C:** Correct - In this case, "should" is the more formal modal verb, while "would" is the less formal, to express preference, desire, offer or inclination. They are completely synonymous in this case; **D:** Incorrect – The use of the passive voice does not direct focus to the awarder, but rather to the prize itself. The focus is on what is to be awarded, not on the giver, nor on the receiver; **E:** Incorrect – The modal verb "will", in this case, does not express an idea of imposition, but rather one of a decision made at the time of speaking which refers to a future action.

Gabarito "C".

This text refers to the next five questions.

1 It may not stir up international outrage like its seminamesake WikiLeaks, but Wikipedia sparks debate. The free online encyclopedia, which celebrates its tenth birthday on
4 January 15th, is a symbol of unpaid collaboration and one of the most popular destinations on the Internet, attracting some 400m visitors a month. It also faces serious charges of elitism.
7 Wikipedia offers more than 17m articles in 247 languages. Every day thousands of people edit entries or add new ones in return for nothing more than the satisfaction of
10 contributing to the stock of human knowledge. Wikipedia relies on its users' generosity to fill its coffers as well as its pages. Recent visitors to the website were confronted with
13 images of Jimmy Wales, a co-founder, and a request for donations. The campaign was annoying but effective, raising $ 16m in 50 days.
16 With its emphasis on bottom-up collaboration and the broad dissemination of knowledge, the online encyclopedia is in many ways an incarnation of the fundamental values of the
19 web. But Wikipedia also reveals some of the pitfalls of the increasingly popular "crowdsourcing" model of content creation. One is maintaining accuracy. On the whole,
22 Wikipedia's system of peer reviewing does a reasonable job of policing facts. But it is vulnerable to vandalism. Several politicians and TV personalities have had their deaths
25 announced in Wikipedia while they were still in fine fettle. Some observers argue the site should start paying expert editors to produce and oversee content, and sell
28 advertising to cover the cost. Problems with accuracy "are an inevitable consequence of a free-labour approach", argues Alex Jannykhin, of WikiExperts, which advises organisations on
31 how to create Wikipedia articles (the very existence of such outfits hints at Wikipedia's importance, as well as its susceptibility to outside influence). The encyclopedia's bosses
34 retort that such concerns are overblown and that taking advertisers would dent its appeal to users.

Wikipedia. The promise and perils of crowdsourcing content. *In:* **The Economist**, January 15th-21st, 2011, p. 69 (adapted).

(Diplomacia 2011) Based on the text, judge if the items below are right (C) or wrong (E).

(1) The basic concepts behind Wikipedia are inconsistent with the usefulness of unhindered access to the Internet.

(2) It is possible to deduce from the text that Wikipedia resorted to an appeal for public monetary contributions.
(3) One of the major concerns regarding the content of the online encyclopedia is its vulnerability to inclusion of imprecise information.
(4) Not all articles in Wikipedia must be submitted by personal individual collaborators.

(Interpretation) 1: Incorrect – On lines 17 to 19, the text confirms that the online encyclopedia incarnates the fundamentals of the web, which are bottom-up collaboration and the broad dissemination of the knowledge. This confirms consistency between the concepts of both systems; 2: Correct – On lines 12 to 15, the text affirms the co-founder's online request for donations. The text even emphasized how annoying the request was; 3: Correct – On lines 28 to 30, one of the WikiExperts admits to problems with accuracy and how they are the inevitable consequence of the free-labour approach. On lines 26 to 27, observers offering solutions confirms that there are concerns over such inaccuracy; 4: Correct – On line 20, the term "crowdsourcing" is the act of making an open request for a job or activity to a wider audience. This audience may consist of individuals or organizations. The latter is also referenced on line 30, where the text confirms that there is a service to help organizations when producing articles for Wikipedia.
Gabarito 1E, 2C, 3C 4C

(Diplomacia 2011) According to the text, judge if the following items are right (C) or wrong (E).

(1) On line 25, "while they were still in fine fettle" can be correctly rewritten as even before their bodies could be prepared for burial, without change in meaning.
(2) On line 23, "But it is vulnerable to vandalism" can be correctly replaced by Furthermore, it falls prey to vandalism, without change in meaning
(3) From the last paragraph, it is correct to infer that volunteer work is inherently slovenly and deceptive.
(4) The terms "stir up" (ℓ.1) and "sparks" (ℓ.2) bear a semantic relationship to the verb to fuel.

(Interpretation) 1: Incorrect – To be in "fine fettle", is to be in excellent condition. The text refers to "living" politicians and TV personalities, whose death was (pre)announced even though they were still alive. "Fine fettle" refers to them as living people, not to their corpses; 2: Incorrect – To be "vulnerable" means there is a chance, in this case, of vandalism. To say they "fall prey" confirms the vandalism, which the text does not; 3: Incorrect – On line 34, Wikipedia bosses find such accusations "overblown", meaning they are exaggerated. On line 33, the "susceptibility to outside influence" does not necessarily confirm slovenly or deceptive work. Such influence could be well-written and well-researched; 4: Correct – Both "stir up" and "spark" connotatively refer to "ignite" or "fuel", all words with a meaning of "provoke".
Gabarito 1E, 2E, 3E, 4C

(Diplomacia 2011) According to what the text states, choose the correct option.

(A) Underlying the idea of Wikipedia is the premise of a profitable approach to the compilation and diffusion of human values and customs.
(B) Contributions to Wikipedia come both in the form of spontaneous inclusion and reviewing of texts as well as of gifts of money.
(C) Advertising would increase the reliability and acceptance of Wikipedia, according to its owners.
(D) The bulk of Wikipedia articles deliberately misguide its users as to the actual death of some celebrities.
(E) Wikipedia is not free of charge, for it launches aggressive worldwide fund-raising campaigns.

(Interpretation) A: Incorrect – On line 4, the text confirms that collaboration is "unpaid" as does the term "free-labour approach". On lines 10 and 11, the text explains that "Wikipedia relies on "its users' generosity to fill its coffers", meaning all inflow of product and money is donated, thus no profit-based system is used; B: Correct – On line 4, the term "unpaid collaboration", together with the information on lines 8 to 10, that people "edit entries or add new ones in return for nothing more than the satisfaction of contributing to the stock of human knowledge" confirms that people spontaneously include and review texts. On lines 12 to 15, the text confirms financial donations were requested and effectively raised "$16m in 50 days"; C: Incorrect – It is not the owners, but rather some "observers" that believe Wikipedia, as cited on lines 26 to 28, "should start paying expert editors to produce and oversee content, and sell advertising"; D: Incorrect – On lines 21 to 23, the text confirms that Wikipedia's peer reviewing system "does a reasonable job of policing facts", meaning that, while some articles are misleading, it is not the bulk (most) of articles that misguide users with false information; E: Incorrect – On lines 13 and 14, the text confirms that the fund-raising campaign was based on "donations". The service is still free to those who choose not to make a donation.
Gabarito "B".

(Diplomacia 2011) In the text, the word "overblown" (ℓ.34) is synonymous with

(A) excessive.
(B) widespread.
(C) fundamental.
(D) grave.
(E) mounting.

(Vocabulary) A: Correct – "Overblown" means "exaggerated" or "overstated", also synonyms of "excessive"; B: Incorrect – This adjective does not refer to the magnitude of the issue, but rather to its reach or range of dissemination; C: Incorrect – This adjective "belittles" the issue, or states that it is "essential" – neither of which are suitable synonyms; D: Incorrect – This adjective refers to the "seriousness" of the issue. On line 34, the text confirms that Wikipedia bosses "retorted", meaning that they disagreed with observers who were "overstating" the problem. Such disagreement with the observers negates the seriousness of the issue; E: Incorrect – This adjective refers to the idea that the issue is "increasing" or "growing". This is not the case.
Gabarito "A".

(Diplomacia 2011) In the text, the expression "peer reviewing" (ℓ.22) refers to

(A) a thorough check of facts and figures carried out by individuals who have spotless academic reputations.
(B) an enforcement of rules similar to that performed by police officers.
(C) the system used by Wikipedia to minimize the publication of false information.
(D) the mounting pressure brought to bear on an individual by his or her colleagues.
(E) a friendly way of going over factual research.

(Vocabulary) A: Incorrect – The text does not confirm who the individuals are that check information. There is no indication in the text that such individuals have spotless academic reputations; **B:** Incorrect – The verb "to police", on line 23, refers to an idea of "verifying" or "checking", and does not involve the law enforcement authorities in any way; **C:** Correct – On lines 22 and 23, the text confirms that Wikipedia uses this system to police (verify) information; **D:** Incorrect – "Peer reviewing" may be inferred as a "pressure" on an individual, but this is not mentioned in this text; **E:** Incorrect – "Peer reviewing" may be inferred as "friendly", but this is not mentioned in this text. The term "peer" merely suggests that reviewers are not necessarily academic experts. It does not mean that it is a friendly approach to verification of facts.

Gabarito "C."

This text refers to the next four questions

1. Remembrance of things past is often dearest to those who are bored or driven to despair by the world around them. To these the contemplation of times gone by brings surcease
4. from current burdens too heavy to bear. "Take not away from me" implored the Emperor Julian, world-weary monarch in another age of disenchantment, "this mad love for that which
7. no longer is. That which has been is more splendidly beautiful than all that is…" To others, concerned as watchers and movers with the challenge of today and the promise or menace
10. of tomorrow, the tale of many yesterdays, reconstructed by the history and the science of living men and women, has another meaning.
13. By revealing what has gone before, it illumines the act of the human adventure now being played and suggests the pattern of acts to come. The drama of earthborn and
16. earthbound humanity, despite all its crises and intermissions, is a continuous story. All the characters are prisoners of time. All the problems of the now are forever shaped by the
19. experiences of a then which extends back in unbroken sequence to the origins of life. Each generation has freedom to choose among alternative designs for destiny, and opportunity
22. to win some measure of mastery over its fate, only to the extent of its comprehension of where it stands in the cavalcade of years, decades, centuries, and millennia ticked off by the
25. spinning planet.

Frederick L. Schuman. **International politics: the destiny of the Western state system.** New York: McGraw-Hill, 1948, p. 1 (adapted).

(Diplomacia 2011) Based on the text, judge if the items below are right (C) or wrong (E).

(1) One can infer from the text that backward or nostalgic views of the world have existed for more than a thousand years.
(2) According to the text, although past events should be taken into consideration, humankind can choose its future and destiny freely.
(3) The author of the text suggests that nostalgia is the preserve of desperate people.
(4) The author's clear intention in the first paragraph is to rightly extol the virtues of extreme political reactionarism.

(Interpretation) 1: Correct – The reference to the nostalgia of Emperor Julian (lines 5-8) allow us to infer this; **2:** Incorrect – On lines 22 to 25, the idea that humanity is free to choose is limited to the understanding of its position over a long stretch of time (comprehension of where it stands in the cavalcade of years, decades, centuries, and millennia). Therefore, the future and destiny cannot be chosen freely; **3:** Correct – On lines 1 and 2, the author confirms that remembrance (nostalgia) is "dearest to those (…) driven to despair", or desperate people; **4:** Incorrect – The first paragraph muses on how the past affects the present, using the example of Emperor Julian. The first paragraph, while making references to political positions ("watchers and movers" lines 8 and 9), does not refer to extreme reactionism, but rather to interpretations of the present and past.

Gabarito 1C, 2E, 3C 4E

(Diplomacia 2011) As far as the semantic and grammar features of the text are concerned, judge if the following items are right (C) or wrong (E).

(1) The word "and" ($\ell.15$) is used as a stylistic device to bring together two synonymous words, "earthborn" ($\ell.15$) and "earthbound" ($\ell.16$).
(2) The pronoun "it" (R13) refers to "another meaning" ($\ell.11$-12)
(3) A more up-to-date manner to convey the notion expressed by "illumines" ($\ell.13$) is sheds light on.
(4) The expression "watchers and movers" ($\ell.8$-9) refers to people who play clearly distinct roles as far as political action is concerned.

(Grammar) 1: Incorrect – While the coordinating conjunction "and" is joining two adjectives, they are not synonymous. The former (earthborn) refers to the origin of humanity, while the latter (earthbound) refers to the limits or limitations of it; **2:** Incorrect – The word "it" refers to "tale of many yesterdays", or, if you prefer, the past. It is not "another meaning", but rather the past that "illumines the act of the human adventure now being played and suggests the pattern of acts to come"; **3:** Correct – "To shed light on" something is synonymous with "to illuminate"; **4:** Correct – "Watchers" refers to those that are responsible for observing and policing political action, while "movers" refers to those that take action.

Gabarito 1E, 2E, 3C 4C

(Diplomacia 2011) Still in the fields of semantics and grammar of the text, judge if the items below are right (C) or wrong (E).

(1) If "ticked off" ($\ell.24$) and "spinning" ($\ell.25$) were replaced respectively by marked off and rotating, there would occur no grammar mistakes in the sentence.
(2) The words "crises" ($\ell.16$) and "millennia" ($\ell.24$), as well as theses and fulcra, can only be found in their plural forms.
(3) In the fragment "All the problems of the now are forever shaped by the experiences of a then" ($\ell.18$-19), the words "now" and "then" can be replaced respectively by here and there without effecting changes in the meaning and the grammatical correction of the passage.
(4) In the first paragraph, the words "world-weary" ($\ell.5$) and "disenchantment" ($\ell.6$) establish a semantic relation which reveals the pessimism which was felt by the "monarch" ($\ell.5$) and characterized his "age" ($\ell.6$)

(Grammar) 1: Correct – "Marked off" and "rotating", respectively, are not only synonyms, but their morphological categories are perfect matches (the former being a subordinating restrictive adjective clause reduced by the past particle, and the latter, a gerund acting as a simple adjective); **2:** Incorrect – "Crisis" is the singular form of "crises"; "millennium" is the singular form of "millennia"; "thesis" is the singular form of "theses", and "fulcrum" is the singular form of "fulcra" (prop or support in the physical sense). Therefore, all four words have singular and plural forms; **3:** Incorrect – "Now" and "then" are adverbs of time, while "here" and "there" are adverbs of place. Therefore, substitution would cause a major change in meaning; **4: Correct** – "World-weary" suggests that the monarch had vast experience in the past and that this had tired him, thus he was old. "Disenchantment", in its turn, suggests that his experience had made him cynical and pessimistic about the world. Also, the fact that this was not his first disenchantment (another age, line 6) places emphasis on his age.

Gabarito 1C, 2E, 3E, 4C

(Diplomacia 2011) The particle "as" (l.8) is used in the text

(A) to express the idea of in the same way..
(B) to describe the purpose or quality of someone or something.
(C) to express the idea of because.
(D) to express the idea of while.
(E) in a comparison to refer to the degree of something.

(Grammar) A: Incorrect – In this case, "as" is not comparing watchers and movers; **B: Correct** – The word "as", in this case, suggest that somebody is "working as", or "acting as", which is a direct reference to purpose/with the aim of; **C: Incorrect** – In this case, "as" is not expressing an idea of reason; **D: Incorrect** – In this case, "as" is not expressing an idea of time; **E: Incorrect** – In this case, "as" is not expressing an idea of intensity, nor is there any comparison made.

Gabarito "B".

This text refers to the next four questions.

Oriana, the agitator

1 Oriana Fallaci, the Italian writer and journalist best known for her abrasive tone and provocative stances, was for two decades, from the mid-nineteen-sixties to the
4 mid-nineteen-eighties, one of the sharpest political interviewers in the world. Her subjects were among the world's most powerful figures: Yasser Arafat, Golda Meir,
7 Indira Ghandi, Haile Selassie, Deng Xiaoping. Henry Kissinger, who later wrote that his 1972 interview with her was "the single most disastrous conversation I have ever had
10 with any member of the press," said that he had been flattered into granting it by the company he'd be keeping as part of Fallaci's "journalistic pantheon." It was more like a collection
13 of pelts: Fallaci never left her subjects unskinned.
Her manner of interviewing was deliberately unsettling: she approached each encounter with studied
16 aggressiveness, made frequent nods to European existentialism (she often disarmed her subjects with bald questions about death, God, and pity), and displayed a
19 sinuous, crafty intelligence. It didn't hurt that she was *petite* and beautiful, with perfect cheekbones, straight, smooth hair that she wore parted in the middle or in pigtails; melancholy
22 blue-grey eyes, set off by eyeliner; a cigarette-cured voice; and an adorable Italian accent. During the Vietnam War, she was sometimes photographed in fatigues and a helmet; her
25 rucksack bore handwritten instructions to return her body to the Italian Ambassador "if K.I.A." In these images she looked slight and vulnerable as a child. Her essential toughness never
28 stopped taking people — men, especially — by surprise. Fallaci's journalism was infused with a "mythic sense of political evil", an almost adolescent aversion to power,
31 which suited the temperament of the times. "Whether," she would say, "it comes from a despotic sovereign or an elected president, from a murderous general or a beloved leader, I see
34 power as an inhuman and hateful phenomenon… I have always looked on disobedience towards the oppressive as the only way to use the miracle of having been born." In her
37 interview with Kissinger, she told him that he had become known as "Nixon's mental wet nurse," and lured him into boasting that Americans admired him because he "always
40 acted alone" — like "the cowboy who leads the wagon train by riding ahead alone on his horse, the cowboy who rides all alone into the town." Political cartoonists mercilessly
43 lampooned this remark, and, according to Kissinger's memoirs, the quote soured his relations with Nixon (Kissinger claimed that she had taken his words out of context). But the
46 most remarkable moment in the interview came when Fallaci bluntly asked him, about Vietnam, "Don't you find, Dr. Kissinger, that it's been a useless war?", and he began his
49 reply with the words, "On this, I can agree."

Internet: <www.newyorker.com> (adapted).

(Diplomacia 2010) From the previous text, it can be inferred that Oriana Fallaci

(A) seemed at times defenceless, vulnerable, and child-like.
(B) had just quit smoking cigarettes.
(C) tried deliberately to use the music-like quality of her mother tongue to lure her interviewers.
(D) grew tired of the Vietnam War.
(E) had become a close friend of the Italian Ambassador in Hanoi at the time of the war.

(Interpretation) A: Correct - Use of the word 'slight' (line 27) (small-frail) and child-like)' support this answer; **B: Incorrect** - (Line 22 – cigarette-cured voice refers to the tone of her voice having changed due to smoking, not that she had quit smoking; **C: Incorrect** - Even though the text states her Italian accent was adorable (line 23), it does not imply that she deliberately used it to seduce (lure) interviewers; **D: Incorrect** – On lines 23 and 24, the word "fatigues", in this text, is a noun meaning "army or military clothing". It is not the adjective "fatigued"; **E: Incorrect** - There is no evidence to suggest a strong relationship with the Ambassador.

Gabarito "A".

(Diplomacia 2010) In the fragment, "lured him into boasting that Americans admired him" (l.38-39), the words "lured" and "boasting" mean, respectively,

(A) pressed and stating.
(B) tempted and denying.
(C) enticed and bragging.
(D) challenged and acknowledging.
(E) coerced and showing off.

(Vocabulary) A: Incorrect - Pressed means to force. To state means to declare; **B: Incorrect** - Tempted works as a synonym for lure; however, deny does not, for boasting; **C: Correct** - To entice means to lure or to seduce. To brag is a close synonym of to boast; **D: Incorrect** - Neither challenge nor acknowledging work as synonyms here; **E: Incorrect** - Coercion has the idea of force or compel. Showing off could work as a synonym for bragging.

Gabarito "C".

(Diplomacia 2010) Based on the text, judge — right (C) or wrong (E) — the items below.

(1) The highly professional sense of Fallaci as a journalist in search of truth made her avoid any sort of tricks in approaching her interviewees, both powerful figures and common people.
(2) Fallaci had either been a heavy smoker or had smoked for a long time.
(3) Fallaci exploited Kissinger's somewhat big ego to trick him into making some public statements he would later regret.

(4) Kissinger seems to suggest that Fallaci was not entirely professionally ethical or honest when dealing with the interview he had granted her.

(Interpretation) 1: Incorrect - No mention in the text about professionalism and it does mention that she was crafty (sneaky or wily) and sinuous (devious) (line 19) in her approach; **2:** Correct - Due to her cigarette-cured (line 22) voice, we can infer this is correct. To cure (verb) is to process or preserve in smoke; **3:** Correct - By suggesting that he was Kissinger's wet-nurse (line 38) (nanny or carer), she played to Kissinger's ego. He clearly states that the interview was his most disastrous interview ever (line 9 and 10), and it negatively affected his relations with Nixon; **4:** Correct - Kissinger said that she took his words out of context (line 45). This would represent unethical and dishonest behavior.
Gabarito 1E, 2C, 3C, 4C

(Diplomacia 2010) Based on the text, judge — right (C) or wrong (E) the following items.

(1) Although fascinated by power, Fallaci was more lenient with democratically elected politicians.
(2) Fallaci, in her interview with Kissinger, praised President Nixon to constraint Kissinger.
(3) Kissinger believed he rightfully belonged to the very select group of world politicians Fallaci had already interviewed.
(4) One of the basic criteria Fallaci adopted to hand-pick her interviewees was gender-based: half of them had to be necessarily women politicians.

(Interpretation) 1: Incorrect - Fallaci treated everyone equally and had a dislike of tyrants and elected politicians alike. She found power to be inhuman and hateful (line 34); **2:** Incorrect - Fallaci never praises Nixon. There is therefore no evidence that she tries to restrain (inhibit or hold back) Kissinger by doing this; **3:** Correct – The use of 'the company he would be keeping' (line 11) allows us to infer that Kissinger felt he should be among the famous people who had been interviewed by Fallaci. It is difficult to say he felt he rightfully belonged to this group, but it can be inferred from the way Kissinger is presented as boasting and acting vain in the rest of the text; **4:** Incorrect - There is no evidence to support this. Men, especially men (line 28), were surprised by her, but that does not allow us to infer how she selected her interviewees.
Gabarito 1E, 2E, 3C, 4E

This text refers to the next four questions.

Amartya Sen

1 Freedom, in the eyes of Amartya Sen, the famous Indian economist and philosopher, does not consist merely of being left to our own devices. It also requires that people have
4 the necessary resources to lead lives that they themselves consider to be good ones. The focus on the individual has led some critics to accuse Sen of "methodological individualism"
7 — not a compliment. Communitarian opponents, in particular, think that he pays insufficient regard to the broader social group. In response, he — usually an unfailingly courteous
10 writer — becomes a bit cross, pointing out that "people who think, choose and act" are simply "a manifest reality in the world". Of course communities influence people, "but
13 ultimately it is individual valuation on which we have to draw, while recognising the profound interdependence of the valuations of people who interact with each other".
16 Nor is Sen easily caricatured as an egalitarian: "capabilities", for example, do not have to be entirely equal. He is a pluralist, and recognises that even capabilities cannot
19 always trump other values. Liberty has priority, Sen insists, but not in an absurdly purist fashion that would dictate "treating the slightest gain of liberty — no matter how small
22 — as enough reason to make huge sacrifices in other amenities of a good life — no matter how large".
Throughout, Sen remains true to his Indian roots. One
25 of the joys of his recently published book entitled **The Idea of Justice** is the rich use of Indian classical thought — the debate between 3rd-century emperor Ashoka, a liberal
28 optimist, and Kautilya, a downbeat institutionalist, is much more enlightening than, say, a tired contrast between Hobbes and Hume.
31 Despite these diverting stories, the volume cannot be said to fall into the category of a "beach read": subtitles such as "The Plurality of Non-Rejectability" provide plenty of
34 warning. But for those who like their summer dinner tables to be filled with intelligent, dissenting discourse, the book is worth the weight. There is plenty here to argue with. Sen
37 wouldn't have it any other way.

Internet: <http://entertainment.timesonline.co.uk> (adapted).

(Diplomacia 2010) Based on the text above, it can be said that the relationship established between the ideas of "unfailingly courteous" ($\ell.9$) and "cross" ($\ell.10$) is one of

(A) contrast.
(B) reiteration.
(C) inclusion.
(D) result.
(E) addition.

(Interpretation) (Vocabulary) A: Correct - Courteous means to be polite, whilst cross is to be angry or in a bad mood. The two behaviors are contrasted; **B:** Incorrect - This means to repeat; **C:** Incorrect - This means to include; **D:** Incorrect - This means there was a cause and effect. There is not; **E:** Incorrect - This means that the two attitudes are similar. They are not.
Gabarito "A".

(Diplomacia 2010) In the fragment, "even capabilities cannot always trump other values" ($\ell.18$-19), the verb "trump" means

(A) to be bracketed with.
(B) to foster.
(C) to vie against.
(D) to prevail over.
(E) to hold on to.

(Vocabulary) A: Incorrect - This means to be placed in the same category; **B:** Incorrect - This means to encourage; **C:** Incorrect - This means to compete against; **D:** Correct - To trump means to get the better of or to prevail over; **E:** Incorrect - This means to secure.
Gabarito "D".

(Diplomacia 2010) According to the text, judge — right (C) or wrong (E) — the items below.

(1) South-east Asian classical economics rather than European philosophy laid the main theoretical and practical foundation for Sen's theses.
(2) Communitarian opponents make up the largest and most vocal group of Sen's critics.
(3) Sen's work, although focused on the individual and on the idea of liberty, does not lose sight of the inherent dynamics of the different communities.
(4) Sen dismisses out of hand the ideas advanced by English philosophers of the XVII and XVIII centuries.

(Interpretation) 1: Incorrect - The second part of the question is correct – Hobbes and Hume are considered European philosophers. The reference on line 26 is not to economics, but to 'classical thought', i.e. that of the political sciences in general; **2:** Incorrect - With reference to line 7, communitarian opponents focus on a particular aspect of Sen's theory. It is too much to infer that they are the most vocal or the largest group of opponents; **3:** Correct - In line 12, Sen states that of course communities influence people – more decisively is the direct quotation in line 14 which acknowledges, "The profound interdependence" and 'those who interact with each other". These views substantiate the view that Sen recognizes the inherent dynamics of different communities; **4:** Incorrect - To dismiss out of hand means to completely disregard or reject. Sen does not do this; rather it is the author of the article that complains about the English philosophers. (line 29 – a tired contrast, i.e. a boring or an overused contrast).

Gabarito 1E, 2E, 3C, 4E

(Diplomacia 2010) Based on the text, judge — right (C) or wrong (E) the following items.

(1) Communitarians' major objection against Sen is based on his vigorous defence of unmitigated individualism.

(2) Sen finds the theses put forward by Ashoka and Kautilya to be more ground-breaking and insightful than those proposed by some major Western philosophers 14 or 15 centuries later.

(3) Even Sen's followers resent the sheer lack of purism in his championing of freedom.

(4) Despite having a usually gentle disposition, Sen often flies into a nasty temper whenever any of his ideas are challenged.

(Interpretation) 1: Incorrect - The major objection of Communitarians is Sen's lack of focus on 'the broader social group' (line 10), but later, on lines 14 and 15, Sen clearly states that we must recognize "the profound interdependence of the valuations of people who interact with each other". And, on line 20, it states that he does not view things in an 'absurdly purist fashion'. These parts show he does not defend "unmitigated" individualism, but a more "relative" individualism; **2:** Incorrect - There is no evidence to support that Sen thinks this. In fact, it is the author's value judgment that Sen's examples are enlightening (insightful) and groundbreaking (new or innovative); **3:** Incorrect - There is no mention of Sen's followers or what they think of his position; **4:** Incorrect - The text does not say he is gentle, but rather that he is unfailingly polite (always with good manners). A nasty temper is an overstatement as becoming 'a bit cross' line 10 is far weaker and shows only mild irritation.

Gabarito 1E, 2E, 3E, 4E

This text refers to the next four questions.

1 "For heaven's sake," *1* my father said, seeing me off at the airport, "don't get drunk, don't get pregnant — and don't get involved in politics." He was right to be concerned.
4 Rhodes University in the late 1970s, with its Sir Herbert Baker-designed campus and lush green lawns, looked prosperous and sedate. But the Sunday newspapers had been
7 full of the escapades of its notorious drinking clubs and loose morals; the Eastern Cape was, after the riots of 1976, a place of turmoil and desperate poverty; and the campus was thought
10 by most conservative parents to be a hotbed of political activity.
 The Nationalist policy of forced removals meant
13 thousands of black people had been moved from the cities into the nearby black "homelands" of Transkei and Ciskei, and dumped there with only a standpipe and a couple of huts
16 for company; two out of three children died of malnutrition before the age of three. I arrived in 1977, the year after the Soweto riots, to study journalism. Months later, Steve Biko
19 was murdered in custody. The campus tipped over into turmoil. There were demonstrations and hunger strikes. For most of us, Rhodes was a revelation. We had been
22 brought up to respect authority. Here, we could forge a whole new identity, personally and politically. Out of that class of 1979 came two women whose identities merge with the
25 painful birth of the new South Africa: two journalism students whose journey was to take them through defiance, imprisonment and torture during the apartheid years.
28 One of the quietest girls in the class, Marion Sparg, joined the ANC's military wing, Umkhonto we Sizwe (MK), and was eventually convicted of bombing two police stations.
31 An Asian journalist, Zubeida Jaffer, was imprisoned and tortured, yet ultimately chose not to prosecute her torturers. Today you can trace the footprints of my classmates
34 across the opposition press in South Africa and the liberal press in the UK — The Guardian, the Observer and the Financial Times. Even the Spectator (that's me). Because
37 journalism was not a course offered at "black" universities, we had a scattering of black students. It was the first time many of us would ever have met anyone who was black and
40 not a servant. I went to hear Pik Botha, the foreign minister, a Hitlerian figure with a narrow moustache, an imposing bulk and a posse of security men. His reception was suitably
43 stormy, even mocking — students flapping their arms and saying, "Pik-pik-pik-P-I-I-I-K!', like chattering hens.
 But students who asked questions had to identify
46 themselves first. There were spies in every class. We never worked out who they were, although some of us suspected the friendly Afrikaans guy with the shark's tooth necklace.

Janice Warman. **South Africa's Rebel Whites.**
In: **The Guardian Weekly**, 20/11/2009 (adapted).

(Diplomacia 2010) Based on the text, judge — right (C) or wrong (E) — the items below.

(1) Of the three journalism students mentioned in the text, it can be said that the most self-effacing and reserved of them all turned out to be the one to deliver a most violent blow against the apartheid security apparatus.

(2) The university the author attended can be described as a place where neither the teaching staff nor school officials exacted blind obedience from students.

(3) The author clearly underscores the striking resemblance the Nationalist Party of South Africa bears to its Nazi counterpart.

(4) Students decided to burlesque Botha's performance as an ineffectual and chicken-hearted foreign minister by doing a ludicrous and crude imitation of a bird.

(Interpretation) 1: Correct - Of the two named journalists, there is no evidence of what they actually did to damage apartheid, only that one joined the ANC and the other was arrested and tortured. The third journalist, the author (line 36 – the Spectator, that's me), went on in her own words to play a part in shaping the liberal press in the UK (line 34). We can assert she was self-effacing (modest) and reserved by the fact that she gives more attention to her other two classmates and not herself and by the use of "even the Spectator" (implying that it is not such an influential newspaper as the other named). We find this to be an extremely difficult question which would require sound knowledge of the vocabulary used, a deep reading of the text, as well as some knowledge of the context (journalism); **2:** Correct - Even though it seemed respectable, the university is described as a 'hotbed' line 10 (breeding ground) of political activity. Line 22 shows that, in contrast to their obedient backgrounds, students could forge new political and personal perspectives, thus showing the lack of control and blind obedience; **3:** Incorrect - Striking resemblance refers to a physical resemblance. Although he had a moustache, Botha is described as having an imposing bulk (i.e. big and strong/burly). The adjective Hitlerian refers to being suggestive of Hitler in style and manner, not look; **4:** Incorrect - To burlesque (to imitate or mock humoursly). Yes, students mocked Botha by parodying his name with the sound of a chicken. It is less clear that this was meant to imply being ineffectual (useless or worthless) or chicken-hearted (cowardly). As Botha was a much feared leader of a violent regime (lines 41 and 42), perhaps it is quite a leap to consider him both ineffectual and a coward.

Gabarito Oficial 1C, 3E, 4C/ Gabarito Nosso 1C, 2C, 3E, 4E

(Diplomacia 2010) The author creates in the reader's mind the distinct impression that her father was

(A) an overprotective and controlling individual who wanted to be an integral part in all aspects of his daughter's life.
(B) prudish parent who persistently demanded that his daughter be or appear to be very prim, proper, modest and righteous at all times.
(C) a paranoid father who refused to let go, and clamped her down with hard and fast rules and strict discipline.
(D) a doting father whose motto could very well be "Spare the rod, spoil the child".
(E) a caring parent who was well-aware of the peculiar atmosphere that pervaded college campuses in the late '70s: permissive, in a state of constant political unrest, and overindulgent in terms of drinking.

(Interpretation) A: Incorrect - Genuine parental advice is given in the opening paragraph – this is not a suggestion of controlling or overprotection; **B:** Incorrect - Too much inference. His advice was parental guidance, but he did not demand modesty or righteousness; **C:** Incorrect - The father in question merely gives advice. If this were the case, his daughter would not be allowed to go away to university; **D:** Incorrect - While the father may be doting (extremely loving), the motto implies the use of physical punishment to discipline children – this is not mentioned in the text; **E:** Correct - The father's advice in lines 1-3 reflects exactly this statement.

Gabarito "E".

(Diplomacia 2010) The overall view the author outlines of late '70s South Africa is

(A) unduly optimistic, coloured by the typically unattainable idealism of young people.
(B) predictably hopelessly distorted by the author's white middle-class background and petit bourgeois values.
(C) inherently flawed and, therefore, pointless for it fails to place the country in a broader regional, African, or world context.
(D) basically descriptive and provides information about a politically, socially, and racially unequal and unfair society poised on the verge of momentous changes.
(E) oddly detached and unemotional due, perhaps, to the fact that she can only sympathize with the oppressed black population's plight up to a point.

(Interpretation) A: Incorrect - Unduly (excessively) is too strong a statement to support; **B:** Incorrect - The author can be said to be white (line 39) and probably middle class as she comes from and obedient background and is a university student; however, the points on 'hopeless distorted' and 'petit bourgeois values' cannot be substantiated by evidence in the text; **C:** Incorrect - No evidence to support this at all. Vague… what about… The author makes several references concerning the importance of the region (lines 8, 14, 17) and how this mattered to the world (33 to 36); **D:** Correct - It is descriptive as it focuses on the author's first hand experiences. The text touches on all the aspects mentioned in this option; **E:** Incorrect - There is no evidence that the author's sympathy with the oppressed black population is limited. To agree with this would be an extreme extrapolation of her position in society.
Note : A difficult question in terms of choosing an option – by elimination it would come down to D or E, with D being the least risky option.

Gabarito "D".

(Diplomacia 2010) In the text,

(1) "hotbed" (*l*.10) is synonymous with **breeding ground**..
(2) "tipped over" (*l*.19) can be replaced by **was plunged**.
(3) "scattering" (*l*.38) can be paraphrased as **an unruly mob**.
(4) "posse" (*l*.42) and **entourage** are interchangeable.

(Vocabulary) 1: Correct - Both good synonyms; **2:** Correct - To tip over (overturn). Plunged means to fall quickly; **3:** Incorrect - Scattering (a small amount) neutral connotation. Unruly mob (riotous group which is difficult to control) pejorative sense; 4: Incorrect - Both mean group, However, posse has the connotation of a gang, whilst entourage has the connotation of an official group surrounding an important person. Synonyms in the broadest sense; but, perhaps, not always when used in context.

Gabarito Oficial 1C, 2C, 3E, 4C/ Nosso Gabarito 1C, 2C, 3E, 4E

This text refers to the next four questions.

1   Fundamentalism has one interesting insight. It perceives the science-based, libertarian, humanist
4   culture of the modern era as being itself a kind of new religion — and its deadly enemy. We fail to see this because we are immersed in it, it dominates more than nine-tenths of our lives, and it is so
7   amorphous. It has no officially recognised scriptures, creeds, prophets or organisation. Rather, it is a loose coalition of many different forces, kept on the move
10 and in constant self-criticism and self-correction by an active and striving ethic derived from Protestantism. So far as this new faith — if that is
13 what it is — has theologians, priests and prophets, they are, respectively, the scientists and scholars whose business it is to criticise and increase
16 knowledge, the artists who refine our perceptions and open up new life-possibilities, and the armies of idealistic campaigners who urge us to become active
19 in hundreds of good causes.
    So seductive and compelling is this new faith that it is somehow impossible to avoid adopting its
22 language and its way of thinking. They are everywhere, and irresistible. That is what makes it like a religion: once we are in the midst of it and do
25 not appreciate how strong and distinctive a flavour it has, we are largely unaware of its awesome, unstoppable, disruptive evangelistic power.

Don Cuppitt. **The sea of faith**. London: British
Broadcasting Corporation, 1985, p. 181
(adapted).

(Diplomacia 2009) It can be concluded from the text that

(A) fundamentalism is more intuitively perceptive than secular culture.
(B) scientists and scholars act the same way as theologians, priests and prophets.
(C) idealism compels people to join good causes.
(D) modern humanist culture is subliminally pervasive.
(E) Protestantism is the backbone of modern humanist culture.

(Interpretation) A: Incorrect - No comparison is made between the perception of secular culture or fundamentalism; **B:** Incorrect - Comparatively they perform a similar function, but they do not act the same way, e.g. do the same things with the same motivations; **C:** Incorrect - It is the campaigners who are idealistic (line 18), not those who get involved in good causes; **D:** Correct – Lines 20-25 support this. It is everywhere (pervasive) and, once in the middle of it, not noticeable (subliminal); **E:** Incorrect - Modern humanist culture is derived from Protestantism, but there is no evidence that it forms the backbone of it.
Gabarito "D".

(Diplomacia 2009) Judge — right (C) or wrong (E) — the following items with reference to the text.

(1) The pronoun "its" (ℓ.4) refers to "humanist culture" (ℓ.2-3).
(2) The word "Rather" (ℓ.8) means **more or less**.
(3) In context, the expression "So far as" (ℓ.12) means **as though**.
(4) The word "business" (ℓ.15) could be appropriately replaced by **concern**.

(Grammar) 1: Incorrect - 'Its' refers to fundamentalism; **2:** Incorrect - In this context, 'rather' means on the contrary; **3:** Incorrect - In this context, it means to the extent that; **4:** Correct – The example – It's none of your business or it's none of your concern illustrates this.
Gabarito 1E, 2E, 3E, 4C

(Diplomacia 2009) Indicate which of the following words or phrases would **not** be an appropriate synonym for the word "once" in the phrase "once we are in the midst of it" (ℓ.24).

(A) because.
(B) since
(C) whenever
(D) as
(E) inasmuch as

(Grammar) A: Correct – This would create a sense of cause or reason between the idea of "being in the midst of it" and "we are largely unaware". This is a possible interpretation of the text. The reason we become "unaware" is because we are "in the midst of it". This is reinforced by the comment on line 5 "we are immersed in it", which suggests that this is not something that happens every now and then, but rather a constant state of being; **B:** Correct – This would create a sense of cause or reason between the idea of "being in the midst of it" and "we are largely unaware". This is a possible interpretation of the text. "Since" (because) we are "in the midst of it", we become "unaware"; **C:** Incorrect - As a form of when, this refers to an idea of a time or moment. The text, on line 5, suggests that we are ALWAYS immersed in the science-based, libertarian, humanist culture. This does not happen every now and then; it is a constant state of being. The word "once", therefore, cannot refer to time. It refers to the fact that we are always in the midst of it, and that is WHY (the reason) we are unaware. In this case, the word "once" carries a sense of cause or reason and not time; **D:** Correct – This would create a sense of cause or reason between the idea of "being in the midst of it" and "we are largely unaware". This is a possible interpretation of the text. "As" (because) we are "in the midst of it", we become "unaware". This is reinforced by the comment on line 5 "we are immersed in it", which suggests that this is not something that happens every now and then, but rather a constant state of being; **E:** Correct – This would create a sense of cause or reason between the idea of "being in the midst of it" and "we are largely unaware". This is a possible interpretation of the text. "Inasmuch as" (because) we are "in the midst of it", we become "unaware". This is reinforced by the comment on line 5 "we are immersed in it", which suggests that this is not something that happens every now and then, but rather a constant state of being.
Gabarito "C".

(Diplomacia 2009) In the phrase "That is what makes it like a religion" (ℓ.23-24), the word "That" refers to

(A) the language and way of thinking being everywhere.
(B) the fact that one cannot avoid adopting its language and rationale.
(C) the pervasiveness of modern humanist culture.
(D) the seductiveness of science-based thinking.
(E) the ubiquitousness of the new faith.

(Grammar) A: Incorrect – It does refer to the idea of being everywhere, but not to the language; **B:** Correct - 'That' referring to the similarities between religion and modern humanist thought in terms of pervasiveness (line 22 – language and rationale are 'everywhere' line 23 and unavoidable (irresistible line 23). "B" is the 'best' option in this case as it provides the most complete description of the phrase; **C:** Incorrect – It does refer to the pervasiveness, but also its rationale; **D:** Incorrect – It does not refer to seductiveness. It is pervasive, but people are unaware (line 26), meaning that it is not seductive but rather deceitful; **E:** Incorrect.
Gabarito "B".

This text refers to the next four questions.

1 German scientists have reconstructed an extraordinarily detailed picture of the domestic life of Martin Luther, the 16th-century reformer and father
4 of Protestantism, by trawling through his household waste uncovered during archaeological digs on sites where he used to live.
7 Despite the widespread belief that Luther lived in poverty, evidence suggests he was a well-fed man — weighing in at a hefty 150 kg when he died in
10 1546 at the age of 63.
   Even Luther's claim that he came from humble circumstances has been dismissed. New
13 evidence has shown that his father owned land and a copper mill besides lending money for interest. His
16 mother meanwhile was born into an upper middle class family and it is unlikely, as Luther suggested, that she "carried all her wood on her back".
   Extensive research carried out at the family
19 home in Wittenberg showed that Luther wrote his celebrated texts with goose quills under lamps lit by animal fat, in a heated room which overlooked the
22 River Elbe. It obviously suited him because he churned out 1,800 pages a year. It debunks something of the Luther myth to know he wrote the
25 95 theses on a stone toilet, which was dug up in 2004.
   But the claim by historians which will
28 arguably be most upsetting for followers is the recently uncovered written evidence that it was not, as thought, a lightning bolt which led to the then 21-
31 year-old's spontaneous declaration he wanted to become a monk. Rather, it was his desperation to escape an impending arranged marriage.

Kate Connolly. **History digs up the dirt on Martin Luther**, *In*: **The Guardian**, Monday, 27 Oct./2008. Internet: <www.guardian.co.uk> (adapted).

(Diplomacia 2009) According to the text, recent archaeological finds

(A) have supplemented and adjusted the portrait of Luther.
(B) have revealed that Luther was not truly religious
(C) have perturbed Lutherans' beliefs.
(D) have proven that Luther misrepresented his parents' financial status.
(E) date back to the year 2004.

(Interpretation) A: Correct – To give more information and to modify or adjust the previous information about Luther; B: Incorrect - It merely questions why he decided to become a monk, not his inherent beliefs; C: Incorrect – The archeological finds may perturb beliefs about him as a person, but not the beliefs he preached; D: Incorrect - Luther's claim was that he came from 'humble circumstances' (line 12). This means unpretentious or modest and does not refer directly to financial status; E: Incorrect - This refers to a previous archeological dig.
Gabarito "A".

(Diplomacia 2009) Indicate which of the following statements is **not** consistent with information the text provides.

(A) Luther's weight belies his supposed poverty.
(B) Luther's parents were relatively well-off.
(C) Luther lived in reasonable comfort at his home in Wittenberg.
(D) Luther's religious calling was not genuine.
(E) Luther's mother probably did not carry "all her wood on her back".

(Interpretation) A: Incorrect - Belies means to misrepresent. It is true he was fat and thus we suppose he ate well. Therefore, he was not poor; B: Incorrect - His father owned land and a mill and was able to lend out money (lines 13 and 14). His mother came from an upper-middle class family (line 17); C: Incorrect - Lines 19-20 show the home comforts Luther enjoyed (light, heat and materials). These items constitute reasonable comforts; D: Correct - We do not know anything about his motivation (calling) to become a monk, only about the reason for the spontaneity of the decision; E: Incorrect - Line 17 uses the word 'unlikely'.
Gabarito "D".

(Diplomacia 2009) The word "digs" ($l.5$) is

(A) a noun referring to excavation.
(B) a noun referring to accommodation.
(C) a verb referring to mocking.
(D) a verb referring to accommodation.
(E) part of an adjectival phrase qualifying sites.

(Grammar) A: Correct; B: Incorrect - A slang British term, but that is not the meaning in this context; C: Incorrect – To take a dig at someone means to mock, but that is not the meaning in this text; D: Incorrect – it is not a verb; E: Incorrect – It is a noun.
Gabarito "A".

(Diplomacia 2009) Based on the text, judge — right (C) or wrong (E) — the following items.

(1) The aim of describing Luther as "weighing in at a hefty 150 kg when he died" ($l.9$) is to suggest a humorous comparison with a heavy-weight boxer.
(2) The phrase "churned out 1,800 pages a year" ($l.23$) suggests that Luther was a careless writer.
(3) Luther's father indulged in usury.
(4) The reference to a "lightning bolt" ($l.30$) was meant to allude to putative divine intervention in Luther's calling.

(Interpretation) 1: Correct - To weight in at – is a phrasal verb from the world of sport (boxing/horse racing). This is humorous as it compares his supposed poverty with the strength and physical presence of a heavyweight boxer. Hefty is informal and means of considerable size; 2: Incorrect - The phrasal verb 'churned out' refers more to quantity of production rather than to quality; 3: Correct - Usury is a synonym for money lending (line 14); 4: Correct - This refers to a dramatic act of nature – lightning striking Luther. It is divine as it represents coming from a celestial force.
Gabarito 1C, 2E, 3C, 4C.

This text refers to the next four questions.

1   It's cold and early and Detlef Fendt repeats a
    morning ritual, heaving himself onto the side of his 28-
    year-old BMW motorbike and jumping with all his
4   might on the kick-start. It takes a few goes, but
    eventually the bike roars into life. After all, this is the
    sort of solid reliable machine that makes German
7   goods a household name for quality. It's that good
    name that means Germany is the world's top exporter.
    China may take the title soon, but for the moment
10 Germany is still a world-beater.
    Detlef is part of that success story. For the last
    40 years he's made machine tools for Daimler cars at
13 the Berlin plant. He started work when he was 16 and
    is now the plant's main union representative for IG
    Metall. But this year, thanks to the world credit crunch,
16 he'll be getting an unwanted seasonal break from his
    early morning ritual. The plant is closing down for an
    extra-long Christmas break, from mid-December to
19 mid-January, because of falling orders.
    He tells me: "At the moment we are in a
    distribution crisis — the automobile industry is not
22 selling enough cars and lorries".
    Consumer confidence was dented in Germany
    long before the credit crunch, and despite his union's
25 recent deal it is not returning.
    Germany is now in recession and the figures
    have been worse than economists were predicting.
28 Equally bad statistics for the whole of the European
    Union are expected today. While consumers in America
    feel cowed, while Asia is jittery, the rest of Europe
31 watches fearfully as the biggest economy in Europe
    continues to shrink.

Mark Mardell. **Germany loses revs**. BBC World News.
At: <www.bbc.co.uk> (adapted).

(Diplomacia 2009) Based on the text, judge — right (C) or wrong (E) — the following items.

(1) Fendt's motorbike starts up immediately because it is a reliable machine.
(2) German manufactures are renowned for their quality and durability.
(3) Fendt is being made redundant.
(4) IG Metall is a subsidiary of BMW.

(Interpretation) 1: Incorrect - Line 4 – 'it takes a few goes (attempts) and line 5 "eventually"; 2: Correct - Line 7 – 'a household name' (commonly known); 3: Incorrect - He is being given a longer Christmas break than usual. Being made redundant or laid off would mean he has no job to go to; 4: Incorrect - IG Metall is the trade union, not a subsidiary (not serving or aiding) of BMW.
Gabarito 1E, 2C, 3E, 4E.

(Diplomacia 2009) Judge — right (C) or wrong (E) — the following items with reference to the text.

(1) In context, the phrase "household name" ($\ell.7$) could be appropriately replaced by **synonym**.
(2) "After all" ($\ell.5$) is equivalent to **Eventually**.
(3) The Berlin factory is closing temporarily owing to a slump in demand
(4) The word "dented" ($\ell.23$) suggests an acute effect.

(Vocabulary) **1**: Correct - But perhaps a better use of collocation would be 'synonymous with'; **2**: Incorrect - In the context, 'eventually' means after some time or in the end. 'After all' means in spite of evidence to the contrary; **3**: Correct - It is possible to assert that the plant is closing down due to a slump (fall/drop/sudden decline) – i.e. falling orders (line 19) in demand. It is stated that time period is from December to mid-January (line 18 and 19) – this reveals it is temporary. They plan to re-open in January; **4**: Incorrect - Dented means to have a diminishing effect. In this case, to dent confidence would mean to negatively affect it. To say that it was acute (sharp or intense) dent would have to be modified with 'severely', i.e. severely dented.
Gabarito 1C, 2E, 3C, 4E

(Diplomacia 2009) In the phrase "consumers in America feel cowed, while Asia is jittery" ($\ell.29$-30), the most appropriate synonyms for "cowed" and "jittery" are respectively

(A) bovine and aggressive.
(B) herded and troubling.
(C) threatened and apprehensive.
(D) confined and alacritous.
(E) bent over and trembling.

(Vocabulary) **A**: Incorrect – Bovine refers to the animal, while aggressive means angry; **B**: Incorrect – Herded refers to grouping of animals, while troubling means worrying; **C**: Correct - Cowed means threatened, frightened or overawed. Jittery means apprehensive or nervy; **D**: Incorrect – Confined refers to restrictions or grouping, while alacritous means willingness; **E**: Incorrect – Bent over refers to a physical position (touching your toes), while trembling means physically shaking.
Gabarito "C".

(Diplomacia 2009) In context, "might" ($\ell.4$) and "kick-start" ($\ell.4$) are respectively

(A) a conditional verb and a noun.
(B) a noun and a verb.
(C) an auxiliary verb and a transitive verb.
(D) an auxiliary verb and a noun.
(E) a noun and a noun.

(Grammar) A, B, C, D e E: Might means weight or power (noun). Kick start is a component on the motorbike (noun).
Gabarito "E".

Text for the next three questions.

European energy

1   The European Union (EU) revealed on January 23rd 1 , 2008, how it plans to save the world. A mammoth climate-change plan spells out in detail how much pain each of its 27 members will have to bear if the EU is to meet ambitious targets set by national leaders last March.
4   The aim is to cut greenhouse-gas emissions by 2020 by at least a fifth, and more than double to 20% the amount of energy produced from renewable sources such as wind or wave power. If fuel from plants proves green enough, 10% of the fuel used in transport must come from biofuels by the same date. The new plan turns
7   these goals into national targets. Cue much grumbling, and no doubt months of horse-trading, as the European Commission's recommendations are turned into binding law by national governments and the European Parliament.
10 Countries with greenery in their veins are being asked to take more of the burden than newer members. Sweden, for example, is being invited to meet 49% of its energy from renewables. At the other end, Malta gets a renewables target of just 10%. It is a similar story when it comes to cutting greenhouse gases: by 2020,
13 Denmark must cut emissions by 20% from 2005 levels; Bulgaria and Romania, the newest members, may let their emissions rise by 20%.
    EU leadership on climate change will not come cheap. The direct costs alone may be i60 billion ($87
16 billion), or about 0.5% of total EU GDP, by 2020, said the commission's president, José Manuel Barroso. But this is still presented as a bargain compared with the cost of inaction, which Mr. Barroso put at ten times as high. Oh, and leading the world in the fight against climate change need not cost jobs, even in the most heavily
19 polluting branches of heavy industry. "We want to keep our industry in Europe", insisted Mr. Barroso.

Internet: <www.economist.com> (adapted).

(Diplomacia 2008) Based on the text, it can be concluded that

(1) the European Union plans to save the world from gas emissions is an easy task.
(2) the targets thought of were set up last year.
(3) greenhouse-gas emissions can be reduced as much as a fifth by 2020 and, along the same period, energy produced from renewable sources should more than double.
(4) "mammoth" ($\ell.1$) means huge.

(Interpretation) **1**: Incorrect – On lines 1 and 2, words such as "mammoth" (referring to the magnitude), "pain" (referring to the difficulty) and "bear" (referring to the suffering) all suggest the task is difficult; **2**: Correct – On line 1, the EU revealed the plan on January 23, 2008. The actual setting up of the plan had to have taken place long before that; **3**: Correct – On lines 4 and 5, the text affirms "the aim to cut greenhouse-gas emission by a fifth by 2020", and "to double the amount of energy produced from renewable sources"; **4**: Correct.
Gabarito Oficial 1E, 2C, 3C, 4E/ Gabarito Nosso 1E, 2C, 3C, 4C

(Diplomacia 2008) Considering the text above, judge — right (C) or wrong (E) — the items below.

(1) 10% of the fuel used in transport ought to come from plants in twelve years' time.
(2) Newer members are now being requested to place more of the burden on themselves.
(3) National Governments won't easily endorse the European Commission's recommendations.
(4) The word "Cue" ($\ell.7$) means queue.

(Interpretation) 1: Incorrect – This is conditioned to the fact that fuel from plants must be proven to be truly "green", as stated on lines 5 and 6. There is no guarantee. "Ought to" in this question is synonymous with "should"; **2:** Incorrect – On line 10, the text affirms that countries with more ecological experience (greenery in their veins) are to take more of the burden than newer members; **3:** Incorrect – On lines 7 to 10, the text affirms that national governments are turning the EC's recommendations into law, but there is no mention of whether this is an easy or difficult task. There is an idea, on line 7, that there will be some complaints and negotiating, but this does not explicitly refer to difficulty or ease; **4:** Incorrect – In this case, "cue" has the meaning of "prompt" or "signal". This word is often used in TV. It is the signal given by the cameraman or director to the actor or presenter that the recording will begin. In this text, the author uses the word to explain that as soon as the targets are to be converted into law, the complaints will start. The word "queue" means a line of people.
Gabarito 1E, 2E, 3E, 4E

(Diplomacia 2008) Based on the text, judge — right (C) or wrong (E) — the following items.

(1) The problem with renewables is the same as that of greenhouse gases.
(2) The cost of inaction is ten times as high as the expenses arisen from the climatic control.
(3) The highest polluting offices will have to dismiss their employees.
(4) In the text, "need not cost" ($\ell.18$) can be correctly replaced by does not need to cost.

(Interpretation) 1: Incorrect – No problem is related to renewable energy in the text. The reader is lead to believe that renewables are still undergoing a testing phase (line 4 and 5 – if fuel from plants proves green enough); **2:** Correct – On line 11, the author quotes Mr. Barroso, who believes the cost ($60 billion) "is still presented as a bargain compared with the cost of inaction", which he believes is ten times as high; **3:** Incorrect – On lines 12 and 13, the author affirms, somewhat ironically, that "polluting branches of heavy industry" will not need to cut jobs; **4:** Correct – The collocation "need not cost" is the use of "need" as a modal (auxiliary) verb. In this case, it maintains the meaning, but the usage requires it to be followed by the infinitive verb without "to" (bare infinitive). It is more commonly used in the negative form "need not" and means "does not need to".
Gabarito Oficial 1E, 2ANULADA, 3E, 4C/ Gabarito Nosso 1E, 2C, 3E, 4C

Text for the next three questions.

1 Two weeks after the Islamists of Hamas toppled the border fence, letting hundreds of thousands of inhabitants of the Gaza Strip spill briefly into Egypt, the situation appears to have returned to what counts as normal. But normal is not good.
4 Gaza's 1.5 million people remain besieged, generally unable to leave, and with imports restricted to minimal amounts of staple food and fuel. The Hamas militants who have run Gaza since ousting their secular-minded Fatah rivals last summer have continued to fire rockets and mortars into
7 Israeli towns and farms.
As a possible harbinger of more violence to come, Hamas has also taken again to sending suicide bombers into Israel. In the first such Hamas operation since blowing up two buses in Beersheba
10 in 2004, a pair of suicide bombers, reportedly former inmates of Israeli prisons from Hebron in the West Bank, killed a 73-year-old woman in the southern Israeli town of Dimona on February 4th 2008. Israel responded the same day with new missile attacks, killing nine armed Hamas men.
13 Now, a fortnight since Hamas forces engineered the Gaza break-out, the Egyptian authorities have resealed and reinforced the border, some 12 km (7.5 miles) long, with thick coils of razor wire and hundreds of extra troops; they say they will resist another attempt to knock a hole in it.
16 Their will was tested this week, when Egyptian security forces clashed with stone-throwing Palestinians.

Internet: <www.economist.com> (adapted).

(Diplomacia 2008) According to the text, judge — right (C) or wrong (E) — the following items.

(1) Gaza's inhabitants can only have access to basic foods which come from abroad.
(2) The Hamas militants joined the Fatah rivals to fire rockets and mortars into Israeli urban and rural areas.
(3) The most recent Hamas suicide operation resulted in the blowing up of two buses.
(4) The word "harbinger" ($\ell.8$) means: a sign that something will happen soon, often something bad.

(Interpretation) 1: Incorrect – On lines 4 and 5, the author explains that imports are restricted to basic foods (staples), but this does not mean that people's access to basic foods is restricted. Some basic food could also come from within the borders; **2:** Incorrect – On lines 5 and 6, the text confirms that Hamas ousted (removed) the Fatah rivals (enemies) last summer. The Hamas, without the Fatah, continued to fire rockets and mortars into Israel; **3:** Incorrect – On line 9, the use of the word "since" reveals that the two buses in Beersheba were blown up before the suicide bombers acted. Their action was the first "since" the bus explosion in Beersheba; **4:** Correct – The word "harbinger" means "omen" or "indication" of something that will happen.
Gabarito Oficial 1ANULADA, 2E, 3E, 4C/ Gabarito Nosso 1E, 2E, 3E, 4C

(Diplomacia 2008) In accordance with the text, judge — right (C) or wrong (E) — the items below.

(1) The two suicide bombers were kept in ordinary prisons.
(2) It took Israel a lot of time to launch a counterattack which killed nine Hamas militants
(3) After a fortnight period the situation in Gaza Strip seems to have become what can be considered as normal.
(4) In the text, "besieged" (*l*.4) means surrounded.

(Interpretation) 1: Incorrect – There is no evidence to suggest the prison was ordinary or special. The assumption is that the statement must be incorrect; 2: Incorrect – On lines 11 and 12, the author confirms the Israeli counterattack occurred the same day; 3: Correct – On lines 2 and 3, the author confirms that "the situation appears to have returned to what counts as normal"; 4: Correct – "Besieged" means "surrounded" or "cornered".
Gabarito 1E, 2E, 3C, 4C

(Diplomacia 2008) Based on the text, it can be deduced that

(1) the Egyptian authorities and Hamas forces both have the same position regarding Egyptian people who want to cross the border to go to Gaza strip.
(2) the border between the Gaza strip and Egypt is about 12 km in length.
(3) a possible title for this article could be: Back to abnormal.
(4) the word "clashed" (*l*.16) is synonymous with fought, in the context.

(Interpretation) 1: Incorrect – On lines 13 and 14, the text reveals that the Egyptian authorities do not want Hamas members to come into Egypt, as they "resealed and reinforced the border". This shows their opposing position to Hamas, which had "toppled the border fence" two weeks earlier; 2: Correct – On line 14, the text explicitly reveals the length of the border (12km/7.5 miles); 3: Correct – On line 3, the author explains that things are back to normal, but counters this by saying "normal is not good". This suggests that "normal" is a bad or unwanted situation. It is normal due to its regularity, but the chaos is, by many, considered abnormal; 4: Correct – "Clash" means "fight", "conflict" or "oppose".
Gabarito 1E, 2C, 3C, 4C

Text for the next three questions.

Nationalisation is becoming rather fashionable. State bailouts of banks are all the rage too. There is just one snag: western institutions are not getting their cash from ministers in London or Washington, but from functionaries in Beijing.

While Britain's chancellor still balks at taking Northern Rock into public ownership, his counterparts in China have no qualms about investing state money in the private sector. This week Beijing bought a 10% stake in the Wall Street blue chip Morgan Stanley; in May it took a slab of the private-equity giant Blackstone. Those two deals, worth just over £4bn, were made by the China Investment Corporation (CIC), a fund set up and run by the government. With over £100bn to burn, it is bound to make more big deals — and big headlines — over the coming year. CIC is one of a new breed of sovereign wealth funds (SWFs) created by nations awash with excess cash from exporting goods or oil. Most oil-producing Arab countries have one, as do Russia, Korea and Singapore, and the funds are estimated to be worth a total of a trillion pounds. The logic behind them is simple: if energy-rich Russia is earning around £425m from exports every day, it naturally wants to invest that money for a higher return. But the impact of these new vehicles is far less straightforward, and it has largely been left to economics wonks to worry about them (even now, a Google search for "SWFs" brings up page after page about some graphic-design software). At last, however, they are entering political debate. The IMF is working on a code of conduct for the funds, while the rich nations' club, the OECD, is coming up with guidelines for recipients. Such users' manuals have their place, but on their own they are not an adequate answer to the issues raised by SWFs.

At their most basic level, these funds (which are projected to be worth £7.5 trillion within a decade) embody a shift of economic power from Europe and America to China, Russia and elsewhere. They sum up one of the global economy's problems too: the west is consuming far more than it is producing. SWFs are also a new and very different kind of investor.

From **The Guardian Weekly**, 4/1/2008 (adapted).

(Diplomacia 2008) According to the text, it can be said that

(A) China would never invest money in dubious bargains.
(B) CIC spent a lot more than £4bn on Morgan Stanley and Blackstone.
(C) most probably, China will put more money in bigger deals.
(D) SWFs were created to avoid exporting excess of goods or oil.
(E) Russia's everyday export earnings are saved so as to be better invested in the long run.

(Interpretation) A: Incorrect – There is nothing in the text that suggests China does not consider dubious investments; B: Incorrect – On lines 6 and 7, the text explicitly reveals that the deals totaled "just over £4bn", which is not the same as "a lot more than £4bn"; C: Correct – On line 8, the author explicitly confirms that China "is bound to make more big deals". "To be bound to do something" refers to the high likelihood or probability of something happening; D: Incorrect – The SWFs were created not to avoid anything. They were created due to the fact that nations were "awash with excess cash" (had extra money) which came from "exporting goods or oil"; E: Incorrect – On line 12, the text shows that Russia is not expected to save the earnings from exports, but rather "invest that money for a higher return".
Gabarito "C".

(Diplomacia 2008) Taking the text into consideration, it can be deduced that

(A) the new economic trends have long been IMF concern.
(B) OECD issued rules to be followed by recipient countries.

(C) the influence of new economic features has almost completely been left to those who work or study too much this subject.
(D) SWFs most probably will follow the guidelines established by OECD
(E) the west is producing more than it is consuming, whereas in the east it is the other way.

(Interpretation) A: Incorrect – On lines 14 and 15, the term "at last" suggests that this economic trend has been happening for a while, but not that the IMF has shown concern. This is reinforced by the fact that the IMF is working on a code of conduct, a new and unfinished project; **B:** Incorrect – On lines 15 and 16, the OECD has not yet issued any rules, but is currently "coming up with the guidelines". "Coming up with" means "creating"; **C:** Correct – On line 13, the text explicitly reveals that the issue "has largely been left to economics wonks to worry about them". "Wonks" are specialists in their field, similar to "pundits"; **D:** Incorrect – There is no explicit mention in the text of the SWFs following or not the OECD guidelines. On line 16 and 17, the author suggest that the rules or manuals may not be enough to resolve problems caused by SWF, but there is no mention that they will most likely follow the guidelines; **E:** Incorrect – On line 20, the text explicitly affirms that the west is "producing more than it is consuming"; however, there is no mention in the text that the east is doing the opposite.

Gabarito "C".

(Diplomacia 2008) A suitable title for this text can be

(A) When Beijing goes lending.
(B) When Beijing goes selling.
(C) When Beijing goes wasting.
(D) When Beijing goes sparing.
(E) When Beijing goes buying.

(Interpretation) A: Incorrect – "Lending" means to "loan" or "to give something to another for a period of time". There is no mention of this in the text; **B:** Incorrect – On line 5, the author explicitly refers to China buying a stake in Wall Street, not selling it; **C:** Incorrect – "Wasting" means "squandering" or "frittering away". All these synonyms refer to the idea of using money unwisely. The author does not suggest that China is being unwise with its money; **D:** Incorrect – "Sparing" means to be "frugal" or "economical"; **E:** Correct – On line 5, the text explicitly refers to China buying a stake in Wall Street, while on lines 7 and 8, the author refers to China having money "to burn".

Gabarito "E".

Text for the next six questions.

No burqa bans

Why is it nearly always wrong to outlaw the wearing of the Muslim veil?

1 What you wear is a statement of who you are. From the old man's cardigan and frayed tie to the youngster's torn jeans plus lip-stud, dress stands for identity. For that reason laws on
4 clothing should be avoided unless there is a compelling case for them. There is no such case for the Dutch government's plan to outlaw the wearing in all public places of the face-covering
7 burqa and niqab by Muslim women.
 As it happens, the plan's announcement by Rita Verdonk, the hardline Dutch immigration minister, was a
10 political stunt aimed at reviving her party's flagging fortunes before this week's election. But a new Dutch government, when one is eventually formed, may still adopt it. And the proposed
13 ban follows a big debate about the Muslim veil in many other European countries.

 In 2004 France passed a law to stop the wearing of the
16 Muslim hijab (headscarf) by girls in state schools. Several German states have banned teachers from wearing the headscarf. One Belgian town has outlawed the burqa and niqab
19 from its streets. Recently a former British foreign secretary, Jack Straw, caused a row by inviting his Muslim constituents to remove their veils when they met him; and a lawsuit confirmed
22 that British schools could sack teachers who wore face-covering garments. Turkey, a mostly Muslim country, has banned the wearing of the veil in public buildings ever since
25 Ataturk established the modern republic in the 1920s.
 Those who favour such bans put forward four main arguments. First, the veil (especially the burqa and niqab)
28 shows a refusal by Muslims to integrate into broader society; Britain's Tony Blair called it a "mark of separation". Second, such clothing is testimony to the oppression of Muslim women;
31 they are said to don veils largely at the behest (or command) of their domineering menfolk. Third, the display of religious symbols is an affront to secular societies (this line resonates
34 especially in France and Turkey). And fourth, there are settings — the schoolroom, the courthouse — in which the wearing of Muslim veils can be intimidating or off-putting to pupils or
37 juries.
 Some of these arguments are stronger than others. But none supports a blanket Dutch-style ban. Muslim dress can
40 indeed appear as a mark of separation, but racial and sectarian discrimination surely counts far more — and bans on religious clothing are likely to aggravate it. Oppression of female
43 Muslims is regrettably common, and should be resisted; but many women choose to wear the veil for cultural reasons, and others do so (as they do in Arab countries) as a sign of
46 emancipation, or even as a fashion statement. France and Turkey have fiercely secular traditions that can be interpreted to justify restrictions on religious symbols; but such restrictions
49 are best applied sparingly, and only in state offices, not in the streets. Similarly, decisions to bar the wearing of Muslim dress _____ courts or by teachers and pupils are surely better left
52 _____ local discretion than imposed nationally.

Adapted from **No burqa bans**. In: **The Economist**, Nov. 25th 2006, p. 15.

(Diplomacia 2007) According to the previous text, judge — right (C) or wrong (E) — each item below.

(1) The Dutch immigration minister has exploited the ban on the Muslim veil for political gain.

(2) The Dutch government's introduction of the ban on the wearing of the burqa and niqab in all public places has had a disastrous impact on the local Muslim community.

(3) The idea conveyed by the proverb in English Clothes make men can be found in this text.

(4) Turkey is the only Muslim country where women have never been allowed to wear veils in public.

(Interpretation) 1: Correct – In line 10, the text refers to a 'political stunt' action to attract attention. In the same line, it refers to the flagging fortunes (declining popularity). Thus, the ban was used to boost the party; **2:** Incorrect – There is no mention of how the Muslim community was affected by the ban; **3:** Correct – In line 1, 'what you wear is a statement of who you are', reflects the meaning of the proverb. The more common version of the proverb is "Clothes maketh the man"; **4:** Incorrect – Turkey is described as 'mostly a Muslim country' (line 23). Furthermore, it is described as having a secular (non-religious) society (line 33).

Gabarito 1C, 2E, 3C, 4E

(Diplomacia 2007) In accordance with the previous text, judge — right (C) or wrong (E) — each statement below.

(1) One of the arguments offered by supporters of the ban on veils is that women are forced by their male relatives to wear them.

(2) The idea that Muslim women are said to don veils largely at the behest (or command) of their domineering menfolk can be summarized as: authoritarian men force their female relatives to cover their heads and faces.

(3) One of the arguments offered by the opponents of the ban on veils is that women are forced by their male relatives to wear them.

(4) The wearing of the veil is an unequivocal and universal symbol of female oppression.

(Interpretation) 1: Correct – Lines 30-31, 'oppression' forced to don (wear) by domineering (controlling) menfolk (males); 2: Correct – Lines 30-31, as above; 3: Incorrect – Those opposed to the ban, i.e. those who support the veil, do not state this; 4: Incorrect – Unequivocal means clear or unambiguous. In line 46, we see that some women voluntarily wear the veil as a sign of emancipation (freedom).
Gabarito 1C, 2C, 3E, 4E

(Diplomacia 2007) The last sentence of the text has been left with two blank spaces. Choose the option below that contains the correct sequence of prepositions that fill in the blanks.

"Similarly, decisions to bar the wearing of Muslim dress _____ courts or by teachers and pupils are surely better left _____ local discretion than imposed nationally."

(A) from – to
(B) to – for
(C) on – for
(D) inside – up
(E) in – to -

(Grammar) A, B, C e D: Incorrect; E: Correct – This is better than option A as it refers to baring (banning) the veil from inside courts as it may intimidate the jury. "In court" and "leave something to somebody's discretion" are common collocations in English.
Gabarito "E".

(Diplomacia 2007) In the fragment "Recently a former British foreign secretary" (l.19-20), the antonym of "former" is

(A) latter.
(B) chief.
(C) actual.
(D) previous.
(E) current.

(Vocabulary) A: Incorrect – This is used to describe the second of two things mentioned; B: Incorrect – The word former means "previous" or "prior"; C: Incorrect - False cognate – In this context, it does not mean present; D: Incorrect – This is the synonym, not the antonym; E: Correct – This is used to contrast who IS now the foreign secretary with who WAS the foreign secretary.
Gabarito "E".

(Diplomacia 2007) In accordance with the previous text, judge — right (C) or wrong (E) — each item below.

(1) In the text, "constituents" (l.20) means the same as voters.
(2) In the text, "constituents" (l.20) means the same as components.
(3) In the text, "secular" (l.47) is the same as non-religious.
(4) In the text, "secular" (l.47) is the same as centuries-old.

(Vocabulary) 1: Correct - Constituents as a resident of an area represent by an elected official; 2: Incorrect – This is an alternative definition of constituents, i.e. constituent parts (components); 3: Correct; 4: Incorrect - Secular can mean this, but not in the context of the text.
Gabarito 1C, 2E, 3C, 4E

(Diplomacia 2007) In the sentence "But none supports a blanket Dutch-style ban" (l.38-39) the word "blanket" can be replaced, with no change in the meaning, by

(A) partial.
(B) temporary.
(C) warm.
(D) protective.
(E) unlimited.

(Vocabulary) A, B, C e D: Incorrect; E: Correct – Blanket, in this case, means encompassing or applying to all areas. Therefore, it is unlimited.
Gabarito "E".

Text for the next four questions

1 Unlike Pombal, who had used the power of the state to ruthlessly force through a crash program of modernization, Salazar froze Portugal's economic and social patterns. "We are
4 antiparliamentarians, antidemocrats, antiliberals", Salazar said in 1936. "We are opposed to all forms of internationalism, communism, socialism, syndicalism." To govern, he said,
7 without apology, "is to protect the people from themselves". Yet Salazar enjoyed sizable support. He had rooted his regime sufficiently in Portuguese social realities to garner for
10 it a small measure of popular approbation. The church and the small landholders of the heavily Catholic north backed him. So did the latifundiários, the owners of big farming estates in the
13 central and southern regions who feared a loss of their holdings if the left took power. The outlawed Portuguese Communist Party, formed in 1921, was especially strong in the south.
16 But Salazar could not freeze the world. In 1961, India seized Goa from a 3,500-man Portuguese garrison that had been ordered to "conquer or die". In Africa, as the French and
19 British were freeing their colonies, African nationalist guerrillas rose up against the Portuguese in Angola (1961), Guinea (1962), and Mozambique (1964).
22 Portugal was the last European power in Africa to cling tenaciously to the panoply of formal domination. This was no accident. For a long time Portugal very successfully disguised
25 the nature of her presence _____ a skilful amalgam of historical mythmaking, claims _____ multiracialism, and good public relations.

Adapted from Kenneth Maxwell. The making of portuguese democracy. CUP, 1997, p.18-9.

(Diplomacia 2007) In accordance with the previous text, judge — right (C) or wrong (E) — each item below.

(1) Land owners feared Salazar would freeze their properties.

(2) The setting free of the French and British colonies took place approximately at the same time as the fight for political freedom in some of the Portuguese African dominions.
(3) Salazar's support in the south of Portugal derived from the fact that landowners believed that if communists came to power they would confiscate their land.
(4) The word "Unlike" (ℓ.1) introduces the notion that Pombal's and Salazar's view on progress differed.

(Interpretation) 1: Incorrect – Not Salazar, but the left-wing parties (Line 14); **2:** Correct – Line 19 'as the French and British'. Here 'as' is a conjunction of time, meaning at roughly the same time; **3:** Correct – In line 14, it discusses the landowners' fear of the left. Holdings refer to properties. Lines 14-15 mention that the Communist party was particularly strong in the south; **4:** Correct – Unlike means different. Lines 1-3 refer to a comparison between Pombal and Salazar in terms of their views on development.
Gabarito 1E, 2C, 3C, 4C

(Diplomacia 2007) In the sentence "He had rooted his regime sufficiently in Portuguese social realities to garner for it a small measure of popular approbation" (ℓ.8-10), "rooted" and "to garner" mean, respectively,

(A) planted and to mirror. Incorrect
(B) sowed and to avoid. Incorrect
(C) approached and to save. Incorrect
(D) established and to gather.
(E) viewed and to reject. Incorrect

(Vocabulary) A, B, C, e E: Incorrect; D: Correct - To root means to become settled or established. Garner means to gather.
Gabarito "D"

(Diplomacia 2007) The last sentence of the text has been left with two blank spaces. Choose the option below that contains the correct sequence of words that fill in the blanks, keeping the main ideas of the text.

"For a long time Portugal very successfully disguised the nature of her presence _____ a skilful amalgam of historical mythmaking, claims _____ multiracialism, and good public relations."

(A) in – with
(B) behind – for
(C) in – for
(D) with – in
(E) behind – of

(Grammar) A, C, D: Incorrect; B: Incorrect – 'Claims for' means to demand or to request; E: Correct – Disguised means hidden or to hide behind. In this case, 'claims of' means declaration or affirmation.
Gabarito "E"

(Diplomacia 2007) In the second line of the text, the word "crash" means

(A) unexpected and notorious.
(B) strong and efficient.
(C) quick and complete.
(D) partial and questionable.
(E) modern and efficient.

(Vocabulary) A, B, D e E: Incorrect; C: Correct – Similar to a 'crash course' it refers to speed and intensity. Whether it means complete is debatable, but it is by far the best option to choose from here.
Gabarito "C"

Read the following text to answer the next three questions.

1 The BBC, Britain's mammoth public-service broadcaster, has long been a cause for complaint among its competitors in television, radio and educational and magazine publishing. Newspapers, meanwhile, have been
4 protected from it because they published in a different medium.
That's no longer the case. The Internet has brought the BBC and newspapers in direct competition — and the BBC looks like coming
7 _____ best.
The success online of Britain's lumbering giant of a public-service broadcaster is largely down to John Birt, a former director-general who
10 "got" the Internet before any of the other big men of British media. He launched the corporation's online operations in 1998, saying that the BBC would be a trusted guide for people bewildered by the variety of online
13 services.
The BBC now has 525 sites. It spends £15m ($ 27m) a year on its news website and another £51m on others ranging from society and culture
16 to science, nature and entertainment. But behind the websites are the vast newsgathering and programme-making resources, including over 5,000 journalists, funded by its annual £2.8 billion public subsidy.
19 For this year's election, the news website offered a wealth of easy-to use statistical detail on constituencies, voting patterns and polls. This week the BBC announced free downloads of several Beethoven symphonies
22 performed by one of its five in-house orchestras. That particularly annoys newspapers, whose online sites sometimes offer free music downloads — but they have to pay the music industry for them.
25 It is the success of the BBC's news website that most troubles newspapers. Newspapers need to build up their online businesses because their offline businesses are flagging. Total newspaper readership has fallen
28 by about 30% since 1990 and readers are getting older as young people increasingly get their news from other sources — principally the Internet. In 1990, 38% of newspaper readers were under 35. By 2002, the figure had
31 dropped to 31%.

Adapted from "Old News and a New Contender", **The Economist**, June 18th 2005, p. 27-8.

(Diplomacia – 2006) Choose the option that fills in the following blank with the correct preposition. "… and the BBC looks like coming ____ best." (ℓ.6-7)

(A) at
(B) on
(C) by
(D) over
(E) off

(Grammar) A: Incorrect – "At best" means "in the best possible hypothesis"; **B:** Incorrect – "To come on" means "to progress". In the text, the emphasis is not on the BBC's progress, but rather its success and achievements; **C:** Incorrect – "To come by" means to "acquire" something or to "find" something by accident; **D:** Incorrect - "To come over" means to "visit" or to "appear" (my remark came over wrong = my remarks sounded bad/offensive). As the sentence structure is "look like", which also means "appear", it would be inappropriate to use another collocation with the same meaning immediately after it; **E:** Correct – "To come off best" is an idiomatic expression that means "to be successful".
Gabarito "E".

(Diplomacia – 2006) In the text,

(A) "mammoth" (ℓ.1) means ancient.
(B) "lumbering" (ℓ.8) means expanding.
(C) "bewildered" (ℓ.12) means angry.
(D) "annoys" (ℓ.22) means upsets.
(E) broadcasting (as in BBC) means journalism.

(Vocabulary) A: Incorrect – "Mammoth" means "large" or "vast"; **B:** Incorrect – "Lumbering" means "massive" or "colossal"; **C:** Incorrect – "Bewildered" means "overwhelmed" or "perplexed"; **D:** Correct – "Annoy" means "upset" or "irritate"; **E:** Incorrect – "Broadcasting" is used for the transmission via TV or radio airwaves of ANY information, not necessarily journalistic, to the general public.
Gabarito "D".

(Diplomacia – 2006) Choose the correct statement, according to the text.

(A) Mr. Birt's headstart made the success of the BBC on the Internet a cinch.
(B) Readership of British newspapers is graying because young cohorts flock to other media.
(C) The BBC's success on the Internet is due to its being a state monopoly.
(D) State ownership of the BBC smothers the competition on the Internet.
(E) The BBC's venture into site creation sought to rein in the Internet's content.

(Interpretation) A: Incorrect – "A cinch" means "very easy". On lines 14 to 18, the text reveals how complex BBC's Internet operations are; **B:** Correct – "Graying" means "losing its advantage", while "cohorts" refers to the percentage of young people that have shown a preference (flock = move in large numbers) for other media. With this, the answer is consistent with the text, on lines 28 and 29, which states that "young people increasingly get their news from other sources — principally the Internet"; **C:** Incorrect – On lines 8 to 10, the BBC's success is not attributed to its status as a state monopoly, but rather to Mr. Birt's commercial foresight; **D:** Incorrect – On lines 25 and 26, the competition, newspapers in this case, are mostly troubled by the success of the BBC's news website and not the fact that it is owned by the state; **E:** Incorrect – On lines 11 to 13, the aim of the venture was not to rein in Internet content, but rather to provide people with a "trusted guide", especially for those "bewildered by the variety of online services."
Gabarito "B".

Read the following text to answer the next three questions.

1 Today, Ramses II's burial site, the Ramesseum, is a vacant and
   rather sad place. The heads have been struck off the Osirian pillars.
   Fallen stones and broken sculptures lie scattered like the cast-off
4 playthings of a young giant.
   "Ozymandias" was one name for Ramses II. It was by this
   name that the Romantic poet Percy Shelley referred to one of the
7 damaged statues, in his sonnet of that title. Shelley describes a stone
   colossus, put up by a mighty ancient emperor in a bid for posterity:
         And on the pedestal these words appear:
10   "My name is Ozymandias, king of kings,
         Look on my works, ye Mighty, and despair!"
         Nothing beside remains. Round the decay
13   Of that colossal wreck, boundless and bare,
         The lone and level sands stretch far away.
   The words of Shelley's broken colossus speak of the fragility
16 and impermanence of empires and manmade things.
   Written in 1818, when Britain's global hegemony was greater
   than ever before, "Ozymandias" expressed a timely and moving
19 indictment of empire. The Napoleonic Wars had left Britain
   triumphant. But they had also left it with massive debts, widespread
   unemployment, huge numbers of demobilized soldiers, industrial
22 discontent, and a visibly unrepresentative Parliament in need of
   reform. The "Peterloo massacre" of 1819, at which soldiers opened
   fire on an apparently peaceful workers' rally at St. Peter's Fields in
25 Manchester, pointed to the uglier possibilities of the peace.
   It looked as if just the things that Napoleon had represented might
   be visited on Britain, too. "Ozymandias" held a mirror up
28 _____ Britain that reflected a frightening image _____

Adapted from Jasanoff, Maya. **Edge of empire: lives, culture, and conquest in the East, 1750-1850**. N. York: Alfred A. Knopf, 2005. p. 261.

(Diplomacia – 2006) In the text, "*level*" (*l.*14) means

(A) barren.
(B) molten.
(C) even.
(D) infinite.
(E) rolling.

(Vocabulary) A: Incorrect – "Barren" means "desolate" and "empty"; **B:** Incorrect – "Molten" is the past participle or "melt", which means "liquefy" or "turn into liquid"; **C:** Correct – "Even" means "smooth", "flat" and "level"; **D:** Incorrect – "Infinite" means "never-ending" or "endless"; **E:** Incorrect – "Rolling" means "hilly" or "undulating".

Gabarito "C".

(Diplomacia – 2006) In the context of the last paragraph, the phrase "visited on Britain, too" (*l.*27) suggests that

(A) the effects of the Napoleonic Terror would extend to Britain.
(B) Napoleon's example would instill hubris into British society.
(C) workers in Manchester would rally around the liberal values Napoleon represented.
(D) the British would fall victim to imperialist overreach.
(E) antiliberal government would take root in Britain.

(Interpretation) A: Incorrect – The effects would not be from his terror, but rather from his style of government; **B:** Incorrect – "Hubris" means "arrogance" or "self-pride". The fact that the soldiers, who represent the State, shot at peaceful workers suggest that Napoleon's form of government was to be instilled, not his arrogance; **C:** Incorrect – The fear was not of workers embracing liberal values, but rather that the State would stifle such values; **D:** Incorrect – On line 24, the text explains that it is "the things that Napoleon had represented" that would be visited on Britain. Napoleon did not run an imperialist administration; Britain did. The fear was of what Napoleon represented, not Britain; **E:** Correct – The fear was that Napoleon's antiliberal style of government would become the norm in Britain.

Gabarito "E".

(Diplomacia – 2006) The last sentence of the text has been left with two blank spaces. Choose the option below that contains the correct sequence of prepositions that fill in the blanks.

"Ozymandias" held a mirror up _____ Britain that reflected a frightening image _____.

(A) at – back
(B) for – over
(C) for – back
(D) to – over
(E) to – back

(Grammar) A: Incorrect – The collocation is not "to hold a mirror up for", but rather "to hold a mirror up to". "Back" is correct; **B:** Incorrect – The collocation is not "to hold a mirror up for", but rather "to hold a mirror up to". Mirrors cannot reflect images "over" something. At best, a mirror can reflect a light over something; **C:** Incorrect – The collocation is not "to hold a mirror up for", but rather "to hold a mirror up to". "Back" is correct; **D:** Incorrect – Mirrors cannot reflect images "over" something. At best, a mirror can reflect a light over something. "To" is correct; **E:** Correct – "To hold a mirror up to" something is a common collocation meaning "to show a mirror to" or "to place a mirror in front of" something. An image is reflected "back" from a mirror – another common collocation.

Gabarito "E".

Religião mestiça

1 Insulado deste modo no país, que o não conhece, em luta aberta com o meio, que lhe parece haver estampado na organização e no temperamento a sua rudeza extraordinária,
4 nômade ou mal fixo à terra, o sertanejo não tem, por bem dizer, ainda capacidade orgânica para se afeiçoar a situação mais alta.
7 O círculo estreito da atividade remorou-lhe o aperfeiçoamento psíquico. Está na fase religiosa de um monoteísmo incompreendido, eivado de misticismo
10 extravagante, em que se rebate o fetichismo do índio e do africano. É o homem primitivo, audacioso e forte, mas ao mesmo tempo crédulo, deixando-se facilmente arrebatar
13 pelas superstições mais absurdas. Uma análise destas revelaria a fusão de estádios emocionais distintos.

Euclides da Cunha. **O homem/Os sertões.** *In*: **Obra completa.** Rio de Janeiro: Nova Aguilar, 1995, p. 197.

(Diplomacia – 2006) É o homem primitivo, audacioso e forte, mas ao mesmo tempo crédulo, deixando-se facilmente arrebatar pelas superstições mais absurdas. Uma análise destas revelaria a fusão de estádios emocionais distintos.

Euclides da Cunha. **Os Sertões**.

Choose the most adequate rendering into English of the above excerpt from Euclides da Cunha's **Os Sertões**.

(A) He is primitive Man, garrulous and strong, but at the same time naïve, prone to be in the grip of the most outrageous superstitions. An analysis of these shall reveal a mix of distinct emotional stages.
(B) He is the primitive individual, bold and strong, but at the same time credulous, readily permitting himself to be led astray by the most absurd superstitions. An analysis of these will reveal a fusion of different emotional stages.
(C) He is man at his most primitive, brazen and strong, but at once credulous, easily beholden to superstitions most absurd, an analysis of which shall reveal a fusion of distinct emotional states.
(D) He is the primitive individual, audacious and strong, but at once naïve, prone to be unwittingly taken in by the most brazen superstitions. An analysis of those will reveal a mix of molten distinct emotional states.
(E) He is the primitive individual, brazen and strong, though at once credulous, prone to be cinched by the most outrageous superstitions. An analysis of these will reveal a fusion of diverse emotional stages.

A: Incorrect – It has the following problems: At once = immediately; Garrulous = talkative; In the grip = controlled by; Shall = contractual language; B: Correct; C: Incorrect - It has the following problems: Most primitive = changes the meaning of the original; Beholden = obliged; Superstitions most absurd = Portuguese structure; D: Incorrect - It has the following problems: At once = immediately; Brazen superstitions = changes the meaning (brazen = audacioso); Those = used to refer to things in a previous paragraph or outside the text; Molten = used for steel or metals; E: Incorrect - It has the following problems: Though = adding words that are not in the original; To be cinched = odd structure with the word "cinch" (cinch = easy task).

Gabarito "B".

Text I

A taxing battle

Nobody wants to pay taxes. No wonders, then, that so many companies spend so much effort trying to avoid them. Almost every big corporate scandal of recent years, from Enron to Parmalat, has involved tax-dodging in one form or another.

In the latest revelation on January 26th, Dick Thornburgh, the man appointed to look at the collapse of World-Com, released a report claiming that, as well as the slew of other crooked dealings of which the bankrupted telecoms company is guilty, it also bilked the Internal Revenue Service (IRS) of hundreds of millions of dollars in taxes through a tax shelter cooked up by KPMG, its auditor.

Tax authorities around the world rightly fret that such cases are the tip of a large iceberg, and they are starting to act. In America, home to many of the best-known corporate-tax scams of recent years, the Bush administration has announced a series of anti-tax-dodging measures in its new budget, which will be presented to Congress on February 2nd, including an extra $300 million to boost enforcement and the shutting of corporate-tax dodges that could bring in, it reckons, up to $45 billion over the next ten years.

The Economist, January 31st – February 6th, 2004, p. 71 (with adaptations).

(Diplomacia – 2004) Judge if each item below presents a correct rewriting of the information contained in lines 6 to 12 of text I.

(1) In the latest revelation on 26th January, Dick Thornburgh, the man nominated to examine the fall of Word-Com, delivered a report saying that, as well as a lot of other dishonest transactions of which the insolvent telecoms company is blameworthy, it also swindled the International Revenue Service (IRS) out of hundreds of millions of dollars in taxes by means of a tax shelter dishonestly invented by KPMG, its auditor.

(2) In the last revelation on 26th, Dick Thornburgh, the man accredited to look into the breach of World-Com, reported that, as well as a slew of other false dealings for which the undetermined telecoms companies are to be criticized, it also defrauded the International Revenue Service (IRS) of heaps of dollars through a tax cover created by KPMG, its accountant.

(3) In the latest revelation, Dick Thornburgh, the man in charge of evaluating the failure of World-Com, issued hearsay evidence stating that, not only many other crooked dealings are to be attributed to broken telecoms company, but that it also deprived the International Revenue Service (IRS) of great sums of dollars using a tax device invented by KPMG, its auditor.

(Vocabulary) 1: Correct – The vocabulary used here reflects that of the original text; dishonest transactions (crooked dealings), blameworthy (guilty), swindled (bilked), dishonestly invented (cooked up); 2: Incorrect – The vocabulary does **not** reflect that of the original text: breach (to tear or to break a rule), undetermined (unknown or undecided); 3: Incorrect – The vocabulary does **not** reflect that of the original text: failure (to not work correctly) this is not a good synonym for bankrupted, hearsay evidence (unverified or based on a rumor). Gabarito 1C, 2E, 3E

(Diplomacia – 2004) Still in relation to text I, judge the following items.

(1) The expression "fret that such cases are tip of a large iceberg" (lines 13-14) means that **many other similar cases have been found**.
(2) The substitution of the phrase "slew of" (line 9) and the verb "boost" (line 19) by **mess of** and **soar** respectively would keep the same semantic and syntactic relations as those presented in the text.
(3) The author's purpose is to show that governments around the world are scrabbling for scarce corporate taxes.
(4) According to the graphic, from 1970 to 2001, accumulated corporate income tax receipts in North American countries displayed better results than European ones.

(Interpretation) 1: Incorrect – This expression means that there may be many more cases to emerge; 2: Incorrect – Slew means a large amount. Boost means to raise or increase. Mess of (noun) means to be in disorder. Soar (verb) means to increase rapidly (intransitive verb); 3: Correct – Scrabbling for scarce corporate taxes means to desperately get hold of limited amounts of corporate taxes. The evidence comes in paragraph 3, 'tax authorities around the world rightly fret……. they are starting to act". "Fret" suggests an idea of desperation. This question relies on knowing the word scrabbling and to assume that they are regarded as scarce; 4: Incorrect – The graph shows that there has been a drop in the US' tax receipts, while Canada has shown no change whatsoever. In Europe, all but Germany showed an increase. Therefore, the accumulated result is higher in Europe. Gabarito 1E, 2E, 3C, 4E

Text II

The world's major economies are _____ (1) and 2004 looks likely to be the best growth year for the United States since the bubble _____ (2). There are signs that Japan and Germany may finally be turning the corner after years of _____ (3). Yet doubt still hangs over the big economies like a cloud, producing an increasingly joyless recovery. As global chieftains gather this week at the World Economic Forum in Davos to mull over the theme of prosperity and security, they are finding that prosperity is returning most brightly outside the major markets, in places like China, Southeast Asia end even parts of Latin America and Africa. There is still plenty of talk of bubbles and overheating in some emerging markets, but not all markets are created equal, and a pack of bulls believes a new golden age is falling on these countries as a whole. "This is turning out to be the best period for emerging markets since 1993," says Ruchir Sharma, co-head of global emerging markets at Morgan Stanley.

The economic forecasters back up the bulls. Southeast Asia is predicted to grow faster than 6 percent, Russia and Poland more than 5 percent, Africa better than 4 percent, and even beleaguered Latin America is expected to rise above 3 percent. According to Global Insight's research, the growth rebound will be most dramatic in current or former pariah economies: Venezuela will snap back from a 10 percent recession in 2003 to top 5 percent this year, and growth in war-torn Iraq will jump from negative 21.2 percent to a positive 39.7 percent.

Newsweek, January 26th, 2004 (with adaptations).

(Diplomacia – 2004) Considering the ideas and expressions found in text II, judge the following items.

(1) Blanks numbered 1, 2 and 3 can be properly filled in with **picking up, burst** and **sluggishness** respectively.
(2) From the text, it can be inferred that the global recovery is oddly joyless in big markets, newly confident in emerging ones.
(3) According to the economic forecasters, in 2004 Southeast Asia will grow faster than Russia, which will grow more than Africa and Latin America. Venezuela will decrease 5 percent this year and Iraq will jump 60.9 percent from 2003 to 2004.

(Interpretation) **1:** Correct – Picking up means improving; burst means collapsed and forms a common collocation with bubble burst. Sluggishness means listless or lacking vitality; **2:** Correct – Oddly means strangely. There is still a cloud over the big economies, i.e. depression or lack of joy. This is strange as one would expect the big economies to be booming. It is made even stranger by the fact that the emerging economies are 'returning most brightly', i.e. performing well; **3:** Incorrect – Southeast Asia will grow faster than Russia and will grow more than Africa and Latin America, but Venezuela will 'top 5%', i.e. exceed 5%. The statement on Iraq is correct.

Gabarito 1C, 2C, 3E

Text III

Every year forests four times the size of Switzerland are lost because of clearing and degradation. In the 1980's, an average of 38 million acres of tropical forest were destroyed each year. Those trends have shown no signs of decreasing in the 1990's. Subsistence farming, unsustainable logging, unsound development of large-scale industrial projects, and national policies that distort markets and subsidize forest conversion to other uses are causing deforestation worldwide, from Cambodia to Colombia, from Cameroon to western Canada and the Western United States.

The loss of forests has major implications for the world. Forests are home to 70 percent of all land-living animals and plants. They replenish the Earth's atmosphere and provide the planet with fresh air by storing carbon and producing oxygen. They help filter pollution out of the water and protect against flooding, mudslides and erosion. Forests provide timber, medicines, food and jobs.

The United States has an enormous stake in the sustainable management of the world's forests. We are a major forest products importer and exporter. Our growing pharmaceutical and food processing industries have a vested interest in protecting the source materials for new medicines, pharmaceuticals, and flood additives. Forests and their ability to absorb carbon dioxide lower the rate of global climate change.

The president of the United States has committed to the goal of achieving sustainable management of our forests by the year 2004. And the State Department and other agencies have been working closely with our global partners to slow deforestation around the world.

Document from the US Sate Department (with adaptations).

(Diplomacia – 2004) In relation to the text above, judge the following items.

(1) In line 6, the world "unsound" means **unheard**.
(2) In line 13, the world "replenish" is synonymous with **fill up**.
(3) In line 18, the phrase "an enormous mistake" indicates that the United States is facing huge financial losses to keep up the sustainable management of the world's forests.
(4) In lines 21-22, the phrase "a vested interest in protecting' can be correctly replaced by **a particular reason to protect**.
(5) The text can be associated with the following statement: "The leaves of the trees are for the healing of the nations".
(6) The main idea of the text can be correctly said to be: The problem of deforestation seems to overcome the human capability of finding a final solution to it. Lots of economic interests prevail over the unquestionable need to control the sensible use of the forests worldwide. Forest management turns out to be a crucial factor not only for rural but also for urban life. The effect of the pharmaceutical industry on forest resources is rather than alarming, and that is the reason why the USA is so keen on trying to maintain the sustainable management of the world's forests.

(Vocabulary) **1:** Incorrect – Unsound means either not strong or not logically valid. Unheard of means not listened to, not heard or unknown (unheard of); **2:** Correct - The phrasal verb fill up is a good synonym for replenish in this context; **3:** Incorrect – The phrase in the text is 'an enormous stake' meaning large scale involvement/ interest in forest management; **4:** Correct – To have a vested interest means to have a special or particular reason for wishing to protect or sustain something as it is to you advantage; **5:** Correct – This is true due to the references to how forests aid the earth's atmosphere and provide fresh strong air. There is a wider idea here that trees compensate for some of the damage nations do to themselves through polluting activities; **6:** Incorrect - The following vocabulary in the statement is incorrect: 'deforestation seems to overcome the human capability of finding a solution to it'. This is overstated. The text discusses how the President is committed to achieving sustainable forest management. The use of 'alarming', i.e. worrying is untrue as it is not stated in the text.

Gabarito 1E, 2C, 3E, 4C, 5C, 6E

Text I

Diplomacy, the conduct of inter-state relations, is an old business, and has remained surprisingly constant across three millennia and five continents. Despite vast changes in its social and economic context, its goals and methods have remained strikingly similar over time, so as the shape of the character of the people active in it.

Perpetually, it has the same core activities: representation, negotiation, observation, reporting, analysis and policy advice. Its meat and drink is politics, trade promotion, economic relations, and consular protection. But nowadays, its scope has widened to cover the whole range of government business in a global society.

The diplomat operates in a field of tensions, between war and peace, depending on the relations between the sending and receiving state. He must be adaptable to both. Psychologically, he is always located somewhere along this spectrum, part man of peace, seeking a productive balance of interests, part man of power, seeking national advantage in the global struggle.

He is by nature ambiguous: a voyager between two worlds, an interpreter between alien cultures, a man who can see both points of view and find common ground. He is a front-line officer who risks being shot in the chest or in the back.

> Internet: <http://www.diplomat21.com/diplomacy/necessity.htm> (with adaptations).

(Diplomacia – 2003) It can be inferred from the text I that

(1) diplomatic concerns are restricted to intra-state relations.
(2) diplomacy has been present all over the world for centuries on end.
(3) diplomacy has never experienced any kind of changes in its activities.
(4) diplomatic activity includes political advice.
(5) the diplomat is always subject to tensions, having to decide between war and peace.

(Interpretation) **1:** Incorrect – In the second paragraph, the text explicitly reveals that the scope of diplomatic concerns "has widened to cover the whole range of government business in a global society", thus they were not restricted; **2:** Correct – In the first paragraph, the text explicitly reveals that diplomacy "has remained surprisingly constant across three millennia"; **3:** Incorrect – In the second paragraph, the widening of the scope is a change to the activities of diplomacy; **4:** Correct – In the second paragraph, politics is considered part of its meat and drinks (essential parts), while policy advice is considered a core activity; **5:** Incorrect – In the third paragraph, diplomats work under tense circumstances, but do not decide between war and peace. Sometimes the context in which they work could be times of war or times of peace, but the decision-making power for war and peace is not, according to this text, up to diplomats.

Gabarito 1E, 2C, 3E, 4C, 5E

(Diplomacia – 2003) Based on text I, judge the following items.

(1) The diplomat sometimes has to face contradictory situations.
(2) The diplomat must be ready to compromise.
(3) Both as man of peace and as a man of power the diplomat has the same goals.
(4) The diplomat should be familiar with foreign cultures.
(5) Diplomacy can be a risky activity.

(Interpretation) **1:** Correct – In the third and fourth paragraph, the text verifies the dichotomy of the nature of the job, oscillating between contradictory issues, such as war and peace, peace and power, risks of being shot in the chest (suggesting confrontation) and shot in the back (dishonesty or deceit); **2:** Correct – In the third and fourth paragraph, respectively, the text confirms compromise (negotiate to reach agreement) for diplomats, as they seek "a productive balance of interests", and "find common ground"; **3:** Incorrect – In the third paragraph, the text shows that the goals as a man of peace are to seek "a productive balance of interests", and that diplomats as men of power seek "national advantage in the global struggle" – both very different goals; **4:** Correct – In the fourth paragraph, the text confirms that a diplomat should be "a voyager between two worlds, an interpreter between alien cultures"; hence, he must have knowledge of foreign (alien) cultures; **5:** Correct – In the fourth paragraph, a diplomat is considered "a front-line officer who risks being shot in the chest or in the back". The risk of being shot makes this a risky activity.

Gabarito 1C, 2C, 3E, 4C, 5C

Text II

It has become clear that preventive diplomacy is only one of a class of actions that can be taken to prevent disputes from turning into armed conflict. Others in this class are preventive deployment of military and(or) police personnel; preventive humanitarian action, for example, to manage and resolve a refugee situation in a sensitive frontier area; and preventive peace-building, which itself comprises an extensive menu of possible actions in the political, economic and social fields, applicable especially to possible internal conflicts.

All these preventive actions share the following characteristics: they all depend on early warning that the risk of conflict exists; they require information about the causes and likely nature of the potential conflict so that the appropriate preventive action can be identified; and they require the consent of the party or parties within whose jurisdiction the preventive action is to take place.

The element of timing is crucial. The potential conflict should be ripe for the preventive action proposed. Timing is also an important consideration in peace-making and peace-keeping. The prevention, control and resolution of a conflict is like the prevention, control and cure of a disease. If treatment is prescribed at the wrong moment in the evolution of a disease, the patient does not improve, and the credibility of both the treatment and the physician who prescribed it is compromised.

> Internet: <http://www.un.org/Docs/SG/SG-Rpt/ch4b.htm> (with adaptations).

(Diplomacia – 2003) From text II, it can be deduced that

(1) preventive diplomacy has just been considered the only possible action to avoid war.

(2) military actions will necessarily lead to armed conflict.
(3) many problems involving refugees occur in frontier areas.
(4) preventive peace-building demands several types of action.
(5) preventive diplomatic actions should rely on previous intelligence.

(Interpretation) 1: Incorrect – In the first paragraph, preventative diplomacy is considered "only one" of a class of actions to prevent war from taking place. There are others; 2: Incorrect – In the first paragraph, the type of military deployment (dispatch or sending) is "preventative", thus suggesting that armed conflict may be avoided; 3: Incorrect – There is nothing in the text that confirms that "many" refugee situations occur in frontier areas. This can be inferred from common knowledge involving refugee situations, but the text has no explicit mention of this; 4: Correct – In the first paragraph, the text explicitly affirms that preventive peace-building "comprises an extensive menu of possible actions in the political, economic and social fields", thus confirming the demand for several types of action; 5: Correct – In the second paragraph, the text explicitly states that preventative diplomatic actions "all depend on early warning that the risk of conflict exists". Early warning suggests previous intelligence.
Gabarito Nosso 1E, 2E, 3E, 4C, 5C
Gabarito Oficial 1E, 2E, 3C, 4C, 5C/

(Diplomacia – 2003) Based on text II, it can be concluded that

(1) preventive diplomacy demands just two conditions to succeed.
(2) preventive diplomacy usually deals with armed conflicts.
(3) in any case, the sooner preventive actions are implemented the better.
(4) the resolution of a conflict can be compared to the cure of a disease.
(5) the physician and the diplomat both play the same role in armed conflicts.

(Interpretation) 1: Incorrect – In the second paragraph, the text lists at least three conditions for success: 1) they all depend on early warning that the risk of conflict exists; 2) they require information about the causes and likely nature of the potential conflict; and 3) they require the consent of the party or parties within whose jurisdiction the preventive action is to take place; 2: Incorrect – In the first paragraph, the texts confirms other issues that preventative diplomacy deals with, such as humanitarian action, for example; 3: Incorrect - In the third paragraph, the text makes several references to "timing", but it does not state that such "timing" should be earlier. Prevention, control and resolution of a conflict at the wrong time could prove risky to those involved, but there is no confirmation that actions should be implemented earlier; 4: Correct – In the third paragraph, such a comparison is actually present in the text, affirming that "If treatment is prescribed at the wrong moment in the evolution of a disease, the patient does not improve, and the credibility of both the treatment and the physician who prescribed it is compromised"; 5: Incorrect – Despite the comparison between preventative action and disease in the third paragraph, in armed conflicts, the text does not affirm that the physician will perform the same role as a diplomat. One can assume that physicians will be focused on healing the injured, while diplomats will be focused on helping restore peace.
Gabarito 1E, 2E, 3E, 4C, 5E

(Diplomacia – 2002) Select the correct sequence of preposition to fill the blanks:

_____ the bottom of French society, the poor sank deeper _____ misery and degradation.

Between a third and a half of the people of France lived _____ the margin of subsistence, spending as much as 80 percent of their income_____ food alone. The numbers of the poor multiplied. Homelessness increased. Public roads were thronged_____ beggars, abandoned children, broken families, and able-bodied men without work.

(A) by / out of / below / for / by.
(B) in / into / at / in / by.
(C) from / under / by / with / for.
(D) at / in / near / on / with.
(E) across / from / over / with / with.

(Grammar) A, B, C e E: Incorrect; D: Correct - This is the only correct pattern possible from the choices available: At the bottom, sank deeper in misery, lived near the margin, spending on, thronged (full of) with.
Gabarito "D".

(Diplomacia – 2002) Select the correct sequence of words to fill the blanks:

In 1739, a bizarre_____ called the War of Jenkins' Ear began between Britain and Spain.

This was a commercial _____ that grew _____ one of the first Jingo-wars in modern History. It started after Spanish officials _____ an English interloper named Captain Robert Jenkins by cutting off his ear. Captain Jenkins presented the _____ ear to Parliament in a handsome mahogany box. It became a cause of war between two great powers.

(A) episode / war / out of / killed / missing.
(B) event / wrangling / towards / disfigured / removed.
(C) conflict / dispute / into / mutilated / severed.
(D) passage / rivalry / through / amputated / amputated.
(E) incident / disagreement / during / offended / other.

(Vocabulary) A, B, D e E: Incorrect; C: Correct – In terms of the best collocation and meaning, this is the only option possible. Grew into means developed.
Gabarito "C".

(Diplomacia – 2002) Select the correct sequence of verbs to fill the blanks:

For most of the past year, investors _____ (assume) that _____ (be) Argentina to default on its debts, Brazil _____ (follow) suit. Yet this week they _____ (appear) to have second thoughts. With Argentina closer than ever to default, Brazil's financial markets and its currency _____ (soar) to their highest levels since before September 11th.

(A) assumed / was / following / were appearing / soar.
(B) Have assumed / is / will follow / are appearing / soar.
(C) Assumed / were / would follow / appear / soaring.
(D) Assumed / were / followed / appear / are soaring.
(E) Have assumed / were / would follow / appeared/ soared.

(Grammar) A, B, C e D: Incorrect; E: Correct – As the text says, 'for most of the past year' implies that the period has not yet finished. Last year would clearly be past; past year can include the current year. This idea requires the present perfect, i.e. I have been busy this week. Were + subject + to infinitive is used as a 2nd conditional inversion and replaces; if + subject + simple past. Would is used again as a conditional - we are imagining a hypothetical situation. The verb appear cannot be used in the present perfect, even though we have the expression – this week – as it a state verb. Soared is used as it reflects an action that is completed.

Gabarito "E".

(Diplomacia – 2002) Select the correct replacements for the words in **bold** type:

The Securities & Exchange Commission has **issued** a warning that it is **investigating** a rumour of fraud in stock trading. A leading London broker apparently **transferred** large quantities of top-performing stock to a partner firm following an attempt by a rival company to **assume** control of the broker. The Commission is calling for those in the know to **volunteer**.

(A) put forward / coming across / turned out / take up / step down.
(B) put out / breaking into / ran across / run down / step out.
(C) given out / looking into / made over / take over / come forward.
(D) turned out / bringing up / made off with / break up / make out.
(E) put out / checking up on / made over / take on / let out.

(Vocabulary) A: Incorrect - Put forward means to propose / coming across means to find accidentally / turned out means to occur, to happen, to be present at an event / take up means to continue, to start / to step down means to leave an important position; **B:** Incorrect - Put out means to extinguish, to issue / breaking into means to enter illegally / ran across means to meet accidentally / to run down means to reduce in size, to lose power / to step out means to leave for a short period; **C:** Correct – In terms of use of language, you do not put forward a warning, put out a warning or turn out a warning. Looking into is the closest definition for investigating. Made over is to transfer ownership, take over is to take control of something and to come forward is to volunteer; **D:** Incorrect - Turned out means to produce / bringing up means to raise a subject, or a person / made off with means to steal / break up means to separate / make out means to understand, to write a cheque; **E:** Incorrect - Put out means to extinguish, to issue / check up on means to verify, supervise / made over means to transfer ownership / to take on means to adopt, to confront / to let out means to slacken, to be allowed to avoid something unpleasant.

Gabarito "C".

Read the following text and complete the exercise:

Inside the valley of fear

The Fergana Valley is sometimes called the tinderbox of Central Asia. In the streets of Namangan, the eye can **pick out** bits of tinder. The Muslim men in their traditional black pillbox hats look down on miniskirted young girls. The dour, functional government offices overlook bustling, sprawling oriental bazaars. This could **pass for** a scene of tolerant multiculturalism, except that at every street corner stand groups of grey--uniformed police. On the 190-mile road from Tashkent, this correspondent's car was **held up** on ten occasions at checkpoints guarded by Kalashnikov-toting soldiers.

After the Soviet Union **broke up** in 1991, there was an explosive religious revival in the valley. Militant Islamic factions following the strict teachings of the Arabian Wahhabi **set up** their own security force, demanding the imposition of sharia law and a share of power. They gained a huge following at the expense of moderate Muslim groups.

The timeless, bucolic appearance of the countryside, with its neat apricot orchards, villages of low white houses and winding roads lined with mulberry trees to feed the silkworms, belies the harsh reality. In return for their produce, farmers are paid by the State up to a year late and then only in grain and cooking oil. The State decides what crops they grow, and the harvest is turned over to officials – a much resented practice retained since Soviet times.

Adapted from The Economist, 10 November 2001

(Diplomacia – 2002) The underlined verbs in the text mean, respectively:

(A) select / represent / stopped / separated / created.
(B) distinguish / be considered / halted / disintegrated / established.
(C) discard / be interpreted as / threatened / fractured / formed.
(D) reject / be mistaken for / investigated / dismembered / instituted.
(E) see / seem / delayed / crumbled / disbanded.

(Vocabulary) A: Incorrect – Select means to choose, while pick out means to identify or distinguish; **B:** Correct - Pick out means distinguish / pass for means to be considered / held up means halted / broke up means disintegrated / established means set up; **C:** Incorrect – Discard means to throw away, while pick out means to distinguish or identify; **D:** Incorrect – Reject means to decline or discard, while pick out means to distinguish or identify; **E:** Incorrect – Disbanded means to separate a group, while set up means to establish.

Gabarito "B".

(Diplomacia – 2002) The text suggests that the Fergana Valley:

(A) is a haven for peaceful cohabitation.
(B) is governed by sharia law.
(C) is run by Muslims.
(D) has a thriving agricultural community.
(E) is a potential trouble spot.

(Interpretation) A: Incorrect - This is contrary to the idea of policemen on every block, rockblocks with soldiers, the rivalries between different Muslim factions and the resentment of the farmers towards the state; **B:** Incorrect - The militant Islamic factions demanded sharia law – it is not stated if this was indeed granted; **C:** Incorrect - Not clear. We know that the area is still controlled by the state. Whether the state is run by Muslims is not clarified in the text; **D:** Incorrect – There is no evidence that agriculture is thriving; **E:** Correct - By referring to 'tinder', which means something inflammatory or dangerous and as the valley is sometimes called the 'tinderbox' of Asia. Tinderbox refers to a potentially explosive place or situation.

Gabarito "E".

COMO GABARITAR – INGLÊS E ESPANHOL PARA CONCURSOS

1. LÍNGUA INGLESA

(Diplomacia – 2002) In the text:

(A) the drab office buildings contrast with the messy markets.
(B) the farmers are paid twice for their produce.
(C) the guards at the roadblocks wave rifles in the air.
(D) the streets of Namangan are dangerous.
(E) the bazaars are not functional.

(Interpretation) A: Correct - The word dour means gloomy or harsh. It gives the idea of being drab (gray or dull). This is contrasted with the sprawling markets. Sprawling means spreading in different directions in an unplanned/messy style; B: Incorrect - Turned over in this context means given to or delivered to; C: Incorrect - Toting means to carry. There is no connotation of them waving the rifles in the air; D: Incorrect - Not necessarily as there are police on every corner to maintain the peace; E: Incorrect - The words bustling means busy with activity, and sprawling means spreading in different directions in an unplanned or messy style.

Gabarito "A".

Read the following text and complete the exercise:

Even before the terrorist attacks, the financial system was under **duress**. Banks were **wobbling** under a pile of bad loans that had doubled in a year to $192 billion. Hedge-fund stars such as George Soros and Julian H. Robertson Jr. had self-destructed. Mutual-fund investors had **deserted** equities. And online brokers were **limping** from the dramatic fall in trading, while their traditional rivals were **struggling** to make profits form dirt-cheap commissions.

(Diplomacia – 2002) Select replacements for the words in **bold** type:

(A) siege / crushed / emptied / hurting / seeking
(B) pressure / staggering / quit / reeling / striving.
(C) pressure / engulfed / abandoned / hurting / trying.
(D) hardship / tottering / quit / faltering / vying
(E) hardship / wavering / abandoned / bankrupt / vying.

(Vocabulary) A: Incorrect - Under siege would be too physical, crushed is too strong, emptied does not mean to leave, seeking does not have the same connotation of effort as striving; B: Correct – Under pressure or under duress, wobbling and staggering meaning to be unsteady, to desert means to leave or to quit, reeling means thrown off balance or staggering, struggling means striving to make great efforts to achieve something; C: Incorrect - Pressure is fine, engulfed (usually engulfed by flames) covered is too strong, abandoned is a good synonym for deserted, hurting can work here as a synonym for limping. Trying does not have the same strength as struggling; D: Incorrect - Hardship means suffering or privation. It is not common to collocate under hardship. Tottering is a good synonym for wobbling, quit can work as a synonym here for deserted. Faltering does not mean damaged or injured it means to be hesitant or unsteady, vying means striving or competing and would work in this context for struggling; E: Incorrect - Hardship means suffering or privation. It is not common to collocate under hardship. Wavering means to be indecisive but is used in the context of making a decision or being resolute and not to be 'wavering under a pile of bad debts'. Abandoned is a good synonym for deserted, bankrupted is too strong here, this would imply they were no longer able to trade at all, vying means striving or competing and would work in this context for struggling.

Gabarito "B".

Read the following text and complete the exercise:

After researchers identify a viral target, they can enlist various techniques to find drugs that are able to perturb it. Drug sleuths can, for example, take advantage of standard genetic engineering (introduced in the 1970s) to produce pure copies of a selected protein for use in drug development. They insert the corresponding gene into bacteria or other types of cells, which synthesize endless copies of the encoded protein.. the resulting protein molecules can then form the basis of rapid screening tests: only substances that bind to them are pursued further.

(Diplomacia – 2002) In the text:

(A) enlist (line 1) means to catalog
(B) sleuths (line 2) means assays.
(C) synthesize (line 6) means to streamline.
(D) screening (line 7) means visualizing.
(E) to pursue (line 8) means to investigate.

(Vocabulary) A: Incorrect - Enlist means to engage the support of. Catalog means to make an itemized list of something; B: Incorrect - Sleuths means detectives (noun). Assays (verb) means to examine or analyze; C: Incorrect - Synthesize means to combine to form a new product. Streamline means to reorganize in a manner which simplifies or makes something appearance or efficiency; D: Incorrect - Screening means an examination done to detect unwanted particles. Visualizing means to form a mental image; E: Correct - To pursue (track, trail) and to investigate are good synonyms in this context.

Gabarito "E".

(Diplomacia – 2002) Select the correct sequence of verbs to fill the blanks:

Using the mouse, I _____ on the area of the video screen where I wanted the robot to go. The machine's motors _____ loudly as they turned the wheels, first pointing the robot in the right direction and then _____ it to the indicated spot. Then I _____ a tougher challenge: I _____ the machine to smash into the wall on the other side of the room. Fortunately for the robot, it stopped just shy of the wall, _____ my destructive intentions.

(A) pushed / banged / casting / plotted / ordered / finishing.
(B) pointed / whirred / sending / proposed / directed / evading.
(C) clicked / whirred / driving / devised / directed / thwarting.
(D) pointed / screeched / driving / invented / told / frustrating.
(E) clicked / buzzed / moving / devised / told / forgetting.

(Vocabulary) A: Incorrect – Push is not commonly collocated with mouse; B: Incorrect – Direct is not collocated this way; C: Correct – Clicked is the most accurate verb for a mouse and it fits with the preposition on. The sound of a motor is most closely associated with whirred. Driving is the most appropriate word in terms of driving the robot in the right direction. Devised meaning invented or came up with is best here. Directed is the best option in terms of directing a

69

mechanical object. Thwarting (preventing) is the best option here in terms of thwarting the driver's intentions; **D:** Incorrect – Point on is not the correct collocation in English; **E:** Incorrect – Forgetting does not collocate with robots.
Gabarito "C".

Read the article below and answer the questions that follow:

To bludge or not to…

Is Helen Clark, New Zealan's Prime Minister, a bludger? Conservative opposition leader Jenny Shipley thinks so. She **bluntly** accuses Labour's leading light of playing silly bludgers with the nation's security. Convinced that New Zealand does not really have any enemies, Ms. Clark plans to abolish most of its air force, including the Skyhawk fighter jets. This is the "bludger's option," says Mrs. Shipley. "Cuts, isolation, and bludging," whinged the National party's Max Bradford. "A peacenik pandering to pacifists." But Ms. Clark was having none of it. The 31-year-old planes had never fired guns in anger, she said, although they once buzzed an errant fishing boat. U.S.-made replacements were far too expensive and not needed, she told parliament. "Is the difference between being a bludger and not being a bludger whether you have 17 clapped-out Skyhawks?"

This is a difficult question to answer without first defining terms. To bludge is to **cadge**, scourge or shirk responsibilities. A bludger is a hanger-on or a loafer. Mrs. Shipley was implying that, under Labour's plan, New Zealand would have to depend on Australia for its defence. The critics recalled the importance of air power during the battle of Crete or **bemoaned** the demotion of the armed services to fishery patrols and other people's peacekeeping. Ms. Clark is probably correct in assuming that no invasion by Indonesia is imminent, and she has set an example in disarmament that Labour leaders the world over might do well to study.

As the debate rages on, a retired defence force chief, Sir Somerford Teagle, summed up New Zealand's dilemma in plaintive terms: "Here we are, sitting in the ocean, all alone." There is no arguing with that.

Adapted from The Guardian Weekly, May 17-23 2001

(Diplomacia – 2002) In the text, **bluntly** means:

(A) ironically.
(B) naturally.
(C) abruptly.
(D) frankly.
(E) candidly.

(**Vocabulary**) A, B, C, D e E: Bluntly means abruptly and disconcertingly frank in speech. The gabarito is incorrect as there is no idea of irony in the accusation. Options E – candidly, D – frankly and C – abruptly seem to be appropriate. The only notion of irony could be the play in words with 'playing silly bludgers'. This is an idiomatic expression well beyond any interpretation of the text.
Gabarito Oficial "A." / Gabarito Nosso "E,", "D," or "C."

(Diplomacia – 2002) In the text, **cadge** means:

(A) get something without paying.
(B) get something at a lower price.
(C) borrow.
(D) buy what is strictly necessary.
(E) pay one's debts.

(**Vocabulary**) **A:** Correct – To cadge a lift means to get a lift for free, to cadge a cigarette is to get one for free by asking someone else for one. It can also mean to beg or to mooch; **B, D** e **E:** Incorrect; **C:** Incorrect – While colloquially people use borrow as a synonym for cadge, there is no idea of returning the item borrowed. Hence, it is only used for petty or intangible items (cigarettes, a lift, a dollar).
Gabarito "A".

(Diplomacia – 2002) In the text, **bemoaned** means:

(A) spoke in pain.
(B) pointed out.
(C) refused.
(D) lamented.
(E) firmly complained.

(**Vocabulary**) A, B, C, e E: Incorrect; D: Correct - Bemoaned means to lament, express grief or to express disapproval.
Gabarito "D".

(Diplomacia – 2002) Max Bradford believes New Zealand's Prime Minister is:

(A) providing what their neighbours want.
(B) acting as a pacifist.
(C) providing what pacifists want.
(D) a genuine pacifist.
(E) advocating word peace.

(**Interpretation**) A, B, D e E: Incorrect; C: Correct – In the phrase, "A peacenik pandering to pacifists." Pandering means to provide for the tastes/desires of others. It is used pejoratively. Peacenik means a pacifist.
Gabarito "C".

(Diplomacia – 2002) The Guardian article states that:

(A) Indonesia is not planning any attack on New Zealand.
(B) Ms. Clark has showed the world what to do in terms of peace.
(C) Labour leaders should follow Ms Clark's example.
(D) Labour leaders may do well to look into Ms. Clark's disarmament plans.
(E) New Zealand needn't fear any attack from other countries.

(**Interpretation**) **A:** Incorrect – It says any attack is not imminent – coming soon. This statement is too categorical; **B:** Incorrect – There is no evidence that her ideas have any worldwide impact; **C:** Incorrect – This is too strong a statement; **D:** Correct – In the phrase, "she has set an example in disarmament that Labour leaders the world over might do well to study", might can be substituted for may and look into can be substituted for study; **E:** Incorrect – It does not state this. Furthermore, it is clearly stated that New Zealand is alone sitting in the ocean and therefore susceptible to attack.
Gabarito "D".

(Diplomacia – 2002) Choose the correct sequence of words to fill the blanks:

Is the Conservative Party _____? Can it ever come back? Not just by June – or even June 2005 - _____? The questions aren't mine: they were _____ long before this election began by Michael Brown, an intelligent, thoughtful ex-Tory MP who lost his _____ in '97. But here they come again, with redoubled force, _____ on the wind of Tapsell.

(A) done / but ever / asked / seat / born.
(B) washed up / but now / posed / place / brought up.
(C) washed up / but ever / posed / seat / born.
(D) finished / but soon / put forward / position / born.
(E) forgotten / but ever / posed / bench / appearing.

(Vocabulary) A: Incorrect – "Done" has too many possible interpretations; **B:** Incorrect – An MP has a seat, not a place. Bring up on has an idea that someone taught them this; **C:** Correct - Washed up means no longer successful. Posed means asked, seat refers to his elected position for a certain constituency, born on the wind is metaphoric and means deriving from; **D:** Incorrect – An MP has a seat, not a position; **E:** Incorrect – Forgotten would only work if the verb tense was present perfect (Have they been forgotten?).
Gabarito "C".

(Diplomacia – 2002) Choose the correct sequence of words to fill the blanks:

The Organization _____ Economic Cooperation and Development (OECD) _____ last week that an international _____ on tax havens was still _____, despite the United States government's decision to _____ its support for central parts of the plan.

(A) of / insisted / attack / being developed / refused.
(B) for / said / law / on track / asunder. Asunder means into separate parts
(C) in / granted / crackdown / on the road / scrap. Scrap is an informal expression to give up a plan.
(D) for / insisted / crackdown / on track / withdraw.
(E) of / published / law / being examined / refuse.

(Vocabulary) A: Incorrect – Refused is in the wrong verb tense; **B:** Incorrect – Asunder is not a verb, but an adjective or adverb meaning separated; **C:** Incorrect – Grant means to offer or give; **D:** Correct – The only option with the specific vocabulary to fit the spaces. Insist is stronger than said, crackdown means an attempt to forcefully restrain or regulate, on track – going a planned, to withdraw support means to recall or retract support; **E:** Incorrect – Publish is a direct transitive verb, making "that" an improbable object.
Gabarito "D".

(Diplomacia – 2002) Choose the correct sequence of words to fill the blanks:

Pirates have provided material for writers _____ so long that one _____ thinks _____ could be any literary treasure _____, but here is a book that proves _____.

(A) for / never / it / left / the opposite.
(B) during / hardly / there / buried / otherwise.
(C) since / rarely / there / still / something else. Rarely is an adverb of frequency.
(D) for / barely / it / left / the opposite.
(E) for / hardly / there / left / otherwise.

(Grammar) A: Incorrect – "It could be any literary treasure left" is impossible in English; **B:** Incorrect – During so long is not the English collocation; **C:** Incorrect – Since so long is not the English collocation; **D:** Incorrect – For opposite to be correct, the original text would require a definite article, i.e., proves **the** opposite; **E:** Correct – For so long is the only correct preposition to use here. Hardly is an adverb meaning the same as barely or just. Otherwise (adverb) means differently.
Gabarito "E".

(Diplomacia – 2002) Choose the correct sequence of words to fill in the blanks:

One of the most explosive ___ in Australian politics is the growing ___ for a government apology for the physical and cultural genocide the Aborigenes ___ since white people ___ on ___ continent.

(A) questions / claims / have gone through / arrived / the new.
(B) problems / clamour / have experienced / reached / their.
(C) issues / clamour / have endured / set foot / their.
(D) complaints / outcry / have undergone / set foot / the.
(E) matters / outcry / have suffered / were introduced / the new.

(Vocabulary) A: Incorrect – Claims (plural) / is the growing (singular) – the concordance would be incorrect; **B:** Incorrect – Reached is not followed by the preposition on; **C:** Correct – An issue can be described as explosive, clamour means outcry. All the options offered work here, but endured is the most appropriate as it has the connotation of suffering. To set foot goes with the preposition on – to set foot on. "Their" is a possessive pronoun referring to the Aborigines; **D:** Incorrect – Complaints seems out of place for the context of politics; **E:** Incorrect – People are not introduced to a place; animals and agriculture are.
Gabarito "C".

Assinale a única resposta certa a cada uma das duas seguintes questões. Leia o texto a seguir e responda às perguntas:

Kosovo: Peace Now?
On the hill near the Serbian village of Drsnik in central Kosovo I counted smoke billowing from eight houses. Or at least I thought they were houses. Some proved to be haystacks. For Albanians taking revenge, even Serbian haystacks must now be burned.
In the northern town of Mitrovica I sat on a wall with Meli Uka, a pretty, twenty-two-year-old student. We sipped Coke as we watched a column of fleeing Serb families packed into cars ands tractor-trailers. They looked no different from the Kosovars I had seen who had been expelled from Kosovo a few weeks earlier.
The New York Review of Books. 12/08/1999.

(Diplomacia – 2000) Com base no texto acima, indique a única afirmação correta:

(A) The author witnessed eight houses burning.
(B) Smoke was rising slowly from the houses.

(C) Less than eight houses were on fire. Correct
(D) The Serbs were burning Albanian property.
(E) It was necessary to burn the haystacks.

(Interpretation) A: Incorrect – In the first paragraph, the author admits to being mistaken. Not all fires were in houses; some were in haystacks; B: Incorrect – The word "billowing" in the first paragraph means that smoke was coming out of the fires quickly and copiously; C: In the first paragraph, the text confirms that the author initially thought there were eight houses, but he quickly realizes his mistake. Not all the eight fires were in houses; some were in haystacks. Thus, there were less than 8 houses on fire; D: Incorrect – In the first paragraph, the texts shows that it was quite the opposite; Albanians were burning Serbian haystacks (and probably their houses); E: Incorrect – There is nothing in the text that confirms the necessity to burn the haystacks. Such fires are attributed to revenge (in the first paragraph).
Gabarito "C".

(Diplomacia – 2000) Na frase we sipped Coke as we watched a column of fleeing Serb families packed into cars.

(A) as significa while.
(B) As significa equally.
(C) Packed significa stored their luggage.
(D) Fleeing é um verbo no gerúndio.
(E) A column é o mesmo que a post.

(Vocabulary) A: Correct – "As", in this case, is a subordinating conjunction of time, used to emphasize the concurrent actions; B: Incorrect – "As", in this case, is not part of a comparative structure. Such a structure requires the use of an adjectives and another "as". (as fast as); C: Incorrect – In this case, "packed into cars" is a no-restrictive adjective clause reduced by the past participle of the verb "to pack" and means "crowded into cars". It suggests that the cars were full to their capacity; D: Incorrect – While "fleeing" is a gerund form derived form the verb "to flee", its role here is not that of a verb, but rather one of an adjective describing the Serbs; E: Incorrect – In this context, a column means a long line.
Gabarito "A".

Leia o texto a seguir e responda as três próximas perguntas:

Fiddling as the Planet Burns

It's a tall order to expect Western politicians to cut the rhetoric, but unless they do something soon to reduce carbon dioxide emissions, the ambitious targets they set at the Kyoto climate change conference in 1997 are likely to be missed.
The consequences for future generations are unclear, but scientists say they could include a further rise in world temperatures, with a variety of adverse, possibly irreversible effects, including severe storms, a rise in the sea level, the spread of disease and the loss of species.
The mere threat of these horrors ought to be enough to make politicians take the issue of greenhouse gases seriously.
Yet to judge by two new studies, they are not doing so. Instead, they are fiddling while the planet burns.

Guardian Weekly, 10/11/1999

(Diplomacia – 2000) Depreende-se do texto que:

(A) Western governments do not intend to cut carbon dioxide emissions.
(B) It is probable people will feel the absence of the Kyoto targets.
(C) World temperatures will inevitably rise.
(D) Many diseases are a direct consequence of pollution.
(E) It is unrealistic to expect Western economies to contain their industrial activities.

(Interpretation) A: Incorrect – In the first paragraph, it is evident that Western governments have the intention to cut carbon dioxide emissions because they set ambitious targets at the Kyoto climate change conference in 1997. While they are in no hurry, by setting targets, their intention is evident; B: Incorrect – "Likely to be missed" in the first paragraph does not mean that people will feel the absence, but rather that the targets will not be reached; C: Incorrect – In the second paragraph, the rising of temperatures is considered a possibility (could include a further rise), but not inevitable; D: Incorrect – While the spread of disease (second paragraph) could be a possible consequence of rising temperatures, there is no reference to the number nor to whether the link is direct or not; E: Correct. – The term "it's a tall order", on the first line, means that something is very difficult, but can be construed as unrealistic. Note: Such interpretation is made in a very wide sense. To be a tall order does not necessarily mean "unrealistic", but it can be inferred.
Gabarito "E".

(Diplomacia – 2000) No texto:

(A) cut the rhetoric significa make shorter speeches.
(B) likely significa positively.
(C) they na frase "scientists say they could include" refere-se a scientists.
(D) mere sugere que the threat is small.
(E) to judge by significa according to.

(Vocabulary) A: Incorrect – In the text, "cut the rhetoric" means to "stop talking and start acting"; B: Incorrect – In the text, "likely" means "probably"; C: Incorrect – "They" in the specific sentence refers to the "consequences". (The consequences could include a further rise in world temperatures); D: Incorrect – "Mere" in the text means "just" or "itself" or "own its own"; E: Correct – "To judge by" in this text means "according to". (According to two new studies,...).
Gabarito "E".

(Diplomacia – 2000) Com relação ao texto:

(A) yet is an adverb of time.
(B) Further is the comparative form of far and means additional.
(C) Soon means not immediately.
(D) Adverse, like possibly, is an adverb.
(E) Rise is a noun derived from the verb raise.

(Grammar) A: Incorrect – In the text, "yet" is a conjuct of contrast, similar to "nevertheless" or "however"; B: Correct – Far / Farther / Farthest – relates to distance. Far / Further / Furthest – relates to additional; C: Incorrect – In the text, "soon" means "immediately" or "almost immediately"; D: Incorrect – In the text, "adverse" is an adjective that describes the effects – adverse effects (adverse [and] possibly irreversible effects); E: Incorrect – "Rise" is an intransitive verb (the sun rises), while "raise" is a transitive verb (the government raises taxes). One is not derived from the other.
Gabarito "B".

Leia o texto a seguir e responda as duas próximas perguntas:

Looking to Tame a Big Neighbor

From its hilltop perch in central Helsinki, a Russian Orthodox church looms over the gleaming, cream-coloured Presidential Palace. It's a reminder of the days when the Grand Duchy of Finland was a jewel in the Russian crown.

With fewer than 100 years of self-rule behind them and the cold war barely over, the Finns hardly need such reminders. But instead of trying to keep plenty of distance between themselves and their neighbor, the Finns want to bring Russia into Europe. And they think natural gas is the way to do it. "It has been possible with nuclear issues, and we think it's possible with other issues as well" says a Finnish Foreign Ministry official.

Business Week, 11/10/1999

(Diplomacia – 2000) Com base no texto, pode-se concluir que:

(A) Finland is a former Soviet Republic.
(B) The Finn's majority religion is the Russian Orthodox Church.
(C) The Finns prefer not to engage their powerful neighbor directly.
(D) The Finns think gas can be a key to Northeastern Europe.
(E) Russia has traditionally disparaged Finland.

(Interpretation) A: Incorrect – In the first paragraph, the Grand Duchy of Finland is revealed as part of the Russian Empire, but not a member of the Soviet Union; **B:** Incorrect – In the first paragraph, the text confirms the presence of a Russian Orthodox church near the Presidential Palace in Helsinki, but this does not confirm the majority religion in the country; **C:** Incorrect – In the second sentence in the second paragraph, the author shows that "instead of trying to keep plenty of distance between themselves and their neighbor, the Finns want to bring Russia into Europe", a form of direct engagement; **D:** Correct – The last two sentences of the second paragraph confirm that the Finns "think natural gas is the way" to bring Russia into Europe; **E:** Incorrect – "To disparage" means to "ridicule". While the author suggests that Finns may not want to remember the past, there is no clear evidence that Russia has poked fun at Finland.
Gabarito "D".

(Diplomacia – 2000) No texto:

(A) hardly significa with difficulty.
(B) Hardly significa do not.
(C) Barely significa incompletely.
(D) Looms significa overlooks.
(E) Natural significa open-air.

(Vocabulary) A: Incorrect – In the text, "hardly" means "almost not" or "do not"; **B:** Correct – In the text, "hardly" means "almost not" or "do not"; **C:** Incorrect – In the text, "barely" means "only just" or "a short time ago"; **D:** Incorrect – In the text, "looms" means "emerges" or "stands threateningly". Special Note – "looms over" means overlooks. The fact that the question omitted the preposition from the phrasal verb complicates the answer. In this case, if "looms" means "overlooks", the sentence, in the case of substitution, would read "a Russian Orthodox church *overlooks over* the gleaming, cream-coloured Presidential Palace", which is not possible; **E:** Incorrect – In this text, "natural" means "unprocessed".
Gabarito "B".

Leia o texto seguinte e responda as três próximas perguntas formuladas:

For all the triumphs of war and peace, the british Empire as it stood in 1763 had many weaknesses. Them in terms of one single design. It was an empire held together by sea power, but that alone was not enough to control it, let alone to govern it. Nor was trading supremacy guaranteed. Asa Briggs, A Social History of England.

(Diplomacia – 1999) Com base no texto acima, pode-se concluir que:

(A) Britain's sea power ensured its trading supremacy.
(B) The Empire was weak owing to the wars.
(C) Britain's naval power was sufficient to control the Empire.
(D) Britain's Navy was the cohesive force sustaining the Empire.
(E) The british empire could not be governed alone.

(Interpretation) A: Incorrect - Sea power is not specifically linked to trade and trading supremacy; **B:** Incorrect - War is not presented as causing weakness. War and peace are in fact presented as positive aspects; **C:** Incorrect - The use of 'that alone', referring to sea power, makes this statement false. The implication is that more than sea power was needed to control the empire; **D:** Correct – The term 'held together by sea power' refers to the role of the Navy in providing cohesion; **E:** Incorrect – The term 'let alone' means much less/not to mention. This refers to the fact that sea power was not enough to control much less govern it.
Gabarito "D".

(Diplomacia – 1999) Na primeira frase, a expressão *For all* significa:

(A) to the benefit of.
(B) because of.
(C) including.
(D) subsequent to.
(E) despite.

(Grammar) A, B, C e D: Incorrect; **E:** Correct – Despite or notwithstanding could be both used in this context to show an idea of contrast, which is the same meaning as 'for all' (specifically in this context).
Gabarito "E".

(Diplomacia – 1999) Na perífrase *the British Empire as it stood in* 1763, a expressão *as it stood* significa:

(A) the way it was.
(B) so long it resisted.
(C) while it resisted.
(D) at the time was established.
(E) when it rose.

(Interpretation) A: Correct – This can always be used as 'the way things stand right now', i.e. the way things are; B, C, D e E: Incorrect.
Gabarito "A".

Leia o texto seguinte e responda as duas próximas perguntas formuladas:

The initial international response to Central America´s tragedy has been generous. The Clinton administration has pledged U$ 80 million and sent troops to help clean up the horrible damage caused by the hurricane Mitch.

But as the long-term impact of this catastrophe becomes clear, so does the inadequacy of the response to date. Honduras and Nicaragua in particular have suffered a once-in-a-century kind of blow.

Governments from Cuba to Sweden have promised help, but what is needed now is a coordinated international response. Private banks, multilateral lenders such as the World Bank and major investors must be involved along with governments.

The International Herald Tribune, 17/XI/98

(Diplomacia – 1999) Como o texto acima avalia a resposta internacional?

(A) Good.
(B) Adequate but not generous.
(C) Excellent.
(D) Insufficient.
(E) U$ 80 million have been sent.

(Interpretation) A, B, C e E: Incorrect; D: Correct – The overall evaluation of the response is of being insufficient. Evidence for this is found in the phrase, 'so does the inadequacy of the response to date'. Inadequate clearly refers to insufficient. Further evidence is found in the last paragraph where the text states, 'what is needed now is a coordinated international response' and also in 'must be involved along with governments'.
Gabarito "D".

(Diplomacia – 1999) No mesmo texto, a expressão once-in-a-century significa:

(A) An event that happens every century.
(B) Something that occurs regularly over a long period of time.
(C) An event that takes place during an entire century.
(D) Something that occurs very often.
(E) An event that occurs very infrequently.

(Vocabulary) A, B, C e D: Incorrect; E: Correct – Once-in-a-century is not a literal expression. It refers to a freak or rare occurrence – such as the extent of the hurricane damage mentioned in the text.
Gabarito "E".

Leia o texto seguinte e responda as duas próximas perguntas formuladas:

"**Under** a government which **bolted** on a women´s minister as an afterthought, women in Britain are doing all right. The new women´s minister, Baroness Jay, has every reason to be proud of her government's record: the new child-care strategy, the **push** to a "family-friendly" work package, social security, reforms that include a big increase in child benefit, and a **sharing** of pensions on divorce. Like most other European states, Britain has seen women making **major** advances in the professions – equal numbers entering law and medicine and even more females taking business studies than men". The Guardian Weekly, 15/XI/98, pg. 12

(Diplomacia – 1999) Com base no texto acima, a única afirmação correta é:

(A) There are more women than men doing law Great Britain.
(B) In all European countries women have equal rights.
(C) The women´s minister was one of the first minister to be appointed.
(D) There are more men doing business studies than women, in Great Britain.
(E) Baroness Jay is doing a good job.

(Interpretation) A: Incorrect – There are equal numbers entering law and medicine; **B:** Incorrect -This is not stated; **C:** Incorrect – The opposite is true, she was 'bolted on as an afterthought', i.e. included as a last thought; **D:** Incorrect – The text clearly states that there are, 'even more females taking business studies than men"; **E:** Correct – In line 2, the text states 'the Baroness has every reason to be proud'. This is reinforced by the statement in line 1 where it says that 'Under a government......women are doing all right'. The implication is that the government in which the Baroness serves is doing a good job.
Gabarito "E".

(Diplomacia – 1999) No mesmo texto,

(A) Under significa below.
(B) Bolted significa moved slowly.
(C) Push significa strong action.
(D) Sharing significa refusing.
(E) Major significa more.

(Vocabulary) A: Incorrect – This means under the auspices of a government or under the mandate of a government. Below is too literal; **B:** Incorrect – Bolted means attached to, or secured to; **C:** Correct – Push refers to a strong action, i.e. in a government push for health reform; **D:** Incorrect – Sharing means to have equal responsibility for doing something, paying for something etc.; **E:** Incorrect – Major means significant.
Gabarito "C".

The Amazon Rainforest

1   The Amazon Rainforest, also known in English as Amazonia or the Amazon Jungle, is a moist broadleaf forest that covers most of the Amazon Basin of South America. This
4   basin encompasses seven million square kilometers, of which five and a half million square kilometers are covered by the rainforest. This region includes territory belonging to nine
7   nations. The majority of the forest is contained within Brazil, with 60% of the rainforest, followed by Peru with 13%, and with minor amounts in Colombia, Venezuela, Ecuador, Bolivia,
10 Guyana, Suriname and France (French Guiana). States or departments in four nations bear the name Amazonas after them. Amazonia represents over half of the planet's remaining
13 rainforests, and it comprises the largest and most species-rich tract of tropical rainforest in the world.
    The basin is drained by the Amazon River, the world's
16 largest river in terms of discharge, and the second longest river in the world after the Nile.
    Wet tropical forests are the most species-rich biome,
19 and tropical forests in the Americas are consistently more animal and plant species rich than the wet forests in Africa and Asia. As the largest tract of tropical rainforest in the Americas,

22 the Amazonian rainforests have unparalleled biodiversity. One in ten known species in the world lives in the Amazon Rainforest. This constitutes the largest collection of living
25 plants and animal species in the world.
   The Amazon Rainforest was short-listed in 2008 as a candidate for one of the New7Wonders of Nature by the New
28 Seven Wonders of the World Foundation. As of February 2009 the Amazon ranked first in Group E, the category for forests, national parks and nature reserves.

The Amazon: the world's largest rainforest. Internet: <http://rainforests.mongabay.com/amazon> and **Amazon Forest**. Internet:<http://en.wikipedia.org/wiki/Amazon_rainforest> (adapted).

(Bolsa-Prêmio/Itamaraty – 2011) Based on the text above, judge the following items.

(1) With an astounding biodiversity, the Amazon Rainforest is home to more species of plants and animals than any other terrestrial ecosystem on the planet.

(2) The expression "are the most species-rich biome" (ℓ.18) could be replaced by **have a great diversity of plant species** without changing the original meaning of the text.

(3) Although the Amazon River basin is home to the largest rainforest on Earth, it is the second most voluminous river on Earth.

(4) The Amazon River basin includes parts of eight South American countries: Brazil, Bolivia, Peru, Ecuador, Colombia, Venezuela, Guyana, and Suriname, as well as French Guiana, a department of France.

(Interpretation) 1: Correct - In line 13, the text says, 'it represents the largest and most species-rich tract (area) of tropical rainforest in the world; 2: Incorrect – In the text, the phrase is a superlative 'the most'. The suggested replacement is not a superlative and, therefore, does not have the same meaning; 3: Incorrect – While the Nile is the longest river (line 18), the Amazon is the most voluminous in terms of its discharge/emission (line 16); 4: Correct – Lines 8-12 identify this. French Guiana is considered to be part of France or an overseas French department.

Gabarito: 1C, 2E, 3E, 4C

Cleaning up after nature plays a trick

1   It was a storm of record consequence, disrupting large swaths of the Northeast in ways large and small: towns were buried in dense snowfalls, closing down streets, schools and
4   even, in some cases, Halloween celebrations.
    By the time the great snowstorm of October 2011 finally ended early Sunday, more than three million customers
7   would find themselves without power and with the prospect of enduring several more days without it. The unseasonably early nor'easter had utility companies struggling to restore electricity
10 to homes and businesses. By early Monday, the number of customers without power was still above 2 million but falling. People emptied stores of generators and chain saws
13 and flocked to town halls to charge phones on emergency power. In Worcester, Mass., a wedding with cranberry dresses and flowers the colors of fall foliage ended up soggy and white.
16 In Glen Rock, N.J., orderly suburban blocks became a maze, with fallen branches draped across nearly every street.
    Communities in New Jersey, Connecticut,
19 Massachusetts and New Hampshire expected schools to remain closed for several days as they cleaned up downed electrical wires and fallen branches. And in Central Park, as many as
22 1,000 trees may be lost — eight times the damage suffered after Tropical Storm Irene.
    But in the most telling sign of how the snow had
25 turned seasons topsy-turvy — throwing an icy and sometimes lethal blanket over trees whose leaves were often still green — the storm threatened to obliterate Halloween.

New York Times. Internet: <www.nytimes.com> (adapted).

(Bolsa-Prêmio/Itamaraty – 2011) Judge the following items based on what is stated in the text above.

(1) Throughout the entire US north and east regions there were hundreds of schools closed, many lacked power and trees littered roads after a surprise snow on Sunday.

(2) In "as they cleaned up downed electrical wires and fallen branches" (ℓ.20-21), the term "downed" (ℓ.20) could be replaced by turned down without changing the original meaning of the text.

(3) Because of the unexpected snowstorm, there was a large power failure in the storm-struck region.

(4) The storm's lingering effects snow were all solved late Sunday.

(5) Despite the snowstorm, many schools in New Jersey, Connecticut and Massachusetts were back to the normal routine the day after.

(Interpretation) 1: Incorrect – In line 2, the text refers to 'swaths'; these represent tracks or paths and do not represent the entire Northeastern area; 2: Incorrect – In this sense, 'downed' means thrown down to the ground. The phrasal verb, 'turned down' refers to lowering the volume – turn down the volume of the radio. It can also refer to rejection – He turned down the job offer (he rejected the job offer); 3: Correct – In lines 7-8, the text refers to unseasonably early nor'easter meaning – weather which was unexpected at that time of the year; and also, in line 7, the text refers to the fact that customers would find themselves without power (this is using 'would' in the sense of recounting a past event – On that day, they would discover the key to the mystery; 4: Incorrect – Lingering, here, means to remain/last. The text clearly states (line 10) that early Monday the number of those without power was still above 2 million. Loss of power was a consequence of the snowfall; 5: Incorrect – (Line 19-20) there was an expectation that schools would remain closed for several days in New Hampshire and Massachusetts. Several – a small number, but more than one day.

Gabarito: 1E, 2E, 3C, 4E, 5E

Obama tries to speed response to shortages in vital medicines

1   President Obama will issue an executive order on Monday that the administration hopes will help resolve a growing number of critical shortages of vital medicines used to
4   treat life-threatening illnesses, among them several forms of cancer and bacterial infections.
    The order offers drug manufacturers and wholesalers
7   both a helping hand and a gloved fist in efforts to prevent or resolve shortages that have worsened greatly in recent years, endangering thousands of lives.
10 It instructs the F.D.A. to do three things: broaden reporting of potential shortages of certain prescription drugs; speed reviews of applications to begin or alter production of
13 these drugs; and provide more information to the Justice Department about possible instances of collusion or price gouging.
16 Such efforts are included in proposed legislation that has been pending in Congress since February despite bipartisan support for its provisions.

19 The order is part of a series of recent executive orders involving such disparate issues as mortgage relief and jobs for veterans. They are intended to show that the president, plagued
22 by low approval ratings, is working to resolve the nation's problems despite a Congress largely paralyzed by partisan disagreements.

New York Times. Internet:<www.nytimes.com> (adapted).

(Bolsa-Prêmio/Itamaraty – 2011) Judge the following items according to the text above.

(1) President Obama signed the executive order without the Congress approval.
(2) Because hospitals are running out of many key drugs, Obama administration is considering creating a stockpile for crucial cancer medicines.
(3) In "the administration hopes will help resolve a growing number of critical shortages of vital medicines" (ℓ.2-3), the verb "resolve" could be replaced by finding the solution for without any changes in meaning.
(4) In "and provide more information to the Justice Department about possible instances of collusion or price gouging" (ℓ.13-15), the expression "price gouging" could be correctly replaced by pricing over market.
(5) In "They are intended to show that the president, plagued by low approval ratings, is working to resolve the nation's problems" (ℓ.21-23), if the verb "plagued" was replaced by pleased it would give the opposite idea to the sentence.
(6) President Obama's executive order aims to address an increasing shortage of prescription drugs that are used to treat cancer and other diseases.

(Interpretation) 1: Incorrect – (In line 17) the legislation has been pending/in the process of being approved/impending, and has bipartisan support; 2: Incorrect – To stockpile is to accumulate a large store for future use. Obama is trying to get medicines to deal with critical shortages (line 3) not to stockpile the medicine; 3: Correct – To resolve means to solve or find a solution for something (to resolve a problem); 4: Correct - Price gouging has a negative connotation of squeezing or wringing out profit through dishonest/ unscrupulous means. In the context, price gouging would mean pricing above the market; 5: Correct – In the text, plagued means annoyed or bothered. Therefore, to be pleased would have the opposite idea; 6: Correct – (Line 3) resolve a growing number of critical shortages, i.e. an increasing number of critical shortages for vital/essential drugs.

Gabarito 1E, 2E, 3C, 4C, 5C, 6C

Text I

1 Slavery in Brazil was not like slavery in the United States of America (US), where slaves were totally debased to the extent that every effort was made to destroy the African
4 language, culture, religion and intellectual capacity. In Brazil, the number of slaves imported was quite large. Moreover, most slaves in Brazil came from parts of Africa
7 with developed culture.
The first system of private education in Brazil was begun by the African Muslim Societies whose members
10 came from West Africa. The African slaves who came from the literary and West African college system were hired to teach the children of the Portuguese slave masters. At the
13 same time, these slaves created their own schools. Brazil has retained many aspects of African culture from the very beginning of its colonial history. The Africans
16 sent to Brazil came from a number of important kingdoms and empires.
Some aspects of African culture that Africans in
19 Africa are allowing missionaries from the European and Arab world to destroy are the traditional African spiritualist religions such as Vadu and Shango. African religions thrive
22 in Brazil, whether it is Umbanda, Candomblé, or the Orisha tradition. These religions are like a steel bond that holds Afro-Brazilians to their African heritage and culture.

Paul Barton. **Brazil's black renaissance is happening**. Internet: <http://www.raceandhistory.com.br>. Access on April/2004 (with adaptations).

(Bolsa-Prêmio/Itamaraty – 2004) Based on text I, it can be correctly inferred that

(1) the main difference between slavery in Brazil and that in the United States is that Brazilian slave owners tried to destroy African culture because its high level of development threatened their domination of the slaves.
(2) slaves who taught the children of Portuguese slave owners had come from an already existing educational system in Africa.
(3) the strength of black culture in Brazil is a result of the origins of slaves in organized African societies.
(4) Brazil is keeping alive cultural traditions that are being threatened in Africa.

(Interpretation) 1: Incorrect – There is no evidence to support this statement. It was in the US that slaves were totally 'debased' (line 2); **2:** Correct – Lines 10-12 "The African slaves who came from the literary and Western African college system were hired to teach the children of the Portuguese slave masters"; **3:** Correct – The text alludes to the fact that the slaves brought to Brazil from Africa already had a 'developed culture', (line 7). In lines 16-17, the author highlights slaves brought to Brazil came from 'important kingdoms and empires.' These facts help to maintain black culture in Brazil; **4:** Correct – Certain African religions thrive (Line 21), i.e. flourish in Brazil such as Candomblé and Umbanda, whereas in Africa they are under threat from European or Arab missionaries (line 19).

Gabarito 1E, 2C, 3C, 4C

(Bolsa-Prêmio/Itamaraty – 2004) Based on text I, judge the following items.

(1) The word "like" (ℓ.1) can be correctly replaced by **alike**.
(2) "Moreover" (ℓ.6) means **also and more importantly**.
(3) The words "who" (ℓ.10) and "hired" (ℓ.11) can be correctly replaced by **that** and **rent** respectively.
(4) In line 14, the word "retained" can be correctly replaced by **restricted**.
(5) The word "thrive" (ℓ.21) can be correctly replaced by **flourish**.
(6) The sentence "These religions are like a steel bond that holds Afro-Brazilians to their African heritage and culture" (ℓ.23-24) can be correctly replaced by: These religions imprison African-Brazilians rigidly within their historical background.

(Grammar) 1: Incorrect – Like in this context means 'in the same way as'. Alike refers to closely resembling something or someone; **2:** Correct - Moreover means in addition to what has been said, similar to in addition and furthermore; **3:** Incorrect – Who is a relative pronoun. If 'that' were used it would imply that we were restricting only slaves coming from a certain area and that there was logically another group that did not come form this area. Hired and rent have different connotations – you can hire staff, a worker, a car. You can rent a car, a house. You cannot rent an employee. Special Note: For restrictive usage, "that" and "who" are interchangeable. By using that, the semantics change slightly, but they are synonymous here; **4:** Incorrect – Retained means to keep, hold or maintain possession of. Restricted on the other hand means to limit or curb; **5:** Correct; **6:** Incorrect – The original sentence is positive. The steel bond is a link. The second sentence by using 'imprison' implies tying or restricting African-Brazilians and is negative.

Gabarito 1E, 2C, 3E, 4E, 5C, 6E

Text II

1 Enslaved Africans transformed the landscapes of tropical America, not merely for plantations but also for subsistence, a process that established many foods of African
4 origin on the other side of the Atlantic. While the plantation economy developed due to the Portuguese, slaves pioneered forms of landscape management that would serve their
7 dietary preferences. In reclaiming swamps for cultivation, they relied upon their sophisticated knowledge of wetland farming to establish rice, a West African food staple.
10 Recognition of botanical families, valued in Africa for medicine and poison, ritual and material culture, similarly led to conscious plant selection and environmental manipulation
13 in the Americas. Such knowledge proved additionally critical in the survival strategies of runaway slaves, whose expertise in tropical farming nurtured their repeated attempts to
16 establish free, independent African communities (quilombos) in the tropical forest hinterlands of Brazil and the Guianas. While the survival strategies of Afro-Brazilians were
19 undoubtedly shaped by Amerindian achievements, the contribution of Brazil's black pioneers remains ignored. Yet their legacy in manipulating plant resources for subsistence,
22 survival, resistance and identity resonates in Afro-Brazilian culture to this day.
There has been a measured willingness, particularly
25 by anthropologists and geographers, to concede that Africans played a significant role in shaping the cultural landscape of the Americas since 1500. Among the long-standing themes
28 in African history in the Americas is the debate over cultural survivals and acculturation. This dates to the 1920s, when anthropologist Melville Herskovits first tried to show that it
31 was a pernicious myth to believe that the African in the Americas had no past. He challenged the notion of sociologist E. Franklin Frazier that slavery had stripped its
34 victims of their African heritage. Over the next decades, Herskovits and his followers searched for the retention of specific African cultural traits in the Americas, emphasizing
37 carry-overs in the arts and especially religion. Much of this research, however, subsequently drew criticism for treating Africa as a single cultural area, a concept of culture very
40 much in fashion at that time, but inaccurate in portraying the diversity and complexity of cultures found in just West Africa alone. The search for vestiges of an African culture in
43 areas where he and his followers worked — Suriname, the Caribbean and the US South — consequently proved so generalized as to provide little understanding of the
46 distinctive black cultures that formed in the Americas.

Judith A. Carney and Robert A. Voeks. **Landscape legacies of the African diaspora in Brazil. In: Progress in human geography,** 2/27/2003, p. 141 (with adaptations).

(Bolsa-Prêmio/Itamaraty – 2004) Based on text II, it can be correctly deduced that

(1) African slaves were forced to drain swamps to create fields for their masters.

(2) African slaves cultivated the wild rice they found in tropical America.

(3) the agricultural skills of African slaves were an advantage in establishing the quilombos.

(4) until the 1920s, it was commonly believed that the history of African slaves had been effectively eliminated when they were brought to the Americas.

(5) Herskovits was criticized for concentrating only on West Africa when searching for African roots in the Americas.

(Interpretation) 1: Incorrect – In line 7, 'reclaiming swamps for cultivation' does not suggest there is an idea of being forced, but rather that the slaves applied their knowledge to create their own food supplies; **2:** Incorrect – In line 9, the text says they established rice using wetland farming techniques. There is no mention of wild rice being found; **3:** Correct – In line 13, 'such knowledge' refers to the agricultural skills of the African slaves. The text then links these skills to being necessary for survival and to establish the quilombos (lines 14 and 15); **4:** Correct – It was in the 1920s that Herskovits challenged this previous view. The previous view held is detailed in lines 32-34; **5:** Incorrect – Herskovits was criticized for portraying African as a single cultural area (line 39).

Gabarito 1E, 2E, 3C, 4C, 5E

(Bolsa-Prêmio/Itamaraty – 2004) Judge if each item below presents a correct re-writing of the information contained in the phrase "There has been a measured willingness, particularly by anthropologists and geographers, to concede (...)" (ℓ.24-25) of text II.

(1) Anthropologists and geographers have cautiously agreed to concede (...).

(2) There has been an enthusiastic willingness, particularly by anthropologists and geographers, to concede (...).

(Interpretation) 1: Correct – The use of 'measured' implies caution; **2:** Incorrect – Enthusiastic is too strong a word to use. They showed a 'measured willingness', not enthusiasm.

Gabarito 1C, 2E

(Bolsa-Prêmio/Itamaraty – 2004) According to text II, judge the following items.

(1) The verb phrase "had stripped" (ℓ.33) can be correctly replaced by had prevented.

(2) In line 34, the word "Over" can be correctly replaced by During.

(3) The phrase "emphasizing carry-overs in the arts" (ℓ.36-37) refers to the artifacts slaves took with them to America.

(Vocabulary) 1: Incorrect – Strip means to deprive or to remove. Prevent means to keep something from happening; **2:** Correct – In this context, both mean throughout a period; **3:** Incorrect – This refers to the cultural traits that spilled over into the arts. There is no mention of any artifacts being brought from Africa.

Gabarito 1E, 2C, 3E

Text III

1 Today Brazil has the largest single population of African-Americans outside of the United States (US). It is, according to some, a population in which at least 60 percent
4 is of African descent. Statistics on the number of slaves imported into Brazil range from 1.025 million: for the rest of South America the figure runs at approximately 400,000. In
7 some parts of colonial Latin America, the ratio of African to European populations was 151, and in some cities, nearly half of the populations were of partial African descent. By
10 independence, two thirds of Brazil's total population of about four million were of African descent. Brazilian society, like a few of the other plantation-dependent colonies of Latin
13 America and the Caribbean, could not have existed without the constant supply of black laborers.
Throughout history, Africans and Afro-Hispanics
16 have been a major force in the development of the cultures, political systems, societies, and economies of the nations of the Iberian Peninsula — Spain and Portugal — and Latin
19 America. Iberian-African relations did not begin with the transatlantic slave trade, nor did it begin in the Americas. African Muslims were involved in the historical development
22 of the political, economic, intellectual, and social structures of the Iberian Peninsula, as rulers and conquerors, centuries before their eventual defeat by the emerging monarchical
25 powers of Spain and Portugal. That experience left long and enduring marks on the course of historical events that led to the emergence of the modern nation-states of Spain and
28 Portugal, and their imperial "conquest" and colonization of the "New World".

Walton Brown. **Democracy and race in Brazil, Britain and the United States.** Internet: <http://www.brazil-brasil.com/blajan99.htm>. Access on April/2004 (with adaptations).

(Bolsa-Prêmio/Itamaraty – 2004) Based on text III, judge the following items.

(1) A close look at the world's population distribution would lead us to conclude that the USA has the largest single number of African-American inhabitants.

(2) Comparing the number of African-Americans who came to Brazil to work basically in agricultural activities with the number of those of the rest of meridian America, it can be seen that Brazil had three times as much the number of those workers.

(3) By 1822, the number of Brazilians of non-African descent was of more than 1 million people.

(4) Undoubtedly, the African culture now found not only on the Iberian Peninsula, but also in the countries colonized by Spain and Portugal can be traced back to the Muslim presence.

(Interpretation) 1: Correct – In lines 1-2, the text states that 'Brazil has the largest single population of African-Americans outside of the US; **2:** Incorrect – In lines 5-6, we can compare the figures: Brazil 1.025 million slaves to the rest of South America 400,000. Therefore, Brazil did not have three times as many slaves; **3:** Correct – In lines 10-11, the text states that by independence (1822) 'two thirds of 'Brazil's population (4 million) were of African descent; **4:** Correct – In line 25, 'that experience' refers to the influence of African culture. The text goes on to detail in lines 25-29 the extent of this in the Iberian Peninsula and the colonies of Spain and Portugal.

Gabarito 1C, 2E, 3C, 4C

(Bolsa-Prêmio/Itamaraty – 2004) Judge if each item below presents a correct re-writing of the information contained in the sentence "Throughout (…) Latin America" (ℓ.15-19) of text III.

(1) All along their stories, American and Afro-Iberian have represented an important strength in the evolution of the cultures, political systems, societies, and economies of the nations of the Iberian Peninsula — Spain and Portugal — and Latin America.

(2) During the whole course of history, African and Afro-Iberian have played a crucial force in the development of the cultures, political systems, societies, and economies of the nations of the Iberian Peninsula — Spain and Portugal — and South America.

(3) Throughout their history, Africans and Afro-Hispanics have played a major role in the evolution of the cultures, political systems, societies, and economies of the nations of the Iberian Peninsula and Latin America.

(Interpretation) 1: Incorrect – The stories or histories of American and Afro-Iberian's dates back much further than those relating to the Iberian Peninsula; **2:** Incorrect – 'During the whole course of history is inaccurate. The use of the word 'crucial' can be seen as an overstatement; **3:** Correct – This accurately reflects the text.

Gabarito 1E, 2E, 3C

Considered the best illustrator of 19th-century Brazil, Jean Baptiste Debret left us a monumental set of masterpieces that, until today, have not been surpassed in Brazilian iconography. Born in Paris in 1768, he studied at Beaux Arts Institute, but received a degree in engineering and in 1814 was invited by Joachin Lebreton to join the French Mission that came to Brazil. Never dreaming he would stay in Brazil for 15 years, Debret landed in Rio in 1816 and was given the title Official Painter of the Emperor. Debret fell in love with the environment he lived in and with everything that happened around him.

Nothing escaped the careful eye of this painter, who made faithful renditions with his sketches of everything he saw: the noblemen, the slaves, animals and costumes, streets and houses. All this work culminated in almost 200 engravings of Rio, São Paulo, Paraná, Santa Catarina and Rio Grande do Sul. His journeys in Brazil produced what is maybe his best work, Voyage Pittoresque et Historique au Brésil, comprising 151 plates in three editions, the first dedicated to Indians and the forest, the second to slaves and craftsmen, and the third to urban costumes and political events. Ironic and sometimes tough, libertarian and conservative, Debret managed to record the enchantment of Brazil with the discipline of a historian and the finesse of an inspired artist. One could write a thesis about every one of Jean Baptiste Debret's pictures.

Internet: <http://www.debret.com/english/debret.asp> (with adaptations).

(Bolsa-Prêmio/Itamaraty – 2004) Based on the text above, it is true to say that

(1) up to now, Debret is, beyond the shadow of any doubt, the best Brazilian painter.
(2) Debret can be considered a popular artist to the extent that he used to portray scenes of everyday Brazilian life in the 19th century.
(3) Debret's interest in imperial Brazil was quite absorbing. Despite being an official appointee of the Brazilian ruler, he included in his works not only Blacks in their daily tasks but also native Brazilians.
(4) Debret most certainly noticed the conditions under which Blacks used to work in Brazil.
(5) Debret's works, if comprehensively analyzed by experts in art and history, can be described as those of a painter endowed with the discipline of a historian and the finesse of an inspired artist.

(Interpretation) 1: Incorrect – Debret was considered the best illustrator of 19th century Brazil. Iconography can be considered a narrower field than all painting in general; 2: Correct – In the definition of 'popular' being representing or coming from the general population; 3: Correct – The first of his plates was dedicated to Indians and the second to slaves and craftsmen; 4: Correct – In the phrase "Nothing escaped the careful eye of this painter", we can assume that while painting slaves, as is made evident in the text, he noticed their working conditions; 5: Correct – The first part of this statement is somewhat vague – no mention is given to art or history experts or careful analysis – this has to be deduced from the statement in the last sentence regarding a thesis. However, the second part is clearly true as the text refers to his discipline (historian) and finesse (inspired artist).

Gabarito 1E, 2C, 3C, 4C, 5C

1 W.E.B. du Bois summed up the black man's ordeal in America eloquently when he wrote, "One ever feels his twoness — an American, a Negro; two souls, two thoughts,
4 two unreconciled strivings; two warring ideals in one dark body, whose dogged strength alone keeps it from being torn asunder". Much has happened since Du Bois wrote these
7 words in 1903, yet they remain relevant to the subject of race relations.
It is not surprising that debates on "twoness" have
10 often led to a discussion of the Brazilian situation. Many observers believed this feeling never disturbed Afro-Brazilians the way they troubled Afro-Americans. They
13 looked excitedly to Brazil as a model of "racial democracy" from which the United States might learn. Robert Allen Christopher summarized the ideal nicely in a 1953 essay,
16 The Human race in Brazil. Said Christopher:
"Perhaps the most poignant illustration of the difference between the United States and Brazil in the matter
19 of race relation is the fact that a Brazilian Negro generally considers himself first and foremost a *brasileiro* and only second a *preto* (black man). Can the equivalent be said for
22 the US Negro? Far too many cannot help thinking of themselves as Negroes first and US citizens second, which is the real meaning of second class citizenship".

Robert Brent Toplin. **Freedom and Prejudice**

(Bolsa-Prêmio/Itamaraty – 2004) Based on the text of Robert Brent Toplin, judge the following items.

(1) The substitution of the phrases "summed up" (ℓ.1) and "black man's ordeal" (ℓ.1) by added up and black man's ordering respectively would keep the same morphological and semantic relations as those presented in the text.
(2) In line 4, "warring ideals" means conflicting ideals.
(3) The phrase "whose dogged strength alone keeps it from being torn asunder" (ℓ.5-6) can be correctly paraphrased as: whose obstinate strength in itself prevents it from being ripped apart.
(4) "poignant" (ℓ.17) means keenly distressing to the feelings.
(5) The situation of Afro-Brazilians could be said to differ from that experienced by the black population in the United States; however, some people think that the "twoness" (ℓ.9) problem also prevails in Brazil.
(6) A striking difference between blacks in the United States and in Brazil can most certainly be said to be that, whereas in the US the former consider themselves first blacks and secondly citizens, the latter see themselves the other way round.
(7) The expression "first and foremost" (ℓ.20) has the same meaning as above all.
(8) Brazilian and American negroes can both be said to hold the same kind of second class citizenship.

(Vocabulary) 1: Incorrect - 'Summed up' means to condense or to capture. 'Add up' means the summation of. Ordeal refers to suffering whereas ordering refers to classification; 2: Correct; 3: Correct – Dogged refers to stubbornness or obstinacy. Torn asunder means to be broken apart or ripped apart; 4: Correct – Poignant means profoundly moving or touching; 5: Correct – This is difficult to surmise. In line 10, the text mentions 'many observers' not all observers. Thus, we could assume there are others who do not share this opinion; 6: Correct – This is clearly stated in lines 19-24; 7: Correct; 8: Incorrect – The whole idea of the text is to show that Brazilian negroes do not experience the same kind of second class citizenship as American negroes (line 24).

Gabarito 1E, 2C, 3C, 4C, 5C, 6C, 7C, 8E

Text I

Brazilian diplomacy

The duties of the diplomat are synthesized in the classic formula: inform, represent and negotiate. The diplomat must keep his (or her) country informed about international affairs, work constantly to mark the presence and spread the image of his country abroad, and be prepared to defend national interests in foreign negotiations of a bilateral or multilateral nature.

A fourth task must be added to this formula that places emphasis on the work of the diplomat overseas, namely, internal coordination. Identifying the interests of the nation lies at the base of the diplomat's work. The diplomat must be permanently articulating with other government employees, members of the Congress, and organized sectors of civil society, in order to be able to define national interests and defend them in proper fashion abroad.

The reality of the diplomatic career is far removed from that other widespread cliché, which claims that this is a professional option for those who want the chance to live in pleasant places overseas. In fact, the great majority of diplomats invariably undergo the experience of living in difficult countries that offer risks to the health and security of both themselves and their family. Furthermore, diplomats must often undergo situations of internal or external conflict in the country to which they are posted. At other times they themselves are the targets of violent actions for political motives. For these reasons, Brazil's diplomatic service is legally bound to endeavour to assign each civil servant to serve alternately in posts where life is agreeable and in others where living conditions are harsher.

Mônica Hirst, João Hermes Pereira de Araújo and Raul Mendes Silva. CD Rom Brazilian Diplomacy: Past and Present. Log On Informática. (with adaptations).

(Bolsa-Prêmio/Itamaraty – 2003) According to text I, it is correct to say that diplomats

(1) should expect to perform complex tasks.
(2) should spread every possible information concerning their country the world over.
(3) may take part in foreign negotiations involving more than two countries.
(4) living outside their own countries have an extra role added to those they have when living in their own countries.
(5) must be perfectly aware of the interests of their countries.

(Interpretation) 1: Correct – In the first paragraph, the text affirms three complex tasks: 1) to keep his (or her) country informed about international affairs; 2) to work constantly to mark the presence and spread the image of his country abroad; and 3) to be prepared to defend national interests in foreign negotiations; **2:** Incorrect – In the first paragraph, the text confirms that diplomats should spread the image of their country, but the text mentions nothing concerning "every possible information". Special Note – "Every possible information" is poor use of English collocation. The correct collocation is "all possible information" because "information" is an uncountable word. The word "every" requires a countable noun in the singular form. E.g. every music – NOT POSSIBLE / every song – POSSIBLE; **3:** Correct – In the first paragraph, the author explicitly shows that diplomats are supposed to "be prepared to defend national interests in foreign negotiations of a bilateral or multilateral nature", thus confirming negotiations involving more than two countries; **4:** Correct – In the last paragraph, the text confirms that diplomats living abroad will often have to "undergo situations of internal or external conflict in the country to which they are posted", thus confirming the extra role; **5:** Correct – In the second paragraph, the author explains that diplomats are expected to "identify the interests of the nation", as well as to "be able to define national interests and defend them", thus confirming the awareness of the country's interests.

Gabarito 1C, 2E, 3C, 4C, 5C

(Bolsa-Prêmio/Itamaraty – 2003) It can be deduced from text I that

(1) the diplomatic career offers a unique chance for those who want to live in the best countries all over the world.
(2) rarely do diplomats have to live in unfavorable conditions.
(3) diplomacy should not always be considered a safe career.
(4) risky countries ought to be avoided by the diplomatic service.
(5) it is illegal to assign diplomats to serve in countries where conditions are unpleasant.

(Interpretation) 1: Incorrect – In the last paragraph, the texts explicitly confirms that the reality of the career is "far removed from that other widespread cliché, (…) that this is a professional option for those who want the chance to live in pleasant places overseas", thus proving that the career offers varying experiences, not only in the best countries all over the world; **2:** Incorrect – In the last paragraph, the text confirms there is a tendency to have diplomats "serve alternately in posts where life is agreeable and in others where living conditions are harsher", and that diplomats "<u>invariably</u> (regularly) undergo the experience of living in difficult countries", thus proving that this is not rare; **3:** Correct – In the last paragraph, the text explicitly reveals that diplomats often "undergo the experience of living in difficult countries that offer risks to the health and security of both themselves and their family" and that diplomats are sometimes "the targets of violent actions for political motives", thus proving the lack of safety that diplomats can often face; **4:** Incorrect – In the last paragraph, the text explains that "diplomatic service is legally bound to endeavor to assign each civil servant serve alternately in posts where life is agreeable and in others where living conditions are harsher", proving that avoiding risky countries is not an option for diplomats. In fact, the great majority of diplomats invariably undergo the experience of living in difficult countries that offer risks to the health and security of both themselves and their family; **5:** Incorrect - In the last paragraph, the text explains that "diplomatic service is legally bound to endeavor to assign each civil servant serve alternately in posts where life is agreeable and in others where living conditions are harsher", proving that assigning diplomats to serve in countries where conditions are unpleasant is, in fact, legal.

Gabarito 1E, 2E, 3C, 4E, 5E

Text II

1 Thank you very much Minister Nkate. Minister Merafhe and Minister Seretse, thank you for inviting us here to open this very important Competitiveness Hub[1].
4 What is this Hub? What is this all about? In October of 2001, president Bush at the AGOA Forum announced that the United States was going to open trade centers to encourage
7 Africans, that is all of Africa, to export goods all over the world. We call these the Competitiveness Hubs and they are in Botswana, where we are going to unveil the plaque today, they
10 are in Ghana and they are in Kenya. And these three Competitiveness Hubs try to, and hopefully will succeed, get all of sub-Saharan Africa to prepare their goods and services for the
13 markets all over the world — Europe, Intra-Africa, North America, and the Far East. This is about getting African business services ready to compete around the world.
16 And you know our belief is, and I believe the Europeans share this belief, that African goods and products can be competitive. They can compete and, given the chance, I think
19 they will compete very effectively. So what does this Hub do? What are we going to try and accomplish? You know we are going to, number one, explain the rules. Trade has rules, the rules
22 to the game. And one of the things that we are going to do is explain the rules to export to the United States. We are going to explain the rules — how to export to Europe, and how to export
25 to the Koreans or to Japan.

[1] Hub — central point of activity, interest or importance, focal point

Internet: <http://www.state.gov/p/af/rls/rm/20401.htm >. Accessed in June/2003 (with adaptations).

(Bolsa-Prêmio/Itamaraty – 2003) Judge the following items related to text II.

(1) The text consists of some oral remarks.
(2) A possible title for this text could be: Sub-Saharan Africa global competitiveness hub: exporting goods
(3) The passage described in the text was marked by a formal ceremony.
(4) President Bush showed interest in African goods in the late 1990's.
(5) Every African country is liable to export goods.
(6) Europeans believe African products are highly competitive.

(Interpretation) 1: Correct – On line 1, the text opens with the speaker thanking people you are present at the speech, a mark of oral remarks; **2:** Correct – On lines 5 to 8, the text (speech) reveals that the competitiveness hubs are aimed at helping African countries to export their goods; **3:** Correct – On lines 2 and 3, the text reveals that it is the opening ceremony for the Competitiveness Hub in Botswana; **4:** Incorrect – The text shows that President Bush's interest in African goods was in 2001, not in the 1990s; **5:** Correct – On lines 11 to 15, the speech reveals that the Hub, if successful, will prepare "all sub-Saharan" African countries to export goods around the world; **6:** Incorrect – On lines 18 and 19, the speaker reveals his belief in African goods becoming highly competitive, but there is nothing that confirms Europeans think the same way.

Gabarito 1C, 2C, 3C, 4E, 5C, 6E

(Bolsa-Prêmio/Itamaraty – 2003) Based on text II, judge the following items.

(1) African countries will not be able to export their goods to Europe.
(2) It seems that in some African countries international export rules still need to be taught.
(3) The rules to export to the United States differ from those to export to Europe.
(4) Asiatic countries are not included in the speaker's comments.

(Interpretation) 1: Incorrect – On lines 23 and 24, the text shows that, provided the rules are followed, Africa will be able to export goods to Europe; **2:** Correct – On lines 21 to 25, the speaker emphasizes that rules must be taught on how to export to other countries, inferring that there is a need for such teachings; **3:** Correct – On lines 22 to 24, the speaker separates the United States from Europe, emphasizing that the rules to each place need to be taught. Such separation suggests the rules are different. This is made even more emphatic when the rules to some Asian countries are further separated; **4:** Incorrect – On line 25, the speaker mentions two Asian countries: Korea and Japan.

Gabarito 1E, 2C, 3C, 4E

(Bolsa-Prêmio/Itamaraty – 2003) In text II,

(1) the first "What" (ℓ.4) can be correctly replaced by Which.
(2) "hopefully" (ℓ.11) means the opposite of hopelessly.
(3) "succeed" (ℓ.11) is synonymous with come after.
(4) "their" (ℓ.12) refers to all African countries.
(5) "around the world" (ℓ.15) is the same as all over the world.
(6) "accomplish" (ℓ.20) is the same as achieve.

(Vocabulary) 1: Incorrect – The word "which" is used when there is a choice or a selection of nouns. In the question "What is this Hub?", no choice is being made; the aim of the question is to define or clarify; **2:** Correct – In this text, the adverb "hopefully" expresses an idea that expectations are high. The adverb "hopelessly" expresses an idea in which expectations are very low or non-existent; **3:** Incorrect – In this text, "succeed" means to "achieve something", while "come after" means to "follow". "Succeed" can have the meaning of to "come after and take the place of" when the context involves a person taking another's position or job; **4:** Incorrect – The word "their" refers to all the countries in sub-Saharan Africa, which is not all African countries; **5:** Correct – The terms "around the world" and "all over the world" are synonymous, as is "the world over"; **6:** Correct – In this text, "accomplish" and "achieve" are synonymous.

Gabarito 1E, 2C, 3E, 4E, 5C, 6C

Text III

1   Preventing nuclear proliferation is an enduring American interest pursued by Presidents and Congresses since 1945. The Senate's October 1999
4   vote against the Test Ban Treaty raised concerns at home and abroad that the United States (US) might be walking away from its traditional leadership of international non-proliferation efforts. I am confident
7   that this was not the intent of the Senate. In my conversations, I have found broad bipartisan support
10 for strengthened US leadership of a comprehensive international campaign against proliferation.
    I recommend that the next Administration work
13 closely with Congress and US allies to mount a more integrated response to the dangers posed by the spread of nuclear weapons, that it appoint a Deputy National
15 Security Advisor for Non-Proliferation to oversee policy coordination and implementation, and that it revisit the Test Ban Treaty in the context of the direct
19 and indirect contributions it can make to this policy.

Internet: <http://www.state.gov/www/global/arms/ctbtpage/ctbt-release.html>. Accessed in June/2003 (with adaptations).

(Bolsa-Prêmio/Itamaraty – 2003) It can be concluded from text III that

(1) the US has been worried about nuclear proliferation for more than half a century.
(2) the American Senate always wanted to ban nuclear weapons of mass destruction.
(3) never have there been international worries in relation to American nuclear policy.
(4) its author is against nuclear test ban treaties.
(5) its author was not considering himself as part of the next US Administration when he wrote it.

(Interpretation) 1: Correct – On line 3, the first sentence mentions "since 1945", making it more than 50 years; **2:** Incorrect – The text does not make it clear that the Senate "always" wanted to ban nuclear weapons of mass destruction. There is no reference to how long this desire has lasted; **3:** Incorrect – On lines 3 to 7, the author identifies "raised concerns at home and abroad" that the Senate could be wavering on its "traditional leadership of international non--proliferation efforts", which suggests that worries on the Senate's intent and efforts to ban nuclear weapons have reached foreign shores; **4:** Incorrect – On lines 16 to 19, the author emphasizes the need to revise the Test Ban Treaty to improve its contributions. He is for improvements, not against the Treaty; **5:** Correct – On lines 12 and 13, the author makes recommendations to the next Administration, suggesting that he would not be part of it.

Gabarito 1C, 2E, 3E, 4E, 5C

(Bolsa-Prêmio/Itamaraty – 2003) In text III,

(1) "this" (ℓ.8) refers back to "traditional leadership" (ℓ.6).
(2) "I have found" (ℓ.9) can be correctly replaced by found.
(3) "comprehensive" (ℓ.10) is the same as understandable.
(4) "appoint" (ℓ.15) can be replaced by appoints.
(5) "oversee" (ℓ.16) means to make certain that it is being done correctly.

(Vocabulary) 1: Incorrect – The reference word "this" refers back to the interpretation that it might be "walking away from traditional leadership of international non-proliferation efforts". It refers more specifically to the "walking away", rather than the "leadership" itself; 2: Incorrect – The sentence does not offer a specific time reference. This reinforces the need to employ the present perfect to emphasize that his conversations have been occurring for some time, even though "for how long" is not made clear. This verb tense also suggests that conversations may still continue. Using the simple past form would suggest that the conversations took place in the past and that there will be no more conversations. Special Note: In modern grammar studies, it is now acceptable to replace the present perfect with the simple past form, although it should be noted that this is predominantly an American style; 3: Incorrect – "Comprehensive" means "broad" or "all-encompassing". Although a derivative of the verb "comprehend", the adjective has a completely different meaning; 4: Incorrect – Taking the beginning of the sentence "I recommend" and joining it with the second item on the list "that it appoint a Deputy National Security Advisor for Non-Proliferation", it becomes evident that the structure is subjunctive. After the verb structure "recommend that" the following verb should take the subjunctive form. For example, "I recommend that he study", not "he studies". In this structure, the verb form for all persons (1st, 2nd, 3rd), both singular and plural, will remain the same: subjunctive (infinitive without "to"); 5: Correct – In this text, "oversee" means to "supervise", "manage" or "make certain that something is being done correctly". As a contrast, "overlook" means to "look, but fail to see", as in "When I was correcting your essay, I overlooked the spelling mistakes" = "I corrected your essay, but I did not correct the spelling mistakes in it".

Gabarito 1E, 2E, 3E, 4E, 5C

Text IV

Explanation of Vote in Security Council by John D. Negroponte, US Representative to the United Nations (UN)

Thank you Mr. President, Mr. Secretary-General. The lifting of sanctions marks a momentous event for the people of Iraq. It is the turning of a historical page that should brighten the future of a people and a region.

My government called for this vote this morning because we firmly believed that each additional day of debate over the language of this important text would further hinder recovery. The gas lines are long, despite blessedly little damage to Iraq's residual infrastructure. After more than a decade of being frozen out of the world economy, it is time for the Iraqi people to benefit from their natural resources.

President Bush and Prime Minister Blair said last month at Hillsborough that the United Nations should play a vital role in rebuilding Iraq. In passing this resolution, we have achieved much for the Iraqi people. By recognizing the fluidity of the political situation and that decisions will be made on the ground, the Security Council has provided a flexible framework under Chapter VII for the Coalition Provisional Authority, member states, the United Nations and others in the international community to participate in the administration and reconstruction of Iraq and to assist the Iraqi people in determining their political future, establishing new institutions, and restoring economic prosperity to the country.

The resolution establishes transparency in all processes and the United Nations participation in monitoring the sale of Iraqi oil resources and expenditure of oil proceeds.

Internet: <http:www.state.gov/p/io/rls/rm/2003/20860.htm>.
Accessed in June/2003 (with adaptations).

(Bolsa-Prêmio/Itamaraty – 2003) Based on text IV, judge the following items.

(1) The suspension of sanctions in Iraq is important for its future.
(2) The vote calling was an American initiative.
(3) The sooner the sanctions are lifted the better for the Iraqis.
(4) Iraqi recent war seriously damaged its oil fields.
(5) Sanctions on Iraq have lasted for more than 10 years.
(6) In Mr. Negroponte's opinion, the Iraqis couldn't benefit from their natural resources.
(7) It is now commonsense that the UN has a crucial task in Iraq's reconstruction.
(8) The UN will help to bring international recognisance to the Iraqi future government.
(9) The UN will act only as an observer on how the Iraqi people will determine their political future.

(Interpretation) 1: Correct – In the first paragraph, the speaker identifies the importance of lifting sanctions (The lifting of sanctions marks a momentous event for the people of Iraq), and how this will effect the future of Iraqis and the region ([It] should brighten the future of a people and a region); 2: Correct – The speaker, Mr. John D. Negroponte, who is a US representative to the UN (see title of text), in paragraph two, explicitly says "my government called for this vote"; 3: Correct – John D. Negroponte explains, in the second paragraph, that "each additional day of debate (...) would further hinder recovery", meaning each additional would make recovery more difficult. Thus, the sooner sanctions are lifted, the sooner recovery (which is a good thing) will be possible; 4: Incorrect – In the second paragraph, the speaker explicitly mentions that the gas lines suffered "blessedly little damage", meaning "happily minimal destruction". The use of the adverb "blessedly" expresses and emphasizes the relief felt that the gas lines were not seriously damaged; 5: Correct – In the second paragraph, the speaker explicitly mentions that Iraq had been "frozen out of the world economy" for "more than a decade"; 6: Correct – In the second paragraph, the speaker explains that now sanctions have been lifted, "it is time for the Iraqi people to benefit from their natural resources", suggesting that before, during sanctions, the Iraqi people were not able to benefit from such resources; 7: Incorrect – In the question, the term "commonsense" seems to be employed incorrectly. The term means "sound practical judgment". For example, it is common sense to cross the street at the traffic lights, rather than jaywalking. In Portuguese, this is best translated as "bom senso". The Portuguese term "senso comum" is best translated as "common knowledge" which would seem more fitting in this case. In spite of this possible mistranslation, in the text, the only people that expressed conviction that the UN has a crucial task in Iraq's reconstruction were "President Bush and Prime Minister Blair", which they did "last month at Hillsborough". This is hardly enough to claim "common sense" or "common knowledge"; **8:** Incorrect – The word "recognisance" is an archaic and obsolete form of "recognition". It is more commonly employed to refer to a "bail bond" (a form of fiança) for people being criminally charged in a court. Furthermore, there is nothing explicit in the text to identify international "recognition". There is international participation and reconstruction, but nothing clearly focused on recognition. The only time "recognition" is mentioned in the text is in the third paragraph when the Security Council recognizes "the fluidity of the political situation and that decisions will be made on the ground", which is not "international" recognition; **9:** Incorrect – In the third paragraph, the speaker reveals that the UN's Security Council has prepared a flexible framework in which the United Nations and others in the international community will participate in the administration and reconstruction of Iraq, this proving that the UN will not merely observe, but will be actively engaged in efforts.

Gabarito Nosso 1C, 2C, 3C, 4E, 5C, 6C, 7E, 8E, 9E /
Gabarito Oficial 1C, 2C, 3C, 4E, 5C, 6C, 7C, 8C, 9E/

(Bolsa-Prêmio/Itamaraty – 2003) The passage "The resolution establishes transparency in all processes and the United Nations participation in monitoring the sale of Iraqi oil resources and expenditure of oil proceeds" in text IV can be replaced by

(1) The resolution sets up transparency in every process and the United Nations participation in keeping track of the sale of Iraqi oil reserves and expenses of oil proceeds.
(2) The resolution settles transparency in all processes and the United Nations participation in watching carefully the sale of Iraqi oil resources and expenditure of oil proceeds.
3) The resolution foresees transparency in each process and the United Nations cooperation in controlling the purchase of Iraqi oil resources and expenditure.
(4) The conclusion settles down transparency in all processes and the UN will take part in monitoring the sale of Iraqi renewable resources and expenditure.
(5) The resolution must establish transparency in all processes and the United Nations participation will be restricted to buying and selling oil resources and proceeds.

(Interpretation) 1: Correct – In the sentence, "establish" is synonymous with "set up", "all" is usually followed by plural nouns, while "every" is followed by nouns in the singular form (no change to meaning); "monitor" is synonymous with "keep track of"; and "expenditure" is synonymous with "expenses"– **2:** Incorrect – "Settle" is not synonymous with "establish". "Settle" can mean "reconcile", "establish a home (not transparency)", "become peaceful", "decide/choose (e.g. settle on a color)", "to pay (a bill)", "to land (a bird settles on a branch)". The use with "transparency" is not the correct collocation; **3:** Incorrect – "Foresee" means to predict, rather than "establish", but it is a possibility, if not the best one. "Cooperation" suggests that others will also monitor the sale, while "participation" suggests that the UN's contribution will be to monitor the sale, which does not suggest it will work in cooperation with another entity. "Controlling" means "to regulate" and "have power over", while "monitor" means to verify and "accompany". This suggests a more aggressive role for the UN, thus changing the meaning of the sentence. "Purchase", in this case, is a reasonable substitute for "sale" as one is not possible without the other; **4:** Incorrect – "Settle down" means to "establish a home and family", not to establish transparency. "Renewable resources" are not the same as "oil resources" as the idea can incorporate other sources of energy, including wind, natural gas, etc.; **5:** Incorrect – "Must" conveys and idea of obligation, which the original sentence did not contain. Changing the idea of monitoring sales to restricted to buying and selling", changes the UN's role in this effort, making this answer incorrect.

Gabarito Oficial 1C, 2C, 3E, 4E, 5E / Gabarito Nosso 1C, 2E, 3E, 4E, 5E

Atenção: Para responder as próximas seis questões, considere o texto abaixo.

During his interview with the Financial Times last Friday, Celso Amorim, Brazil's foreign minister, admitted to feeling tired, frustrated and as if he had a bad hangover. "If the party has been good, a hangover is OK," he said. "But if it's been a bad party and your girlfriend has left with somebody else…"

Mr Amorim has every reason to look back on the collapse of the Doha round of talks at the World Trade Organisation in Geneva last week as a grim episode. Brazil's leadership of the G20 group of developing nations, which briefly showed so much promise, has come to nothing. Deep splits in the group emerged during the final days of the talks, with India, China and even Argentina putting protection of their own manufacturers and producers ahead of the interests of global free trade.

Mr Amorim, his team, Brazil and the world all deserved (A)_____ , and even in failure and frustration Mr Amorim deserves recognition for the statesmanlike role he played throughout the talks. Brazil's farmers are among the most efficient in the world and they have achieved that status with none of the coddling handed out to their competitors in developed nations. Brazil has the expertise and land – most of it far away from the Amazon and other sensitive areas – to supply the world with the food it so badly needs. Instead, as Mr Amorim warns, what the world will get is more starvation and destabilisation.

Jonathan Wheatley
(http://www.brazilmax.com/forum/message.cfm?MID=1005)

(Oficial de Chancelaria - 2009 - FCC) A palavra que preenche corretamente a lacuna **A**, no texto, é

(A) good.
(B) best.
(C) better.
(D) worse.
(E) worst.

(Vocabulary) A: Incorrect – This does not form a recognized collocation. Another way to look at this is that "deserve" is a transitive verb, which means it requires a noun (object). The comparative adjective "better" can represent a noun in some specific cases, such as this one. "Good" is not used in this fashion; B: Incorrect – The superlative form of good. Not appropriate here and would require 'the' definite article – the best; C: Correct - The comparative form of good. This forms the correct collocation – to deserve better. The verb "deserve" is transitive, which means it requires a noun (object). The comparative adjective "better" can represent a noun in some specific cases, such as this one; D: Incorrect - The comparative form of bad. This does not make sense within the context of the text; E: Incorrect- The superlative form of bad. Not appropriate here and would require 'the' definite article – the worst.
Gabarito "C".

(Oficial de Chancelaria - 2009 - FCC) In the text, 'their' refers to

(A) India, China and Argentina.
(B) India.
(C) China.
(D) India and China.
(E) Argentina.

(Grammar) A, B, C, D e E: "Their" is a possessive adjective and refers to all three countries (India, China and Argentina.). Possessive adjectives are governed by the word they refer in terms of ownership: manufacturers and producers = their – belonging to the three countries.
Gabarito "A".

(Oficial de Chancelaria - 2009 - FCC) A synonym for *Instead* in the above text is

(A) In spite of.
(B) Likewise.
(C) Therefore.
(D) However.
(E) In addition.

(Grammar) A: Incorrect – Variant of despite. Prepositional phrase showing contrast or surprise; B: Incorrect – Adverb – similar to similarly, equally; C: Incorrect – Adverb – showing a logical conclusion – similar to thus, consequently; D: Correct – Conjunction – similar to although, on the other hand, yet. The best option in terms of instead meaning in the text – in place of something; E: Incorrect – Adverb – similar to moreover, furthermore, besides.
Gabarito "D".

(Oficial de Chancelaria - 2009 - FCC) O verbo *warns*, no texto, indica

(A) confirmação.
(B) sugestão.
(C) probabilidade.
(D) necessidade.
(E) alerta.

(Vocabulary) A, B, C, D e E: Celso Amorim notifies of the negative consequences that will occur. In this sense, he alerts.
Gabarito "E".

(Oficial de Chancelaria - 2009 - FCC) According to the text, Mr Amorim

(A) believes that due to the failure of the Doha round of talks the world will be in greater need of food.
(B) is exhilarated by the outcome of the Doha round of talks.
(C) was frustrated because he only played a minor role in the Doha round of talks.
(D) had a bad hangover during a party at the Doha round of talks.
(E) failed to grant Brazilian farmers the customs protection developed countries enjoy.

(Interpretation) A: Correct – Mr Amorim warns that the world will see more starvation, i.e. a greater need for food; B: Incorrect – Exhilarated is to feel happy and energetic. The text explicitly says Mr Amorim felt tired and frustrated; C: Incorrect – He was frustrated about the outcome of the talks, not about his role in the talks. On the contrary, the text states he had a statesman-like role in the talks; D: Incorrect – Mr Amorim uses the idea of a hangover figuratively. 'As if he had a bad hangover'; E: Incorrect – There is no suggestion that this was Mr Amorim's objective in the talks. It is true that other farms are portrayed as being overly protected – (coddled).
Gabarito "A".

(Oficial de Chancelaria - 2009 - FCC) Infere-se do texto que

(A) grande parte dos alimentos de que o mundo precisa chega a seu destino em más condições de consumo.
(B) grande parte da terra produtiva do Brasil encontra-se próxima à região amazônica.
(C) os fazendeiros do Brasil, caso tivessem os subsídios de seus concorrentes dos países desenvolvidos, poderiam tornar-se os mais eficientes do mundo.
(D) a rodada de Doha falhou porque alguns países colocaram seus próprios interesses acima dos interesses globais.
(E) o Brasil, como líder do grupo G20, teve um desempenho bastante frustrante na rodada de Doha.

(Interpretation) A: Incorrect – No evidence to support this; B: Incorrect – The text states most agricultural land is far away from the Amazon; C: Incorrect – The text says Brazilian farmers are **among** the most efficient farmers – not the most efficient. The text does not allow inference about what would happen if they received more subsidies; D: Correct – The Doha round did fail. As the text states, countries put their own interests ahead of global free trade (paragraph 2) – i.e. countries prioritised their own individual interests; E: Incorrect – This is too strong to state. The text says that Brazil's leadership came to nothing, i.e. had no result. However, the blame for the failure of the talks is other countries, not Brazil.
Gabarito "D".

Instruções: Para responder as próximas quatorze questões, considere o texto abaixo.

Brazil's foreign policy: ___TITLE___

Brazil is bidding for big-power status.
What sort of power does it want to be?

It is a small force, but of huge symbolic significance. This month, 1,200 Brazilian troops arrived in Haiti, the country's biggest foreign military deployment since the Second World War. Brazil is commanding a United Nations peacekeeping force of 6,700 mainly Latin American troops and 1,600 police which is taking over from American and French forces in the Caribbean island. This marks a new departure. Brazil has long been a gentle and introverted giant, content to be a bystander on the world stage. **34.**

Luiz Inácio Lula da Silva, the country's left-leaning president, is carving out a role for Brazil as spokesman for poor countries, most notably by founding the G20 group which lobbies for rich countries to open up farm trade. His government is playing a more active role across South America. And it is seeking a permanent seat on the UN Security Council. "Brazil has begun to flex its muscles as a regional superpower," says Miguel Díaz of the Centre for Strategic and International Studies, a Washington-based think-tank.

If so, it is a paradoxical one. On the one hand, Brazil's fondest wish is to mitigate the United States' dominance of global affairs and thereby to enhance Brazil's influence. The foreign minister, Celso Amorim, calls for "a more balanced world" and justifies the Haiti mission in part as a step towards it. "You can't be a supporter of multilateralism and when it comes to act say it's [too] dangerous," says Mr Amorim.

On the other hand, Brazil's new activism often, though **B**, coincides with the interests of the United States. Both countries want democracy and stability in places in the Américas where these seem fragile. In some of those places, Lula's Brazil has more friends and influence than George Bush's more abrasive United States. The two sometimes back rivals in these countries, but that is one source of Brazil's usefulness.

Lula did not start Brazil's international activism. In recent years, Brazilian troops have joined UN missions in East Timor and Angola. In 1996, Brazil acted with Argentina and the United States to forestall a coup in Paraguay – recognition that the defence of democracy in the region should take precedence over a tradition of non-intervention in the affairs of neighbours.

The search for a stable South America has long been an axiom of Brazil's foreign policy, but demographics have given it greater urgency. Brazilians, once described as clinging to the coast like crabs, have scurried westwards and northwards. The building of Brasília, which replaced Rio de Janeiro as the capital in 1960, helped to spark development of the interior, a process accelerated by an agricultural boom in such western states as Mato Grosso. The Amazon, Brazil is learning, is both a resource and weak spot, vulnerable to guerrillas, drug traffickers and land-grabbers.

For most of its history as an independent country, Brazil saw Argentina as its chief rival and strategic threat. That changed with the formation of Mercosur, an incipient customs union also involving Paraguay and Uruguay. This has allowed Brazil to shift much of its army from its southern border to the north-western jungles near Colombia and Peru.

Brazil's sense of neighbourhood may be widening. Yet, argues Mr Valladão, Brazil has not decided what sort of neighbour to be. At times, it portrays itself as a team player. In theory, it negotiates on trade as a member of Mercosur. But Brazil also sees itself as a "whale", with the heft and appetite to act on its own. Mr Amorim's answer is that, in a world likely to be dominated by blocks, Brazil's best option is to co-operate as much as possible with its neighbours and other developing countries. Whales, he notes, "are gregarious animals."

(Adapted from **The Economist**, June 11, 2004)

(Oficial de Chancelaria - 2009 - FCC) A synonym for *taking over from* in the text is

(A) bringing together.
(B) joining.
(C) replacing.
(D) defeating.
(E) wiping out.

(**Vocabulary**) A: Incorrect - To connect, unite; B: Incorrect – To unite, connect; C: Correct – Taking over means to assume control or take responsibility, i.e. to replace; D: Incorrect - To bet, to win over; E: Incorrect – To completely destroy.
Gabarito "C".

(Oficial de Chancelaria - 2009 - FCC) Considerando o sentido do texto, a melhor tradução para *This marks a new departure* é:

(A) Isso sinaliza uma nova atitude.
(B) Este é o marco de uma nova partida.
(C) Este é um sinal de sucesso.
(D) Essa é a marca do novo governo.
(E) Isso indica um novo rompimento.

(**Vocabulary**) A: Correct – Departure – deviation, divergence – showing in this context that Brazil is taking a new position; B: Incorrect – Departure, here, has nothing to do with leaving; C: Incorrect – Departure, here, has nothing to do with success; D: Incorrect – Departure, here, has nothing to do with a new government; E: Incorrect – Departure, here, has nothing to do with a rupture of ideas.
Gabarito "A".

(Oficial de Chancelaria - 2009 - FCC) The alternative that correctly completes the first paragraph of the above text is

(A) And so it will remain.
(B) At last it is playing a minor role.
(C) As usual, a Latin American leader.
(D) Now that is changing.
(E) No more troops for Haiti.

(**Interpretation**) A: Incorrect – This is illogical by what follows in paragraph 2; B: Incorrect - This is illogical by what follows in paragraph 2; C: Incorrect – This neither concludes the first paragraph nor links into the second paragraph; D: Correct – This phrase logically concludes paragraph 1, discussing Brazil's previous attitude, and provides a link to the second paragraph, which goes on to discuss the change that Brazil has made; E: Incorrect – Paragraph one states that the large number of troops will be in charge of in Haiti.
Gabarito "D".

(Oficial de Chancelaria - 2009 - FCC) *In the text, the pronoun one refers to*

(A) UN Security Council.
(B) the country's left-leaning president.
(C) active role.
(D) farm trade.
(E) G20 group.

(Grammar) A, B, C, D e E: active role refers back to paragraph 2 – the text says this government is playing a more active role in South America. This should remind students to read both texts above the target language to help identify what the pronoun refers to.
Gabarito "C".

(Oficial de Chancelaria - 2009 - FCC) Preenche corretamente a lacuna B, no texto:

(A) not seldom.
(B) usually.
(C) sometimes.
(D) never.
(E) not always.

(Interpretation) A: Incorrect – Seldom, rarely – this would be illogical; B: Incorrect - This would not be logical as 'though' demands a contrast to often; C: Incorrect – This would not be logical as 'though' demands a contrast to often; D: Incorrect – This would not form a logical phrase; E: Correct – This combines with the previous phrase – often, though not always – to provide a restriction to the phrase.
Gabarito "E".

(Oficial de Chancelaria - 2009 - FCC) In the text, these refers to

(A) places.
(B) democracy and stability.
(C) both countries.
(D) friends and influence.
(E) the Americas.

(Grammar) A, B, C, D e E: In the sentence, this is what both countries want – these – plural of this. This demonstrative pronoun refers back to the plural that comes immediately before, which, in this case, is democracy and stability.
Gabarito "B".

(Oficial de Chancelaria - 2009 - FCC) A synonym for back in the text is

(A) command.
(B) enhance.
(C) support.
(D) deploy.
(E) mitigate.

(Vocabulary) A; Incorrect – To command rivals in this context does not make sense; B: Incorrect – To enhance/improve rivals in this context does not make sense; C: Correct – To back (verb) means to support; D: Incorrect – You cannot deploy rivals – normal use is to deploy troops; E: Incorrect – You cannot mitigate rivals – normal use it to mitigate the effects of something.
Gabarito "C".

(Oficial de Chancelaria - 2009 - FCC) Infere-se, pelo texto, que

(A) os países ricos estão empenhados em abrir suas fronteiras aos produtos do grupo G-20
(B) o Brasil tem enviado tropas ao Haiti desde a Segunda Guerra Mundial.
(C) um dos objetivos do grupo G-20 é fazer os países ricos abdicarem do protecionismo aos seus produtos agrícolas.
(D) o grupo G-20 foi criado para incentivar a comercialização dos produtos agrícolas entre seus membros.
(E) o Presidente Lula pretende ser o porta-voz dos países pobres da América do Sul.

(Interpretation) A: Incorrect – There is no information to suggest the position of the rich countries on trade with the G20 group; B: Incorrect – The Haiti operation is the biggest mission for Brazilian troops since the Second World War; C: Correct – (Paragraph 2) the G20 group which lobbies for rich countries to open up farm trade. (To lobby – to try to influence), (to open up – to ease restrictions.); D: Incorrect – This is not stated; E: Incorrect – The role is for Brazil, not Lula (paragraph 2, line 1).
Gabarito "C".

(Oficial de Chancelaria - 2009 - FCC) According to the text, Mr Amorim

(A) concedes that Brazil should not support Haiti.
(B) believes Brazil should not get involved in regional disputes.
(C) claims that it is too dangerous to side with multilateralism.
(D) does not think a "balanced world" will ever be possible.
(E) believes Brazil's mission in Haiti will contribute to a more balanced world.

(Interpretation) A: Incorrect – The opposite is true. Brazil is taking an active role in Haiti; B: Incorrect – No evidence to support this; C: Incorrect – (Paragraph 3) the opposite is true. If you support multilateralism, you must be willing to act even when it is dangerous; D: Incorrect – No evidence to support this; E: Correct – (Paragraph 3) Mr Amorim justifies that the peace mission in part as a step towards it. In this case, 'it' represents a more balanced world.
Gabarito "E".

(Oficial de Chancelaria - 2009 - FCC) One can infer from the text that

(A) Brazil may be more influential in South America than the U.S. due to President Lula's friends in the region.
(B) Brazil and the U.S. have always had the same interests in Latin America.
(C) the U.S. are not really interested in promoting democracy in South America.
(D) Brazil and the U.S. are, in fact, rivals in South America.
(E) Brazil is useful in the international scene due to its alliances with the United States.

(Interpretation) A: Correct – (Paragraph 4) – In some of these places, Lula has more friends and influence than George Bush's abrasive/rough/annoying United States; B: Incorrect – (Paragraph 4) - The two (i.e. Brazil and the U.S.) sometimes back rivals. This shows the countries sometimes support rival parties/political stances in Latin American countries; C: Incorrect – No evidence to support this; D: Incorrect – This is too strong a statement to support. Sometimes they differ, but Paragraph 4 shows that their interests often, though not always, coincide; E: Incorrect – No evidence to support this.
Gabarito "A".

(Oficial de Chancelaria - 2009 - FCC) De acordo com o texto, o objetivo prioritário da política externa do Brasil é

(A) a participação ativa em organizações internacionais multilaterais.
(B) a estabilidade política da América do Sul.
(C) a não intervenção nos assuntos de outros países.
(D) a segurança de suas fronteiras.
(E) o apoio aos governos democráticos dos países vizinhos.

(Interpretation) A: Incorrect – The text suggests this is an interest, but it is not a priority; B: Correct – (Paragraph 6) the search for a stable South America has long been an axiom of Brazil's foreign policy. Axiom = an established rule; C: Incorrect – Mr Amorim even says that you can not back out when things become too dangerous. This suggests that "non-intervention" is not the policy; D: Incorrect – No evidence that this is a priority of Brazilian foreign policy; E: Incorrect - The text suggests this is an interest, but it is not a priority.

Gabarito "B".

(Oficial de Chancelaria - 2009 - FCC) According to the text,

(A) although Brasilia has encouraged many Brazilians to move inland, most of its population still lives along the coast.
(B) the creation of Mercosur allowed Brazil to move a large part of its troops to more troublesome regions like the Amazon.
(C) in spite of the Mercosur, Argentina is still viewed as a strategic threat to Brazil.
(D) Paraguay has always been a threat to the democracy in South America.
(E) the sudden agricultural boom of the state of Mato Grosso has contributed to a more balanced demographic distribution.

(Interpretation) A: Incorrect – No evidence to support where the majority of the population now lives; B: Correct – Yes, it has moved its troops to these areas (Paragraph 7) and (in Paragraph 6) the text mentions the Amazon jungle as a weak spot, vulnerable to guerillas, drug traffickers and land-grabbers – therefore, a troublesome region; C: Incorrect – The contrary is true. (Paragraph 7) Brazil has shifted much of its army to the north-western jungles near Columbia and Peru; D: Incorrect – The text only mentions an intervention in 1996 (Paragraph 5) to forestall/prevent a coup. Therefore, it has not always been a threat to democracy; E: Incorrect – This is too strong to support. Yes, there has been development and population growth in Mato Grosso, but to say it is more balanced is an exaggeration.

Gabarito "B".

(Oficial de Chancelaria - 2009 - FCC) One can infer from the text that

(A) the "whale", as suggested by Mr Valadão, is a perfect metaphor, not only for Brazil but also for all Mercosur members.
(B) Mr Valadão and Mr Amorim agree that Brazil has been a responsible neighbour in South America.
(C) Mr Amorim endorses the idea that Brazil is a whale, acting on its own.
(D) the future of Brazil's foreign policy will be to side with a larger number of developing countries, even beyond South America's borders.
(E) Brazil is willing to cooperate with developed countries in order to widen its influence in South America

(Interpretation) A: Incorrect – The whale metaphor is suitable only for Brazil as it refers to its 'heft', i.e. size/power and aspirations. The metaphor cannot be extended to the other Mercosur countries; B: Incorrect – There is no evidence to show an agreement between the Mr Valadão and Mr Amorim; C: Incorrect – Mr Amorim says that, like whales, Brazil should be co-operative and sociable/gregarious; D: Correct – Paragraph 8 – Mr Amorim states that Brazil's best option is to co-operate as much as possible with its neighbours and other developing countries; E: Incorrect – No evidence to support this.

Gabarito "D".

(Oficial de Chancelaria - 2009 - FCC) The phrase that completes the TITLE of the text in the best way is:

(A) We are the world
(B) Dwindling light
(C) Playing second fiddle.
(D) The UN wakes up
(E) A giant stirs

(Interpretation) A: Incorrect - No relevance; B: Incorrect - Dwindling means to lessen gradually – the sense in the text is of Brazil's expanding, not reducing role; C: Incorrect – To play second fiddle means to perform a minor/secondary role – this is not the focus of the text; D: No evidence that the UN is doing this; E: Correct - This is the most appropriate as the giant is Brazil and to stir means to awaken/arouse and to take action.

Gabarito "E".

Instruções: Para responder as próximas cinco questões, considere o texto abaixo.

The best of enemies

On a surprising range of foreign-policy issues, the rivals have morphed into each other. But differences remain.

*Vin Weber, a former Republican congressman for Minnesota, once joked that Americans treat foreign policy much as they treat dentistry – something they would rather not think about unless they have to. The first three presidential elections after the end of the cold war, in 1992, 1996 and 2000, saw **C** discussion of the world beyond America's borders. The economy trumped international affairs, the culture wars diplomacy. Even in 2004, when America was really at war, values seemed to matter much more than abroad did.*

This year will be different. Foreign policy will define the election almost as much as America's troubled economy. The next American president will inherit the most difficult international situation since Richard Nixon won power in 1968: two nasty wars, in Iraq and Afghanistan, in their fifth and seventh year respectively; an Iran bent on acquiring nuclear weapons; instability in Pakistan; deeply strained relations with a prickly Russia; rivalry with booming China; a catastrophic drop in America's standing around the world; and a backlash against globalisation.

The candidates, Barack Obama and John McCain, are the products of different worlds. Nevertheless, they see eye-toeye on many big issues. First, both genuinely understand that the next president must strive to improve America's global image. A big majority of Americans agree that their country's reputation has been badly damaged in the Bush years. This not only makes it difficult for America to exercise moral leadership; it also hinders its exercise of hard power. In the run up to the invasion of Iraq the Turkish government felt obliged to refuse American troops permission to operate from its soil.

Things can only get better

The good news is that either candidate is well-placed to improve America's image. And if you are in the business of improving America's brand, there is no better way to start than by replacing the current president. That said, Mr Obama would clearly do a lot more to rebuff America's image than Mr McCain ever could. Some 250,000 people turned out to see him in Berlin in July; Mr McCain's earlier visit to Europe went virtually unnoticed.

Both candidates also advocate specific policies that are designed to clear some of the blemishes on America's image. They both propose a policy of cap-and-trade to deal with global warming, an issue on which American leadership has been sorely lacking for the past eight years. They both oppose the use of torture – Mr McCain with the authority of a man who was himself tortured by the Vietnamese. They both want to close Guantánamo Bay.

The second area where the two men have more in common than one might expect is the "war on terror". They have plenty of disagreements, to be sure: Mr Obama does not go as far as Mr McCain in describing it as the defining struggle of the time, and he sounds less preoccupied with state sponsors of terrorism. But whoever wins the presidency will continue to place militant Islam at the centre of his foreign policy.

But for all that they agree on the need for a fresh, more multilateral approach, there remain some hefty differences between the two men, even if the pressures of the campaign have narrowed them a little. Most simply put, Mr McCain remains significantly more hawkish than Mr Obama. No voter should doubt that, as president, he would be more inclined to favour a robust approach, whether that be the use of military means, or the use of tougher diplomatic ones.

The second big difference is over diplomacy. Mr Obama hopes to use the power of negotiation to tackle some of the world's most intractable problems. During the primary He promised to hold unconditional talks with America's enemies, including the theocratic government of Iran. He promised to back talks between Israel and Syria in a bid to break Damascus's military alliance with Tehran. He also put a lot of emphasis on using diplomatic tools to solve the impasse over Israel and Palestine. Mr McCain gives the impression that he thinks talk has its limits.

(Adapted from **The Economist**, October 2nd 2008)

(Oficial de Chancelaria - 2009 - FCC) A palavra que preenche a lacuna C, no texto, corretamente é

(A) many.
(B) few.
(C) such.
(D) little.
(E) much.

(Grammar) A: Incorrect – "Many" is a quantifier used with countable words. In this text, the word "discussion" is being used as an uncountable noun; B: Incorrect – "Few" is a quantifier used with countable words. In this text, the word "discussion" is being used as an uncountable noun; C: Incorrect – "Such" is a determiner used to refer back to a previously mentioned idea. In the sentence prior to the one in question, the author argues that there was no discussion. Thus, "such" would refer back to an idea that was not given; D: Correct – "Little" is a quantifier used with uncountable words. In this text, the word "discussion" is being used as an uncountable noun. "Little" also reinforces the idea that is given in the previous sentence, i.e. Americans "would rather not think about" foreign policy. This is reinforced in the following sentence, when the author argues that "values seemed to matter much more than abroad did"; E: Incorrect – "Many" is a quantifier used with countable words. In this text, the word "discussion" is being used as an uncountable noun.
Gabarito "D".

(Oficial de Chancelaria - 2009 - FCC) Segundo o texto,

(A) o resultado das eleições americanas já é previsível face às posições antagônicas advogadas pelos dois candidatos.
(B) a política externa proposta pelos candidatos será um dos fatores determinantes do resultado das eleições americanas.
(C) a política externa sempre foi uma das maiores preocupações dos presidentes eleitos após a Guerra Fria.
(D) os problemas internacionais atuais dos Estados Unidos são decorrentes, em grande parte, do governo Nixon.
(E) foi graças ao fim da Guerra Fria que as relações entre os Estados Unidos e a Rússia tornaram-se amistosas.

(Interpretation) A: Incorrect – The last sentence in the sixth paragraph clearly shows that no foreseeable outcome is offered in the text. *"But whoever wins the presidency will continue to place militant Islam at the centre of his foreign policy"*; B: Correct – The beginning of the second paragraph clearly states that *"Foreign policy will define the election almost as much as America's troubled economy"*; C: Incorrect – The first paragraph clearly states that *"the first three presidential elections after the Cold War (...) saw little discussion of the world beyond America's borders"*; D: Incorrect – The second paragraph mentions: *"The next American president will inherit the most difficult international situation **since** Richard Nixon won power in 1968"*. The word since in this sentence offers a comparison between the government that Nixon inherited and the one that the next president will inherit. No blame is attributed; E: Incorrect – There is no mention of this in the text. In the second paragraph, reference is made to *"deeply strained relations with a prickly Russia"*, but no reference to friendly relations.
Gabarito "B".

(Oficial de Chancelaria - 2009 - FCC) According to the text,

(A) Mr Obama is better suited to improve America's image abroad.
(B) the US has always set a moral example to the international community in spite of resorting to hard power occasionally.
(C) due to the positive views the US enjoys around the world, it was allowed to base its troops in Turkey before an attack on Iraq.

(D) Mr McCain enjoyed a large audience during his visit to Europe.
(E) Mr Bush can't be blamed, alone, for America's damaged image.

(Interpretation) A: Correct – In the fourth paragraph, the text clearly states "*Mr Obama would clearly do a lot more to rebuff America's image than Mr McCain ever could.*" In this context, the word "rebuff" has the idea of shine, revive; B: Incorrect – In the third paragraph, the text clearly states: "*This not only makes it difficult for America to exercise moral leadership; it also hinders its exercise of hard power*", proving that the US has NOT always set the moral example; C: Incorrect – In the fourth paragraph, the text clearly states: "*In the run up to the invasion of Iraq the Turkish government felt obliged to **refuse** American troops permission to operate from its soil*"; D: Incorrect – At the end of the fifth paragraph, the text clearly states "*Mr McCain's earlier visit to Europe went virtually **unnoticed**"; E: Incorrect – In the fourth paragraph, blame is attributed to Mr. Bush: "*A big majority of Americans agree that their country's reputation has been badly damaged in the Bush years.*" However, there is no mention of blame being attributed to him alone, nor to another president.
Gabarito "A".

(Oficial de Chancelaria - 2009 - FCC) O trecho American leadership has been sorely lacking for the past eight years significa que a liderança americana

(A) vem sendo injustamente criticada há oito anos.
(B) está gravemente ameaçada há oito anos.
(C) foi bastante comprometedora durante oito anos.
(D) tem sido extremamente ativa nesses últimos oito anos.
(E) tem sido praticamente inexistente nesses últimos oito anos.

(Vocabulary) A: Incorrect – There is no reference to "criticism"; B: Incorrect – There is no reference to "threats"; C: Incorrect – There is no reference to the leadership being "compromising", in the sense of "a risk"; D: Incorrect – There is no reference to "activity"; E: Correct – The collocation "sorely lacking" means "extreme inexistence" or "major absence".
Gabarito "E".

(Oficial de Chancelaria - 2009 - FCC) Segundo o texto, os dois candidatos à presidência dos Estados Unidos têm pontos de vista divergentes em relação

(A) à posição que deve ocupar a guerra ao terrorismo islâmico na política externa.
(B) ao uso do poder militar para resolver impasses diplomáticos.
(C) à política relativa ao aquecimento global.
(D) ao fechamento da Baía de Guantanamo.
(E) à tortura de prisioneiros.

(Interpretation) A: Incorrect – In the sixth paragraph, the text clearly states: "*The second area where the two men have more **in common** than one might expect is the "war on terror"*"; B: Correct – In the last paragraph, the author shows how "*Mr Obama hopes to use the power of negotiation*". This is reiterated in the following sentences when he refers to the "*talks*" Mr. Obama plans to have with several countries. The author emphasizes the difference between the candidates in the last sentence "*Mr McCain gives the impression that he thinks talk has its limits*"; C: Incorrect – In the fifth paragraph, the text clearly states: "*They **both propose** a policy of cap-and-trade to deal with **global warming**"; D: Incorrect – In the fifth paragraph, the text clearly states: "*They both want to close Guantanamo Bay*"; E: Incorrect – In the fifth paragraph, the text clearly states: "*They both oppose the use of torture*".
Gabarito "B".

1 As a new form of international diplomacy develops to deal with a number of emerging issues in which science and technology play a central role, the United Nations (UN)
4 risks being relegated to the sidelines. The influence and effectiveness of diplomats and international civil servants will increasingly depend on the extent to which they can
7 mobilize scientific and technical expertise in their work. This need not require the UN to acquire extensive in-house scientific competence, but the organization — especially the
10 office of the secretary general — must learn to tap advisory services to identify, mobilize, and use the best available expertise.
13 Although a large number of UN agencies, programs, and treaties rely on scientific and technological expertise for their work, they are not designed to receive systematic
16 science advice as a key component of effective performance. In most cases, science is used in the UN to support special interests and political agendas that do not necessarily
19 advance the goals of the organization. But this should not come as a surprise. The UN was founded and grew to prominence in the era of the Cold War, when much of
22 diplomacy was devoted to dealing with threats arising from external aggression. Today, attention is turning to issues such as infectious diseases, environmental degradation, electronic
25 crimes, weapons of mass destruction, and the impacts of new technologies, which in the past would have been the concern of individual nations but have now grown to international
28 stature. The UN's capacity to deal with these questions must also grow.
   What is notable about the UN is that it includes
31 organizations that cater to a wide range of jurisdictions but not to the growing community of science advisors. Even agencies such as the UN Educational, Scientific and Cultural
34 Organization (UNESCO) have done little to provide a platform for the world's science advisors. Specialized agencies such as UNESCO, the Food and Agriculture
37 Organization, the World Health Organization, and the UN Industrial Development Organization relate to the UN secretary general's office through a bureaucratic hierarchy
40 that is not responsive to timeliness. They are generally accountable to their governing bodies and are heavily influenced by the interests of activist states.

University of Texas at Dallas (with adaptations).

(Oficial de Chancelaria – 2006 – CESPE) Based on the text, judge the following items.

(1) Science and technology now play an important role in international diplomacy the same way as uncountable other emerging matters do.

(2) Diplomats and international civil servants must now increase their technical and scientific knowledge to cope with the new demands coming from emerging issues.

(3) Numerous UN agencies depend upon scientific and technological advice to carry out their tasks, however they are yet to be ready to receive systematic science consultancy as a crucial component of effectual performance.

(4) The present use of science by UN does not in every case act in its best interest so as to enforce its goals.

(5) When the UN began its activities, its sole concern had to do with dealing with issues concerning the Cold War.

(6) Problems that once were coped with by individual nations have now become international subjects which led the UN to devote its time to them.

(7) Due to the lack of world's science consultants, the UN specialized agencies would rather report to their governing staff to escape being influenced by the interest of the activist states.

(8) The gist of the text above can be said to be the importance of specialized advice to the UN in a new globalized era.

(Interpretation) 1: Incorrect – There is no clear evidence to substantiate this claim. "Other uncountable emerging matters" is so vague it's impossible to say they play the same role as science and technology; 2: Incorrect – In the first paragraph, the text clearly states the issue is about how diplomats and civil servants "*mobilize scientific and technical expertise in their work*". It is not about increasing knowledge, but rather about how they use and organize the scientific knowledge they have and receive; 3: Correct – In the second paragraph, the text clearly states that a large number of UN agencies "**are not designed** to receive systematic science advice as a key component of effective performance"; 4: Correct – In the second paragraph, the text clearly states that "science is used in the UN to support special interests and political agendas that **do not necessarily advance** the goals of the organization"; 5: Incorrect – In the second paragraph, the text clearly states that the "UN was **founded** (began) and grew to prominence (grew in important) in the era of the Cold War, when much of diplomacy was devoted to dealing with threats arising from **external aggression**". "External aggression", in this context, is not contained to issues related to the Cold War; 6: Correct – In the second paragraph, the text clearly states that the UN's attention is now on issues "which **in the past** would have been **the concern of individual nations** but have **now grown to international stature**"; 7: Incorrect – In the third paragraph, the text states that the specialized agencies are, in fact, "*accountable to their governing bodies*", but the text does not confirm that this is due to the lack of the scientists, nor that it is to escape influence from activist states; 8: Correct – The gist, or the general idea, conveyed in the text involves specialized information (scientific and technological) and the importance of dealing with it as the circumstances have become more international (new globalized era).

Gabarito 1E, 2E, 3C, 4C, 5E, 6C, 7E, 8C

(Oficial de Chancelaria – 2006 – CESPE) In the text,

(1) the word "little" (ℓ.34) means **not much**.
(2) the word "heavily" (ℓ.41) is the opposite of **roughly**.

(Vocabulary) 1: Correct – The collocation "to do little" means "not to do much"; 2: Correct – Within the context, the expression "heavily influenced" means "influenced a great deal" or "very much influenced". When "roughly" is used together with "influenced", it means "somewhat influenced", or "more or less influenced", taking on an aspect of opposition.

Gabarito 1C, 2C

---

1 A personal expression of regret from Pope Benedict XVI over a speech which offended Muslims has proved partially successful in stemming a torrent of anti-Christian
4 anger, and in some places violence, in the Islamic world. Speaking from the balcony of his residence at Castel Gandolfo outside Rome, the pontiff used his Sunday blessing
7 on September 17th to say he was "deeply sorry" for the "reactions in some countries" to a speech he gave on Tuesday last week.
10 He insisted that the words of a medieval text he quoted — an outburst against Islam by a late Byzantine emperor — "do not in any way express my personal
13 thought". In Turkey, where a papal visit planned for November has now been called into question, the top Muslim official said the Pope's expression of respect for Islam
16 amounted to a "civilised position". But in many Muslim nations people grumbled that the Pope appeared to be regretting the reactions to the speech, but not the speech
19 itself.
   The Muslim Brotherhood, a powerful international association whose offshoots include the Palestinian
22 movement Hamas, said the Pope's statement of regret was welcome but would not satisfy all Muslims. A wave of small protests and some violence continued over the weekend in
25 several Muslim countries. On Sunday an Italian nun in Mogadishu, Somalia's capital, was shot dead at the entrance to a hospital; many feared a link to the papal row. Half a
28 dozen churches in the West Bank were attacked, as the Palestinian prime minister, Ismail Haniya, appealed for restraint.

Internet: <www.economist.com> (adapted).

(Preparação Oficial de Chancelaria – 2006 – CESPE) Based on the text, judge the following items.

(1) Pope Benedict XVI succeeded in stopping the angry reaction against Christians.
(2) Many countries reacted against the Pope's speech.
(3) The Byzantine Emperor mentioned is still alive.
(4) The Pope's visit to Turkey has been questioned.
(5) For many the Pope's apology refers to people's reaction against his speech.
(6) Several Muslim countries reacted violently to Pope Benedict's speech during the weekend.

(Interpretation) 1: Incorrect – In the first paragraph, the text clearly states: "*A personal expression of regret from Pope Benedict XVI over a speech which offended Muslims has proved **only partially successful** in stemming a torrent of anti-Christian anger*". There was some success, but not total success; 2: Incorrect - In the first paragraph, the text clearly states that the Pope was "*deeply sorry for the reactions in **some countries***", not many countries; 3: Incorrect – In the second paragraph, the text clearly states: "*an outburst against Islam by a **late** Byzantine emperor*". In this context, the word "late" means deceased or departed; 4: Correct – In the second paragraph, the text clearly states: "*In Turkey, where a papal visit planned for November **has now been called into question**"*. In this context, the collocation "to call something into question" is synonymous with "to question"; 5: Correct - In the second paragraph, the text clearly states: "*But in **many Muslim nations** people grumbled that the Pope appeared to be **regretting the reactions** to the speech, **but not the speech itself**"*; 6: Correct – In the third paragraph, the text clearly states: "*A wave of small protests and some **violence** continued **over the weekend** in several Muslim countries*".

Gabarito 1E, 2E, 3E, 4C, 5C, 6C

(Preparação Oficial de Chancelaria – 2006 – CESPE) In the text,

(1) "deeply sorry" (ℓ.7) is the same as **dreadfully sorry**.
(2) "was shot dead" (ℓ.26) means **was killed**.

(Vocabulary) 1: Correct – Within the context, "dreadfully" has the meaning of "extremely", which is synonymous with "deeply"; 2: Correct – The collocation "to be shot dead" means that somebody shot the victim, and that the shot killed the victim.

Gabarito 1C, 2C

---

1 Raymond Mikesell, a professor of economics at the University of Oregon, died on Thursday September 14th at the age of 93. Mr Mikesell's old age brought with it a
4 noteworthy achievement. He was thought to be the last surviving economist present at the conference in 1944 at Bretton Woods, New Hampshire, which saw the

7   establishment of the post-war economic regime and with it
    the birth of the International Monetary Fund (IMF) and the
    World Bank. As the annual autumn meeting of the two
10 institutions gets underway in Singapore, Mr Mikesell's death
    is a reminder to the ageing figures of international finance
    that they may also have a natural lifespan.
13 The organisations were born into a world torn apart
    by war. The economists meeting at Bretton Woods also had
    sharp memories of the international financial crisis of the
16 1930s, when mercantilist policies and the failure of the
    international-payments system devastated world trade. They
    hoped to avert future crises by setting up multilateral
19 institutions to act as a stabilising influence during the postwar
    reconstruction. The bank's first job was rebuilding
    Europe; the IMF oversaw the fixed exchange-rate system
22 established at Bretton Woods. Later on the pair sought new
    roles as the stewards of global economic development and
    financial stability.
25 Now the IMF and World Bank have fewer jobs to
    do. Markets work better, as do other financial institutions.
    Helped by improved economic theory, the world has grown
28 richer and more stable. As for helping the poorest, a
    multilateral model of giving poor countries money and
    advice for running their economies is under fire from both
31 left and right. Conservatives argue that such interventions
    cause more problems than they solve. The left complains that
    developing nations get too little money and not enough
34 control over how it is spent. Both sides fear that the
    institutions' structures are outdated, hinting, increasingly
    loudly, that retirement is due.

Idem, ibidem.

(Preparação Oficial de Chancelaria – 2006 – CESPE) According to the text, it can be deduced that

(1) Professor Mikesell was 41 when he attended the Bretton Woods' Conference.
(2) the Bank's sole job was to rebuild Europe.
(3) the world richness and stability were supported by economic theory.

(Interpretation) 1: Incorrect – If Professor Mikesell died in 2006 (date of the text) at the age of 93, he was born in 1913. In 1944, when he attended the Bretton Woods' Conference, he would have been **31**, not 41; 2: Incorrect – In the second paragraph, the text clearly states *"The bank's **first** job was rebuilding Europe"*. Rebuilding Europe was the "first" job, not the "only" job; 3: Correct – In the third paragraph, the text clearly states: "***Helped by improved economic theory***, the world has **grown richer** and **more stable**".
Gabarito 1E, 2E, 3C

(Preparação Oficial de Chancelaria – 2006 – CESPE) According to the text, the IMF and the World Bank

(1) began their activities in the late 40's..
(2) meet once a year.
(3) were born to solve the international financial crisis of the 1930's.
(4) were created to avoid new crises.

(Interpretation) 1: Incorrect – Essentially, these two institutions began work at the conference held in 1944, i.e. **before** the middle of the decade. Therefore, they did **NOT** start in the late 40's; 2: Correct – In the first paragraph, the text clearly states: *"As the annual autumn meeting of the two institutions gets underway in Singapore,…"* The word "annual" means "once a year"; 3: Incorrect –The institutions were set up in 1944. It was too late to solve the 1930's crisis; 4: Correct – In the second paragraph, the text affirms that the institutions "*hoped to **avert future crises** by setting up multilateral institutions to act as a stabilising influence

during the postwar reconstruction". The initial job was to rebuild Europe, but the institutions became *"the stewards of global economic development and **financial stability**"*, meaning they would manage the economy to avoid financial crises.
Gabarito 1E, 2C, 3E, 4C

(Preparação Oficial de Chancelaria – 2006 – CESPE) In the text,

(1) "economic" (ℓ.7) is synonymous with economical.

(Vocabulary) 1: Incorrect – "Economic" is related to the economy, while "economical" is related with the idea of saving or not spending money.
Gabarito 1E

(Preparação Oficial de Chancelaria – 2006 – CESPE) Mrs. Green calls at the Bank:

— I'd like to cash this check for fifty dollars for me, please.

— Have you an account with us?

— Yes, my husband and I have a checking account. I also want to deposit these other checks in our account at the same time.

— I see. Have you made out a deposit slip?

(Mrs Green hands teller deposit slip with checks for deposit) — I hope that I have made it out correctly.

— It seems to me all right. How do you want this other check cashed, Mrs. Green? Will five tens be all right?

— That will be fine. (Accepts bills) I also want to ask you about starting a savings account. My husband and I have been thinking of opening a small savings account in which we could perhaps put aside a few dollars each week.

— The procedure is very simple. You can open a savings account at any time with an initial deposit of five dollars or more. Five dollars is the minimum original deposit. After that you deposit or withdraw money as you wish. You bring your bank book with you each time and the deposit or withdrawal is entered in your book. The amount carries interest of 2••• % and the interest is added to your account every six months. That's about all there is to it. If you'd like to open an account you can talk with the manager or with one of his assistants. They will be glad to take care of you.

Dixson, **Everyday Dialogues**, p. 1-2 (adapted).

From the text above, it can be concluded that

(1) Mrs Green has already started a savings account.
(2) to start a savings account you cannot deposit more than five dollars.
(3) savings accounts carry interest of 21/2 % every other six months.
(4) the teller couldn't open the savings account.

(Interpretation) 1: Incorrect – Mrs. Green clearly asks about starting a savings account: *"I also want to ask you about **starting a savings account**"*; 2: Incorrect – The bank teller clearly explains that to start a savings account, the initial deposit is five dollars. The issue of depositing more is not mentioned, but, "five dollars is the **minimum original deposit**"; 3: Incorrect – The teller clearly explains that "inte-

*rest is added to your account every six months", which translates into two interest payments per year. The expression "every other six months" carries the idea that interest payments are made only once a year; 4: Correct – The teller clearly states that "If you'd like to open an account you can **talk with the manager** or with one of his assistants." Candidates should infer that his referral to the manager or one of his assistants means that he himself could not open the savings account.*

Gabarito 1E, 2E, 3E, 4C

(Preparação Oficial de Chancelaria – 2006 – CESPE) Juan Gonzales visits New York City and has to ask his way around:

```
1   — I'm sorry, sir. I'm trying to find my way to Columbia
    University. Can you direct me? This is my first time in New
    York City.
4   (Passerby, looking bewildered) — Let's see! Columbia
    University? That's in the Bronx, isn't it?
    — I haven't the faintest idea. The only thing I know is
7   that someone told me it was "uptown".
    — Yeah! That's right. It's in the Bronx. Well, you take
    the subway here. There's a station on the next corner. You
10  have to walk down the stairs and take the uptown train.
```

According to the text above, it can be deduced that

(1) Juan Gonzales had already been to New York.
(2) the passerby was sure that Columbia University was in the Bronx.
(3) "faintest" (l.6) is synonymous with **slightest**.
(4) "subway" (l.9) is the same as **underground**.

*(Vocabulary) 1: Incorrect – Juan clearly states "This is my **first time** in New York City"; 2: Incorrect – The passerby uses a tag question (isn't it?), which suggests a level of uncertainty concerning what he has said. "That's in the Bronx, **isn't it**?"; 3: Correct – Within this context, the word "faintest" means almost none. "Slightest" means a small amount, or almost none. Hence, they are synonymous; 4: Correct – "Subway" is the American term for "underground". The British use two terms: the "underground", and the "tube".*

Gabarito 1E, 2E, 3C, 4C

```
1   The experience of sending the Strykers to Baghdad
    indicates that more troops could help in the short term.
    A growing number of analysts in Washington, including
4   some conservative supporters of the Bush Administration,
    have called for a substantial increase in U.S. troop levels to
    stop Iraq's slide into civil war. But expanding the total U.S.
7   force in Iraq remains unlikely — military officials
    interviewed by TIME say that the U.S. command remains
    reluctant to make a major manpower boost. To some, that
10  reluctance is indicative of the leadership's broader failure to
    heed complaints about U.S. troop strength that have been
    voiced by officers in Iraq for more than three years. "I know
13  I could have used more forces," says a Lieut. Colonel who
    served in Iraq. "We could have held more territory... I asked,
    but I'm not sure the request ever made it."
```

Internet: <www.time.com> (adapted).

(Preparação Oficial de Chancelaria – 2006 – CESPE) Based on the text, it can be said that

(1) it is easy to know who was the "Lieut. Colonel" (l.13) mentioned.
(2) the Lieut. Colonel is in doubt whether he is going to get more troops.
(3) to solve Iraq's problem is just a matter of sending more troops.
(4) increasing US troop level is thought to be able to prevent a civil war in Iraq.
(5) the United States commanders hesitate about increasing man power in Iraq.

*(Interpretation) 1: Incorrect – The title "Lieut. Colonel" is a reference to his rank, not to his name. He served in Iraq, but so did many other Lieut. Colonels. Who this Lieut. Colonel is remains a mystery; 2: Correct – The Lieut. Colonel clearly states that he asked for more troops, "but I'm **not sure** the request ever made it"; 3: Incorrect – "A substantial increase in U.S. troop levels" is an idea sustained by some analysts in Washington, but military officials have proved to be "reluctant to make a major manpower boost." There is no clear answer to solve Iraq's problem; 4: Correct – The text clearly states that some analysts in Washington think that "A substantial increase in U.S. troop levels **stop Iraq's slide into civil war**"; 5: Correct – The text clearly states that military officials have proved to be "**reluctant** to make a major manpower **boost**." Within this context, being "reluctant" is synonymous with "hesitate", while "increase" and "boost" have similar meanings.*

Gabarito 1E, 2C, 3E, 4C, 5C

(Preparação Oficial de Chancelaria – 2006 – CESPE) In the text,

(1) "in the short term" (l.2) is the opposite of in the long run.
(2) "have called" (l.5) is the same as have asked.
(3) "boost" (l.9) is the same as decrease.

(Vocabulary) 1: Correct – The collocation "in the long run" is synonymous with "in the long term", the opposite of "in the short term"; 2: Correct – The phrasal verb "call for" can mean "ask for". Within the context of this text, the meanings are the same; 3: Incorrect – The word "boost" in a synonym for "increase", not "decrease".

Gabarito 1C, 2C, 3E

```
1   The idea of the triumph of one people being the
    tragedy of another is eloquently captured in Sandy Tolan's
    book, The Lemon Tree — essential reading for anyone
4   seeking to understand the difficulty in resolving the Israeli-
    Palestinian conflict. Tolan chronicles the true story of Dalia
    Eshkenazi, whose family flees post-Holocaust Bulgaria in
7   1948 to live the Zionist dream of building a Jewish state in
    the Holy Land. The new Israeli government provides them
    with an abandoned Arab house in the town of Ramla, in
10  which she grows up. One summer morning in 1967, she's
    sitting in the garden near the old lemon tree, when Bashir
    Khairi knocks on the gate. Khairi is the son of the man who
13  planted the lemon tree; he was born in the house and lived
    there until age 4, when he and his family, and hundreds of
    others, were forced onto buses by Israeli soldiers and driven
16  to the West Bank, where they have lived as refugees ever
    since.
```

Idem, ibidem.

(Preparação Oficial de Chancelaria – 2006 – CESPE) According to the text, judge the following items.

(1) Reading Sandy Tolan's book is basic for those interested in solving the Israeli and Palestinian conflict.
(2) Sandy Tolan deals with the victory of Israel and the tragedy of Palestine.
(3) Bashir and Dalia were born in the same house.
(4) Bashir and Dalia have nothing in common.
(5) Bashir's father used to live in Dalia's house.
(6) Khairi's family abandoned their house in 1967.

(Interpretation) 1: Incorrect – The text states that Sandy Tolan's book is "**essential** reading for anyone seeking to understand the difficulty in resolving the Israeli-Palestinian conflict." This suggests that the book can help people understand and it is highly recommended. However, there is no reference to its level of difficulty, i.e., whether it is basic or complex; 2: Correct – The text clearly states that "the idea of the **triumph of one people** being the **tragedy of another** is eloquently captured in Sandy Tolan's" book. The triumph is clearly attributed to the Israeli people later in the text, when it states Bashir Khairi and his family "were **forced onto buses by Israeli soldiers**"; 3: Incorrect – The text clearly states that Bashir Khairi "**was born in the house** and lived there until age 4", but Dalia, after fleeing post-Holocaust Bulgaria with her family, moves in and grows up there. She was not born there; 4: Incorrect – The text clearly states that they grew up in the same house, albeit at different moments; 5: Correct – The text affirms that Bashir Khairi lived in the house with his family, including his father, who planted the lemon tree there; 6: Incorrect – The text clearly states that Bashir Khairi's family did not abandon the house; they were forced to leave. This happened well before 1967, because that is the year he returns and meets Dalia who, at this time, is living in the house. "*One summer morning **in 1967**, **she's sitting** in the garden near the old lemon tree, **when Bashir Khairi knocks on the gate**.*"

Gabarito 1E, 2C, 3E, 4E, 5C, 6E

(Preparação Oficial de Chancelaria – 2006 – CESPE) In the text,

(1) "chronicles" (ℓ.5) is the plural of **chronicle**.
(2) "he" (ℓ.13) refers to "Khairi" (ℓ.12).

(Grammar) 1: Incorrect – In this text, the word "chronicles" is being used as a verb, not a noun. It is in the 3rd person singular "*Tolan chronicles the true story*"; 2: Correct – The word "he" is the subject of a secondary clause. The word "he" refers back to the subject in the first clause. The use of the semi-colon in this sentence creates a syntactic-semantic link between the two clauses, reinforcing the reference back to the first subject. "**Khairi** is the son of the man who planted the lemon tree; **he** was born in the house …".

Gabarito 1E, 2C

---

1 The democratic race has never seemed so intriguing or so close, with each election's results closely watched and delegates agreed, each vote really does seem to count this time around. Numbers of those turning out to the polls have reached new highs for a primary election, and one of the main drivers is the head-to-head race between Obama and Clinton. After Super Tuesday,
4 Clinton was in the lead and sitting pretty. But since then, election after election has turned to Obama's favor. Some big elections coming up include Texas and Ohio, both of which have Hillary in the lead.
    But how different are these two candidates? People seem passionate about their candidates, but when looking at the two
7 side by side, they are overall very similar. There are some who hate Hillary, and would not want her to be president, but the same is not true for Obama. At the same time, if my candidate of choice wasn't elected president, I think I wouldn't be opposed to the other winning the nomination. Which raises the question of a joint ticket[1] between the two.
10 In the recent California debate Obama and Clinton were asked if they would consider a joint ticket, and both said yes. It seems interesting. They are both strong and successful and wouldn't back down[2] if the other didn't see eye-to-eye with them. That's the kind of relationship I want between my President and Vice President, if you pick a pair who agree on everything, what good
13 does that serve? What if no one is looking at the issue from another angle?
    However, I would be worried about the two partnering together with the red states, I think together they can seem too liberal and might not be the winning ticket. I still think a middle of the road white male would be the best ticket for both. Although,
16 personally I would be all for a joint ticket.

[1] joint ticket – agreement.
[2] back down – to stop supporting a position.

Internet: <2008myvote.wordpress.com> (adapted).

(Assistente de Chancelaria – 2008 – CESPE) According to the text, judge the following items.

(1) It is the first time that the democratic elections look so interesting.
(2) Never before has every single vote been so important for the democratic party.
(3) Clinton remains in the lead election after election.
(4) Obama and Clinton don't seem to share any characteristics.
(5) People hate both candidates the same way.
(6) It is indifferent for the author whether either Clinton or Obama wins the election.
(7) According to the author, it would be a good idea to have two candidates with the same point of view.

(Interpretation) 1: Correct – In the first sentence, the text clearly states that "*The democratic race **has never seemed so intriguing** or so close…*" The word "never" implies that the democratic elections that were held before were not as interesting as these [ones]. Therefore, this is the first time they seem so interesting; 2: Correct – In the first sentence, the text clearly states that "**each vote** really does seem **to count** this time around". The importance is reiterated in the second sentence when the author uses the term "**head-to-head race**", showing how close the election is and, consequently, how important each vote is; 3: Incorrect – The text clearly states that "*election after election **has turned to Obama's favor***", meaning Obama has been in the lead election after election; 4: Incorrect – The text clearly states "…*but when looking at the two side by side, they are overall **very similar**". The similarities are reiterated later in the text, when the author claims "They are **both strong and successful**"; 5: Incorrect - Some hate Hillary and do not want her to be president, whereas others hate Obama, but do not state they don't wish him to be president (lines 7-8); 6:
Gabarito Oficial – ANULADA / Nosso
Gabarito – Correct – The author affirms that "…*if my candidate of choice wasn't elected president, I think I **wouldn't be opposed to the other winning the nomination**.*" The author's lack of opposition to the other candidate can be construed as indifference; 7: Incorrect – The author shows that he is against the idea of two candidates with the same point of view when he writes "*if you pick a pair who agree on everything, **what good does that serve**?*"

Gabarito Oficial 1C, 2C, 3E, 4E, 5E, 6ANULADA, 7E

(Assistente de Chancelaria – 2008 – CESPE) In the text,

(1) "both of which" (*l*.5) refers to "Texas and Ohio" (*l*.5).
(2) "coming up" (*l*.5) is synonymous with **happening soon**.
(3) "who" (*l*.7) can be correctly replaced by **whom**.

(Vocabulary) 1: Correct – The collocation "both of which" works as a non-restrictive relative pronoun that refers back to a two-noun phrase (both = two). The only two-noun phrase in the sentence is Texas and Ohio; 2: Correct – The phrasal verb "coming up" means "looming", "on the agenda", or "happening soon"; 3: Incorrect – The word "who" in the sentence "*There are some **who** hate Hillary*" functions as a relative pronoun referring back to the word or idea "*some (people)*". However, it also functions as the subject of the verb "*hate*". The relative pronoun "whom" can never function as a subject, but rather as an object, e.g. an unpopular politician is Hillary, whom many people hate. In the example, "many people" is the subject of the transitive verb "hate". "Whom" represents the object of the transitive verb "hate" (Many people hate Hillary).

Gabarito 1C, 2C, 3E

The Golden State Gets Greener

1 Governor Arnold Schwarzenegger has signed Executive Order S-3-05 which establishes greenhouse gas (GHG) emission reduction targets for California. The California
4 Air Resources Board, which oversees the state's pollution, has announced a sweeping plan designed to cut the state's current greenhouse gas emissions 30% by 2020.
7 The proposed rules come after two years of debate, public meetings, and consultations with scientists, economists, and policy experts from around the world. After accepting
10 comments on the plan, the California Air Resources Board will vote on it 1 January 2009. If they approve it, regulations could be in place as early as January 2010. For his part, California
13 Governor Arnold Schwarzenegger said at a Florida climate conference that he wants his state's citizens to prepare for the long haul. "America did not get into this mess overnight, and we
16 are not going to get out of this mess overnight. We need to change our energy policies and our thinking, and stick with it". Its emission reduction goals put California in the forefront of
19 efforts to regulate greenhouse gases.
  The signature proposal is the greenhouse gas cap. It would target 85% of California's carbon dioxide and other
22 greenhouse gas emissions, mainly from power plants, oil refineries, and factories. The reductions are roughly three times more aggressive than the eight-state Regional Greenhouse Gas
25 Initiative adopted in the U.S. northeast, which goes into force next year.
  If the rules are enacted, the state's greenhouse pollution
28 in 2020 will equal its 1990 emissions. Over time, the plans could create jobs and tax revenue by growing new green industries like solar power, energy-efficient appliance
31 manufacture, or alternative fuel development.
  California also wants to contribute to global efforts to avert potential catastrophes such as sea level rise.

Eli Kintisch. **Science NOW. Daily News**. Internet: <www.sciencenow.sciencemag.org.> (adapted).

(Preparação Assistente de Chancelaria – 2008 – CESPE) According to the text, it can be inferred that

(1) California's Air Resources Board is the state agency responsible for monitoring and regulating greenhouse gas emission sources in California.
(2) the proposal aims to improve air quality and reduce greenhouse gas emissions throughout the United States of America.
(3) one proposal goal is to reduce California greenhouse gas emissions to 1990 levels by 2010.
(4) the standards will reduce greenhouse gas emissions by 85 per cent relative to current models.
(5) reducing greenhouse gas emissions will be enough to avoid sea level rise.

(Interpretation) 1: Correct – In the first sentence, the California Air Resources Board is clearly stated as the agency "*which **oversees the state's pollution**"* and which is responsible for the "***plan** designed to cut the state's current **greenhouse gas emissions** 30% by 2020*"; 2: Incorrect – In the third paragraph, the text clearly states that the proposal "*would target 85% of **California's** carbon dioxide and other greenhouse gas emissions*". In the third paragraph, the proposal is also compared to "*the **eight-state** Regional Greenhouse Gas Initiative adopted **in the U.S. northeast**"*, suggesting that the proposal is not nationwide; 3: Incorrect – In the fourth paragraph, the text clearly states that "*the state's greenhouse pollution **in 2020** will equal its 1990 emissions*", and not in 2010; 4: Incorrect – In the third paragraph, the text states that the standards "*would **target 85%** of California's carbon dioxide and other greenhouse gas emissions*". Targeting 85% of the state's emissions does not mean an 85% reduction. It means that 85% of the sources for emissions will be targeted by the standards, but there is no guarantee that they will all be reduced; 5: Incorrect – In the fourth paragraph, the text clearly states that "*California also wants to **contribute to global efforts** to avert potential catastrophes such as sea level rise*", which means that the state will help. It does not mean that the state alone will be able to avoid the sea level rise.

Gabarito 1C, 2E, 3E, 4E, 5E

(Preparação Assistente de Chancelaria – 2008 – CESPE) It is correct to conclude from the text that

(1) the Greenhouse Gas Initiative adopted in the U.S. northeast is more radical than California's plan for GHC reduction.
(2) California's plan to cut greenhouse gas emissions could create new jobs in coming years.
(3) global warming is expected to raise temperatures between 8 and 10.4 degrees in California if greenhouse gas emissions are not cut.
(4) greenhouse gas emissions are mainly from power plants.
(5) "**The Golden State**", in the title, refers to the State of California.

(Interpretation) 1: Incorrect – In the third paragraph, the text clearly states that "*The reductions [planned in California] are roughly **three times more aggressive than** the eight-state Regional Greenhouse Gas **in the U.S. northeast**"*; 2: Correct – In the fourth paragraph, the text clearly states that "*Over time, the **plans** could **create jobs** and tax revenue by growing new green industries*"; 3: Incorrect – In the text, there is no mention of how much global warming would raise temperatures; 4: Incorrect – In the third paragraph, the text clearly states that greenhouse gas emissions are "*mainly from power plants, **oil refineries**, and **factories**"*, thus including more than just power plants; 5: Correct – In the first paragraph, the only state mentioned in California, thus making the connection. Also, California is famously known as the Golden State.

Gabarito 1E, 2C, 3E, 4E, 5C

(Preparação Assistente de Chancelaria – 2008 – CESPE) In the text,

(1) "which" (*l*.2) refers to "Arnold Schwarzenegger" (*l*.1).
(2) "has announced" (*l*.4-5) can be replaced by **talked about**.
(3) "forefront" (*l*.18) means the same as **leading position**.

(4) "roughly" (ℓ.23) could be replaced by **approximately**.
(5) "enacted" (ℓ.27) means **not approved**.

(Vocabulary) 1: Incorrect – In the first paragraph, the text clearly states that "*Arnold Schwarzenegger signed the **Executive Order S-3-05** which establishes greenhouse gas emission reduction targets for California*". The word "*which*" is a relative pronoun referring back to "*the Executive Order S-3-05*" and a subject for the verb "*establishes*". Schwarzenegger signed the Executive Order, but the order establishes the targets. This is a grammar question. Obviously, Schwarzenegger and his advisors wrote the order, but the word "which" tells you where they have been established; 2: Incorrect – "The verb "to announce" means to proclaim to a large audience, to "publicize" or "make known". Meanwhile, "talk about" merely means to discuss, but not necessarily with a large audience; 3: Correct – The word "forefront" comes from the combination of the word "fore" (before) and "front". Together, it is a synonym for "leader", or "leading position"; 4: Correct – The word "roughly" is an informal synonym for the word "approximately"; 5: Incorrect – The word "enact" means to "ratify" or "endorse". In Portuguese, this is often translated as "promulgar", which is, essentially, the opposite of "not approved".

Gabarito 1E, 2E, 3C, 4C, 5E

The election of 1864

1 Dissatisfaction over the Civil War split the Democratic Party. In the elections of 1864, many Democrats joined the Republicans to form the Union
4 Party. This party chose the Republican Lincoln for the Presidency and Andrew Johnson of Tennessee, a former Democratic member of Congress but an opponent of the
7 Confederacy, for the Vice-Presidency. The Democratic Party responded by naming General George B. McClellan as its candidate for the Presidency.
10 Antiwar feeling was running so high in 1864 that President Lincoln fully expected to be defeated. "We are now on the brink of destruction, and I can hardly see a ray
13 of hope" he wrote to a friend.
   The Union of northern states was fighting the Confederacy of southern states. The tide of the war turned
16 in favor of the North shortly before the election. As a result, Lincoln won an overwhelming victory.

This cartoon from the 1864 election seems to favor McClellan, who tries to keep his opponent, Lincoln, and Jefferson Davis from pulling the Union apart. But the voters gave Lincoln 212 electoral votes to McClellan's 21.

Lewis Paul Todd. **Rise of the American Nation**. Liberty Edition, 1982 (adapted).

(Preparação Assistente de Chancelaria – 2008 – CESPE) Based on the information given by the text and shown in the picture above, judge the following items.

(1) The election of 1864 was conducted before the Civil War.
(2) In early 1864 Lincoln felt he would easily win re-election.
(3) The Confederates defeated the states located in the South of the United States.
(4) President Lincoln formed a new group called the National Union Party that included Republicans and Democrats.

(Interpretation) 1: Incorrect – In the third paragraph, the text clearly states that "*The tide of the war turned in favor of the North **shortly before** the election*", showing that the war had already begun before the elections were held. This is reinforced in the political cartoon, showing the obvious conflict between the North and South **at the same time** the elections were being held; 2: Incorrect – In the second paragraph, the text clearly states that "*Antiwar feeling was running so high **in 1864** that **President Lincoln fully expected to be defeated**"*; 3: Incorrect – In the third paragraph, the text clearly states that "*The Union of northern states **was fighting** the Confederacy of southern states.*" The Confederates were the southern states; 4: Incorrect – In the first paragraph, the text clearly states that "*many Democrats joined the Republicans **to form the Union party**. This party **chose the Republican Lincoln** for the Presidency*". Hence Lincoln did not form the party.

Gabarito 1E, 2E, 3E, 4E

(Preparação Assistente de Chancelaria – 2008 – CESPE) In the text,

(1) "Dissatisfaction" (ℓ.1) means Not happy.
(2) "chose" (ℓ.4) is the simple past form of the verb to chase.
(3) "its candidate" (ℓ.9) refers to the candidate of the Republican Party.
(4) "fully" (ℓ.11) can be correctly replaced by completely.
(5) The suffix -ern in "northern" (ℓ.14) and "southern" (ℓ.15) occur with names of directions like North and South.
(6) "overwhelming" (ℓ.17) is the opposite insignificant.

(Vocabulary) 1: Gabarito Oficial ANULADA / Nosso Gabarito – While the essence of the word "dissatisfaction" means "not happy", the different morphological classification may have been the reason this question was annulled. "Dissatisfaction" is a noun, while "not happy" is an adjective. Had the option been "unhappiness" or "disappointment", the question would have been correct; 2: Incorrect – The word "chose" is the simple past form of the verb "to choose". The verb "chase" is a regular verb, and its simple past form is "chased"; 3: Incorrect – In the first paragraph, the text clearly states that "*The **Democratic Party responded** by **naming General George B. McClellan as its candidate** for the Presidency*", showing that McClellan was the Democratic Party's candidate, and not the Republican candidate; 4: Correct – In this context, the meaning of "fully" is synonymous with the meaning of "completely"; 5: Correct – The suffix "-ern" is typically used with nouns of direction to make them adjectives. All the directions can receive the suffix: "eastern", "western". These words are usually capitalized when they are acting as names of places; when they are acting as directions, do not capitalize; 6: Gabarito Oficial ANULADA / Nosso Gabarito – Incorrect – The word "overwhelming" in this context means "significant". The poor wording of the question may have been the reason it was annulled (...is the opposite **of** insignificant).

Gabarito 1ANULADA, 2E, 3E, 4C, 5C, 6ANULADA

1   Parents and guardians are bestowed with the
    responsibility of protecting and educating children from all the
    hazards that abound. It is not strange that children are often
4   injured in a familiar environment, such as the home and its
    surroundings. Accidents could not be completely avoided, but
    their occurrence could be prevented. Home accidents can be
7   avoided by child-proofing your home, as there are so many
    different home safety products available today.
       Reasonable supervision by an adult, and the use of
10 ordinary precautions against accidents, are outstanding as
    means of prevention. The pictures below illustrate some general
    instructions for parents and older children in order to prevent
13 home accidents.

• Children should never play on stairs.
• Furniture must be moved away to prevent children placing
16 tep-stones such as a chair next to a window, climbing up
   and falling out.
• Prevent the child from sticking his small fingers in electric
19 sockets and electric fires.
• Keep matches and lighters where young children can't see
   them or reach them, and also install proper cover to sockets.
22 Children, being less aware of danger, are one of the
   most vulnerable groups. Younger children are more vulnerable
   indoors, while older ones are more at risk outdoors. There
25 appear to be gender types of accidents; males tend to have more
   accidents outdoors while females tend to have accidents
   indoors.

Internet: <www.familymagazinegroup.com> (adapted).

(Preparação Assistente de Chancelaria – 2008 – CESPE) According to text, judge the items below.

(1) At their first years of age, children are more protected from accidents that typically happen in the interior of a house or building.
(2) Children injuries caused by domestic accidents are very common.
(3) Prevention of children injuries and accidents can be successfully achieved when home safety measures are taken.
(4) In general, children under adult supervision will suffer fewer injuries.
(5) Male and female do not usually have the same types of accidents.

(Interpretation) 1: Incorrect – In the last paragraph, the text clearly states that "*Younger children are **more vulnerable indoors**,* while older ones are more at risk outdoors"; 2: Correct – In the first paragraph, the text clearly states that "*It is not strange that children are **often injured in a familiar environment, such as the home** and its surroundings*"; 3: Correct – In the first paragraph, the text clearly states that "*Home accidents can be avoided by child-proofing your home*". This is reinforced in the second paragraph, where the text also clearly states that "Reasonable **supervision by an adult**, and the **use of ordinary precautions against accidents**, are outstanding as means of prevention." These ideas are given as ways to successfully prevent children from injuries and accidents; 4: Correct – In the second paragraph, the text clearly states that "*Reasonable **supervision by an adult** (...) are **outstanding as means of prevention**"*; 5: Correct – In the last sentence, the text clearly states that "***males** tend to have **more accidents outdoors** while **females** tend to have **accidents indoors**.*"

Gabarito 1E, 2C, 3C, 4C, 5C

(Preparação Assistente de Chancelaria – 2008 – CESPE) In the text,

(1) "ordinary" (ℓ.10) could be replaced by **special** without any change in meaning.
(2) "their" (ℓ.6) is a possessive pronoun related to occurrence.
(3) "being less aware of danger" (ℓ.22) can be replaced by **not perceiving danger as readily**.
(4) both "Younger" (ℓ.23) and "older" (ℓ.24) indicate comparisons.
(5) "gender" (ℓ.25) refers to the kinds of accidents: indoor and outdoor accidents.

(Vocabulary) 1: Incorrect – The word "ordinary" is the opposite of "special"; 2: Incorrect – "The word "their" is a possessive adjective, and it is related to the word "accidents" at the beginning of the sentence. Possessive adjectives are governed by the word they refer in terms of ownership: the occurrence of accidents = their occurrence; 3: Correct – The expression "being less aware of danger" means "not noticing" or "not perceiving danger". The word "readily" means "easily"; 4: Correct – The words "younger" and "older" contain the suffix "-er", which is used in English to make comparisons; 5: Incorrect – The word "gender" in English is strictly used when referring to the "sex" (masculinity or femininity) of something or somebody. It is not used to discriminate whether things are "indoor" or "outdoor".

Gabarito 1E, 2E, 3C, 4C, 5E

This text refers to the following items.

Blazing a trail with solar power

1   In a hangar outside Zurich, engineers are paring away at the obstacles to a very 21st century challenge: flying a plane around the world powered by nothing but the rays of
4   the sun. If the Solar Impulse project goes to plan, in 2011 a gangly aircraft with the wingspan of an Airbus A380 and the weight of a compact car will attempt to circle the globe in
7   about a month at an average speed of 43 m.p.h. (70 km/h), landing only five times along the way.
    The challenge, says Piccard, is to keep going until
10 the next sunrise before the batteries are empty: "We have very little margin of error from night into day. Each dawn will be a moment of incredible suspense." For the 2011
13 flight, he and Boschberg will do alternating stints of five days and five nights between landings. A day on the ground spent charging in the sunlight should be enough to get the
16 plane back into the air the next morning for another stage in its globe-girdling journey.
    It's a delicate enterprise, complicated by
19 meteorological challenges and the ungainliness of a plane this big and light. Even Piccard doesn't envision solar planes replacing today's airliners anytime soon, but that's not the
22 point. To reduce emissions, he believes, aviation will eventually need to wean itself from fossil fuels. "To make reasonable use of any alternative," he says, "we have to
25 become lighter and more aerodynamic to reduce consumption." Solar Impulse promises to generate an array of futuristic insights – and some old-fashioned thrills along
28 the way.

Internet: <www.time.com> (adapted).

(Técnico – ANAC – 2009 – CESPE) Judge the following items according to the text.

(1) A plane that can fly on solar power has been fully developed.

(2) The aircraft will fly powered only by the rays of the sun.

(3) The aircraft prototype, which is made of low--density carbon fiber, will be able to circle the globe in about a month.

(4) Despite being big, the airplane is quite heavy.

(5) Due to its aerodynamics, the airplane will reduce emissions.

(6) Solar planes will replace today's airliners in the future.

(7) The aircraft will fly at around 43 m.p.h.

(Interpretation) 1: incorrect – In line 1 the text states that engineers are, **'paring away at the obstacles to a very 21st century challenge'.** To pare away means to reduce or decrease bit by bit. Therefore the obstacles or problems still need to be overcome; 2: correct – In line 2 the text states that the challenge is,**'flying a plane around the world powered by nothing but the rays of the sun'**. Nothing but the rays of the sun means using only the sun's rays; 3: incorrect – The text does not mention what material the plane is made from; 4: incorrect – The plane is big, (wingspan of an airbus – line 5) but it is in fact light (line 20); 5: incorrect – The plan will reduce emissions due to what it uses for fuel i.e. solar power; 6: incorrect – The text states in lines 20-24 that solar planes are not predicted to replace airliners any time soon and that the key issue is for airliners to reduce their reliance on fossil fuels; 7: correct – (Line 7) An average speed of 43 m.p.h.

Gabarito 1E, 2C, 3E, 4E, 5E, 6E, 7C

(Técnico – ANAC – 2009 – CESPE) In the text,

(1) the expression "**Blazing a trail**" in the title can figuratively mean avant garde or inventive work in arts or sciences, evoking the literal meaning of going into new territory which has no marked paths.

(2) the adjective "gangly" (ℓ.5) means **too big** or **long**.

(3) the word "stints" (ℓ.13) refers to **an unbroken period of time doing a certain job or activity**.

(Vocabulary) 1: correct – to blaze a trail or to be a trailblazer refers to being innovative or pioneering; 2: correct – It can mean tall, long or slender; 3: correct – Stints means this.

Gabarito 1C, 2C, 3C

1   Foodborne illnesses* are a serious public health threat. Each year, approximately 76 million cases of foodborne illness occur in the United States alone, according
4   to the Centers for Disease Control and Prevention (CDC). Of those cases of foodborne illness, more than 325,000 people are hospitalized and about 5,000 deaths occur.
7   Why Be Food Safe?
    Preventing foodborne illness is one of the U.S. Department of Agriculture's (USDA's) top priorities. For
10 more than 100 years, the USDA's Food Safety and Inspection Service (FSIS) has worked with our Nation's commercial suppliers to ensure that meat, poultry, and egg
13 products are safe, wholesome, and correctly labeled and packaged for public consumption. And because research shows that improper handling, preparation, and storage of
16 food can cause foodborne illness, FSIS has conducted – and is a key stakeholder in – many public education programs to prevent foodborne illness.
19 What is the Be Food Safe Campaign?
    USDA developed the Be Food Safe Campaign in cooperation with the Partnership for Food Safety Education,
22 FDA, and CDC because research shows that Americans are aware of food safety, but they need more information to achieve and maintain safe food handling behaviors. The Be
25 Food Safe Campaign, which is grounded in social marketing, behavior change, and risk communications theories, is designed to provide educators with the tools to inform
28 consumers about foodborne illness and raise the level of awareness of the dangers associated with improper handling and undercooking of food.

* *Foodborne illnesses are defined as diseases, usually either infectious or toxic in nature, caused by agents that enter the body through the ingestion of food.*

Internet: <www.fsis.usda.gov> (adapted).

(Técnico – ANVISA – 2007 – CESPE) According to the text above, judge the following items.

(1) Americans are perfectly conscious of the danger of undercooked food.

(2) Foodborne sicknesses are the most serious public health problem.

(3) The CDC estimates that more than 50 million cases of foodborne illness are found in the USA every year.

(4) Foodborne disease prevention is among the most important concerns of the USDA.

(5) For more than a century, the FSIS has been concerned about three particularly important nutritional items.

(6) Public education programs are all that is required to prevent illness coming from food handling, preparation and storage.

(7) The Be Food Safe Campaign aims at making Americans aware of food safety problems.
(8) The Be Food Safe Campaign intends to provide more information to users about the diseases that can be caused by food.

(Interpretation) 1: incorrect – The text states in line 28 that the campaign seeks, 'to raise the level of awareness of the dangers associated with improper handling and undercooking of food'. This statement and the fact that 5,000 people die per year illustrate that Americans are nto perfectly conscious about these dangers; 2: incorrect – They are one of the U.S Department of Agriculture's top priorities but not necessarily the top priority (line 8); 3: correct – (Line 2) According to the CDC approximately 76 million cases are found every year in the U.S.; 4: correct – They are one of the U.S Department of Agriculture's top priorities. (line 8); 5: correct – (line 9) 'For more than 100 years, the USDA's Food Safety and Inspection Service (FSIS) has worked with our Nation's commercial suppliers to ensure that meat, poultry, and egg products are safe, wholesome, and correctly labeled and packaged for public consumption'; 6: incorrect – Don't all these come back to forms of education; 7: incorrect – It aims at giving educators they tools to help people change their habits; 8: correct – 'to raise the level of awareness associated with the improper handling and undercooking of food'. (line 28).

Gabarito 1E, 2E, 3C, 4C, 5C, 6E, 7E, 8C

(Técnico – ANVISA – 2007 – CESPE) In the text,

(1) "to ensure" (ℓ.12) means to make (something) certain to happen.
(2) "which" (ℓ.25) can be correctly replaced by what.

(Vocabulary) 1: correct – to ensure means to make sure or to guarantee something will happen; 2: incorrect – 'Which' refers to the subject of the sentence 'the campaign'. What could not be used in this type of construction.

Gabarito 1C, 2E

Read the text below in order to answer the questions:

The Latin American Economies

For decades, the economies of Latin America were heavily protected. Government ownership of industry was widespread. Foreign investment was minimal. The theory was that to end dependence on basic commodities (coffee, sugar, copper), industries had to be protected against bigger – usually U.S. – companies. Nationalism and economics made a marriage of convenience.

But beginning in the 1980s, Latin governments changed, because economic performance was dismal and Asia's example was instructive. The phrase "Washington consensus" was soon coined by economist John Williamson of the Institute for International Economics to denote the policies that the U.S. government and Washington-based institutions (the World Bank, the International Monetary Fund) were advocating: lower tariffs, higher foreign investment, tighter budgets, less inflation.

Brazil exemplified the shift. In 1985, tariffs averaged 80 percent; by 2000, they were 15 percent. Privatization of nationalized companies exploded; from 1996 to 2001, Brazil received nearly $150 billion in foreign direct investment. As The Economist notes, the changes have benefited Brazil. Hyperinflation (exceeding 1,000 percent annually) was conquered. But there was no permanent boom, and since 1999, the economy has slowed.

(Analista – BACEN – 2002 – FCC) According to the author, Latin America's economic situation

(A) served as a model for the Asian countries.
(B) has shown no significant shift since 1980.
(C) was poor in the 1980s, thus requiring change.
(D) has remained unquestionable since 1980.
(E) should not have been influenced by the World Bank.

(Interpretation) A: incorrect – Asian countries served as a model for Latin America; B: incorrect – Paragraph 3, line 1 – shows the significant shifts that took place; C: **correct** – This answer is correct as much by elimination as by clear evidence. The presence of hyperinflation, lack of foreign investment and dismal economic performance are not positive but just by removing these factors does not in itself eliminate poverty; D: incorrect – Since 1980s there have been significant positive developments; E: incorrect – the text sets out that as part of the Washington Consensus the World Bank has assisted Latin America attract investment and overcome hyperinflation.

Gabarito "C".

(Analista – BACEN – 2002 – FCC) The text mentions

(A) a set of policies derived from certain institutions.
(B) the recent urge to raise international tariffs.
(C) Argentina's economic and social turmoil.
(D) Asia's lack of trade with the Latin American region.
(E) the lack of economic changes in South America.

(Interpretation) A: correct – The Washington Consensus from the World Bank, IMF and US government; B: incorrect – this is not mentioned in the text; C: incorrect – Argentina is not specifically mentioned; D: incorrect – Trade between these two continents is not discussed; E: incorrect – The text focuses on the economic changes that have taken place in South America.

Gabarito "A".

(Analista – BACEN – 2002 – FCC) According to the text, Brazil

(A) symbolizes the refusal to promote economic changes.
(B) has been unable to fight inflation.
(C) has rejected the free-market model.
(D) became dependent on Asian investments.
(E) has promoted economic renewal within its borders.

(Interpretation) A: incorrect – the contrary is true; B: incorrect – Brazil conquered hyperinflation; C: incorrect – In paragraph 3, Brazil is the example of a country embracing the free-market model; D: incorrect – This is not mentioned; E: correct – In paragraph 3, Brazil is the example of a country embracing the free-market model in order to promote economic growth.

Gabarito "E".

(Analista – BACEN – 2002 – FCC) The author says that **hyperinflation was conquered**, which means it

(A) ought to be controlled.
(B) was controlled.
(C) was achieved.

(D) must have been foreseen.
(E) might have been avoided.

(Vocabulary) A: incorrect – ought to – implies duty or obligation – conquered does not have this connotation; B: correct – to conquer means to defeat or secure control of; C: incorrect – the idea was to be rid of hyperinflation not to achieve it; D: incorrect – foreseen means to predict; E: incorrect – to conquer does not have this connotation.
Gabarito "B".

(Analista – BACEN – 2002 – FCC) In the main, the text deals with

(A) the North-American countries.
(B) the Asian policies in the world.
(C) the undeniable Brazilian nationalism.
(D) economic shifts in Latin America.
(E) the unchanged economic scenario.

(Interpretation) A: incorrect – Only mentioned as the source of the policy which were adopted by Latin America; B: incorrect – Asian countries/polices are only briefly mentioned; C: incorrect –It does not focus on Brazilian nationalism; D: **correct** – The title of the text and its content reflects this; E: incorrect – The opposite is true, the economic scenario has changed.
Gabarito "D".

Read the text below in order to answer the questions:

Capitalism reconsidered

Remember the triumph of Anglo-Saxon capitalism? Not many do. The nations that inspired the late-20th--century boom in global trade and profited most greatly from its advance no longer define its rules. What the radical individualists of the United States and Britain failed to recognize was how few poor nations had joined the global system by the turn of the millennium: two dozen at best. More than 100 were left out. Now, as more poor nations join the international trading game, they have increased their share of world trade by more than half. They are demanding a greater say in the global system, led by nations that most opposed the "Americanization" of global trade and culture: India, China, Brazil.

This new force looks to Europe for inspiration. As a result, the governors of globalization – the International Monetary Fund, World Bank and World Trade Organization – are no longer led by the United States, but by consensus, similar to the EU (European Union). The global rules are cracking down on multinationals that order mass layoffs or grow too powerful for local comfort. Global capitalism is now truly continental.

(Analista – BACEN – 2002 – FCC) According to the text, poor nations

(A) currently influence decisions in relation to global trade.
(B) no longer play a major role within the global trade context.
(C) have been leading the global trade boom for the last decade.
(D) will probably participate in the international trade game.
(E) have slowed the growth of international trade.

(Interpretation) A: correct – (paragraph 2) **'They are demanding a greater say in the global system'**. Paragraph 3 also states that the governors of globalization are no longer led by the United States but by consensus; B: incorrect – The opposite is true; C: incorrect – It cannot be said they lead the boom or for how long; D: incorrect – They already participate in it; E: incorrect – No evidence that they slow international trade growth.
Gabarito "A".

(Analista – BACEN – 2002 – FCC) According to the author, global capitalism

(A) was born in Asia.
(B) is undergoing changes.
(C) should exclude certain regions.
(D) encourages the monopoly.
(E) was refused by the USA.

(Interpretation) A: incorrect – This is not affirmed in the text; B: **correct** – The title of the text – 'Capitalism Reconsidered' shows that it is undergoing/experiencing changes. The context of the text provides details about the changes that are happening; C: incorrect – This is not affirmed in the text; D: incorrect – This is not affirmed in the text; E: incorrect – This is not affirmed in the text.
Gabarito "B".

(Analista – BACEN – 2002 – FCC) The text refers to the emerging role played by

(A) the USA along with Asia.
(B) India along with the USA.
(C) Africa along with the USA.
(D) the poor nations as well as by Europe.
(E) the USA along with Brazil.

(Interpretation) A: incorrect – The US has a declining role; B: incorrect – India is given as an example with Brazil and China as a country which rejected Americanization of global trade'; C: incorrect – Africa is not mentioned in the text; D: correct – **'Now, as more poor nations join the international trading game, they have increased their share of world trade by more than half'**, and **'This new force looks to Europe for inspiration'**; E: Brazil is given as an example with India and China as a country which rejected Americanization of global trade'.
Gabarito "D".

(Analista – BACEN – 2002 – FCC) According to the text,

(A) consensus has been achieved since the early 90s.
(B) Brazil kept its leading role during the 1980s and 1990s.
(C) rules might have been defined in relation to global trade.
(D) Americanization is unavoidable in the poorest regions.
(E) the EU serves as a model within the global trade context.

(Interpretation) A: incorrect – There is no evidence about consensus beign achieved since the early 90s; B: incorrect – This is not explicitly stated; C: incorrect – This is not stated in the text; D: incorrect – The contrary is true – India, China, and Brazil rejected Americanization; E: correct – **'This new force looks to Europe for inspiration'** The phrasal verb 'looks to' means to seek inspiration or guidance from someone/something.
Gabarito "E".

(Analista – BACEN – 2002 – FCC) The text mentions **mass layoffs**, which means

(A) the hiring of under-qualified employees.
(B) the huge increase of certain trade tariffs.
(C) the dismissal of numerous employees.
(D) the disregard for environmental issues.
(E) the disrespect for local legal requirements.

(**Vocabulary**) A: incorrect – No mention of workers having low levels of qualifications; B: incorrect – Layoffs does not mean this; C: correct – 'layoffs' means dismissing or suspending employees due to changes in company structure or lack of work. Mass layoffs would be large scale layoffs or redundancies. This is different form being fired or sacked – both of which carry a connotation of improper employee conduct; D: incorrect – Layoffs does not mean this; E: incorrect – Layoffs does not mean this.
Gabarito "C".

Read the text below in order to answer the questions:

Lower interest rates

Stockmarkets rose in expectation of the Federal Reserve's half-point cut in interest rates on November 6th to 1.25%, the lowest rate for more than 40 years. The following day, the European Central Bank (ECB) and the Bank of England decided not to cut their rates, but they are still expected to ease next month. However, investors' exuberance is odd, for interest rates are coming down because the world economy is in worse shape than had been hoped.

America's recovery is stalling, as consumers tighten their belts. In the euro area, consumer and business confidence are both on the wane. Although euro-area inflation is above the 2% ceiling set by the ECB, weak demand will push inflation down next year. The case for interest-rate cuts in both America and the euro area was strong, even though the ECB has not yet moved. But will rate cuts work?

(Analista – BACEN – 2002 – FCC) The text refers to the Federal Reserve's

(A) initiative to lower interest rates.
(B) future decision to reduce interest rates.
(C) intention to increase interest rates.
(D) 1.25% cut in interest rates.
(E) refusal to decrease interest rates.

(**Interpretation**) A: correct – Line 1 – **Stockmarkets rose in expectation of the Federal Reserve's half-point cut in interest rates on November 6th to 1.25%;** B: incorrect – The decision was not to be made in the future; C: incorrect – to cut rates means to decrease them; D: incorrect – The new rate was 1.25%. The cut was half a point; E: incorrect – The Federal Reserve was cutting/decreasing rates.
Gabarito "A".

(Analista – BACEN – 2002 – FCC) According to the text, "America's recovery is **stalling**", which means it is

(A) exuberant.
(B) amazing.
(C) miraculous.
(D) speedy.
(E) delayed.

(**Vocabulary**) A: incorrect – exuberant means unrestrained enthusiasm; B: incorrect – amazing means wonder; C: incorrect – miraculous means astounding; D: incorrect – speedy means swift; E: **correct** – to stall means to delay or cause to delay.
Gabarito "E".

(Analista – BACEN – 2002 – FCC) The expression "**on the wane**" in relation to consumer and business confidence means it is

(A) lost.
(B) invigorated.
(C) weakening.
(D) strengthened.
(E) endorsed.

(**Vocabulary**) A: incorrect – lost is the past tense of – to lose; B: incorrect – invigorate means to animate to give vigor or strength; C: **correct** – a period of decrease, decline or weakening; D: incorrect – waning means decreasing; E: incorrect – endorsed means to support or give approval.
Gabarito "C".

(Analista – BACEN – 2002 – FCC) The European Central Bank

(A) has been able to revive the international demand.
(B) might reduce its own interest rates.
(C) should have increased the interest rates.
(D) has prevented an increase in the interest rates.
(E) is likely to establish an inflation ceiling.

(**Interpretation**) A: incorrect – There is no mention of the ECB and international demand; B: correct – '**The European Central Bank (ECB) and the Bank of England decided not to cut their rates, but they are still expected to ease next month'**. – To ease in this context means to reduce interest rates. Still expected means there is an expectation they might do it; C: incorrect – This would imply they ought to have already done it; D: incorrect – No evidence to support this; E: incorrect – The ceiling/upper limit has already been established by the ECB. It is not an action that will take place in the future as this statement suggests.
Gabarito "B".

(Analista – BACEN – 2002 – FCC) The author

(A) predicts higher demand over the next years.
(B) analyses the need to cut bank loans.
(C) encourages the adoption of a looser fiscal policy.
(D) questions the effectiveness of rate cuts.
(E) looks into the increase in real debt burdens.

(**Interpretation**) A: incorrect – The opposite is true – the author is gloomy about business and consumer confidence; B: incorrect – The author analyses interest rates not bank loans; C: incorrect – This is too wide an assertion to say that this is correct; D: correct – '**But will rate cuts work?**' – this questions how effective they will be; E: incorrect – This is not raised in the text.
Gabarito "D".

Read the text below in order to answer the questions:

The world's three largest economies are limping. Emerging markets are drifting into financial crisis.

Emerson: Are we sliding into global recession?

Hormats: The risk is growing, but we are not there yet. Almost every economy on the globe is slowing down. We haven't seen this kind of sharp, synchronized downturn for years.

E: Is this the dark side of globalization?

H: You could say that. With the rapid increase in global trade and investment flows, growth in one country has a greater probability of contributing to growth in others. But the reverse is also true. When the world's largest economy experiences a sharp drop, that inevitably drags down others.

E: There are twin worries now: global recession and financial contagion in emerging markets. Is this more dangerous than the financial contagion of 1997-1998?

H: In 1997, a financial crisis in emerging markets led to recession in those economies. But most were able to export their way out, because the US and Europe were growing. Now all major economies are slowing down, as Argentina and Turkey are facing financial crisis. So yes, this situation is more dangerous for them. Even for the industrialized countries there is no locomotive. Countries cannot count on restoring growth by exporting a lot more to one another.

(Analista – BACEN – 2001 – FCC) According to the text,

(A) a slowdown in the US economy does not affect the global economy.
(B) the three largest economies are insulated from this global downturn.
(C) the economies of the world are closely linked and interdependent.
(D) globalization prevents financial contagion and global recession.
(E) emerging countries have constantly had the foresight to cut taxes.

(Interpretation) A: incorrect – The text states that economies are now interlinked and affect each other; B: incorrect – Insulated means protected. The text does not state this; C: **correct** – '**With the rapid increase in global trade and investment flows, growth in one country has a greater probability of contributing to growth in others. But the reverse is also true**'; D: incorrect – This is not stated in the text; E: incorrect –Taxes are not mentioned in the text.
Gabarito "C".

(Analista – BACEN – 2001 – FCC) The headline of the article states that "The world's three largest economies are limping", which means they are

(A) currently experiencing difficulties.
(B) exporting to emerging markets.
(C) finding domestic solutions.
(D) underpinning global growth.
(E) experiencing a high-tech investment boom.

(Interpretation) A: correct – to limp means to lack strength or firmness. This reflects that the economies are suffering and are not flourishing; B: incorrect – This is not reflected in the statement; C: incorrect – This is not reflected in the statement; D: incorrect – To underpin means to provide a foundation – limping contradicts this idea; E: incorrect – There is no mention of this in the text.
Gabarito "A".

(Analista – BACEN – 2001 – FCC) According to the interviewee,

(A) emerging countries are the ones which steer global economy.
(B) Argentina and Turkey have restored their internal growth.
(C) Europe has remained insulated from the actual global downturn.
(D) globalization has both its advantages and its drawbacks.
(E) the threat of financial contagion has been overcome.

(Interpretation) A: incorrect – to steer means to direct – In the context of globalization no single country is directing or steering the global economy; B: incorrect – The opposite is true. Both countries are facing financial crises; C: incorrect – The text says all major economies are slowing down, therefore Europe has not remained protected; D: **correct** – '**With the rapid increase in global trade and investment flows, growth in one country has a greater probability of contributing to growth in others. But the reverse is also true**'. Drawbacks means disadvantages; E: incorrect – overcome means to defeat. The financial disease has not been defeated.
Gabarito "D".

Read the text below in order to answer the questions:

Fed steers US rates lower by quarter point

The US Federal Reserve last night demonstrated its determination to steer the American economy away from recession when it cut its key interest rate for the seventh time this year and signalled that borrowing costs could fall again.

The Fed announced it was cutting its funds rate by a quarter of a point to 3.5 per cent, its lowest for seven years, and also reduced its largely symbolic discount rate. The discount rate fell a quarter of a point to 3 per cent, matching lows seen in the early 1990's.

In a statement released alongside the rate decision, the Fed reiterated its so-called "easing bias", a signal that rates are more likely to fall than rise, saying that the risks to the US economy remained "weighted mainly toward economic weakness".

The Fed said: "Business profits and capital spending continue to weaken and growth abroad is slowing, weighing on the US economy".

(Analista – BACEN – 2001 – FCC) According to the text, the US Federal Reserve

(A) might reduce its interest rate for the 7th time.
(B) has been cutting its interest rate 7 times a year.
(C) has been trying to guide the US economy towards recession.
(D) may soon announce its willingness to reduce interest rates.
(E) has decided to reduce its interest rates.

(Interpretation) A: incorrect – Might suggests possibility. In this case the action has already taken place; B: incorrect – It has cut its rates on seven separate occasions this year. Not seven times a year – which would suggest a habitual yearly practice; C: incorrect – It is trying to guide the U.S away from recession; D: incorrect – the action will not take place in the future; E: correct – It has already decided – '**it demonstrated its determination**' and '**when it cut its funds rate**'.
Gabarito "E".

(Analista – BACEN – 2001 – FCC) According to the author, such lows in the interest rates

(A) have occurred before.
(B) have weakened the world's economy.
(C) are likely to cause global recession.
(D) might resolve Europe's recession.
(E) have underpinned global growth.

(Interpretation) A: correct – '**The discount rate fell a quarter of a point to 3 per cent, matching lows seen in the early 1990's'.**; B: incorrect – No mention of weakening the world's economy; C: incorrect – There is no link made between interest rate lows and global recession; D: incorrect – Not stated in the text; E: incorrect – No link is made between interest rates and supporting global growth.
Gabarito "A".

(Analista – BACEN – 2001 – FCC) In connection with recession in the American economy, the aim of the Fed is to

(A) sustain it.
(B) bide its time.
(C) avert it.
(D) restore it.
(E) interpret it.

(Interpretation) A: incorrect – Sustain means to maintain or keep in existence; B: incorrect – This means to wait for further developments. The Fed is taking action; C: **correct** – avert means to prevent from occurring. The Fed is trying to steer or direct the economy away from recession; D: incorrect – The Fed is not trying to bring back a recession; E: incorrect – The Fed is taking action not trying to understand it.
Gabarito "C".

Shocks to the system

At the start of the year, it was not uncommon to hear businessmen saying that Brazil was enjoying its best economic conditions for a generation. The country appeared to be well on the way to a period of sustained economic expansion. Most economists were looking to another strong year of growth, with gross domestic product expanding by 4.5 per cent in 2001, on top of 4 per cent in 2000. Real interest rates were about to fall to single digits for the first time in decades.

However, within just a few months, the outlook for the Brazilian economy has deteriorated dramatically. A whole series of unexpected factors are to blame. "We have been confronted by a series of shocks", admits Armínio Fraga, president of the central bank.

The main cause of this turnaround has been the energy crisis. It had been well known for several years that Brazil ran the risk of power shortages because the expansion of capacity was not accompanying growth in demand, leaving the reservoirs that fuel the power stations precariously low. Yet, even with so much advance warning, the introduction of rationing still came as a surprise.

(Analista – BACEN – 2001 – FCC) The text suggests that businessmen

(A) have succeeded in importing foreign energy.
(B) have remained optimistic up until now.
(C) are to blame for the energy crisis.
(D) have been accompanying the steady Brazilian growth.
(E) expressed their optimism concerning Brazil's economy.

(Interpretation) A: incorrect – the text does not refer to foreign energy, or the import of it, at any moment. Energy is mentioned in the third paragraph, but the reference is about Brazilian energy and the shortage of it; B: incorrect – In the second paragraph, the text suggests that businessmen lost their optimism due to the "**series of shocks**" that have deteriorated the outlook of the Brazilian economy; C: incorrect – the text does not explicitly place blame for the energy crisis. It suggest that the reason for the crisis lies in the lack of capacity to meet demand, but no direct blame is given to businessmen. Such an inference would be too subjective in this case; D: incorrect – Businessmen have commented on the steady growth in Brazil. No evidence to say they have coexisted or acted a companion to the growth; E: correct – In the first sentence, the text clearly states that *"it was **not uncommon to hear businessmen** saying that Brazil was enjoying its best economic conditions for a generation."* If we could **hear** them talking about Brazil's economy, then it is obvious they were **expressing** themselves.
Gabarito "E".

(Analista – BACEN – 2001 – FCC) Concerning the Brazilian economy, the year 2001 has been

(A) disappointing.
(B) predictable.
(C) invaluable.
(D) satisfactory.
(E) profitable.

(Interpretation) A: correct – In the second paragraph, the text clearly states that "**within a few months**" – that is, early in the year – "*the outlook for the Brazilian economy has deteriorated dramatically*". Thus, the economy in 2001 did not live up to expectations; B: incorrect – In the second and third sentences, the language used suggests that expectations were for a positive outcome – *"The country **appeared** to be well on the way"* / *"Most economists **were looking** to another strong year"*–, but the outcome was negative (as stated in the second paragraph); C: incorrect – The word "invaluable" can be misleading as it means "impossible to establish a price" or "helpful". On the other hand, the word "valueless" means to have none or little value; D: incorrect – In the second paragraph, the quote from Armínio Fraga, *"we **have been confronted** by a series of shocks"* clearly shows that no one was satisfied with the situation; E: incorrect – In the second paragraph, the text refers to *dramatic deterioration*, which does not suggest any idea of profit.
Gabarito "A".

(Analista – BACEN – 2001 – FCC) Which aspect is not mentioned in the text?

(A) Power shortages.
(B) Environmental impact.
(C) Rationing.
(D) Economic expansion.
(E) Gross domestic product.

(Interpretation) A: incorrect – In the third paragraph, the second sentence explicitly mentions "power shortages"; B: correct – There is no mention of environmental impact in the text; C: incorrect – In the third paragraph, the last sentence explicitly mentions "rationing"; D: – incorrect – In the first paragraph, the second sentence explicitly mentions "economic expansion"; E: incorrect – In the first paragraph, the third sentence explicitly mentions "gross domestic product".
Gabarito "B".

(Analista – BACEN – 2001 – FCC) According to the text,

(A) the energy crisis made interest rates decrease.
(B) the president of the central bank predicted the crisis.
(C) Brazil was able to avert the energy crisis.
(D) more than one element affected Brazil's economy.
(E) advance warning could have avoided the crisis.

(Interpretation) A e B: incorrects; C: incorrect – In the third paragraph, the last sentence, *"Yet, even with so much advance warning, **the introduction of rationing still came as a surprise**"* shows that the problem was not averted. It was a surprise, but Brazil did in fact suffer from rationing; D: correct – In the second paragraph, the quote from Armínio Fraga, *"we have been confronted by **a series** of shocks"* clearly shows that Brazil's economy was affected by more than one element; E: incorrect – In the third paragraph, the last sentence, *"Yet, **even with so much advance warning**, the introduction of rationing still came as a surprise"* shows that the crisis was inevitable. The collocation *"even with"* is equivalent to "despite", which does not suggest that the advance warning could have changed the outcome, but rather that the advance warning had no chance of preventing the crisis.

Gabarito "D".

"I had never thought of archiving websites..."

August 5, 2009 – Following a successful pilot program during the spring of 2008, the Library of Congress, Internet Archive and California Digital Library initiated a web archiving program that explored archiving
5 websites from the perspective of students in elementary, middle and high schools. Two Library activities supported the pilot: the National Digital Information Infrastructure and Preservation Program and the Teaching with Primary Sources program.
10 The Web Archiving Program gives students the opportunity to think about history by selecting sources for ongoing research use. Teens and younger students select and capture web content using Internet Archive's Archive-It service, creating "time capsules" of what is
15 important to them to represent their current lives. During the 2008-09 school year, students from ten different schools in nine states participated in the program. Over 1,700 websites and 233 million URLs, or objects, were collected during the year, totaling 11.7
20 terabytes of data. The Internet Archive noted that 96 percent of the websites selected by students have not been archived by any other Archive-It partner, and 24 percent of the websites are not in the Internet Archive's general archive. Examples include websites for the Iowa
25 Farm Bureau, Women's Adventures in Science, and How to Make a Sock Monkey. In total, 68 web collections were created – including a Dancing Guide and Historical Black College Search collection – and immediately accessible on the Archive-It website.
30 Students and teachers alike found the program eyeopening. Student comments included "choosing the websites was really fun because it let everyone be creative and really think about what teenagers enjoy today," and "I had never thought of archiving websites,
35 even though in this day and age we use them as much as and more than books." Teacher Emily Patterson of George Washington High School in Charleston, West Virginia said, "I think it was certainly an enriching experience. I like that it allowed them to see and examine
40 their lives and Internet content as history in the making." "Most of the decisions being made about what gets archived have been made by adults," said Cheryl Lederle, educational resources specialist at the Library of Congress. "Student users are arguably one of the largest
45 users of the Internet proportionately, and their voices weren't being heard."

The benefits of their work might not be felt for generations to come, when 21st century adolescent culture and society are being researched. However, the
50 project has served as an informative psychological tool to some degree. "We have this image of kids just going on the Internet and cruising all these sites. The project has shown that students visit a select number of sites frequently, as opposed to browsing everything that's out
55 there. The Web sites that students put in, people can research 20 years from now."
According to Lederle, the variety in the types of sites chosen by the 10 classrooms has more to do with age than geography, meaning students in the same age
60 groups are likely to preserve similar sites.
The student archive is not being widely used yet, "but by the end of this year we'll have a total of 11 partnerships," Lederle said. That's "a pretty robust offering, and then we can step back and see what its
65 value is to researchers."

Adapted from: http://www.digitalpreservation.gov/news/2009/20090805news_article_k-12_archiving_program.html
http://www.zwire.com/site/tab1.cfm?newsid=20290909&BRD=2755&PAG=461&dept_id=592709&rfi=6

(Técnico – BNDES – 2010 – CESGRANRIO) The main purpose of this article is to

(A) analyze adolescents' interest in the Internet.
(B) contrast adults' and youngsters' choices of websites.
(C) prove that students in each location will navigate in different sites.
(D) explain the web archiving program and its relevance.
(E) justify the need for a psychological study of students' Internet use.

(Interpretation) A: incorrect – According to the text, the archiving program is aimed at recording adolescents' interest in the Internet for future researchers. The article, however, does not analyze their interest. The article explains the program, how it works and its relevance. Maybe in the future, researchers will analyze their interests; B: incorrect – The text does not contrast choices of websites, but rather focuses on the choices made by adolescents. The only contrast mentioned is that concerning decisions on what gets archived (lines 41-46), but this has no specific reference to choices of websites; C: incorrect – In the last paragraph, the text clearly states that "the variety of types of sites (...) has more to do with age than geography" (lines 57-59); D: correct – The first and second paragraphs explain the program, while its relevance is mentioned in the third paragraph, specifically talking about "*history in the making*" (line 40) and the students' voices being heard (line 45-46); E: incorrect – The article does not clearly state that there is an actual "need for a psychological study of students' Internet use". In the fourth paragraph, the text mentions that "*the project has served as an informative psychological tool*" (lines 49-50), but there is not reference to the need for a study. The needs and the value of the project are being left for researchers to define in the future (lines 64-65).

Gabarito "D".

(Técnico – BNDES – 2010 – CESGRANRIO) Websites are considered 'time capsules' because

(A) they reveal what the adolescents of this generation are like and what they value.
(B) they will expose that teenagers from the early 21st century could not use the web for research.
(C) the children will be adults in the next century and their past habits will not interest historians.

(D) the content of the web pages has lasted for many centuries, so it is correct to use the expression.
(E) the early 21st century kids research about journeys to past eras and learn historical events in general.

(Interpretation) A: correct – In the second paragraph, the text clearly states that *"creating 'time capsules' of **what is important to them to represent their current lives**"* (lines 14-15); B: incorrect – In the third paragraph, one of the examples of student comments clearly states that *"I had never thought of archiving websites, even though **in this day and age we use them as much as and more than books**."* This shows that websites are able to use the Internet as a research tool; C: incorrect – In the fifth paragraph, the text clearly states that in the "*21st century adolescent culture and society*" will be undergoing research (lines 48-49). Historians are of the professions that usually studies culture and society in a specific timeframe; D: incorrect – In the fifth paragraph, the text clearly references the use of the "time-capsule" for future research; E: incorrect – While the second paragraph mentions some of the archives that 21st century kids research, there is nothing explicitly in the text concerning journeys to the past.
Gabarito "A".

(Técnico – BNDES – 2010 – CESGRANRIO) In terms of reference, it is correct to affirm that

(A) "Over 1,700 websites…" (line 18) – refers to the number of websites visited by college students in the US.
(B) "…11.7 terabytes…" (lines 19-20) – refers to the volume of memory used in archiving the chosen websites.
(C) "…96 percent of the websites…" (lines 20-21) – refers to the share of websites that were eliminated by students.
(D) "…24 percent of the websites…" (lines 22-23) – refers to the websites considered extremely relevant by educational specialists.
(E) "…68 web collections…" (line 26) – refers to the number of sites that were included in the archive.

(Interpretation) A: incorrect – In the second paragraph, the text clearly states that this is the number of websites that were collected – *"Over **1,700 websites** and 233 million URLs, or, objects, **were collected** during the year"*, not the number visited by college students; B: correct – The measurement "terabytes" has this specific meaning; C: incorrect – In the second paragraph, the text clearly states that this number refers to the *"percent of websites selected by students that **have not been archived** by any Archive-it partner"* (lines 21-22). They "have not been archived" – this does not mean they have been eliminated; D: incorrect – In the second paragraph, the text clearly states that this number refers to the percent of websites that *"are not in the Internet Archive's general archive"* (lines 23-24). This does not refer to relevance of the websites in any way; E: incorrect – In the second paragraph, the text clearly states that this number refers to the number of "web collections", not to the number of websites (lines 26-27).
Gabarito "B".

(Técnico – BNDES – 2010 – CESGRANRIO) The sentence "Students and teachers alike found the program eye-opening." (lines 30-31) means that

(A) students and teachers considered that having new instructors opened their minds.
(B) students and teachers were happy to be able to use websites and not books.
(C) neither students nor teachers enjoyed the innovative experience.
(D) not all students liked searching the web for educational sites.
(E) both students and teachers considered the program a revealing experience.

(Vocabulary) A: incorrect – The excerpt makes no reference to new instructors; B: incorrect – the excerpt does not mention a preference for the Internet over the use of books; C: incorrect – The word "*alike*" is not an antonym of 'like'. It means "in a similar fashion". The excerpt states that both students and teachers like the program more or less equally; D: incorrect – The word "*alike*" is not an antonym of 'like'. It means "in a similar fashion". The excerpt states that both students and teachers like the program more or less equally; E: correct – The word "eyeopening" means that something is a revelation, hence, a revealing experience. Author's Note: The term (noun) "eyeopener" is much more common than the gerund form.
Gabarito "E".

(Técnico – BNDES – 2010 – CESGRANRIO) According to Cheryl Lederle, the web archiving program has proved that

(A) students did not like to be forced to search the web for new information.
(B) students from the 10 classrooms analyzed showed a clear preference for researching geography sites.
(C) students usually consult a limited number of preferred websites when browsing the Internet.
(D) the benefits of this project will certainly be felt soon in the educational system and in society in general.
(E) the websites which the Library of Congress selected for archiving were not adequate for researchers.

(Interpretation) A: incorrect – In the third paragraph, the text shows that students enjoyed searching the web for new information. *"(…) choosing the websites was **really fun** because it **let** everyone be creative"* (lines 31-33). Nobody was forced to do anything; B: incorrect – In the last paragraph, the text clearly states that *"sites chosen by the 10 classrooms has more to do with age than geography, meaning students **in the same age groups are likely to preserve similar sites**"* (lines 58-60). This means that geography was not a focus of the research, and that student preferences were connected to age, not geography; C: correct – In the fourth paragraph, Lederle is quoted as saying *"The project has shown that students visit **a select number of sites** frequently, **as opposed to browsing everything that's out there**."* This clearly shows that the number of sites visited is limited; D: incorrect – Lederle, in the fourth paragraph, clearly states that *"the benefits of their work **might not be felt for generations to come, when 21st century adolescent culture and society are being researched**"* (lines 47-49). This means that there is no certainty concerning when the benefits will be felt. Also, the benefits will not necessarily be felt in the educational system or in society in general. There is no mention of what area will benefit from the program; E: incorrect – In the third paragraph, Lederle, who works for the Library of Congress, clearly states that *"Most of the decisions being made about what gets archived have been **made by adults**"* (lines 41-42). This does not suggest that the sites were not adequate for researchers. This means that Lederle believes that other people, in this case students, should be involved in the decisions on what sites to archive.
Gabarito "C".

(Técnico – BNDES – 2010 – CESGRANRIO) Based on the meanings in the text, mark the only option in which the two words are synonymous.

(A) "...successful..." (line 1) – unprofitable.
(B) "...capture..." (line 13) – release.
(C) "...accessible..." (line 29) – available.
(D) "...certainly..." (line 38) – doubtfully.
(E) "...preserve..." (line 60) – throw away.

(Vocabulary) A: incorrect – The word "successful" has a positive meaning, while "unprofitable" is generally used in a negative sense; B: incorrect – The word "capture" means to "seize" or "take ownership/control of", while "release" means "liberate" or "let go of something"; C: correct – Both these words mean "easy to reach" or "reachable"; D: incorrect – These two words are almost direct opposites: "certainly" means "with no doubt", while "doubtfully" means "full of doubt"; E: incorrect – These two words are almost direct opposites: "preserve" means "keep", while "throw away" means "discard".
Gabarito "C".

(Técnico – BNDES – 2010 – CESGRANRIO) Check the only alternative in which the **boldfaced** expression does NOT add a contrastive idea to the sentence.

(A) "...**even though** in this day and age we use them..." (line 35)
(B) " '...we use them **as much as** and more than books.' " (lines 35-36)
(C) "**However**, the project has served as an informative psychological tool..." (lines 49-50)
(D) "The student archive is not being widely used **yet**," (line 61)
(E) " ...'**but** by the end of this year we'll have a total of 11 partnerships,' " (lines 62-63)

(Grammar) A: incorrect – The expression "even though" is a subordinating conjunction used to show concession or contrast. Here, it contrasts the idea that archiving websites has never crossed the student's mind (previous clause) with the current usefulness of websites; B: correct – The expression "as much as" is a comparison of quantity which expresses "equality", not a contrast; C: incorrect – "however" is a word used to show contrast. Here, it contrasts the idea that the project has not been useful yet (previous sentence) and the fact that it has been useful in some way (as an informative psychological tool); D: Gabarito Oficial – incorrect / Nosso Gabarito – correct – In this sentence, the word "yet" has a meaning of "continuity", similar to "still". In this sentence, the word "yet" does not have a contrastive idea, but it can have a contrastive meaning when used in a similar way to "but" or "however" in coordinated clauses. E.g. The student archive is not being widely used; **yet, it will be soon**; E: incorrect – The word "but" is usually used to show contrast. In this sentence it shows a contrast between the archive not being used, and when it will be used.
Gabarito "B".

(Técnico – BNDES – 2010 – CESGRANRIO) The quote in the title, "I had never thought of archiving websites..." can be attributed to

(A) Emily Patterson, who was teaching students about the importance of books.
(B) Cheryl Lederle, Library of Congress specialist who created the archiving program.
(C) a teacher from George Washington High School, when commenting on the psychological effects of the project.
(D) an educational specialist who worked for the Library of Congress and participated in the project.
(E) one of the enthusiastic teenagers who was involved in collecting varied material for the program.

(Interpretation) A, B, C, D e E: In the third paragraph, the text clearly states that this comment was made by students: "**Student comments** included 'choosing...today' and 'I had never thought of archiving websites'" (lines 31-34)
Gabarito "E".

Social innovation: Good for you, good for me

Ethical Corporation, 10 April 2008 World Business Council for Sustainable Development

Big firms are joining the queue to follow in Muhammad Yunus's footsteps by developing businesses designed to fix social ills.
Muhammad Yunus has for more than 30 years
5 challenged business leaders to find radical ways of creating new markets in poor countries. The Nobel Peace Prize winner's latest book, explores how big companies can invest in external partners to develop products and services that will benefit the poor. Yunus outlines the concept of a
10 "social business", which he defines as a "no loss, no dividend" company with social objectives. Social business ventures are set up by a "social entrepreneur", who combines the risk-taking of enterprise with an explicit mission to address urgent problems, such as access to
15 healthcare, sanitation, education and so on. The new products and services that these inventive individuals devise are examples of "social innovation".
Unlike charities, social businesses do not need to keep applying to governments or foundations for grants.
20 They support themselves by selling goods and services at cost, or at a small profit – all of which is reinvested to fund their expansion. But to do this, social entrepreneurs must find investors willing to help take a new idea to scale. Now multinational companies are emerging as an important
25 source of funding for social innovation. Big companies are looking for exciting and potentially lucrative new ways to meet their sustainability goals.
The archetypal social business is Danone Grameen Foods, a joint venture set up two years ago between
30 Yunus's own Grameen group and the French food and drink multinational Danone. The partners have developed an affordable, fortified yoghurt for poor children in Bangladesh. The yoghurt is high in calcium and other nutrients that children lack. It is cheap because it is
35 produced locally, cutting down on expensive refrigeration. As a social business, Danone Grameen Foods measures its success in terms of "social dividend" or "social return on investment" – its positive impact on the rate of market failure that it was set up to redress. In this case,
40 the dividend and return are the improvement in child health in Bangladesh and the number of jobs its activities supports. The first yoghurt processing plant in Bogra will in three to four years support 1,600 jobs, while the company plans to build 50 plants over the next ten years.
45 Investing in social entrepreneurs can boost a company's reputation for being responsible in a way that limits the risks of investing in new products, especially when these could take years to become commercially viable.
50 Alternatively, big companies can buy up innovative firms that have already done the groundwork on products with social benefits and commercial potential. Dow Chemical, for example, in 2006 added three water purification technologies to its Dow Water Solutions
55 portfolio when it acquired Chinese firm Zhejiang Omex Environmental Engineering. Dow backs up this work with its sponsorship of Blue Planet Run, a non-profit group

that raises money for clean drinking water projects in developing countries.

One reason why partnerships between companies and social entrepreneurs are yet to take off could be mutual ignorance of each other. "This is quite new territory for business," says International Business Leaders' Forum director Ros Tennyson, who advises companies on partnerships. "Most do not know what the term 'social entrepreneurship' means." She says business must listen to social entrepreneurs "if it is to get beyond simply philanthropic funding of a good idea". However, she adds, social entrepreneurs, too, must be flexible and understanding of companies. "They need to develop a genuine interest in business drivers and priorities in order to conduct purposeful and equitable conversations."

Disponível em: http://www.wbcsd.org/plugins/DocSearch/details.asp?type=DocDet&ObjectId=Mjk1MTI

(Técnico – BNDES – 2008 – CESGRANRIO) The main purpose of this text is to

(A) introduce examples of highly prosperous industrial plants.
(B) complain against Muhammed Yunus's idea of social innovation.
(C) explain the concept of social business and introduce its main characteristics.
(D) discuss the innovative water purification technologies developed in China.
(E) describe how to increase jobs and put an end to famine in Bangladesh in four years.

(Interpretation) A: incorrect – Two examples (Danone and Dow) are given to sustain the argument for social business. This is not the main purpose of the text, but rather supporting ideas aimed at sustaining the main argument; B: incorrect – The text does not complain about Yunus's ideas. It offers some constructive criticism in terms of what is necessary for it to prosper; C: correct – The text, especially the second paragraph, gives an overview of what "social business" is. The other paragraphs use examples to introduce its main characteristics; D: incorrect – The water technology in China is used as an example to support the main idea of the text: social business; E: incorrect – This is given as an example of the result of good social business. It is a supporting idea, not the main purpose. Gabarito "C".

(Técnico – BNDES – 2008 – CESGRANRIO) It is NOT true that Muhammad Yunus

(A) wrote a book to explain how some companies can partner with larger corporations to produce goods or services that will help the needy.
(B) has been a leader in creating innovative products or services for poor nations for more than three decades.
(C) has long been devoted to social businesses in order to help poor communities in relevant areas as healthcare and education.
(D) was awarded the Nobel Peace Prize for his efforts in improving the life of poor citizens through business ventures.
(E) is the archetype of an investor who is looking for high profits in exploring the poor.

(Interpretation) A: incorrect – In the second paragraph, the text clearly states that "**The Nobel Peace Prize winner's** latest book **explores how big companies can invest in external partners to develop products and services that will benefit the poor**" (lines 6-9); B: incorrect – In the second paragraph, the text states that "Muhammad Yunus has for **more than 30 years** challenged business leaders to find radical ways of creating new markets in poor countries" (lines 4-6) and "(...) **to develop products and services that will benefit the poor**" (lines 6-9); C: incorrect – In the second paragraph, the text states that "Muhammad Yunus has for **more than 30 years** challenged business leaders to find radical ways of creating new markets in poor countries" (lines 4-6) and "(...) an explicit mission **to address urgent problems**, such as access to **healthcare**, sanitation, **education** and so on" (lines 13-15); D: incorrect – In the second paragraph, the text clearly states that "**The Nobel Peace Prize winner's** latest book **explores how big companies can invest in external partners to develop products and services that will benefit the poor**" (lines 6-9). Given the work and efforts made by Muhammad Yunus, it is reasonable to infer and understand that the Nobel Prize was awarded for these reasons, even though this is not explicit in the text; E: correct – Muhammad Yunus is not an archetypal investor. He seeks archetypal investors. In the fourth paragraph, the text states that "The **archetypal social business is Danone Grameen Foods**, a joint venture set up two years ago between drink multinational Danone" (lines 28-31). This does not mean that Muhammad Yunus is an archetypal investor, but rather that the joint venture represents an archetypal social business. Gabarito "E".

(Técnico – BNDES – 2008 – CESGRANRIO) According to the text, social businesses

(A) need to be supported by grants or government funding to be able to survive.
(B) have often small margins of earnings because they aim at making a positive impact on the social environment of the region invested in.
(C) have multinational companies as important partners to support potentially lucrative ways to explore social misery.
(D) provide very costly products and services because the businessmen are only interested in material gains.
(E) should only be implemented in Asian countries, where the governments are incapable of providing the necessary access of poor citizens to healthcare, sanitation and education.

(Interpretation) A: incorrect; B: Gabarito Oficial correct / Nosso Gabarito incorrect – In the third paragraph, the text states that "They support themselves by selling goods and services at cost, or **at a small profit** – all of which is reinvested to fund their expansion" (lines 20-22), which makes the first part of the question correct. However, the text is not explicit as to why they have small profits. It is not explicit that this is "because they aim at making a positive impact on the social environment of the region invested in." This affirmation is contradicted even further by the sentence "Big companies are looking for exciting and potentially lucrative new ways to meet their sustainability goals" (lines 25-27). This suggests that big companies are not aimed "at making an impact on the social environment of the region invested in", but rather that they will happily invest as long as it becomes profitable. Compared to the options available, this answer is somewhat correct, but not entirely; C: incorrect – In the third paragraph, the text states that "Big companies **are looking for** exciting and potentially lucrative new ways to meet their sustainability goals" (lines 25-27). This means that multinationals are not yet partners; D: incorrect – In the third paragraph, the text states that "They support themselves by selling goods and services **at cost**, or **at a small profit** – all of which is **reinvested to fund their expansion**" (lines 20-22). This suggests that products are sold with no profit (at cost), or with very little profit. It also suggests that businessmen are not only interested in material gains; they are interested in expanding their social business; E: incorrect – The two examples given in the text, Bangladesh and China, are located in Asia; however, the text does not suggest that social businesses should concentrate in these areas; nor does the text suggest that governments in Asian countries are "incapable of providing the necessary access of poor citizens to healthcare, sanitation and education".

Gabarito "B".

(Técnico – BNDES – 2008 – CESGRANRIO) Danone Grameen Foods is a good example of social business because it

(A) produces yoghurt, which is children's favorite food, in assorted flavors.
(B) opened an yoghurt processing plant in Bangladesh that will impact the nutritional needs of the children in the region.
(C) was very successful in changing the official politics for adult healthcare in Bangladesh.
(D) is showing positive results in the market and will soon pay dividends to the investors.
(E) will soon employ millions of people living in Bogra and in other 50 Bangladeshi cities.

(Interpretation) A: incorrect – Danone Grameen Foods does in fact produce yoghurt, but the text does not mention the children's preference for yoghurt, nor the flavors available; B: correct – In the fourth paragraph, the text states "The partners have developed an affordable, fortified **yoghurt for poor children in Bangladesh**. The yoghurt is **high in calcium and other nutrients that children lack**" (lines 31-34); C: incorrect – The text makes no reference to adult healthcare in Bangladesh; D: incorrect – In the fourth paragraph, the text states "The first yoghurt processing plant in Bogra will in three to four years **support 1,600 jobs, while the company plans to build 50 plants** over the next ten years" (lines 42-44). To measure positive results, social business uses "its **success** in terms of "social dividend" or "social return on investment" – its **positive impact on the rate of market failure that it was set up to redress**" (lines 37-39). With these two sentences, we can infer that there are positive results (more jobs). However, there is no mention of dividend payments to investors; E: incorrect – In the fourth paragraph, the text states "The first yoghurt processing plant in Bogra will in three to four years **support 1,600 jobs, while the company plans to build 50 plants** over the next ten years" (lines 42-44). This shows that there are no plans to employ millions of people. The 50 plants are not necessarily going to be built in different cities.

Gabarito "B".

(Técnico – BNDES – 2008 – CESGRANRIO) Ros Tennyson, International Business Leaders' Forum director, believes that

(A) the majority of businessmen are familiar with the term 'social entrepreneurship' but have refused to do business in this new territory.
(B) it is important to see social entrepreneurship exclusively as a means of philanthropy without any intention of earning profit.
(C) most social entrepreneurs are not ready to develop an interest in original business partnerships because they do not believe in new priorities.
(D) social entrepreneurs and investors should learn more about each other so as to establish fruitful partnerships.
(E) social businesses must only emerge in developing countries where no other companies exist, with the aim of developing the nation's economy.

(Interpretation) A: incorrect – In the last paragraph, Ros Tennyson is quoted as saying "This is quite new territory for business (...). **Most [businesses] do not know what the term 'social entrepreneurship' means.**" (lines 62-66). This confirms that the majority of businessmen are **not** familiar with the term 'social entrepreneurship'; B: incorrect – In the last paragraph, the text affirms that Ros Tennyson said that "business must listen to social entrepreneurs "**if it is to get beyond simply philanthropic funding** of a good idea" (lines 66-68). The term "**get beyond**" suggest that philanthropic funding is **not desirable** in this context. Hence, it is important to see social entrepreneurship as something **different from philanthropic funding**; C: incorrect – In the last paragraph, Ros Tennyson is quoted as saying "**They [social entrepreneurs] need to develop a genuine interest in business drivers** and priorities in order to conduct purposeful and equitable conversations" (lines 70-72). This suggests what social entrepreneurs should do. It does not confirm that social entrepreneurs are not ready to develop partnerships; D: correct – In the last paragraph, Ros Tennyson is quoted as saying "She says **business must listen to social entrepreneurs** "if it is to get beyond simply philanthropic funding of a good idea" (lines 66-68). This idea is complemented when she is quoted as saying "However, she adds, **social entrepreneurs, too, must be flexible and understanding of companies**" (lines 68-70). This confirms that social entrepreneurs and investors should learn more about each other; E: incorrect – In the text, Ros Tennyson is not quoted as saying where she believes social businesses should be induced, nor does she say anything about the purpose of their businesses. She merely talks about how to approach the idea of negotiating a partnership, an area in which she is a specialist.

Gabarito "D".

(Técnico – BNDES – 2008 – CESGRANRIO) Which option expresses an accurate relationship between the items?

(A) "address" (line 14) and *deal with* are antonyms.
(B) "expansion" (line 22) is the opposite of *growth*.
(C) "looking for" (line 26) means the same as *searching for*.
(D) "affordable" (line 32) and *expensive* are synonymous.
(E) "cutting down on" (line 35) and *reducing* reflect contradictory ideas.

(Vocabulary) A: incorrect – "address" and "deal with" are synonyms; B: incorrect – "expansion" and "growth" are synonyms; C: correct – "looking for" and "searching "for" are synonyms; D: incorrect – "affordable" and "expensive" are antonyms; E: incorrect – "cutting down" and "reducing" are synonymous.

Gabarito "C".

(Técnico – BNDES – 2008 – CESGRANRIO) The **boldfaced** item introduce a purpose in

(A) "They need to develop a genuine interest in business drivers and priorities **in order to** conduct purposeful and equitable conversations." (lines 70-72)
(B) "**Alternatively**, big companies can buy up innovative firms that have already done the groundwork on products with social benefits and commercial potential." (lines 50-52)
(C) "It is cheap **because** it is produced locally, cutting down on expensive refrigeration." (lines 34-35)
(D) "**But** to do this, social entrepreneurs must find investors willing to help take a new idea to scale." (lines 22-23)
(E) "**Unlike** charities, social businesses do not need to keep applying to governments or foundations for grants." (lines 18-19).

(Grammar) A: correct – The term "**in order to**" is aimed at showing the purpose for the need to develop a genuine interest in business drivers". This is a common term to show purpose; B: incorrect – The adverb "**Alternatively**" is not used to show purpose, but rather a contrast; C: incorrect – The term "**because**" shows the reason it is cheap, not the purpose; D: incorrect – the word "**but**" is used to show a contrast rather than a purpose; E: incorrect – The word "**unlike**" shows the idea of difference or dissimilarity, not purpose.

Gabarito "A".

(Técnico – BNDES – 2008 – CESGRANRIO) Mark the sentence in which "take off" has the same meaning as in "One reason why partnerships between companies and social entrepreneurs are yet to **take off** could be mutual ignorance of each other." (lines 60-62)

(A) Take off your coat and stay for a while.
(B) He took 20 percent off the original price as I had a discount card.
(C) I'm taking Thursday off because I'm moving to a new house.
(D) She just took off without saying goodbye to anyone in the room.
(E) That actor's career took off after that successful movie.

(Vocabulary) A: incorrect – The phrasal verb "**take off**" in the sentence on lines 60-62 has the meaning of "**to be successful**". The use of the phrasal verb in question A means "**to remove**". That is, "**Remove** your coat…"; B: incorrect – The phrasal verb "**take off**" in the sentence on lines 60-62 has the meaning of "**to be successful**". The use of the phrasal verb in question B means "**to deduct**". That is, "He **deducted** 20 percent off the original price…"; C: incorrect – The phrasal verb "**take off**" in the sentence on lines 60-62 has the meaning of "**to be successful**". The use of the phrasal verb in question C means "**to not work**". That is, "**I will not work on** Thursday because…"; D: incorrect – The phrasal verb "**take off**" in the sentence on lines 60-62 has the meaning of "**to be successful**". The use of the phrasal verb in question D means "**to leave**". That is, "She **left** without saying goodbye…"; E: correct – The phrasal verb "**take off**" in the sentence on lines 60-62 has the meaning of "**to be successful**", as it does when referring to the actor's career. That is, "That actor's career **was successful** after that …".

Gabarito "E".

Read text I and answer the questions.

Nutrition and Older Persons in Brazil:
A Human Rights Perspective

Brazil, along with many other countries in the developing world, faces an epidemiological transition in a scenario characterized by gross fertility rates as low as 2.3 and a continually rising life expectancy to 67 years (63 for men and
5 71 for women). On the one hand, this is good news; on the other hand, however, it translates into a fast-growing older population which presents society with major social challenges. Foremost among these challenges is to guarantee that older persons have access to adequate food and nutrition
10 – their basic and fundamental human right.

(http://www.unsystem.org/scn/archives/scnnews19/ch20.htm)

(Técnico Legislativo – Senado – 2008 – FGV) The text informs that life expectancy in Brazil is

(A) going down.
(B) going back.
(C) going up.
(D) going still.
(E) going away.

(Interpretation) A: incorrect – The expression "going down" is used to refer to decrease, not an idea of increase; B: incorrect – The expression "going back" is used to refer to return, not an idea of increase; C: correct – On line 4, the text clearly states that there is a "continually **rising** life expectancy to 67 years". "Rising", here, means "going up"; D: incorrect – The expression "going still" is used to refer to continuity, not an idea of increase; E: incorrect – The expression "going away" is used to refer to departure, not an idea of increase.

Gabarito "C".

(Técnico Legislativo – Senado – 2008 – FGV) The news reported is

(A) mostly irrelevant.
(B) both good and bad.
(C) neither fresh nor old.
(D) totally unwelcome.
(E) definitely reassuring.

(Interpretation) A: incorrect – The text argues in favor of providing older people "basic and fundamental human rights" in the form of "food and nutrition". In the text, this is a considered a major social challenge. Thus, it is not irrelevant; B: correct – The expressions "on the one hand" and "on the other hand" are used to show two sides of an argument. The positive side is the rising life expectancy, while the negative side is the fast-growing society; C: incorrect – There is no reference to the date the text was published. While the content seems up-to-date, it would be a risk to affirm the "age" of this text; D: incorrect – The fact the text presents good news means that it is most probably welcomed by older people; E: incorrect – While a continuously rising life expectancy is most definitely reassuring, the negative aspect of the text removes any guarantees and reduces the weight of the "reassuring" news. The text is equally reassuring and disheartening. Hence, answer B is a better option.

Gabarito "B".

(Técnico Legislativo – Senado – 2008 – FGV) According to the text, the most important challenge is to see that old people have

(A) proper nourishment.
(B) warm clothing.
(C) good housing.
(D) instant help.
(E) quality medicare.

(Interpretation) A: correct – On line 8-9, the text clearly states that "**Foremost** among these challenges is to guarantee that older persons **have access to adequate food and nutrition**". The word "**foremost**" means "most important"; B: incorrect – The text mentions nothing about "warm clothing"; C: incorrect – The text mentions nothing about "good housing"; D: incorrect – The text mentions nothing about "instant help"; E: incorrect – The text mentions nothing about "quality medicare".

Gabarito "A".

(Técnico Legislativo – Senado – 2008 – FGV) In "major social challenges" (lines 7-8) challenges implies an action that is

(A) easy.
(B) fast.
(C) slow.
(D) angry.
(E) difficult.

(Vocabulary) A: incorrect – The word "challenges", in the quoted section, does not suggest the level of difficulty (easy) of the action; B: incorrect – The word "challenges", in the quoted section, does not suggest the speed (fast) of the action; C: incorrect – The word "challenges", in the quoted section, does not suggest the speed (slow) of the action; D: incorrect – The word "challenges", in the

(Técnico Legislativo – Senado – 2008 – FGV) In "on the other hand, however, it translates…" (lines 5-6) on the other hand brings an idea of

(A) opposition.
(B) similarity.
(C) consequence.
(D) addition.
(E) control.

(Grammar) A: correct – The expression "on the other hand" is used to show the other side, or the "opposite" side of an argument; B: incorrect – The expression "on the other hand" is used to show the other side, or the "opposite" side of an argument. The word "similarity" is an antonym for opposition; C: incorrect – The expression "on the other hand" is used to show the other side, or the "opposite" side of an argument. The word "consequence" has an idea of result; D: incorrect – The expression "on the other hand" is used to show the other side, or the "opposite" side of an argument. The word "addition" has an idea of inclusion; E: incorrect – The expression "on the other hand" is used to show the other side, or the "opposite" side of an argument. The word "control" has an idea of restraint.
Gabarito "A".

Read text II and answer the questions.

Department of Sociology

Sociology is the study of the way humans influence each other through groups, organizations, and societies.
Sociologists investigate social change as well as the causes and consequences of human behavior in a variety of contexts,
5 from families to political movements to hospitals. Often combining scientific and humanistic perspectives, sociologists analyze survey data, carry out in-depth interviews, ethnographic studies and content analyses. The Sociology major at Pomona College emphasizes social theory and
10 research, culminating in the senior exercise, which allows each student to carry out an original research project with the advice of one or two faculty members.
Many sociology majors are able to study abroad for a semester during their junior year, for example, in Spain, Brazil,
15 Greece, South Africa, and the Dominican Republic.

(http://www.sociology.pomona.edu)

(Técnico Legislativo – Senado – 2008 – FGV) This text may be found in a(n)

(A) manual.
(B) outdoor.
(C) journal.
(D) letter.
(E) diary.

(Interpretation) A: correct – The details offered towards the end of the text are typical of a brochure or manual. This information is usually provided for those interested I attending the college; B: incorrect – The language and details in the text are not typical for large-scale advertising. OBS: The word "outdoor" has been incorrectly employed here. It is a false cognate in Portuguese. The correct word is "billboard". The word "outdoor" is an adverb (not a noun) that refers to an external place (not inside). In Portuguese, "outdoor" could be translated as "lá fora"; C: incorrect – The language and details in the text are not typical for journal writing. OBS: The word journal can be misleading. It is more often employed to refer to a personal diary, or an academic magazine. Some parts of the world use this word to refer to a newspaper, but it is the least common usage; D: incorrect – The language and details in the text are not typical for letter writing. Texts in letters are usually more personal or directly aimed at a specific reader; the large-scale approach to detail in the text is not typically found in letters; E: incorrect – The language and details in the text are not typical for diary entries. OBS: The word diary is often substituted with the word journal.
Gabarito "A".

(Técnico Legislativo – Senado – 2008 – FGV) In "as well as the causes and consequences…" (lines 3-4) as well as is used to indicate

(A) manner.
(B) time.
(C) addition.
(D) consequence.
(E) cause.

(Grammar) A: incorrect – The expression "as well as" is not related to manner or the way things are done; B: incorrect – The expression "as well as" is not related to time; C: correct – The expression "as well as" is synonymous with "and", "besides", "in addition to", which all carry an idea of addition; D: incorrect – The expression "as well as" is not related to consequence or the result of any action; E: incorrect – The expression "as well as" is not related to cause or the reason something is done.
Gabarito "C".

(Técnico Legislativo – Senado – 2008 – FGV) The underlined word in "Often combining…." (lines 5-6) is the opposite of

(A) always.
(B) seldom.
(C) also.
(D) never.
(E) somewhat.

(Grammar) A: incorrect – The word "always" is similar to "often", not an opposite; B: correct – The word "seldom" is a direct opposite of "often". It is a synonym of "rarely"; C: incorrect – The word "also" carries an idea of addition. This is not the opposite of seldom or rarely; D: incorrect – The word "never" is the opposite of "always". This is not the opposite of seldom or rarely; E: incorrect – The word "somewhat" carries an idea of "quite a lot" or "rather". This is not the opposite of seldom or rarely.
Gabarito "B".

(Técnico Legislativo – Senado – 2008 – FGV) The underlined expression in "each student to carry out" (line 11) can be replaced by

(A) finish.
(B) undertake.
(C) support.
(D) continue.
(E) spread.

(Vocabulary) A: incorrect – The word "finish" can mean "complete" or "accomplish", not "carry out"; B: correct – The word "undertake" is a synonym of "**do**", "**perform**" and "**carry out**"; C: incorrect – The word "support" can mean "defend" or "help", not "carry out"; D: incorrect – The word "continue" can mean "carry **on**" or "be persist", not "carry out"; E: incorrect – The word "spread" can mean "distribute" or "multiply", not "carry out".
Gabarito "B".

(Técnico Legislativo – Senado – 2008 – FGV) The verb form in "Many sociology majors are able to…" (line 13) can be replaced by

(A) must.
(B) should.

(C) will.
(D) could.
(E) can.

(Grammar) A: incorrect – The word "must" is usually employed to show obligation. As the expression "to be able to" usually holds the meaning of ability, this is not a good replacement; B: incorrect – The word "should" is usually employed to show suggestions. As the expression "to be able to" usually holds the meaning of ability, "should" is not a good replacement; C: incorrect – The word "will" is used to show a future time. The expression "to be able to" usually holds the meaning of ability. If this is to show the future, it is used together with "will" – We will be able to leave soon; D: incorrect – The verb form "could" can be the past of the modal verb "can". As the sentence in question refers to ability, this would change the sense. It could refer to what students were able to do in the past, but not able to do now. The word "could" is also used to show politeness and possibilities (neither necessarily in the past). E.g. Could I offer you some tea? We could try another route. Either way, this is not a good replacement; E: correct – The verb form "to be able to" usually holds the meaning of ability, which is generally expressed in English with the modal verb "can".

Gabarito "E".

Off the radar screen

1 Days after Air France's ill-fated Airbus A330 plunged mysteriously into the southern Atlantic Ocean four hours after leaving Rio de Janeiro for Paris on May 31st, rescuers were still
4 searching for debris.
   The wreckage is thought to lie up to some 3,700 metres below the waves, possibly in one of the many trenches that riddle
7 the rocky undersea mountain range west of the Mid-Atlantic Ridge. Its exact location may not be known for several weeks. One of the hazards of flying over oceans is the lack of
10 radar coverage. Even the latest radar equipment can reach out no more than 550 kilometres (300 nautical miles) from land. Once out of radar range, pilots flying intercontinental routes make
13 scheduled radio contact every half an hour or so with air-traffic control stations, behind or ahead of them, to report their positions. The rest of the time, no one knows exactly where they
16 are.
   A number of countries, especially those surrounded by oceans or by vast expanses of rugged wilderness are none too
19 happy with this. America, Australia and Canada have been among the most active proponents of satellite navigation for commercial aircraft.
22 The Canadian authorities began operation of such a system in January. It uses what is known in aviation circles as ADS-B, short for automatic dependent surveillance-broadcast.
25 The technology combines the precise position of the aircraft, as identified by global-positioning satellites, with data about its flight number, speed, direction and attitude (whether it is
28 climbing, descending or turning).
   Although ADS-B would not have prevented the crash into the Atlantic Ocean, it might well have helped locate the
31 debris more quickly. Knowing the exact location of the accident would allow rescue craft to be on the scene within hours, pulling any survivors from the water. That too would be a great benefit
34 of the new air-traffic-control technology.

Internet: <www.economist.com> (adapted).

(Analista – ANAC – 2009 – CESPE) Judge the following items about the ideas and the linguistic structures of the text above.

(1) America, Australia and Canada, which are surrounded either by oceans or rough wilderness are the most active proponents of satellite navigation for commercial aircraft.
(2) The automatic dependent surveillance broadcast would not have prevented the crash into the Atlantic, notwithstanding its technology which combines the precise position of the aircraft with data about its flight number, speed, direction as well as attitude.
(3) The word "ill-fated" (ℓ.1) is synonymous with doomed.
(4) The verb to plunge in "Airbus A330 plunged mysteriously into the southern Atlantic Ocean" (ℓ.1-2) means to thrust or throw (something or oneself) forcibly or suddenly downwards.
(5) The word "wreckage" (ℓ.5) refers to the remaining parts of something that has been wrecked.
(6) The wreckage exact location is already known.

(Interpretation) 1: incorrect – The text states in lines 19-20 that 'America, Australia and Canada have been among the most active proponents', this signifies they were not the only countries active; 2: correct – The text states clearly in line 29 – the technology would not have prevented the crash. **Notwithstanding** means the same as **In spite of** and shows contrast or surprise; 3: correct – Both have the meaning of being destined for misfortune; 4: correct – To plunge is defined in the dictionary exactly in this way. Possible synonyms would be: to drop or to fall; 5: correct – Wreckage (noun) derives from something that has been wrecked; 6: incorrect – In lines 4-5, the text says rescuers are still searching for the debris/wreckage. In line 5, the text states 'the wreckage is thought to lie' or that there is no certainty as to where it lies.

Gabarito 1E, 2C, 3C, 4C, 5C, 6E

Shifting gears

1 That jet engines have evolved over the past few decades will be apparent to any seasoned air traveller. Early jet engines had narrow inlets and were very noisy,
4 but as the diameter of the fans at the front increased, the engines became quieter. Compared with a rowdy 1960s jet, a modern turbofan is some 80% quieter and burns as
7 little as half as much fuel – thus producing fewer greenhouse gases.
   The aviation industry has set itself a tough
10 target: a 50% reduction in fuel consumption by 2020, to cut CO_2 emissions in half. The solution devised by Pratt & Whitney (P&W), a division of United Technologies,
13 is a "geared turbofan" engine called the PurePower PW1000G.
   Some airlines, however, are wary of gearboxes.
16 They worry that replacing a simple shaft with a complex gearbox will increase maintenance costs and make it more likely that something will go wrong.

Internet: <www.economist.com> (adapted).

(Analista – ANAC – 2009 – CESPE) Judge the following items about the ideas and the linguistic structures of the text above.

(1) The aviation industry will have a 50% reduction in fuel consumption by 2020, thus cutting CO_2 emissions in half.
(2) Besides producing fewer greenhouse gases, a modern turbofan is about 80% quieter than 1960 jets.
(3) The word "rowdy" (ℓ.5) is synonymous with quiet.
(4) In "Some airlines, however, are wary of gearboxes" (ℓ.15), "wary" is synonymous with cautious.

(Interpretation) 1: incorrect – 'Will have' implies it is a certainty. Line 9 of the text states "**the aviation industry has set itself a tough target.**" This means the target is desired, but not a certainty; 2: correct – Besides means also or in addition. The turbofan will produce fewer gases in addition to being quieter; 3: incorrect – Rowdy means loud or disorderly. Rowdy is an antonym of quiet; 4: correct – To be wary means to be cautious.

Gabarito 1E, 2C, 3E, 4C

USS Constitution under sail in Massachusetts Bay, 21 July 1997.

1   USS Constitution is a wooden-hulled, three-masted heavy frigate of the United States Navy. Named after the Constitution of the United States of America by President George Washington, she is the oldest commissioned vessel afloat in the world. Constitution, launched in 1797, was one of the six original frigates authorized for construction by the Naval Act of 1794 to be
4   the Navy's capital ships, and so Constitution and her sisters were larger and more heavily armed than the standard run of frigate. Built in Boston, Massachusetts, her first duty with the newly formed United States Navy was to provide protection for American merchant shipping during the Quasi War with France and to defeat the Barbary pirates in the First Barbary War.
7   Her most famous era of naval warfare was the War of 1812 against Great Britain, when she defeated five British warships. From the battle with Guerriere, she earned the nickname of "Old Ironsides" because cannon balls glanced off her thick hull. She continued to actively serve the nation as flagship in the Mediterranean and African squadrons and circled the world in the 1840s.
10 From 1853 to 1855 she patrolled the coast of Africa searching for illegal slave traders. During the American Civil War, the sailing frigate gave way to the progress of shipbuilding. For several years "Old Ironsides" was used as a training ship for the United States Naval Academy. Considered unfit to sea, the USS Constitution was rescued from destruction when Oliver Wendell Holmes's poem
13 "Old Ironsides" launched a preservation movement in 1830. Retired from active service in 1881, she served as a receiving ship until designated a museum ship in 1907, and in 1931 she made a three year 90-port tour of the nation. The frigate was completely overhauled for its bicentennial in 1997 and it sailed under its own power, drawing international attention.
16 Now the oldest U.S. warship still in commission, Constitution remains a powerful reminder of the nation's earliest steps into dominance of the sea. The Naval Historical Center Detachment of Boston is responsible for planning and performing her maintenance, repair and restoration, keeping her as close to her 1812 configuration as possible. She is berthed at Pier 1 of the
19 former Charlestown Navy Yard, at one end of Boston's Freedom Trail, and she is open to the public year round.

Internet: <www.wikipedia.org> (adapted).

(Analista – ANATEL – 2009 – CESPE) Based on the text above, judge the following items.

(1) Throughout the last 200 years as Constitution's purpose and function changed from fighting warship, to training vessel, to receiving ship, to dock side exhibit.
(2) USS Constitution was the first ship of line built in the United States to defend the young American nation.
(3) After minor repair USS Constitution celebrated its 200th birthday in 1997 making passage under her own sail in Massachusetts Bay.
(4) USS Constitution returned in 1931after a three-year world circumnavigation scheduled journey.
(5) Because of an inspirational poem, the USS Constitution was reported unseaworthy and condemned to be broken up, but the museum helped to raise funds for her overhauling.
(6) In 1934, Old Ironsides returns to her place of honor in Boston harbor after a national cruise to ninety American different cities.
(7) "wooden-hulled" (ℓ.1) and "three-masted" (ℓ.1), related to "USS Constitution", are examples of modifying compounds that are often hyphenated when preceding a noun.
(8) In the text, "glanced" (ℓ.8) can be replaced by bounced without any change in meaning.
(9) "actively serve" (ℓ.9) means assist at work.
(10) "was used" (ℓ.11) can be substituted by served, maintaining the same tense.

(Interpretation) 1: correct – All of the above purposes and functions are detailed in chronological order in the text above; 2: incorrect – Line 4 states that the USS constitution was one of six original ships authorized for construction; therefore, she was not the first. In line 4 there is mention of the USS Constitution not being a standard run of frigate – this implies there were already standard frigates in operation; 3: incorrect – The ship was **'completely overhauled'** line 5 – this signifies major not minor repairs; 4: incorrect – The 1931 tour was of the nation i.e. the United States, not of the world; 15: incorrect – The poem had no impact on considering the ship unseaworthy. The poem served to inspire a preservation movement: lines 13-14; 6: correct – Line 14 – The three year national cruise began in 1931; therefore, 1934 was the end. The text does not mention any other destination after this apart from Boston; 7: When compounded modifiers precede a noun, they are often hyphenated: part-time teacher, fifty-yard-wide field, fire-resistant curtains, high-speed chase. When those same modifying words come after the noun, however, they are not hyphenated: a field fifty yards wide, curtains that are fire resistant, etc. The second-rate opera company gave a performance that was first rate – Gabarito Oficial – Errado/ Nosso Gabarito – Correto; 8: correct – To glance off as used in the text means the same as to bounce off; 9: correct – To be in active service or actively serve means to assist at work, usually in the context of military operations; 10: correct – Served can mean to act in a specific capacity – to serve as proxy/ to be used as a proxy.

Gabarito 1C, 2E, 3E, 4E, 5E, 6C, 7C, 8C, 9C, 10C

This text refers to the following items.

Japan and Korea are outstanding markets in terms of the world's advances in cellular telephony, where multimedia applications have surged into feverish popularity. Users in these countries have demanded velocity and high quality data transmission – such as images, videos and sounds – as the principal distinctive features for the cellular telephone. Although the industry in Brazil is not yet experiencing the same phase as in the Asian countries, innovative third generation services, aligned with world-class technology, are already present, with data transmission speeds of up to 2.4 Mbps.

In fact, in some cases, Brazil has held multimedia application launches simultaneously with the United States, tremendously increasing the economic and digital inclusion that cellular telephony has fomented in recent years. The heavy impact of mobile communication on Brazilian society can be measured by the expansion of the customer base, which has been growing at historic rates of 30% a year and now serves over 50 million customers. In other words, four out of every ten Brazilians have a cellular telephone.

The importance of mobile telephony has already surpassed that of the traditional fixed telephone system, because the cell phone actually fulfills the function of taking communication to all levels of the population. Its widespread network has opened gateways to regions that formerly had not been benefited by the implementation of a fixed telephone system, such as, for example, many rural areas that are now mobile telephone customers.

The responsibility that cellular telephony carries as an instrument for transforming people's lives tends to increase enormously in the short term. In Brazil, third generation CDMA 3G EVDO service is already offered and is able to provide handheld resources, similar to CD, DVD and TV, anywhere and at any time, based on Qualcomm's cutting edge CDMA technology.

Internet: <www.wirtel.co.uk> (with adaptations).

(Analista – ANATEL – 2006 – CESPE) Based on the text above, judge the following items.

(1) Japan and Korea are the two most important countries as far as mobile telephony market is concerned.

(2) All that Japanese and Korean peoples request in cellular telephony are images, video and sound.

(3) In terms of cellular telephony, Brazil is far behind the two Asian countries mentioned in the text.

(4) There are cases when Brazil and USA have launched multimedia applications at the same time.

(5) Six out of ten Brazilians don't have a cellular phone yet.

(Interpretation) 1: incorrect – The use of 'outstanding' means these markets are prominent or remarkable. These countries are great examples of the popularity of mobile phones, but not necessarily the most important; 2: incorrect – Images, video and sound are given as examples of what people in Japan and Korea demand, which is velocity and high quality data transmission (line 5); 3: incorrect – The text states, in line 8, that Brazil is not yet at the same phase as in Asian countries; it cannot be argued that Brazil is far behind. Indeed, examples are given throughout the text of the Brazilian market being highly developed; 4: correct – Line 13 – Brazil has held simultaneous launches with the U.S.; 5: correct – As line 20 states, 4 out of ten Brazilians have a mobile phone; it is possible to deduce this;
Gabarito 1E, 2E, 3E, 4C, 5C

(Analista – ANATEL – 2006 – CESPE) Judge the following items.

(1) The mobile phone system aims at reaching every Brazilian social class.
(2) Cellular phones have substituted for the fixed telephone system.
(3) The more people use the cellular telephony the more responsibility it takes.

1: correct – In lines 24-25, the text states, **'the cell phone actually fulfills the function of taking communication to all levels of the population'**; 2: incorrect – To substitute or replace the fixed telephone system is too strong a statement. Cellular phones have increased access to phones, not replaced fixed telephones; 3: correct – Lines 30-32 – **The responsibility that cellular telephony carries as an instrument for transforming people's lives tends to increase enormously in the short term.** This can interpreted as when there is huge growth in the number of cellular phone users the companies bear more responsibility;
Gabarito 1C, 2E, 3C

(Analista – ANATEL – 2006 – CESPE) In the text,

(1) "In fact" ($\ell.12$) means As a matter of fact.
(2) "is already offered" ($\ell.33$) can be replaced by has already been offered without changing the meaning.

1: correct – These are synonymous. Actually can also be used although with a slightly less formal register; 2: incorrect – "is already offered" uses simple present tense; whereas 'has already been offered' uses present perfect and carries the idea that the services were offered in the past and continues to be offered. M – I tend to think that this could be correct. The tenses are different, but I think the present perfect wouldn't changed the meaning. In essence, the service is available. The present perfect, in fact, tends to suggest that it was offered, but there is no reference to the present (It has been offered some time in the past). The simple present tense suggests that it is constantly offered. IN terms of meaning, I think they would be interchangeable.
Gabarito 1C, 2E

Your answers to questions must be based on the text below which is entitled "And the winners are…":

And the winners are…

Source: The Economist/ Technology Quarterly
(Adapted) Dec 8th 2005

This newspaper was established in 1843 to take part in "a severe contest between intelligence, which presses forward, and an unworthy, timid ignorance obstructing our progress". One of the chief ways in which intelligence presses forward is through innovation, which is now recognized as one of the most important contributors to economic growth. Innovation, in turn, depends on the creative individuals who dream up new ideas and turn them into reality.

The Economist recognizes these talented people through our annual Innovation Awards, presented in seven fields, including energy and the environment – whose winner is:

Stanford Ovshinsky, president and chief scientist and technologist, Energy Conversion Devices, for developing the **nickel-metal-hydride battery**. This is the battery technology found in hybrid cars, laptop computers and many other devices, and is just one of the many innovations devised by Mr Ovshinsky, a self-taught inventor who pioneered the field of amorphous materials in the 1950s. He is now focusing on solar panels and hydrogen-powered cars.

(Analista – ANEEL – 2006 – ESAF) In paragraph 1, the author refers to innovation and its

(A) lack in current society.
(B) main drawbacks.
(C) uninspiring role.
(D) harmful consequences.
(E) invaluable contribution.

(Interpretation) A: incorrect – Lack refers to absence. There is no mention of its absence in society; B: incorrect – Drawbacks are disadvantages; C: incorrect – On the contrary, innovation is presented as being positive and inspiring; D: incorrect – No harmful or negative consequences are mentioned; E: correct – Invaluable meaning means having great value/priceless and contributing to economic growth.
Gabarito "E".

(Analista – ANEEL – 2006 – ESAF) The field of energy and the environment

(A) makes up the set of fields awarded by the newspaper.
(B) was mentioned as the least relevant among other areas.
(C) has been excluded due to its questionable contributions.
(D) has its main researchers and specialists listed and assessed.
(E) should have been included as well as highlighted.

(Interpretation) A: correct – Energy and the Environment is one of seven different fields where awards are given. correct – This question is correct by means of elimination of the other options; B: incorrect – The field of energy and the environment is not given any more or less prestige than other areas; C: incorrect – The field of energy and the environment is not excluded; D: incorrect – There is not concentration on "main" researchers; E: incorrect – The field of energy and the environment is included and highlighted.
Gabarito "A".

(Analista – ANEEL – 2006 – ESAF) The text mentions Stanford Ovshinsky,

(A) whose inventions derive from a solid academic background.
(B) who is said to have developed some of his skills by himself.
(C) who might be awarded a prize for his scientific breakthroughs.
(D) whose innovative scientific approach has been underestimated.
(E) who used to research key scientific areas such as solar panels.

(Interpretation) A: incorrect – He is a self-taught inventor; B: correct – He is a self-taught inventor; C: incorrect – He has already been awarded the prize; D: incorrect – No mention that he has been underestimated; E: incorrect – Solar panels are a current area of research, not a past one.
Gabarito "B".

Your answers to questions must be based on the text below which is entitled "The politics of power":

The politics of power

Source: www.economist.co.uk
Feb 9th 2006 (Adapted)

There is an intense debate over the future of energy and its impact on Europe's economy. On the one hand is a longstanding project for lower prices led by the European Commission designed to liberalize the market and enable producers and distributors to compete freely within and across national borders. On the other is a camp that argues with growing confidence against further freeing the market. In its view, long-term security and stable prices can best be preserved in managed national markets that are dominated by strong quasi-monopolistic companies which can withstand bullying producers and sudden shifts in demand and supply.

This tension has implications for businesses across Europe. Today business customers in different countries pay prices that vary as much as 100% across what is supposed to be a single European market. A freer market in energy promises to reduce prices back to something like a Europe-wide clearing level. Energy is a critical input to businesses, especially manufacturing, and rising prices are putting unwelcome pressure on already tight margins, as companies try to compete with emerging low-wage economies in Asia.

(Analista – ANEEL – 2006 – ESAF) Paragraph 1 reports a debate on the future of energy and its impact on Europe's economy which

(A) has been closed.
(B) must be opened.
(C) is currently taking place.
(D) has been postponed.
(E) might be officially addressed.

(Interpretation) A: incorrect – The debate is current; B: incorrect – The debate is already open; C: correct – **Line 1 – 'there is an intense debate'**; D: incorrect – Postponed means delayed; E: incorrect – The debate is current, not something that might happen.
Gabarito "C".

(Analista – ANEEL – 2006 – ESAF) In paragraph 2, the author refers to a single European market whose prices

(A) are just the same.
(B) may soon equal.
(C) are set by officials.
(D) presently differ.
(E) ought to be increased.

(Interpretation) A: incorrect – There is a great variation in prices; B: incorrect – No evidence to suggest this; C: incorrect – This is what some want – a state controlled system, but it does not exist yet; D: correct – The text states, **'prices vary as much as 100% across what is supposed to be a single European market'**. Vary means to differ; E: incorrect – ought to – suggestion that it should be increased. This is against the tone of the text, which discussed reducing energy costs.
Gabarito "D".

(Analista – ANEEL – 2006 – ESAF) The author

(A) portrays the present reality of the European energy industry.
(B) analyses the on-going deregulation of the energy sector.
(C) foresees steep price increases and fears over supply.
(D) advertises the creation of a European chain of energy companies.
(E) defends the past European market position and behavior.

(Interpretation) A: correct – Use of present tense throughout the text and in paragraph 2 reference to 'Today' suggest the text is about the present reality of the European energy industry; B: incorrect – De-regulation is contrary to liberalization as mentioned in the text; C: incorrect – To foresee is to predict. There is no prediction of steep increases or supply, but rather over existing price discrepancies; D: incorrect – No mention of the creation of this chain; E: incorrect – There is no mention of defending past positions or behavior. Longstanding in paragraph 1 – i.e. having existed for a long time – refers to "project for lower prices", but it is not defended by the author.
Gabarito "A".

Your answers to questions must be based on the text below which is entitled "The Knowledge Race":

The Knowledge Race

Source: Newsweek Special Edition
Dec 2006 – Feb 2006 (Adapted)

There are losers in every race, but let not the worries over who is winning and losing the knowledge race obscure the more powerful underlying dynamic: knowledge is liberating. It creates the possibility for change and improvement everywhere. It can create amazing devices and techniques, save lives, improve living standards and spread information. Some will do well on one measure, others on another. But on the whole, a knowledge-based world will be a healthier and richer world.

The caveat I would make is not about one or another country's paucity of engineers or computers. These problems can be solved. But knowledge is not the same thing as wisdom. Knowledge can produce equally powerful ways to destroy life, intentionally and unintentionally. It can produce hate and seek destruction. Knowledge does not by itself produce good sense, courage, generosity and tolerance. And most crucially, it does not produce the farsightedness that will allow us all to live together – and grow together – on this world without causing war, chaos and catastrophe. For that we need wisdom.

(Analista – ANEEL – 2006 – ESAF) The author intends to make a caveat in relation to the distinction between knowledge and wisdom. Thus, he is posing

(A) a threat.
(B) a problem.
(C) a risk.
(D) a challenge.
(E) a warning.

(Interpretation) A: incorrect – To pose a threat would imply to actually threaten. Instead the author warns about a possible threat; B: incorrect – He poses a warning about a possible problem; C: incorrect – The warning he gives is about possible risks; D: incorrect – A challenge would demand action; E: correct – He is giving advice to beware.
Gabarito "E".

(Analista – ANEEL – 2006 – ESAF) In the author's point of view,

(A) knowledge undoubtedly hinders progress and development.
(B) considering the future results of an action is of critical importance.
(C) there has been an alarming paucity of engineers and computers.
(D) destruction ought to be sought by wise and knowledgeable leaders.
(E) the knowledge race fortunately obscured the value of wisdom.

(Interpretation) A: incorrect – To hinder means to hold back or to curb; B: correct – We need to be **farsighted**/ to consider the consequences of out actions; C: incorrect – On the contrary the scarcity of engineers and computers is not the worrying/arming issue for the author; D: incorrect – Destruction will be avoided not sought/pursued by wise and knowledgeable leaders; E: incorrect – 'Let not' means we should not allow the knowledge race to obscure the value of wisdom.
Gabarito "B".

Your answers to questions must be based on the text below, which is entitled "The technologies to halt global warming":

The technologies to halt global warming

Source: www.mg.co.za
August 17, 2004 (Adapted)

The technologies to halt global warming for 50 years already exist, according to research published this week in the journal Science. The study's authors, Stephen Pacala and Rob Socolow, say that implementing them should begin immediately.

The researchers identified 15 technologies that store carbon, provide energy without producing carbon emissions or improve the efficiency of carbon-based energy suppliers. They say the large-scale use of any one of any of these has the potential to reduce global carbon emissions by at least one billion tons a year by 2054.

Options available include renewable energy sources such as wind and solar power, switching of fuel from coal to nuclear or natural-gas supplies, storage of carbon dioxide produced by power plants, more efficient use of car fuel and electricity, increasing the global forested area, and the use of "biomass" fuels, such as ethanol.

(Analista – ANEEL – 2004 – ESAF) According to the article, "The technologies **to halt global warming** for 50 years already exist." In other words, global warming may be

(A) researched.
(B) successfully mapped.
(C) gradually increased.
(D) decreased.
(E) stopped.

(Vocabulary) A: incorrect – The idea is to stop global warming, not to research it; B: incorrect – This is not the definition given by 'to halt'; C: incorrect – The opposite is true; D: incorrect – The idea of halt is stronger than to merely decrease, or reduce global warming; E: correct – The dictionary definition of **'to halt' is to stop**.
Gabarito "E".

(Analista – ANEEL – 2004 – ESAF) According to the text,

(A) 15 technologies will have been implemented up to 2054.
(B) global carbon emissions might be decreased.
(C) renewable energy sources must have been forbidden.
(D) researchers ought to identify the sources of global warming.
(E) global carbon emissions have been halted.

(Interpretation) A: incorrect – 'will have been implemented' suggests a definite action. The text says that 15 technologies have been identified and that **'use of any one of any of these has the potential to reduce global carbon emissions….'**; B: correct – The text states, in paragraph 2, **'They say the large-scale use of any one of any of these has the potential to reduce global carbon emissions by at least one billion tons a year by 2054'**. Having potential means we can say emissions might be decreased – There is a possibility or potential; C: incorrect – There is no suggestion of renewable energy sources being forbidden or prohibited; D: incorrect – The use of ought is a polite suggestion or recommendation – The text states that researchers have already identified options to reduce emissions; presumably they have thus identified the sources of emissions; E: incorrect – Emissions have not yet been halted/stopped – the text states there is the potential to halt emissions not that they have already been halted.
Gabarito "B".

Your answers to questions must be based on the text below, which is entitled "Latest Distribution News":

Latest Distribution News

Source: www.energyinforsource.com
August 17, 2004 (Adapted)

Florida Power & Light Company (FPL) remains determined to do whatever is needed as safely and as quickly as possible to restore electrical power to all customers whose lives and neighborhoods were impacted by Hurricane Charley.

Since the state began to feel the effects of the Category 4 hurricane, FPL has restored power to 577,000 customers of the 874,000 that were originally left without electricity.

"We at FPL appreciate the patience of our customers as we continue our around-the-clock efforts," said Geisha Williams, vice-president of electrical distribution. The logistical challenges posed by this massive rebuilding and restoration effort are compounded for the electrical workers by many of the same challenges confronted by residents of the damaged areas: hot and humid weather, long days and nights and limited services.

(Analista – ANEEL – 2004 – ESAF) The text refers to Hurricane Charley, which

(A) is said to have been a man-made catastrophe.
(B) has been looked into as well as foreseen by FPL.
(C) has hit an American state.
(D) will be researched so as to be categorized.
(E) had been predicted by the American government.

(Interpretation) A: incorrect – Man-made means to be made by humans as opposed to nature; B: incorrect – There is no evidence to suggest that Hurricane was 'looked into' i.e. researched/investigated or that it was foreseen or predicted; C: correct – **'To feel the effects of'** means to effect or to suffer the consequences of something. The state is specifically mentioned in paragraph 2, and it can be deduced the state may be Florida from the mention of Florida Power and Light Company (paragraph 1); D: incorrect – No evidence to suggest that it will be researched. The only action will be to reestablish power supplies; E: incorrect – No evidence to suggest the hurricane had been predicted.
Gabarito "C".

(Analista – ANEEL – 2004 – ESAF) According to the text,

(A) efforts have been made all day and all night.
(B) electrical power might no longer be supplied by FPL.
(C) customers have called off their contracts with FPL.
(D) residents and customers have decided to join hands.
(E) federal financial assistance may be pivotal.

(Interpretation) A: correct – **'As we continue our around-the-clock efforts'** – this infers the efforts are continuous; B: incorrect – In paragraph one, the company is said to be determined to restore power quickly and safely. Thus, there is no suggestion FPL will no longer supply power, nor that customers are canceling/calling off their contracts; C: incorrect – In paragraph one, the company is said to be determined to restore power quickly and safely. Thus there is no suggestion FPL will no longer supply power nor that customers are canceling/calling off their contracts; D: incorrect – There is nothing in the text that they will join hands; E: incorrect – 'Pivotal' means of crucial importance. Although this sounds sensible as the scale of the disaster is huge, there is no evidence to support this in the text.
Gabarito "A".

(Analista – ANEEL – 2004 – ESAF) Florida Power & Light Company (FPL) is determined to

(A) minimize the extensive environmental damage.
(B) assess the vast local electricity supplies.
(C) provide shelter for its potential customers.
(D) keep on working despite the practical difficulties.
(E) file a lawsuit against the local government.

(Interpretation) A: incorrect – No evidence to support this. The **'restoration efforts'** mentioned are related to power supplies not environmental damage; B: incorrect – No evidence that the company will assess/estimate the electricity supply; C: incorrect – No evidence that the company will provide shelter or accommodation for customers; D: correct – The text states in paragraph one that, "Florida Power & Light Company (FPL) **remains determined to do whatever is needed as safely and as quickly as possible to restore electrical power to all customers whose lives and neighborhoods were impacted by Hurricane Charley'**. Furthermore, in paragraph three, logistical challenges are mentioned. Both parts of the above information make this option correct; E: incorrect – There is no suggestion of legal action in the text.

Gabarito "D".

GLOBAL PETROLEUM

The outlook for oil supply and demand fundamentals over the next two years points to an easing of the oil market balance in 2009. Higher non-OPEC production and planned additions to OPEC
5 capacity should more than offset expected moderate world oil demand growth, and relieve some of the tightness in the market. As a result, surplus production capacity could grow from its current level of under 2 million to over 4 million barrels per day by the end of
10 2009. This balance suggests some price softening, although delays or downward revisions in capacity additions in both OPEC and non-OPEC nations could alter the outlook, as could OPEC production decisions.
World oil consumption is expected to rise by
15 1.6 million barrels per day in both 2008 and 2009 compared with the estimated 1 million barrels per day increase recorded last year. The larger volume gains expected in 2008 and 2009 compared with 2007 mainly reflect higher consumption expected in the
20 Organization for Economic Cooperation and Development (OECD), particularly Europe, where weather factors constrained oil consumption last year. Projections of continued strong world economic growth will spur oil consumption gains in a number of non-
25 OECD markets, including China, non-OECD Asia, and the Middle East countries, over the next 2 years.
OPEC members' production decisions and the pace and timing of capacity additions in a number of countries will play a key role in determining oil market
30 trends over the next 2 years. The Energy Information Administration projects that OPEC crude oil production will average about 32.6 million barrels per day in 2008 and 31.8 million barrels per day in 2009 compared with the 31.7 million barrels per day seen during the fourth
35 quarter of 2007. Increased production from Angola, Saudi Arabia, Kuwait, and Iraq boosted OPEC's crude output during the fourth quarter 2007.
Non-OPEC production is expected to rise by about 0.9 million barrels per day in 2008 and by 1.6
40 million barrels per day in 2009. This compares with a gain of 0.6 million barrels per day recorded last year. Azerbaijan, Russia, Canada, Brazil, the United States, China, Sudan, and Kazakhstan account for a large share of the gain in non-OPEC production growth in
45 2008 and 2009. Increases in these nations will more than offset expected declines in production in a number of countries including Mexico, the United Kingdom, and Norway.

EIA – Energy Information Administration Short-Term
Energy Outlook, January 8, 2008

(Analista – ANP – 2008 – CESGRANRIO) The purpose of the first paragraph is to

(A) announce that world oil production capacity will soon increase to 4 million barrels per day.

(B) criticize both OPEC and non-OPEC countries for causing unexpected delays in production.

(C) discuss the prospects for global oil supply and demand until the end of the year 2009.

(D) predict increasing losses in the oil markets if the surplus production capacity remains unaltered.

(E) report what will certainly happen in the international oil market over the next two years.

(Interpretation) A: incorrect – The text refers to surplus capacity growing to 4 million barrels per day. The text also states 'could grow', not "will grow" as asserted here; B: incorrect – There is no form of criticism; rather, there is a caveat that production may not be as high as expected; C: correct – The text mentions **the outlook for oil fundamentals**. Outlook means prediction or forecast; D: incorrect – There is no mention of losses occurring if capacity remains unchanged; E: incorrect – To say it will certainly happen is too strong. The texts states 'points to' – this means estimates a broad trend, not that is guaranteed to happen.

Gabarito "C".

(Analista – ANP – 2008 – CESGRANRIO) According to Paragraph 2, oil consumption

(A) achieved a record-breaking increase in the world last year.
(B) fell sharply in Europe in 2007 due to weather factors.
(C) is likely to speed economic growth in a number of markets.
(D) may increase in 2008-2009 at a higher rate than in 2007.
(E) will certainly grow in OECD countries for the next 2 years.

(Interpretation) A: incorrect – No evidence to say it was a record-breaking increase – i.e. better than ever before. The text merely says it was recorded or noted; B: incorrect – Oil consumption in Europe is said to be 'constrained' i.e. restrained – this is not as strong as falling sharply; C: incorrect – To spur means to speed up, however, the text refers specifically to non-OECD markets not a number of markets; D: correct – **'World oil consumption is expected to rise by 1.6 million barrels per day in both 2008 and 2009 compared with the estimated 1 million barrels per day recorded last year'**; E: incorrect – The use of the word 'expected' means we cannot assert OECD oil consumption will certainly grow in the next 2 years.

Gabarito "D".

(Analista – ANP – 2008 – CESGRANRIO) Concerning the oil production of both OPEC and non-OPEC members the text informs that

(A) OPEC crude oil production is expected to grow steadily over the next two years.
(B) the oil output of Mexico and Norway, among other countries, decreased last year.
(C) non-OPEC countries' daily production averaged six hundred thousand barrels of oil in 2007.
(D) an upward trend in oil production of non-OPEC nations is expected in 2008-2009.
(E) Angola, Saudi Arabia, Kuwait and Iraq could not pump any oil in the first three quarters of 2007.

(Interpretation) A: incorrect – Decisions, pace and timing will all affect OPEC production over the next two years; B: incorrect – there are expected declines for these countries (line 46) – it cannot be stated that output decreased last year; C: incorrect – Six hundred thousand barrels refers to a gain in production in 2007. There was normal production plus the gain; D: correct – **'Non-OPEC production is expected to rise by about 0.9 million barrels per day in 2008 and 1.6 million barrels per day in 2009'**; E: incorrect – There will be **increased production** from these countries in the fourth quarter, but that does not allow inference that they could not pump oil in the first three quarters of 2007.

Gabarito "D".

(Analista – ANP – 2008 – CESGRANRIO) The sentence in which "should" is used in the same sense as in "... planned additions to OPEC capacity should more than offset..." (lines 4-5) is:

(A) I should say that the salaries make up very nearly two thirds of the budget
(B) If you should be fired, your health benefits will not be automatically cut off.
(C) In such cases the officer should first give notice to those in the house.
(D) Should he go back to the office and wait for you to telephone?
(E) This year's treasury deficit should be six billion dollars or more.

(Grammar) A: incorrect – Used to moderate bluntness or directness of a statement; B: incorrect – Expresses conditionality; C: incorrect – Expresses obligation or duty; D: incorrect – Expresses obligation or duty; E: correct – Expresses a probability or expectation.

Gabarito "E".

(Analista – ANP – 2008 – CESGRANRIO) The statement which describes accurately the meaning relationship between the pair of words is

(A) "offset" (line 5) means *compensate for*.
(B) "softening" (line 10) is the opposite of *reduction*.
(C) "constrained" (line 22) and *restrained* are antonyms.
(D) "spur" (line 24) could be replaced by *discourage*.
(E) "boosted" (line 36) and *hindered* are synonyms.

(Vocabulary) A: correct – To compensate or counterbalance; B: incorrect – To make gentler, less harsh; C: incorrect – They are considered synonyms; D: incorrect – To spur (verb) means to encourage; E: incorrect – To boost (verb) means to increase, to hinder (verb) means to curb or hamper. Both words have opposite meanings and could be considered antonyms.

Gabarito "A".

The year 2004 may be characterized as a year of extremes, which witnessed record prices for crude oil and gasoline, a severe hurricane season, and world energy markets that were disturbed by unexpectedly high oil
5 demand in China and continued volatility in the Middle East. West Texas Intermediate (WTI) crude oil prices for the near-term futures contract on the New York Mercantile Exchange soared and closed at an all-time record of more than $55 per barrel on October 22, a level about two-thirds
10 above the $33.78-per-barrel price of crude oil at the beginning of the year. Since the October peak, WTI crude oil prices have fluctuated downward to about $42 per barrel as of December 28, 2004. Although the record high crude oil price this year can be attributed to a number of factors,
15 the most influential of those were: low U.S. crude oil inventories held in commercial storage, particularly during the early months of the year; uncertainty about the flow of Iraqi oil exports in the face of the high level of turmoil within that country; the damage inflicted on Gulf Coast
20 and offshore oil installations following hurricanes Charley, Frances, and Ivan; unexpectedly strong world oil demand, particularly in China; and capacity constraints. Moreover, Venezuelan political instability, Nigerian labor strikes, and internal strife between the Russian government and Yukos,
25 the giant oil company, contributed as well to keep crude oil and other petroleum prices higher this year.
Rising crude oil prices also pushed most petroleum product prices higher during 2004, including retail regular gasoline. Another noteworthy item during 2004 was record
30 distillate fuel demand, which measured nearly 4.1 million barrels per day. Even high diesel fuel prices, reaching a record (unadjusted for inflation) 221.2 cents per gallon on October 25, 2004, were not sufficient to temper strong demand that was in part fueled by a still strong U.S.
35 economy.

(Analista – ANP – 2005 – CESGRANRIO) The main purpose of the text is to:

(A) explain how the political situation in Venezuela and in Nigeria can affect petroleum prices.
(B) discuss the role of the New York Mercantile Exchange in the establishment of crude oil prices.
(C) criticize the Russian government for its turbulent relationship with the oil giant Yukos.
(D) summarize the main events and factors that caused a record rise in crude oil prices in 2004.
(E) analyze in detail why a robust U.S. economy was responsible for last year's record rise in diesel fuel prices.

(Interpretation) A: incorrect – These are examples within the text and not the main purpose of the text; B: incorrect – This is an example within the text and not the main purpose of the text; C: incorrect – This is an example within the text and not the main purpose of the text; D: correct – The use of the word – **characterized** – gives the idea of a series of broad events and factors; E: incorrect – These are examples within the text and not the main purpose of the text.

Gabarito "D".

(Analista – ANP – 2005 – CESGRANRIO) Classify the statements as true (T) or false (F), according to the ideas presented in the first paragraph.

( ) In the last days of 2004 crude oil prices were lower than in October but higher than in the beginning of the year.
( ) American crude oil inventories were very low in 2004 due chiefly to the unexpected oil demand in China.
( ) The three hurricanes that hit the world last year caused a lot of damage to oil installations.
( ) The rise in crude oil prices in 2004 was caused by conflicts between major oil companies and national governments.

Mark the option that correctly classifies the statements.

(A) T, T, T and F.
(B) T, F, T and F.
(C) T, F, F and T.
(D) F, F, F and T.
(E) F, T, F and F.

(Interpretation) 1: True – Lines 10-13. ($33.78 beginning of the year; $55 in October; $42 December 2004); 2: False – Unexpected Chinese demand and low inventories were contributory factors to the record high price of crude oil; 3: True – Lines 19-21 '**..the damage inflicted on Gulf Coast and offshore oil installations following hurricanes Charley, Frances, and Ivan; unexpectedly strong world oil demand.**"; 4: False – This was only one of a number of contributing factors and cannot be stated as being the only cause of a rise in crude oil prices in 2004.
Gabarito "B".

(Analista – ANP – 2005 – CESGRANRIO) It can be inferred from paragraph 2 that:

(A) the increase in crude oil and high diesel prices results from strong demand.
(B) all petroleum product prices reached an unprecedented record in 2004.
(C) there has been a decline in fuel consumption because of the high oil prices.
(D) oil price rises and excessive consumption have pushed up inflation in 2004.
(E) the powerful US economy is partially responsible for the intense oil demand.

(Interpretation) A: incorrect – The increase in price related to both supply and demand side factors; B: incorrect – Only record prices for gasoline and crude oil (lines 2-3); C: incorrect – Demand for diesel continued even in the face of high prices – Line 33 – to temper means to moderate; D: incorrect – No mention in the text of any increases in inflation; E: correct – "**..were not sufficient to temper strong demand that was in part fueled by a still strong U.S. economy**", (lines 33-35).
Gabarito "E".

(Analista – ANP – 2005 – CESGRANRIO) In the sentence "Since the October peak, WTI crude oil prices have fluctuated downward ...December 28, 2004." (lines 11-13), the expression "fluctuated downward" can be best replaced by:

(A) declined unsteadily.
(B) risen suddenly.
(C) dropped dramatically.
(D) increased slightly.
(E) decreased sharply.

(Vocabulary) Downward means to decrease. Unsteadily gives the impression that the drop was neither dramatic nor sharp, but rather it moved downwards in an erratic manner. Fluctuated also has an idea of an erratic or unsteady change.
Gabarito "A".

(Analista – ANP – 2005 – CESGRANRIO) Identify the correct statement about reference.

(A) "Which" (line 2) refers to "extremes".
(B) "That" (line 4) refers to "record prices".
(C) "Those" (line 15) refers to "crude oil inventories".
(D) "Which" (line 30) refers to "retail regular gasoline".
(E) "That" (line 34) refers to "strong demand".

(Grammar) A: incorrect – 'Which' refers to the year 2004; B: incorrect – 'That' refers to world energy markets; C: incorrect – 'Those' refers to a number of factors; D: incorrect – 'Which' refers to distillate fuel demand; E: correct – 'That' refers to strong demand.
Gabarito "E".

The need to transport large volumes of low-value loads across long distances while facing up to harsh competition in the international market led the Brazilian agricultural sector to be punished the hardest by the high costs of transportation and port fees. In 1995, for example, shipping a ton of soy from New Orleans cost just US$ 3.00 whereas the cost to ship the same product from the Brazilian port of Paranaguá exceeded US$ 14.00 and the cost to transport the product between the production regions of the US and the same port (an average of 2,000 km) by waterways was just US$ 16/t. In Brazil it exceeded US$ 80/t. In order to overcome the problem, the Brazilian Federal Government has decided to encourage the development of multimode transportation corridors based on the use of some waterways and on the privatization of railroads and ports.
Considering the prospects for the expansion of agricultural borders, plus the existing trade flows of production, and the main consumer markets (including potential markets) in developing and implementing the transportation policy, the Government has decided to establish five corridors: the Northwest, the Central-North, the Northeast, the Central-East, and the Southwest. The Government had already embarked on a process of rationalisation of the management of port labour (one of the lobbies responsible for the high port charges) and has accelerated concessions of private terminals in the main outlet ports. Since the enactment of the Harbour Law in 1993, more than 100 concessions of private and hybrid terminals have been granted.

Internet: <http://www.mre.gov.br/cdbrasil/itamaraty/web/ingles/economia/agric/logist/apresent.htm>
(with adaptations).

(Analista – ANTAQ – 2005 – CESPE) Based on the text above, it can be concluded that

(1) the Government has already rationalized the control of harbor work.
(2) ten years ago, shipping soy from the port of Paranaguá was more expensive than doing it from New Orleans.
(3) "prospects" (ℓ.17) means likelihood.
(4) the cost of transportation is the only setback for the delivery of agricultural products.
(5) the use of waterways as a means of transportation of goods can be a costly initiative.

(Interpretation) 1: incorrect – (Line 23), '**The Government had already embarked on a process of rationalisation of the management of port labour**' This means the government has begun the process, but not that it has necessarily completed it; 2: correct – Line 5 – In **1995, for example, shipping a ton of soy from New Orleans cost just US$ 3.00 whereas the cost to ship the same product from the Brazilian port of Paranaguá exceeded US$ 14.00**; 3: correct – In this usage, these words can be considered synonyms; 4: incorrect – Port fees are also considered a setback. A setback is a frustration or obstacle; 5: correct Line 11 – The text clearly states that in the US, waterway transportation costs "US$ 16/t", while "in Brazil it exceeded US$ 80/t."
Gabarito 1E, 2C, 3C, 4E, 5C

The U.N. and the sea grab of today

It was the Maltese delegate to the United Nations (U.N.) who spoke up first, in November 1967, to urge the members of the U.N. to use their collective clout to come to an agreement on fair and responsible use of the world's oceans. It took 15 years, but an agreement was eventually struck from a nine-year conference that produced the U.N. Convention on the Law of the Sea.

The treaty was completed in 1982 and came into force in 1994. Essentially, it codified already established customs, like the Law of the Sea. International waters remained international, "the common heritage of all mankind". Limitations were set on how much coastal water and seafloor a nation could claim as its own.

Other legislation determined by the convention included creating the concept of exclusive economic zones (EEZ). Territorial waters are extensions of a state's laws and right of defense; EEZs are extensions of a state's rights to resources offshore. The boundaries of an EEZ go well beyond territorial waters, extending 200 miles (322 km) from shore. All of the organic and mineral resources found in these waters are the exclusive domain of the coastal nation it belongs to.

Josh Clark. **Who owns the oceans?** Internet: <geography.howstuffworks.com> (adapted).

(Analista – ANTAQ – 2009 – CESPE) According to the text, judge the following items.

(1) According to the U.N. Convention on the Law of the Sea, the boundaries of an exclusive economic zone exceed territorial waters.
(2) It has taken nine years for an agreement on fair and responsible use of the world's oceans to be struck since the Maltese delegate to the United Nations spoke about it.
(3) The treaty on fair and responsible use of the world's oceans was struck in 1982 and came into force right away.
(4) Legislation determined by the U.N. Convention on the Law of the Sea included limitations on how much coastal water a nation could claim as its own.

(**Interpretation**) 1: correct – In paragraph 3, the text states, '**The boundaries of an EEZ go well beyond territorial waters**'. To exceed means to be more than, and to go well beyond means to be more than; 2: incorrect – Paragraph 1 – It took 15 years for the agreement to be struck/made; 3: incorrect – Although struck in 1982, the treaty came into force in 1994 (paragraph 2); 4: correct – '**Limitations were set on how much coastal water and seafloor a nation could claim as its own**'. (Paragraph 2).

Gabarito 1C, 2E, 3E, 4C

Text for the next items.

Sharks in the water

In the last year, Somalia's pirates have attacked 120 vessels in the Gulf of Aden, choking commerce in a critical shipping lane (the transit route for 20 percent of the world's oil), blocking aid supplies and driving up transport costs.

The last few weeks have shown how hard it will be to defeat the pirates on the high seas, which seems like the international community's approach. When British Marines tried to board a captured fishing dhow on Nov. 11, they had to go in with guns blazing and killed one possible hostage in the process. A week later, an Indian warship opened fire on what it thought was a pirate mother ship. But the target turned out to be a Thai fishing vessel. When pirates seized their most valuable prize ever on Nov. 15 – the Sirius Star supertanker holding 2 million barrels of Saudi crude – everyone kept their distance.

As this suggests, Somalia's seaborne bandits are making a mockery of all efforts to stop them. Pirates have only increased their efforts, ranging across an area bigger than the Mediterranean. The Sirius Star was taken 450 nautical miles southeast of Kenya, and with it, the Somalis now hold 300 hostages and 15 ships.

The Somalia's internationally recognized transitional government has invited foreign navies to do what's necessary to stop the pirates, even attacking them ashore if need be. The Security Council has affirmed that option. Moreover, nearly all of Somalia's pirates come from one region (Puntland), live in a single town (Boosaaso) and stash captured vessels in one of three ports (Eyl, Hobyo or Haradhere) – making interdiction that much easier. Andrew Linington of Nautilus UK, a seaman's union that has had many of its members taken hostage, says the international community "knows where the pirates are, they know the ports they use, they know the mother ships. Stopping them could be done," he says. But that would be expensive at a time when U.S. resources are tied up in Afghanistan and Iraq.

Rod Nordlant. **Sharks in the water**.
Internet: <www.newsweek.com> (adapted).

(Analista – ANTAQ – 2009 – CESPE) According to the text, it is correct to affirm that

(1) a supertanker was the pirates' most valuable capture.
(2) British Marines tried to board a captured pirate ship on Nov 11. In this process, a possible hostage was killed.
(3) an Indian warship attacked a supposed pirate mother ship which was, nevertheless, a fishing vessel.
(4) All of Somalia's pirates come from one region, what makes their interdiction quite easy.
(5) The efforts to stop the attacks have forced the pirates to shrink the area of their activities.
(6) Although the international community may know where the pirates are or the ports they use, interdicting them would be quite expensive for the U.S. at this moment.

(**Interpretation**) 1: correct – '**When pirates seized their most valuable prize ever on Nov. 15 – the Sirius Star supertanker holding 2 million barrels of Saudi crude.**' (paragraph 2); 2: incorrect – Not clear that it was a pirate ship. The text states it was a fishing dhow (a traditional broad hulled fishing vessel); 3: correct – '**...what it** thought was a pirate mother ship. But the target turned out to be a Thai fishing vessel'. Turned out, here, means found to be; 4: incorrect – The text states, 'nearly all pirates come from one region'. Therefore, it cannot be affirmed that they all do; 5: incorrect – 'Pirates have only increased their efforts, ranging across an area bigger than the Mediterranean.' (paragraph 2); 6: correct – Interdicting them means to prevent/prohibit or destroy. The last line of the text states, 'Stopping them could be done," he says. But that would be expensive at a time when U.S. resources are tied up in Afghanistan and Iraq'. Tied up means to be occupied or engaged for other purposes.

Gabarito 1C, 2E, 3C, 4E, 5E, 6C

Text for the next items.

Food control systems: integrated farm-to-table concept

1   The objective of reduced risk can be achieved most effectively by the principle of prevention throughout the production, processing and marketing chain. To achieve
4   maximum consumer protection, it is essential that safety and quality be built into food products from production through to consumption. This calls for a comprehensive and
7   integrated farm-to-table approach in which the producer, processor, transporter, vendor, and consumer all play a vital role in ensuring food safety and quality.
10   It is impossible to provide adequate protection to the consumer by merely sampling and analyzing the final product. The introduction of preventive measures at all
13   stages of the food production and distribution chain, rather than only inspection and rejection at the final stage, makes better economic sense, because unsuitable products can be
16   identified earlier along the chain. The more economic and effective strategy is to entrust food producers and operators with primary responsibility for food safety and quality.
19   Government regulators are then responsible for auditing performance of the food system through monitoring and surveillance activities and for enforcing legal and regulatory
22   requirements.
     Food hazards and quality loss may occur at a variety of points in the food chain, and it is difficult and
25   expensive to test for their presence. A well-structured, preventive approach that controls processes is the preferred method for improving food safety and quality. Many but not
26   all potential food hazards can be controlled along the food chain through the application of good practices *i.e.* agricultural, manufacturing and hygienic.

Internet: <http://www.fao.org> (with adaptations).

(Analista – ANVISA – 2004 – CESPE) According to the text above, judge the following items.

(1) In the farm-to-table approach, products are sold directly by farmers to consumers.
(2) Transporters and vendors won't play any significant role along the food production and distribution chain.
(3) Primary responsibility for food safety and quality should rest with producers and operators.
(4) Prevention eliminates all potential food hazards.

(Interpretation) 1: incorrect – The farm-to-table approach refers to an approach in which, **"the producer, processor, transporter, vendor, and consumer all play a vital role in ensuring food safety and quality'**. (line 7); 2: incorrect – As in the question above, the farm-to-table approach identifies a clear role for transporters and vendors; 3: correct – **'The more economic and effective strategy is to entrust food producers and operators with primary responsibility for food safety and quality'**. (line 16); 4: incorrect – In line 25, the text states, **'many but not all potential food hazards can be prevented'.**

Gabarito 1E, 2E, 3C, 4E

(Analista – ANVISA – 2004 – CESPE) Judge the following items, related to the text above.

(1) The sentence "it is essential that safety and quality be built into food products" (*l*.4-5) follows the same structure as **it's vital that he go straight to the house**.
(2) "their presence" (*l*.25) refers to food hazards and quality loss.

(Grammar) 1: correct – this is using a subjunctive form where – 'he go' and 'be built' use the bare infinitive form of the verb. This is brought about by the structures "It is vital that" and "it is essential that"; 2: correct – Line 23 is where we find the subject of 'their presence'.

Gabarito 1C, 2C

(Analista – ANVISA – 2004 – CESPE) In the text above,

(1) "achieve" (*l*.3) is to **accomplish** as "hazards" (*l*.23) is to **security**.
(2) "calls for" (*l*.6) means **requires**.
(3) "rather than" (*l*.13-14) could be correctly replaced by **instead of** with no change in meaning.

(Vocabulary) 1: incorrect – Achieve and accomplish can be synonymous. However, hazard means a possible source of danger and security means to free from risk; 2: correct – To call for action means to need or require action; 3: correct – In this context, they can be correctly replaced.

Gabarito 1E, 2C, 3C

Freedom of IMFormation

By Reza Moghadam

Posted on September 17, 2009 by iMFdirect

With the global financial crisis, the world is increasingly looking to the International Monetary Fund– not just for financing but as the global institution charged with overseeing members' economies and policies (what
5   we call surveillance). It's easy to forget that only 10 years ago the Fund was a secretive institution. That's no longer the case. Communicating and engaging with the world at large is now a normal and essential part of the Fund's business.
10   The IMF today is a very open institution. The vast majority of our reports are published. The public can search the IMF's archives. And we are making lots of effort to reach out to external stakeholders.
     The benefits of this increased transparency, both
15   for the Fund's surveillance and lending activities, are indisputable. Transparency allows us to engage with the public and to build a broader understanding and support of what we do. It benefits the *quality* of our advice by subjecting our analysis to outside scrutiny. And more
20   generally, it makes us more *accountable* for our advice and financial decisions. In all, it makes us a more *effective* and *legitimate* institution.
     Frankly, the Fund cannot be a genuine leader on economic policy issues unless it is seen as transparent.
25   We certainly would not have been able to achieve the major reforms of our lending frameworks and the increase in our financial resources had we not been seen as an open and transparent institution. Rightly, the public expects to know what we are up to.

30 At the same time, certain aspects of transparency remain controversial. Some believe that publication undermines candor in the reports, the frankness of discussions between staff and country authorities, and the Fund's role as trusted advisor.
35 Communicating and engaging with the world at large is now a normal and essential part of the Fund's business. We are gearing up to review the Fund's transparency policy, as part of our efforts to increase our effectiveness.
40 The IMF has come a long way over the last 10 years, and publication rates of reports are high. Raising them further is not the main issue, nor one that can easily be resolved without changes much of our membership would consider revolutionary (such as making publication
45 mandatory). Rather, further efforts should focus on making progress on a broad front, on issues that may catch fewer headlines, but are nevertheless crucial:
• Reducing long publication lags. How can we simplify the cumbersome procedure for obtaining consent?
50 • *Maintaining the integrity of reports.* The IMF's analysis and advice must be, and be seen to be, convincing, candid, and independent. To this end, there is a long-standing and fundamental principle that Fund reports are not "negotiated" documents.
55 • *Making the Fund's archives more accessible.* The current setup for searching the archives – in particular the need to travel to Washington to gain full access to them–is outdated. We should also consider whether we can make some archived material available more
60 quickly to the public.

http://blog-imfdirect.imf.org/2009/09/17/
freedom-of-imformation/

(Analista – BACEN – 2010 – CESGRANRIO) The wordplay in the title refers to the fact that the

(A) IMF has not dared to open its reserved archives in Washington to the public in general.
(B) IMF has been adopting a transparency policy so as to enhance its credibility and legitimacy.
(C) IMF must be freed from the impositions of the world leaders on its financial decisions.
(D) once secret information kept by the IMF is not freely discussed nor is it easily negotiable.
(E) world economies are trying to get rid of the excessive control of the IMF over their financial systems.

(Interpretation) A: incorrect – In the last paragraph, the text clearly states that *"The current setup for searching the archives – in particular **the need to travel to Washington to gain full access to them** – is outdated"* (lines 55-58). The author recognizes that access is possible, even though it is difficult; B: correct – In the first paragraph, the text clearly states that *"It's easy to forget that only 10 years ago the Fund **was a secretive institution. That's no longer the case**"* (lines 5-7); C: incorrect – The text makes no reference to impositions from world leaders; D: incorrect – In the fourth paragraph, the text makes reference to the idea of discussions – **"Some believe that publication undermines** candor in the reports, **the frankness of discussions between staff and country authorities**, and the Fund's role as trusted advisor" (lines 31-35). These discussions involve once-secret information, even though some people are not in favor of them. In the seventh paragraph, the text clearly states that *"(...) that Fund reports **are not "negotiated" documents**"* (lines 53-54). This does not mean that information is easily negotiated (or not), but rather that the report must be based on fact and not negotiated information; E: incorrect – In the first paragraph, the text clearly states that *"With the global financial crisis, **the world is increasingly looking to the International Monetary Fund** – not just for financing but **as the global institution charged with overseeing members' economies and policies** (what we call surveillance)"* (lines 1-5). This shows that world economies are not trying to get rid of the IMF, but rather seeking it to oversee their economies.
Gabarito "B".

(Analista – BACEN – 2010 – CESGRANRIO) The only argument that **CANNOT** be considered supportive of publishing the IMF documents is that the

(A) public must be made aware of what the IMF has been doing and the support it is giving to economic policy issues.
(B) IMF will be regarded as a more trustworthy institution if it releases its documents and financial decisions to the public at large.
(C) language used in documents that circulate publicly is usually more controlled and therefore less frank and direct in exposing opinions and facts.
(D) lack of access of external stakeholders to the issues the IMF supports and the actions it takes makes the institution more vulnerable and less effective.
(E) relevant changes made to the financing structure of the institution were only effected in recognition of the IMF as a reputable and candid organization.

(Interpretation) A: incorrect – In the third paragraph, the text clearly states that *"Frankly, the Fund cannot be a genuine leader on economic policy issues **unless it is seen as transparent**"* (lines 23-24). This shows that the IMF is supportive of making its economic policy transparent, or public. In the same paragraph, the text clearly states that *"**Rightly**, **the public expects to know** what we are up to"* (lines 28-29). This means that the IMF is supportive of public awareness; B: incorrect – In the second paragraph, the text clearly states that *"**Transparency** allows us to engage with the public and to build **a broader understanding and support of what we do**"* (lines 16-18). *"(...) it makes us more **accountable for our advice and financial decisions**. In all, it makes us a more **effective** and **legitimate** institution"* (lines 20-22). These 2 sections prove the supportiveness of the idea to release documents and financial decisions; C: correct– In the fourth paragraph, the text clearly states that *"**Some believe that publication undermines candor in the reports**, the frankness of discussions between staff and country authorities, and the Fund's role as trusted advisor"* (lines 31-35). This shows that IMF reports use "careful language", which means they may not expose all opinions and facts in the most earnest manner. This is not supportive of the plan to release information; D: incorrect – In the fifth paragraph, the text clearly states that *"We are gearing up to review the **Fund's transparency policy, as part of our efforts to increase our effectiveness**"* (lines 37-39). This links the idea of transparency and effectiveness as supportive ideas; E: incorrect – In the third paragraph, the text clearly states that "*We certainly would not have been able to achieve **the major reforms of our lending frameworks and the increase in our financial resources had we not been seen as an open and transparent institution**"* (lines 25-28). This shows that the financing structure was affected due to its transparency.
Gabarito "C".

(Analista – BACEN – 2010 – CESGRANRIO) In terms of meaning, it is correct to affirm that

(A) "...charged with..." (lines 3-4) and *endowed with* are synonyms.
(B) "...reach out to..." (line 13) and *get in touch with* are antonyms.

(C) "...scrutiny." (line 19) and *inquiry* have opposite meanings.
(D) "...gearing up to." (line 37) and *getting ready for* express contradictory ideas.
(E) "...come a long way..." (line 40) and *made considerable progress* express similar ideas.

(Vocabulary) A: incorrect – "to be charged with" means to be *attributed the task of doing* something. "To be endowed with" has an idea of *being given something*, usually a skill or a gift; B: incorrect – These two expressions are in fact synonyms; C: incorrect – These two words have similar meanings, although not exactly the same. They both suggest an idea of *inspection*; D: incorrect – The two expressions have similar meanings, although not exactly the same. They both suggest a meaning of *getting prepared for* something; E: correct – The expression "to come a long way" suggest an idea of *substantial evolution*.
Gabarito "E".

(Analista – BACEN – 2010 – CESGRANRIO) The expression in **boldtype** and the item in parenthesis are semantically equivalent in

(A) "**In all**, it makes us a more *effective* and *legitimate* institution." – lines 21-22. (all things considered).
(B) "the Fund cannot be a genuine leader on economic policy issues **unless** it is seen as transparent." – lines 23-24. (given that).
(C) "**Rather,** further efforts should focus on making progress on a broad front, on issues that may catch fewer headlines," – lines 45-47. (moreover).
(D) "**To this end**, there is a long-standing and fundamental principle that Fund reports are not 'negotiated' documents." – lines 52-54. (last but not least).
(E) "We should also consider **whether** we can make some archived material available more quickly to the public." – lines 58-60. (while).

(Vocabulary) A: correct – "In all" is semantically equivalent to "all things considered"; B: incorrect – "Unless" carries an idea of *condition*, while "given that" carries an idea of *reason*, much like "because"; C: incorrect – "Rather" carries an idea of "instead of", while "moreover" carries an idea of *addition*; D: incorrect – "To this end" means "(In order) to achieve the previously stated goal", while "last but not least" means "the last topic to be covered"; E: incorrect – "Whether" carries an idea of *condition*, whereas the word "while" carries an idea of *contrast* or *concession*.
Gabarito "A".

(Analista – BACEN – 2010 – CESGRANRIO) "I agree wholeheartedly with these transparency initiatives. I would also urge the IMF to keep going further forward particularly in regards to archives, as well as releasing country reports as part of a regular pattern of their activities, and to move to a system of releasing mandatory reports. In order for us not to repeat the same mistakes over and over again, we must be able to discern patterns from real world data. Secrecy is to be shunned since it promotes an imbalance in power and always leads to abuses."

Rahim, on December 14th, 2009 at 12:41 am http://blog-
    -imfdirect.imf.org/2009/09/17/freedom-of-imformation/
    #comment-579

The comment above is in tune with Moghadam's ideas, because Rahim states that

(A) secret reports are not welcome in the IMF any more because they actually distort real world data.
(B) some concealment measures should be preserved so as to protect IMF archives and country reports.
(C) no country reports should be mandatory to avoid the imbalance of power among the world's leading nations.
(D) the transparency initiatives promoted by the IMF may eventually lead to mistakes and to an abuse of power.
(E) the IMF should regularly publish reports in order to keep the world informed on financial and economic issues the institution has adopted.

(Interpretation) A: incorrect – In the third sentence, the text states that *"(...) we must be able **to discern patterns from real world data**."* This does not suggest a distortion of real world data, but rather a separation of patterns and data; B: incorrect – In the first sentence, the text clearly states that *"I **agree wholeheartedly with these transparency initiatives**."* and in the last sentence, the text also clearly states *"**Secrecy is to be shunned** (...)"*. These two excerpts prove that Rahim does not believe in concealment; C: incorrect – In the second sentence, the text clearly states that *"(...)and to **move to a system of releasing mandatory reports**,"* which shows that Rahim thinks reports should be mandatory; D: incorrect – In the last sentence, the text clearly states that *"**Secrecy is to be shunned since it promotes an imbalance in power and always leads to abuses**."* This shows that Rahim believes that it is secrecy (not transparency) that leads to mistakes and abuses of power; E: correct – In the second sentence, the text clearly states that *"(...)as well as releasing country reports as part of **a regular pattern of their activities** (...), and to move to a system of **releasing mandatory reports**,"* thus showing that Rahim believes in the regularity of reports.
Gabarito "E".

The difference between saying what you mean and meaning what you say is obvious to most people. To computers, however, it is trickier. Yet getting them to assess intelligently what people mean from what they
5 say would be useful to companies seeking to identify unhappy customers and intelligence agencies seeking to identify dangerous individuals from comments they post online.
   Computers are often inept at understanding the
10 meaning of a word because that meaning depends on the context in which the word is used. For example, "killing" is bad and "bacteria" are bad but "killing bacteria" is often good (unless, that is, someone is talking about the healthy bacteria present in live yogurt, in which case,
15 it would be bad).
   An attempt to enable computers to assess the emotional meaning of text is being led by Stephen Pulman of the University of Oxford and Karo Moilanen, one of his doctoral students. It uses so-called "sentiment
20 analysis" software to assess text. The pair have developed a classification system that analyses the grammatical structure of a piece of text and assigns emotional labels to the words it contains, by looking them up in a 57,000-word "sentiment lexicon" compiled by people. These
25 labels can be positive, negative or neutral. Words such as "never", "failed" and "prevent" are tagged as "changing" or "reversive" words because they reverse the sentiment of the word they precede.

The analysis is then broken into steps that progressively take into account larger and larger grammatical chunks, updating the sentiment score of each entity as it goes. The grammatical rules determine the effect of one chunk of text on another. The simplest rule is that positive and negative sentiments both overwhelm neutral ones. More complex syntactic rules govern seemingly conflicting cases such as "holiday hell" or "abuse helpline" that make sense to people but can confuse computers.

By applying and analysing emotional labels, the software can construct sentiment scores for the concepts mentioned in the text, as a combination of positive, negative and neutral results. For example, in the sentence, "The region's largest economies were still mired in recession," the parsing software finds four of the words in the sentiment lexicon: largest (positive, neutral or negative); economies (positive or neutral); mired (negative); and recession (negative). It then analyses the sentence structure, starting with "economies" and progressing to "largest economies", "region's largest economies" and "the region's largest economies". At each stage, it computes the changing sentiment of the sentence. It then does the same for the second half of the sentence.

Instead of simply adding up the number of positive and negative mentions for each concept, the software applies a weighting to each one. For example, short pieces of text such as "region" are given less weight than longer ones such as "the region's largest economies". Once the parser has reassembled the original text ("the region's largest economies were still mired in recession") it can correctly identify the sentence as having a mainly negative meaning with respect to the concept of "economies".

As well as companies seeking to better understand their customer, intelligence agencies are also becoming interested in the sentiment analysis. But the software can only supplement human judgment – because people don't always mean what they say.

Oct 6th 2009 from Economist.com
http://www.economist.com/sciencetechnology/tm/
displayStory.cfm?story_id=14582575
&source=hptextfeature

(Analista – BNDES – 2010 – CESGRANRIO) The best title for this text is

(A) Killing Bacteria Can Be Bad.
(B) The Wrong Emotional Response.
(C) Software Reveals Emotions in Text.
(D) Computerized Emotional Analysis Fails.
(E) New Computer Software Frauds Text Analysis.

(Interpretation) A: incorrect – In the second paragraph, the text provides examples as in introduction to the topic. However, the introduction (killing bacteria) is merely an anecdote for the introduction. The text does not focus on bacteria at all, but rather on the software that can attribute emotional weight to words and language; B: incorrect – In the sixth paragraph, the text clearly states that *"Once the **parser has reassembled the original text** ("the region's largest economies were still mired in recession") **it can correctly identify the sentence** as having a mainly negative meaning with respect to the concept of "economies"* (lines 59-63). This shows that the software has not provided the wrong response, but rather the correct one; C: correct – In the third paragraph, the text clearly states that *"It uses so-called **"sentiment analysis" software to assess text**."* (lines 19-20). This idea is expanded throughout the text, but it is the essence of the text; D: incorrect – In the sixth paragraph, the text clearly states that *"Once the **parser has reassembled the original text** ("the region's largest economies were still mired in recession")*

it can correctly identify the sentence as having a mainly negative meaning with respect to the concept of "economies" (lines 59-63). This shows that the software has not failed; E: incorrect – There is no mention of "fraud" or "fraudulent" activities in the text.
Gabarito "C".

(Analista – BNDES – 2010 – CESGRANRIO) According to the text, the software developed by Pulman and Moilanen

(A) should be widely tested before being commercially used.
(B) is now able to precisely interpret what people mean from what they say.
(C) might be considered risky if used to analyse dangerous individuals.
(D) can classify all English words into grammatical categories.
(E) can be particularly relevant for companies and intelligence agencies.

(Interpretation) A: incorrect – The text makes no reference to the commercialization of the software; B: incorrect – In the last paragraph, the text clearly states that *"But the software can only supplement human judgment – because **people don't always mean what they say**"* (lines 66-68). This shows that the software is unable to interpret what people mean from what they say because they do not always mean what they say; C: incorrect – The software is not used to analyze individuals, but rather language; D: incorrect – In the third paragraph, the text clearly states that *"The pair have developed a classification system that **analyses the grammatical structure of a piece of text and assigns emotional labels to the words it contains**, by looking them up in a 57,000-word "sentiment lexicon" compiled by people"* (lines 20-24). This shows that the software does not analyze grammar, but rather attributes sentimental values to words in a grammatical structure; E: correct – In the last paragraph, the text clearly states that *"As well as **companies seeking to better understand their customer, intelligence agencies are also becoming interested in the sentiment analysis**"* (lines 64-66).
Gabarito "E".

(Analista – BNDES – 2010 – CESGRANRIO) Which of the following statements is **NOT** true about how the software processes emotional analysis?

(A) Words receive positive, negative or neutral labels.
(B) Words with reversed sentiments are excluded.
(C) The words are always seen in context.
(D) The grammatical structure of each segment is analysed.
(E) A list of nearly sixty thousand words is consulted.

(Interpretation) A: incorrect – In the third paragraph, the text clearly states that *"These labels can be **positive, negative or neutral**"* (lines 24-25); B: correct – In the third paragraph, the text clearly states that *"Words such as "never", "failed" and "prevent" **are tagged as "changing" or "reversive" words** because they reverse the sentiment of the word they precede"* (lines 25-28). This shows that reversed sentiments are not excluded, but "are tagged as "changing" or "reversive"."; C: incorrect – In the second paragraph, the text clearly states that *"Computers are often **inept at understanding the meaning of a word because that meaning depends on the context** in which the word is used"* (lines 9-11). The rest of the text shows how the software does the exact opposite, that is, analyzes words in context by attributing emotional value to the words. Therefore, the words are seen in context; D: incorrect – In the third paragraph, the text clearly states that *"The pair have developed a classification system that **analyses the grammatical structure of a piece of text** and assigns emotional labels to the words it contains, by looking them up in a 57,000-word "sentiment lexicon" compiled by people" (lines 20-24); E: incorrect – In the third paragraph, the text clearly states that *"The pair have developed a classification system that analyses the grammatical structure of a piece of text and assigns emotional labels to the words it contains, by **looking them up in a 57,000-word "sentiment lexicon"** compiled by people"* (lines 20-24).

Gabarito "B".

(Analista – BNDES – 2010 – CESGRANRIO) "holiday hell" and "abuse helpline" (lines 36-37) are quoted in the text to illustrate cases in which the computers will

(A) readily identify the clear meaning of such phrases.
(B) easily deduce the writer's primary negative feelings.
(C) doubt people's capacity of expressing their feelings intelligently.
(D) have difficulty in understanding the writer's original emotional meaning.
(E) be able to immediately interpret the text's underlying sarcastic intentions.

(Interpretation) A: incorrect – In the fourth paragraph, the text clearly states that *"More complex syntactic rules govern seemingly conflicting cases such as **"holiday hell" or "abuse helpline"** that make sense to people but **can confuse computers**"* (lines 35-38); B: incorrect – In the fourth paragraph, the text clearly states that *"More complex syntactic rules govern seemingly conflicting cases such as **"holiday hell" or "abuse helpline" that make sense to people but can confuse computers**"* (lines 35-38); C: incorrect – There is no mention in the text of computers doubting people's capacity; D: correct – In the fourth paragraph, the text clearly states that *"More complex syntactic rules govern seemingly conflicting cases such as **"holiday hell" or "abuse helpline"** that make sense to people but **can confuse computers**"* (lines 35-38); E: incorrect – In the fourth paragraph, the text clearly states that *"More complex syntactic rules govern seemingly conflicting cases such as **"holiday hell" or "abuse helpline"** that make sense to people but **can confuse computers**"* (lines 35-38).

Gabarito "D".

(Analista – BNDES – 2010 – CESGRANRIO) Check the option that contains a correct correspondence of meaning[1].

(A) "…seeking…" (line 5) and 'refusing' have similar meanings.
(B) "…inept…" (line 9) and 'skillful' express contrastive ideas.
(C) "…assigns…" (line 22) could not be replaced by 'attributes'.
(D) "…tagged…" (line 26) and 'labelled' are antonymous.
(E) "…reassembled…" (line 59) and 'split up' are synonymous.

(Vocabulary) A: incorrect – The word "seeking" means "looking for" or "in search of", while "refusing" means "rejecting". These words do not have similar meanings; B: correct – The word "inept" means "a lacking ability", while "skillful" means to have abilities. These are contrastive in meaning; C: incorrect – Both words "assign" and "attribute" mean to "allocate" or to "name". Therefore, "attribute" could replace "assign" in the text; D: incorrect – These two words are synonymous; E: incorrect – These two words/phrases are antonymous.

Gabarito "B".

---

1 The enunciation of the question is misleading. Each individual part of the question had its own enunciation.

(Analista – BNDES – 2010 – CESGRANRIO) Mark the alternative that contains an expression that is a correct replacement for the boldfaced item(s).

(A) "**Yet** getting them to assess intelligently what people mean from what they say…" (lines 3-5) – For that reason.
(B) "(**unless**, that is, someone is talking about the healthy bacteria …)" (lines 13-14) – nevertheless.
(C) "Words **such as** 'never', 'failed', and 'prevent' are tagged as 'changing' or 'reversive' words…" (lines 25-27) – Inasmuch as.
(D) "…**because** they reverse the sentiment of the word they precede." (lines 27-28) – Since.
(E) "**Instead of** simply adding up the number of positive and negative mentions for each concept," (lines 54-55) – While.

(Interpretation) A: "The word "yet" is used to show an idea of *contrast* or *concession*, while the phrase "for that reason" is used to show *cause* or *reason*. Therefore, "for that reason" cannot replace "yet" correctly; B: incorrect – The conjunction "unless" is used to show an idea of *condition*, while the conjunct "nevertheless" is used to show an idea of *contrast* or *concession*. Therefore, the word "nevertheless" cannot replace "unless" correctly; C: incorrect – The phrase "such as" is used to *introduce examples*, while the phrase "inasmuch as" is used to show an idea of *cause* or *reason*. Therefore, "inasmuch as" cannot replace "such as" correctly; D: correct – The conjunctions "since" and "because" can both be used to show an idea of *cause* or *reason*. Therefore, "since" can replace "because" correctly; E: incorrect – The prepositional phrase "instead of" is used to show an idea of *alternative*, whereas the adverb "while" is used either to show an idea of *time* or *contrast*. Therefore, "while" cannot replace "instead of" correctly.

Gabarito "D".

(Analista – BNDES – 2010 – CESGRANRIO) The only fragment in which 'it' refers to "software" is

(A) "To computers, however, **it** is trickier." (lines 2-3)
(B) "**it** would be bad." (line 15)
(C) "**It** uses so-called 'sentiment analysis' software to assess text." (lines 19-20)
(D) "…assigns emotional labels to the words **it** contains," (lines 22-23).
(E) "At each stage, **it** computes the changing sentiment of the sentence." (lines 51-52)

(Grammar) A: incorrect – The pronoun "it", in this sentence, refers back to the obviousness mentioned in the previous sentence: "The difference between saying what you mean and meaning what you say is obvious to most people" (lines 1-2). "It" could be replaced with "understanding the difference between saying what you mean and meaning what you say". Therefore, "it" does not refer to software; B: incorrect – The pronoun "it", in this sentence, refers back to "killing bacteria" (line 12) *"(…) but **killing bacteria**" is often good (unless, that is, someone is talking about the healthy bacteria present in live yogurt, in which case, it **would be bad**)* (lines 12-15). Therefore, "it" does not refer to software; C: incorrect – The pronoun "it", in this sentence, refers back to the subject of the previous sentence: *"**An attempt to enable computers to assess the emotional meaning of text** is being led by Stephen Pulman of the University of Oxford and Karo Moilanen, one of his doctoral students"* (lines 16-19). The pronoun "it" can be replaced as follows: **Pulman and Moilanen's attempt** *"uses so-called 'sentiment analysis' software to assess* text." Therefore, "it" does not refer to software; D: incorrect – The pronoun "it", in this sentence, refers back to "a piece of text" (line 22). Although extremely repetitive, if the pronoun "it" were to be replaced with "a piece of text", the sentence would read as follows: *"The pair have developed a classification system that analyses the grammatical structure of **a piece of text** and assigns emotional labels to the words **that piece of text** contains"*. Therefore, "it" does not refer to software; E: correct – The pronoun "it", in this sentence, refers back to "***the parsing software***" mentioned on line 44: "***the parsing software*** *finds four of the words in the sentiment lexicon:*" The "***the parsing software***" is also the reference for the pronoun "it" in the following sentence that begins on line 47: "***It*** *then analyses the sentence structure (…)*" and then again for the pronoun in the sentence that begins on line 52: "***It*** *then does the same for (…).*" Therefore, "it" does refer to software.

Gabarito "E".

(Analista – BNDES – 2010 – CESGRANRIO) In the example given in paragraphs 5 and 6 (lines 39-63), the author explains that the

(A) emotional meanings are attributed to words in isolation and not to the sentence structure.
(B) emotional scores of each word may change according to the topic discussed in the text.
(C) length of segments and emotional tags of each word are considered in scoring emotional concepts.
(D) word 'recession' is not analyzed because it is hard to identify its emotional meaning.
(E) mere arithmetic sum of the scores indicated for each word will reveal the emotional content of the text analysed.

(Interpretation) A: incorrect – In the fifth paragraph, the text clearly states that "***It*** *then **analyses the sentence structure** (…)*" (lines 47-48); B: incorrect – In the fifth paragraph, the sentence *"For example, in the sentence, "The region's largest economies were still mired in recession," the parsing software finds four of the words in the sentiment lexicon:* ***the words in the sentiment lexicon****: largest (positive, neutral or negative); economies (positive or neutral); mired (negative); and recession (negative)"* (lines 42-45) suggest that emotional scores are attributed based on their own meaning, not on what the topic of the text is. Later, the text clearly states that "***It*** *then **analyses the sentence structure** (…)*" (lines 47-48). This does not mean, however, that the topic of the text is taken into consideration; C: correct – In the sixth paragraph, the text clearly states that *"For example,* ***short pieces of text*** *such as "region" are given less weight than **longer ones** such as "the region's largest economies"* (lines 56-59). This shows that length of text is considered. In the fifth paragraph, the text clearly states that *"For example, in the sentence, "The region's largest economies were still mired in recession,"* ***the parsing software finds four of the words in the sentiment lexicon***: *(…)"* (lines 42-45), thus proving that the emotional tags of each word are also considered; D: incorrect – In the fifth paragraph, the word "recession" is analyzed: *"For example, in the sentence, "The region's largest economies were still mired in recession," the parsing software finds four of the words in the sentiment lexicon: (…)* ***and recession (negative)****"* (lines 42-47); E: incorrect – In the sixth paragraph, the text clearly states that "***Instead of simply adding up the number*** *of positive and negative mentions for each concept,* ***the software applies a weighting to each one***" (lines 54-56). This proves that a mere arithmetic sum is not used.

Gabarito "C".

(Analista – BNDES – 2010 – CESGRANRIO) Check the alternative in which the expression is precisely explained, according to its meaning in the text.

(A) "…'killing' (…) 'bacteria'…" (line 12) – bacteria that can kill.
(B) "…the emotional meaning of text…" (lines 16-17) – the meaning of a sentimental text.
(C) "…complex syntactic rules…" (line 35) – difficult language regulations.
(D) "…seemingly conflicting cases…" (line 36) – cases that are apparently doubtful.
(E) "…('the region's largest economies…' " (line 60) – economies of highly populated regions.

(Interpretation) A: incorrect – The word "bacteria" on line 12 refers to bad bacteria, but not necessarily to bacteria that can kill. The explanation is too precise and extrapolates the meaning in the text; B: The adjective "sentimental" is used when talking about people's feeling or sensitiveness. It is not used to talk about the emotional charge of a word. The meaning of the noun "sentiment" is quite different from the adjective "sentimental". "Sentiment" means "opinion", "attitude" or "specific view". The explanation is wrong and not in accordance with the meaning in the text; C: incorrect – Language has rules/conventions, not regulations; D: correct – The word "seemingly" is synonymous with "apparently"; the word "conflicting" in this case means "incompatible", which is similar to "doubtful". The explanation is precise and in accordance with the meaning in the text; E: incorrect – The collocation "largest economies" does not refer to the size of the population within a given economy, but rather to the monetary size of that economy. The explanation is wrong and not in accordance with the meaning in the text.

Gabarito "D".

(Analista – BNDES – 2010 – CESGRANRIO) From the fragment "But the software can only supplement human judgement – because people don't always mean what they say." (lines 66-68), we may infer that the author

(A) does not believe the software can be totally trusted.
(B) complains that human judgement is never fair enough.
(C) pressuposes that computer sentiment analysis is fully reliable.
(D) rejects human analysis of feelings and supports technological sentiment analysis.
(E) criticizes companies that intend to use the new software to analyse potentially dangerous clients.

(Interpretation) A: correct – The use of the adverb "only" in this sentence diminishes the author's trust in the software's ability. The adverb here carries a meaning of "merely". This can lead to an inference that the author feels the software is quite limited and, therefore, cannot be totally trusted; B: incorrect – The author does not mention fairness; C: incorrect – The use of the adverb "only" in this sentence diminishes the author's trust in the software's ability. The adverb here carries a meaning of "merely". This can lead to an inference that the author feels the software is quite limited and, therefore, not fully reliable; D: incorrect – The author refers to the unreliability of what people say, but there is no clear rejection of the human analysis. The use of the adverb "only" in this sentence diminishes the author's trust in the software's ability. The adverb here carries a meaning of "merely". This can lead to an inference that the author feels that technological sentiment analysis the software is quite limited; E: incorrect – the author makes no criticism of companies in this sentence, or in the text.

Gabarito "A".

Green is the hot topic these days, and the concept is having an impact on the way people think about datacenters. Companies around the world are announcing ways to save energy and reduce costs by buying new hardware and services. Yet, there is little guidance on how you can take action to control energy costs. In the past, electricity has been treated as an overhead expense, like the cost of space. But with rising power costs and issues regarding reliability, supply, and capacity, electricity requires its own specific strategy. Projects regarding performance optimization and cost reduction are a part of everyday best practices in nearly every area of business. So why not treat energy cost in the same way?

As Information Technologies (IT) pros, many of us make decisions about the configuration and setup of servers, the specifications on the equipment our organizations purchase, and the requirements for datacenter upgrades and construction. We even provide early design input during application development. When it comes to these projects, we obviously have a golden opportunity to be green and influence the energy efficiency of any datacenter.

The first part of any strategy is to know your current energy usage. You need to know where your energy is used and by what specific equipment, as well as what usage is efficient and what is wasteful in the datacenter. Unfortunately, it's rare to find power-consumption metering in place that can break down usage to a level where people can see the results of their actions. Most organizations typically only see a monthly power bill that rolls up consumption into an overall bottom line. This offers little incentive for saving energy since individuals never see the impact of their decisions, and there is no way for them to prove that their changes have actually saved energy.

One of the first issues people confront when considering a green datacenter initiative is whether they have executive support. For the purpose of the article, I am going to assume the answer is "not yet." Executive support requires a serious commitment that provides resources and budget for your initiative. And while there is a lot of talk about green datacenters, the reality is that there is still often a lack of serious support at the executive level. If you did already have such executive support, you would probably be running a green datacenter right now.

Still, even assuming you are not getting the support you need, there is a great deal you can do to push your green datacenter initiative forward. So how do you determine effective actions to take in achieving your goals? Fortunately, energy efficiency is not a new concept and there is a lot that IT pros can learn from other industries. [...]

Anyway, for whichever direction you choose, planning an energy efficiency program for your datacenter will require collaboration across groups in IT. Until recently, the typical approach to planning IT solutions has been to ignore power costs early on during the design phase, focusing on the hardware and software being purchased, along with the labor and hosting costs of the solution. When power is buried in the overhead cost of running solutions in a datacenter, energy efficiency is a low priority. Exposing the actual power being consumed by solutions is the first critical step in changing the behavior of your organization.

By Dave Ohara *TechNet Magazine*, October 2007

(Analista – BNDES – 2008 – CESGRANRIO) All the statements below refer to ideas expressed in the first paragraph, **EXCEPT** one. Mark it.

(A) It is important to develop a strategy to control energy costs in datacenters.
(B) Companies can reduce energy consumption by changing computer hardware.
(C) The current concern with protection of natural resources affects datacenters.
(D) Formerly, both space and electricity costs used to be considered overhead expenses.
(E) Instructions about how to reduce costs through hardware replacement are scarce.

(Interpretation) A: incorrect – In the first paragraph, the text clearly states that *"Green is the hot topic these days, and the concept is having **an impact on the way people think about datacenters**"* (lines 1-3) and that *"Projects regarding performance optimization and **cost reduction** are a part of **everyday best practices in nearly every area of business**"* (lines 11-13). This shows that it is important for datacenters to control energy costs; B: incorrect – In the first paragraph, the text clearly states that "Companies around the world are announcing ways to save energy and reduce costs by **buying new hardware** and services" (lines 3-5); C: incorrect – In the first paragraph, the text clearly states that *"**Green is the hot topic** these days, and the concept is having an impact on the way people think about datacenters"* (lines 1-3); D: incorrect – In the first paragraph, the text clearly states that "**In the past, electricity has been treated as an overhead expense, like the cost of space**" (lines 7-8); E: correct – In the first paragraph, the text mentions nothing about instructions on how to reduce costs, nor does it mention how readily available or scarce these instructions are.

Gabarito "E".

(Analista – BNDES – 2008 – CESGRANRIO) The main purpose of the second paragraph is to:

(A) explain in detail the early decisions that all information technologies experts have already made.
(B) show the key role of information technologists in helping datacenters become energy-efficient.
(C) blame IT professionals for any problems with equipment specifications and with configuration and setup of servers.
(D) present the author of the article as an Information Technology pro, responsible for making all the decisions described.
(E) criticize information technologists who fail to influence the energy efficiency of the datacenters in which they work.

(Interpretation) A: incorrect – While the paragraph mentions early design input, the focus is not detailed; B: correct – The second paragraph clearly states that *"When it comes to these projects, we obviously have **a golden opportunity** to be green and **influence the energy efficiency of any datacenter**"* (lines 20-23); C: incorrect – There is no blame attributed in the second paragraph; D: incorrect – The second paragraph focuses on the opportunity that pros have to influence energy efficiency, not on the author's decision-making powers; E: incorrect – The second paragraph does not offer criticism of technologists, but rather focuses on their influence in energy saving issues.

Gabarito "B".

(Analista – BNDES – 2008 – CESGRANRIO) The correct opposites for the words "hot" (line 1) and "wasteful" (line 27) as they are used in the text are, respectively:

(A) out of fashion – imprudent
(B) unpopular – economical.
(C) outdated – excessive.
(D) cool – unnecessary.
(E) trendy – thrifty.

(Vocabulary) A: incorrect – Within the context of the text, "out of fashion" (not in fashion) does not figure as a collocation for "topic". "Imprudent" does not necessarily suggest "does not waste", thus it is not an exact opposite of "wasteful."; B: correct – "A hot topic" means a very popular topic, while "wasteful" means "careless with cost-related issues" – both opposites of the words "unpopular" and "economical"; C: incorrect – Within the context of the text, "outdated" (not currently in fashion) does not figure as a collocation for "topic". While the word "excessive" collates well in the sentence, it does not necessarily suggest "does not waste"; thus, it is not an exact opposite of "wasteful."; D: incorrect – Within the context of the text, "cool" (not hot, as in temperature, or in fashion) is not suitable. "Unnecessary" does not necessarily suggest "does not waste;" thus, it is not an exact opposite of "wasteful."; E: incorrect – Within the context of the text, "trendy" (in fashion) is not suitable. "Thrifty" does not necessarily suggest "does not waste", but rather "try to save". Thus, it is not an exact opposite of "wasteful."

Gabarito "B".

(Analista – BNDES – 2008 – CESGRANRIO) In Paragraph 3, the author:

(A) gives advice on measures to be taken by organizations and regrets that the energy-saving efforts of datacenter workers cannot be verified.
(B) warns about what is wasteful in corporate datacenters and criticizes employees for not engaging in energy-saving programs.
(C) encourages the use of power-consumption metering in datacenters and claims that this is the only possible way of saving energy in an office.
(D) reveals that most organizations do not stimulate the reduction in energy consumption and blames office workers for wasting energy in datacenters.
(E) describes the importance of monthly power bills for energy-efficient programs and justifies why this strategy has been adopted by most organizations.

(Interpretation) A: correct – In the paragraph, the text clearly states that "**You need to know where your energy is used and by what specific equipment**, as well as what usage is efficient and what is wasteful in the datacenter. **Unfortunately, it's rare to find power-consumption metering in place that can break down usage** to a level where people can see the results of their actions" (lines 25-30); B: incorrect – There is no criticism of employees in this paragraph; C: incorrect – While the paragraph does encourage metering in datacenters, it does not state that this is the only way to save energy; D: incorrect – In the paragraph, the text mentions the idea of stimulating the reduction of energy consumption – "This offers **little incentive for saving energy** since individuals never see the impact of their decisions" (lines 33-34); however, there is no blame attributed to workers; E: incorrect – In the paragraph, the text clearly states that "Most organizations typically **only see a monthly power bill** that rolls up consumption into an overall bottom line" (lines 30-32). The author does not glorify this issue, but rather criticizes it.

Gabarito "A".

(Analista – BNDES – 2008 – CESGRANRIO) Mark the sentence in which the idea introduced by the word in **bold type** is correctly described.

(A) "**Yet**, there is little guidance on how you can take action to control energy costs." (lines 5-7) – addition
(B) "**So** why not treat energy costs in the same way?" (lines 13-14) – contrast
(C) "This offers little incentive for saving energy **since** individuals never see the impact of their decisions," (lines 33-34) – reason
(D) "One of the first issues people confront … is **whether** they have executive support." (lines 37-39) – exemplification.
(E) "And **while** there is a lot of talk about green datacenters", (lines 42-43) – cause

(Grammar) A: incorrect – The conjunct "yet", here, carries a meaning of contrast; B: incorrect – The conjunction "so", here, carries a meaning of consequence; C: incorrect – The conjunction "since", here, carries a meaning of cause or reason; D: The word "whether" is merely placed at the beginning of the subject complement (predicativo do sujeito). It is not the word "whether" that construes the idea of "exemplification", but rather the structure of the sentence (subject + linking verb + subject complement) that can accept the word "whether", which is, in fact, a conjunction used to show alternatives (whether or not); E: incorrect – The conjunction "while", here, carries a meaning of contrast (similar to "even though").

Gabarito Oficial "D" / Nosso Gabarito: todas incorretas.

(Analista – BNDES – 2008 – CESGRANRIO) The sentence in which "can" is used in the same sense as in "there is a great deal you can do to push your green datacenter initiative forward." (lines 49-50) is:

(A) The employees will ask the manager if they can give their opinion on the issue.
(B) You can read my final report on energy consumption if you want to.
(C) Stockholders can hardly wait to read the company's balance sheet.
(D) Can you tell me how many laptops the company has?
(E) I don't think you can find a solution for this problem.

(Grammar) A: incorrect – The modal verb "can", here, carries a meaning of permission; B: incorrect – The modal verb "can", here, carries a meaning of permission; C: incorrect – The modal verb "can", here, carries a meaning of possibility, which is negated by the adverb "hardly", making it an impossibility; D: incorrect – The modal verb "can", here, carries a meaning of possibility, or a request; E: correct – The word "can", here, carries a meaning of ability as does the use in the enunciation.

Gabarito "E".

(Analista – BNDES – 2008 – CESGRANRIO) Check the correct pair of synonyms.

(A) early (line 20) – quick.
(B) actually (line 36) – presently.
(C) provides (line 41) – supplies.
(D) lack (line 44) – loss.
(E) achieving (line 51) – planning.

(Vocabulary) A: incorrect – "Early" means in the beginning of a process, while "quick" means "rapidly"; B: incorrect – The word "actually" is a false cognate (atualmente) and is not used with a sense of time in this case. On line 36, it carries the meaning of "true" or "real"; C: Gabarito Oficial incorrect / Nosso Gabarito correct – The verb "supply" is a synonym for the word "provide" on line 41; D: incorrect – The word "lack" carries a meaning of "shortage" or "scarcity", while "loss" means you no longer have something you originally had; E: incorrect – The word "achieving" means "being successful", while "planning" means "making strategies".

Gabarito "C".

(Analista – BNDES – 2008 – CESGRANRIO) If you "push your ... initiative forward" (lines 49-50) you:

(A) try to get people to pay attention to it.
(B) use all available means to impose it.
(C) take steps to implement it forcefully.
(D) postpone its execution to a later time.
(E) transfer the responsibility for it to other people.

(Vocabulary) A: correct – The collocation "push your ... initiative forward" carries a sense of *making it publicly known*, or *advertising*; B: incorrect – The collocation "push your ... initiative forward" does not carry a sense of *imposition*; C: incorrect – The collocation "push your ... initiative forward" does not carry a sense of *forcefully implementing* something; D: incorrect – The collocation "push your ... initiative forward" does not carry a sense of *postponing*; E: incorrect – The collocation "push your ... initiative forward" does not carry a sense of *transference*.
Gabarito "A".

(Analista – BNDES – 2008 – CESGRANRIO) The final message of the text (lines 55-66) is that:

(A) to change company behavior you must proceed step by step.
(B) it is only during the design phase that power costs have to be considered.
(C) it is important to discriminate power consumption by IT equipment in companies.
(D) energy efficiency will ensure close collaboration between teams of IT experts.
(E) energy experts ought to invest more time in planning IT solutions.

(Interpretation) A: incorrect – The text makes reference to what has been happening up until now, but no suggestion to take a step-by-step approach is made; B: incorrect – The text reveals that power costs were ignored during the design phase, but it does not suggest that this is the only phase when power costs should be given attention; C: correct – The text clearly states that "*Exposing the actual power being consumed by solutions is the first critical step in changing the behavior of your organization*" (lines 64-66). These solutions are specified earlier in the paragraph as IT solutions; D: incorrect – The text suggests that energy efficiency will **require** close collaboration between teams of IT experts, not ensure it; E: incorrect – It is exactly the opposite. The text suggests that **IT experts** ought to invest more time in planning **energy solutions**.
Gabarito "C".

(Analista – BNDES – 2008 – CESGRANRIO) The title that best summarizes the content of the article is:

(A) The importance of executive support.
(B) How to improve datacenter capacity.
(C) Technology experts and their decisions.
(D) Building a green datacenter.
(E) Learning to deal with waste.

(Interpretation) A: incorrect – This is an aspect of the datacenter that is questioned, but it is not the core of the article; B: incorrect – The issue is cost and energy reduction, not building capacity; C: incorrect – These are aspects of the datacenter that are questioned, but it is not the core of the article; D: correct – This title best summarizes the text; E: incorrect – The text focuses very little on waste.
Gabarito "D".

Professional-Client Relationships: Rethinking Confidentiality, Harm, and Journalists' Public Health Duties

by Renita Coleman, Louisiana State University; Thomas May, Medical College of Wisconsin *Journalists seldom consider the layers of those affected by their actions; third parties such as families, children, and even people unlucky enough to be in the wrong place at the wrong time. This paper argues for consideration of the broader group, considering a range of options available for doing their duty to inform the public while also minimizing harm to others. Journalists might compare themselves with other professions that have similar roles; anthropologists, for one on such issues as confidentiality and disclosure. A broader lesson is the value of applying different views, theoretical frameworks, and starting points to the ethical issues in any profession.*

(**Journal of Mass Media Ethics**, 2002: volume 17.2
Special Issue: Codes of Ethics)

(Analista Legislativo – Câmara dos Deputados – 2007 – FCC) No texto, *the broader group* refere-se a

(A) the anthropologists.
(B) the public.
(C) journalists in general.
(D) third parties.
(E) other professions.

(Interpretation) A: incorrect – The term refers to those affected by journalists; the paper compares anthropologists, but this is not broader group; B: incorrect – Journalists generally write for the public; however, the first sentence clearly states that journalists do not "***consider the layers of those affected by their actions***", meaning that the reach of the effect is broader than the public that reads (it goes beyond the immediate readers), including children, who can be classified as third parties; C: incorrect – The term refers to those affected by journalists, not the journalists themselves; D: correct –The first sentence clearly states that journalists do not "***consider the layers of those affected by their actions***", meaning that the reach of the effect is broader than the public that reads (it goes beyond the immediate readers), including children, who can be classified as third parties; E: incorrect – The term refers to those affected by journalists; the paper references other professions, but this is not broader group.
Gabarito "D".

(Analista Legislativo – Câmara dos Deputados – 2007 – FCC) Infere-se do resumo do artigo que

(A) qualquer relação entre o exercício da profissão de jornalista e a saúde pública é inaceitável.
(B) o respeito à confidencialidade de suas fontes é o princípio maior que deve reger a ética do jornalista.
(C) o jornalista deve levar em conta o lado humano ao cumprir o dever de informar o público.
(D) mesmo um jornalista responsável acabará, inevitavelmente, afetando a saúde de pessoas não envolvidas no evento que estiver cobrindo.
(E) jornalistas e antropólogos só têm em comum o fato de trabalharem diretamente com o público.

(Interpretation) A: incorrect – The text makes no reference to public health care; B: incorrect – Confidentiality is mentioned when comparing the role of journalists with that of anthropologists, but the text does not place this as the main principle of the jobs; C: correct – The sentence "*This paper argues for consideration of the broader group, considering a range of options available for **doing their duty to inform the public while also minimizing harm to others**"* clearly states that the human factor is the core of the article; D: incorrect – The text does not talk about the affect on health, nor does it mention any difference between types of journalists (responsible or irresponsible). The text does mention that journalists could affect the lives of third parties, but not specifically their health; E: incorrect – The text clearly states that common factors between anthropologists and journalists include "***confidentiality and disclosure***".

Gabarito "C".

E-9.025 Patient Advocacy for Change in Law and Policy

Physicians may participate in individual acts, grassroots activities, or legally permissible collective action to advocate for change, as provided for in the AMA's Principles of Medical Ethics. Whenever engaging in advocacy efforts, physicians... ensure that the health of patients is not jeopardized and that patient care is not compromised.

Formal unionization of physicians, and including physicians-in-training, may tie physicians' obligations to the interests of workers who may not share physicians' primary and overriding commitment to patients and the public health. Physicians should not form workplace alliances with those who do not share these ethical priorities.

Strikes and other collective action may reduce access to care, eliminate or delay necessary care, and interfere with continuity of care. Each of these consequences raises ethical concerns. Physicians should refrain from the use of the strike as a bargaining tactic. In rare circumstances, individual or grassroots actions, such as brief limitations of personal availability, may be appropriate as a means of calling attention to needed changes in patient care. Physicians are cautioned that some actions may put them or their organizations at risk of violating antitrust laws. Consultation with legal counsel is advised.

Physicians and physicians-in-training should press for needed reforms through the use of informational campaigns, non-disruptive public demonstrations, lobbying and publicity campaigns, and collective negotiation, or other options that do not jeopardize the health of patients or compromise patient care.

(Adapted from htpp://www.ama-assn.org/ama1/pub/upload/mm/38/a-05ceja.pdf)

(Analista Legislativo – Câmara dos Deputados – 2007 – FCC) A palavra que preenche a lacuna corretamente é

(A) can.
(B) must.
(C) may.
(D) might.
(E) could.

(Grammar) A: incorrect – The modal verb "can" refers to ability or permission. The context of the sentence does not refer to the physicians' abilities or their permission. It establishes the obligations of physicians during advocacy efforts; B: correct – The modal verb "must" refers to obligation. The context of the sentence refers to the obligations of physicians during advocacy efforts; C: incorrect – The modal verb "may" refers to possibility or probability. The context of the sentence does not refer to these ideas. It establishes the obligations of physicians during advocacy efforts; D: incorrect – The modal verb "might" refers to possibility or probability. The context of the sentence does not refer to these ideas. It establishes the obligations of physicians during advocacy efforts; E: incorrect – The modal verb "could" refers to possibility, ability or permission. The context of the sentence does not refer to these ideas. It establishes the obligations of physicians during advocacy efforts.

Gabarito "B".

(Analista Legislativo – Câmara dos Deputados – 2007 – FCC) Um sinônimo para *not jeopardized*, no texto, é

(A) not put at risk.
(B) not delayed.
(C) limited.
(D) destroyed.
(E) reduced.

(Vocabulary) A: correct – The word "jeopardize" means to put something at risk; B: incorrect – The word "delay" means to postpone the timing, while "jeopardize" means to put something at risk; C: incorrect – The word "limit" means to restrict, while "jeopardize" means to put something at risk; D: incorrect – The word "destroy" means to damage, while "jeopardize" means to put something at risk; E: incorrect – The word "reduce" means to minimize, while "jeopardize" means to put something at risk.

Gabarito "A".

Read the text below entitled "Another one bites the dust" in order to answer the questions:

Another one bites the dust

Source: www.economist.com Apr 27th, 2012 (Adapted)

Less than three months after it took office, Romania´s government has fallen. The centre-right administration lost a no-confidence vote filed by the left-wing opposition. When the motion was originally filed few thought the government was in danger. But in recent weeks it has been weakened by a series of defections.

"Today there was justice," celebrated Victor Ponta, leader of the centre-left Social-Liberal Union (USL), after securing 235 votes in favour of his motion, four more than he needed. "We don´t want any more dubious firms, no more selling under the market price and huge bribes," he said in a five-hour long debate that preceded the vote.

Traian Basescu, the president and main political player in Romania, proposed Mr Ponta as prime minister back in February when the previous government, led by Emil Boc, resigned after three weeks of street protests denouncing party cronyism, incompetence and harsh austerity measures. Mr Ponta refused, but now he seems more willing to step in thanks to the fair-weather politicians who have flocked to his party from the centre-right.

The International Monetary Fund (IMF), which began an official visit to Romania earlier this week to review the country's performance linked to a 5 billion euro credit line it was granted last year, announced it would suspend its mission until a new government is in place. That may not take long. But with Romanian governments showing the longevity of mayflies, and the European Union (EU) weary of a country that seems unable or unwilling to make serious progress on the corruption problems that continue to plague it five years after it was accepted into the club, it will take a good deal longer for Romania to acquire the clout that should come naturally to an EU country with 22m people.

(Analista – CGU – 2012 – ESAF) According to paragraph 1, Romania's government

(A) is on the verge of taking office.
(B) has been defeated.
(C) is likely to fall.
(D) has strengthened its political support.
(E) will leave office in three months.

(Interpretation) A: incorrect – In the first sentence, the text clearly states that "(…) Romania's government *has fallen*", meaning that they are not about to take office, but are leaving it; B: correct – In the second sentence, the text clearly states that "The centre-right administration *lost a no-confidence vote* filed by the left-wing opposition"; C: incorrect – In the first sentence, the text clearly states that "(…) Romania's government *has fallen*", meaning that they are not about to fall, but have already fallen; D: incorrect – In the second sentence, the text clearly states that "The centre-right administration *lost a no-confidence vote* filed by the left-wing opposition", meaning that there is very little support or confidence in the government; E: incorrect – In the first sentence, the text clearly states that "Less than three months *after it took office*, Romania's government *has fallen*", meaning that it took office three months ago and that now it is leaving.
Gabarito "B".

(Analista – CGU – 2012 – ESAF) At the opening of paragraph 2, the leader of the centre-left USL, Victor Ponta, expressed his

(A) contentment.
(B) resentment.
(C) rage.
(D) hopelessness.
(E) disappointment.

(Interpretation) A: correct – In the sentence "Today there was justice," *celebrated* Victor Ponta, leader of the centre-left Social-Liberal Union (USL), after *securing 235 votes in favour of his motion*, four more than he needed", the text clearly shows that Mr. Ponta was contented; B: incorrect – The word "resentment" means anger and bitterness; C: incorrect – The word "rage" means anger or fury; D: incorrect – The word "hopelessness" means despair and desperation; E: incorrect – The word "disappointment" means discontent and dissatisfaction.
Gabarito "A".

(Analista – CGU – 2012 – ESAF) According to paragraph 3, Mr Ponta

(A) took office as prime minister in February.
(B) unfortunately resigned as prime minister.
(C) may soon join a centre-right party.
(D) might still run for a political post.
(E) led decisive street protests for weeks.

(Interpretation) A: incorrect – In the first sentence in the third paragraph, the text clearly states that "Traian Basescu, the president and main political player in Romania, *proposed Mr Ponta as prime minister back in February*", which shows that it was a proposal. Mr. Ponta did not take office in February; B: incorrect – In the first sentence in the third paragraph, the text clearly states that "Traian Basescu, the president and main political player in Romania, proposed Mr Ponta as prime minister back in February *when the previous government, led by Emil Boc, resigned* after three weeks of street protests", which shows that it was Emil Boc that resigned, not Mr. Ponta; C: incorrect – In the last sentence in the third paragraph, the text clearly states that "Mr Ponta refused, but now he seems more willing to step in thanks to the fair-weather *politicians who have flocked to his party from the centre-right.*" This shows that he will remain in his centre-left Social-Liberal Union (USL), but that politicians *from the centre-right* have joined him; D: correct – In the last sentence in the third paragraph, the text clearly states that "Mr Ponta refused, but now *he seems more willing to step in* thanks to the fair-weather politicians who have flocked to his party from the centre-right." This shows the possibility of his candidacy; E: incorrect – In the first sentence in the third paragraph, the text clearly states that "Traian Basescu, the president and main political player in Romania, proposed Mr Ponta as prime minister back in February *when the previous government, led by Emil Boc, resigned after three weeks of street protests*", which shows that the street protests were not led by Mr. Ponta. The text does not reveal who led the protests.
Gabarito "D".

(Analista – CGU – 2012 – ESAF) In paragraph 4, the European Union is said to be "weary" as regards Romania's attitude towards corruption. In other words,

(A) hopeful.
(B) not certain.
(C) very tired.
(D) quite optimistic.
(E) rather doubtful.

(Vocabulary) A: incorrect – The word "hopeful" means expectant; B: incorrect – The phrase "not certain" means unsure; C: correct – The word "weary" means very tired; D: incorrect – The phrase "quite optimistic" means confident and positive; E: incorrect – The phrase "rather doubtful" means quite suspicious.
Gabarito "C".

(Analista – CGU – 2012 – ESAF) According to paragraph 4,

(A) Romanians have succeeded in their struggle against corrupt practices.
(B) the IMF has denied the 5 billion euro credit line agreed upon.
(C) the new government will have to be recognized by the IMF.
(D) the EU recognizes the steps taken by Romania so as to fight corruption.
(E) Romania has still not obtained the political influence it could.

(Interpretation) A: incorrect – In the last sentence, the text clearly states that "(…) and the European Union (EU) weary of *a country that seems unable or unwilling to make serious progress on the corruption problems* (…)", meaning that the EU is tired of Romania's lack of progress against corruption; B: incorrect – In the first sentence of the fourth paragraph, the text clearly states that *"**The International Monetary Fund** (IMF), which began an official visit to Romania earlier this week to **review the country's performance linked to a 5 billion euro credit line** it was granted last year, announced it would suspend its mission until a new government is in place."* This means that the loan has not been canceled, but rather that it is under review; C: incorrect – In the first sentence of the fourth paragraph, the text clearly states that *"**The International Monetary Fund** (IMF), which began an official visit to Romania earlier this week to review the country's performance linked to a 5 billion euro credit line it was granted last year, **announced it would suspend its mission until a new government is in place**."* This means that the IMF will wait until a new government is in power before sending a team to the country. This does not suggest that the government require recognition from the IMF; D: incorrect – In the last sentence, the text clearly states that *"(...) and the European Union (EU) weary of **a country that seems unable or unwilling to make serious progress on the corruption problems** (...)"*, meaning that the EU believes the steps are futile or that the steps have not really been taken; E: correct – In the last sentence, the text clearly states that *"(...) **it will take a good deal longer for Romania to acquire the clout that should come naturally** to an EU country with 22m people"*, showing that Romania is behind in acquiring the political sway it could have.

Gabarito "E".

Your answers to questions must be based on the text below entitled "Land of Promise":

Land of Promise

Source: www.economist.com/specialreports
April 12th 2007 (Adapted)

In 2003 Goldman Sachs, an investment bank, selected Brazil, along with Russia, India and China, as one of the "BRICs"– the developing countries that would share dominance of the world economy by 2050.

In some ways Brazil is the steadiest of the BRICs. Unlike China and Russia it is a full-blooded democracy; unlike India it has no serious disputes with its neighbours. It is the only BRIC without a nuclear bomb. The Heritage Foundation's "Economic Freedom Index", which measures such factors as protection of property rights and free trade, ranks Brazil ("moderate free") above the other BRICs ("mostly unfree"). One of the main reasons why Brazil's growth has been slower than China's and India's is that Brazil is richer and more urbanized.

The survey will argue that disgruntlement persists because Brazil is a battleground between progress and inertia. Since independence was proclaimed by the son of the Portuguese king, Brazil has been adding layer upon layer of change rather than sweeping away the old and starting afresh.

(Analista – CGU – 2008 – ESAF) In paragraph 1, four countries are referred to as

(A) unlikely to play a key role in the world economic scenario.
(B) the slowest-growing economies of the present.
(C) likely to dominate the world economy in the future.
(D) the fastest-growing economies over the past 50 years.
(E) being today's richest and most prosperous economies.

(Interpretation) A: incorrect – The sentence clearly states that *"the developing countries that would **share dominance of the world economy by 2050**."*; B: incorrect – The text does not mention the speed of growth; C: correct – The sentence clearly states that *"the developing countries that would **share dominance of the world economy by 2050**."*; D: incorrect – The text does not mention the speed of growth; E: incorrect – The sentence clearly states that *"the developing countries that would **share dominance of the world economy by 2050**."* It makes reference to the future, not today.

Gabarito "C".

(Analista – CGU – 2008 – ESAF) In paragraph 2, the author compares Brazil's growth to China's and India's and, therefore, defines it as

(A) not being as fast.
(B) dependent on the latter.
(C) unexpectedly higher.
(D) not as stable.
(E) the least steady.

(Interpretation) A: correct – In the last sentence in the second paragraph, the text clearly states that *"One of the main reasons why **Brazil's growth has been slower than China's and India's** is that Brazil is richer and more urbanized."*; B: incorrect – The text show no dependence of any country on another; C: incorrect – In the last sentence in the second paragraph, the text clearly states that *"One of the main reasons why **Brazil's growth has been slower than China's and India's** is that Brazil is richer and more urbanized."*; D: incorrect – In the first sentence of the second paragraph, the text clearly states that *"In some ways **Brazil is the steadiest of the BRICs**."*; E: incorrect – In the first sentence of the second paragraph, the text clearly states that *"In some ways **Brazil is the steadiest of the BRICs**."*

Gabarito "A".

(Analista – CGU – 2008 – ESAF) In paragraph 3, progress and inertia are cited as the two

(A) complementary forces in Brazil's promising future.
(B) opposing forces in the Brazilian battleground.
(C) foes of Brazil's past growth as a world economy.
(D) forces that triggered Brazil's economic growth.
(E) realities which are likely to coexist in Brazil's economic scenario.

(Interpretation) A: incorrect – The text clearly states that *"The survey will argue that disgruntlement persists because **Brazil is a battleground between progress and inertia**."* This shows these two issues are opposing ideas; B: correct – The text clearly states that *"The survey will argue that disgruntlement persists because **Brazil is a battleground between progress and inertia**."*; C: incorrect – The text clearly states that *"**Since independence was proclaimed** by the son of the Portuguese king, **Brazil has been adding layer upon layer of change** rather than sweeping away the old and starting afresh."* This does not mean that progress and inertia are foes, but rather the reasons underpinning Brazil's slow progress; D: incorrect – The word "trigger" is too positive for this meaning. Brazil's growth has been slow, not fast; E: incorrect – The word "likely", here, suggests that this has not been proven. The text clearly states that *"**The survey** will argue that disgruntlement persists because Brazil is a battleground between progress and inertia."* The existence of a survey makes the word "likely" inappropriate.

Gabarito "B".

Your answers to questions must be based on the text below entitled "Brazil's president is wildly popular":

Brazil's President is Wildly Popular

Source: Special Double Issue Newsweek
Dec 31st, 2007/ Jan 7th, 2008 (Adapted)

For Brazilian President Luiz Inácio Lula da Silva, 2007 has been a good year. The economy is surging, even as the United States shows signs of weakness. Rising real wages, school enrollments and life expectancy have finally nudged Brazil into the United Nations' elite of "high human development" nations. One by one Lula has seen top aides and allies fall to corruption scandals, but so far nothing seems to dim his aura. Now some of Lula's most ardent devotees in the ruling Workers Party (PT) are even pushing to change the Constitution to allow him to run for a third consecutive term in office. "All the stars are aligned," says Walter Molano, a specialist in emerging markets with BCP Securities.

(Analista – CGU – 2008 – ESAF) The opening sentence of the text refers to the year of 2007 as having been

(A) challenging.
(B) lost.
(C) positive.
(D) negative.
(E) gloomy.

(Interpretation) A: incorrect – The word "challenging" means difficult; B: incorrect – The word "lost" means off course; C: correct – The text clearly states that *"(...) 2007 has been a **good** year."*; D: incorrect – The word "negative" means bad; E: incorrect – The word "gloomy" means depressing.
Gabarito "C".

(Analista – CGU – 2008 – ESAF) The text reports that the Brazilian economy **is surging**. In other words,

(A) its scenario had urged caution.
(B) its growth has been slowing down.
(C) it will emerge in the near future.
(D) it is undergoing a process of growth.
(E) its development has been hindered.

(Vocabulary) A: incorrect – The phrase "to urge caution" means to recommend carefulness; B: incorrect – The phrase "slow down" means to reduce speed; C: incorrect – The phrase "to emerge in the near future" means to become known soon; D: correct – The word "surge" means to rise; E: incorrect – The word "hinder" means to hold back.
Gabarito "D".

(Analista – CGU – 2008 – ESAF) According to the text, the Brazilian President

(A) could have run for a third consecutive term.
(B) might have to face a second consecutive term in office.
(C) must have run for a third term.
(D) ought to have faced a second election round.
(E) is not currently allowed to run for a third consecutive term.

(Interpretation) A: incorrect – The word "could" suggests that the Constitution would allow this. It did not; B: incorrect – The phrase "might have to face a second (...) term" suggests that Lula had not already run a second time for office. He had already done so; C: incorrect – The phrase "must have run" suggests that the only logical conclusion is that he had already run for office for the third consecutive time. This cannot be true as the Constitution did not allow it – Lula's supporters wanted to change this; D: incorrect – The phrase "ought to have faced a second election" suggests that he did not do this. Lula did and this is evident because his supporters were seeking a **third** election; E: correct – The text clearly states that *"(...) Lula's most ardent devotees in the ruling Workers Party (PT) are even pushing to **change the Constitution to allow him to run for a third consecutive term in office**."*
Gabarito "E".

Read text I and answer the questions.

The web makes waves in Brazil

There is no doubt that the web has caught on in Brazil as its web-using population has doubled in just three years In July 2008 more than 23.7 million Brazilians went online according to figures gathered by web statistics firm
5 IBOPE/NetRatings. The figure is up 28% on the same time in 2007 and continues the trend of booming net use. Proof that it has caught on can be seen in statistics which suggest Brazilians spend the longest time surfing from home than any other nationality.
10 By contrast, North Americans spend 20 hours 30 minutes and Germans 21 hours browsing the web every month. While net access is popular in the homes of Brazilians, with 35.4 million homes connected to the web in July 2008, internet cafes, or Lan houses as they are known in Brazil, are
15 becoming hugely popular.
So popular that they are springing up in underground stations and fast food restaurants...
The dark side
The internet has a reputation for harbouring some dark
20 areas and for that reason, a rigorous check is done before anyone can use a computer in a Lan house.

(adapted from http://news.bbc.co.uk/2/hi/
technology/7642224.stm)

(Analista Legislativo – Senado – 2008 – FGV) The title of this article refers to a movement that is

(A) swaying.
(B) sweeping.
(C) swindling.
(D) swerving.
(E) swinging.

(Vocabulary) A: incorrect – The word "sway" means to influence; B: correct – Of the choices offered, this is the most plausible. However, the informal expression "to make waves" is commonly used to show an idea of disturbing the status quo; causing trouble, usually by questioning or resisting the accepted rules, procedures. The other options are inappropriate, making this only plausible option; C: incorrect – The word "swindle" means to deceive; D: incorrect – The word "swerve" means to turn sharply; E: incorrect – The word "swing" means to move to and from.
Gabarito "B".

(Analista Legislativo – Senado – 2008 – FGV) The underlined word in "<u>While</u> net access is popular" (line12) can be replaced by

(A) Whereas.
(B) Wherefore.
(C) Whenever.

(D) Whence.
(E) Whereby.

(Vocabulary) A: correct – This conjunction is used to show contrast, as the word "while" is doing in the phrase; B: incorrect – This archaic conjunction means "what for?" or "why?"; C: incorrect – This conjunction is used to show time, not contrast; D: incorrect – This conjunction means "from where?"; E: incorrect – This archaic conjunction means "by what means?"
Gabarito "A".

(Analista Legislativo – Senado – 2008 – FGV) When the article informs that it "has a reputation for harbouring some dark areas" (lines 19-20), this implies the Internet can be used for

(A) exquisite ends.
(B) sober objectives.
(C) genuine aims.
(D) sensible reasons.
(E) grim purposes.

(Interpretation) A: incorrect – The word "exquisite" means superb; B: incorrect – The word "sober" means serious or calm; C: incorrect – The word "genuine" means real or true; D: incorrect – The word "sensible" means rational or prudent; E: correct – The sense of the phrase to "harbour some dark areas" suggest some macabre or gruesome ideas, which is synonymous with "grim".
Gabarito "E".

Read text II and answer the questions.

Meet the new neighbours

The empty house, in a middle-class corner of southern California, is two storeys high and boasts a three-car garage. Roses bloom around a kidney-shaped swimming pool, which is green with algae. Bill Bobbitt, a county inspector, dips a
5 ladle into the water and brings up half a dozen wriggling larvae. Mosquitoes, and the West Nile virus that some of them carry, are thriving in California's plunging property market. West Nile virus arrived in America in 1999 and made it to California three years later. Since then it is known to have
10 infected 2,300 people in the state, of whom 76 have died... In theory, owners are supposed to keep their properties in decent shape whether they live there or not. California has even passed a bill fining banks and mortgage companies that seize properties and then allow pools to fester. But Mr. Bobbitt
15 isn't waiting for the lawyers. He has treated the pool in Santa Ana with oil and synthetic growth hormones, which will keep the mosquitoes adolescent, preventing breeding. Then he tips in a few dozen mosquito fish (Gambusia affinis), which begin happily munching larvae. You can buy a lot of the fish for what
20 a lawyer charges per hour, and some authorities, with commendable creativity, even provide them free to help control the pests.

(from The Economist, August 2d, 2008, p. 34)

(Analista Legislativo – Senado – 2008 – FGV) The tone of the title is

(A) tragic.
(B) sympathetic.
(C) ironic.
(D) wailing.
(E) enthusiastic.

(Interpretation) A: incorrect – The word "tragic" means sad; B: incorrect – The word "sympathetic" means compassionate; C: correct – As the neighbors are mosquitoes, or even fish, the tone is one of irony; D: incorrect – The word "wailing" means crying; E: incorrect – The word "enthusiastic" means keen.
Gabarito "C".

(Analista Legislativo – Senado – 2008 – FGV) According to the text, the market for buying and selling houses in California is

(A) dropping.
(B) stable.
(C) rising.
(D) sky-rocketing.
(E) inflated.

(Interpretation) A: correct – The text clearly states that *"Mosquitoes, and the West Nile virus that some of them carry, are thriving in California's **plunging property market**"* (lines 6-7); B: incorrect – The word "stable" means secure; C: incorrect – The word "rising" means increasing; D: incorrect – The word "sky-rocketing" means increasing; E: incorrect – The word "inflated" means over-priced.
Gabarito "A".

(Analista Legislativo – Senado – 2008 – FGV) A kidney-shaped swimming-pool is

(A) triangular.
(B) square.
(C) rectangular.
(D) trapezoid.
(E) curved.

(Vocabulary) A: incorrect – This shape has corners and flat sides, making it impossible to be similar to the shape of a kidney; B: incorrect – This shape has corners and flat sides, making it impossible to be similar to the shape of a kidney; C: incorrect – This shape has corners and flat sides, making it impossible to be similar to the shape of a kidney; D: incorrect – This shape has corners and flat sides, making it impossible to be similar to the shape of a kidney; E: correct – The phrase "kidney-shaped" literally means has the shape of a kidney, the body organ.
Gabarito "E".

(Analista Legislativo – Senado – 2008 – FGV) The underlined word in "<u>wriggling</u> larvae" (lines 5-6) means that the larvae are

(A) growing.
(B) migrating.
(C) reproducing.
(D) twisting.
(E) dying.

(Vocabulary) A: incorrect – The word "growing" means increasing; B: incorrect – The word "migrating" means moving to another place; C: incorrect – The word "reproducing" means procreating; D: correct – The word "wriggle" means to move about, as does the word "twist"; E: incorrect – The word "dying" means terminating.
Gabarito "D".

(Analista Legislativo – Senado – 2008 – FGV) The expression "boasts a three-car garage" (line 2) reveals an attitude which is

(A) humble.
(B) haughty.
(C) hopeful.
(D) hospitable.
(E) holy.

(Vocabulary) A: incorrect – The word "humble" means modest and unassuming; B: correct – The word "boast" suggests a sense of "showing off" and self-importance, which is the meaning of haughty; C: incorrect – The word "hopeful" means optimistic; D: incorrect – The work "hospitable" means welcoming and generous; E: incorrect – The word "holy" means sacred.
Gabarito "B".

(Analista Legislativo – Senado – 2008 – FGV) When "mortgage companies seize properties" (lines 13-14) this means they

(A) take them down.
(B) take them off.
(C) take them away.
(D) take them out.
(E) take them apart.

(Vocabulary) A: incorrect – This transitive phrasal verb means to remove something from a high place, to dismantle something, to humble somebody; B: incorrect – This transitive phrasal verb means to remove something (usually clothing), or to imitate somebody; C: correct – Of the choices offered, this is the closest in meaning to "***seize properties***". In fact, the mortgage companies take the properties away "***from the previous owners***". The phrasal verb "take something away" can be misleading without the complement (adverbial phrase) and may mean "arrest somebody", or "remove from a place", neither of which are suitable in this context; D: incorrect – This transitive phrasal verb means to extract something, or to go out with somebody (on a date, for example); E: incorrect – This transitive phrasal verb means to dismantle something, or to criticize somebody.
Gabarito "C".

(Analista Legislativo – Senado – 2008 – FGV) In "provide them free" (line 21) them refers to

(A) lawyers.
(B) larvae.
(C) authorities.
(D) pests.
(E) fish.

(Grammar) A: incorrect – Authorities do not provide lawyers for free, and they do not help control pests; B: incorrect – Authorities do not provide larvae for free, and they are the pests; C: incorrect – Authorities do not provide themselves for free, and they do not help control pests; D: incorrect – Authorities do not provide pests for free; E: correct – In the last sentence, the text clearly states that "You can **buy** a lot of ***the fish*** for what a lawyer charges per hour, and some authorities, with commendable creativity, even **provide them** free to help control the pests" (lines 19-22). The object of the transitive verb "buy" in the first part of the sentence is "the fish". So, in the second part, the object of the transitive verb "provide" refers back to the previous object (parallelism).
Gabarito "E".

Read the text below entitled "Currency disunion" in order to answer the questions:

Currency disunion

Source: www.economist.com (Adapted) Apr 7th, 2012

The Irish left the sterling zone. The Balts escaped from the rouble. The Czechs and Slovaks left each other. History is littered with currency unions that broke up. Why not the euro? Had its fathers foreseen turmoil, they might never have embarked on currency union.

The founders of the euro thought they were forging a rival to the American dollar. Instead they recreated a version of the gold standard abandoned by their predecessors long ago. Unable to devalue their currencies, struggling euro countries are trying to regain competitiveness by "internal devaluation", ie, pushing down wages and prices. That hurts: unemployment in Greece and Spain is above 20%. And resentment is deepening among creditors. So why not release the yoke? The treaties may declare the euro "irrevocable", but treaties can be changed.

One reason the euro holds together is fear of financial and economic chaos on an unprecedented scale. Another is the impulse to defend the decades-long political investment in the European project. So, despite many bitter words, Greece has a second rescue. So the euro zone remains vulnerable to new shocks.

Markets still worry about the risk of sovereign defaults, and of a partial or total collapse of the euro. Common sense suggests that leaders should think about how to manage a break-up.

(Analista – MDICE – 2012 – ESAF) In paragraph 1, the author claims that if the euro´s fathers had foreseen turmoil, they would never have

(A) begun a currency union.
(B) replaced the euro.
(C) maintained the euro zone currencies.
(D) turned down a currency union.
(E) devalued the euro.

(Interpretation) A: correct – The text clearly states that "(...) they might never have embarked on currency union". Here, "embark" means the same as "begin"; B: incorrect – The word "replace" means to substitute. In the text, "embark" means the same as "begin"; C: incorrect – The word "maintained" means to keep. In the text, "embark" means the same as "begin"; D: incorrect – The phrasal verb "turned down" means refuse. In the text, "embark" means the same as "begin"; E: incorrect – The word "devalued" means depreciated. In the text, "embark" means the same as "begin".
Gabarito "A".

(Analista – MDICE – 2012 – ESAF) In paragraph 2, the author points out that "struggling euro countries" are

(A) steadily recuperating competitiveness.
(B) currently devaluing their currencies.
(C) expected to value their currencies.
(D) incapable of devaluing their currencies.
(E) not allowed to push down wages and prices.

(Interpretation) A: incorrect – In the third sentence of the second paragraph, the text clearly states that "Unable to devalue their currencies, ***struggling euro countries*** are ***trying to regain competitiveness*** by "internal devaluation". This suggests that these countries are not steadily recuperating; B: correct – In the third sentence of the second paragraph, the text clearly states that "***Unable to devalue their currencies, struggling euro countries*** are trying to regain competitiveness by "internal devaluation". This shows that the countries are unable to do so; C: incorrect – There is no mention in the text of "valuing" their currencies. The word "value" is misleading in this question as it is a false cognate which is easily confused with the Portuguese word "valorizar". The word "value" only means "valorizar" in the figurative sense, and not in the monetary sense. A currency does not value; it appreciates. However, a person can value a friendship; D: correct – In the third sentence of the second paragraph, the text clearly states that "***Unable to devalue their currencies, struggling euro countries*** are trying to regain

competitiveness by "internal devaluation"; E: incorrect – In the third sentence of the second paragraph, the text clearly states that "Unable to devalue their currencies, struggling euro countries are trying to regain competitiveness by "internal devaluation", ie, **pushing down wages and prices**." Although it is not helping countries like Greece and Spain, they are allowed to do this.
Gabarito "D".

(Analista – MDICE – 2012 – ESAF) In paragraph 2, the author argues that treaties

(A) might have been ratified.
(B) may be altered.
(C) should have been negotiated.
(D) ought to bring about changes.
(E) must be urgently approved.

(Interpretation) A: incorrect – The text does not mention the ratification of treaties; B: correct – In the last sentence of the second paragraph, the text clearly states that "The treaties may declare the euro "irrevocable", but **treaties can be changed**"; C: incorrect – In the last sentence of the second paragraph, the text clearly states that "The treaties may declare the euro "irrevocable", but **treaties can be changed**". This suggests that the author believes they should be negotiated, but not that this has already happened; D: incorrect – In the last sentence of the second paragraph, the text clearly states that "The treaties may declare the euro "irrevocable", but **treaties can be changed**". This does not suggest that the author believes the treaties are expected to cause change; E: incorrect – The text does not mention the approval of treaties.
Gabarito "B".

(Analista – MDICE – 2012 – ESAF) In paragraph 3, the author tries to explain why the euro

(A) recovered.
(B) devalued.
(C) values.
(D) collapsed.
(E) remains.

(Interpretation) A: incorrect – In the last sentence of the third paragraph, the text clearly states that "So the euro zone **remains vulnerable to new shocks**", showing that it has not recovered; B: incorrect – In the third sentence of the second paragraph, the text clearly states that "**Unable to devalue their currencies**, struggling euro countries are trying to regain competitiveness by "internal devaluation"; C: incorrect – In terms of values, the only mention in the text refers to desired depreciation and not appreciation. The word "value" is misleading in this question as it is a false cognate which is easily confused with the Portuguese word "valorizar". The word "value" only means "valorizar" in the figurative sense, and not in the monetary sense. A currency does not value; it appreciates. However, a person can value a friendship; D: incorrect – The collapse of the euro is expressed as a concern, not a fact; E: correct – The text clearly states that "**One reason the euro holds together** is fear of financial and economic chaos on an unprecedented scale. **Another** is the impulse to defend the decades-long political investment (...)".
Gabarito "E".

(Analista – MDICE – 2012 – ESAF) According to the text, currency unions

(A) have invariably strengthened markets.
(B) are not supposed to break up.
(C) have previously proved unsuccessful.
(D) restructure regional markets.
(E) prevent long-term damages.

(Interpretation) A: incorrect – The text mentions nothing about strengthening markets; B: incorrect – In the last sentence of the text, the author explicitly recommends that "*Common sense suggests that leaders should think about **how to manage a break-up***". This suggests that the break-up of currency unions is common sense and, therefore, can happen; C: correct – In the first paragraph, the text clearly states that "**History is littered with currency unions that broke up**."; D: incorrect – The text mentions nothing about restructuring regional markets; E: incorrect – The text mentions nothing about long-term damages.
Gabarito "C".

Text for the next items.

Law of public biddings

1   According to the Brazilian Federal Constitution, article 37, item XXI: "With the exception of the cases specified in law, public works, services, purchases and disposals shall be contracted by public bidding proceedings that ensure equal conditions to all bidders, with clauses that establish payment obligations, maintaining the effective conditions of the bid, as the law provides,
4   which shall only allow the requirements of technical and economic qualifications indispensable to guarantee the fulfilling of the obligations." The regulatory law is Law Number 8666, 21st June, 1993.
    The Law forbids preference to or differential treatment between Brazilian and foreign companies. However, when local
7   and foreign competitors offer equivalent conditions in terms of price, quality and delivery time, the law ensures preference for: goods produced or supplied by a Brazilian firm of national capital; locally produced; and produced or supplied by Brazilian firms. The comments below are a very superficial highlight of some important topics of the law.
10 • Article 1 mentions the entities subject to the law: all the three branches; all the three levels of government (Federal, State, and Municipal); all agencies and foundations; all public companies, including those with private participation (this means that big businesses like PETROBRAS, Banco do Brasil and others are subject to the law).
13 • Article 3 mentions that the nationality of the bidders will be considered only as a tie-breaking criterion: otherwise, Brazilian and foreign companies compete equally. Also, article 3 states that all the bidding process is open to the public, except, of course, for the value of bidding while not disclosed.
16 • Article 4: all bids are in national currency, except in the cases prescribed in article 42 (international purchases).
    • Article 24 states the situations where bidding is not mandatory. Some examples: purchases of small value (as defined by law); emergency situations which put people or premises in risk; when previous bidding processes had no bidders; to purchase
19 or rent specific buildings; several others.
    • Article 25 states situations when a bidding process is not feasible. Examples: there is only one possible contractor for a given product or service (electricity supply, for example); a professional is so outstandingly better than all the others that a
22 bidding competition would be meaningless.
    • Article 45 states that, besides the price bid, technical factors may also define the winner.

Internet: <www.V-brazil.com/business> (adapted).

(Analista – TCU – 2009 – CESPE) Based on the above text, judge the following items about biddings regulated by Law Number 8666, 21st June, 1993.

(1) Contracts to deal with emergency situations may be awarded without a bidding process.
(2) However low a price bid may be, it still may not be the winner if technical factors are not up to standards.
(3) The Portuguese word for public biddings is alienações.
(4) In a public bidding, all conditions being the same, Brazilian companies have preference over foreign ones if there is a tie.

(Interpretation) 1: correct – The text in Article 24 (lines 17-18) clearly states that bidding is not mandatory in *"emergency situations which put people or premises in risk"*; 2: correct – The text in Article 45 (line 23) clearly states that *"besides the price bid, technical factors may also define the winner"*; 3: incorrect – The term "public biddings" is the informal term for government procurement; both are translated as "licitações" in Portuguese. "Alienações", depending on the area and the context, can be translated as "mortgage liens", "disposal/sale of assets", "divestment/divestiture" among many others; 4: correct – The text clearly states that "The Law forbids preference to or differential treatment between Brazilian and foreign companies. However, **when local and foreign competitors offer equivalent conditions in terms of price, quality and delivery time, the law ensures preference for: goods produced or supplied by a Brazilian firm of national capital**; locally produced; and produced or supplied by Brazilian firms" (lines 6-8);
Gabarito 1C, 2C, 3E, 4C

(Analista – TCU – 2009 – CESPE) Judge the following items.

(1) Public companies are exempt from the bidding process.
(2) Only bidders are allowed in all of the bidding process.
(3) By no means shall any bids be expressed in foreign currency.

(Interpretation) 1: incorrect – The text in Article 1 (lines 10-12) clearly mentions *"the entities subject to the law: all the three branches; all the three levels of government (Federal, State, and Municipal); all agencies and foundations; **all public companies**, including those with private participation (this means that big businesses like PETROBRAS, Banco do Brasil and others are subject to the law)."*; 2: incorrect – The text in Article 3 (line 14-15) clearly states that *"Also, article 3 states that all the bidding process is **open to the public**, except, of course, for the value of bidding while not disclosed."*; 3: incorrect – The text in Article 4 (line 16) clearly states that *"all bids are in national currency, **except in the cases prescribed in article 42 (international purchases)**."*
Gabarito 1E, 2E, 3E

(Analista – TCU – 2009 – CESPE) In the text,

(1) "others" ($\ell.12$) stands for other big businesses.
(2) "premises" ($\ell.18$) means the building and land that a business or organization uses.
(3) "besides" ($\ell.23$) can be correctly replaced by in addition to.
(4) "shall" ($\ell.2$) can be correctly replaced by might.
(5) "those" ($\ell.11$) refers to "public companies" ($\ell.11$).

(Vocabulary) 1: correct – The word "others" refers back to **big businesses** which precedes the example: *"including those with private participation (this means that **big businesses** like PETROBRAS, Banco do Brasil and **others** are subject to the law)."*; 2: incorrect – The word "premises" has two meanings: 1) the building and land that a business or organization uses; and 2) a basis or argument for reasoning – in the text, the second meaning is correct; 3: correct – In the context of the sentence, these two adverbs are synonymous and interchangeable; 4: incorrect – The modal verb "shall" in the text is used in the legal sense, meaning "must". In contractual language, "shall" is used to establish obligations. The modal verb "might" expresses an idea of probability, which is not common in this kind of text; 5: correct – In the text, the plural pronoun "those" is used to refer back to the plural noun "public companies": *"(…) all **public companies**, including **those** with private participation".*
Gabarito 1C, 2E, 3C, 4E, 5C

For the following questions, choose the best answer in accordance with this Text

Brazil's exports

Trade barriers imposed by Argentina on imports in general have resulted in a drop of 16% in Brazil's exports to its neighbor in the first half of this year. Between January and June last year, Brazil sold goods worth US$ 10.43 billion to Argentina. This year, during the same period, the value of goods sold to Argentina is US$ 1.6 billion less.

In spite of the trade barriers, the executive secretary at the Ministry of Development, Industry and Foreign Trade, Alessandro Teixeira, blames the international crisis for the situation. "The cause of these problems is the international crisis. It affects Argentina and it affects us, too," he declared. Teixeira noted that negotiations have improved the relationship with Argentina, that there has been a more positive dialogue.

Brazil's exports to Eastern Europe are down 38% and down 8% to the European Union in the first half. On the other hand, they have risen by over US$ 2 billion to China during the same period.

From: Brazil Magazine July 2012 [adapted]

(Auditor Fiscal da Receita Federal – 2012 – ESAF) In 2012, Brazil's exports

(A) have all been reduced in comparison with last year..
(B) to Argentina have increased due to positive dialogue.
(C) have decreased with Eastern Europe but gone up with the European Union.
(D) are expected to show an increase by the end of the year.
(E) have generally declined, except for goods sent to China.

(Interpretation) A: Incorrect – Exports to China have gone up, B: Incorrect – There has been positive dialogue but it has not influenced the overall drop in exports to Argentina this year, C: Incorrect – Exports to both areas have gone down, D: Incorrect – There is no evidence to support this, E: Correct – Argentina, Eastern Europe and the European Union are down. Exports to China have risen (i.e. have gone up).
Gabarito "E".

(Auditor Fiscal da Receita Federal – 2012 – ESAF) Argentina has

(A) placed restrictions on most imports.
(B) discriminated against Brazil more than others.

(C) encouraged the entry of goods from abroad.
(D) allowed Brazil to export more than last year.
(E) blamed the international crisis for it imports.

(Interpretation) A: Correct – 'Trade barriers imposed by Argentina on imports in general' – 'Trade barriers' refers to restrictions. B: Incorrect – No evidence is given suggesting specific discrimination against Brazil. C: Incorrect – On the contrary it has imposed trade barriers on goods from abroad, D: Incorrect – No evidence is given suggesting this is the case, E: Incorrect – Reference to the international crisis comes from the Brazilian executive secretary Teixeira. Gabarito "C" Obs.: apesar do gabarito oficial, a alternativa "A" é claramente a correta.
Gabarito oficial "C" / Gabarito nosso "A".

(Auditor Fiscal da Receita Federal – 2012 – ESAF) Alessandro Teixeira's comments on Argentina's position could best be described as

(A) hostile.
(B) cowardly.
(C) diplomatic.
(D) unfriendly.
(E) pessimistic.

(Interpretation) A: Incorrect – On the contrary, his tone and words are conciliatory and optimistic. B: Incorrect – No information is given suggesting he is being a coward, C: Correct – Teixeira describes a negative situation for Brazil in terms of exports in a positive light and talks about future relations with Argentina positively, D: Incorrect – His tone is positive and optimistic, E: Incorrect – On the contrary, he is optimistic.
Gabarito "C".

For the following questions, choose the best answer in accordance with this Text

South Korea banks in rate-rigging investigation

A South Korea financial regulator has started an investigation into alleged interest rate rigging by some of the country's banks. The Fair Trade Commission is looking at possible collusion over setting certificates of deposit (CD), used as a benchmark to set lending rates. It follows the Libor-rigging scandal involving Barclays and possibly several other UK banks.

A CD is a way of saving with a fixed interest rate and maturity sold by banks and circulated in the secondary market by brokerages. Financial firms benefit from high CD rates as many household loans are linked to them. They are frequently used to help South Koreans buy homes. The possible rigging of CD can help flatter companies' financial health.

The indebtedness of South Koreans has become a particular worry to the authorities as the economy slows.

From: www.bbc.com/news [slightly adapted]

(Auditor Fiscal da Receita Federal – 2012 – ESAF) The opening paragraph suggests that some South Korean banks may have

(A) acted dishonestly.
(B) deserved commendation.
(C) been unfairly attacked..
(D) started an investigation.
(E) moved to the UK.

(Interpretation) A: Correct – Rigging – 'to rig' means to manipulate in a fraudulent manner for profit. Some banks have allegedly (supposedly) rigged interest rates, B: Incorrect – 'To receive a commendation' means to receive an award or favorable opinion, C: Incorrect – The accusation of illegal activity is only alleged. We cannot infer there was an attack or that it was fair or unfair, D: Incorrect – The Fair Trade Commission has started the investigation. It is a separate body from the banks in question, E: Incorrect – 'follows' in this case means: comes after as a consequence. There is no idea of physical movement.
Gabarito "A".

(Auditor Fiscal da Receita Federal – 2012 – ESAF) In paragraph 2 line 3, the word "brokerages" refers to

(A) second class financial deals.
(B) companies that buy and sell financial assets.
(C) firms perceived as likely to go bankrupt.
(D) large accountancy enterprises.
(E) risky exchange rate transactions.

(Vocabulary) A: Incorrect – There is no inference that the deals are inferior or second-class. The secondary market refers to a market where securities are traded after their initial market offering, B: Correct – A brokerage is defined as a firm buying stocks and shares on behalf of its clients, C: Incorrect – No inference is made that the firms will go bust or bankrupt, D: Incorrect – Brokerages does not refer to accountancy firms, E: Incorrect – No inference is made that the transactions are risky.
Gabarito "B".

(Auditor Fiscal da Receita Federal – 2012 – ESAF) Officials in South Korea are concerned about

(A) high levels of personal debt in a sluggish economy.
(B) poor credit-ratings and economic over-heating.
(C) rising household expenditures and house prices.
(D) broken homes and inability to support flattery.
(E) the national debt and how to pay it off.

(Interpretation) A: Correct – 'The indebtedness of South Koreans has become a particular worry to the authorities as the economy slows'. Indebtedness refers to the state of being in debt. A sluggish economy is one which is slowing or lacking in vigor, B: Incorrect – Neither of these factors are mentioned in the text, C: Incorrect – Neither of these factors are mentioned in the text, D: Incorrect – 'Broken homes' refers to families which have split up (divorced). 'To flatter' in this case means to make firms accounts look healthy, E: Incorrect - This is not mentioned in the text.
Gabarito "A".

For the following questions, choose the best answer in accordance with this Text

Rio+20: reasons to be cheerful

Read the commentaries from Rio+20, and you'd think a global disaster had taken place. The UN multilateral system is said to be in crisis. Pundits and NGOs complain that it was "the greatest failure of collective leadership since the first world war", "a bleak day, a disastrous meeting" and "a massive waste of time and money".

Perspective, please. Reaction after the 1992 Rio summit was uncannily similar. Countries passed then what now seem far-sighted treaties and embedded a slew of aspirations and commitments into international documents – but NGOs and journalists were still distraught. In short, just like Rio 2012, the meeting was said to be a dismal failure of governments to co-operate.

I was pretty downhearted then, too. So when I returned I went to see Richard Sandbrook, a legendary environmental activist who co-founded Friends of the Earth, and profoundly influenced a generation of governments, business leaders and NGOs before he died in 2005. Sandbrook made the point that NGOs always scream blue murder because it is their job to push governments and that UN conferences must disappoint because all views have to be accommodated. Change, he said, does not happen in a few days' intense negotiation. It is a long, muddled, cultural process that cannot come from a UN meeting. Real change comes from stronger institutions, better public information, promises being kept, the exchange of views, pressure from below, and events that make people see the world differently.

Vast growth in global environmental awareness has taken place in the past 20 years, and is bound to grow in the next 20.

[From The Guardian PovertyMatters blog - adapted]

(Auditor Fiscal da Receita Federal – 2012 – ESAF) According to the text, the general reaction to the Rio+20Conference was

(A) generally optimistic.
(B) absolutely singular.
(C) relatively cheerful.
(D) extremely gloomy.
(E) remarkably sanguine.

(Interpretation) A: Incorrect – The opposite is true. It was generally pessimistic, B: Incorrect – It was strangely similar – uncannily similar to the reaction after the 1992 conference, C: Incorrect – 'Cheerful' means positive and upbeat, D: Correct – 'Gloomy' means depressing, pessimistic and dark. The choice for words in paragraph 1 (disaster, crises, failure, bleak) reflects this, E: Incorrect – This means very optimistic.
Gabarito "D."

(Auditor Fiscal da Receita Federal – 2012 – ESAF) The author of the article believes that immediately after the 1992 environmental conference

(A) his only hope was to visit a famous environmentalist.
(B) the response to the event was much the same as now.
(C) the United Nations failed to foster any agreements.
(D) everybody praised the far-sighted accords reached.
(E) the climate began to change all around the world.

(Interpretation) A: Incorrect – It is true he went to visit the famous environmentalist but to say it was his 'only hope' is dramatic and an exaggeration, B: Correct – The author states the response was 'uncannily similar' – strangely or weirdly similar, C: Incorrect – 'to foster' means to nurture or to develop. No evidence is given with respect to this statement, D: Incorrect - The treaties mentioned in the text are now seen as far-sighted; at the time, the overall tone was negative, E: Incorrect – Results of a conference would have no immediate impact on the earth's climate.
Gabarito "B."

(Auditor Fiscal da Receita Federal – 2012 – ESAF) The main aim of the third paragraph is to report on

(A) the views of a well-known environmentalist on how change occurs.
(B) the failure of the UN to achieve any significant results in 1992.
(C) the life and work of a late-lamented UN environmental activist.
(D) the author's despondent mood in 1992 and the reasons for it.
(E) the similarities between the conference results in 2012 and 1992.

(Interpretation) A: Correct – The entire paragraph relates to the specific views of Richard Sandbrook, B: Incorrect – This is not the main aim of the paragraph, C: Incorrect – The focus is on Sandbrook's views, not his life and work, D: Incorrect – 'Down-hearted' means despondent, but this is not the aim nor content of the paragraph; E: Incorrect – This was mentioned indirectly but was not the main aim of the paragraph.
Obs.: entendemos que a alternativa "A" é claramente a correta.
Gabarito oficial "D." / Gabarito nosso "A."

(Auditor Fiscal da Receita Federal – 2012 – ESAF) The expression "scream blue murder" in paragraph 3 line7 means

(A) feel severely threatened.
(B) call out for protection.
(C) commit environmental crimes.
(D) shout about their mistreatment.
(E) raise an indignant outcry.

(Vocabulary) A: Incorrect – The feeling of being threatened is too strong to assert here, B: Incorrect – This cry refers to indignation not as to a cry for help, C: Incorrect – It means to scream loudly in protest, D: Incorrect – To mention mistreatment is too much of an extrapolation from the text, E: Correct – 'To scream blue murder' means to make an extremely loud cry in protest about something.
Gabarito "E."

For the following questions, choose the best answer in accordance with this Text

Brazil's economy

Government spending and exports of commodities like soy beans and metals to fast-growing countries in Asia, have propelled Brazil's economy to sixth place in the world. But red-hot growth when Latin America's largest economy clocked in a 7.5% growth rate in 2010 appears to have fizzled out.

The economy stalled in May following an unexpected drop in retail sales. That heightened fears for what was one of the few bright spots of the world economy, making it the worst performer among Brics nations. GDP grew just 0.2% in the first quarter year-on-year, marking the third straight quarter of near-zero growth.

There seem to be few signs that GDP growth will head backup above the 2.6% posted last year. The Bank of Brazil expects growth to be lower than 2.5%. The drop in retail sales raised worries over Brazil's consumer-led growth model, which was fuelled by rising incomes and easy credit. In fact, the amount of loans that could not be paid back hit an all-time high in May, underlining how Brazilians are increasingly struggling to keep debt under control. That prompted banks to tighten lending, and the central bank cut interest rates for the eighth straight time in July to 8%.

[From: BBC.co.uk/news/business July 13 2012 - adapted]

(Analista-Tributário da Receita Federal – 2012 – ESAF) The phrase "in the first quarter year-on-year" refers to

(A) January-March 2012 compared to the same period of 2011.
(B) the last nine months of the current year.
(C) the last trimester of 2011 and the first of 2012.
(D) annual economic figures for successive years.
(E) the period April-June two years running.

(Vocabulary) A: Correct – 'First quarter' refers to the first three months of the year. 'Year-on-year' or the phrase 'on the year' refers to a comparison with the same time the previous year, B: Incorrect – It refers to the first three months of the current year, C: Incorrect – See B, D: Incorrect – The figures are for successive years but this answer is not as specific as option A, E: Incorrect – This refers to the first period of the financial year.
Gabarito "A".

(Analista-Tributário da Receita Federal – 2012 – ESAF) Paragraph 3 suggests that Brazil's economy has grown due to

(A) increased exports to Asia.
(B) international loans.
(C) foreign direct investment.
(D) high prices and inflation.
(E) domestic consumption.

(Interpretation) A: Incorrect – No evidence is given to suggest this, B: Incorrect – No evidence is given to suggest this, C: Incorrect – No evidence is given to suggest this, D: Incorrect – No evidence is given to suggest this, E: Correct – Paragraph 3 refers to a Consumer-led growth model. The economy has grown due to internal spending by Brazilian consumers.
Gabarito "E".

For the following questions, choose the best answer in accordance with this Text

A Coup in Paraguay

On June 22, 2012, the Paraguayan Senate invoked a clause in the constitution which authorized it to impeach the president for "poor performance in his duties." The President was Fernando Lugo, who had been elected some three years earlier and whose term was about to end in April 2013. Under the rules, Lugo was limited to a single term of office.

Lugo charged that this was a coup, and if not technically illegal, certainly illegitimate. Almost every Latin American government agreed with this analysis, denouncing the destitution, and cutting relations in various ways with Paraguay.

The removal of Lugo had the negative consequence for those who made the coup of making possible the one thing the Paraguayan Senate had been blocking for years. Paraguay is a member of the common market Mercosur, along with Brazil, Argentina and Uruguay. Venezuela had applied to join. This required ratification by the legislatures of all five member states. All had long since given their assent except the Paraguayan Senate. After the coup, Mercosur suspended Paraguay, and immediately welcomed Venezuela as a member.

[From: International Herald Tribune 18-7-12]

(Analista-Tributário da Receita Federal – 2012 – ESAF) President Lugo of Paraguay was removed from office in a process he considered to be

(A) a poor performance of his duties.
(B) premature and destitute.
(C) of dubious legality and legitimacy.
(D) unfair after a full three years in office.
(E) technically unnecessary in view of 2013 elections.

(Interpretation) A: Incorrect – The president made no comment about how his duties had been carried out, B: Incorrect – 'Destitute' means without resources or impoverished. This is not mentioned in the text, C: Correct – He charged (accused) that the process was a coup, and if not technically illegal, certainly illegitimate, D: Incorrect – No mention of unfairness, E: Incorrect – Not mentioned as being what the President considered.
Gabarito "C".

(Analista-Tributário da Receita Federal – 2012 – ESAF) As a result of Lugo's impeachment, many Latin American governments

(A) applauded the move.
(B) severed ties with Paraguay.
(C) changed their analysis.
(D) impeached their own authorities.
(E) charged Lugo with illegitimacy.

(Interpretation) A: Incorrect – They cut relations indicating disagreement with the coup, B: Correct – 'Cutting relations' means the same as 'severing ties', C: Incorrect - This is too vague to be a better answer than option B, D: Incorrect – This is not mentioned in the text, E: Incorrect – On the contrary, the idea is given that they felt the process of his impeachment was illegitimate.
Gabarito "B".

(Analista-Tributário da Receita Federal – 2012 – ESAF) The unexpected result of the overthrow of President Lugo was

(A) the blocking of Venezuela's membership of Mercosur..
(B) the Paraguayan Senate's ratification of Venezuela's entry into Mercosur.
(C) the permanent expulsion of Paraguay from Mercosur.
(D) the admission of Venezuela to Mercosur in Paraguay's absence.
(E) Venezuela's denunciation of the coup at a Mercosur meeting.

(Interpretation) A: Incorrect – This was not an unexpected result of the overthrow of the president. This had previously been Paraguay's position, B: Incorrect – No mention of this in the text, C: Incorrect – Paraguay's membership was suspended, D: Correct – Paraguay had blocked Venezuela's admission. With Paraguay suspended, Venezuela was welcomed into Mercosur, E: Incorrect – This is not mentioned in the text.
Gabarito "D".

For the following questions, choose the best answer in accordance with this Text

Armenia: prisoner of history

ARMENIA tends to feature in the news because of its problems (history, geography, demography and economics to name but a few). But a new report says not all is doom and gloom. The parliamentary elections in May showed significant improvement. Media coverage was more balanced, and the authorities permitted greater freedom of assembly, expression and movement than in previous years. That bodes well for the future.

The economy is still recovering from the global financial crisis, which saw GDP contract by 14.2% in 2009. In the same period, the construction sector contracted by more than 40%. Remittances from the diaspora dropped by 30%. That led Forbes magazine to label Armenia the world's second worst performing economy in 2011. Over one-third of the country lives below the poverty line. Complaints of corruption are widespread, and inflation is high.

Low rates of tax collection-19.3% of GDP, compared with a 40% average in EU countries—limit the government's reach. Cracking down on tax evasion could increase government revenue by over $400 million, says the World Bank. A few, high-profile businessmen dominate the economy. Their monopolies and oligopolies put a significant brake on business development. Their influence also weakens political will for the kind of reforms that the country sorely needs.

[From The Economist print edition June 24, 2012]

(Analista-Tributário da Receita Federal – 2012 – ESAF) With regard to the political situation in Armenia, the opening paragraph of the text is

(A) unnecessarily pessimistic.
(B) wildly enthusiastic.
(C) depressingly frank.
(D) remarkably despondent.
(E) mildly optimistic.

(Interpretation) A: Incorrect – 'not all is doom and gloom', that is, the outlook is not completely pessimistic, B: Incorrect – This is too strong. The tone of the text is neither too enthusiastic nor too negative, C: Incorrect – The text is balanced and frank (to the point) but not depressing, D: Incorrect – 'despondent' means without hope – The text discusses positive aspects as well, E: Correct – Paragraph 1 is fairly optimistic – 'not all is doom and gloom' and 'that bodes well for the future' i.e. that is a hopeful sign.
Gabarito "E".

(Analista-Tributário da Receita Federal – 2012 – ESAF) The international economic adversities of 2009 had multiple effects on Armenia, including

(A) a massive boom in the country's construction industry.
(B) attempts to control the country's endemic corruption.
(C) critical acclaim of the country's economy in Forbes magazine.
(D) poverty-reduction plans to bring people into line.
(E) a drop in funds sent home by Armenians working abroad.

(Interpretation) A: Incorrect – The construction sector 'contracted' i.e. shrank. This is opposite to a boom, which means to expand, B: Incorrect – Corruption is widespread i.e. endemic but there is no evidence of attempts to control it, C: Incorrect – Forbes magazine criticized Armenia severely. 'Critical acclaim' is to give a positive review, D: Incorrect – Cracking down on tax evasion means to bring people into line/make them adhere to laws, however this is not related to poverty reduction and is a national World Bank recommendation not a consequence of economic adversities, E: Correct – Remittances from the Diaspora dropped by 30% - this refers to money sent home by Armenians working abroad.
Gabarito "E".

(Analista-Tributário da Receita Federal – 2012 – ESAF) According to the World Bank, the government could raise money by

(A) taking steps to repress tax dodging.
(B) joining the European Union soon.
(C) making the rich pay more for business.
(D) raising tax rates for high-profile businessmen.
(E) introducing reforms in all sectors.

(Interpretation) A: Correct – Tax dodging – refers to tax avoidance/evasion. The World Bank estimates $400 million could be raised this way, B: Incorrect – No mention of this, C: This is not suggested by the text, D: Incorrect - The issue mentioned about high-profile businessmen relates to oligopoly not taxation rates, E: Incorrect – Not mentioned and it is too vague to say reforms are needed in all sectors.
Gabarito "A".

(Analista-Tributário da Receita Federal – 2012 – ESAF) In paragraph 3 line 8, the word "sorely" could best be replaced by

(A) usually.
(B) obviously.
(C) scarcely.
(D) badly.
(E) painfully.

(Vocabulary) A: Incorrect – 'usually' means commonly/regularly, B: 'obviously' means clearly, C: Incorrect – 'scarcely' means hardly/barely, D: Correct – 'Badly' (adverb) is a synonym for 'sorely' meaning extremely/greatly, E: Incorrect – 'painfully' (adverb) means unpleasant.
Gabarito "D".

Read the text below entitled "The long climb" so as to answer the questions:

The long climb

Source: www.economist.com
st Oct, 2009 (Adapted)

The world economy is fitfully getting back to normal, but it will be a "new normal". This phrase has caught on, even if people disagree about what it means. In the new normal, as defined by Pimco's CEO, Mohamed El-Erian, growth will be subdued and unemployment will remain high. "The banking system will be a shadow of its former self," and the securitization markets, which buy and sell marketable bundles of debt, will presumably be a shadow of a shadow. Finance will be costlier and investment weak, so the stock of physical capital, on which prosperity depends, will erode.

The crisis invited a forceful government entry into several of capitalism's inner sanctums, such as banking, American carmaking and the commercial-paper market. Mr El-Erian worries that the state may overstay its welcome. In addition, national exchequers may start to feel some measure of the fiscal strain now hobbling California. America's Treasury, in particular, must demonstrate that it is still a "responsible shepherd of other countries' savings."

(Auditor Fiscal da Receita Federal – 2010 – ESAF) In paragraph 1, growth in the new order is defined as

(A) both real and active.
(B) absolutely extraordinary.
(C) not very active or busy.
(D) sustainable and rapid.
(E) unpredictable.

(Vocabulary) A: Incorrect – 'fitfully' means in irregular bursts – we cannot say growth is active, B: Incorrect – 'Extraordinary' means beyond the usual, yet the banking system is described as a shadow of its former self, C: Correct – Both the ideas of 'fitfully' and 'shadow of its former self' indicate growth being neither very active nor halted, D: No evidence is given that growth will be sustainable, only evidence that growth will be irregular, E: Incorrect – No evidence is given of not being able to forecast growth. The text uses 'will' to say that growth will be 'subdued' i.e. less intense.
Gabarito "C".

(Auditor Fiscal da Receita Federal – 2010 – ESAF) In paragraph 1, finance is referred to as

(A) remaining low throughout the crisis.
(B) having been affected by the crisis.
(C) having eroded throughout the process.
(D) likely to be considered in a future analysis.
(E) likely not to be hit by this scenario.

(Interpretation) A: Incorrect – Finance is referred to as getting 'costlier', becoming 'a shadow of its former self'. The text refers to the future not the present crisis, B: Correct – As a consequence of the crisis, finance saw government interference (paragraph 2 – 'forceful government entry'), C: It will be eroded/diminished due the effects of the crisis not during/throughout the crisis, D: Incorrect – No evidence of this, E: finance' is mentioned throughout the text as having been negatively affected.
Gabarito "B".

(Auditor Fiscal da Receita Federal – 2010 – ESAF) In paragraph 2, the author mentions "the fiscal strain now hobbling California". In other words, the fiscal

(A) policies which have been favouring California's growth.
(B) pressure currently preventing California's development.
(C) programs successfully espoused by California.
(D) measures which have steadily gained acceptance.
(E) incentives recently promoted by the Californian government.

(Vocabulary) A: Incorrect – 'hobbling' means to hamper/impede/hold back. This is the opposite of favoring, B: Correct – 'fiscal strain' refers to fiscal pressure and 'hobbling' refers to holding back development. C: Incorrect – No mention of successful programs being promoted in California, D: Incorrect – No evidence that policies (measures) have been gaining acceptance, E: No evidence to support that measures where recent. The policies in California were not incentives.
Gabarito "B".

Read the text below entitled "Taxation Trends in the European Union" so as to answer the questions:

Taxation Trends in the European Union

Source: www.ec.europa.eu
2009 Edition (Adapted)

This year's edition of the Taxation Trends in the European Union appears at a time of upheaval. The effects of the global economic and financial crisis have hit the European Union (EU) with increasing force from the second half of 2008. Given that the last year for which detailed data are available is 2007, this year's report cannot yet analyze the consequences of the recession on tax revenues. Nevertheless, the report takes stock of the tax policy measures taken by EU governments in response to the crisis up to spring 2009.

The European Union is, taken as a whole, a high tax area. In 2007, the overall tax ratio, i.e. the sum of taxes and social security contributions in the 27 Member States amounted to 39.8% of GDP. This value is about 12 percentage points above those recorded in the United States and Japan.

The high EU overall tax ratio is not new, dating back essentially to the last third of the 20th century. In those years, the role of the public sector became more extensive, leading to a strong upward trend in the tax ratio in the 1970s, and to a lesser extent also in the 1980s and early 1990s.

(Auditor Fiscal da Receita Federal – 2010 – ESAF) According to paragraph 1, the global economic and financial crisis

(A) has impacted on the EU.
(B) may still hit the European Union.
(C) has caused tax reductions in the EU.
(D) could have affected the EU.
(E) might bring about growth in the EU.

(Interpretation) A: Correct – In lines 1-2 – The effects of the crisis 'have hit' – use of present perfect suggests an action in the past with consequences to the present time, B: Incorrect - The text in line 2 is explicit that the crisis that has hit the EU and with increasing force – 'may' suggests a possibility to occur, C: Incorrect – 'this year's report cannot yet analyze the consequences of the recession on tax revenues', D: Incorrect – Could have – suggests a possibility of something happening – this is not the case here – it did affect the EU, E: Incorrect – There is no evidence to support this.
Gabarito "A".

(Auditor Fiscal da Receita Federal – 2010 – ESAF – adaptada) In relation to the EU´s overall tax ratio, it

(A) must hit 39.8% of GDP.
(B) is likely to reach 39.8% of GDP.
(C) is soon to be defined.
(D) exceeds half the GDP.
(E) reached 39.8% of GDP in 2007.

(Interpretation) A: Incorrect – This would imply a future event, yet the text refers to 2007, B: Incorrect – This again would imply the probability of a future event, C: Incorrect – It has already been defined, D: Incorrect – 39.8% is not half of GDP, E: Correct – 'amounted to 39.8% of GDP' – This shows the figure was reached in 2007. Alteramos a alternativa E, que consignava, originalmente, "equals to 39.8% of GDP" [equivale a 39,8% do PIB]. Não havia resposta correta, razão pela qual a questão foi anulada. Com nossa adaptação, ficou claro que esse nível de tributação foi atingido no ano de 2007, especificamente, de modo que a alternativa passou a ser correta.
Gabarito "E".

(Auditor Fiscal da Receita Federal – 2010 – ESAF) According to paragraph 3, the role played by the public sector

(A) widened.
(B) lessened.
(C) diminished.
(D) faded.
(E) decreased.

(Vocabulary) A: Correct – To widen = to increase in size. Paragraph 3 –Tthe role of the public sector has become more extensive. B: Incorrect – 'to lessen' means to get smaller, C: Incorrect – 'to diminish' means to make smaller, D: Incorrect – 'to fade' means to be less clear, to lose strength, E: Incorrect – 'to decrease' means to lessen. As alternativas B a E indicam diminuição, razão pela qual são incorretas.
Gabarito "A".

Read the interview below entitled "Reason with him" so as to answer the questions:

Reason with him

Source: www.newsweek.com
22nd Sep, 2009 (Adapted)

Question (Q) 1: Margolis: When you took office, Brazil was regarded as an underachiever, and the last among the BRIC nations. Now Brazil is considered a star among emerging countries. What´s happened?

Lula: No one respects anyone who doesn´t respect themselves. And Brazil always behaved like a second-class country. We always told ourselves we were the country of the future. But we never transformed these qualities into anything concrete. In a globalized world you cannot sit still. You have to hit the road and sell your country. So we decided to make strengthening Mercosul (the South American trading bloc) a priority, and deepened our relations with Latin America in general. We prioritized trade with Africa and went into the Middle East aggressively. Our trade balance today is diversified. This helped us cushion the blow of the economic crisis.

Q2: Margolis: Has Brazil´s success in navigating the economic crisis changed investors´views?

Lula: There was no miracle. We had a strong domestic market. We had consumers who wanted to buy cars. We reduced part of the sales tax and asked the companies to offer consumers credit on affordable items. It´s the same case with refrigerators, stoves, washing machines, and with computers and the housing construction.

Q3: Margolis: What are the lessons for other countries?

Lula: The great lesson is that the state has an important role to play, and has great responsibility. We don´t want the state to manage business. But it can be an inducer of growth and can work in harmony with society.

(Auditor Fiscal da Receita Federal – 2010 – ESAF) In his answer to question 1, Brazil´s president refers to "strengthening Mercosul as a priority." In other words, a measure he considered

(A) risky.
(B) unattainable.
(C) pivotal.
(D) unnecessary.
(E) advisable.

(Vocabulary) A: Incorrect – 'risky' means incurring lots of risk, B: Incorrect – 'unattainable' means unachievable, C: Correct – 'pivotal' means of central importance, as a priority, D: Incorrect – 'unnecessary' means unneeded, E: Incorrect – 'advisable' is too weak. The text is much clearer and thus makes option C a much better answer.
Gabarito "C".

(Auditor Fiscal da Receita Federal – 2010 – ESAF) In his answer to question 2, Luiz Inácio Lula da Silva says that

(A) the Brazilian domestic market was frail.
(B) a miracle did come about in Brazil.
(C) credit on affordable items was halved.
(D) part of the sales tax was lowered.
(E) consumers were not willing to spend.

(Vocabulary) A: Incorrect – 'frail' means weak, B: Incorrect - Lula states there was no miracle in Brazil. 'come about' means happened, C: Incorrect - Credit was extended, not halved (reduced by 50%), D: Correct – 'to reduce' means to lower, E: Incorrect – Lula states there was a strong domestic market.
Gabarito "D".

(Auditor Fiscal da Receita Federal – 2010 – ESAF) Brazil´s president refers to the country´s diversified trade balance as having

(A) contributed to worsen the global economic crisis.
(B) resulted from trade with one sole strategic partner.
(C) been prevented by internal regulations.

(D) been considered as an unattainable goal.
(E) minimized the adverse effects of the world crisis.

(Interpretation) A: Incorrect – The diversified trade balance protected Brazil from the crisis, B: Incorrect – Tthe trade balance is diversified i.e. across different sectors and with different countries, C: Incorrect – No evidence to support this, D: Incorrect – The idea of it not being achievable was not mentioned, E: Correct – The trade diversification – 'cushioned the blow' of the crisis i.e. limited the negative effects of the crisis.
Gabarito "E".

(Auditor Fiscal da Receita Federal – 2010 – ESAF) In his answer to question 3, Brazil´s president

(A) emphasizes the role played by the private sector.
(B) criticizes initiatives derived from private ownership.
(C) sees the private sector as an inducer of growth.
(D) affirms the significance of the state.
(E) disregards duties attributed to the state.

(Interpretation) A: Incorrect – His answer deals specifically with the public sector and the state, B: Incorrect – No criticism of private initiatives, C: Incorrect – Tthe opposite is true; the state is the inducer (agent) of growth, D: Correct – 'the state has an important role to play and has great responsibility'. E: Incorrect – 'to disregard' means to pay no attention to – this is not mentioned and is opposite to the overall tone of the text.
Gabarito "D".

Read the text and answer the questions.

Companies in the rich world are confronted with a rapidly ageing workforce. Nearly one in three American workers will be over 50 by 2012, and America is a young country compared with Japan and Germany. China is also ageing rapidly, thanks to its one-child policy. This means that companies will have to learn how to manage older workers better.

Most companies are remarkably ill-prepared. There was a flicker of interest in the problem a few years ago but it was snuffed out by the recession. The management literature on older workers is a mere molehill compared with the mountain devoted to recruiting and retaining the young.

Companies are still stuck with an antiquated model for dealing with ageing, which assumes that people should get pay rises and promotions on the basis of age. They have dealt with the burdens of this model by periodically "downsizing" older workers or encouraging them to take early retirement. This has created a dual labour market for older workers, of cosseted insiders on the one hand and unemployed or retired outsiders on the other.

But this model cannot last. The number of young people, particularly those with valuable science and engineering skills, is shrinking. And governments are raising retirement ages and making it more difficult for companies to shed older workers, in a desperate attempt to cope with their underfunded pension systems.

Feb 4th 2010 | From *The Economist* print edition [adapted]

(Auditor Fiscal do Trabalho – 2010 – ESAF) According to the text, businesses

(A) are fully prepared to deal with an ancient workforce.
(B) cannot cope with an influx of elderly workers.
(C) are incapable of growing old gracefully.
(D) must get rid of older workers through streamlining operations.
(E) must learn to deal with the need to keep older staff employed.

(Interpretation) A: Incorrect – This is contrary to the subject of the entire text. 'Ancient' is too strong of a word to use, B: Incorrect – The text is about managing existing elderly workers not an influx of new elderly workers, C: Incorrect – This expression means to behave appropriately – no relevance to the text, D: Incorrect – 'streamlining' or 'downsizing' are seen as bad things in the text, E: Correct – 'companies will have to learn how to manage older workers better'.
Gabarito "E".

(Auditor Fiscal do Trabalho – 2010 – ESAF) In paragraph 2, the author claims that the recent economic recession has

(A) awakened an interest in science and engineering among younger workers.
(B) caused the number of young people seeking jobs in business to increase.
(C) extinguished what little interest firms had shown in how to manage an older staff.
(D) made a mountain of business management out of a managerial molehill.
(E) led many firms to dismiss older workers in their periodic staff reductions.

(Interpretation) A: Incorrect – On the contrary, there is a shrinking number. B: Incorrect – No evidence given of this, C: Correct – 'snuffed out by the recession' means the interest was destroyed completely, D: Incorrect – This is a play on the expression – to make mountains out of molehills – to exaggerate – no relevance here, E: Incorrect – There is no connection in the text between the recession and dismissals of older workers.
Gabarito "C".

(Auditor Fiscal do Trabalho – 2010 – ESAF) The text suggests that the governments of industrialized countries are

(A) trying to stop companies dismissing older members of their workforce.
(B) refusing to employ younger workers because of their expensive pensions.
(C) cutting the retirement pensions of valuable workers on the basis of age.
(D) making desperate attempts to cope with an inefficient labour market.
(E) regretting their generosity to workers who have taken early retirement.

(Interpretation) A: Correct – 'And governments are raising retirement ages and making it more difficult for companies to shed older workers, in a desperate attempt to cope with their under funded pension systems', B: Incorrect - Not stated in the text, C: Incorrect – No mention of cutting pensions of valuable workers, D: Incorrect – Perhaps true in a wide sense, but not as specific as option A, E: Incorrect – No mention of regret of generosity for early retirees.
Gabarito "A".

Read the text and answer the questions.

Minister calls for wider flexible working rights

British government ministers are considering giving all employees the right to ask for flexible working hours "from the beginning" of a new job as part of plans to encourage a fundamental shift in working habits.

The Work and Pensions Secretary, Yvette Cooper, says her office is working with employers and organisations such as the federation of small businesses to draw up new ways of supporting men as well as women and non-parents as well as parents working more flexible hours.

The current rules are limited to parents of children under 16 and carers, and Cooper wants to extend them. "You want people to offer flexible working from the beginning and we need to look again at how the legislation can support different ways of doing that," she said.

"There will be some areas where it's not possible to fit round particular school hours or particular things where the nature of the business makes it hard – but what you need is the cultural change for everybody to think differently." Cooper's proposals come as the government announced that fathers will be given the right to six months' paternity leave.

There will be a legal right to take the mother's place at home for the last three months of a nine-month maternity break; they would receive £123 a week in statutory pay. Fathers would then be entitled to take a further three months' unpaid leave. The move was criticised by some business leaders.

(From: *The Guardian*, Friday 29 January 2010 - slightly adapted)

(Auditor Fiscal do Trabalho – 2010 – ESAF) According to the text, current British laws on working timetables are designed mainly for

(A) women who work as secretaries for the government.
(B) parents of young children and teenagers, as well as care workers.
(C) men who have been in their current jobs for some time.
(D) women extending their maternity leave with unpaid work.
(E) those who want a change in the cultural mentality of businesses.

(Interpretation) A: Incorrect – The Work and Pensions Secretary mentioned is an official government position, B: Correct – 'The current rules are limited to parents of children under 16 and carers', C: Incorrect – Not mentioned in the text, D: Incorrect – The extension mentioned refers to who the legislation covers, E: Incorrect – Current or present laws do not reflect the change in mentality that is being sought.
Gabarito "B".

(Auditor Fiscal do Trabalho – 2010 – ESAF) With regard to paternity leave, the government has given men the right to

(A) take six months' paid leave as soon as their baby is born.
(B) care for a baby if the mother returns to work within three months.
(C) receive their full salary to look after the baby for three out of the first six months.
(D) take a three-month break receiving payment when the baby is six months old.
(E) stay at home with the baby's mother on unpaid leave for six months.

(Interpretation) A: Incorrect – The leave would happen after six months of a mother's maternity leave, B: Incorrect – The period is for the last three months of a mother's nine month maternity leave, C: Incorrect – Fathers would receive a fixed amount not their full salary, D: Correct - Fathers would receive 123 pounds for three months at the end of 6 months of mothers maternity leave, E: Incorrect – Fathers would receive payment and would not be at home as they same time as mothers.
A alternativa D é correta, pois, de acordo com o texto, "Haverá direito legal de substituir a mãe em casa pelos últimos três meses da licença maternidade de nove meses", ou seja, após 6 meses do início da licença da mãe, a partir do nascimento do bebê.
Gabarito "D".

(Auditor Fiscal do Trabalho – 2010 – ESAF) The Work and Pensions Secretary

(A) has been personally attacked by company bosses who dislike her plans.
(B) believes flexible working hours are a drawback for many workers.
(C) is seeking employers' cooperation for new proposals on working hours.
(D) shows scant regard for the needs of parents wanting flexible timetables.
(E) wants pensions to be paid to fathers who care for their neonate infants.

(Interpretation) A: Incorrect – The policy not the secretary herself was criticized, B: Incorrect – 'drawback' means disadvantage, C: Correct – It is explicitly mentioned that they are working together to draw up new plans. 'to draw up' means to write, D: Incorrect – 'scant regard' means to show little regard, E: Incorrect – No mention of wishing pensions for fathers of very young children.
Gabarito "C".

(Auditor Fiscal do Trabalho – 2010 – ESAF) Ms Cooper hopes her new proposals will give more flexible working hours

(A) from the outset, to workers of both genders.
(B) to fathers of babies, concurrently with mothers.
(C) after six months, to those established in their jobs.
(D) to senior staff who want to start a family.
(E) to parents and youth workers up to the age of sixteen.

(Interpretation) A: Correct – 'from the outset' means from the very beginning. This is the overall meaning of the text, B: Incorrect – 'concurrently' means at the same time. Fathers would replace mothers as carers after 6 months, C: Incorrect – No mention of people being established in their jobs, D: Incorrect – No mention of staff seniority – experienced staff, E: Incorrect – The assistance is for those caring for people under 16 years of age.
Gabarito "A".

Read the text and answer the questions.

The International Labour Organization

The International Labour Organization (ILO) is devoted to advancing opportunities for women and men to obtain decent and productive work in conditions of freedom, equity, security and human dignity. Its main aims are to promote rights at work, encourage decent employment opportunities, enhance social protection and strengthen dialogue in handling work-related issues.

Origins and history

The ILO was founded in 1919, in the wake of a destructive war, to pursue a vision based on the premise that universal, lasting peace can be established only if it is based upon decent treatment of working people. The ILO became the first specialized agency of the UN in 1946.

ILO's vision of decent work

Work is central to people's well-being. In addition to providing income, work can pave the way for broader social and economic advancement, strengthening individuals, their families and communities. Such progress, however, hinges on work that is decent. Decent work sums up the aspirations of people in their working lives.

Tripartism and social dialogue

The ILO is the only 'tripartite' United Nations agency in that it brings together representatives of governments, employers and workers to jointly shape policies and programmes. This unique arrangement gives the ILO an edge in incorporating 'real world' knowledge about employment and work.

Source: http://www.ilo.org/global/About_the_ILO/lang-en/index.htm

(Auditor Fiscal do Trabalho – 2010 – ESAF) The International Labour Organization seeks to

(A) encourage social equality at international level.
(B) foster workers' rights and good working practices.
(C) stamp out protectionism and restrictive practices.
(D) promote national wealth through higher productivity.
(E) overturn protective practices in the workplace.

(Vocabulary) A: Incorrect – It seeks social protection in the workplace not social equality, B: Correct – 'to foster' means to develop. C: Incorrect – 'stamp out' means to eradicate, this is not mentioned in the text, D: Incorrect – No mention of national wealth. Economic enhancement is mentioned at an individual level, E: Incorrect – 'to overturn' means to abolish. No mention of abolishing protective practices.
Gabarito "B".

(Auditor Fiscal do Trabalho – 2010 – ESAF) The founders of the ILO believed that

(A) the people must wake up again after a damaging war.
(B) decent social rights must be promoted by advanced countries.
(C) individuals' mercenary aims reinforce community life.
(D) good working conditions are essential to maintain world peace.
(E) the ILO favours tripartite progress between men, women and the UN.

(Interpretation) A: Incorrect – 'in the wake of' means 'immediately after', B: Incorrect – Social rights are not just restricted to advanced countries, C: Incorrect – 'mercenary' meaning 'motivated solely by material gain' has a pejorative connotation, D: Correct – Lasting peace is based on decent working conditions and treatment of workers, E: Incorrect – The tripartite relations in the text refer to employers, workers and governments.
Gabarito "D".

(Auditor Fiscal do Trabalho – 2010 – ESAF) The phrase "gives the ILO an edge" [paragraph 4 line 4] means

(A) offers the ILO a shove.
(B) cuts the ILO to the quick.
(C) sends the ILO to the rearguard.
(D) lumps the ILO together with.
(E) provides the ILO with an advantage.

(Vocabulary) A: Incorrect – 'a shove' means 'a push'; this is not directly related to having an edge, B: Incorrect – 'to cut to the quick' means to cut to the core of something, to be extremely damaging emotionally, C: Incorrect – 'rearguard' means a defensive action – this does not apply to a proactive lobbying group, D: Incorrect – 'lumps together' means to treat various elements as a unit, E: Correct – 'to have an edge' or 'to give someone the edge' means to give them an advantage.
Gabarito "E".

Read the text entitled "The case for flat taxes" in order to answer the questions:

The case for flat taxes

Source: The Economist (adapted) Apr 14th 2005

Estonia's economy has grown impressively since its 1994 reform. Growth reached double digits in 1997, and has since settled at around 6% annually, after a slump at the turn of the century. Repealing its high tax rate on the rich did not erode the country's tax base as some might have feared. In 1993, general government revenues were 39.4% of the gross domestic product (GDP); in 2002, they were 39.6%. Estonia now plans to cut its flat tax from 26% to 20% by 2007. How much do Estonia's robust revenues owe to its flat income tax? Perhaps less than is frequently advertised. In 1993, the year before its reform, Estonia's multiple personal income taxes raised revenues amounting to 8.2% of GDP. In 2002, its flat income tax raised revenues worth just 7.2%.

Indeed, the flat income tax that generated so much excitement abroad seems to be carrying less weight than Estonia's old-fashioned value-added tax (VAT), which raised 9.4% of GDP in revenues in 2002. VAT is, of course, the flattest tax of all. It levies a uniform rate on the goods you buy, taking a constant cut of your money when it is spent as opposed to when it is earned. Estonia's VAT is also quite broad, leaving relatively few things out (hydropower and windpower were two curious exceptions).

(Técnico da Receita Federal – 2006 – ESAF) In paragraph 1, the author provides a brief outline of

(A) Estonia's growth in 1994.
(B) a country's reform attempt.
(C) Estonia's burdensome tax system.
(D) a country's growth and fiscal policy.
(E) a country's upcoming interest rates.

(Interpretation) A: Incorrect – The text is not just restricted to 1994, B: Incorrect – The text is more specific than just mentioning a general reform, C: Incorrect – 'burdensome' means onerous. This is too specific and in fact, it states some of its tax laws are not as onerous as thought, D: Correct – This captures the overall theme and tone of the article, E: Incorrect – 'upcoming' means future. The text is mainly about past events.
O início do texto descreve brevemente o crescimento econômico da Estônia a partir de 1994 e o perfil de sua arrecadação tributária com os impostos de alíquota única.
"Gabarito "D".

(Técnico da Receita Federal – 2006 – ESAF) The author mentions a slump in Estonia's growth at the turn of the century which characterizes

(A) a much less successful period.
(B) a remarkable period of prosperity.
(C) a slightly better fiscal period.
(D) a landmark in Estonia's growth.
(E) the beginning of Estonia's growth.

(Vocabulary) A: Correct – A slump refers to a period of economic decline, B: Incorrect – The opposite is true, C: Incorrect – The period was negative not positive, D: Incorrect – 'landmark' means an important event. It was a period without growth, E: Incorrect – It refers to a period of decline not growth.
O autor se refere a uma brusca queda do índice de crescimento, que estava em dois dígitos, para a média em que se estabilizou a partir de então (6%). Ver a frase que se inicia em "O crescimento atingiu dois dígitos...".
Gabarito "A".

(Técnico da Receita Federal – 2006 – ESAF) In paragraph 2, the role played by Estonia's flat income tax in relation to its "robust revenues" is

(A) ignored.
(B) questioned.
(C) omitted.
(D) not mentioned.
(E) disregarded.

(Interpretation) A: Incorrect – The text specifically deals with this issue, B: Correct – To question in this case means to dispute. 'Perhaps less than is frequently advertised' shows an element of questioning, C: Incorrect – It is not left out or omitted, D: Incorrect – It is mentioned, E: Incorrect – It is not ignored.
O autor indica que as receitas do imposto de renda estoniano são menos representativas do que se imagina, inferiores às do IVA.
Gabarito "B".

(Técnico da Receita Federal – 2006 – ESAF) In paragraph 3, the author refers to VAT, a tax which

(A) is about to be raised.
(B) may frequently be dodged.
(C) might be repealed.
(D) will be simplified.
(E) has already been set.

(Interpretation) A: Incorrect – No mention that is about to be raised i.e. increased, B: Incorrect – 'to dodge' means to avoid - In this case, to avoid paying tax. This is not possible as the tax is paid as part of the price of goods. C: Incorrect – 'to repeal' means to revoke a law. This is not stated in the text. D: Incorrect – No mention of VAT being simplified. E: Correct - VAT is an old-fashioned tax which levies a uniform rate i.e. a fixed rate.
O autor descreve a incidência ampla e constante do IVA, incidente com alíquota única sobre a aquisição de praticamente todos os bens.
Gabarito "E".

Read the text entitled "The prices of sin" in order to answer the questions:

The prices of sin

Source: The Economist (adapted)
Aug 25th 2005

Much ministerial brow-sweat has been devoted to turning Britons into healthier, better-adjusted citizens, but the public has a nasty habit of spoiling the party. New figures provoked hand-wringing this week when they suggested that British alcohol consumption is rising even as the French and the Germans are drinking less. Alcohol fuelled crime is on the increase and smoking rates, which the government has promised to reduce, are stuck. To economists, the solution is obvious: just raise taxes on the goods in question. Successive governments have taken this advice to heart, leaving Britain with some of the highest "sin taxes" in Europe. Yet Labour has abandoned fiscal tinkering for a sort of social engineering that comes over as inconsistent: liberal laws that allow pubs to open around the clock in the hope of curing Britain's drink culture sit oddly with authoritarian plans to forbid smoking in public places.

(Técnico da Receita Federal – 2006 – ESAF) The author

(A) describes the successful health service in Germany.
(B) looks into the increase in alcohol consumption in France.
(C) comments on the politics of alcohol in Britain.
(D) praises the effectiveness of some British social policies.
(E) sets up policies concerning alcohol consumption in Britain.

(Interpretation) A: Incorrect – No mention of the German health service, B: Incorrect – Alcohol consumption in France is decreasing, C: Correct – Alcohol consumption and alcohol related crime are the main topics of the text, D: Incorrect – There is no praise given to British social policies, E: Incorrect – 'to set up' means to establish. The author comments on existing policies not on trying to establish new policies.
O texto refere-se às políticas relacionadas ao consumo de álcool na Grã-Bretanha, especialmente à tributação mais pesada como ferramenta para sua inibição.
Gabarito "C".

(Técnico da Receita Federal – 2006 – ESAF) In paragraph 1, the new figures related to the British alcohol consumption are said to have caused

(A) worries.
(B) consternation.
(C) relief.
(D) disbelief.
(E) mistrust.

(Interpretation) A: Correct – 'hand-wringing' means distress of worry, B: Incorrect – 'consternation' means paralysing dismay – Actions are being taken therefore it cannot be said to be paralyzing, C: Incorrect – The opposite of relief was felt on seeing the new figures, D: Incorrect – No mention that the figures were not believed, E: Incorrect – 'hand-wringing' does not mean mistrust.
Ver a frase que se inicia com "Novos dados provocaram preocupação...".
Gabarito "A".

(Técnico da Receita Federal – 2006 – ESAF) According to the text, the "sin taxes"

(A) are likely to be adopted in Britain.
(B) have been proposed by the German authorities.
(C) should have been implemented in Britain.
(D) must be forbidden by the European Union.
(E) have been put into practice by British governments.

(Interpretation) A: Incorrect – The use of 'successive governments' reveals that this had already been adopted in Britain, B: Incorrect – No mention of this in the text, C: Incorrect – They have already been implemented in Britain, D: Incorrect - No mention of prohibition by the European Union, E: Correct – 'Successive governments have taken this advice to heart' i.e. previous governments have listened to this idea and implemented policies relating to it.
Ver a frase que se inicia com "Sucessivos governos têm adotado...".
Gabarito "E".

Read the interview below entitled "When should you start to worry?" in order to answer the questions:

When should we start to worry?

Source: Newsweek (adapted)
Oct 17, 2005

I'm concerned about the long-term risks of drinking a lot of caffeine (two or more cups of coffee a day). I have no family history of heart disease and no history of heart trouble. Am I at risk?
Dr. Thomas H. Lee: I wouldn't worry about the caffeine in a few cups of coffee. Lots of caffeine can rev up your heart and make it beat faster, occasionally even launching into prolonged periods of a racing heart. You will almost surely feel palpitations if you get these abnormal heartbeats, and then you should heed your body's advice to cut back on the caffeine. Heavy coffee drinkers don't have a higher risk of cardiomyopathy (damaged heart muscle) or heart attacks. If you do decide to cut back on caffeine, you may experience headaches during the transition.

Until recently, vitamin E was touted as a good-heart supplement. Now several studies indicate that vitamin E supplements can increase the risk of heart disease or stroke. Does the medical community agree?
Dr. Thomas H. Lee: You have it right. In the 1990's, vitamin E was very promising – but controversial. Epidemiological studies showed that regular vitamin E users had 20 to 40 percent lower rates of heart disease than nonusers. Since then, larger experiments have not shown any benefit from taking vitamin E.

(Técnico da Receita Federal – 2006 – ESAF) In his answer to question 1, Dr. Lee warns against drinking lots of caffeine since it

(A) might cause a sudden faint.
(B) can slow the heartbeats.
(C) may accelerate the heartbeats.
(D) will surely increase the heartbeats.
(E) damages the heart muscle.

(Interpretation) A: Incorrect – No mention of fainting in the text, B: Incorrect – The opposite is true, C: Correct – Coffee is said to rev up (speed up) your heart and make it beat faster, D: Incorrect – The author uses the modal verb 'can' (rev up your heart rate), thus, it is possible but not certain, E: Incorrect – Heavy coffee drinkers don't have higher rates of damage to heart muscles.
Leia a frase que se inicia com "Muita cafeína pode acelerar seu coração...".
Gabarito "C".

(Técnico da Receita Federal – 2006 – ESAF) According to Dr. Lee, we should listen to our body's advice to "cut back on the caffeine". In other words, our body advises us

(A) not to stop drinking it.
(B) to reduce our caffeine intake.
(C) to increase caffeine consumption.
(D) to regularly consume caffeine.
(E) to quit caffeine consumption.

(Interpretation) A: Incorrect – 'to cut back' means to reduce, B: Correct – 'to cut back on caffeine' means to reduce caffeine intake, C: Incorrect – The opposite of cut back, D: Incorrect – 'cut back' does not mean to relate to regular consumption, it refers rather to the quantity of intake, E: Incorrect – Not to quit or stop completely, instead simply to reduce.
Ao entendermos o significado de "cut back on the caffeine", a resposta torna-se evidente. Leia a frase que se inicia com "Você irá, muito provavelmente...".
Gabarito "B".

(Técnico da Receita Federal – 2006 – ESAF) In his answer to question 2, Dr. Lee

(A) prescribes the intake of vitamin E supplements.
(B) points out the risks of taking vitamin E.

(C) bears out the claim that supplements are risky.
(D) demystifies the benefits from taking vitamin E.
(E) corroborates the benefits of vitamin E intake.

(Interpretation) A: Incorrect – 'to prescribe' means to order the use of a medicine – this is not stated in the text, B: Incorrect – The doctors position is neutral, he does not highlight potential risks, C: Incorrect – The doctor does not confirm or deny that supplements are risky, D: Correct – The doctor provides information that shows benefits of vitamin E have not been proved, E: Incorrect – 'to corroborate' means to strengthen with evidence. The doctor does not do this.
O Dr. Lee afirma que os estudos mais recentes não demonstraram benefício no consumo da vitamina E.
„Gabarito "D".

Your answers to questions must be based on the text below entitled "A dip in the middle":

A dip in the middle

Source: The Economist (adapted) Sep 8th 2005

Income tax has been paid in Britain for more than two centuries. First introduced by William Pitt the Younger to finance the war against Napoleonic France, it is the Treasury's biggest source of revenue, raising 30% of tax receipts. It arouses strong political emotions, regarded as fair by some because it makes the rich pay a bigger share of their income than the poor, but unfair by others because it penalizes enterprise and hard work. During the past 30 years, income tax has been subject to sweeping changes, notably the cut in the top rate from 98% to 40% under Margaret Thatcher between 1979 and 1988. Now another Conservative politician, George Osborne, is floating a radical reform to match that earlier exploit. The shadow chancellor announced on September 7th that he was setting up a commission to explore the possible introduction of an income tax in Britain. Introducing an income tax into Britain would involve two main changes. At present, there are three marginal tax rates. These three rates would be replaced by a single rate, which would be considerably lower than the current top rate. At the same time there would be an increase in the tax-free personal allowance, currently worth 4,895 pounds.

(Auditor Fiscal da Receita Federal – 2005– ESAF) According to the text,

(A) a commission introduced an income tax into Britain.
(B) a war once justified the payment of income tax.
(C) an income tax would be made up of three tax rates.
(D) the reform would yield many economic benefits.
(E) George Osborne has managed to introduce the single rate.

(Interpretation) A: Incorrect – The commission mentioned is being set up i.e. established, it has not yet introduced the tax, B: Correct – It was introduced to finance the war against France, C: Incorrect – The income tax would be a single rate, D: Incorrect – No mention of the economic benefits it would yield or produce, E: Incorrect – The use of 'to explore' is not evidence that he has managed to introduce the rate.
Ver a frase que se inicia com "Introduzido por William Pitt...".
„Gabarito "B".

(Auditor Fiscal da Receita Federal – 2005– ESAF) According to paragraph 2, Margaret Thatcher's government brought in

(A) major alterations to British income tax rates.
(B) measures that made cosmetic changes only.
(C) a tax system that discourages hard work.
(D) proposals imitated by a shady politician.
(E) a substantial increase in top taxation rates.

(Interpretation) A: Correct – 'sweeping changes' means radical alterations, B: Incorrect – The changes were sweeping i.e. radical, C: Incorrect – This comment refers to the tax system as a whole not the changes under Thatcher, D: Incorrect – 'shadow chancellor' refers to the chancellor in the main opposition party of the government, E: Incorrect – The opposite is true, the top rate was cut dramatically.
Ver a frase que se inicia com "Durante os últimos 30 anos...".
„Gabarito "A".

(Auditor Fiscal da Receita Federal – 2005– ESAF) The flat income tax

(A) is intended to hinder enterprise and hard work.
(B) would be below the present top rate.
(C) ought to please low-earners and high-fliers.
(D) must generate a cut in public spending.
(E) might be financed by increases in other taxes.

(Interpretation) A: Incorrect – Although it is considered "unfair by others because it penalizes enterprise and hard work", this is not the intention of the tax, B: Correct – 'considerably lower than the current top rate', C: Incorrect – No mention of who it should please, D: Incorrect - Not mentioned in the text, E: Incorrect – Not mentioned in the text.
Ver a frase que se inicia com "Essas três alíquotas teriam...".
„Gabarito "B".

(Auditor Fiscal da Receita Federal – 2005– ESAF) In paragraph 3, the author notes that the present tax-free personal allowance would

(A) remain unchanged.
(B) be cut.
(C) rise.
(D) be abolished.
(E) be phased out.

(Interpretation) A: Incorrect – 'there would be an increase in the tax-free personal allowance', B: Incorrect – It would increase not be decreased i.e. cut, C: Correct – It would increase, D: Incorrect – It would still exist, E: Incorrect – It would increase not be slowly taken away.
Ver a frase que se inicia com "Ao mesmo tempo, haveria um aumento...".
„Gabarito "C".

Your answers to questions must be based on the text below entitled "Flight of the French":

Flight of the French

Source: Newsweek (adapted) Sept 26th/Oct 3rd 2005

The Belgians call them "fiscal refugees", but these refugees wear Channel. They are runaways from high taxes in France. Officially, France has lost, on average, one millionaire or billionaire tax payer per day for tax reasons since 1997, when the government started trying to track capital flight. Privately, economists say the number is much higher. "The statistic is stupid," holds French economist Nicolas Baverez. "It's as if, to count contraband, you only counted what people declared at the border." While much of Europe has revised its tax codes, France's fiscal inertia is virtually begging its rich to leave. Holding dear its commitment to *égalité* and *fraternité*, France has bucked the trend in the European Union, where most member states have dropped the wealth tax since the mid-1990s. France went the opposite way in 1997 by abolishing a cap that limited the wealth-tax bill, which kicks in at incomes over 720,000 euros to 85% of a taxpayer's income. The result: some pay more taxes than they earn in income.

(Auditor Fiscal da Receita Federal – 2005– ESAF) The text refers to France's

(A) historic decision to drop its wealth-tax.
(B) recent proposal to suppress the wealth-tax.
(C) commitment to prevent the so-called capital flight.
(D) current fiscal policy in relation to the rich.
(E) controversial attempt to penalize its fiscal refugees.

(Interpretation) A: Incorrect – No such decision has been made, B: Incorrect – 'to suppress' means to end. This is not mentioned, C: Incorrect – It does not talk about commitment by France to stop this, D: Correct – This covers the broad theme of tax policy and the rich in France, E: Incorrect – No mention of attempts to penalize the fiscal refugees.
O texto se refere à alta tributação sobre os ricos franceses, em relação a boa parte da Europa.
Gabarito "D".

(Auditor Fiscal da Receita Federal – 2005– ESAF) The so-called 'fiscal refugees' are the

(A) fleeing taxpayers.
(B) successful shareholders.
(C) well-known tax attorneys.
(D) notorious smugglers.
(E) top company executives.

(Vocabulary) A: Correct – 'to flee' means to run from trouble or danger, B: Incorrect – No evidence the refugees are shareholders, C: Incorrect – No mention of tax attorneys, D: Incorrect – There is a mention of contraband which relates to smuggling but this has nothing to do with the fiscal refugees, E: Incorrect – This is too specific.
Ver a frase que se inicia com "Eles são fugitivos...".
Gabarito "A".

(Auditor Fiscal da Receita Federal – 2005– ESAF) According to the author, France

(A) might change its fiscal system.
(B) must preserve its wealth tax.
(C) has not changed its fiscal policy.
(D) ought to slash its public spending.
(E) could lose from a tax reform.

(Interpretation) A: Incorrect – No indications that it will do this, B: Incorrect – Use of 'must' implies a strong assertion – This is not the tone of the text which is slightly critical of France, C: Correct – France's fiscal inertia – i.e. it has done nothing, D: Incorrect – 'to slash' means to cut dramatically. This is not in the text, E: Incorrect – The opposite is true as current law encourages the rich to leave a tax reform could be a good thing.
A rigor, o texto diz que a França trilhou sentido contrário em relação à maioria dos países europeus, ampliando a tributação sobre a riqueza (não houve simples manutenção da política fiscal, mas recrudescimento em relação aos maiores rendimentos). Ver a frase que se inicia com "A França foi pelo caminho oposto...". De qualquer forma, a alternativa C é a que mais se aproxima do texto, até por exclusão das demais.
Gabarito "C".

Your answers to questions must be based on the text below entitled "The real medicine":

The real medicine

Source: Newsweek (adapted) Oct 17th 2005

People who survive a heart attack often describe it as a wake-up call. But for a 61-year old executive I met recently, it was more than that. This man was in the midst of a divorce when he was stricken last spring, and he had fallen out of touch with friends and family members. The executive's doctor, unaware of the strife in his life, counseled him to change his diet, start exercising and quit smoking. He also prescribed drugs to lower cholesterol and blood pressure. It was sound advice, but in combing the medical literature, the patient discovered that he needed to do more. Studies suggested that his risk of dying within six months would be four times greater if he remained depressed and lonely. So he joined a support group and reordered his priorities, placing relationships at the top of the list instead of the bottom. His health has improved steadily since then, and so has his outlook on life. In fact he now describes his heart attack as the best thing that ever happened to him. "Yes, my arteries are more open," he says. "But even more important, *I´m* more open."

(Auditor Fiscal da Receita Federal – 2005– ESAF) According to the text, the executive

(A) actually refused to eat right, exercise and avoid smoking.
(B) seems to have increased his risk of early death.
(C) agrees that medicine should focus primarily on drugs.
(D) declined new choices and priorities in his life.
(E) went further in his search for recovery and health.

(Interpretation) A: Incorrect – The executive did not refuse to eat right. He is quoted at the end of the text as saying, "My arteries are more open", which suggests he followed his doctor's advice; B: Incorrect – The text explicitly says, "His health has improved steadily since then"; C: – Incorrect – The fact that he realized his loneliness could shorten his life suggests he does not believe medicine should focus on drugs; D: Incorrect – The executive drastically changed his life, joining support groups and placing relationships as a priority in his life; E: Correct – The executive discovered, while combing the medical literature, that he needed to do more than take drugs, and he did much more (joined support groups, prioritized relationships). Veja as frases que se iniciam com "Foram conselhos ótimos, mas...".
Gabarito "E".

(Auditor Fiscal da Receita Federal – 2005– ESAF) The advice given by the doctor is defined as sound. In other words, it

(A) might be effective.
(B) is reliable and effective.
(C) is questionable.
(D) should be looked into.
(E) must be deeply researched.

(Vocabulary) A: Incorrect – The word "sound" in this context does not suggest possibility or probability, as does "might"; B: Correct – "sound" means reliable and effective; C: Incorrect – "questionable" is almost an antonym of "sound"; D: Incorrect – The modal verb "should" is used for making suggestion, not guaranteeing reliability and effectiveness; E: Incorrect – The modal verb "must" is related to obligations, which is not the case here. "Sound", além do significado mais conhecido (som), indica também algo eficaz e confiável.
Gabarito "B".

(Auditor Fiscal da Receita Federal – 2005– ESAF) The text focuses on the relevance of

(A) current scientific and technological advances.
(B) studies carried out by obscure scientists.
(C) preventive medicine in relation to some ailments.
(D) a desirable change of attitude to life.
(E) leading a healthy life in spite of loneliness.

(Interpretation) A: Incorrect – The text does not mention anything about advances in medicine; B: Incorrect – The text does not focus on obscure scientists, but rather on a combination of techniques and the executive's choices; C: Incorrect – As the executive had a heart attack, the focus was on getting better, not preventing his problem; D: Correct – The text focuses on how the executive changed his attitude to life (joining support groups, prioritizing relationships); E: Incorrect – The text talks about living a healthy life and avoiding loneliness, not "in spite of" it.
O texto refere-se à mudança de atitude do executivo em relação à vida, com uma reorganização de suas prioridades. Ver as frases que se iniciam com "Ele, então, juntou-se a um grupo de apoio...".
Gabarito "D".

Read the text below in order to answer the questions:

Analysis: Brazil's Lula faces new phase

In a speech last week from the capital, Brazil's president Luiz Inácio Lula da Silva appeared to balloon with pride over his accomplishments and gloated over achieving in months what his predecessor Fernando Henrique Cardoso could not do during his eight years in office.

"I am pleased and the Brazilian people are satisfied that we have done something in seven months that has taken other countries years to do," said Lula on the pension reform amendment. "The last president of Brazil spent eight years trying to get a social security reform bill through Congress."

While the president is riding high over his win with pensions, analysts see a much tougher field to hoe in the coming months.

Next on the Lula administration agenda is taxes, a fight that will not only be waged in the capital, but at the state and local levels as well. Governors, who backed Lula's pension proposal in Congress, want to see additional revenue tickle down to the local levels. The president, however, insists on "tax reform designed to stimulate production, not to boost revenue" for the states, as he put it on Monday.

(Auditor Fiscal da Receita Federal – 2003– ESAF) According to the text, Brazil's president Luiz Inácio Lula da Silva

(A) pretends to have revoked an amendment proposed by the former Brazilian president.
(B) might submit a controversial amendment that revamps the nation's pension policy.
(C) has postponed a major political battle related to the nation's pension policy.
(D) conceals his feeling of pride in relation to his accomplishments.
(E) did not conceal his elation concerning a political accomplishment.

(Interpretation) A: Incorrect – The then-president did not pretend to revoke an amendment. He compares his success in passing a bill to the failure of the previous president in doing so; B: Incorrect – In the text, the bill on pension reform is said to have already passed (it took seven months to do so); C: Incorrect - In the text, the bill on pension reform is said to have already passed (it took seven months to do so). Nothing has been postponed, in the text; D: Incorrect – The text explicitly says he "ballooned with pride over his achievements"; E: Correct – The text explicitly says he "ballooned with pride over his achievements".
Ver o primeiro parágrafo do texto.
Gabarito "E".

(Auditor Fiscal da Receita Federal – 2003– ESAF) According to the author, analysts

(A) foresee difficulties.
(B) predict victories.
(C) forecast gains.
(D) praise Lula's victory.
(E) triggered political reactions.

(Interpretation) A: Correct – The text explicitly says, "analysts see a much tougher field to hoe in the coming months." A "tougher field to hoe" suggests that the work ahead will be more difficult; B: Incorrect – The text does not mention analysts predicting victories; C: Incorrect - The text does not mention analysts forecasting gains; D: Incorrect - The text does not mention analysts praising Lula's victory. The only one praising Lula's victories, in the text, is himself; E: Incorrect - The text does not mention analysts triggering political reactions. There may be political reaction to the tax reform, but analysts are not triggering this.
Ver o terceiro parágrafo do texto.
Gabarito "A".

(Auditor Fiscal da Receita Federal – 2003– ESAF) Brazil's president intends to

(A) deregulate production.
(B) slash the budget.
(C) increase revenue.
(D) fight another war.
(E) state legal requirements.

(Interpretation) A: Incorrect – The then-president is quoted as insisting on "tax reform designed to stimulate production", not to deregulate it; B: Incorrect – The then-president is quoted as wishing to stimulate production and not boost revenue for states. This does not suggest that he wishes to slash (cut) the budget; C: Incorrect - The then-president is quoted as wishing to stimulate production

and not boost revenue for states; D: Correct – The text explicitly says that the next fight, taxes, will not only be fought in the capital, but also at state and municipal levels. The war will be against high taxes; E: Incorrect – 'legal requirements' are not mentioned in this text.
Segundo o texto, a próxima batalha do presidente seria a reforma tributária. Ver o quarto parágrafo do texto.
Gabarito "D".

Read the text below in order to answer the questions:

Tax Strategies for 2003 and Beyond

Even the accountants are having a hard time keeping all the phase-ins and phase-outs straight after the last tax law change (the Jobs and Growth Tax Relief Reconciliation Act of 2003, which was signed by President Bush on May 28, 2003). Our Tax Act Timeline can help you take maximum advantage of income, gift, and estate tax laws.

Almost everyone will see a decrease in overall tax paid in 2003. The ordinary income tax brackets that were due to decrease gradually over time until 2006 have been accelerated into 2003. The top tax bracket is now 35%.

Watch out for how those income tax brackets change over time, however. For example, in 2003-2004 the 10% bracket applies to $0-$7,000 of income for single filers and $0-$14,000 for married filing jointly. But in 2005, the brackets shrink and only $0-$6,000 (single) will quality for the 10% tax and $0-$12,000 for married filing jointly. The brackets change again (back to the higher levels) in 2008.

(Auditor Fiscal da Receita Federal – 2003– ESAF) The author refers to the Jobs and Growth Tax Relief Reconciliation Act of 2003 as
(A) likely to be signed.
(B) an achievable change.
(C) officially accepted.
(D) a changeable tax law.
(E) having been changed.

(Interpretation) A: Incorrect – The text explicitly says that the "Jobs and Growth Tax Relief Reconciliation Act… was signed by President Bush on May 28"; therefore, it is not "likely" to be signed. It has been signed; B: Incorrect – The text explicitly says that the "Jobs and Growth Tax Relief Reconciliation Act… was signed by President Bush on May 28", suggesting that this 'change' has already been achieved; C: Correct - The text explicitly says that the "Jobs and Growth Tax Relief Reconciliation Act… was signed by President Bush on May 28"; therefore, it has already been officially accepted; D: Incorrect – This is a misleading question. The law itself is not referred to as being "changeable"; however, the tax brackets within the law are changeable; E: Incorrect – This is a misleading question. The use of the present perfect, together with the passive voice, creates a sense in which the change has happened, but we are unsure as to who made that change. While answer C is correct, this answer is plausible, as the text explicitly says that accountants were having trouble understanding things "straight after the last tax law change", which suggests that it has been changed.
Esse Ato foi oficialmente aprovado, no momento da assinatura pelo presidente Bush em 2003. Ver o primeiro parágrafo do texto.
Gabarito "C".

(Auditor Fiscal da Receita Federal – 2003– ESAF) According to the author, in 2003 almost everybody's total tax bill will show
(A) a sharp fall.
(B) a reduction.
(C) a steep rise.
(D) a balance.
(E) an increase.

(Interpretation) A: Incorrect – The text explicitly says that "Almost everyone will see a decrease in overall tax paid in 2003"; however, it does not mention this reduction as being "sharp"; B: Correct – The text explicitly says that "Almost everyone will see a decrease in overall tax paid in 2003"; C: Incorrect - The text explicitly says that "Almost everyone will see a decrease in overall tax paid in 2003". There is a mention of some changes back to "higher levels" in 2008, but they are not mentioned as being 'steep'; D: Incorrect - The text explicitly says that "Almost everyone will see a decrease in overall tax paid in 2003", as well as a possible rise to "higher levels" in 2008. This is not a balance; E: Incorrect - The text explicitly says "Almost everyone will see a decrease in overall tax paid in 2003". There is a mention of some changes back to "higher levels" in 2008, but they are not mentioned as being for everyone.
Ver o segundo parágrafo do texto.
Gabarito "B".

(Auditor Fiscal da Receita Federal – 2003– ESAF) The author points out
(A) the difficulties faced by accountants in setting sensible tax brackets.
(B) the urgent need to change the last tax law.
(C) the government's decision to increase tax brackets in 2005.
(D) a certain number of changes concerning tax brackets.
(E) the need to be married so as to qualify for the 10% tax bracket.

(Interpretation) A: Incorrect – The text talks about accountants difficulties, but they do not set tax brackets; the government does; B: Incorrect - The text explicitly says that the tax law has already changed ("straight after the last tax law change"). The need is no longer urgent, nor mentioned; C: Incorrect – The text explicitly says that "in 2005, the brackets shrink", but this does not mean that the government plans to raise taxes; D: Correct - The text explicitly says "Watch out for how those income tax brackets change over time"; E: Incorrect - Text explicitly says, "the brackets shrink and only $0-$6,000 (single) will quality for the 10% tax".
O autor se refere às alterações nas alíquotas progressivas do imposto de renda e, especialmente, às faixas de rendimento a que se aplica a alíquota mínima de 10%. Ver o segundo e o terceiro parágrafos do texto.
Gabarito "D".

Read the text below in order to answer the questions:

EU Law Taxes Overseas Net Firms

They've survived the bursting of the tech bubble, a global economic downturn and the occasional virus, but now overseas Internet retailers may see their European profit push derailed by one of the oldest drags on business: tax.

On July 1, a new EU (European Union) directive goes into effect requiring all Internet firms to account for value-added tax, or VAT, on "digital sales".

The law adds a 15 to 25 percent levy on select Internet transactions such as software and music downloads, monthly subscriptions to an Internet service provider and on any product purchased through an online auction anywhere in the 15-member bloc of nations.

The VAT tax is nothing new for some Net firms. European dot-coms have been charging customers VAT since their inception. Their overseas rivals though have been exempt, making foreign firms an obvious choice for the bargain-hunting consumer.

(Auditor Fiscal da Receita Federal – 2003– ESAF) The opening paragraph of the text

(A) emphasizes the need to tax digital sales.
(B) foresees a global economic downturn.
(C) refers to tax as something annoying.
(D) defines a future increase in digital sales.
(E) outlines the profit globally made.

(Interpretation) A: Incorrect – The opening paragraph of the text says there is a possibility that profits will suffer from taxes. No 'need' is emphasized; B: Incorrect – The opening paragraph of the text says there is a possibility that profits will suffer from taxes. There is no forecast of a global downturn. The text mentions that it has been surpassed; C: Correct – The text explicitly says that tax is "one of the oldest drags on business". 'Drag' here means 'burden' or something annoying; D: Incorrect - The opening paragraph of the text says there is a possibility that profits will suffer from taxes. There is no reference to a future increase in digital sales; E: Incorrect – The opening paragraph of the text does not outline global profit. It mentions that specific retailers will see their profit diminish. O primeiro parágrafo, em seu final, descreve a tributação como um dos mais antigos empecilhos aos negócios.
„Gabarito "C".

(Auditor Fiscal da Receita Federal – 2003– ESAF) According to the text, all Internet firms are required to

(A) obey a new EU official order.
(B) prevent taxation in certain cases.
(C) save in tax payments.
(D) relocate their headquarters.
(E) apply for tax exemption.

(Interpretation) A: Correct – The second paragraph of the text explicitly says "On July 1, a new EU (European Union) directive goes into effect requiring all Internet firms to account for value-added tax, or VAT, on "digital sales"; B: Incorrect – The text explicitly says that in some cases, taxes will be higher ("The law adds a 15 to 25 percent levy on select Internet transactions"); C: Incorrect – The text does not mention savings for any firms; D: Incorrect – The text mentions that the law now affects companies in Europe, but not that they will relocate. Customers prefer to buy overseas, but there is nothing in the text to suggest firms relocating; E: Incorrect – The text mentions the fact that up until now some overseas rivals have enjoyed tax exemption ("Their overseas rivals though have been exempt"). It does not say that Internet firm must apply for such exemption.
O texto se refere a uma nova diretiva normativa da UE, que deverá ser observada por todas as empresas que atuam na internet, inclusive aquelas que operam a partir de outros países (sujeição de suas operações ao IVA).
„Gabarito "A".

(Auditor Fiscal da Receita Federal – 2003– ESAF) The author states that the VAT (value-added tax) has been

(A) lowered.
(B) lifted.
(C) forbidden.
(D) reduced.
(E) charged.

(Interpretation) A: Incorrect – The text explicitly talks about charging VAT and even mentions extra charges in some cases, but there is no mention of "lowering" it; B: Incorrect – The text explicitly says that "all Internet firms to account for value-added tax, or VAT, on "digital sales". This means that VAT is to be charged, not lifted; C: Incorrect - The text explicitly says "all Internet firms to account for value-added tax, or VAT, on "digital sales". This means that VAT is to be charged, not forbidden; D: Incorrect - The text explicitly talks about charging VAT and even mentions extra charges in some cases, but there is no mention of "reducing" it; E: Correct – The text explicitly says that "The VAT tax is nothing new for some Net firms", suggesting that VAT has been charged. Now foreign companies will also be charged VAT.
O último parágrafo do texto deixa claro que o IVA já vem sendo recolhido pelas empresas europeias que atuam na internet. A nova diretiva vem apenas submeter as empresas estrangeiras ao mesmo tratamento tributário.
„Gabarito "E".

(Auditor Fiscal da Receita Federal – 2003– ESAF) Concerning the European profit made by the overseas Internet retailers, it

(A) may be re-invested.
(B) may be affected.
(C) must be spent.
(D) shall be cut.
(E) might remain high.

(Interpretation) A: Incorrect – The opening paragraph of the text says there is a possibility that profits will suffer from taxes, not that it will be re-invested; B: Correct – The opening paragraph of the text says there is a possibility that profits will suffer from taxes; C: Incorrect - The opening paragraph of the text says there is a possibility that profits will suffer from taxes, not that it must be spent; D: Incorrect - The opening paragraph of the text says there is a possibility that profits will suffer from taxes. To cut profit would be too strong in this case; E: Incorrect - The opening paragraph of the text says there is a possibility that profits will suffer from taxes, not that it might remain high. If profit is taxed, then it will reduce.
O primeiro parágrafo do texto deixa claro que os lucros dessas empresas poderão ser reduzidos, por conta da tributação. É uma possibilidade (*may, might*) não uma certeza, um dever a ser cumprido ou um conselho a ser seguido (*must, shall*).
„Gabarito "B".

For questions below, choose the answer which best fits the ideas in the text.

Brazil: One Growth Obstacle after Another

After just eight months in office, President Luiz Inácio Lula da Silva of the left-wing Workers' Party has won congressional approval for economically critical and politically controversial pension and tax reforms. Now, however, da Silva faces a bigger challenge: reviving Brazil's economy.

In 2003's first half, Brazil's economy fell into recession. Most economists expect growth for the entire year to be a miserly 1%. And a government linked research group recently embarrassed ministers by predicting growth of just 0.5% in 2003.

Taxes are a serious obstacle to growth. Brazil's tax burden is among the highest in the world, equal to 41.7% of salaries. Reforms now proceeding through Congress will simplify the tax system, but won't reduce the total burden. That will be possible only if interest rates fall and the government can keep spending in check, thereby reducing the amount of money needed to pay its own debts. For now, Brazil's economy is going nowhere.

(By Jonathan Wheatley in São Paulo – adapted. From: ***Business Week*** September 10, 2003)

(Técnico da Receita Federal – 2003 – ESAF) The picture of the current Brazilian economy given by this article is

(A) highly optimistic.
(B) guardedly hopeful.
(C) unremittingly positive.
(D) faintly negative.
(E) distinctly bleak.

(Interpretation) A: Incorrect – The text explicitly says, "In 2003's first half, Brazil's economy fell into recession" and "For now, Brazil's economy is going nowhere", quite the opposite of 'highly optimistic'; B: Incorrect – 'guardedly hopeful' means 'cautiously optimistic'. The text explicitly says, "In 2003's first half, Brazil's economy fell into recession" and "For now, Brazil's economy is going nowhere", the opposite of 'optimistic'; C: Incorrect – 'unremittingly positive' means 'continuously optimistic'. The text explicitly says, "In 2003's first half, Brazil's economy fell into recession" and "For now, Brazil's economy is going nowhere", the opposite of 'optimistic'; D: Incorrect – 'faintly negative' means 'slightly' or 'a little bit negative'. The text explicitly says, "In 2003's first half, Brazil's economy fell into recession" and "For now, Brazil's economy is going nowhere", which is not slightly or a little bit; E: Correct - The text explicitly says, "In 2003's first half, Brazil's economy fell into recession" and "For now, Brazil's economy is going nowhere", showing a distinctly bleak view.
A frase final ("Por enquanto, a economia do Brasil não está indo a lugar algum") indica o tom claramente pessimista do texto em relação à situação da economia.
Gabarito "E".

(Técnico da Receita Federal – 2003 – ESAF) According to the text, a think tank recently caused the government some embarrassment by predicting

(A) lower growth than most other economists had forecast.
(B) cynicism over the government's tax reform program.
(C) one of the highest tax burdens in the world.
(D) stubbornly high interest rates for bank loans.
(E) further cuts in the national interest rates for loans.

(Interpretation) A: Correct – The text explicitly says, "Most economists expect growth for the entire year to be a ***miserly 1%***. And a government linked research group recently embarrassed ministers by predicting growth of ***just 0.5%*** in 2003"; B: Incorrect – The think tank only forecast lower growth. There was no cynicism or sarcasm on their part; C: Incorrect - The think tank only forecast lower growth. The author mentions that Brazil has one of the highest tax burdens in the world, but not the think tank; D: Incorrect - The think tank only forecast lower growth. Interest rates are mentioned, but they are not referred to as "stubbornly high"; E: Incorrect - The think tank only forecast lower growth. Interest rates are mentioned, but the think tank did not predict a cut in them.
A maioria dos economistas previa taxa de crescimento de 1%, enquanto o instituto de pesquisa ligado ao governo previu índice de apenas 0,5%. Ver as frases que se iniciam com "A maioria dos economistas espera...".
Gabarito "A".

(Técnico da Receita Federal – 2003 – ESAF) The advantage of the proposed tax reform measures is

(A) particularly fast progress through Congress.
(B) a proposed 41.7% reduction in taxation.
(C) a welcome simplification of the tax system.
(D) the prospect of controlling high inflation.
(E) further political support for the government

(Interpretation) A: Incorrect – The text does not say that reform measures will move fast through Congress; B: Incorrect – The text explicitly says that Brazil's "tax burden is among the highest in the world, equal to 41.7% of salaries", not that taxes will be reduced by this percentage; C: Correct – The text explicitly says, "Reforms now proceeding through Congress will simplify the tax system"; D: Incorrect – The tax reform measures are not aimed at controlling high inflation, but rather to lighten the tax load so that the government can reduce its debt load; E: Incorrect – The text does not mention political support from the government.
Ver a frase que se inicia com "Reformas em andamento no Congresso irão simplificar...".
Gabarito "C".

(Técnico da Receita Federal – 2003 – ESAF) According to the last section of the text, taxation will only be reduced if

(A) there are strong signs of growing inflation.
(B) Congress passes the new taxation reform bill.
(C) Brazil's economy goes nowhere soon.
(D) the sum needed to meet public debt is reduced.
(E) income tax bills cease to be such a heavy burden.

(Interpretation) A: Incorrect – The text does not say that taxation will only be reduced if inflation takes off. Inflation is not explicitly mentioned in the text; B: Incorrect – The text explicitly says that congressional approval has been given "for economically critical and politically controversial pension and tax reforms". If it has already been given, then taxation does not need to wait for more congressional approval; C: Incorrect – A reduction in taxation is not conditioned to Brazil's economic growth, but rather to interest rates falling, government spending, and "reducing the amount of money needed to pay its own debts"; D: Correct - Reduction in taxation is conditioned to interest rates falling, government spending, and "reducing the amount of money needed to pay its own debts"; E: Incorrect – 'income tax' is not explicitly mentioned in the text. The tax in question is a generic idea of taxation, and not a specific tax, such an income tax.
Ver a frase que se inicia com "Isso será possível apenas se...".
Gabarito "D".

For questions below, choose the answer which best fits the ideas in the text.

How the world's poor changed dynamics of global politics

A new alliance of some of the world's poorest countries forged during the last week's global trade talks has changed the entire dynamics of world politics, the foreign minister of Brazil told *The Independent* yesterday.

In an exclusive interview, Celso Amorim said the formation of the Group of 21 nations (G21) had "reshuffled the cards" by creating a powerful counterweight to Washington and Brussels. The creation of the G21 has been one of the most significant developments of the World Trade Organisation meetings that have dominated the Mexican beach resort of Cancun since Wednesday.

Thanks to tough negotiating by the G21, analysts believe that the world's two most powerful economic blocs have been prevented from riding roughshod over the 100-plus countries that make up the developing world. It has also enhanced the reputation of Brazil - the leading voice in the G21 and the country with the largest democratic support for any left-wing government in the world - and the administration led by the uneducated steelworker Lula da Silva. "We have gained the political initiative," said Mr Amorim on the fringes of the conference.

(From: *The Independent* September 15th 2003 – slightly adapted.)

(Técnico da Receita Federal – 2003 – ESAF) The expression "forged" in the first paragraph of the text could best be defined as

(A) misled.
(B) broken down.
(C) set up.
(D) made off with.
(E) falsified.

(**Vocabulary**) A: Incorrect – 'forge' means to form, make or set up through a concentrated effort; 'misled' (past participle of 'mislead') means 'lead into error'; B: Incorrect – 'forge' means to form, make or set up through a concentrated effort; 'broken down' (past participle of 'break down') means 'dissolve' or 'itemize'; C: Correct – 'forge' means to form, make or set up through a concentrated effort; D: Incorrect – 'forge' means to form, make or set up through a concentrated effort; 'made off with' (past participle of 'make off with') means 'to steal'; E: Incorrect - 'forge' means to form, make or set up through a concentrated effort; 'falsified' (past participle of 'falsify') means 'make something false'.
Note: 'forge' can have the meaning of 'falsify', but this meaning is only used with real objects (money, a signature), not an alliance (as is the case in the text).
O texto refere-se a uma nova aliança formada por países em desenvolvimento, o G21.
Gabarito "C".

(Técnico da Receita Federal – 2003 – ESAF) According to the text, G21 is a group involved in trade talks, and it aims to

(A) bring up new trump cards in Mexico negotiations.
(B) offset the bargaining power of the USA and the EU.
(C) shore up the power of the WTO to do deals.
(D) lead over 100 countries to victory in the talks.
(E) enhance the power of Brazil internationally.

(**Interpretation**) A: Incorrect – The text says that the G21 was created during the Mexican negotiations, but not that it would 'bring up trump cards'. The expression 'reshuffle(d) the cards' means that the political game has changed; B: Correct – 'offset' means 'compensate' or 'counterbalance', which carries the idea that the G21 is "a powerful counterweight to Washington and Brussels"; C: Incorrect – 'shore up' means 'provide support for'. The text does not say that the formation of the G21 necessarily 'provides support for' the WTO, but rather that the formation happened within the WTO negotiations. The strength of the 21 countries forming the new bloc has been 'shored up'; D: Incorrect – The text says that the G21 aims to protect over 100 countries from the two most powerful economic blocs (the world's two most powerful economic blocs have been prevented from riding roughshod over the 100-plus countries), but there is no mention of victory; E: Incorrect – The text says that the formation of the G21 did in fact enhance Brazil's international influence, but that was not the aim. It was a consequence.
Segundo Celso Amorim, o G21 criou "um poderoso contrapeso em relação a Washington [EUA] e a Bruxelas [UE]".
Gabarito "B".

(Técnico da Receita Federal – 2003 – ESAF) In relation to Brazil, the G 21 is expected to

(A) reinforce the President's left-wing tendencies.
(B) override national decisions of smaller powers.
(C) make it the leading voice in the WTO.
(D) leave it on the fringes of the conference.
(E) bring additional prestige to the country.

(**Interpretation**) A: Incorrect – The text says that Brazil was "the country with the largest democratic support for any left-wing government in the world". It does not say that the G21 will enhance any tendencies; B: Incorrect – The text says that the G21 aims to **protect** over 100 countries from the two most powerful economic blocs (the world's two most powerful economic blocs have been prevented from riding roughshod over the 100-plus countries), not that the group will override smaller powers; C: Incorrect – The text says that Brazil will be a leading voice in the G21, not in the WTO; D: Incorrect – The text says that Ceslo Amorim commented on the new group while "on the fringes of the conference", meaning he did not comment while negotiating, but rather in interviews outside the negotiating arena; E: Correct - The text explicitly says that the formation of the G21 "has also enhanced the reputation of Brazil - the leading voice in the G21".
Ver a frase que se inicia com "Também ampliou a reputação...".
Gabarito "E".

For questions below, choose the answer which best fits the ideas in the text.

Virtues of vice

The rewards from investing in politically incorrect companies

REGRETTABLE though it may be, the wages of sin can be well worth having. Vice Fund, a mutual fund started 14 months ago by Mutuals.com, a Dallas investment company, is profiting nicely from what some would consider the wickedest corners of the legitimate economy: alcohol, arms, gambling and tobacco. So far this year, Vice Fund has returned 17.2% to investors, beating both the S&P 500 (15.2%) and the Dow Jones industrial average (13.2%) by a few points.

In fact, all four vice-ridden sectors have outperformed the overall American market during the past five years. "No matter what the economy's state or how interest rates move, people keep drinking, smoking and gambling," says Dan Ahrens, a portfolio manager at the self-described "socially irresponsible" fund. With President George Bush pursuing a muscular foreign policy, the outlook for defence spending is also bright.

(From: *The Economist* October 30th 2003)

(Técnico da Receita Federal – 2003 – ESAF) According to the text, Vice Fund

(A) is concerned with stamping out illegal vices.
(B) deals with illicit assets in the grey economy.
(C) has attracted 17.2% of the legitimate investors.
(D) profits from human addictions and conflicts.
(E) is barely worth serious attention from investors.

(Interpretation) A: Incorrect – The text says that Vice Fund "is profiting nicely from (...) alcohol, arms, gambling and tobacco". There is no mention if illegal vices in the text; B: Incorrect – Vice Fund deals with "alcohol, arms, gambling and tobacco assets", which are "what some would consider the wickedest corners of the legitimate economy". These vices are legal and the assets are legitimate; C: Incorrect – The text explicitly says, "Vice Fund has returned 17.2% to investors", meaning that investors have gained 17.2% profit on their investments; D: Correct – The text says that "Vice Fund has returned 17.2% to investors", meaning there was profit, and that Vice Fund is a "self-described 'socially irresponsible' fund"; E: Incorrect - The text says that "Vice Fund has returned 17.2% to investors, and that this return was better than "the S&P 500 (15.2%) and the Dow Jones industrial average (13.2%)".
O Fundo do Vício investe em empresas que exploram os vícios humanos. Há também boas perspectivas em relação aos conflitos bélicos. Ver as frases que se iniciam com "Fundo do Vício, um fundo mútuo iniciado..." e "Com o Presidente George Bush...".
Gabarito "D".

(Técnico da Receita Federal – 2003 – ESAF) The text points out that Vice Fund has

(A) proved a good investment for its shareholders.
(B) outperformed smoking, drinking and gambling.
(C) had mutually regrettable fund results.
(D) found popularity with portfolio managers.
(E) been promoted in wicked corners of Dallas.

(Interpretation) A: Correct – The text says that Vice Fund "is profiting nicely" and that return was 17.2% for investors; B: Incorrect – The text says that Vice Fund profited from 'smoking, drinking and gambling', not that it outperformed them. These are the activities that provide gains to Vice Fund. The text says that "four vice-ridden sectors have outperformed the overall American market", meaning the other areas of the market gained less; C: Incorrect - The text says that Vice Fund "is profiting nicely" and that return was 17.2% for investors. What is regrettable is the fact that people gain money from other people's vices; D: Incorrect – The text talks about the profitability of the fund, not its popularity; E: Incorrect – The text says that the wickedest corners are the legitimate vices, or legally permitted actions, in the economy as a whole, not only in Dallas.
Ver a frase que se inicia com "Até o momento neste ano...".
Gabarito "A".

(Técnico da Receita Federal – 2003 – ESAF) The word "muscular" (paragraph 2, last line) implies that US foreign policy is

(A) peaceable.
(B) belligerent.
(C) athletic.
(D) protective.
(E) well-formed.

(Vocabulary) A: Incorrect – The word 'muscular' means 'forceful'; 'peaceful' is the opposite; B: Correct – The word 'muscular' means 'forceful'; 'belligerent' means 'aggressive'. This is the best match from the options available; C: Incorrect – The word 'muscular' means 'forceful'; 'athletic' means 'physically strong and agile'. This does not collocate with 'foreign policy'; D: Incorrect - The word 'muscular' means 'forceful'; 'protective' means 'watchful' or 'vigilant'; E: Incorrect - The word 'muscular' means 'forceful'; 'well-formed' means 'well-structured'.
A expressão refere-se à política beligerante do governo Bush, que abriria boas perspectivas para investimentos ligados à defesa.
Gabarito "B".

Read the text below in order to answer the questions.

Election fears harm Brazilian economy

Brazil's presidential election does not take place until October, but investors are already voting with their feet at the prospect of victory for the leftwing opposition candidate, Luiz Inácio Lula da Silva.

The presidential contender from the Workers' Party, better known simply as Lula, holds a commanding lead over José Serra, the ruling Social Democratic party candidate. The possibility that Lula, a former metalworker, will become leader of Latin America's most important economy has got the markets – which consider him a leftwing firebrand – rattled.

Stocks have tumbled and the currency, the real, has slumped in recent weeks. Last week, credit rating agencies – which access the ability of borrowers to repay their debt – downgraded Brazilian debt.

Investors fear that if Brazil goes off the rails, the rest of Latin America will descend into chaos as the economic contagion spreads. Although Argentinians are suffering terribly from economic turmoil and a once-proud country is reverting to a barter economy, Argentina's problems have not spread to the rest of the continent so far.

(Auditor Fiscal da Receita Federal – 2002.2 – ESAF) According to the text, Lula's possible victory in Brazil's upcoming presidential election

(A) would avoid economic turmoil.
(B) might relieve the economic pressure.
(C) would hardly impact the national economy.
(D) already worries the markets.
(E) would underpin the national growth.

(Interpretation) A: Incorrect – The text explicitly says, "The possibility that Lula (…) will become leader of Latin America's most important economy **has got the markets** – which consider him a leftwing firebrand – **rattled**', and "Investors fear that if Brazil goes off the rails, **the rest of Latin America will descend into chaos as the economic contagion spreads**" meaning economic turmoil could be a consequence of Lula's election. Argentina is already suffering from political turmoil; B: Correct – The text explicitly says, "The possibility that Lula (…) will become leader of Latin America's most important economy **has got the markets** – which consider him a leftwing firebrand – **rattled**', and "Investors fear that if Brazil goes off the rails, **the rest of Latin America will descend into chaos as the economic contagion spreads**" meaning economic pressure would not be relieved; C: Incorrect – The possibility that Lula could be elected has already impacted the market (Stocks have tumbled and the currency, the real, has slumped in recent weeks. Last week, credit rating agencies – which access the ability of borrowers to repay their debt – downgraded Brazilian debt); D: Correct - The text explicitly says, "The possibility that Lula (…) will become leader of Latin America's most important economy **has got the markets** – which consider him a leftwing firebrand – **rattled**"; E: Incorrect – 'underpin' means 'support'. The text suggests the opposite.
A perspectiva de vitória já estaria preocupando os mercados. Esse é o teor do texto.
Gabarito "D".

(Auditor Fiscal da Receita Federal – 2002.2 – ESAF) The author says that the Brazilian currency **has slumped in recent weeks**, which means it

(A) has suddenly fallen.
(B) has rallied.
(C) has not been hit.
(D) could have been depreciated.
(E) has reached its highest quotation.

(Vocabulary) A: Correct – 'to slump' means to 'fall heavily'; B: Incorrect – 'to slump' means to 'fall heavily'; 'to rally' means in this context 'to recover'; C: Incorrect - 'to slump' means to 'fall heavily'; 'has not been hit' means 'has not been affected'; D: Incorrect – 'could have been depreciated' suggests that it was not depreciated, when in fact, it was; E: Incorrect – 'to slump' means to 'fall heavily'; 'highest quotation' means 'highest level'.
O texto informa que "Ações caíram e a moeda, o real, desvalorizou-se nas últimas semanas."
Gabarito "A".

(Auditor Fiscal da Receita Federal – 2002.2 – ESAF) Argentina's present economic situation is referred to as

(A) affluent.
(B) harrowing.
(C) thriving.
(D) smooth.
(E) impeccable.

(Vocabulary) A: Incorrect – The text explicitly says, "Argentineans are suffering terribly from economic turmoil"; 'affluent' means 'wealthy'; B: Correct – 'harrowing' means 'distressing'; C: Incorrect – 'thriving' means 'flourishing' or 'growing'; D: Incorrect – 'smooth' means 'steady' or 'stable'; E: Incorrect – 'impeccable' means 'perfect'.
A imagem da Argentina, no texto, é negativa, indicando distúrbios e retrocessos econômicos. Ver seu último parágrafo.
Gabarito "B".

Read the text below in order to answer the questions.

High level of protectionism

As a member of the Southern Cone Common Market (MERCOSUR), Argentina maintains relatively low trade barriers with Brazil, Paraguay, and Uruguay but applies a high tariff on all goods and services coming into Argentina from countries outside MERCOSUR. This year, the common external tariff rate for MERCOSUR is 13.5 percent. Because the common external tariff rate is applied to most of the world's countries, Argentina's average tariff rate is 13.5 percent this year, up from 7.5 percent last year. As a result, its trade policy score is 1 point worse this year. In an effort to stimulate the economy, MERCOSUR has allowed Argentina to raise tariffs on consumer goods, in some cases up to 35 percent, while eliminating tariffs on capital goods. Argentina maintains some non-tariff barriers, such as quotas on automobiles. According to the U.S. Department of State, "Customs procedures are opaque and time-consuming, thus raising the cost for importers".

(Auditor Fiscal da Receita Federal – 2002.2 – ESAF) According to the text, Argentina

(A) intends to become a member of the MERCOSUR.
(B) has exempted Brazil from paying tariffs on its goods.
(C) might soon implement some aggressive market reforms.
(D) has been given a lower score in relation to its trade policy.
(E) has kept low trade barriers with the American countries.

(Interpretation) A: Incorrect – That text explicitly says "As a member of the Southern Cone Common Market (MERCOSUR), Argentina"; B: Incorrect – The text explicitly says "Argentina maintains relatively low trade barriers with Brazil", but nothing about exemptions: C: Incorrect - The text explicitly says that "In an effort to stimulate the economy, MERCOSUR has allowed Argentina to raise tariffs on consumer goods". Any market reforms have already been implemented; D: Correct – The text explicitly says, "As a result, its trade policy score is 1 point worse this year"; E: Incorrect – The text explicitly says that Argentina "applies a high tariff on all goods and services coming into Argentina from countries outside MERCOSUR", which includes North America and Canada, for example.
Ver a frase que se inicia com "Como resultado, a pontuação (nota) para...".
Gabarito "D".

(Auditor Fiscal da Receita Federal – 2002.2 – ESAF) Argentina's customs procedures are considered by the U.S. Department of State as

(A) sluggish and transparent.
(B) transparent, but obsolete.
(C) obscure and sluggish.
(D) innovative, but time-consuming.
(E) both well-defined and efficient.

(Vocabulary) A: Incorrect – "opaque and time-consuming" mean 'unclear and slow'; 'sluggish and transparent' mean 'slow and clear; B: Incorrect – "opaque and time-consuming" mean 'unclear and slow'; 'transparent, but obsolete' mean 'clear, but out-of-date'; C: Correct - "opaque and time-consuming" mean 'unclear and slow'; 'obscure and sluggish' mean 'unclear and slow'; D: Incorrect - "opaque and time-consuming" mean 'unclear and slow'; 'innovative, but time-consuming' mean 'inventive, but slow',; E: Incorrect - "opaque and time-consuming" mean 'unclear and slow'; 'well-defined and efficient' mean 'precise and slow'.

O Departamento de Estado americano descreve os procedimentos aduaneiros da Argentina como opacos (não-transparentes) e demorados. Ver a última frase do texto.

Gabarito "C".

(Auditor Fiscal da Receita Federal – 2002.2 – ESAF) In the main, the text deals with

(A) Argentina's wages and prices.
(B) Argentina's trade policy.
(C) Paraguay's high fiscal deficit.
(D) Brazil's financial institutions.
(E) Brazil's regulation score.

(Interpretation) A: Incorrect – The text does not mention wages; B: Correct – The text focuses on Argentina's trade tariffs; C: Incorrect – The text explicitly says, "Argentina maintains relatively low trade barriers with (…) Paraguay"; D: Incorrect – The text only mentions the low trade barriers with Brazil. Brazil is not mentioned in any other part of this text; E: Incorrect – The text explicitly talks about Argentina's trade score (As a result, its [Argentina's] trade policy score is 1 point worse this year), not Brazil's.

O texto trata da política da Argentina em relação ao comércio exterior.

Gabarito "B".

Read the text below in order to answer the questions.

US tax evasion probe extends to Singapore

The reach of Uncle Sam's taxman in pursuit of unpaid revenue has apparently extended even to Singapore, despite the banking secrecy laws here in the U.S.

The Republic has reportedly become involved in an attempt by the United States tax authorities to identify tax evaders among an estimated one to two million American citizens who have opened offshore bank accounts.

The fact the taxman is going to this extent may seem astonishing to Singaporeans. But it makes sense when you realize that all income earned by US citizens is taxable, whether it is held locally or in other countries.

The information, which the US Internal Revenue Service (IRS) hopes will stem the loss of between US$20 billion and US$40 billion each year in tax revenues, is being sought from MasterCard International. This is because offshore bank account holders often use credit cards issued by MasterCard, Visa, American Express and other payment specialists to gain access to their funds from the US.

But whether the IRS will succeed in obtaining information such as the names and transaction records of such account holders is still an open question, because of the present US banking secrecy laws.

(Auditor Fiscal da Receita Federal – 2002.2 – ESAF) The expression "to stem the loss" means to

(A) stop it.
(B) bring it about.
(C) sum it up.
(D) take it over.
(E) make it out.

(Vocabulary) A: Correct – 'to stem', in this context, means 'to go against or 'to stop'; B: Incorrect – 'to stem', in this context, means 'to go against or 'to stop'; 'to bring it about' means 'to cause'; C: Incorrect - 'to stem', in this context, means 'to go against or 'to stop'; 'to sum it up' means to 'to total' or 'to calculate'; D: Incorrect - 'to stem', in this context, means 'to go against or 'to stop'; 'to take it over' means to 'to take control of it'; E: Incorrect - 'to stem', in this context, means 'to go against or 'to stop'; 'to make it out' means 'to decipher' or 'to endorse' (make a check out to somebody).

"To stem" (verbo) significa, literalmente, retirar o cabo de uma fruta, por exemplo. É utilizado no texto no sentido de eliminar, acabar, excluir.

Gabarito "A".

(Auditor Fiscal da Receita Federal – 2002.2 – ESAF) The aim of the US tax authorities

(A) could have been to pursue tax evaders.
(B) has been to restrain the issue of credit cards.
(C) is to root out tax evaders.
(D) is to target all the tax haven countries.
(E) has been to forbid offshore bank accounts.

(Interpretation) A: Incorrect – The 'aim of the US tax authorities' is not a possibility. 'Could have been' suggests that it is unclear what their aim is. The text explicitly says, "The reach of Uncle Sam's taxman in pursuit of unpaid revenue"; B: Incorrect – The text says that the US tax authorities are seeking information from MasterCard, not that it plans to restrain the use of their cards; C: Correct - The text explicitly says, "The reach of Uncle Sam's taxman in pursuit of unpaid revenue"; D: Incorrect – The text focuses on Singapore as a tax haven and a target of the US tax authorities. However, the question could be misleading as the text does open up the possibility to interpret the part "an estimated one to two million American citizens who have opened offshore bank accounts" more broadly. It is not totally clear whether these one or two million US citizens necessarily have accounts in Singapore, or whether this is the global number; E: Incorrect – The text does not say that the aim of the US tax authorities is to forbid offshore accounts. They want access to these accounts in order to tax people. They are seeking access to bank details, not a prohibition of accounts.

O texto indica a intenção de o fisco federal americano identificar aqueles que evadem tributos, por meio de informações a respeito das movimentações bancárias no exterior.

Gabarito "C".

(Auditor Fiscal da Receita Federal – 2002.2 – ESAF) According to the text,

(A) one or two million American citizens are, in fact, tax evaders.
(B) deposits made by American citizens abroad are eligible for tax reductions.
(C) there is a set of laws which determine that bank accounts cannot be surrendered.
(D) purchases made by credit card may benefit from tax exemption.
(E) Singaporeans might have their accounts disclosed by US tax authorities.

(Interpretation) A: Incorrect – The text explicitly says the US tax authorities want "to identify tax evaders among an estimated one to two million American citizens who have opened offshore bank accounts", meaning that some of them may be tax evaders, not all of them; B: Incorrect – The text explicitly says "all income earned by US citizens is taxable, whether it is held locally or in other countries". This does not necessarily mean all deposits; only those coming from income; C: Correct – The text explicitly says, "But whether the IRS will succeed in obtaining information such as the names and transaction records of such account holders is still an open question, because of the present US banking secrecy laws". The banking secrecy laws is the set mentioned in the question; D: Incorrect – The text does not mention exemption at all; E: Incorrect – The text says that the US tax authorities seeks information on US citizens that hold accounts in Singapore. The local people's accounts are not mentioned.

O texto refere-se às leis que garantem o sigilo bancário nos Estados Unidos.

Gabarito "C".

(Auditor Fiscal da Receita Federal – 2002.2 – ESAF) The main subject of the text is

(A) the impact of fiscal adjustments in the United States.
(B) a considerable drop in tax revenues due to the American recession.
(C) a significant increase in tax revenues in the United States.
(D) the unsustainable pension system adopted by the United States.
(E) a procedure adopted by the IRS in order to identify tax evaders.

(Interpretation) A: Incorrect – The text does not mention fiscal adjustments; B: Incorrect – The text says that the "loss of between US$20 billion and US$40 billion each year" arises from tax evasion, not the recession; C: Incorrect – The text explicitly talks about losses, not increases in tax revenue; D: Incorrect – Pensions are not mentioned in the text; E: Correct – The text focuses on what the US tax authorities (IRS) are doing to identify tax evaders (an attempt by the United States tax authorities to identify tax evaders).

O texto indica a intenção de o fisco federal americano identificar aqueles que evadem tributos, por meio de informações a respeito das movimentações bancárias no exterior.

Gabarito "E".

Read the text below in order to answer the questions.

Britain's budget

When the New Labour government first came to power in 1997, Gordon Brown, the Chancellor of the Exchequer (or finance minister), was tightfisted. He bolted down public spending and increased the tax burden. In 2000 the dividends arrived, as Mr Brown ladled out money for public services. The ever-more--powerful Chancellor promised targeted giveaways in the 2001 budget.

This year's budget focused on reviving the perpetually troubled National Health Service. Mr Brown vowed to raise taxes—National Insurance contributions, more precisely—to bring British health spending to European levels. In his mid-year spending review, delivered in July, he showered still more money on other services, education in particular. But pouring money into an unreformed system may not be his cleverest idea.

(Técnico da Receita Federal – 2002.2 – ESAF) With regard to public spending, the British finance minister was

(A) first parsimonious, then more generous.
(B) generous at first, then more cautious.
(C) first anxious to please, then more objective.
(D) popular in the early stages, but now unpopular.
(E) first concerned with education, now with health.

(Vocabulary) A: Correct – The text explicitly says, "Gordon Brown, (…) finance minister, was *tightfisted*. (…) Mr Brown *ladled out* money for public services", meaning he was 'parsimonious' or 'tightfisted', then, later, 'more generous' or 'openhanded' (ladling out money); B: Incorrect – The text explicitly says he was first 'tightfisted' (stingy, not generous), then generous later; C: Incorrect – The text explicitly says he "increased the tax burden", which does not aim to please people, but rather charge them more; D: Gordon Brown's popularity is not mentioned in the text; E: Incorrect – The text explicitly says that Mr. Brown controlled pending first, then "focused on reviving the (…) National Health Service".

O texto relata que Gordon Brown, então ministro das finanças, foi parcimonioso ("tight-fisted", mão-fechada) em um primeiro momento. Posteriormente, a partir de 2000, passou a despejar ("ladled out") dinheiro para a prestação de serviços públicos.

Gabarito "A".

(Técnico da Receita Federal – 2002.2 – ESAF) The text says that, as a minister, George Brown is becoming

(A) more and more impotent.
(B) increasingly pro-European.
(C) stronger and stronger.
(D) less and less influential.
(E) more and more tight-fisted.

(Interpretation) A: Incorrect – The text does not mention oscillation in the level of Mr. Brown's power; B: Incorrect – The text does not connect Mr. Brown's approach to his nationality; the text mentions that Mr. Brown wanted to increase spending on health to the same level as Europe; C: Incorrect – The text does not mention his political power; D: Incorrect - The text does not mention his political power; E: Incorrect – The text shows how he went from being tightfisted to being more generous with public services. ANULADA

(Técnico da Receita Federal – 2002.2 – ESAF) Gordon Brown's plans for the National Health Service aims to

(A) provide more patients with low-cost free treatment.
(B) permit European countries to imitate Britain's health care system.
(C) help health services to reach the same standards as those of education.
(D) allow for progressive privatization of health care, on European lines.
(E) catch up with spending on health care in other European countries.

(Interpretation) A: Incorrect – The text does not mention the cost of health care to patients; B: Incorrect – The text says that Mr. Brown wants to imitate the European system in terms of spending; C: Incorrect – The standards of health and education are not compared in the text. Mr. Brown showered money on both areas; D: Incorrect – The text says nothing about privatizing health care in Britain; E: Correct – The text explicitly says Mr. Brown raised taxes "to bring British health spending to European levels".

Segundo o texto, "O Sr. Brown prometeu aumentar a tributação (...) para elevar os gastos britânicos com saúde aos níveis europeus."

Gabarito "E".

(Técnico da Receita Federal – 2002.2 – ESAF) Improvements in the British National Health system are to be financed by

(A) European direct investment.
(B) increases in income tax.
(C) outsourcing of some services.
(D) higher national insurance contributions.
(E) Borrowing money from public coffers.

(Interpretation) A: Incorrect – The text does not mention any investment from Europe; B: Incorrect – The text explicitly says, "Mr. Brown vowed to raise taxes — National Insurance contributions, more precisely", not income tax; C: Incorrect – The text says nothing about outsourcing services; D: Correct – The text explicitly says, "Mr. Brown vowed to raise taxes — **National Insurance contributions**, more precisely"; E: Incorrect – The text says nothing about borrowing money.
Segundo o texto, as melhorias serão financiadas pelo aumento da tributação, "contribuições para o Seguro Nacional, mais precisamente".
Gabarito "D".

(Técnico da Receita Federal – 2002.2 – ESAF) The writer of the article has reservations about whether increased spending on public services

(A) can be effective without first reforming them.
(B) is advisable in times of global recession.
(C) has ever been a viable economic target.
(D) can lead to more equality with Europe.
(E) can really be achieved before mid year.

(Interpretation) A: Correct – The text explicitly says, "But **pouring money into an unreformed system** may not be his cleverest idea", meaning the author may be suggesting that reform should have been done before pouring all the money into the services; B: Incorrect – The text says nothing about global recession; C: Incorrect – The author does not consider past economic targets; D: Incorrect – The text explicitly says Mr. Brown raised taxes "to bring British health spending to European levels", but nothing suggests the author has reservation about equality with Europe; E: Incorrect – The text explicitly says, "In his mid-year spending review, delivered in July, he showered still more money on other services", meaning that a report was delivered in the mid-year, but there is nothing about reservations as to whether it can be achieved.
Segundo o texto, "despender dinheiro em um sistema não-reformado pode não ser sua [de Gordon Brown] ideia mais inteligente".
Gabarito "A".

Read the text below in order to answer the questions.

(Re) Brand You

This marketing expert and author will help you reboot yourself after a layoff.

by Cecilia Rothenberger

Late last year, as the tide of layoffs in the dotcom sector reached a groundswell, a certain bravado still characterized the newly unemployed. Pink-slip parties were all the rage in Manhattan and San Francisco. Internet castoffs were using their severance checks to travel or just to recover from a massive dotcom hangover.

But as the winter dragged on, reality began to sink in: Job = Money = Rent. And with Internet job losses totaling more than 50,000 people in the past 12 months, people who were courted enthusiastically a few months ago are now finding the job market excruciatingly tight.

Small wonder that armies of dotcom refugees are now feeling a little dispirited, wondering how to regroup and reposition themselves, especially with a layoff or two sullying their résumés.

Robin Fisher Roffer says not to worry. The marketing veteran wants people to build brands strong enough to survive a dotcom flop. Roffer translates the rules of product marketing into a personal arena that helps people find their "big idea" and go after it.

Lose the Guilt

Above all, promote your authentic self – your specialized set of talents and the vital strengths that you bring to the table, inside and outside of a job. Create a personal mission statement and tag line. Your slogan shouldn't hinge on your company or job title. Get to know your audience's taste and package yourself accordingly. "As with any product, it is vital that your personal brand resonates with your audience and its specific needs," Roffer says.

(Técnico da Receita Federal – 2002.2 – ESAF) The purpose of this article is to

(A) express confidence in the resurgence of the technology sector.
(B) teach people about the commercial advertising industry.
(C) offer helpful advice to people who have lost their jobs.
(D) suggest how people can help the authorities tackle unemployment.
(E) promote better sales techniques through new technology.

(Interpretation) A: Incorrect – The text does not mention a possible resurgence of the technology sector; B: Incorrect – The text explicitly says, "Roffer translates the rules of product marketing into a personal arena", meaning this is not about commercial advertising; C: Correct – The text talks about job losses ("Internet job losses totaling more than 50,000 people in the past 12 months"), and ties this in with how to "promote your authentic self – your specialized set of talents and the vital strengths that you bring to the table, inside and outside of a job", thus showing the purpose of the text is to help those who have lost their job; D: Incorrect – The text says nothing about helping authorities to fight unemployment; E: Incorrect – The text says nothing about sales techniques. The specialist Roffer says that to get the great job, one must package oneself, but this is not a sales technique.
O artigo refere-se a dicas para o reposicionamento de pessoas que perderam o emprego no setor ponto-com.
Gabarito "C".

(Técnico da Receita Federal – 2002.2 – ESAF) According to the article, people took some time to realize that

(A) they might have to leave their country.
(B) drinking would have bad effects on health.

(C) they might need new boots after a layoff.
(D) some bosses are unenthusiastic about technology.
(E) it might be quite difficult to find another job.

(Interpretation) A: Incorrect – The text says nothing about leaving the country; B: Incorrect – The text uses the word 'hangover' as a metaphor in which the booze-filled party would represent the dotcom era, and the hangover would represent the layoffs. The text says nothing about the effects of drinking; C: Incorrect - The term "reboot" in the title is used as wordplay (pun) to mean 'start again'. 'Reboot' is the term used when the computer has a problem and the only way to fix it is to 'restart' the computer; D: Incorrect – The text says nothing about bosses; E: Correct – In the first paragraph, the text refers to "a certain bravado still characterized the newly unemployed. Pink-slip parties were all the rage in Manhattan and San Francisco. Internet castoffs were using their severance checks to travel or just to recover from a massive dotcom hangover", which suggests that while people were losing their job (receiving the pink slip = lose your job), they were partying, travelling or recovering from the parties. They were not concerned about unemployment. The second paragraph then starts with "But as the winter dragged on, reality began to sink in: Job = Money = Rent", meaning that it took some time to realize the problem (unemployment).
Ver a frase que se inicia com "E com as perdas de postos de trabalho da internet totalizando...".
Gabarito "E".

(Técnico da Receita Federal – 2002.2 – ESAF) It can be deduced from Paragraph 1 of the text that "pink slip parties" are for

(A) rich socialites in Manhattan.
(B) women's underwear manufacturers.
(C) bosses planning to dismiss staff.
(D) people notified of their dismissal.
(E) workers in the car industry.

(Vocabulary) A: Incorrect – The expression 'pink-slip' refers to the official document that was used to advise an employee that (s)he was being dismissed. A 'pink-slip party' refers to the celebration that followed, as there is usually a payout. It does not mean they are socialites; B: Incorrect – The expression 'pink-slip' refers to the official document that was used to advise an employee that (s)he was being dismissed. The word 'slip' is also used to refer to an underskirt worn by women if their skirts were made of see-through material. This is not the case here; C: Incorrect - The expression 'pink-slip' refers to the official document that was used to advise an employee that (s)he was being dismissed. The party is held after the pink slips have been delivered to the employees, not before; D: Correct - The expression 'pink-slip' refers to the official document that was used to advise an employee that (s)he was being dismissed. A 'pink-slip party' refers to the celebration that followed, meaning the employee had already been notified of dismissal; E: Incorrect - A 'pink-slip party' refers to the celebration that followed, as there is usually a payout. This has nothing to do with the car industry.
"Pink slip" é o aviso de demissão. "Pink slip parties" é uma expressão bem humorada que indica festas realizadas por pessoas nessa situação.
Gabarito "D".

(Técnico da Receita Federal – 2002.2 – ESAF) The meaning of "with a layoff or two sullying their résumés" (Paragraph 3) means

(A) with one or more dismissals from jobs spoiling their work record.
(B) with a few notable professional successes to their credit.
(C) bringing summaries of their achievements for their CVs.
(D) with plans to help refugees and displaced persons settle down.
(E) having a criminal record which might cause future problems.

(Vocabulary) A: Correct – The word 'layoff' means 'dismissal'; the word 'sully' means 'spoil' or 'tarnish'; the word 'résumé' is used in British English for 'CV' or 'work record'; B: Incorrect – 'success' and 'sully' are almost opposites; C: Incorrect – 'resume' is a false cognate in English. It means 'start again', while résumé, in French, is borrowed by the British for 'CV'. In Portuguese, the word *'resumo'* means 'summary'; D: Incorrect – see A. The text makes no reference to 'refugees'. E: Incorrect – 'sully', which means 'spoil' or 'tarnish'; it may be used to talk about a criminal record, but it is not only used in this context. The text says nothing about criminal records.
Ver o final da frase que se inicia com "Não surpreende que exércitos de refugiados ponto-com...".
Gabarito "A".

(Técnico da Receita Federal – 2002.2 – ESAF) The marketing expert Robin Fisher Roffer advises people to

(A) market almost everything they own.
(B) sell themselves like a brand of goods.
(C) re-launch a product on the market.
(D) use new technology to boost sales.
(E) avoid using any kind of sales jargon.

(Interpretation) A: Incorrect – The text explicitly says that Roffer suggests promoting "promote your authentic self – your specialized set of talents and the vital strengths", not what you own, but rather your skills; B: Correct – Roffer is quoted as saying "As with any product, it is vital that your personal brand resonates with your audience and its specific needs", thus confirming that people should sell themselves like a brand of goods; C: Incorrect – Roffer suggests repackaging yourself ("Get to know your audience's taste and package yourself accordingly"), but not re-launching a product; D: Incorrect – Roffer says nothing about boosting sales; E: Incorrect – Roffer says, "Your slogan shouldn't hinge on your company or job title", meaning your skills should not rely on a company name or a job title. He says nothing about sales jargon.
Segundo o texto, o especialista adapta o marketing de produtos para a reinserção do profissional no mercado.
Gabarito "B".

Atenção: As questões a seguir, referem-se ao texto abaixo.

History of the Income Tax in the United States

The nation had few taxes in its early history. From 1791 to 1802, the United States government was supported by internal taxes on distilled spirits, carriages, refined sugar, tobacco and snuff, property sold at auction, corporate bonds, and slaves. The high cost of the War of 1812 brought about the nation's first sales taxes on gold, silverware, jewelry, and watches. In 1817, however, Congress did away with all internal taxes, relying on tariffs on imported goods to provide sufficient funds for running the government.

In 1862, in order to support the Civil War effort, Congress enacted the nation's first income tax law. It was a forerunner of our modern income tax in that it was based on the principles of graduated, or progressive, taxation and of withholding income at the source. Additional sales and excise taxes were added, and an "inheritance" tax also made its debut.

The Act of 1862 established the office of Commissioner of Internal Revenue. The Commissioner [TO GIVE] the power to assess, levy, and collect taxes, and the right to enforce the tax laws through seizure of property and income and through prosecution. The powers and authority remain very much the same today.

In 1868, Congress again focused its taxation efforts on tobacco and distilled spirits and eliminated the income tax in 1872. It had a short-lived revival in 1894 and 1895. In the latter year, the U.S. Supreme Court decided that the income tax was unconstitutional because it was not apportioned among the states in conformity with the Constitution.

In 1913, the 16th Amendment to the Constitution made the income tax a permanent fixture in the U.S. tax system. The amendment gave Congress legal authority to tax income and resulted in a revenue law that taxed incomes of both individuals and corporations. The withholding tax on wages was introduced in 1943 and was instrumental in increasing the number of taxpayers to 60 million and tax collections to $43 billion by 1945.

In 1981, Congress enacted the largest tax cut in U.S. history, approximately $750 billion over six years. The tax reduction, however, was partially offset by two tax acts, in 1982 and 1984, that attempted to raise approximately $265 billion.

(Adapted from http://w w w .infoplease.com/ipa/A0005921.html)

(Agente Fiscal de Rendas/SP – 2006 – FCC) The correct conjugation of [*TO GIVE*], in the text is:

(A) *gave*.
(B) *gives*.
(C) was given.
(D) was giving.
(E) has given.

(Grammar) A: Incorrect – The previous sentence, "The Act of 1862 established the office of Commissioner of Internal Revenue", establishes that the tense should be past. The structure, however, must be passive voice, because it is the Commissioner that received the power from the Act. He did not give power to anyone; B: Incorrect – The previous sentence, "The Act of 1862 established the office of Commissioner of Internal Revenue", establishes that the tense should be past; C: Correct - The previous sentence, "The Act of 1862 established the office of Commissioner of Internal Revenue", establishes that the tense should be past. It was the Act that gave power to the Commissioner; therefore, he 'was given' power; D: Incorrect – The Act gave the Commissioner power; therefore, he 'was given' power. 'Was giving' suggest that he was actively distributing power, which is not the case; E: Incorrect - The previous sentence, "The Act of 1862 established the office of Commissioner of Internal Revenue", establishes that the tense should be past; therefore, present perfect would be unacceptable.
A construção correta é "The Commissioner **was given** the power to…", cuja tradução é "**[Ao]** Comissário **[foi dado]** o poder de...".
Gabarito "C."

(Agente Fiscal de Rendas/SP – 2006 – FCC) No texto, a expressão *latter year* refere-se a
(A) 1862.
(B) 1868.
(C) 1872.
(D) 1894.
(E) 1895.

(Vocabulary) A: Incorrect; B: Incorrect; C: Incorrect; D: Incorrect; E: Correct – The previous sentence, "It had a short-lived revival in 1894 and 1895", ends with the year 1895. The word 'latter' is a reference word used in text to refer back to the 'last item mentioned', which in this case is the year 1895.
Note que a frase anterior indica dois anos (1894 e 1895): "It had a short-lived revival in 1894 and 1895." A expressão "latter year", a seguir, significa "este último ano", ou seja, 1895.
Gabarito "E."

(Agente Fiscal de Rendas/SP – 2006 – FCC) Um sinônimo para *offset*, no texto, é

(A) upgraded.
(B) held up.
(C) taken off.
(D) cancelled out.
(E) overcome.

(Vocabulary) A: Incorrect – 'upgraded' means 'improved'; 'offset' means 'compensated' or 'annulled'; B: Incorrect – 'held up' means 'delayed' or 'robbed'; 'offset' means 'compensated' or 'annulled'; C: Incorrect – 'taken off' means 'removed' or 'left'; 'offset' means 'compensated' or 'annulled'; D: Correct – 'cancelled out' means 'annulled'; E: Incorrect – 'overcome' means 'conquer' or 'prevail over'; 'offset' means 'compensated' or 'annulled'.
"Offset" foi utilizado no texto para indicar que o corte de impostos em 1981, de $ 750 bilhões, foi parcialmente compensado (ou anulado, cancelado) por normas que buscaram ampliar a arrecadação em $ 265 bilhões.
Gabarito "D."

(Agente Fiscal de Rendas/SP – 2006 – FCC) Segundo o texto, nos Estados Unidos,

(A) os impostos sobre venda de jóias e similares existem desde os primórdios de sua história.
(B) o ouro começou a ser taxado para fazer face aos gastos decorrentes da Guerra de 1812.
(C) além de impostos sobre produtos importados, foram instituídos mais impostos internos a partir de 1817.
(D) a primeira versão do imposto de renda foi instituída após a Guerra Civil.
(E) já havia retenção de imposto de renda na fonte antes da Guerra Civil.

(Interpretation) A: Incorrect – Tax on jewelry was only implemented in 1812, after the Civil War, not from the beginning of US history; B: Correct – The text explicitly says, "The high cost of the War of 1812 brought about the nation's first sales taxes on gold, silverware, jewelry, and watches."; C: Incorrect – The text explicitly says, "In 1817, however, Congress did away with all internal taxes", meaning internal taxes were eliminated; D: Incorrect – The text explicitly says, "In 1862, in order to support the Civil War effort, Congress enacted the nation's first income tax law", meaning it was not after the civil war, but during it; E: Incorrect – The text explicitly says that there were "internal taxes on distilled spirits, carriages, refined sugar, tobacco and snuff, property sold at auction, corporate bonds, and slaves", but not income tax. This could be misleading in that tax on property sold at an auction or on corporate bonds could be construed as income tax. Nevertheless, the text seems to be clear that those first taxes were not considered income tax. See D.

A e B: a tributação sobre a venda de ouro, joias e similares começou apenas em 1812; C: em 1817 foram abolidos os tributos federais internos, permanecendo apenas as tarifas sobre bens importados; D e E: o imposto de renda americano, com a retenção na fonte, foi criado para fazer frente às despesas da Guerra Civil, em 1862 (não antes, nem depois da guerra).

Gabarito "B".

(Agente Fiscal de Rendas/SP – 2006 – FCC) Ainda segundo o texto,

(A) com a retenção do imposto de renda sobre salários na fonte, o número de contribuintes subiu para 60 milhões em dois anos.
(B) a maior arrecadação na história dos Estados Unidos deu-se em 1981.
(C) a tabela progressiva de imposto de renda só entrou em vigor em 1943.
(D) o Agente Fiscal de Rendas, quando o cargo foi criado nos Estados Unidos, não tinha autoridade para processar o infrator.
(E) a 16a Emenda à Constituição Americana não passou de mais uma tentativa frustrada de fazer o imposto de renda incidir tanto sobre os ganhos de pessoas físicas quanto jurídicas.

(Interpretation) A: Correct – The text explicitly says, "The withholding tax on wages was introduced in 1943 and was instrumental in *increasing the number of taxpayers to 60 million*"; B: Incorrect – The text explicitly says, "In 1981, Congress enacted the largest tax *cut* in U.S. history"; C: Incorrect – The text explicitly says, "In 1862, (…) Congress enacted the nation's first income tax law. (…) it was based on the principles of graduated, or progressive, taxation"; D: Incorrect – The text explicitly says, "The Commissioner [TO GIVE] the power to (…) enforce the tax laws (...) through prosecution"; E: Incorrect – The text explicitly says, "In 1913, the 16th Amendment to the Constitution made the income tax *a permanent fixture* in the U.S. tax system".

A: ver a frase que se inicia com "A retenção tributária nos salários..."; B: em 1981 ocorreu o maior corte de impostos na história dos Estados Unidos; C: o texto salienta que o precursor do atual imposto de renda já previa a progressividade, em 1862; D: a autoridade fiscal federal ("Commissioner of Internal Revenue") tinha (e tem) amplos poderes para "avaliar, impor e cobrar impostos e o direito de fazer cumprir as leis tributárias por meio de apreensão de propriedade e rendas e por meio de execução judicial"; E: a 16ª Emenda à Constituição Americana possibilitou a cobrança do imposto de renda americano, na forma atual.

Gabarito "A".

Atenção: As questões a seguir, referem-se ao texto abaixo.

Avoidance and evasion compared:
The United States example

The use of the terms tax avoidance and tax evasion can vary depending on the jurisdiction. In the United States, for example, the term "tax evasion" (or, more precisely, "attempted tax evasion") generally consists of criminal conduct, the purpose of which is to avoid the assessment or payment of a tax that is already legally owed at the time of the criminal conduct. (The term "assessment" is here used in the technical sense of a statutory assessment: the formal administrative act of a duly appointed employee of the Internal Revenue Service who records the tax on the books of the United States Treasury after certain administrative prerequisites have been met. In the case of Federal income tax, this act generally occurs after the close of the tax year – and usually after a tax return has been filed.) By contrast, the term "tax avoidance" is used in the United States to describe lawful conduct, the purpose of which is to avoid the creation of a tax liability. Tax evasion involves breaking the law; tax avoidance is using legal means to avoid owing tax in the first place. An evaded tax remains a tax legally owed. An avoided tax (in the U.S. sense) is a tax liability that has never existed. A simple example of tax avoidance in this sense is the situation where a business considers selling a particular asset at a huge gain but, after consulting with a tax adviser, decides not to [VERB] the sale. KK 97 no sale occurs, no gain is realized. The additional income tax liability that [TO GENERATE] by the inclusion of the gain on the sale in the computation of taxable income is simply not incurred, as there was no sale and no realized gain.

(Adapted from Wikipedia: en.wikipedia.org/wiki/Tax_evasion)

(Agente Fiscal de Rendas/SP – 2006 – FCC) O verbo que substitui corretamente [*VERB*] é

(A) enhance.
(B) refuse.
(C) put an end to.
(D) go through with.
(E) get away with.

(Interpretation) A: Incorrect – 'enhance' means 'increase' or 'improve'; this verb does not commonly collocate with 'sale'; B: Incorrect – The phrase says, "…decides not to [VERB] the sale". The negative form of 'decide' would make the phrase "…decides not to refuse the sale", which is not the sense. The idea is that the company decides not to 'make' the sale; C: Incorrect – 'put an end to' means to 'stop'. The idea is to continue and finalize the sale, not stop it; D: Correct – 'got through with' a sale means 'finalize or complete' the sale; E: Incorrect – 'get away with' means 'do something wrong but not be held responsible for it'. The sale is not wrong in this context. D: A frase complementada adequadamente fica: "...but, after consulting with a tax adviser, decides not to **[go through with]**", cuja tradução é "...mas, após conversar com um consultor tributário, decide **[não ir adiante (não realizar a venda)]**."

Gabarito "D".

(Agente Fiscal de Rendas/SP – 2006 – FCC) A palavra que preenche corretamente a lacuna é

(A) However.
(B) Therefore.
(C) Because.
(D) Despite.
(E) Although.

(Interpretation) A: Incorrect – 'However' suggests an idea of contrast; the sentence requires an idea of cause or reason; B: Incorrect – 'Therefore' suggest and idea of conclusion or consequence; the sentence requires an idea of cause or reason; C: Because' suggests an idea of cause or reason; D: Incorrect – 'Despite' suggests an idea of contrast; the sentence requires an idea of cause or reason; E: Incorrect – 'Although' suggests an idea of contrast; the sentence requires an idea of cause or reason.

A frase complementada adequadamente fica: "[**Because**] no sale occurs, no gain is realized", cuja tradução é "[**Como (porque)**] não ocorreu venda, nenhum ganho é realizado."

Gabarito "C".

(Agente Fiscal de Rendas/SP – 2006 – FCC) A forma verbal correta de [*TO GENERATE*] no texto é

(A) will be generated.
(B) was generated.
(C) generates.
(D) has been generating.
(E) would have been generated.

(Grammar) A: Incorrect – The topic is a sale that did not occur, thus turning any suggestion of its actually happening into a hypothetical situation. 'Will be generated' confirms that something will happen, that is, not hypothetical, but real; B: Incorrect – The topic is a sale that did not occur, thus turning any suggestion of its actually happening into a hypothetical situation. 'Was generated' confirms that something already happened, when in fact it did not; C: Incorrect – The existence of the word 'by' after the verb suggests that it should be in the passive voice form, thus an active voice form (generates) would sound odd; D: Incorrect - The existence of the word 'by' after the verb suggests that it should be in the passive voice form, thus an active voice form (has been generating) would sound odd; E: Correct – 'Would have been' is used to talk about hypothetical ideas in the past (that did not really happen, such as the sale). The passive voice structure also matches the use of 'by'.

A frase complementada adequadamente fica: "The additional income tax liability that [**would have been generated**] by the inclusion of the gain...", cuja tradução é "A obrigação tributária relativa à renda adicional que [**teria sido gerada**] pela inclusão do ganho...".

Gabarito "E".

(Agente Fiscal de Rendas/SP – 2006 – FCC) No texto, *after a tax return has been filed* pode ser traduzido como

(A) depois de ter sido entregue a declaração de imposto de renda.
(B) depois da restituição do imposto de renda.
(C) depois do preenchimento da guia de recolhimento do imposto de renda.
(D) depois de a declaração de imposto de renda ter sido processada.
(E) depois de retificada a declaração do imposto de renda.

(Interpretation) A: Correct – 'file' in this context has the idea of 'submit' or 'hand in'. 'A tax return' is the form that is handed in, or delivered, to the tax authorities; B: Incorrect – 'restituição' in the tax area is usually translated as 'rebate'; C: Incorrect – 'preenchimento' means to fill in a tax return (form). Note: 'fill' and 'file' can easily be confused. The former means 'preencher', while the latter means 'entregar'; D: Incorrect – 'processada', in this context, means to be 'processed' or 'handled'; 'file' only refers to the idea of submitting the tax return.; E: Incorrect – 'retificada' means 'corrected' or 'fixed'. "Tax return" é como os americanos se referem à declaração anual do imposto de renda. A frase "after a tax return has been filed" pode ser traduzida como "após uma declaração do imposto de renda ter sido entregue".

Gabarito "A".

(Agente Fiscal de Rendas/SP – 2006 – FCC) O texto pode ser sintetizado na seguinte oposição:

(A) Tax evasion is acceptable conduct. Tax avoidance is contravention.
(B) Tax evaded remains due. Tax avoided is not due.
(C) Tax evasion implies fiscal debt. Tax avoidance implies legally reduced debt.
(D) Tax evasion is tax paid. Tax avoidance is tax not paid.
(E) Tax evaded can be returned. Tax avoided cannot be returned.

(Interpretation) A: Incorrect – The text explicitly says, "Tax evasion involves **breaking the law**"; B: Correct – The text explicitly says, "An evaded tax **remains a tax legally owed**"; and "An avoided tax is a tax liability **that has never existed**; C: Incorrect – The text explains the difference between the two terms; it does not compare forms of debt; D: Incorrect – The text explicitly says, "An evaded tax **remains a tax legally owed**", meaning it has not been paid; E: Incorrect – The text explicitly says, "An evaded tax remains a tax legally owed"; therefore, as it has not been paid, it cannot be returned.

O texto refere-se à distinção entre elisão fiscal, ou planejamento tributário [tax avoidance], que é legítima, e evasão fiscal [tax evasion], que é conduta criminosa. No caso da elisão fiscal, não há obrigação tributária, ou seja, nenhum tributo é devido. Já no caso de evasão fiscal, a dívida perante o fisco existe e, enquanto não for paga, permanece devida.

Gabarito "B".

Text I

A Day in the Life of the Women of O&G

by Jaime Kammerzell
From Rigzone Contributor. Tuesday, February 14, 2012

Although far fewer women work in the oil and gas (O&G) industry compared to men, many women find rewarding careers in the industry. Five women were asked the same questions regarding their career
5 choices in the oil and gas industry.
Question 1: Why did you choose the oil and gas industry?
Woman 1: Cool technology, applying science and money.
10 **Woman 2:** It seemed interesting and the pay was good.
Woman 3: They offered me a job! I couldn't turn down the great starting salary and a chance to live in New Orleans.
15 **Woman 4:** I did not really choose the oil and gas industry as much as it chose me.
Woman 5: I chose the oil and gas industry because of the challenging projects, and I want to be part of our country's energy solution.
20 **Question 2: How did you get your start in the oil and gas industry?**
Woman 1: I went to a university that all major oil companies recruit. I received a summer internship with Texaco before my last year of my Master's degree.
25 **Woman 2:** I was recruited at a Texas Tech Engineering Job Fair.
Woman 3: At the time, campus recruiters came to the geosciences department of my university annually and they sponsored scholarships for
30 graduate students to help complete their research. Even though my Master's thesis was more geared toward environmental studies, as a recipient of one of these scholarships, my graduate advisor strongly encouraged me to participate when the time came for
35 O&G Industry interviews.

Woman 4: I was working for a company in another state where oil and gas was not its primary business. When the company sold its division in the state where I was working, they offered me a position at the company's headquarters in Houston managing the aftermarket sales for the company's largest region. Aftermarket sales supported the on-highway, construction, industrial, agricultural and the oil and gas markets. After one year, the company asked me to take the position of managing their marine and offshore power products division. I held that position for three years. I left that company to join a new startup company where I hold the position of president.

Woman 5: My first job in the oil and gas industry was an internship with Mobil Oil Corp., in New Orleans. I worked with a lot of smart, focused and talented geoscientists and engineers.

Question 3: Describe your typical day.

Woman 1: Tough one to describe a typical day. I generally read email, go to a couple of meetings and work with the field's earth model or look at seismic.

Woman 2: I talk with clients, help prepare bids and work on getting projects out the door. My days are never the same, which is what I love about the job I have.

Woman 3: I usually work from 7:30 a.m. – 6:30 p.m. (although the official day is shorter). We call the field every morning for an update on operations, security, construction, facilities and production engineering activities. I work with my team leads on short-term and long-term projects to enhance production (a lot of emails and Powerpoint). I usually have 2-3 meetings per day to discuss/prioritize/review ongoing or upcoming work (production optimization, simulation modeling, drilling plans, geologic interpretation, workovers, etc.). Beyond our team, I also participate in a number of broader business initiatives and leadership teams.

Woman 4: A typical day is a hectic day for me. My day usually starts well before 8 a.m. with phone calls and emails with our facility in Norway, as well as other business relationships abroad. At the office, I am involved in the daily business operations and also stay closely involved in the projects and the sales efforts. On any given day I am working on budgets and finance, attending project meetings, attending engineering meetings, reviewing drawings and technical specifications, meeting with clients and prospective clients, reviewing sales proposals, evaluating new business opportunities and making a lot of decisions.

Woman 5: On most days I work on my computer to complete my projects. I interpret logs, create maps, research local and regional geology or write documents. I go to project meetings almost every day. I typically work only during business hours, but there are times when I get calls at night or on weekends from a rig or other geologists for assistance with a technical problem.

Adapted from URL: <http://www.rigzone.com/news/article.asp?a_id=11508>.
Retrieved on February 14, 2012.

(ADVOGADO – PETROBRÁS – 2012 – CESGRANRIO) According to Text I, when asked about their choice of the oil and gas industry,

(A) all the interviewees pointed out the relevance of having a green job.
(B) all the women felt really committed to solving the nation's energy problems.
(C) all the interviewees mentioned that the challenges of the field attracted them.
(D) just one of the women commented that she was attracted by the location of the job.
(E) no interviewee considered the salary an important factor for accepting the job.

(Interpretation) A: Incorrect – None of the women mention the relevance of having a green job; B: Incorrect – Only Woman 5, on lines 18 and 19, expresses such a commitment to solving the nation's energy problems; C: Incorrect – Only Woman 5, on lines 17 and 18, expresses the challenges of the field as a reason the oil industry attracted her; D: Correct – The text, on lines 12-15, explicitly says "They offered me a job! I couldn't turn down the great starting salary and *a chance to live in New Orleans*"; E: Incorrect - The text, on lines 12-15, explicitly says, "They offered me a job! **I couldn't turn down the great starting salary** and a chance to live in New Orleans".

Gabarito "D".

(ADVOGADO – PETROBRÁS – 2012 – CESGRANRIO) In Text I, using the interviewees' experience, it can be said that getting a job in the O&G industry can result from all the following situations, EXCEPT

(A) participating in a job fair.
(B) taking part in O&G Industry interviews.
(C) applying to specific job ads via internet sites.
(D) attending a university where major oil companies look for prospective employees.
(E) getting previous experience in an internship program with an O&G organization.

(Interpretation) A: Incorrect – Woman 2, on lines 25 and 26, explicitly says, "I was recruited at a Texas Tech Engineering *Job Fair*"; B: Incorrect – **The text, on lines 34 and 35, explicitly says,** "encouraged me to participate when the time came for O&G Industry interviews"; C: Correct – None of the women mention job ads on internet sites as a way of getting a job in the field; D: Incorrect – The text, on lines 27 and 28, explicitly says, "At the time, **campus recruiters came to the geosciences department of my university** annually"; E: Incorrect – The text, on lines 23 and 24, explicitly says, "**I received a summer internship with Texaco** before my last year of my Master's degree", meaning that the internship was the doorway to getting a job in the field.
NOTE: This question is worded in a misleading manner. The idea is to find the answer that is **NOT** mentioned in the text.

Gabarito "C".

(ADVOGADO – PETROBRÁS – 2012 – CESGRANRIO) In Text I, according to the answers to the third question in the interview,

(A) Woman 1 implies that every day is the same for her, since she performs exactly the same tasks routinely.
(B) Woman 2 complains against her very boring schedule at the office, dealing with strictly technical issues.
(C) Woman 3 always works off hours and does not get involved with the operations in the field.
(D) Woman 4 has negotiations with the international branches and gets involved in commercial and technical issues.
(E) Woman 5 does not need to worry about preparing written materials nor deciding on last-minute technical issues at nights or on weekends.

(Interpretation) A: Incorrect – Woman 1, on line 54, says, "*Tough one to describe a typical day*", meaning that she may not do the same thing every day; B: Incorrect – Woman 2, on lines 58 and 59, says, "My days are *never the same*", meaning that her schedule is not boring; C: Incorrect – Woman 3, on lines 68-71, explicitly says, "(…) to discuss/prioritize/review ongoing or upcoming work (*production optimization, simulation modeling, drilling plans, geologic interpretation, workovers*, etc.)", meaning she is involved with operations in the field; D: Correct – Woman 4, on lines 75-77, explicitly says, "with *phone calls and emails with our facility in Norway*, as well as *other business relationships abroad*"; E: Incorrect – Woman 5, on line 92, explicitly says, "I get calls *at night or on weekends*".
Gabarito "D".

(ADVOGADO – PETROBRÁS – 2012 – CESGRANRIO) Based on the meanings of the words in Text I,

(A) major (line 22) and **main** express opposite ideas.
(B) headquarters (line 40) could be substituted by **main office**.
(C) smart (line 51) and **intelligent** are antonyms.
(D) enhance (line 66) and **reduce** express similar ideas.
(E) prospective (line 84) and **former** are synonyms.

(Vocabulary) A: Incorrect – 'major' and 'main' are synonymous in this context, both meaning large and important; B: Correct – 'headquarters' is a synonym for 'main office' and, therefore, can replace it; C: Incorrect – 'smart' and 'intelligent' are synonyms, not antonyms; D: Incorrect – 'enhance', in this context, means 'increase', while 'reduce' is the opposite; E: Incorrect – 'prospective' means 'potential', which is intrinsically linked to an idea of future, while 'former' is used to refer to things in the past.
Gabarito "B".

(ADVOGADO – PETROBRÁS – 2012 – CESGRANRIO) The sentence, in Text I, in which the **boldfaced** expression introduces an idea of **addition** is

(A) "**Although** far fewer women work in the oil and gas (O&G) industry compared to men, many women find rewarding careers in the industry." (lines 1-3)
(B) "I chose the oil and gas industry **because of** the challenging projects," (lines 17-18)
(C) "**Even though** my Master's thesis was more geared toward environmental studies," (lines 31-32)
(D) "**as well as** other business relationships abroad." (lines 76-77)
(E) "**but** there are times when I get calls at night or on weekends from a rig or other geologists for assistance with a technical problem." (lines 91-94)

(Grammar) A: Incorrect – 'Although', in this context, is a conjunction used to show contrast, not addition; B: Incorrect – 'because of', in this context, is a conjunction used to show reason or cause, not addition; C: 'Even though', in this context, is a conjunction used to show contrast, not addition; D: Correct – 'as well as', in this context, is a conjunction used to show addition. It is synonymous with 'and'; E: Incorrect – 'but', in this context, is a conjunction used to show contrast, not addition.
Gabarito "D".

(ADVOGADO – PETROBRÁS – 2012 – CESGRANRIO) In Text I, the expression "turn down" in "I couldn't **turn** down the great starting salary and a chance to live in New Orleans" (lines 12-14) could be replaced, without change in meaning, by

(A) refuse
(B) take
(C) accept
(D) request
(E) understand

(Vocabulary) A: Correct – 'turn down', in this context, is a phrasal verb that means 'refuse' or 'reject'; B: Incorrect – 'take', in this context, means 'seize' or 'accept'; C: Incorrect – 'accept', in this context, means 'agree to receive'; D: Incorrect – 'request' in this context, means 'ask for'; E: Incorrect – 'understand', in this context, means 'comprehend'.
Gabarito "A".

(ADVOGADO – PETROBRÁS – 2012 – CESGRANRIO) The only fragment from Text I that presents a series of actions exclusively performed in the past is

(A) "I chose the oil and gas industry because of the challenging projects, and I want to be part of our country's energy solution." (lines 17-19)
(B) "I held that position for three years. I left that company to join a new startup company where I hold the position of president." (lines 46-48)
(C) "My first job in the oil and gas industry was an internship with Mobil Oil Corp., in New Orleans. I worked with a lot of smart, focused and talented geoscientists and engineers." (lines 49-52)
(D) "At the office, I am involved in the daily business operations and also stay closely involved in the projects and the sales efforts." (lines 77-80)
(E) "On most days I work on my computer to complete my projects. I interpret logs, create maps, research local and regional geology or write documents." (lines 87-90)

(Grammar) A: Incorrect – The verb 'chose' represents an action in the past, but 'want' refers to the present; B: Incorrect – The verbs 'held' and 'left' represent actions in the past, but 'hold' refers to the present; C: Correct – All verbs are in the past tense; D: Incorrect – All actions refer to the present (I *am* involved in…); E: Incorrect – All actions refer to the present (I *work*….*interpret*, *create*, *research*, *write*).
Gabarito "C".

Text II

How To Start A Career In The Oil And Gas Industry: What Employers Say

By Katie Weir

From Talent Acquisition Specialist, Campus

Talisman Energy

How to start your career, step by step
Fix up your résumé – take it to your career centre at your university and they'll help you.
Write a compelling cover letter that speaks to
5 **your best qualities** – save the pretentious language for your English papers.
Join a professional association and attend their events – if you feel uncomfortable attending alone, try volunteering at them. By having a job to do,
10 it gives you an excuse to interact with the attendees, and an easy way to start up a conversation the next time you see them.
Do your research – I can't stress this enough. I want students to apply to Talisman, not because we
15 have open jobs, but because they actually have an interest in what we're doing, and want to be a part of it.
Be confident, but stay humble – it's important

to communicate your abilities effectively, but it's also important to be conscious of the phrase: "sense of entitlement." This generation entering the workforce has already been branded with the word "entitlement," so students will need to fight against this bias from the very beginning of any relationship with people in the industry – be aware that you will need to roll up your sleeves and work hard for the first couple years, and you will be rewarded in the end.

Retrieved and adapted from URL: <http://talentegg.ca/incubator/2010/11/29/how-to-start-a-career-in-the-oil-and-gas-industry-what-employers-say/>.
Access on: February 14, 2012.

(ADVOGADO – PETROBRÁS – 2012 – CESGRANRIO) The main purpose of Text II is to

(A) teach prospective workers how to prepare cover letters to impress employers.
(B) advise the readers about the importance of researching for open jobs in institutional websites.
(C) criticize job candidates who are excessively confident and feel that the world owes them something.
(D) alert the readers to the importance of joining a professional association to have free access to their events.
(E) list relevant hints for those interested in entering the job market and building a successful professional life.

(Interpretation) A: Incorrect – Preparing cover letters is only one of the issues mentioned in the text; it is not the main purpose of the text; B: Incorrect – International websites are not mentioned in the text; C: Incorrect – While a part of the text mentions the idea of excessive confidence (This generation entering the workforce has already been branded with the word "***entitlement***"), this is not the main purpose of the text; D: Incorrect – The text suggests joining a professional association (lines 7 to 12), but not with the purpose of free access to events; E: Correct – The text lists 5 relevant steps for those interested in entering the job market and building a successful professional life. On line 1, the text explicitly introduces the main purpose (**How to start your career, *step by step*)**.
Gabarito "E".

(ADVOGADO – PETROBRÁS – 2012 – CESGRANRIO) The fragment that closes Text II, "be aware that you will need to roll up your sleeves and work hard for the first couple years, and you will be rewarded in the end." (lines 23-25), implies that one must

(A) make an effort to commit totally to one's job in the initial phase, in order to reach success in the future.
(B) wear formal clothes to work so that, as years go by, a couple of top-rank officers can recognize one's worth.
(C) accept jobs with severe routines only in order to obtain early promotions.
(D) avoid postponing assigned tasks and wearing inappropriate clothes in the working environment.
(E) show commitment to the working routine and demand the rewards frequently offered to senior employees.

(Interpretation) A: Correct – '***roll up your sleeves*** and **work hard for the first couple years***'* means to 'make an effort to commit totally to one's job in the initial phase', while 'you will be ***rewarded in the end***' means 'success in the future'; B: Incorrect – 'wear formal clothes' refers to the way you dress, not commitment to the job; C: Incorrect – 'accept jobs with severe routines' means 'agree to do work with little variation', not that it is hard work; 'early promotions' means to be given a better position in a short amount of time', while the text suggest this may take more time; D: Incorrect – 'avoid postponing assigned tasks' means 'to try not delaying your work until a future time'; 'wearing inappropriate clothes' means wearing clothes that are not suitable for that environment; E: Incorrect – 'demand the rewards' means to 'forcefully request compensation'. In the text, 'you will be rewarded in the end' does not refer to 'demands'.
Gabarito "A".

(ADVOGADO – PETROBRÁS – 2012 – CESGRANRIO) Concerning Texts I and II, it is possible to affirm that

(A) neither text points out ways to get rewarding jobs in the O&G industry.
(B) both texts discuss strategies to ask for promotion in the O&G industry.
(C) both texts present ways of starting successful careers in the O&G industry.
(D) only Text I encourages prospective employees of O&G industries to plan their careers in advance.
(E) only Text II provides hints on how to give up highly--paid jobs in the O&G industry.

(Interpretation) A: Incorrect – The title for Text II is '***How To Start A Career In The Oil And Gas Industry***', meaning it shows ways to get rewarding jobs in the O&G industry; B: Incorrect – While both texts mention the idea of promotions, they do not discuss strategies for this; C: Correct – Text I presents examples of ways of starting successful careers in the O&G industry, while Text II makes suggestions on how to do this; D: Incorrect – Text II suggests revising your résumé and writing a cover letter, both related to planning a career; E: Incorrect – 'give up' means 'abandon' or 'renounce'. Neither text mentions this.
Gabarito "C".

Happy 150th, Oil! So Long, and Thanks for Modern Civilization

By Alexis Madrigal
WIRED SCIENCE, August 27, 2009

One hundred and fifty years ago on Aug. 27, Colonel Edwin L. Drake sunk the very first commercial well that produced flowing petroleum. The discovery that large amounts of oil could be found underground marked the beginning of a time during which this convenient fossil fuel became America's dominant energy source.

But what began 150 years ago won't last another 150 years — or even another 50. The era of cheap oil is ending, and with another energy transition upon us, we've got to extract all the lessons we can from its remarkable history.

"I would see this as less of an anniversary to note for celebration and more of an anniversary to note how far we've come and the serious moment that we're at right now," said Brian Black, an energy historian at Pennsylvania State University. "Energy transitions happen and I argue that we're in one right now. Thus, we need to aggressively look to the future to what's going to happen after petroleum."

When Drake and others sunk their wells, there were no cars, no plastics, no chemical industry. Water power was the dominant industrial energy source. Steam engines burning coal were on the rise, but the nation's energy system — unlike Great Britain's — still used fossil fuels sparingly. The original role for oil was as an illuminant, not a motor fuel, which would come decades later.

Oil, people later found, was uniquely convenient. To equal the amount of energy in a tank of gasoline, you need 200 pounds of wood. Pair that energy density with
30 stability under most conditions and that, as a liquid, it was easy to transport, and you have the killer application for the infrastructure age.

In a world that only had a tiny fraction of the amount of heat, light, and power available that we do
35 now, people came up with all kinds of ideas for what to do with oil's energy: Cars, tractors, airplanes, chemicals, fertilizer, and plastic.

The scale of the oil industry is astounding, but it's becoming clear the world's oil supply will peak soon, or
40 perhaps has peaked already. People discuss about the details, but no one argues that oil will play a much different role in our energy system in 50 years than it did in 1959.

The search for alternatives is on. If that search goes poorly — as some Peak Oil analysts predict —
45 human civilization will fall off an energy cliff. The amount of energy we get back from drilling oil wells in the middle of the Gulf of Mexico continues to drop, and alternative sources don't provide usable energy for humans on the generous terms that oil long has.
50 Yet humans with an economic incentive to be optimistic become optimists, and the harder we look, the more possible alternatives we find. The big question now is whether the cure for our oil addiction will come with a heavy carbon side effect.
55 Over the next 20 years, synthetic fuels made from coal or shale oil could conceivably become the fuels of the future. On the other hand, so could advanced biofuels from cellulosic ethanol or algae. Or the era of fuel could end and electric vehicles could be deployed in mass, at
60 least in rich countries.

With the massive injection of stimulus and venture capital money into alternative energy that's occurred over the past few years, the solutions for replacing oil could already be circulating among the labs and office parks
65 of the country. To paraphrase technology expert Clay Shirky talking about the media, nothing will work to replace oil, but everything might.

If history tells us anything, it's that energy sources can change, never tomorrow, but always some day.
70 "What is required is to operate without fear and to take energy transitions on as a developmental opportunity," Black said.

slightly adapted from: http://www.wired.com/wiredscience/
2009/08/oilat150/#ixzz0gW1mC0Zm,
access on Feb. 10, 2010.

(ADVOGADO – PETROBRÁS DISTRIB. – 2010 – CESGRANRIO)
The author's intention in this text is to

(A) complain about the useless efforts and investments in new sources of energy.
(B) celebrate the fact that oil has been the world's cheapest form of energy ever known.
(C) support the worldwide view that oil is the only possible source of energy for the future.
(D) prove that oil production is large enough to supply all the world's energy needs for the next 150 years.
(E) stress the relevance of oil in the history of civilization and the need for alternative energy sources.

(Interpretation) A: Incorrect – The text explicitly says, "the solutions for replacing oil *could already be circulating among the labs and office parks* of the country" (lines 63-65), meaning that efforts are not useless; B: Incorrect – The text says, "The era of *cheap oil is ending*", but the author does not suggest celebrating oil prices; C: Incorrect – The text explicitly says, "If history tells us anything, *it's that energy sources can change*, never tomorrow, but always

some day" (lines 68 and 69), meaning that the author recognizes how oil may not be the only source of energy; D: Incorrect – The text explicitly says, "But what began 150 years ago **won't last another 150 years — or even another 50**" (lines 7 and 8), meaning that oil production will not last even 50 years; E: Correct – The author covers several aspects of oil to emphasize its importance in the history of civilization, while suggesting the need for new energy sources.
Gabarito "E".

(ADVOGADO – PETROBRÁS DISTRIB. – 2010 – CESGRANRIO)
Alexis Madrigal comments that oil was

(A) initially used to supply energy for lighting purposes.
(B) less important as an energy source in the last century than biofuels.
(C) a cheap fuel for most industrial uses and will certainly continue to be so.
(D) found to be inappropriate to replace wood in providing energy for motors.
(E) relatively important due to its by-products, for pharmaceuticals, fertilizers and plastics.

(Interpretation) A: Correct – The text explicitly says, "The *original role for oil was as an illuminant*, not a motor fuel" (lines 25-26); B: Incorrect – The text explicitly says, "alternative sources *don't provide usable energy* for humans on the generous terms that oil long has (lines 47-49), meaning that oil was the most important fuel in the last century; C: Incorrect - The text explicitly says, "The era of *cheap oil is ending*", meaning oil prices will not continue cheap; D: Incorrect – The text explicitly says, "Oil, people later found, was *uniquely convenient*. To equal the amount of energy in a tank of gasoline, you need *200 pounds of wood*" (lines 27-29), meaning that oil was rather appropriate in replacing wood as a fuel; E: Incorrect – The text says, "people came up with all kinds of *ideas for what to do with oil's energy*. Cars, tractors, airplanes, *chemicals*, *fertilizer*, and *plastic*" (lines 35-37), meaning that people found other ways of using oil, but the author does not emphasize the importance of such by-products.
NOTE: Option E is worded in a misleading manner. It could be inferred that the author implies a certain amount of importance to these by-products, merely by including them in his text.
Gabarito "A".

(ADVOGADO – PETROBRÁS DISTRIB. – 2010 – CESGRANRIO)
According to Brian Black in paragraphs 3 (lines 12-19) and 13 (lines 70-72), energy transitions should be

(A) understood as phases of uncertainty when historians become more serious and aggressive.
(B) celebrated as a special event that represents the end of non-lucrative periods in oil production.
(C) seen as opportunities to reflect on past achievements and evaluate the right investments for the future.
(D) taken as fearful periods in which people feel hopeless about the unstable supply and distribution of energy.
(E) considered serious moments in history since they always bring unexpected and dangerous consequences.

(Interpretation) A: Incorrect – Black does not mention uncertainty, nor aggressive historians; B: Incorrect – Black, in paragraphs 3 and 13, does not mention the lucrative aspects of oil; C: Correct – Black explicitly says, "*an anniversary to note how far we've come*", meaning a chance to reflect on past achievements, and "*take energy transitions on as a developmental opportunity*", meaning

the chance to assess the best way to invest in the future; D: Incorrect – Black, in paragraphs 3 and 13, does not mention feelings of hopelessness; E: Incorrect - Black, in paragraphs 3 and 13, does not mention dangerous consequences.
Gabarito "C".

(ADVOGADO – PETROBRÁS DISTRIB. – 2010 – CESGRANRIO) In the fragments "…people **came up with** all kinds of ideas for what to do with oil's energy…" (lines 35-36) and "The amount of energy we **get back** from drilling oil wells…" (lines 45-46), the phrases "came up with" and "get back", can be replaced without change in meaning by, respectively,

(A) prevented – miss
(B) proposed – recover
(C) supplied – destroy
(D) suggested – invest
(E) discarded – collect

(Vocabulary) A: Incorrect – 'prevented' means 'stopped', while 'miss' means 'yearn for' or 'fail to find or see'; B: Correct – 'came up with' means 'invented' or 'suggested' or 'proposed'; 'get back' means 'receive' or 'recover'; C: Incorrect – 'supplied' means 'gave'; 'destroy' means 'damage'; D: Incorrect – 'suggested' is a possible answer here; 'invest' means 'intentionally give money in search of profit'; E: Incorrect – 'discarded' means 'threw away'; 'collect' means accumulate (the meaning is similar to 'get back', but the collocation is odd).
Gabarito "B".

(ADVOGADO – PETROBRÁS DISTRIB. – 2010 – CESGRANRIO) The pair of words that express opposing ideas is

(A) "…remarkable…" (line 11) – *extraordinary* .
(B) "…sparingly." (line 25) – *economically*.
(C) "…tiny…" (line 33) – *huge*.
(D) "…drop," (line 47) – *fall*.
(E) "…deployed…" (line 59) – *used*.

(Vocabulary) A: Incorrect – 'remarkable' means 'extraordinary' or 'amazing' (synonyms); B: Incorrect – 'sparingly' means 'economically' or 'in moderation' (synonyms); C: Correct – 'tiny' means 'small', while 'huge' means 'big' (opposing ideas); D: Incorrect – 'drop' means 'fall' or 'dive' (synonyms); E: Incorrect – 'deployed', in this context, means 'used' or 'employed'.
Note: 'deploy' is more commonly used as 'send' as in 'send military troops and equipment to a place'.
Gabarito "C".

(ADVOGADO – PETROBRÁS DISTRIB. – 2010 – CESGRANRIO) The expression in **bold type** introduces a consequence in

(A) "**But** what began 150 years ago…" (line 7)
(B) "**Thus**, we need to aggressively look to the future…" (lines 17-18)
(C) "**If** that search goes poorly —" (lines 43-44)
(D) "**Yet** human with an economic incentive to be optimistic…" (lines 50-51)
(E) "**On the other hand**, so could advanced bio-fuels…" (line 57)

(Grammar) A: Incorrect – 'But', in this context, is a conjunction used to show contrast, not consequence; B: Correct – 'Thus', in this context, is an adverb used to show consequence, similar to 'therefore' or 'consequently'; C: Incorrect – 'If', in this context, is a conjunction used to show condition, not consequence; D: Incorrect – 'Yet', in this context, is a conjunction used to show contrast, not consequence; E: Incorrect – 'On the other hand', in this context, is a conjunction used to show contrast, not consequence.
Gabarito "B".

(ADVOGADO – PETROBRÁS DISTRIB. – 2010 – CESGRANRIO) In the fragment "nothing will work to replace oil, but everything might." (lines 66-67) the verbs 'will' and 'might', respectively, convey the idea of

(A) possibility, doubt.
(B) fact, high probability.
(C) probability, suspicion.
(D) future possibility, certainty.
(E) certainty, remote probability.

(Grammar) A: Incorrect – 'could' is a modal verb that expresses possibility; to express doubt with a modal verb, usually the use of the negative form is required; B: Incorrect – Fact is usually expressed with auxiliary verbs such as 'do/does', 'did', 'has' (done); 'might' expresses a low probability; C: Incorrect - Probability is usually expressed with modal verbs such as 'may' or might', not 'will'; suspicion can be expressed with the modal verb 'might', but not in this context; D: Incorrect - 'will' can express an idea of future possibility, but not in this context; 'certainty' is not expressed with the modal verb 'might'; E: Correct – 'will', in this context, is a modal verb affirming the certainty that nothing will work; while 'might', in this context, is a modal verb used to express the 'remote possibility' that every other product has the chance of replacing oil.
Gabarito "E".

(ADVOGADO – PETROBRÁS DISTRIB. – 2010 – CESGRANRIO) In paragraph 9 (lines 50-54), Alexis Madrigal shows concern for the

(A) convenient implications of oil addiction to the ecological balance.
(B) choice of heavy carbon as an easy alternative fuel to substitute oil.
(C) few alternative sources of energy that would effectively replace oil.
(D) environmental impact of the sources of energy that might replace oil.
(E) optimistic human beings who pay incentives to choose alternatives to oil.

(Interpretation) A: Incorrect – 'convenient' implies a positive aspect. The author expresses concern, not a positive outlook; B: Incorrect – The author does not express that heavy carbon is an easy alternative, but rather that it may bring problems; C: Incorrect – The author does not express concern over numbers of alternatives, but rather the severity of the consequences; D: Correct – The text explicitly says, "The big question now is whether **_the cure_** for our oil addiction will **_come with a heavy carbon side effect_**" (lines 52-54), meaning that the replacement for oil (the cure) may be environmentally problematic (come with a heavy carbon side effect); E: Incorrect – The author does not mention payment of incentives in this paragraph.
Gabarito "D".

(ADVOGADO – PETROBRÁS DISTRIB. – 2010 – CESGRANRIO) The fragment "…energy sources can change, never tomorrow, but always some day." (lines 68-69) implies that

(A) energy sources may eventually change.
(B) energy sources will certainly change overnight.
(C) it is highly unlikely that energy sources will change one day.
(D) it is possible to predict when the energy sources should change.
(E) it is possible to anticipate the changes energy sources have to go through and their timing.

(Interpretation) A: Correct – '***can change*** (...) ***some day***' suggests that the change can happen at anytime, that is, eventually; B: Incorrect – 'will certainly' means that the change is guaranteed; C: Incorrect – 'highly unlikely' means almost no chance of it happening; D: Incorrect – 'possible to predict' means that we can know when the change will happen; E: Incorrect – 'possible to anticipate the changes' means that we can calculate the kinds of changes that will happen and when (timing).
Gabarito "A".

(ADVOGADO – PETROBRÁS DISTRIB. – 2010 – CESGRANRIO) The title of this text is a reference to all of the facts below EXCEPT for

(A) the high return on investments in drilling oil in the last 150 years.
(B) the anniversary of the discovery of the first commercial oil source.
(C) all of the modern developments that the finding of oil made possible.
(D) a need to say goodbye to oil as new energy sources must be developed.
(E) the long history of oil as a major economic industry in the modern world.

(Interpretation) A: Correct – The titles makes no reference to profit from investments in oil; B: Incorrect – 'Happy 150th' refers to the anniversary of the discovery of oil; C: Incorrect – 'Modern Civilization' refers to the modern developments oil made possible; D: Incorrect – 'So Long" means goodbye; E: Incorrect – 'Happy 150th' refers to the long history of oil.
Note: This question is worded in a misleading manner. The idea is to identify the reference that is ***NOT*** made in the title.
Gabarito "A".

Happy 150th, Oil! So Long, and Thanks for Modern Civilization

World Oil Reserves at 'Tipping Point'

ScienceDaily (Mar. 26, 2010) — The world's capacity to meet projected future oil demand is at a tipping point, according to research by the Smith School of Enterprise and the Environment at Oxford University.
5 There is a need to accelerate the development of alternative energy fuel resources in order to ensure energy security and reduce emissions, says a paper just published in the journal *Energy Policy*.
The age of cheap oil has now ended as demand
10 starts to outstrip supply as we head towards the middle of the decade, says the report. It goes on to suggest that the current oil reserve estimates should be downgraded from between 1150-1350 billion barrels to between 850-900 billion barrels, based on recent
15 research. But how can potential oil shortages be mitigated?
Dr Oliver Inderwildi, Head of the Low Carbon Mobility centre at the Smith School, said: 'The common belief that alternative fuels such as biofuels could
20 mitigate oil supply shortages and eventually replace fossil fuels is pie in the sky. There is not sufficient land to cater for both food and fuel demand. Instead of relying on those silver bullet solutions, we have to make better use of the remaining resources by improving
25 energy efficiency. Alternatives such as a hydrogen economy and electric transportation are not mature and will only play a major role in the medium to long term.'
Nick Owen, from the Smith School of Enterprise and the Environment, added: 'Significant oil supply
30 challenges will be compounded in the near future by rising demand and strengthening environmental policy. Mitigating the oil crunch without using lower grade resources such as tar sands is the key to maintaining energy stability and a low carbon future.'
35 The Smith School paper also highlights that in the past, political and financial objectives have led to misreporting of oil reserves, which has led to contradictory estimates of oil reserve data available in the public domain.
40 Sir David King, Director of the Smith School, commented: 'We have to face up to a future of oil uncertainty much like the global economic uncertainty we have faced during the past two years. This challenge will have a longer term effect on our economies unless
45 swift action is taken by governments and business. We all recognize that oil is a finite resource. We need to look at other low carbon alternatives and make the necessary funding available for research, development and deployment today if we are to mitigate the tipping
50 point.'
The report also raises the worrying issue that additional demand for oil could be met by nonconventional methods, such as the extraction of oil from Canada's tar sands. However, these methods have a
55 far higher carbon output than conventional drilling, and have been described as having a double impact on emissions owing to the emissions produced during extraction as well as during usage.

Available in http://www.sciencedaily.com/releases/2010/03/100324225511.htm. Access on April 6, 2010

(ADVOGADO – PETROBRÁS BIO. – 2010 – CESGRANRIO) The author reports that world oil reserves are at a 'tipping point' because oil

(A) is already being replaced by alternative fuels in most uses of the fuel.
(B) is now in shortage and will not supply global needs in the near future.
(C) has already been substituted by alternative energy fuel resources worldwide.
(D) has been misreported as non-abundant to satisfy political interests of non-producing nations.
(E) has reached a peak in off-shore wells and is now abundantly extracted from tar sand reserves.

(Interpretation) B: Correct – To 'be at the tipping point' means to be at the critical point of a situation beyond which significant or unstoppable changes can take place. Option B refers to the current shortage of oil reserves, which will soon not meet global demand.
Gabarito "B".

(ADVOGADO – PETROBRÁS BIO. – 2010 – CESGRANRIO) Based on the meanings of the words in the text, it can be said that

(A) "...ensure..." (line 6) and *guarantee* are antonyms.
(B) "...outstrip..." (line 10) and e*xceed* are synonyms.
(C) "...downgraded..." (line 13) and *subsidized* express similar ideas.
(D) "...highlights..." (line 35) and *underlines* express contradictory ideas.
(E) "...owing to..." (line 57) and *as a result of* have opposite meanings.

(Vocabulary) A: Incorrect – 'ensure' means to guarantee – they are synonyms, B: Correct – 'outstrip' means to exceed, C: Incorrect – 'downgraded' means revised downwards: to minimize the value of something, D: Incorrect – 'highlights' means the same as underlines. E: Incorrect – 'owing to' and 'as a result of' are similar in meaning and show consequence.
Gabarito "B".

(ADVOGADO – PETROBRÁS BIO. – 2010 – CESGRANRIO) The word in parentheses describes the idea expressed by the word in **boldtype** in

(A) "...a need to accelerate the development of alternative energy fuel resources **in order to** ensure energy security and reduce emissions," - lines 5-7 (contrast)
(B) "'The common belief that alternative fuels **such as** biofuels..." - lines 18-19 (result)
(C) "**Instead of** relying on those silver bullet solutions,"- lines 22-23 (consequence)
(D) "**However**, these methods have a far higher carbon output than conventional drilling," - lines 54-55 (reason)
(E) "...the emissions produced during extraction **as well as** during usage." - lines 57-58 (addition)

(Grammar) A: 'in order to' means 'for the purpose of', B: Incorrect – 'such as' refers to exemplification, C: Incorrect – 'Instead of' refers to contrast, D: Incorrect – 'However' refers to contrast, E: Correct – 'as well as ' refers to addition.
Gabarito "E".

(ADVOGADO – PETROBRÁS BIO. – 2010 – CESGRANRIO) Dr. Oliver Inderwildi supports all of the following statements EXCEPT

(A) Alternative energy sources, like hydrogen, are still not foreseen as productive in the immediate future.
(B) It is illusory to believe that the production of alternative fuels will make up for the decline in oil supply.
(C) There is enough soil available in the world for the production of agricultural products to meet the needs of both food and energy.
(D) It is more advisable to start using energy more efficiently than to depend on alternative solutions that are not yet entirely developed.
(E) Using electricity for transportation and reducing the dependence on oil are unripe strategies that still have a minor impact in the current scenario.

(Interpretation) C: Correct – Line 21 "There is not sufficient land to cater for both food and fuel demand'. To cater means to provide or to meet (the demand).
Gabarito "C".

(ADVOGADO – PETROBRÁS BIO. – 2010 – CESGRANRIO) Nick Owen believes that

(A) stricter environmental regulations will impose even more restrictions on the already heavy challenges in oil supply.
(B) more demand for oil will certainly not interfere with the current support for ecological programs to reduce carbon emissions.
(C) further investments in newly found oil reserves will be the only alternative to help maintain future energy stability in the world.
(D) shifting to fuel production from tar sands can reduce the oil problems, since tar sands are more abundant and less expensive to drill.
(E) the exploration of lower grade resources seems to be the best solution to conform to the environmental policies in favor of low carbon emissions.

(Interpretation) A: Correct – Line 29: "Significant oil supply challenge will be compounded in the near future by rising demand and strengthening environmental policy". To compound means to add or to increase.
Gabarito "A".

(ADVOGADO – PETROBRÁS BIO. – 2010 – CESGRANRIO) In the text, 'contradictory estimates of oil reserve data available in the public domain.' (lines 38-39) refers to the fact that

(A) the figures on the probable amount of remaining oil in reserves known have been inaccurately announced.
(B) researchers in the Smith School have reached conclusions on the use of energy alternatives that confirm the opinion of political leaders.
(C) oil reserves estimates should be readjusted to indicate that around twelve hundred billion barrels are available for consumption.
(D) political and financial concerns have led to the announcement of precise data on oil production available to the public.
(E) only 850-900 billion barrels will be produced by the middle of the current decade.

(Interpretation) A: Correct – Meaning publicly available data give different levels of estimates and are therefore contradictory.
Gabarito "A".

(ADVOGADO – PETROBRÁS BIO. – 2010 – CESGRANRIO) In paragraph 7 (lines 40-50), Sir David King's main comment is that

(A) other low carbon alternatives are not available to replace the finite oil resources.
(B) the tipping point in oil production will not affect the underdeveloped economies of the world.
(C) business and governments are not expected to take quick measures to face the world economic problems.
(D) more money has to be spent on financing new fuel technologies that produce low carbon emissions.
(E) research, development and deployment of low carbon alternatives are the sole responsibility of university researchers.

(Interpretation) D: Correct – He states we need to face up to – i.e. acknowledge the problems and to spend more money on producing low carbon alternatives.
Gabarito "D".

(ADVOGADO – PETROBRÁS BIO. – 2010 – CESGRANRIO) "This challenge" in "This challenge will have a longer term effect on our economies..." (lines 43-44) refers to the

(A) uncertainty about the future of the global economy.
(B) unclear estimation of oil reserves reported by the government.
(C) low carbon emissions resulting from conventional oil extraction.
(D) political and financial interests of the world's economic leaders.
(E) confrontation of the unpleasant situation of oil shortage in the near future.

(Interpretation) E: Correct – 'This challenge' refers to oil uncertainty in the near future.
Gabarito "E".

(ADVOGADO – PETROBRÁS BIO. – 2010 – CESGRANRIO) In "...additional demand for oil could be met by non-conventional methods," (lines 52-53) the verb form could expresses

(A) certainty.
(B) necessity.
(C) possibility.
(D) obligation.
(E) permission.

(Grammar) C: 'Could be' refers to a possibility; i.e. it is possible to meet the demand for oil using nonconventional methods.
Gabarito "C".

(ADVOGADO – PETROBRÁS BIO. – 2010 – CESGRANRIO) According to the text, extracting oil from the Canadian tar sands

(A) can be harmful to the environment because it generates an additional demand for oil.
(B) requires unconventional drilling methods that cause lower impact on the nation's carbon footprint.
(C) is not feasible since it will require non-conventional financing to make up for the lower output rates.
(D) produces higher carbon emissions resulting from both the extraction and the deployment of fuel from this source.
(E) has not been authorized since Canada's governmental authorities have passed strict laws against the exploration of such reserves.

(Interpretation) D: Correct – 'double impact': carbon emissions are caused both from extraction and deployment from this source.
Gabarito "D".

The importance of discovering your plan B

By John W. Mullins and Randy Komisar

If the founders of Google, Starbucks, or PayPal had stuck to their original business plans, we'd likely never have heard of them. Instead, they made radical changes to their initial models, became household
5 names, and delivered huge returns for their founders and investors. How did they get from their Plan A to a business model that worked? Why did they succeed when most new ventures crash and burn?
Every aspiring entrepreneur, whether they
10 desire to start a new company or create something new within an existing company, has a Plan A — and virtually all of these individuals believe that their Plan A will work. They can probably even imagine how they'll look on the cover of *Fortune* or *Inc.*
15 magazine. Unfortunately, they are usually wrong. But what separates the ultimate successes from the rest is what they do when their first plan fails to catch on. Do they lick their wounds, get back on their feet, and morph their newly found insights into great businesses
20 or do they doggedly stick to their original plan?
Let's face an uncomfortable fact: the typical startup process, largely driven by poorly conceived business plans based on untested assumptions, is seriously flawed. Most new ventures, even those
25 with venture capital backing, share one common characteristic. They fail. But there is a better way to launch new ideas — without wasting years of your time and loads of investors' money. This better way is about discovering a business model that really works:
30 a Plan B, like those of Google and Starbucks, which grows out of the original idea, builds on it, and once it's in place, enables the business to grow rapidly and prosper.
Most of the time, breaking through to a better
35 business model takes time. And it takes error, too — error from which you learn. For Max Levchin, who wanted to build a business based on his cryptography expertise, Plans A through F didn't work, but Plan G turned out to be the ubiquitous PayPal we know today.

40 **Getting to Plan B in Your Business**

How can you break through to a business model that will work for your business? First, you'll need an idea to pursue. The best ideas resolve somebody's pain, some customer problem you've identified for which you
45 have a solution that might work. Alternatively, some good ideas take something in customers' lives that's pretty boring and create something so superior it provides true customer delight, as was the case for the Walkman and the iPod.
50 Next, you'll need to identify some analogs, portions of which you can borrow or adapt to help you understand the economics and various other facets of your proposed business and its business model. And you'll need antilogs, too. As we have seen from the Apple story,
55 analogs and antilogs don't have to only be from your own industry, though. Sometimes the most valuable insights come from rather unusual sources.
Having identified both analogs and antilogs, you can quickly reach conclusions about some things that
60 are, with at least a modicum of certainty, known about your venture. But it is not what you know that will likely scupper your Plan A, of course. It's what you don't know. The questions you cannot answer from historical precedent lead to your leaps of faith — beliefs you
65 hold about the answers to your questions despite having no real evidence that these beliefs are actually true.
To address your leaps of faith, you'll have to leap! Identify your key leaps of faith and then test
70 your hypothesis. That may mean opening a smaller shop than you aspire to operate, just to see how customers respond. It may mean trying different prices for your newly developed gadget to see which price makes sales pop. By identifying your leaps of
75 faith early and devising ways to test hypotheses that will prove or refute them, you are in a position to learn whether or not your Plan A will work before you waste too much time and money.

The European Business Review
Available at: http://www.europeanbusinessreview.com/?p=1608 -retrieved on July 4th, 2010.

(ADVOGADO – BNDES – 2010 – CESGRANRIO) According to the authors,

(A) businesses only prosper if they strictly adopt their Plan A.
(B) most famous companies fail because their leaders never stick to their original plan.
(C) it is necessary to be faithful to the first business plan and wait for customers to respond.
(D) some currently successful companies had to give up their initial plans for alternative business models.
(E) companies always fail when they decide to adopt their Plan B as a shortcut to their original business strategy.

(Interpretation) D: Correct – The author cites Starbucks, Google and PayPal as examples of this.
Gabarito "D".

(ADVOGADO – BNDES – 2010 – CESGRANRIO) Google, Starbucks and PayPal are mentioned in paragraph 1 (lines 1-8) since they

(A) are the only well-known companies in America nowadays.
(B) represent companies which have never delivered high returns to the investors.
(C) are examples of companies which made significant alterations to their original business plans.
(D) illustrate the kind of businesses that remained loyal to their original plans and fought for results.
(E) have founders who have been on the cover of *Fortune* magazine and are the world's richest men.

(Interpretation) C: Correct – These companies are said to have had a plan B or in the case of PayPal a plan F.
Gabarito "C".

(ADVOGADO – BNDES – 2010 – CESGRANRIO) Mulins and Komisar, in paragraph 3 (lines 21-33), state that the typical business startup process is usually unsuccessful because it

(A) does not invest rich sums or waste years on precise planning to design an elaborate business model.
(B) shares common characteristics with traditional businesses that have survived crises.
(C) expects the business to grow rapidly and prosper faster than all other companies in the market.
(D) rejects venture capital funding and does not expect immediate returns.
(E) is based on inadequately designed business plans and on market hypothesis that are not previously tested.

(Interpretation) E: Correct – Line 22 - "largely driven by poorly conceived business plans based on untested assumptions'. This reflects the lack of testing and bad design of business plans.
Gabarito "E".

(ADVOGADO – BNDES – 2010 – CESGRANRIO) Max Levchin, mentioned in paragraph 4 (lines 34-39), can be considered a(an)

(A) persistent businessman who fought for success.
(B) careless worker who didn't take time to build a business model.
(C) foolish entrepreneur who insisted on opening his own company.
(D) expert in cryptography who failed as a businessman.
(E) impatient investor who did not believe PayPal would prosper.

(Interpretation) A: Correct – He tried repeatedly to make his company a success and it is even said to have had a plan F. This illustrates persistence and a fighting spirit, B: Incorrect – No evidence is given that suggests he was careless or that he had no business model, C: Incorrect – No evidence is given to support that he was foolish, D: Incorrect – He was an expert in cryptography who eventually became a very successful businessman, E: Incorrect – He was very patient and had a great deal of belief that PayPal would succeed.
Gabarito "A".

(ADVOGADO – BNDES – 2010 – CESGRANRIO) The term in parentheses expresses the idea introduced by the term in **bold** in

(A) "**Instead**, they made radical changes to their initial models," – lines 3-4 (replacement).
(B) "**Unfortunately**, they are usually wrong." – line 15 (reason).
(C) "**Alternatively**, some good ideas take something in customers' lives that's pretty boring…" – lines 45-47 (cause).
(D) "**Next**, you'll need to identify some analogs," – line 50 (exemplification).
(E) "beliefs you hold about the answers to your questions **despite** having no real evidence…" – lines 64-66 (consequence).

(Grammar) A: Correct – 'Instead' refers to replacement, B: Incorrect – "Unfortunately' refers to regret, C: Incorrect - 'Alternatively' refers to substitution, D: Incorrect – 'Next' refers to a process, E: Incorrect – 'despite' refers to contrast or surprise.
Gabarito "A".

(ADVOGADO – BNDES – 2010 – CESGRANRIO) In the fragments "…their first plan fails to catch on." (line 17) and "How can you break through to a business model…" (line 41), the expressions "catch on" and "break through to" mean, respectively,

(A) arrange; find.
(B) work; discover.
(C) capture; give in.
(D) pick up; destroy.
(E) triumph; deteriorate.

(Vocabulary) B: Correct – 'to catch on' means 'to work', 'to breakthrough' means 'to discover'. A breakthrough is a discovery.
Gabarito "B".

(ADVOGADO – BNDES – 2010 – CESGRANRIO) The expression "…leaps of faith" (line 64) refers to

(A) a religious conviction that the business project is definitely going to prosper.
(B) confidence on the various concrete evidences that your business model will surely be successful.
(C) everything you do not know about the returns of your investment and should not worry about.
(D) knowledge about historical precedents that are applicable to your company's current situation.
(E) assumptions about the aspects of the business you propose that are carefully thought of but not tested.

(Vocabulary) E: Correct – A leap of faith is to believe or trust in something that cannot be proven by fact.
Gabarito "E".

(ADVOGADO – BNDES – 2010 – CESGRANRIO) The word "might" in "… you have a solution that might work." (lines 44-45) can be replaced without change in meaning by

(A) must surely.
(B) will certainly.
(C) may probably.

(D) can eventually.
(E) should definitely.

(Grammar) A: Incorrect – 'must surely' implies certainty, B: Incorrect – 'will' implies certainty, C: Correct – 'might' implies probability. D: Incorrect – 'can' implies ability, E: Incorrect – should implies obligation or certainty.
Gabarito "C".

(ADVOGADO – BNDES – 2010 – CESGRANRIO) The pair of expressions that express opposing ideas is

(A) "...stuck to..." (line 2) – abandoned.
(B) "...grows out of... " (line 31) – develops from.
(C) "...pursue." (line 43) - follow.
(D) "...scupper..." (line 62) – ruin
(E) "...devising..." (line 75) – elaborating.

(Vocabulary) A: Correct – 'to stick to' means 'to remain committed to something'. 'To abandon' means 'to give up' and is therefore the opposite in meaning.
Gabarito "A".

(ADVOGADO – BNDES – 2010 – CESGRANRIO) The sentence "It may mean trying different prices for your newly developed gadget to see which price makes sales pop." (lines 72-74) implies that

(A) higher product pricing will certainly lead to more market sales.
(B) sales are determined solely by the characteristics of the gadget.
(C) the most appropriate price should be defined by the competitors.
(D) the cheaper the product is, the more profitable the company will be.
(E) previous testing of price ranges will help find the one which will boost sales.

(Vocabulary) E: Correct – 'to make sales pop' means 'to make sales increase'. The meaning here is that different price ranges must be tried before finding out which will be successful in terms of boosting sales.
Gabarito "E".

2. Língua Espanhola

Rodrigo Goyena Soares

Texto 1

Internacional

Obama expondrá en el G-20 su reforma financiera como «modelo» a seguir

Obama culpa a los bancos de desatar la peor crisis financiera en 80 años

El País - ESPAÑA

Día 26/06/2010 - 10h56

El presidente de Estados Unidos, Barack Obama, pidió el viernes al resto de los líderes mundiales reunidos en la cumbre del G-20 que sigan sus pasos a la hora de reformar el sistema financiero, al
5 tiempo que otros países alabaron sus progresos en la lucha contra las elevadas deudas que amenazan la recuperación global. Un día después de que los legisladores estadounidenses alcanzaron un acuerdo histórico sobre una reforma al sistema financiero del
10 país, Obama animó a sus colegas del G-20 a cumplir sus propias promesas para acabar con las maniobras arriesgadas de los bancos, a las que ya ha culpado de desatar la peor crisis financiera en 80 años. "Espero que este fin de semana en Toronto podamos
15 aprovechar estos progresos coordinando nuestros esfuerzos para promocionar el crecimiento económico, conseguir la reforma financiera y fortalecer la economía global", dijo el mandatario poco antes de salir de Washington para ir a Canadá. "Necesitamos
20 actuar concertados por una simple razón: esta crisis demostró y los acontecimientos continúan afirmando que nuestras economías nacionales están inseparablemente relacionadas", añadió.
Los países miembros del G-20, que conforman
25 dos tercios de la población mundial, se reúnen el sábado y el domingo en Toronto. El G-8, formado por Alemania, Canadá, Estados Unidos, Francia, Italia, Japón, Reino Unido y Rusia, se reúne el viernes y el sábado, centrándose sobre todo en ayuda al desarrollo
30 para los países más pobres. Mientras Obama puede reclamar el liderazgo en la reforma regulatoria, Estados Unidos va por detrás de Alemania, Reino Unido y otros países que priorizan los recortes en el gasto para reducir los déficit. Otros posibles motivos
35 de conflicto son el comercio y la divisa china, el yuan. Ya al comienzo de la reunión del G-8, la canciller alemana, Angela Merkel, negó que hubiera divisiones, y aseguró que no hay contradicción entre recortar los gastos e impulsar un crecimiento sostenible. Además
40 declaró que Estados Unidos no mostró una visión opuesta a la política europea de reducción del déficit.

El primer ministro británico, David Cameron, quitó importancia a la división transatlántica, pero dijo que para reducir los desequilibrios entre los países
45 más exportadores y aquellos con más deudas también haría falta que Estados Unidos se apriete el cinturón.
"Parte de la gestión de los desequilibrios es que los países con más déficit se arremanguen, hagan el trabajo y se aseguren de que están viviendo con sus
50 medios", afirmó. El año pasado, el G-20 se comprometió a coordinar una serie de reformas a finales del 2012. Mientras Estados Unidos ha cumplido la mayor parte de estos compromisos, Europa todavía no ha aportado unas normas amplias al acuerdo. Además,
55 países como Canadá o Japón, cuyos bancos tuvieron un mejor rendimiento durante la crisis, han puesto objeciones a algunas de las propuestas de reformas, argumentando que castigan de manera injusta a los bancos que no contribuyeron a la misma. El primer
60 ministro japonés, Naoto Kan, dijo que el debate de las reformas debería tener en cuenta la situación de cada país.

Disponible en: <http://www.abc.es/20100626/internacional/obama-reforma-fi nanciera-201006260257.html>.

(Advogado – BNDES – 2010 – CESGRANRIO) Indique la opción que coincide con las ideas presentes em el texto.

(A) El presidente americano impuso a los jefes de Estado, reunidos en la cumbre, su modelo de reforma económica.
(B) Todos los líderes allí reunidos han decidido adoptar como reto las orientaciones de Barack Obama.
(C) Para Obama, todos deben unir esfuerzos para solucionar la crisis, ya que las economías se encuentran compaginadas.
(D) Han sido considerados los motivos principales del conflicto el comercio y la moneda china.
(E) Muchos representantes de los países no estaban de acuerdo con echar la culpa por la crisis a los bancos.

(Interpretación) A: Incorrecta. El mandatario americano no impuso, pero pidió a los jefes de Estado, reunidos en la cumbre, que sigan sus pasos a la hora de reformar el sistema financiero. No se trata de una imposición, pero de una solicitación (líneas 1 a 5).
B: Incorrecta. En las líneas 43 a 45, se lee que David Cameron, primer ministro británico, "quitó importancia a la división transatlántica", con la cual se infiere que no todos los líderes allí reunidos han decidido adoptar las orientaciones de Barack Obama. En efecto, en las líneas 30 a 43, se sostiene que hay divisiones entre líderes por lo que a cuales medidas adoptar se refiere.

C: Correcta. Se trata precisamente de la afirmación de Barack Obama que encontramos en las líneas 19 a 23 del fragmento. Textualmente, el mandatario americano declaró que "necesitamos actuar concertados por una simple razón: esta crisis demostró y los acontecimientos continúan afirmando que nuestras economías nacionales están inseparablemente relacionadas", o "compaginados", término sinónimo, en lenguaje connotativo, a "relacionadas".

D: Incorrecta. El comercio y la divisa china, el yuan, son "otros posibles motivos de conflicto" (línea 34-35), y no los motivos principales del conflicto.

E: Incorrecta. Fueron pocos los representantes de los países que no estaban de acuerdo con echar la culpa por la crise a los bancos. En la línea 55, se lee que Canadá y Japón "han puesto objeciones a algunas de las propuestas de reformas, argumentando que castigan de manera injusta a los bancos que no contribuyeron a la misma".

Gabarito "C".

(Advogado – BNDES – 2010 – CESGRANRIO) Según lo que se advierte en el texto,

(A) la situación de los países debería evaluarse de forma equivalente, según el ministro japonés.
(B) la canciller alemana afirmó que no existen contradicciones entre disminuir los gastos y estimular el crecimiento sostenible.
(C) el liderazgo por la reforma regulatoria fue defendido tanto por Obama como por los demás jefes de Estado.
(D) el enfoque del desarrollo para los países pobres es prioritario tanto para el G-20 como para el G-8 allí reunidos.
(E) Canadá y Japón aceptaron sin restricciones las normas sugeridas por los demás representantes en ló que atañe a la reforma bancaria.

(Interpretación) A: Incorrecta. El mandatario japonés advirtió que "el debate de las reformas debería tener en cuenta la situación de cada país" (líneas 60 a 62), y no que la situación de los países debería evaluarse de forma equivalente.

B: Correcta. Angela Merkel, canciller de Alemania, "aseguró que no hay contradicción entre recortar los gastos e impulsar un crecimiento sostenible" (líneas 37 a 39).

C: Incorrecta. "Mientras Obama puede reclamar el liderazgo en la reforma regulatoria, Estados Unidos va por detrás de Alemania, Reino Unido y otros países que priorizan los recortes en el gasto para reducir los déficits (líneas 30 a 34). Se deduce, por consiguiente, que los recortes en el gasto fueron motivos de conflicto, con el cual el liderazgo estadounidense no fue defendido por los demás jefes de Estado.

D: Incorrecta. En ningún momento de explicita que el enfoque del desarrollo para los países pobres es prioritario para el G-20. Además, según se lee en las líneas 29 y 30, los países del G-8, y no del G-20, se reúnen para centrarse sobre todo en ayuda al desarrollo a los países más pobres, lo que no quiere decir que el enfoque del desarrollo sea prioritario.

E: Incorrecta. En la línea 55, se lee que Canadá y Japón "han puesto objeciones a algunas de las propuestas de reformas, argumentando que castigan de manera injusta a los bancos que no contribuyeron a la misma".

Gabarito "B".

(Advogado – BNDES – 2010 – CESGRANRIO) En lo que se refiere al G-20 se asevera que

(A) cumplió con todos los compromisos concernientes a la reforma.
(B) representa cerca de un treinta por cien de la población mundial.
(C) visa fundamentalmente al desarrollo de los países pobres.
(D) busca minimizar los perjuicios ocasionados por la crisis bancaria.
(E) se plantea como reto castigar a los bancos que no contribuyan con la reforma.

(Interpretación) D: Correcto. La alternativa correcta es la letra D. En las líneas 10 a 14, se entiende que Obama instó sus homólogos del G-20 a "cumplir sus promesas para acabar con las maniobras arriesgadas de los bancos", con lo cual se deduce que el G-20 busca minimizar los perjuicios ocasionados por la crisis bancaria. Las demás alternativas no encuentran respaldo en el texto.

Gabarito "D".

(Advogado – BNDES – 2010 – CESGRANRIO) La expresión **al tiempo** en el primer párrafo (líneas 4-5) identifica

(A) simultaneidad.
(B) conformidad.
(C) semejanza.
(D) exclusión.
(E) transitoriedad.

(Vocabulario) A: Correcto. La alternativa correcta es la letra A. En este caso, l a expresión "al tiempo que" (líneas 4-5) identifica simultaneidad. En otras palabras, se podría escribir el fragmento indicado de esta forma: "el presidente de Estados Unidos [ ] pidió [ ], simultáneamente al hecho que otros países alabaron [ ]". Por lo tanto, no se trata de una expresión de conformidad, de semejanza, de exclusión o de transitoriedad.

Gabarito "A".

(Advogado – BNDES – 2010 – CESGRANRIO) "Mientras Estados Unidos ha cumplido la mayor parte de estos compromisos, Europa todavía no ha aportado unas normas amplias al acuerdo." (líneas 52-54)

Considerando de forma aislada el fragmento anterior, El término "todavía" **NO** se podría sustituir por

(A) aún.
(B) no obstante.
(C) sin embargo.
(D) al contrario.
(E) de igual modo.

(Vocabulario) E: Incorrecto. La alternativa incorrecta es la letra E. En este caso, el término "todavía" es equivalente a "aún". Indica, por lo tanto, hasta un momento determinado desde el tiempo anterior. Al igual que en portugués, en castellano, el término "todavía" puede tener valor de concesión y de negación, siendo posible su substitución por "no obstante", "sin embargo" o "al contrario". Decir que el término se podría substituir no equivale a inferir identidad semántica; por consiguiente, las alternativas A, B, C y D están correctas.

Gabarito "E".

(Advogado – BNDES – 2010 – CESGRANRIO) De acuerdo con el texto, **SE EXCLUYE** de los planes para la recuperación de la economía la(el)

(A) lucha contra la amenaza de las altas deudas.
(B) exclusión de maniobras bancarias arriesgadas.
(C) actuación conjunta y coordinación de esfuerzos entre todos.
(D) corte de gastos para disminuición de déficit.
(E) decisión de cada país por sus propios caminos.

(Interpretación) E: Incorrecto. La alternativa incorrecta es la letra E. A lo ancho y a lo largo del texto, se hace hincapié en el hecho que los planes para la recuperación de la economía deben excluir la decisión de cada país por sus propios caminos. Debido a la interdependencia entre economías nacionales, se advogan soluciones concertadas, coordinadas y harmónicamente tomadas.

Gabarito "E".

Texto 2

La cumbre de la hamburguesa

27/06/10 – Por Gustavo Sierra

Barack Obama y el presidente ruso Dimitri Medvedev se llevan muy bien. En el último año y medio se vieron siete veces. Esta semana estuvieron nuevamente juntos en Washington. Y la química entre
5 los dos fue tan compatible que el estadounidense lo llevó a comer a su restaurante favorito, la hamburguesería Ray´s Hell de Arlington, a diez minutos de la Casa Blanca. Y allí, con sendos "cuarto de libra" en la mano, discutieron y llegaron a un acuerdo sobre el
10 tema que más los preocupaba: el nivel del cloro utilizado en la desinfección de los pollos que se exportan a Rusia.

Para entonces ya habían acordado sobre las sanciones a Irán y Norcorea, los detalles del histórico
15 tratado de no proliferación nuclear que firmaron a principios de año en Praga y la entrada de Rusia en la Organización Mundial de Comercio. Incluso se aventuraron en las ríspidas aguas de la invasión rusa a Georgia, un aliado de Washington. Ese conflicto
20 ocurrido en agosto del 2008 había degradado las relaciones entre las otrora superpotencias a su nivel más bajo desde el fin de la Guerra Fría.

Tanta es la estima que se tienen estos dos líderes que Medvedev dijo que recientemente habían
25 tenido una conversación telefónica que se extendió por una hora y 45 minutos. "Me quedó la oreja colorada", expresó el ruso. Y hasta encontraron una solución para evitar estos malestares. Dijeron que a partir de ahora se enviarían mensajes a través de Twitter.
30 Después se sacaron los sacos para aguantar los 33 grados de la media tarde y cruzaron el Parque Lafayette, frente a la Casa Blanca, para ir a la Cámara de Comercio, con un andar de actores franceses de la Nouvelle Vague.
35 Pero el tema crucial lo trataron mientras le ponían ketchup a la hamburguesa. En enero, Rusia adoptó un nuevo código de sanidad alimenticia y descubrió que los pollos que viene comiendo su población desde hace 15 años ahora contienen un nivel de cloro
40 más elevado el adecuado. Las productoras estadounidenses perdieron el negocio.

Hamburguesa de carne vacuna mediante, Obama y Medvedev acordaron reanudar el comercio de pollo. Algo que jamás se podía haber arreglado a través
45 del teléfono rojo.

Disponible en: http://www.clarin.com/mundo/cumbre-hamburguesa_0_287971343.html

(Advogado – BNDES – 2010 – CESGRANRIO) La opción en la cual **NO** hay coincidencia de sentido entre la definición expuesta y la palabra en el texto es

(A) **Sanciones** – penas que una ley o un reglamento establece para sus infractores. (línea 14)

(B) **Estima** – consideración que se hace de alguien por su calidad y circunstancias. (línea 23)

(C) **Hamburguesa** – tortita de carne picada, con diversos ingredientes, frita o asada. (línea 36)

(D) **Negocio** – utilidad o interés que se logra en lo que se trata, comercia o pretende. (línea 41)

(E) **Vacuna** – virus o principio orgánico que se inocula a una persona o a un animal. (línea 42)

(Vocabulario) E: Incorrecto. La alternativa correcta es la letra E. Todas las definiciones de los términos seleccionados corresponden a las expuestas, con excepción de la alternativa E. El término "vacuno", en este caso, equivale a "bovino", en portugués, y nada tiene que ver con un virus o principio orgánico que se inocula a una persona o a un animal.

Gabarito "E".

(Advogado – BNDES – 2010 – CESGRANRIO) "Incluso se aventuraron en las ríspidas aguas de La invasión rusa a Georgia, un aliado de Washington." (líneas 17-19)

Tras la lectura del fragmento arriba se comprende que em ese momento, según el enunciador, los presidentes trataron de un tema

(A) parcial.
(B) polémico.
(C) insoluble.
(D) prescindible.
(E) inmejorable.

(Interpretación) B: Correcto. La alternativa correcta es la letra B. La metáfora "ríspidas aguas" equivale, en este caso, a un asunto polémico, delicado y de difícil solución. Otra alternativa seria la expresión "por aguas turbulentas". Por lo tanto, la metáfora no tiene relación con la parcialidad, la insolubilidad, la característica prescindible o inmejorable de un asunto.

Gabarito "B".

(Advogado – BNDES – 2010 – CESGRANRIO) Aunque el texto trate de un tema importante en el escenario mundial, es posible identificar en él rasgos de ironía, como

(A) algunas mentiras que se presentan como verdad y establecen una relación con la ficción.
(B) el vocabulario típico de la política, como si su interlocutor fuera uno de ellos.
(C) las expresiones que en general se relacionan a parejas enamoradas.
(D) las palabras no adecuadas a la formalidad del tema, como jergas y palabrotas.
(E) las opiniones parciales relación a uno de los lados de la pelea, de forma caricaturesca.

(Interpretación) C: Correcto. La alternativa correcta es la letra C. Las expresiones que en general se relacionan a parejas enamorados son las siguientes: "se llevan muy bien" (línea 2), "se vieron siete veces" (línea 4), "la química entre los dos" (líneas 4 y 5) y "una conversación telefónica que se extendió por una hora y 45 minutos" (líneas 24 y 25).

Gabarito "C".

(Advogado – BNDES – 2010 – CESGRANRIO) Según el texto, afirmase que

(A) las dos potencias, Estados Unidos y Rusia, restablecieron el comercio de la carne de pollo.
(B) las sanciones a Irán y Norcorea continúan como punto de desacuerdo entre los dos países.
(C) las hamburguesas de carne vacuna rusa tenían uma cantidad de cloro nociva a la salud.

(D) el actual código de sanidad alimenticia rusa condeno la salsa de tomate norteamericana.
(E) una gran parte de los malestares entre las dos potencias se soluciona por el teléfono rojo.

(Interpretación) A: Correcta. En las líneas 42 a 45 se afirma que Obama y Medvedev "acordaron reanudar el comercio de pollo", es decir, el comercio de dicho bien fue reanudado.
B. Incorrecta. Las sanciones a Irán y a Norcorea ya habían sido acordadas antes del encuentro de los dos mandatarios en la hamburguesería.
C: Incorrecta. Eran los pollos, y no las carnes vacunas, que contenían un nivel de cloro más elevado que el adecuado (líneas 39).
D: Incorrecta. No hay registro en el texto al respecto de esta afirmación.
E: Incorrecta. No se afirma en el texto que gran parte de los malestares entre las dos potencias se soluciona por el teléfono rojo, pero que se solucionó el problema del nivel de cloro en el pollo ruso, "algo que jamás se podía haber arreglado a través del teléfono rojo" (línea 44-45).
Gabarito "A".

¿En qué consiste una intervención light de la economía?

La situación de España en estos momentos se parece mucho a una madeja en la que cada hilo está tan enredado con los demás que distinguirlos es casi imposible. Es cierto que cada uno tiene un color, pero al final casi es preferible tejer una bufanda que incluya todos los tonos antes de esforzarse en separar cada uno de ellos. Claro que cuando la metáfora se traslada a la alta política europea, la bufanda se convierte en un nido de polémica y buscar el inicio de cada hilo se vuelve materia fundamental. Y las preguntas se disparan. ¿Está intervenida España? ¿A qué nivel? ¿Por qué concepto? España ahora mismo se enfrenta a dos procesos ligados entre sí. Por un lado está su déficit, excesivo a todas luces e inmerso en una senda obligada de rebaja para ajustarse a las exigencias comunitarias. Y por otro está el rescate a la banca nacional, que requiere el cumplimiento estricto de la disciplina fiscal del país para que pueda recibirlo: un nudo perfectamente elaborado... e indisoluble.

En el centro, un Gobierno que necesitaba con urgencia ayuda de Bruselas para obtener una flexibilización de los objetivos de reducción del déficit –logró una mejora de un punto en el objetivo para este año (hasta el 6,3%) y el retraso de un año en la reducción al 3% (que ahora pasa a 2014)– y disponer cuanto antes del dinero del rescate a la banca (una ayuda de 30.000 millones) o al menos de parte de él. Y eso costará. Al estar tan ligados ambos procesos, es complicado saber qué implica qué. Pero al menos hay dos núcleos claros de condicionalidad: la economía en general y el sector financiero. A finales de mayo, la Comisión Europea publicó sus recomendaciones para España en materia de cumplimiento fiscal y en ellas quedan claras varias cosas que tendrá que hacer el Gobierno (meter en cintura a las Comunidades Autónomas, la subida del IVA, el retraso en la edad de jubilación al acompasarlo a la esperanza de vida, la reforma de la recién acometida reforma laboral, la eliminación de la deducción por compra de vivienda...). Y los bancos que requieran auxilio deberán tener una ratio de capital específica y estarán sometidos a una estricta supervisión financiera por parte de la troika (El triunvirato entre Bruselas, el BCE y el FMI)

CincoDias, 10/07/2012. Disponible en: <http://www.cincodias.com/articulo/mercados/exdirectivos-banco-valencia--investigados-presuntaestafa/20120710cdscdsmer_6/>.

(Auditor Fiscal da Receita Federal – 2012 – ESAF) De acuerdo con el texto, ni el rescate a la banca ni el periodo de gracia para el déficit:

(A) serán gratis.
(B) tienen que ver con asuntos tributarios.
(C) se relacionan entre sí.
(D) paliarán la crisis española.
(E) tranquilizan el mercado.

(Interpretación) A, B, C, D, E: La alternativa correcta es la letra A. En el segundo párrafo, se afirma que ni el rescate a la banca –"y disponer cuanto antes del dinero del rescate a la banca"–, ni el periodo de gracia para el déficit –"y el retraso de un año en la reducción"–, será gratis –"Y eso costará". Las demás alternativas no tienen respaldo en el texto.
Gabarito "A".

(Auditor Fiscal da Receita Federal – 2012 – ESAF) En el texto se dice que la situación de España:

(A) se parece a una barahúnda.
(B) incluye factores diversos e interrelacionados.
(C) es bien común.
(D) está controlada.
(E) se restringe a los bancos.

(Interpretación) A: Incorrecto. La metáfora empleada es la de una bufanda, y no la de una barahúnda, que quiere decir "ruidos y confusiones de gran porte", según la Real Academia Española.
B: Correcto. Los factores diversos e interrelacionados están expuestos en el primer párrafo, precisamente, cuando se afirma que "la situación en España [...] se parece mucho a una madeja en la que cada hilo está tan enredado con los demás que distinguirlos es casi imposible". El término "madeja" quiere decir un conjunto de hilos recogidos en vueltas idénticas, para que luego se puedan devanar con facilidad. Se trata, por lo tanto, de la metáfora de la bufanda, expuesta en las líneas siguientes.
C: Incorrecto. No hay mención a la idea de bien común en el texto.
D: Incorrecto. La metáfora de la madeja y de la bufanda permite inducir que la situación en España no está controlada.
E: Incorrecto. La situación en España no se restringe a los bancos. Al final del primer párrafo, se admite que España, por un lado, debe ajustarse a las exigencias comunitarias para solucionar el déficit y, por otro lado, debe confrontar el problema del rescate a la banca nacional.
Gabarito "B".

(Auditor Fiscal da Receita Federal – 2012 – ESAF) La expresión "meter en cintura" que aparece en la línea 33/34 del texto significa:

(A) matarlas en el aire.
(B) meter a todas una trola.
(C) flexibilizar la administración comunitaria.

(D) dejar más independiente la gestión propia.
(E) someter a una conducta que se considera correcta.

(Vocabulario) A, B, C, D, E: La alternativa correcta es la letra E. La expresión "meter en cintura" significa reconducir un comportamiento; en otras palabras, quiere decir someter a una conducta que se considera correcta. Las demás alternativas no tienen relación cualquier con la expresión en consideración.
Gabarito "E".

(Auditor Fiscal da Receita Federal – 2012 – ESAF) Según el texto, la ayuda de la Comisión Europea a España supone:

(A) invertir recursos en sus reservas internacionales.
(B) conducir con independencia la economía.
(C) reducir el déficit fiscal en un punto este año.
(D) expandir los recursos estatales en 30 mil millones.
(E) cumplir un entramado de requisitos.

(Interpretación) A, B, C, D, E: La alternativa correcta es la letra E. La ayuda de la Comisión Europea a España, conforme se lee en el segundo párrafo, supone cumplir un entramado de requisitos, entre ellos, "meter en cintura a las Comunidades Autónomas, la subida del IVA, el retraso en la edad de jubilación al acompasarlo a la esperanza de vida, la reforma de la recién acometida reforma laboral, la eliminación de la deducción por compra de vivienda". Sabemos que son esos los requisitos, dado que la frase previamente referida está antecedida por la siguiente afirmación: "a finales de mayo, la Comisión Europea publicó sus recomendaciones para España en materia de cumplimiento fiscal y en ellas quedan claras varias cosas que tendrá que hacer el Gobierno".
Gabarito "E".

$18,5 millardos suman pagos de deuda interna para año y medio

Desde el año 2009 el nivel de endeudamiento está en ascenso y eso impacta en las cuentas, debido a que el Ejecutivo Nacional tiene que orientar más recursos a los pagos a futuro de la deuda pública. Los datos del Ministerio de Planificación y Finanzas proyectan en 27,9 millardos de dólares el servicio de deuda que deberá efectuar el Gobierno central en año y medio, y el mayor peso en las cancelaciones lo representarán las obligaciones internas, que al cierre del primer trimestre del año absorbieron 3,3 millones de dólares y para el resto de 2012 y todo 2013 el servicio será de 18,5 millardos de dólares. Por la aceleración de las emisiones, al término de marzo, el saldo de la deuda interna llegó a 42,9 millardos de dólares (184,5 millardos de bolívares), un aumento de 58% en 12 meses. Las cifras del despacho de las finanzas públicas detallan que al cierre de marzo el servicio de deuda externa fue de 4,4 millardos de dólares y para el resto de 2012 y 2013 se estima en 9,4 millardos de dólares. Para el término del primer trimestre el saldo de las obligaciones externas fue de 43,5 millardos de dólares, un repunte en 12 meses de 17%.

Aunque el precio del crudo promedio se mantiene por encima de los 100 dólares, igual la administración venezolana se endeuda para incrementar sus disponibilidades. El Gobierno, más allá de lo previsto en la Ley de Endeudamiento, ha creado nuevas vías para colocar instrumentos de deuda y esquemas como el Fondo de Desarrollo Nacional y el Fondo Simón Bolívar para la Reconstrucción, autorizados para hacer operaciones de crédito público. A ello se añade, la reforma a la Ley Orgánica de Administración Financiera del Sector Pública que faculta al primer mandatario nacional a emitir bonos para atender "el financiamiento del servicio de deuda pública así como las circunstancias sobrevenidas, no previstas o difíciles de prever para el momento de entrada en vigencia de la Ley de Endeudamiento Anual".

El Universal, 11/07/12.
Disponible en: <http://www.eluniversal.com/economia/120711/185-millardos-suman-pagos-de-deuda-interna-para-ano-y-medio>

(Auditor Fiscal da Receita Federal – 2012 – ESAF) De acuerdo con el texto, la deuda pública venezolana:

(A) asciende a 27,9 millardos de dólares.
(B) se explica por la expansión de la economía local.
(C) ha crecido en los últimos tres años.
(D) incide poco en las cuentas públicas.
(E) la impulsa el precio del crudo.

(Interpretación) A: Incorrecto. No es la deuda pública venezolana que ascienda a 27,9 millardos de dólares, pero el servicio de deuda que asciende a esa suma (línea 3).
B: Incorrecto. No hay relación establecida en el texto entre la expansión de la economía local y el crecimiento de la deuda pública venezolana.
C: Correcto. En la primera línea del fragmento, se afirma que "desde el año de 2009 el nivel de endeudamiento está en ascenso" en Venezuela. Teniendo en cuenta que el artículo fue publicado en 2012, se puede concluir que la deuda venezolana ha crecido en los últimos tres años.
D: Incorrecto. Al contrario de lo que se afirma en la alternativa, la deuda pública venezolana incide substancialmente en las cuentas públicas. Para llegar a esa conclusión, podemos valernos de la penúltima línea del primer párrafo, según la cual se afirma que "al cierre de marzo el servicio de deuda externa fue de 4,4 millardos de dólares y para el resto de 2012 y 2014 se estima en 9,4 millardos de dólares". El aumento de la deuda indica que hay incidencia substancial en las cuentas públicas.
E: Incorrecto. Al contrario de lo que se afirma en la alternativa, la deuda pública venezolana crece, aunque el precio del crudo, es decir, del petróleo crudo, "se mantiene por encima de los 100 dólares" (línea 1 del segundo párrafo). La relación de concesión nos permite deducir que el aumento del precio del crudo debería funcionar como freno al crecimiento de la deuda pública venezolana.
Gabarito "C".

(Auditor Fiscal da Receita Federal – 2012 – ESAF) Según el texto, el gobierno venezolano:

(A) se valdrá de diferentes fondos para pagar la deuda.
(B) confía en las ventas de petróleo para enfrentar la deuda.
(C) dejará de hacer pagos internos por valor de 18,5 millardos de dólares.
(D) administra la deuda pública en un marco legal.
(E) ha creado nuevas vías y mecanismos para reducir la deuda.

(Interpretación) A, B, C, D, E: La única alternativa que encuentra respaldo en el texto es la D. El gobierno venezolano administra la deuda pública en marco legal, según se lee la última frase del segundo párrafo: "a ello se añade, la reforma a la Ley Orgánica de Administración Financiera del Sector Pública que faculta al primer mandatario nacional a emitir bonos para atender *el financiamiento del servicio de deuda pública así como las circunstancias sobrevenidas, no previstas o difíciles de prever para el momento de entrada en vigencia de la Ley de Endeudamiento Anual*". Si la reforma de la Ley Orgánica de Administración Financiera permite al mandatario nacional administrar la deuda pública; y si la Ley Orgánica es en marco legal de gestión de cuentas públicas, se concluye que la deuda pública venezolana es manejada en marco legal.
Gabarito "D".

(Auditor Fiscal da Receita Federal – 2012 – ESAF) En el texto se dice que, en materia de deuda pública:

(A) la interna ha crecido menos que la externa.
(B) la externa aumentó 17% desde 2009.
(C) se proyecta el pago de 27 mil 900 millones de dólares.
(D) la interna sumaba 42 millones 900 mil dólares en marzo.
(E) se observó un descenso de las obligaciones externas.

(Interpretación) A: Incorrecto. En el primer párrafo se afirma que la deuda interna alcanzó 42,9 millardos de dólares, y que la deuda externa fue de 4,4 millares de dólares. Además, si tenemos en cuenta que la deuda interna creció 58% en 12 meses y que la deuda externa tuvo un "repunte en 12 meses de 17%" (primer párrafo), no se puede afirmar que la deuda interna creció menos que la externa.
B: Incorrecto. El "repunte en 12 meses de 17%" (primer párrafo) de la deuda externa concierne al periodo que va del primer trimestre de 2011 al primer trimestre de 2012. No se puede afirmar, por lo tanto, que la deuda externa aumentó de 17% desde 2009.
C: Correcto. En el primer párrafo, se afirma que el "Ministerio de Planificación y Finanzas proyect[a] en 27,9 millardos de dólares el servicio de deuda que deberá efectuar el Gobierno central en año y medio"; el punto neurálgico de la alternativa reside en saber que 27,9 millardos de dólares equivalen a 27 mil 900 millones de la misma moneda.
D: Incorrecto. Por el mismo artificio matemático que el de la alternativa D, sabemos que 42,9 millardos de dólares no equivalen a 42 millones 900 mil de la misma moneda, pero a 42 mil 900 millones.
E: Incorrecto. Por lo contrario, según se lee en la última frase del primer párrafo, hubo un repunte de las obligaciones externas, y no un descenso.
Gabarito "C".

Hay que firmar un acuerdo con la UE, pero acorde con el Modelo de Desarrollo Ecuatoriano

Analizar la firma de un acuerdo con la Unión Europea (UE), requiere de una revisión de las estadísticas de esta relación comercial y, por ende, de la posición del Gobierno ecuatoriano. Las cifras revelan que el crecimiento de las exportaciones de nuestro país a la UE, en los últimos 7 años, ha sido importante; escenario pese al cual el Ejecutivo ha expresado su negativa de firmar un acuerdo bajo las mismas condiciones de Perú y Colombia, y más bien ha planteado un Acuerdo Comercial de Desarrollo (ACD). El Coordinador de Investigaciones Socioeconómicas de la Escuela Superior Politécnica del Litoral (ESPOL), Fabricio Zanzzi, coincide en que firmar un acuerdo así no está acorde con el Modelo de Desarrollo Ecuatoriano; de ahí, que sugiera estudiar a fondo el caso y luego firmar.

Mientras el aumento de las ventas ecuatorianas a la UE es de aproximadamente un 19% anual; actualmente, nuestro país exporta alrededor de US$2,630 millones a este mercado, es decir, más de 2.4 veces de lo que le vendía en el 2003; realidad que lo convierte en el tercer destino de nuestros productos, después de Estados Unidos y la Comunidad Andina (CAN). El 93% de estas exportaciones son denominadas no petroleras, siendo los productos primarios los de mayor importancia. El Banano es el principal de ellos, de acuerdo a las cifras de Eurostat, el mayor proveedor es Colombia con el 26%, seguido de Ecuador con el 24% del mercado, lo que represento aproximadamente US$864 millones, en el 2010.

Ambito.com, 19.07.12.
Disponible en: <http://www.ambito.com/noticia.asp?id=646118>.

(Auditor Fiscal da Receita Federal – 2012 – ESAF) En el contexto del texto, "por ende" (línea tercera) conserva su sentido al sustituirse por:

(A) es decir.
(B) por supuesto.
(C) en tanto.
(D) por tanto.
(E) en cambio.

(Gramática) A, B, C, D, E: La alternativa correcta es la D. La locución adverbial "por ende" tiene característica consecutiva y, en consecuencia, equivale a "por (lo) tanto". Otras locuciones consecutivas substituibles en este caso son: por ello/eso, por ese/tal/dicho motivo/razón/causa, por consiguiente, pues, así pues.
Gabarito "D".

(Auditor Fiscal da Receita Federal – 2012 – ESAF) De acuerdo con el texto, Fabricio Zanzzi recomienda estudiar en profundidad la cuestión del tratado antes de firmarlo:

(A) porque concuerda con el gobierno.
(B) para garantizar condiciones iguales a las peruanas y colombianas.
(C) debido al crecimiento de las exportaciones desde 2003.
(D) en función de un intercambio comercial equilibrado.
(E) y revisar las estadísticas de la relación comercial con la UE.

(Interpretación) A: Correcto. El primer párrafo nos indica que "analizar la firma [o sanción] de un acuerdo con la Unión Europea, requiere de una revisión […] de la posición del Gobierno ecuatoriano". En la última frase del primer párrafo, se lee que "Fabricio Zanzzi "coincide [con el gobierno] que firmar en acuerdo así no está acorde con el Modelo de Desarrollo Ecuatoriano".
B: Incorrecto. El texto indica, en el primer párrafo, que "el Ejecutivo ha expresado su negativa de firmar un acuerdo bajo las mismas condiciones de Perú y Colombia".
C: Incorrecto. No hay indicaciones en el texto que respalden esta afirmación.
D: Incorrecto. Nada se dice al respecto de un intercambio comercial equilibrado entre Ecuador y la Unión Europea.

E: Incorrecto. La revisión de las estadísticas de la relación comercial entre Ecuador y la Unión Europea requiere una revisión de la posición del Gobierno ecuatoriano (línea 1). Fabricio Zanzzi "sugiere estudiar a fondo el caso y luego firmar" (última línea del primer párrafo). Nada se dice, por lo tanto, al respecto de una supuesta recomendación de Zanzzi en revisar las estadísticas de la relación comercial con la Unión Europea.
Gabarito "A".

(Auditor Fiscal da Receita Federal – 2012 – ESAF) Según el texto, las exportaciones de Ecuador hacia la UE:

(A) acusan un déficit en la balanza comercial.
(B) han crecido bastante.
(C) son fundamentalmente petroleras.
(D) excluyen los productos primarios.
(E) tienen similar volumen que las destinadas a la CAN.

(Interpretación) A, B, C, D, E: La alternativa correcta es la B. Todos las respuestas as demás alternativa, con excepción de la A, que no tiene respaldo en el texto, se encuentran en las 4 primeras líneas del segundo párrafo: "mientras el aumento de las ventas ecuatorianas a la UE es de aproximadamente un 19% anual; actualmente, nuestro país exporta alrededor de US$2,630 millones a este mercado, es decir, más de 2.4 veces de lo que le vendía en el 2003; realidad que lo convierte en el tercer destino de nuestros productos, después de Estados Unidos y la Comunidad Andina (CAN)".
Gabarito "B".

Sube Rajoy IVA a 21% en España y aumenta recorte al gasto público

El presidente del gobierno español, Mariano Rajoy, anunció nuevas medidas de ajuste destinadas a reactivar la economía del país, que incluyen una reforma de la administración que debería permitir ahorrar 3 mil 500 millones de euros y un incremento del Impuesto al Valor Agregado (IVA). Lo primero prevé una reducción del número de empresas públicas y una disminución del 30 por ciento el número de concejales por tramos de población. Rajoy también anunció que dadas las circunstancias excepcionales de la economía, en 2012 suspenderá el abono del aguinaldo a funcionarios y altos cargos de la administración. La segunda medida será un aumento del IVA, cuyo tipo pasará del 18 al 21 por ciento, después que el gobierno hubiera rechazado durante mucho tiempo tomar tal decisión, pedida por la Comisión Europea y el Fondo Monetario Internacional (FMI). El IVA reducido para algunos productos subirá del 8 al 10 por ciento, mientras que se mantendrá el tipo súper reducido del 4 por ciento sobre productos de primera necesidad, que incluyen los alimentarios básicos.

Estas condiciones fueron impuestas a España por Bruselas a cambio de una suavización del objetivo de reducción del déficit al 6.3 por ciento del PIB en este año, al 4.5 por ciento en 2013 y al 2.8 por ciento en 2014.Paralelamente, los ministros de Finanzas de la zona euro lograron acuerdo sobre el plan de ayuda a los bancos españoles, que incluye la entrega antes de fin de mes de 30 mil millones de euros.

La Jornada 11/07/2012. Disponible en: <http://www.jornada.unam.mx/ ultimas/2012/07/11/73315925-espana-rajoy-sube-el-iva-a-21-y-recorta-elgasto- publico>.

(Analista-Tributário da Receita Federal – 2012 – ESAF) En el texto se dice que entre las medidas de ajuste anunciadas por el presidente del gobierno español está:

(A) la suspensión de la paga extraordinaria a funcionarios públicos.
(B) el ahorro de 3,5 millones de euros durante el año 2012.
(C) la creación de nuevos impuestos al consumo.
(D) el préstamo de 30 millones de millones a la banca local.
(E) la disminución del número de habitantes por concejal.

(Interpretación) A: Correcto. La frase del texto que nos permite confirmar la validez de la alternativa A es la siguiente: "Rajoy también anunció que dadas las circunstancias excepcionales de la economía, en 2012 suspenderá el abono del aguinaldo a funcionarios y altos cargos de la administración". Según la Real Academia Española, "aguinaldo" quiere decir "regalo que se oferta en el período de las navidades".
B: Incorrecto. La afirmación no tiene respaldo en el texto.
C: Incorrecto. Conforme se lee en el título y en el primer párrafo, no se trata de la creación de un nuevo impuesto, pero del aumento de un impuesto ya existente, el IVA (Impuesto sobre el Valor Agregado).
D: Incorrecto. La afirmación no tiene respaldo en el texto.
E: Incorrecto. La palabra "concejal" quiere decir "persona que ha sido elegida para formar parte del ayuntamiento o gobierno municipal", según la Real Academia Española. En el primer párrafo, no se afirma que habrá un disminución del número de habitantes por concejal, pero "una disminución del 30 por ciento el número de concejales por tramos de población".
Gabarito "A".

(Analista-Tributário da Receita Federal – 2012 – ESAF) De acuerdo con el texto, el socorro a los bancos y la suavización del objetivo de reducción del déficit público español:

(A) parecen suficientes para reactivar la economía.
(B) permitirán ahorrar recursos financieros estatales.
(C) se rechazaron durante mucho tiempo.
(D) garantizan un aumento de los ingresos públicos.
(E) supusieron diversos condicionamientos.

(Interpretación) A, B, C, D, E: La única alternativa que encuentra respaldo en el texto es la E. Los diversos condicionamientos a los cuales se refiere la alternativa están explicitados en la siguiente afirmación del texto: "estas condiciones fueron impuestas a España por Bruselas a cambio de una suavización del objetivo de reducción del déficit al 6.3 por ciento del PIB en este año, al 4.5 por ciento en 2013 y al 2.8 por ciento en 2014" (primera línea del segundo párrafo).
Gabarito "E".

El FROB cifró la maniobra en 137 millones de euros

El Fondo de Reestructuración Ordenada Bancaria (FROB) ha acusado al exconsejero delegado del Banco de Valencia, Domingo Parra, de los presuntos delitos de estafa, apropiación indebida y administración desleal, según un informe pericial al que ha tenido acceso Cadena SER. También acusa a su socio Aurelio Izquierdo, que presidió la entidad y fue director comercial de Bankia, de participar en los hechos "a título lucrativo". Según el FROB, los exdirectivos utilizaron el Banco de Valencia para realizar diversas operaciones financieras e inmobiliarias a través de sociedades instrumentales sin el conocimiento del consejo de administración. Y se las considera como generadoras de grave perjuicio para la entidad y una estafa por cerca de 137 millones de euros.

El informe del FROB ha sido presentado ante la Audiencia Nacional y la investigación será asumida por el magistrado Santiago Pedraz. Se trata de la segunda causa en que se encuentran implicados exdirectivos del banco, que ya cuenta con una investigación iniciada en el Juzgado nº 3 de Valencia, tras la denuncia de pequeños accionistas de la entidad.

CincoDias, 10/07/2012. Disponible en: <http://www.cincodias.com/articulo/ mercados/exdirectivos-banco-valencia--investigados-presuntaestafa/ 20120710cdscdsmer_6/>.

(Analista-Tributário da Receita Federal – 2012 – ESAF) Dentro del texto, la palabra "estafa" significa:

(A) cohecho.
(B) soborno.
(C) desfalco.
(D) perjurio.
(E) proprina.

(Vocabulario) A, B, C, D, E: La alternativa correcta es la letra C. El término "estafa" significa desfalco, o pedir y sacar dinero o cosas de valor con engaño. Según la Real Academia Española, además da la definición previa, "estafa" también quiere decir "dar a alguien menos o cobrarlo más de lo justo", o, en sentido figurado, "defraudar, no ofrecer lo que se espera de algo".
Gabarito "C".

(Analista-Tributário da Receita Federal – 2012 – ESAF) En el texto se dice que la causa en que están implicados el exconsejero delegado del Banco de Valencia (BV) y su socio:

(A) incluye a pequeños accionistas de esa entidad.
(B) envuelve graves prejuicios.
(C) es inédita en relación a esa institución.
(D) la desconocía el consejo de administración del banco.
(E) es la segunda contra exdirectivos del BV.

(Interpretación) A, B, C, D, E: La única alternativa que tiene respaldo en el texto es la letra E. La afirmación del fragmento que nos permite así concluir es la siguiente: "el informe del FROB ha sido presentado ante la Audiencia Nacional y la investigación será asumida por el magistrado Santiago Pedraz. *Se trata de la segunda causa* en que se encuentran implicados exdirectivos del banco, que ya cuenta con una investigación iniciada en el Juzgado nº 3 de Valencia, tras la denuncia de pequeños accionistas de la entidad".
Gabarito "E".

Informe de EU sobre HSBC desnuda vulnerabilidad de banca mexicana

El informe del congreso estadounidense sobre la forma como la filial mexicana del banco británico HSBC transfirió más de 7 mil millones de dólares, que en parte a lo mejor corresponden al narcotráfico, expone la debilidad de México para frenar el flujo de dinero ilícito. El presidente la Comisión Nacional Bancaria y de Valores de México restringió a menos de 7 mil dólares el monto máximo mensual de las transacciones que pueden realizarse en efectivo en esa moneda ante bancos y casas de cambio. El Congreso tramita otra iniciativa para frenar el blanqueo mediante compras de joyas, casinos, bienes inmuebles y autos.

El informe estadounidense halló por ejemplo que el HSBC México opera 50 mil cuentas y fondos por 2 mil 100 millones de dólares en Islas Caimán, donde no tiene oficinas ni empleados. Para el experto argentino en crimen organizado, Edgardo Buscaglia, que trabaja en México y es investigador invitado de la universidad de Columbia en Estados Unidos, las denuncias muestran que México se ha transformado en un "bazar" para el flujo de dinero ilícito.

La jornada, 18/07/12. Disponible en: <http://www.jornada.unam.mx/ ultimas/2012/07/18/16327554-informe-de-eu-sobre-hsbc-desnudavulnerabilidad-de-banca-mexicana-cnbv>.

(Analista-Tributário da Receita Federal – 2012 – ESAF) De acuerdo con las declaraciones del presidente de la CNBV, recogidas en el texto, existen fallas en el sistema financiero local:

(A) de carácter legal y técnico.
(B) aun cuando se tomaron medidas para su fortalecimiento.
(C) por falta de control estatal sobre la actividad bancaria.
(D) debido al volumen de transacciones en efectivo.
(E) atribuibles a negocios en especie.

(Interpretación) A, B, C, D, E: La única alternativa que tiene respaldo en el texto es la letra B. Las medidas tomadas para el fortaleciendo del sistema financiero mexicano están expuestas en la afirmación siguiente: "el presidente la Comisión Nacional Bancaria y de Valores de México restringió a menos de 7 mil dólares el monto máximo mensual de las transacciones que pueden realizarse en efectivo en esa moneda ante bancos y casas de cambio. El Congreso tramita otra iniciativa para frenar el blanqueo mediante compras de joyas, casinos, bienes inmuebles y autos" (últimas dos frases del primer párrafo).
Gabarito "B".

(Analista-Tributário da Receita Federal – 2012 – ESAF) Según el texto, la filial mexicana del banco británico HSBC:

(A) opera todas sus cuentas dentro del territorio de México.
(B) transfirió dinero del narcotráfico a Estados Unidos.
(C) realizó transacciones con bienes muebles e inmuebles.
(D) carece de fuertes controles de prevención del lavado de dinero.
(E) fue sancionada por blanqueo entre 2002 y 2009.

(Interpretación) A, B, C, D, E: La única alternativa que tiene respaldo en el texto es la letra D. Según lo que se lee en primera línea del texto, "el informe del congreso estadounidense sobre la forma como la filial mexicana del banco británico HSBC transfirió más de 7 mil millones de dólares, que en parte a lo mejor corresponden al narcotráfico, expone la debilidad de México para frenar el flujo de dinero ilícito".
Gabarito "D".

(Analista-Tributário da Receita Federal – 2012 – ESAF) La locución "a lo mejor" que aparece en la tercera línea del texto significa:

(A) tal vez.
(B) sin duda.
(C) de preferencia.
(D) difícilmente.
(E) a todas luces.

(Vocabulario) A, B, C, D, E: La alternativa correcta es la letra A. La locución "a lo mejor" significa "tal vez"; indica, por lo tanto, características de probabilidad.

Gabarito "A".

Del sueño a la pesadilla

Si bien la actual crisis europea tiene un evidente componente económico, su principal factor de desajuste parecería ser la acelerada pérdida de credibilidad en el proyecto. Por primera vez los inversores, los ciudadanos y hasta los mismos políticos han comenzado a dudar seriamente de la irreversibilidad del proceso de la eurozona y se ha comenzado a pensar en que la eurozona no funcione y que sus actores tengan que dar marcha atrás. Algo para lo que nadie estaba preparado.

La unificación monetaria del espacio europeo fue sin duda un golpe visionario como pocos en la historia, el paso obligado una vez consolidado un mercado comercial gigantesco. Sin embargo, la sustitución de las monedas nacionales por una continental no vino de la mano de un mecanismo igualmente unificado de manejo fiscal. Los estados miembros quedaron simplemente obligados a cumplir ciertas metas fiscales pero nada más. La Unión Europea no asumió mecanismos efectivos de administración fiscal, ni de control de las cuentas públicas, de cada uno de los miembros. Y este desfase monetario fiscal tiene una explicación política. Si el régimen de hacienda pública dejaba de estar en manos de los estados miembros y pasaba a manos de un organismo supranacional, en ese momento los bancos centrales, los ministros de finanzas, pero más importante, los propios parlamentos nacionales prácticamente dejarían de tener su razón de ser. La política dejaría de ser entonces un asunto "local" para convertirse en una actividad europea en plenitud. El actual parlamento europeo –que carece de iniciativa legislativa– tendría que convertirse en la fuente directa de legitimidad de todo el andamiaje político de la actual Unión Europea. Habría un electorado auténticamente europeo y la Unión Europea dejaría entonces de ser tal para convertirse en un Estado federal. Y este es el salto que nadie está dispuesto a dar. Cierto es que en los últimos años el proyecto de una federación ha venido discutiéndose. Sin embargo, hay sociedades como la francesa, por ejemplo, que requerirían de algún tiempo para aceptarla. Y tiempo es lo que menos tiene hoy la eurozona. Y decisión política es lo que más le está haciendo falta.

El Universo, 17/07/12. Disponible en: <http://www.eluniverso.com/2012/07/17/1/1363/ sueno-pesadilla.html>.

(Analista-Tributário da Receita Federal – 2012 – ESAF) En el texto se dice que la actual crisis europea tiene un evidente componente económico:

(A) vinculado a la consolidación del comercio.
(B) pero apenas monetario.
(C) y otro político.
(D) como única causa.
(E) resultante de la unificación monetaria.

(Interpretación) A, B, C, D, E: La alternativa correcta es la letra C. La primera frase del primer párrafo deja claro que "si bien la actual crisis europea tiene un evidente componente económico, su principal factor de desajuste parecería ser la acelerada pérdida de credibilidad en el proyecto". Una pérdida de credibilidad en el proyecto europeo es un componente político de explicación de la crisis de dicho continente. Las demás alternativas están incorrectas, dado que no se apoyan el texto.

Gabarito "C".

(Analista-Tributário da Receita Federal – 2012 – ESAF) Según el texto, en el marco del proyecto de unión de Europa la unificación monetaria

(A) fue una imposición de algunos países.
(B) debió acompañarse de un mecanismo de administración fiscal unificado.
(C) ha supuesto un golpe para algunos estados miembros.
(D) ha conservado la credibilidad en el proyecto.
(E) garantiza la irreversibilidad del proceso de la eurozona.

(Interpretación) A: Incorrecto. No hay oración en el texto que permita afirmar que la unión monetaria fue una imposición de algunos países.
B: Correcto. Según el texto, la unión monetaria debería haber sido acompañada de un mecanismo de administración fiscal unificado. Las afirmaciones que nos permite así concluir son las siguientes: "la unificación monetaria del espacio europeo fue sin duda un golpe visionario como pocos en la historia, el paso obligado una vez consolidado un mercado comercial gigantesco. Sin embargo, la sustitución de las monedas nacionales por una continental no vino de la mano de un mecanismo igualmente unificado de manejo fiscal" (líneas 2 y 3 del segundo párrafo).
C: Incorrecto. No hay frase en el texto que permita afirmar un supuesto golpe para algunos estados miembros.
D: Incorrecto. La pérdida de credibilidad en el proyecto está enunciado en las afirmaciones siguientes: "por primera vez los inversores, los ciudadanos y hasta los mismos políticos han comenzado a dudar seriamente de la irreversibilidad del proceso de la eurozona y se ha comenzado a pensar en que la eurozona no funcione y que sus actores tengan que dar marcha atrás. Algo para lo que nadie estaba preparado" (dos últimas frases del primer párrafo).
E: Incorrecto. La reversibilidad del proyecto queda elucidada en la frase siguiente del texto: "por primera vez los inversores, los ciudadanos y hasta los mismos políticos han comenzado a dudar seriamente de la irreversibilidad del proceso de la eurozona y se ha comenzado a pensar en que la eurozona no funcione y que sus actores tengan que dar marcha atrás" (primer párrafo).

Gabarito "B".

(Analista-Tributário da Receita Federal – 2012 – ESAF) De acuerdo con el texto, el desfase entre lo monetario y lo fiscal:

(A) es el resultado de la crisis.
(B) es un problema insoluble.
(C) responde al descontrol de las cuentas públicas.

(D) se debe a la falta de una plena integración política.
(E) ha venido discutiéndose los últimos años.

(Interpretación) A, B, C, D, E: La única alternativa correcta es la letra D. Las oraciones del texto que nos permiten afirmar que el desfase entre lo monetario y lo fiscal se debe a la falta de una plena integración política es la siguiente: "los estados miembros quedaron simplemente obligados a cumplir ciertas metas fiscales pero nada más. La Unión Europea no asumió mecanismos efectivos de administración fiscal, ni de control de las cuentas públicas, de cada uno de los miembros. Y este desfase monetario fiscal tiene una explicación política" (segundo párrafo).

Gabarito "D".

Estilo casual

La tendencia se afirma en las oficinas, pero con reglas

La moda informal gana seguidores en las oficinas. Una tendencia que comenzó en Estados Unidos a fines de la década del 90 de la mano de las puntocom, y que hace un par de años se instaló definitivamente en la Argentina.
5 "Fue un estilo que se puso de manifiesto en las compañías dedicadas a la tecnología, que privilegiaron la comodidad para enfrentar las presiones laborales y la gran cantidad de horas de trabajo", dice Gisella Gulli, asesora de imagen y fundadora junto a María Pínola de la agencia Making Of,
10 empresa dedicada al asesoramiento de imagen.
Bill Gates, fundador de Microsoft, y Steve Jobs, presidente de Apple, se convirtieron involuntariamente en iconos de este nuevo vestir, alejado del traje y la corbata. A ellos, años más tarde, se sumaron los jóvenes empresarios
15 surgidos de esa generación, que trasladaron esa filosofía del vestir a sus propios emprendimientos.
El nuevo estilo se impuso poco a poco en otras empresas multinacionales y bancos nacionales e internacionales. "Así establecieron el código *casual friday* –dice la asesora
20 de imagen Josefina Posse–. Una forma de darles a sus empleados libertad y cierto relax a la hora de comenzar el fin de semana, un anticipo del bienestar que vendrá ".
Así lo confirma Santiago Batlle, director de recursos humanos de Standard Bank Argentina: "En este banco se
25 inició tímidamente hace ocho años con una propuesta llamada *Viernes sport*, que permitió reconfirmar los viernes como el mejor día de la semana, pero actualmente el uso de vestimenta *sport* está permitido todos los días del año".
El rubro tarjetas de crédito también se subió a esta nueva
30 tendencia, como es el caso de American Express. Así lo afirma Sergio Sosa, director de recursos humanos. "Desde 1999 se implementa la política del *casual day every day*, con un claro objetivo: enfatizar el concepto *the best place to work*, a través del cual se brinda a los empleados
35 un entorno de informalidad y comodidad en cuanto a la indumentaria que pueden usar durante todo el año".
En esa misma sintonía, la empresa Coca-Cola hizo lo suyo: "Nos alineamos a las tendencias del momento, y con la búsqueda de una mayor flexibilidad y dinamismo
40 en nuestra cultura organizacional", destaca Silvina Kippke, gerente de compensaciones y beneficios y *HR business partner* de la marca de gaseosa.
Para evitar lo sucedido en Estados Unidos (donde al comienzo los empleados se extralimitaban en el vestuario,
45 usando bermudas y ojotas, los hombres, y microminis y escotes pronunciados, las mujeres), las empresas establecieron límites.
"Es algo que está muy regulado –dice Alejo Estebecorena, de la firma de diseño masculino más personal Hermanos
50 Estebecorena–. Hay memos internos en los que figuran lo que está permitido (como remeras tipo polo) y lo prohibido (bermudas y jeans). De algún modo es un nuevo uniforme".
Kippke agrega: "En realidad, lo que se pide es discreción, y tomar como base el papel y el tipo de interacción, de

55 manera de evitar prendas que puedan incomodar a otras personas. Por eso recomendamos un elegante *sport*".
Hay otras restricciones. Tanto American Express Argentina como Standard Bank reconocen que esta política no se aplica a empleados que tienen contacto con el público
60 en forma personalizada ni para los que deban mantener alguna reunión de trabajo importante con profesionales de otras empresas. "Porque en esos casos están representando a la compañía", explica Batlle.
Cómo mostrarse
65 Lejos de solucionar un problema, para muchos esta nueva moda sumó una preocupación a sus vidas y un nuevo interrogante: ¿*Qué me pongo hoy?*
"El traje y la corbata es un uniforme que no permite pensar ni proponer nada –dice Estebecorena–. Por eso, este
70 paso de moda formal a informal hizo que al principio la comodidad pasara a segundo plano. Ahora el problema es saber cómo mostrarse." El sastre Alfredo Marino coincide con Estebecorena y agrega: "Vestir casual exige un mínimo de sensibilidad, saber elegir las prendas, las texturas
75 y sus combinaciones".
Esto llevó a que muchos clientes se acercaran en busca de asesoramiento. "Me preguntaban: ¿*Cómo hago para no parecer un payaso?* ", comenta el Estebecorena. Algo parecido sucedió en Mc Taylor, así lo cuenta Germán
80 Fernández, CEO de la firma. "El cliente buscaba los consejos de nuestros asesores de moda, y justamente por escucharlos e interpretar sus necesidades creamos una línea *sport* metropolitana o urbana, más fresca que el traje tradicional, pero poniendo foco en la elegancia que
85 implica la acertada combinación de saco *sport*, camisa – abierta, aunque no tanto, claro–, pantalón y calzado de diseño al tono".
Juan José Bertolino, hijo de un sastre y creador de Pato Pampa, marca de ropa masculina que, como él sostiene,
90 "interpreta al nuevo hombre urbano", notó otro fenómeno. "En este período, aumentaron notablemente los clientes y se dedican a casi todas las profesiones. El cambio más importante es que los industriales y comerciantes dejaron de lado la corbata".
95 **Sentido común + ideas**
Las mujeres no quedaron fuera de esta nueva preocupación al momento de vestirse para ir a trabajar. "El típico traje de falda o pantalón más blazer es una tendencia que está desapareciendo, y justamente el 90 por ciento de las
100 mujeres que asiste a Making Of es para saber cómo deshacerse de ese *look* y crear algo que parezca formal, pero que sea desestructurado."
Como sostiene la asesora de imagen Claudia Servino, una regla es indispensable: "Hay que saber que los límites
105 entre lo que es y no es equivocado también los impone la mirada de los demás. Lo esencial es no dejar de ser uno mismo, pero adecuándose a ciertas reglas de vestimenta esenciales para un trabajo. Y, por supuesto, adaptarse a cada ambiente. No es lo mismo trabajar en una agencia
110 de diseño gráfico que en una oficina de la Corte Suprema". Sentido común y creatividad, una combinación necesaria también para equipos acertados.

Disponible en: <http://www.lanacion.com.ar/ Edicion Impresa/ suplementos/modaybelleza>.
Consulta del 13 mar. 2008.

(Advogado – BNDES – 2008 – CESGRANRIO) "Así establecieron el código *casual friday* –dice la asesora de imagen Josefina Posse–." (líneas 19 y 20) La acción señalada en el fragmento es

(A) presente.
(B) pasada.
(C) futura.
(D) imperativa.
(E) reflexiva.

(Gramática) A, B, C, D, E: La alternativa correcta es la A. El verbo decir está conjugado en el presente del indicativo, "dice", en la tercera persona del singular.
Gabarito "A".

(Advogado – BNDES – 2008 – CESGRANRIO) "…un entorno de informalidad y comodidad en cuanto a la indumentaria que pueden usar…" (líneas 35 y 36) Lo señalado equivale a

(A) por lo visto.
(B) por lo que toca.
(C) cuando.
(D) empero.
(E) mientras tanto.

(Gramática) A, B, C, D, E: La alternativa correcta es la B. La locución "en cuanto" es sinónimo de "por lo que toca". Otra posibilidad seria la expresión "por lo que se refiere a".
Gabarito "B".

(Advogado – BNDES – 2008 – CESGRANRIO) "la empresa Coca-Cola hizo lo suyo:" (líneas 37 y 38) Por lo señalado se comprende que la empresa

(A) no se sujeta a nadie.
(B) creó su propio estilo.
(C) cumplió con su parte.
(D) rechazó el estilo casual.
(E) sigue buscando cosa mejor.

(Vocabulario) A, B, C, D, E: La alternativa correcta es la C. La expresión "hizo lo suyo" significa "cumplió con su parte".
Gabarito "B".

(Advogado – BNDES – 2008 – CESGRANRIO) El fragmento que expresa una acción reflexiva es

(A) "En este banco se inició tímidamente…" (líneas 24 y 25)
(B) "…se implementa la política…" (línea 32)
(C) "…se brinda a los empleados…" (línea 34)
(D) "…los empleados se extralimitaban…" (línea 44)
(E) "lo que se pide…" (línea 53)

(Gramática) A, B, C e E: Incorrectas. En estos casos, la partícula "se" indica indeterminación del sujeto. D: Correcta. En este caso, la partícula "se" indica que se trata de un verbo reflexivo.
Gabarito "D".

(Advogado – BNDES – 2008 – CESGRANRIO) El texto ennumera algunas prendas. Las palabras jeans, remeras y faldas pueden ser sustituidas, respectivamente, por

(A) chaquetas, medias y chalecos.
(B) calcetines, chanclas y bufandas.
(C) bragas, sostenes y cazadoras.
(D) vaqueros, camiseta y polleras.
(E) guantes, calzoncillos y chalecos.

(Vocabulario) A, B, C, D, E: La única alternativa correcta es la letra D. "Jeans", "remera" y "pollera", en castellano de Argentina, son equivalentes a "vaqueros", "camiseta" y "falda", en castellano de España.
Gabarito "D".

(Advogado – BNDES – 2008 – CESGRANRIO) "…la comodidad pasara a segundo plano." (líneas 70 y 71) Se puede sustituir lo señalado, sin cambio de significado, por

(A) pase.
(B) pasase.
(C) pasaría.
(D) pasaba.
(E) pasó.

(Gramática) A, B, C, D, E: La única alternativa correcta es la letra B. El verbo "pasar" conjugado en el imperfecto del subjuntivo, asume las formas, en tercera persona del singular, "pasara" o "pasase", que son substitutos perfectos.
Gabarito "B".

(Advogado – BNDES – 2008 – CESGRANRIO) "…cómo mostrarse." (línea 72) El uso de la tilde se justifica porque se trata de

(A) palabra aguda.
(B) frase afirmativa.
(C) comparación.
(D) posición en final de frase.
(E) cuestionamiento indirecto.

(Gramática) A, B, C, D, E: La única alternativa correcta es la letra E. En este caso, el uso de la tilde se justifica debido a que se trata de un cuestionamiento indirecto. Recuérdense, por lo que se refiere a la acentuación en castellano, las tres reglas principales. 1) Se acentúan todas palabras agudas que terminan en vocal, o en *n o s* solas; 2) Las palabras agudas que no terminan en vocal, o en *n o s* solas, nunca se acentúan; 3) Todas las palabras esdrújulas se acentúan.
Gabarito "E".

(Advogado – BNDES – 2008 – CESGRANRIO) La afirmativa que exprime idea de necesidad es

(A) "…hace un par de años…" (líneas 3 y 4)
(B) "Así establecieron…" (línea 19)
(C) "…está permitido…" (línea 28)
(D) "Hay otras restricciones." (línea 57)
(E) " 'Hay que saber…" (línea 104)

(Gramática) A: Incorrecto. La alternativa indica característica espacio temporal. B: Incorrecto. La alternativa indica conformidad. C y la D: Incorrectas. Indican veracidad. E: Correcto. La alternativa indica necesidad.
Gabarito "E".

(Advogado – BNDES – 2008 – CESGRANRIO) "… los límites entre lo que es y no es equivocado también los impone la mirada de los demás." (líneas 104 - 106) Lo señalado en la frase se refiere a

(A) límites.
(B) los demás.
(C) las mujeres.
(D) ideas.
(E) gerentes.

(Gramática) A, B, C, D, E: La única alternativa correcta es la letra A. El término "los", en la oración señalada, se refiere a "los límites". Se podría reescribir la oración de esta manera sin pérdida de identidad: "la mirada de los demás impone los límites entre lo que es y no es equivocado".
Gabarito "A".

(Advogado – BNDES – 2008 – CESGRANRIO) Considerando el contenido del texto en lo que se refiere a oficina, personas y el estilo casual, NO se puede afirmar que

(A) Bill Gates y Steve Jobs fueron referencia de la moda sin traje.
(B) Hermanos Estebecorena considera el estilo casual un nuevo "uniforme".

(C) Coca-cola está alienada con la tendencia del estilo casual.
(D) American Express adoptó el estilo informal hace algunos años.
(E) Standard Bank Argentina ha adoptado la moda informal poco a poco.

(Interpretación) A: Incorrecta. Las líneas 11 a 14 indican que "Bill Gates, fundador de Microsoft, y Steve Jobs, presidente de Apple, se convirtieron involuntariamente en iconos de este nuevo vestir [...]".
B: Incorrecta. En las líneas 52 y 53, se indica que Kippke, y no Hermanos Estecorena, agrega que, "de algún modo, es un nuevo uniforme".
C: Correcta. En las líneas 37 a 40, se afirma que "en la misma sintonía, la empresa Coca-Cola hizo lo suyo: "nos alineamos a las tendencias del momento, y con la búsqueda de una mayor flexibilidad y dinamismo en nuestra cultura organizacional", destaca Silvina Kippke".
D: Incorrecta. En la línea 30, se indica que American Express también adoptó la nueva tendencia, desde 1999 (línea 33).
E: Incorrecta. En la línea 25, se afirma que el banco Standard Bank Argentina "inició tímidamente hace ocho años con una propuesta llamada Viernes sport".
Gabarito "C".

Texto I

Escaladores de Greenpeace en el Corcovado de Río de Janeiro piden inmediata protección de bosques y océanos

Acción de Greenpeace a tres días de la Cumbre sobre Biodiversidad (CBD)

Activistas de Greenpeace despliegan una pancarta en el Cristo de Corcovado para pedir a los 188 gobiernos participantes en la Cumbre de la Biodiversidad protección inmediata para la biodiversidad.

Río de Janeiro, Brasil – Activistas de Greenpeace han desplegado una gran pancarta desde una mano del famoso Cristo de Corcovado, en Río de Janeiro, Brasil, con la leyenda "El futuro del planeta está en vuestras manos" para demandar a los gobiernos que tomen medidas para proteger la vida en la Tierra y asegurar un futuro más seguro para el planeta. El mensaje iba dirigido a los representantes de 188 gobiernos que se van a reunir en Brasil para discutir la protección de la biodiversidad a escala global.

En el decimocuarto aniversario de la primera Cumbre sobre Biodiversidad (CBD) (1), que se inicia el próximo día 20, las delegaciones gubernamentales de todo el mundo negociarán una serie de asuntos cruciales para alcanzar los "Objetivos de Biodiversidad" para 2010 que frenarían la dramática pérdida de biodiversidad en el planeta. Los responsables de Medio Ambiente de 188 países llegarán a Curitiba el 26 de marzo para una recepción con el presidente brasileño Luis Inacio "Lula" da Silva.

"No podemos esperar otros catorce años para que los gobiernos actúen. Tienen que detener la extinción masiva de animales y plantas para todo el planeta inmediatamente, de lo contrario se negarán los beneficios económicos, sociales y culturales de un planeta sano a las generaciones futuras", comentó Paulo Adario, coordinador de la campaña de Greenpeace en la Amazonia.

La diversidad tanto de la vida terrestre como de la marina está siendo destruida a un ritmo sin precedentes. La tasa actual de extinción de plantas y animales es, aproximadamente, 1.000 veces mayor que en épocas anteriores a la aparición del ser humano y las predicciones apuntan a que en 2050 esta tasa sea de 10.000 veces mayor. Esta pérdida de biodiversidad impide a los ecosistemas funcionar adecuadamente.

"La degradación de los ecosistemas es un problema cada vez mayor y por ello se hace urgente la necesidad de establecer una red global de áreas protegidas en las que se incluyan espacios naturales que abarquen grandes superfícies y que estén interconectados entre sí", ha afirmado Miguel Ángel Soto, responsable de la campaña de Bosques de Greenpeace España.

Mientras los gobiernos discuten en Brasil, equipos de activistas de Greenpeace están trabajando en el corazón de la Amazonia y los bosques de Papúa Nueva Guinea para detener la destrucción de las selvas tropicales provocada por el cultivo de productos agrícolas como la soja.

Greenpeace hace un llamamiento a todos los gobiernos para que cumplan sus promesas de establecer una red global de áreas protegidas tanto continentales como en los océanos para preservar la biodiversidad en la Tierra.

Notas:

1 - La CBD, junto con la Convención sobre el Cambio Climático de la ONU, nacieron de la Cumbre de la Tierra que tuvo lugar en 1992 en Río de Janeiro. La CBD es el único acuerdo global que trata la necesidad de conservación, uso responsable y reparto equitativo de la biodiversidad, tanto la marina como la terrestre. También es el primero que reconoce que la conservación de la biodiversidad es "una preocupación común de la humanidad" y una parte integral del desarrollo sostenible. Así mismo incluye la necesidad de proteger los conocimientos de los pueblos indígenas y las comunidades locales y fomenta el uso tradicional de los recursos naturales (como la extracción de caucho, por ejemplo).

Disponible en: <http://www.greenpeace.org/espana/news/escaladores-de-en-e>.

(Advogado – BNDES – 2006 – CESGRANRIO) Al desplegar una pancarta con leyenda, en el Corcovado de Río de Janeiro, los activistas de Greenpeace tienen como objetivo:

(A) celebrar el día del medio ambiente.
(B) divulgar la Cumbre sobre Biodiversidad.
(C) llamar la atención de los mandatarios del mundo.
(D) clamar a los gobernantes brasileños.
(E) festejar el aniversario de la Cumbre.

(Interpretación) A, B, C, D, E: La alternativa correcta es la C, dado que es la única que tiene respaldo en el texto. La afirmativa que nos permite así concluir es: "activistas de Greenpeace han desplegado una gran pancarta desde una mano del famoso Cristo de Corcovado, en Río de Janeiro, Brasil, con la leyenda "El futuro del planeta está en vuestras manos" para demandar a los gobiernos que tomen medidas para proteger la vida en la Tierra y asegurar un futuro más seguro para el planeta" (primer párrafo).
Gabarito "C".

(Advogado – BNDES – 2006 – CESGRANRIO) Donde se lee "y por ello se hace urgente" (5º párrafo), el uso de "ello", en relación a lo dicho anteriormente, sirve para:

(A) explicar.
(B) retomar.
(C) aclarar.
(D) enfatizar.
(E) orientar.

(Gramática) A, B, C, D, E: La alternativa correcta es la B. En este caso, el uso de "ello" sirve para retomar lo que se dijo anteriormente. En la afirmativa "la degradación de los ecosistemas es un problema cada vez mayor y por ello se hace urgente la necesidad de [...]", ello retoma y se refiere a "la degradación de los ecosistemas".
Gabarito "B".

(Advogado – BNDES – 2006 – CESGRANRIO) Los conectores mientras (último párrafo) y así mismo (Notas), en el texto, encierran, respectivamente, idea de:

(A) adversidad / exclusión.
(B) suposición / adversidad.
(C) concordancia / conclusión.
(D) finalización / afirmación.
(E) concomitancia / inclusión.

(Gramática) A, B, C, D, E: La alternativa correcta es la E. Los conectores "mientras" (último párrafo) y "así mismo" (Notas) encierran idea de concomitancia e inclusión. Podrían ser substituidos, respectivamente, por "simultáneamente" y "inclusive".
Gabarito "E".

(Advogado – BNDES – 2006 – CESGRANRIO) Tras leer las afirmaciones del texto uno concluye que:

(A) los gobernantes suelen actuar con vistas al futuro.
(B) las reservas naturales están protegidas en definitiva.
(C) CBD tiene objetivos con fecha determinada para alcanzarlos.
(D) la pérdida de la biodiversidad es algo reciente.
(E) le toca a Greenpeace organizar la Cumbre sobre Biodiversidad.

(Interpretación) A, B, C, D, E: La alternativa correcta es la C, dado que es la única que tiene respaldo en el texto. Los párrafos que permiten así concluir son: "en el decimocuarto aniversario de la primera Cumbre sobre Biodiversidad (CBD) (1), que se inicia el próximo día 20, las delegaciones gubernamentales de todo el mundo negociarán una serie de asuntos cruciales para alcanzar los "Objetivos de Biodiversidad" para 2010 que frenarían la dramática pérdida de biodiversidad en el planeta. Los responsables de Medio Ambiente de 188 países llegarán a Curitiba el 26 de marzo para una recepción con el presidente brasileño Luis Inacio "Lula" da Silva". Y; "no podemos esperar otros catorce años para que los gobiernos actúen. Tienen que detener la extinción masiva de animales y plantas para todo el planeta inmediatamente, de lo contrario se negarán los beneficios económicos, sociales y culturales de un planeta sano a las generaciones futuras", comentó Paulo Adario, coordinador de la campaña de Greenpeace en la Amazonia".
Gabarito "C".

(Advogado – BNDES – 2006 – CESGRANRIO) Respecto a la Cumbre sobre Biodiversidad se puede afirmar que:

(A) surgió a partir de la Cumbre de la Tierra.
(B) tendrá lugar en Río de Janeiro.
(C) fue creado por un organismo internacional.
(D) refleja la preocupación con los países pobres.
(E) actúa exclusivamente en la Amazonia.

(Interpretación) A, B, C, D, E: La alternativa correcta es la A, dado que es la única que tiene respaldo en el texto. El párrafo que nos permite así concluir es: "la CBD, junto con la Convención sobre el Cambio Climático de la ONU, nacieron de la Cumbre de la Tierra que tuvo lugar en 1992 en Río de Janeiro. La CBD es el único acuerdo global que trata la necesidad de conservación, uso responsable y reparto equitativo de la biodiversidad, tanto la marina como la terrestre. También es el primero que reconoce que la conservación de la biodiversidad es "una preocupación común de la humanidad" y una parte integral del desarrollo sostenible. Así mismo incluye la necesidad de proteger los conocimientos de los pueblos indígenas y las comunidades locales y fomenta el uso tradicional de los recursos naturales (como la extracción de caucho, por ejemplo)" (Notas).
Gabarito "A".

(Advogado – BNDES – 2006 – CESGRANRIO) La CBD - Cumbre sobre Biodiversidad - se caracteriza por ser un(a):

(A) organismo criado para fiscalizar lo relativo a la biodiversidad.
(B) contrato firmado entre gobernantes de varias naciones.
(C) junta gubernamental de ámbito global.
(D) ONG que objetiva preservar la biodiversidad.
(E) fundación que objetiva la preservación del ecosistema.

(Interpretación) A, B, C, D, E: La alternativa correcta es la B, dado que es la única que tiene respaldo en el texto. El párrafo que nos permite así concluir es: "la CBD es el único acuerdo global que trata la necesidad de conservación, uso responsable y reparto equitativo de la biodiversidad, tanto la marina como la terrestre. También es el primero que reconoce que la conservación de la biodiversidad es "una preocupación común de la humanidad" y una parte integral del desarrollo sostenible. Así mismo incluye la necesidad de proteger los conocimientos de los pueblos indígenas y las comunidades locales y fomenta el uso tradicional de los recursos naturales (como la extracción de caucho, por ejemplo)" (Notas).
Gabarito "B".

(Advogado – BNDES – 2006 – CESGRANRIO) En la expresión "desarrollo sostenible" (Nota), lo subrayado puede ser sustituido por:

(A) crecimiento.
(B) detención.

(C) empobrecimiento.
(D) acercamiento.
(E) programación.

(Vocabulario) A, B, C, D, E: La alternativa correcta es la A. El único substituto posible es "crecimiento". Nota de la edición: si tuviésemos que mantener un estricto rigor de conceptos, no podríamos decir que "desarrollo sostenible" es lo mismo que "crecimiento sostenible", pero teniendo en cuenta que las otras alternativas encierran ideas más dispares, concluimos que la alternativa correcta es la A.
Gabarito "A".

Texto II

Fracasa el intento de un acuerdo mundial para frenar la pérdida masiva de especies

El enfrentamiento entre países ricos y pobres frustra el objetivo de la Cumbre de la Biodiversidad. El objetivo de la cumbre de Río de Janeiro de 1992 tendrá que esperar. A falta del documento oficial, que se elaborará el viernes, la octava Conferencia de las Partes sobre Biodiversidad que se celebra en Curitiba (Brasil acabará sin un acuerdo para detener la pérdida de especies en 2010. La falta de sistemas de financiación y los intereses contrapuestos entre países biodiversos (los del sur, que tienen la mayoría de las especies) y los industrializados (que, una vez acabada con su riqueza ambiental, buscan formas para explotar la de los demás) son las causas de este fracaso anunciado.

El tramo ministerial de la cumbre concluyó ayer con la convicción de que la sexta extinción de las especies es actualmente imparable. En 1992 parecía factible frenar la pérdida de biodiversidad en 2010. Hoy, los 122 representantes de los 198 países firmantes del protocolo de Río de Janeiro – salvo Estados Unidos, Irak y Corea del Norte admitieron que no se podrá conseguir. Ni siquiera fueron capaces de fijar una nueva fecha que sustituya a la de 2010. El problema no es menor. Sólo entre 2000 y 2002 la lista de especies animales amenazadas pasó de las 10.000 a casi las 16.000. En total, y contando las plantas, hay 76.000 especies amenazadas (el 4% del total).

La financiación internacional topa con dificultades. El Fondo Mundial Ambiental (GEF, en sus siglas en inglés) es incapaz de aportar recursos, y lo obstaculiza el anuncio de EEUU de reducir a la mitad su aportación, que es casi la cuarta parte de los 12.500 millones de euros que maneja.

Sin embargo, tras 14 años de reuniones y siete cumbres, en algunos temas se vislumbran avances. Uno de ellos, según el secretario general español para la Biodiversidad, Antonio Serrano, es el acceso y distribución de los beneficios genéticos. Esto incluye el pago a los indígenas y a los países ricos ambientalmente (llamados en la conferencia biodiversos) de una compensación por el uso de sus recursos. "Ha sido un día satisfactorio. Por primera vez nadie se opone a discutir la regulación internacional de este sistema", dijo Serrano en una rueda de prensa para los medios españoles organizada por la Fundación Biodiversidad, dependiente del ministerio.

Aunque se trata de un acuerdo para empezar a establecer la regulación es "poner la primera pica", dijo Serrano. Un optimismo que no comparten las organizaciones ecologistas presentes en la cumbre, como Greenpeace, que el martes dio su anti-premio Pelota Desinflada (representada por un globo terráqueo vacío) a la UE por demorar al menos dos años la puesta en marcha de este sistema de compensación.

El País, 30 de marzo de 2006.

(Advogado – BNDES – 2006 – CESGRANRIO) Hay equivalencia semántica entre la expresión "puesta en marcha" (último párrafo) y:
(A) finalizar.
(B) aportar.
(C) reglamentar.
(D) arrancar.
(E) mantener.

(Vocabulario) A, B, C, D, E: La alternativa correcta es la D. En este caso, el único equivalente semántico a la expresión "puesta en marcha" es "arrancar". Se trata de una analogía con el motor de coche, o de cualquier otro mecanismo que necesita arrancar para ponerse en marcha.
Gabarito "D".

(Advogado – BNDES – 2006 – CESGRANRIO) En este texto de El País, respecto a la CBD (Cumbre sobre Biodiversidad), el periódico señala que entre los participantes del encuentro hubo:
(A) acuerdos financieros para la protección de las especies.
(B) convicción de todos de que se puede parar la pérdida de biodiversidad.
(C) coincidencia de todos sobre el acceso indígena a los beneficios genéticos.
(D) discusión unánime sobre los indicios de avances.
(E) aprobación de la nueva fecha acordada para reemplazar el año 2010.

(Interpretación) A, B, C, D, E: La alternativa correcta es la C, dado que es la única que tiene respaldo en el texto. El penúltimo párrafo nos permite así concluir: "esto incluye el pago a los indígenas y a los países ricos ambientalmente (llamados en la conferencia biodiversos) de una compensación por el uso de sus recursos. "Ha sido un día satisfactorio. Por primera vez nadie se opone a discutir la regulación internacional de este sistema", dijo Serrano en una rueda de prensa para los medios españoles organizada por la Fundación Biodiversidad, dependiente del ministerio".
Gabarito "C".

(Advogado – BNDES – 2006 – CESGRANRIO) El fracaso anunciado por el titular de la noticia, según el texto, se debe a varios motivos señalados a seguir, con EXCEPCIÓN de:
(A) ausencia de sistemas de financiación.
(B) intereses contrapuestos entre países biodiversos y los industrializados.
(C) rechazo de parte de las organizaciones ecologistas a la acción lenta y optimista.
(D) incapacidad del Fondo Mundial Ambiental para aportar recursos.
(E) anuncio de EE.UU. sobre la reducción a la mitad de su aportación.

(Interpretación) A: Incorrecta. El tercer párrafo nos permite afirmar la ausencia de sistemas de financiación: "La financiación internacional topa con dificultades. El Fondo Mundial Ambiental (GEF, en sus siglas en inglés) es incapaz de aportar recursos, y lo obstaculiza el anuncio de EEUU de reducir a la mitad su aportación, que es casi la cuarta parte de los 12.500 millones de euros que maneja."
B: Incorrecta. El primer párrafo indica que hay intereses contrapuestos entre los países biodiversos y los industrializados: "La falta de sistemas de financiación y los intereses contrapuestos entre países biodiversos (los del sur, que tienen la mayoría de las especies) y los industrializados (que, una vez acabada con su riqueza ambiental, buscan formas para explotar la de los demás) son las causas de este fracaso anunciado."
C: Correcta. El último párrafo afirma lo contrario: "Aunque se trata de un acuerdo para empezar a establecer la regulación es "poner la primera pica", dijo Serrano. Un optimismo que no comparten las organizaciones ecologistas presentes en la cumbre, como Greenpeace, que el martes dio su anti-premio Pelota Desinflada (representada por un globo terráqueo vacío) a la UE por demorar al menos dos años la puesta en marcha de este sistema de compensación."
D: Incorrecta. El tercer párrafo nos permite afirmar la ausencia de sistemas de financiación: "La financiación internacional topa con dificultades. El Fondo Mundial Ambiental (GEF, en sus siglas en inglés) es incapaz de aportar recursos, y lo obstaculiza el anuncio de EEUU de reducir a la mitad su aportación, que es casi la cuarta parte de los 12.500 millones de euros que maneja."
E: Incorrecta. El tercer párrafo nos permite afirmar la ausencia de sistemas de financiación: "La financiación internacional topa con dificultades. El Fondo Mundial Ambiental (GEF, en sus siglas en inglés) es incapaz de aportar recursos, y lo obstaculiza el anuncio de EEUU de reducir a la mitad su aportación, que es casi la cuarta parte de los 12.500 millones de euros que maneja."

Gabarito "C".

Texto I

Inmigrantes imprescindibles

La llegada de inmigrantes a los países ricos continúa imparable pese a la ralentización de la actividad económica y el estallido de la burbuja tecnológica en los últimos años. Ésta es una de las
5 conclusiones del informe de la Organización de Cooperación y desarrollo Económico (OCDE) titulado *Tendencias en la migración internacional*. El informe se centra no sólo en la inmigración que llena las páginas de sucesos –los desesperados que mueren en las
10 costas de España e Italia o en la oscuridad del túnel del Canal de la Mancha–, sino sobre todo en los inmigrantes, regulares o irregulares, que cuidan de niños y ancianos, construyen casas, trabajan en la agricultura...; en definitiva, en aquellos que "están
15 cambiando la estructura de las sociedades desarrolladas y permiten la movilidad social y profesional de los nacionales", como dice el estudio.
La condición de los inmigrantes también ha cambiado. Ahora, la mayoría son personas que buscan
20 sobre todo trabajo, incluso ha aumentado el número de los que tienen alguna calificación profesional, principalmente en los sectores sanitario y tecnológico.
En contrapartida, el descenso de los solicitantes de asilo o refugiados es notable. El fin de las guerras
25 balcánicas y la introducción de medidas restrictivas por numerosos Gobiernos tras el 11-S han provocado una caída en picado de su número. Y aquí es donde está el verdadero reto. La contribución de la inmigración al crecimiento demográfico y a la fuerza laboral de los
30 países ricos ha sido decisiva. Al margen de las naciones con tradición en la acogida de inmigrantes (Australia, Canadá, EEUU), el porcentaje de extranjeros en los países europeos ha crecido exponencialmente en los últimos años: 8,9% de la población en Alemania, 6,2% en
35 Francia, 4,6% en Suecia, e incluso ¡un 5,6%! en Irlanda, un país históricamente de emigrantes.
Los nacimientos registrados entre la población inmigrante alivian los efectos del envejecimiento de Europa, pero el informe advierte que "ésta no será una
40 solución permanente porque el índice de fertilidad de las mujeres extranjeras tiende a converger con las de las nacionales con el tiempo".

El País, 04 feb. 2004 (adaptado)

(Advogado – BNDES – 2004 – CESGRANRIO) Términos como *ralentización* y *burbuja tecnológica* (líneas 2-4) conllevan percepciones aguzadas de una realidad poco compatible con:

(A) el dinamismo de la migración europea.
(B) los propósitos tecnológicos de la UE.
(C) las tendencias de la migración internacional.
(D) la conclusión del informe de la OCDE.
(E) la llegada de inmigrantes a los países ricos.

(Interpretación) A, B, C, D, E: La única alternativa correcta es la E. El término "ralentización" quiere decir disminución de velocidad en determinado proceso, y el sentido de la expresión "estallido de la burbuja tecnológica" es de ruptura con un orden insostenible. En ese sentido, esos términos son poco compatibles que el atractivo económico que impulsa la llegada de inmigrantes a los países ricos.

Gabarito "E".

(Advogado – BNDES – 2004 – CESGRANRIO) Los *sucesos* mencionados en el primer párrafo del texto (líneas 7-11) se refieren a:

(A) las frecuentes victorias de los inmigrantes irregulares que llegan a la UE.
(B) los episodios más significativos para el informe de la OCDE.
(C) los accidentes más comunes entre los inmigrantes regulares.
(D) algunas circunstancias que provocan la muerte de los inmigrantes.
(E) acontecimientos de poca importancia que registran los inmigrantes.

(Interpretación) A, B, C, D, E: La única alternativa correcta es la D. En castellano, el término "suceso" reviste dos sentidos: 1) lo que sucede cuando reviste cierta importancia; 2) hecho desgraciado o delictivo. Lo que nos permite afirmar que los sucesos mencionados en el primer párrafo del texto se refieren a algunas circunstancias que provocan la muerte de los inmigrantes es la afirmativa siguiente: El informe se centra no sólo en la inmigración que llena las páginas de sucesos "los desesperados que mueren en las costas de España e Italia o en la oscuridad del túnel del Canal de la Mancha [...]".

Gabarito "D".

(Advogado – BNDES – 2004 – CESGRANRIO) En el Texto I, la conjunción sino (línea 11) establece con la oración anterior una relación de:

(A) coordinación disyuntiva.
(B) coordinación distributiva.
(C) coordinación adversativa.
(D) subordinación adversativa.
(E) subordinación circunstancial.

(Interpretación) A, B, C, D, E: La única alternativa correcta es la C. La conjunción "sino" (línea 11) tiene relación de coordinación y de adversidad con la oración anterior: "El informe se centra no sólo en la inmigración que llena las páginas de sucesos "los desesperados que mueren en las costas de España e Italia o en la oscuridad del túnel del Canal de la Mancha", sino sobre todo en los inmigrantes, regulares o irregulares, que cuidan de niños y ancianos, construyen casas, trabajan en la agricultura […]".
Gabarito "C".

(Advogado – BNDES – 2004 – CESGRANRIO) La preocupación principal del informe de la OCDE es:

(A) establecer nuevos patrones para la migración internacional.
(B) relatar la situación de la inmigración, regular o irregular, en Europa.
(C) reconocer la importancia de la migración para los países en desarrollo.
(D) poner en tela de juicio la necesidad de contratar a extranjeros.
(E) proponer la utilización de la mano de obra extranjera.

(Interpretación) A, B, C, D, E: La única alternativa que tiene respaldo en el texto es la letra B. Las líneas del texto que nos permiten así concluir son: "La llegada de inmigrantes a los países ricos continúa imparable pese a la ralentización de la actividad económica y el estallido de la burbuja tecnológica en los últimos años informe de la Organización de Cooperación y desarrollo Económico (OCDE) titulado *Tendencias en la migración internacional*. El informe se centra no sólo en la inmigración que llena las páginas de sucesos "los desesperados que mueren en las costas de España e Italia o en la oscuridad del túnel del Canal de la Mancha", sino sobre todo en los inmigrantes, regulares o irregulares, que cuidan de niños y ancianos, construyen casas, trabajan en la agricultura…; en definitiva, en aquellos que "están cambiando la estructura de las sociedades desarrolladas y permiten la movilidad social y profesional de los nacionales", como dice el estudio".
Gabarito "B".

(Advogado – BNDES – 2004 – CESGRANRIO) La expresión *en definitiva* (línea 14), se sustituye en el contexto por:

(A) en conclusión.
(B) en la realidad.
(C) asimismo.
(D) finalmente.
(E) también.

(Vocabulario) A, B, C, D, E: La única correcta es letra A. Se podría substituir, sin pérdida de valor semántico, "en definitiva" por "en conclusión": "[…] en definitiva, en aquellos que "están cambiando la estructura de las sociedades desarrolladas y permiten la movilidad social y profesional de los nacionales", como dice el estudio" (línea 14 y 15).
Gabarito "A".

(Advogado – BNDES – 2004 – CESGRANRIO) El pronombre complemento los, en la línea 23, se refiere concretamente a los:

(A) solicitantes de asilo.
(B) miembros de la OCDE.
(C) refugiados notables de las guerras.
(D) nacimientos registrados en notaría.
(E) inmigrantes cuya condición ha cambiado.

(Gramática) A, B, C, D, E: La única correcta es la letra E. El pronombre complemento "los" se refiere a los inmigrantes cuya condición ha cambiado: "La condición de los inmigrantes también ha cambiado. Ahora, la mayoría son personas que buscan sobre todo trabajo, incluso ha aumentado el número de los que tienen alguna calificación profesional, principalmente en los sectores sanitario y tecnológico" (líneas 22 y 23).
Gabarito "E".

(Advogado – BNDES – 2004 – CESGRANRIO) La "…introducción de medidas restrictivas por numerosos Gobiernos…" (líneas 25-26) se debe:

(A) al miedo de que les acometan ataques terroristas como les acometió a los americanos.
(B) al fin de las guerras balcánicas y a la inestabilidad política de las naciones que promueven las guerras.
(C) a la perfidia de los países pobres que contribuyen a la inmigración de los pordioseros.
(D) a la disminución irremediable de la actividad económica en los países desarrollados.
(E) a la disminución demográfica y de la fuerza laboral de los países en desarrollo.

(Interpretación) A, B, C, D, E: La única alternativa que encuentra respaldo en el texto es la A. Las líneas 25 y 26 nos permiten afirmar que la "introducción de medidas restrictivas por numerosos Gobiernos se debe al miedo de que les acometan ataques terroristas como les acometió a los americanos": "El fin de las guerras balcánicas y la introducción de medidas restrictivas por numerosos Gobiernos tras el 11-S han provocado una caída en picado de su número". La mención al 11-S es una referencia a los atentados contra las Torres Gemelas el 11 de septiembre de 2001, en Nueva York.
Gabarito "A".

(Advogado – BNDES – 2004 – CESGRANRIO) Cuando se menciona en el texto el *verdadero reto* (línea 28), se aclara la importancia de la inmigración en cuanto a la/al:

(A) cuestión laboral.
(B) supervivencia de los nacionales.
(C) movilidad social y profesional de los inmigrantes.
(D) crecimiento demográfico y económico.
(E) cuidado de los niños.

(Interpretación) A, B, C, D, E: La única alternativa que encuentra respaldo en el texto es la D. Las líneas que nos permiten así concluir son las 26 y 27: "Y aquí es donde está el verdadero reto. La contribución de la inmigración al crecimiento demográfico y a la fuerza laboral de los países ricos ha sido decisiva".
Gabarito "D".

(Advogado – BNDES – 2004 – CESGRANRIO) La convergencia a la que se refiere el Texto I (último párrafo) se convertirá en un problema para:

(A) el rejuvenecimiento de Europa.
(B) la fertilidad de las mujeres europeas.
(C) la concienciación de la mujer.
(D) la población inmigrante.
(E) los nacimientos oriundos de la migración.

(Interpretación) A, B, C, D, E: La única alternativa que encuentra respaldo en el texto es la A. Las líneas del último párrafo que nos permiten así concluir son las siguientes: "Los nacimientos registrados entre la población inmigrante alivian los efectos del envejecimiento de Europa, pero el informe advierte que "ésta no será una solución permanente porque el índice de fertilidad de las mujeres extranjeras tiende a converger con las de las nacionales con el tiempo."
Gabarito "A".

Texto II

El gasto social y la inversión en infraestructura, dos de las prioridades que se ha fijado el gobierno de Néstor Kirchner, podrían aumentarse por un programa de créditos del Banco Interamericano de Desarrollo
5 (BID) de hasta US$ 5500 millones para el período 2004/2008, si este organismo lo aprueba. El presidente del BID declaró que se dará el visto bueno, y altas fuentes del banco admitieron que la cifra solicitada son US$ 5000 millones, "que pueden ser más si se
10 ejecutan bien los US$ 2800 millones del anterior programa y si se presentan suficientes proyectos".
La llamada estrategia de financiamiento se discute entre el presidente del BID y el ministro de Economía argentino en Lima, donde han comenzado las reuniones
15 preliminares de la 45ª reunión anual de la asamblea de gobernadores del BID.
Argentina ya ha solicitado al Banco Mundial la aprobación de un programa de créditos por otros US$ 5000 millones, pero el directorio de esa entidad aún
20 no lo ha votado, ante las disputas entre el país y el Fondo Monetario Internacional (FMI) por la negociación de la deuda en default. En cambio, el BID, del que 50,3% de las acciones está en manos de los países latinoamericanos, se diferenciará del Banco Mundial
25 (BM), dominado por el grupo de los siete países más ricos del mundo (G-7), y agilizará el tratamiento del programa solicitado por el Gobierno, según fuentes de la delegación argentina. Además, el estudio de la estrategia presentada al BID comenzó más tarde, en el gobierno de
30 Néstor Kirchner, mientras que el pedido al BM fue en el de Eduardo Duhalde.
Los fondos pedidos al BID irán destinados a la Nación y a las provincias, tal como se viene haciendo desde 1996. Pese a varios otros proyectos, los distritos
35 también pretenden recursos para la modernización del Estado en la recaudación tributaria. Cada provincia recibirá entre US$ 80 millones y US$ 250 millones.
La Nación espera para fines de año un crédito de US$ 500 millones para la mejora de la gestión y de la
40 transparencia del gasto social y del sector público en general. Estos fondos contribuirán a la implementación de las tarjetas sociales para los beneficiarios del plan Jefes y Jefas de Hogar. Por ahora, sólo se especificarán los créditos solicitados para los próximos 12 meses y no
45 todos los que se ejecutarán hasta 2008.
El BID concede a los países préstamos de emergencia, de políticas de Estado y de inversión, pero la Argentina ya no quiere usar los primeros porque van en detrimento de los otros. Sin embargo, el país debió
50 echar mano de ellos en 2003, cuando recibió US$ 1900 millones que deberá cancelar en cinco años. El horizonte de vencimientos con el BID está despejado de grandes pagos hasta 2006.
Si el Gobierno ejecuta "razonablemente" los
55 US$ 2800 millones pendientes, entre los que figuran el financiamiento al sector agrícola para promover exportaciones e infraestructuras, se cubrirán todos los vencimientos con el BID de este año. Mientras tanto sigue subiendo la partida de la entidad para la Argentina.
60 "Al FMI no podéis tenerlo como caja chica de donde se saca cuando necesitáis, pero los bancos de desarrollo deberían ir incrementando su exposición en el país a lo largo del tiempo y es lo que viene sucediendo con altibajos tanto con el BID como con el Banco Mundial",
65 manifestó una fuente de la delegación argentina.

Alejandro Rebossio. **La Nación Line**.
26 marzo 04 (adaptado)

(Advogado – BNDES – 2004 – CESGRANRIO) En la línea 7, "el visto bueno" al cual se refiere el primer párrafo significa que:

(A) la cifra solicitada no está correcta.
(B) el BID aprobará el préstamo solicitado.
(C) el gasto social estará condicionado al BID.
(D) se permiten nuevas inversiones en el BID.
(E) se reconoce la validez del gobierno.

(Vocabulario) A, B, C, D, E: La única alternativa correcta es la letra B. "El visto bueno" al cual se refiere el primer párrafo significa que el BID aprobará el préstamo solicitado: "El presidente del BID declaró que se dará el visto bueno, y altas fuentes del banco admitieron que la cifra solicitada son US$ 5000 millones, "que pueden ser más si se ejecutan bien los US$ 2800 millones del anterior programa y si se presentan suficientes proyectos" (líneas 6 y 7).
Gabarito "B".

(Advogado – BNDES – 2004 – CESGRANRIO) La lectura correcta del numeral 5.000.000.000 es:

(A) cinco millones.
(B) cinco billones.
(C) cinco mil millones.
(D) cinco millones de millones.
(E) cinco billones de millones.

(Vocabulario) A, B, C, D, E: La única alternativa correcta es la letra C. La lectura correcta del numeral 5.000.000.000 es cinco mil millones, o cinco millardos. Por otro lado, millones equivale 1.000.000; billones, a 1.000.000.000.000.
Gabarito "C".

(Advogado – BNDES – 2004 – CESGRANRIO) La principal razón por la cual el Banco Mundial no ha aprobado todavía un nuevo programa de créditos para el referido país (3er párrafo) es que:

(A) la falta del reintegro al FMI le inhibe al BM aprobar nuevos préstamos.
(B) las coyunturas internacionales no son favorables a nuevos préstamos.
(C) el FMI no lo permite hasta que se salden las deudas con este organismo.
(D) el BID no aprueba nuevos créditos para los países en default.
(E) los nuevos programas de créditos están prohibidos hasta el 2008.

(Interpretación) A, B, C, D, E: La única alternativa que tiene respaldo en el texto es la letra A. Las líneas que nos permiten así afirmar son las 18,19, 20 y 21: "Argentina ya ha solicitado al Banco Mundial la aprobación de un programa de créditos por otros US$ 5000 millones, pero el directorio de esa entidad aún no lo ha votado, ante las disputas entre el país y el Fondo Monetario Internacional (FMI) por la negociación de la deuda en default".
Gabarito "A".

(Advogado – BNDES – 2004 – CESGRANRIO) El verbo comenzar (línea 29) sufre en los tiempos del presente las mismas irregularidades que los verbos:

(A) mentir y soler.
(B) servir y mover.
(C) apretar y volver.
(D) empezar y entender.
(E) colgar y cocer.

(**Gramática**) A, B, C, D, E: La única alternativa correcta es la letra D. El verbo "comenzar", en los tiempos del presente, sufre las mismas irregularidades que los verbos "empezar" y "entender". Vea: *Empezar*: yo empiezo/tú empiezas/él, ella, Ud. empieza/nosotros empezamos/vosotros empezáis/ellos, ellas, Uds. empiezan/vos empezás. *Comenzar*: yo comienzo/tú comienzas/él, ella, Ud. comienza/ nosotros comenzamos/vosotros comenzáis/ellos, ellas, Uds. comienzan/vos comenzás. *Entender*: yo entiendo/tú entiendes/él, ella, Ud. entiende/nosotros entendemos/vosotros entendéis/ellos, ellas, Uds. entienden/vos entendés.
Gabarito "D".

(**Advogado – BNDES – 2004 – CESGRANRIO**) La expresión *pese a* (4º párrafo), al referirse a la recaudación tributaria, señala la:
(A) posibilidad de rehusarse otros proyectos para concretarse la recaudación.
(B) importancia de las provincias cuando el tema es la modernización.
(C) distancia existente entre el deseo de los distritos y su concreción.
(D) incapacidad del Gobierno para amortizar sus deudas tributarias.
(E) prioridad de la modernización sobre varios otros proyectos.

(**Interpretación**) A, B, C, D, E: La única alternativa correcta es la letra E. En este caso, la expresión "pese" significa "a pesar de". Substitúyase, entonces, en la línea 34, "pese" por "a pesar de": *a pesar de* "varios otros proyectos, los distritos también pretenden recursos para la modernización del Estado en la recaudación tributaria. Cada provincia recibirá entre US$ 80 millones y US$ 250 millones".
Gabarito "E".

(**Advogado – BNDES – 2004 – CESGRANRIO**) De la oración: "El horizonte de vencimientos con el BID está despejado de grandes pagos hasta 2006." (líneas 51 a 53), se infiere que, hasta el año de 2006, las deudas de Argentina con el BID:
(A) ya estarán quitadas.
(B) se convertirán en un estorbo.
(C) son relativamente bajas.
(D) no se conseguirán pagar.
(E) no estarán libres de intereses.

(**Interpretación**) A, B, C, D, E: La única alternativa correcta es la letra C. Los términos "horizonte" y "despejado" funcionan, en este caso, como metáforas para establecer comparación con un cielo sin nubes. En otras palabras, se podría entender la expresión como un porvenir sin problemas. En ese sentido, de la oración "El horizonte de vencimientos con el BID está despejado de grandes pagos hasta 2006" (líneas 51 a 53) se infiere que las deudas de Argentina con el BID son relativamente bajas.
Gabarito "C".

EL LÍO DE LAS TASAS

Revive el debate por el costo de los créditos que otorgan las entidades financieras. ¿Qué hay en el fondo de este nuevo 'round' entre banqueros y gobierno? Hace dos semanas el ministro de Desarrollo, Eduardo Pizano, llamó la atención del país sobre un hecho aritmético muy sencillo pero de grandes implicaciones económicas y políticas. Quien se acerca a un banco a solicitar, por ejemplo, un crédito de consumo, debe pagar una tasa cercana al 33 por ciento. Ese mismo banco, sin embargo, a la hora de remunerar los depósitos de los ahorradores apenas reconoce una tasa que se acerca al 12 por ciento. La diferencia, 21 puntos, es lo que se conoce como el margen de intermediación financiera, que no es otra cosa que la remuneración que reciben los bancos por los servicios que prestan. Aunque podría considerarse un tecnicismo financiero reservado para las discusiones de los entendidos, el margen de intermediación se ha convertido en objeto de una acalorada discusión pública en el país. La queja de muchos usuarios y de algunos miembros del gobierno es que los bancos están cobrando unas tasas excesivamente altas por los créditos que otorgan. Algo que, en opinión de los críticos de los bancos, en nada contribuye al propósito de reactivar la economía, pues es bien sabido que una condición indispensable para que ésta despegue es que el crédito vuelva a fluir a las empresas y los hogares.

(Adaptado de **Revista Nación**, Colombia, septiembre de 2001.)

(**Advogado – BNDES – 2001 – VUNESP**) En cuanto al tipo de préstamo mencionado en el texto, su tasa es
(A) superior al 33%.
(B) inferior al 33%.
(C) exactamente de 33%.
(D) de aproximadamente 33%.
(E) del 12% al 33%.

(**Vocabulario**) A, B, C, D, E: La única alternativa correcta es la letra D. La expresión "una tasa cercana" equivale a "apropiadamente". Por lo tanto, se podría substituir, en la línea 4, "una tasa cercana al 33 por ciento" por "de aproximadamente 33%".
Gabarito "D".

(**Advogado – BNDES – 2001 – VUNESP**) La remuneración de los depósitos citada en el texto se refiere a
(A) cuentas de ahorro.
(B) cuentas corrientes.
(C) acciones del banco.
(D) fondos de inversión.
(E) cualquier inversión.

(**Interpretación**) A, B, C, D, E: La única alternativa correcta es la letra A. Lo que nos permite así concluir es la oración siguiente: "Ese mismo banco, sin embargo, a la hora de remunerar los depósitos de los ahorradores apenas reconoce una tasa que se acerca al 12 por ciento".
Gabarito "A".

(**Advogado – BNDES – 2001 – VUNESP**) Según la opinión de los críticos de los bancos,
(A) los bancos colombianos están cobrando tasas muy altas.
(B) las alzas en las tasas de los créditos perjudican la reactivación de la economía.
(C) las altas tasas contribuyen para la inflación de la economía.
(D) las tarifas en los préstamos concedidos son excesivas.
(E) con la disminución de las tarifas bancarias habrá más préstamos.

(Interpretación) A, B, C, D, E: La única alternativa correcta es la letra B. Lo que nos permite así concluir son las oraciones siguientes: "La queja de muchos usuarios y de algunos miembros del gobierno es que los bancos están cobrando unas tasas excesivamente altas por los créditos que otorgan. Algo que, en opinión de los críticos de los bancos, en nada contribuye al propósito de reactivar la economía, pues es bien sabido que una condición indispensable para que ésta despegue es que el crédito vuelva a fluir a las empresas y los hogares".
Gabarito "B".

(Advogado – BNDES – 2001 – VUNESP) Las expresiones "sencillo", "se ha convertido" y "despegue" podrían sustituirse, según el sentido del texto y respectivamente, por:

(A) complicado – se ha transformado – crezca
(B) difícil – se ha fijado – evolucione
(C) simple – se ha transformado – evolucione
(D) simple – se ha vuelto – disminuya
(E) complicado – se ha fijado – disminuya

(Vocabulario) A, B, C, D, E: La única alternativa correcta es la letra C. En el texto, "sencillo" equivale a "simple", "se ha convertido" a "se ha transformado" y "despegue" a "evolucione".
Gabarito "C".

Córdoba: De la Sota juró la nueva Constitución

El gobernador de Córdoba, José Manuel de la Sota, juró ayer la nueva Constitución provincial y se insinuó como presidenciable. La reforma redujo a la mitad la cantidad de legisladores; además, achicó el gasto político legislativo y consolidó la hegemonía institucional del oficialismo. Otra vez, no hubo representantes de la oposición en la sesión. Entre los invitados estuvo el senador menemista Eduardo Bauzá. Luego, De la Sota encabezó un acto con la presencia de unas 2.000 personas.

(Extraído de **Diario Clarín**, Argentina, septiembre de 2001.)

(Advogado – BNDES – 2001 – VUNESP) La reforma en el sistema administrativo de la provincia argentina de Córdoba, con la toma de posesión del Sr. De la Sota,

(A) ha consolidado la hegemonía institucional del oficialismo a pesar del aumento del gasto con el legislativo.
(B) ha reducido a la mitad el número de legisladores, aunque haya aumentado el gasto político.
(C) ha consolidado la hegemonía institucional del oficialismo aun con la reducción de los legisladores.
(D) ha reducido a la mitad el número de legisladores, además de haber disminuido el gasto legislativo.
(E) ha disminuido a la mitad el número de legisladores y encima ha conseguido mantener el mismo gasto político.

(Interpretación) A, B, C, D, E: La única alternativa correcta es la letra D. En el texto, lo que nos permite así concluir es la oración siguiente: "La reforma redujo a la mitad la cantidad de legisladores; además, achicó el gasto político legislativo y consolidó la hegemonía institucional del oficialismo".
Gabarito "D".

(Advogado – BNDES – 2001 – VUNESP) La forma del verbo "haber" (hubo) que aparece en el texto, podría sustituirse, en el caso de que el verbo fuera el "estar", por

(A) estuvo
(B) estuvieron
(C) ha estado
(D) estuve
(E) estuvimos

(Gramática) A, B, C, D, E: La única alternativa correcta es la letra B. En este caso, la forma del verbo haber conjugada en el pretérito perfecto – "hubo"- no existe en forma plural. Así, su substitución por el verbo "estar", que sí admite plural en el pretérito perfecto, flexiona el verbo en la forma "estuvieron".
Gabarito "B".

Reubicación rápida en Nueva York

"En los próximos días, todo el mundo podrá tener ya su nueva ubicación", dijo Raymond O'Keefe, director de Grubb & Ellis. En este momento, los únicos escollos que todavía quedan para que una empresa empiece a operar en una nueva ubicación son las comunicaciones y las funciones informatizadas, explicó O'Keefe. Además de las torres gemelas, los edificios destruidos son 4, 5, 6 y 7 World Trade Center. One Liberty Plaza sufrió un derrumbe parcial. Entre los edificios con daños se cuentan tres del World Financial Center, 1 Bankers Trust Plaza, 140 West St., 90 Church St. y 195 Broadway.

(Adaptado de Diario Clarín, Argentina, septiembre de 2001.)

(Advogado – BNDES – 2001 – VUNESP) Con respecto al texto Reubicación rápida, el director de la empresa Grubb & Ellis dice que en los próximos días, las empresas

(A) tendrán nuevas perspectivas para un futuro cercano.
(B) van a tener que reorganizarse y revisar sus objetivos.
(C) tendrán nuevas metas profesionales que alcanzar.
(D) podrán presentar nuevas funciones informatizadas.
(E) podrán tener nuevas direcciones para operar.

(Interpretación) A, B, C, D, E: La única alternativa correcta es la letra E. La frase del texto que nos lo indica es: "En los próximos días, todo el mundo podrá tener ya su nueva ubicación", dijo Raymond O'Keefe, director de Grubb & Ellis (línea 1).
Gabarito "E".

(Advogado – BNDES – 2001 – VUNESP) Basándose en el texto Reubicación rápida, las palabras "escollo", "todavía" y "quedan" significan, respectivamente:

(A) dificultad – aún – permanecen
(B) escombro – aun – hay
(C) desecho – encima – permanecen
(D) obstáculo – encima – hay
(E) escombro – aún – hay

(Vocabulario) A, B, C, D, E: La única alternativa correcta es la letra A. Respectivamente, los equivalentes semánticos de "escollo", "todavía" y "quedan" podrían ser "dificultad", "aún" y "permanecen".
Gabarito "A".

"Camino a casa" aborda la relación del país nórdico con la Alemania nazi

El islandés Ólafur Ólafsson acaba de publicar en España "Camino a casa" (RBA), una novela traducida ya a varios idiomas que narra el viaje de regreso de una mujer, Dísa, a Islandia tras pasar muchos años en Inglaterra. El libro, del que la productora norteamericana Palomar Pictures ha comprado los derechos para el cine, es una excelente ocasión para acercarse a una literatura poco conocida en nuestro país. En la novela, Ólafsson aborda el escabroso asunto de las relaciones de Islandia con la Alemania nazi. En "Camino a casa", explica Ólafsson, "Dísa cierra el ciclo entre pasado y presente y recupera la paz. Al principio del libro dice que ha planeado este viaje muchas veces y que siempre lo ha aplazado; esta vez, no. En este sentido, la novela relata un viaje heroico en el que una mujer se enfrenta a su pasado".

Uno de los temas de la novela, las relaciones de Islandia con la Alemania nazi, suele pasarse por alto en su país. "A veces olvidamos que en Islandia hubo gente que simpatizó con los nazis. Desde Alemania se contemplaba a Islandia con una luz romántica, como un lugar de puros arios. Cuando, durante la II Guerra Mundial, las tropas británicas se instalaron allí, parece que se adelantaron por unas semanas a los planes alemanes. Islandia no fue independiente hasta 1944, y hasta entonces dependía de Dinamarca, que ya estaba ocupada por Alemania".

(Adaptado de **El País**, España, septiembre de 2001.)

(Advogado – BNDES – 2001 – VUNESP) "Camino a Casa", según las declaraciones de su autor, es

(A) una obra cuya protagonista es una mujer que solía aplazar el regreso a su tierra.
(B) una telenovela islandesa ya doblada en varios idiomas.
(C) un libro que cuenta la historia de Dísa y su vuelta a Inglaterra.
(D) una película cuyos derechos fueron comprados por una productora estadounidense.
(E) una obra que habla del apoyo islandés a la Alemania nazista.

(**Interpretación**) A, B, C, D, E: La única alternativa que tiene respaldo en el texto es la letra A. En el texto, de dice que "Al principio del libro dice que ha planeado este viaje muchas veces y que siempre lo ha aplazado; esta vez, no. En este sentido, la novela relata un viaje heroico en el que una mujer se enfrenta a su pasado". Sinónimos posibles de la palabra "aplazar" son: postergar, prorrogar, demorar, diferir, dilatar, posponer, retardar, retrasar, preterir, tardar, suspender.
Gabarito "A."

(Advogado – BNDES – 2001 – VUNESP) El principal tema abordado en "Camino a Casa" es

(A) el refugio de alemanes en lugares altos de Islandia.
(B) la independencia de Islandia, en el año de 1944
(C) las relaciones germanoislandesas en la época del nazismo.
(D) la ocupación alemana en países como Dinamarca.
(E) la instalación de tropas británicas en Islandia.

(**Interpretación**) A, B, C, D, E: La única alternativa que tiene respaldo en el texto es la letra C. Lo que nos permite así afirmar es la oración: "En la novela, Ólafsson aborda el escabroso asunto de las relaciones de Islandia con la Alemania nazi".
Gabarito "C."

Texto I

ELPAÍS.com | **Deportes**

"Adiós a nuestro complejo de perros callejeros"

Los brasileños consideran, como destaca Lula, que ya son "ciudadanos respetados del mundo"

Tras las lágrimas de emoción por el sueño cumplido, Río de Janeiro y todo Brasil se despertaron ayer con la conciencia de haber conseguido ser reconocidos como un país con el que hay que contar.
5 "Hemos recibido nuestro carnet de identidad como ciudadanos respetados del mundo", dijo el presidente, Lula da Silva. "Es el fin de nuestro complejo de perros callejeros", escribió ayer uno de los más importantes analistas políticos, Merval Pereira.
10 Quizás por esta conciencia de que Brasil ya es alguien que cuenta no sólo en el continente latinoamericano, sino en todo el planeta, ayer mismo comenzaron los análisis "para transformar la victoria en oportunidad", como escribía Myriam Leitão *(O Globo)*,
15 quien ha recordado que los Juegos Olímpicos son más que un momento de fiesta deportiva, ya que representan la ocasión "para que se amalgamen deportes, economía, educación, política, cultura y cuestiones sociales".
Ahora todos los ojos están puestos en lo que los
20 Juegos podrán hacer en la transformación de Río, clave económica, cultural y emblemática de Brasil, y la repercusión que podrán tener en el resto del país. Por ello, Lula –contó ayer que Barack Obama, su homólogo de Estados Unidos le telefoneó para felicitarle
25 y le demostró su agrado por ser los Juegos en Suramérica– confesó que "no le había importado llorar" de emoción, ya que la elección de Río supone para Brasil "un nuevo camino de futuro".
Los teléfonos quedaron colapsados porque la
30 gente no se conformaba con saborear el triunfo con quien tenía al lado, sino que quiso compartirlo con amigos y familiares lejanos. Hasta a los corresponsales españoles les llamaban para preguntarles, antes del resultado, si estaban apostando por Río o por Madrid. La euforia fue
35 generalizada.
La clase política ha hecho al día siguiente un esfuerzo para entender más racionalmente el por qué de la victoria. Se recuerda que no ha sido un capricho ni un arbitrio del COI, sino que se enamoró de las bellas imágenes
40 de esta ciudad mágica. Recuerdan que ha sido el fruto de 16 años de esfuerzos acumulativos para transformar Brasil en una potencia económica en la que ya se puede confiar. Comenzó, tras la dictadura militar, el largo viaje democrático con el Gobierno de Itamar Franco, con la
45 institución del *Plan Real*, que acabó con la inflación de tres cifras que acogotaba al país y hacía más pobres si cabe a millones de personas que vivían en la miseria.
Continuó su trabajo el ejecutivo socialdemócrata de Fernando Henrique Cardoso con su política de
50 privatizaciones que atrajo a los grandes inversores y ha continuado con Lula, que no sólo mantuvo los logros de una economía controlada y sin inflación, sino que con su carisma, su popularidad y su agudo y pragmático sentido político, ayudó a dar a conocer mejor al mundo lo que ya

55 se estaba forjando en una nación en pleno desarrollo. Ahora, el gran reto es demostrar a los que han confiado en que Brasil es capaz de llevar a cabo una Copa del Mundo de fútbol en 2014 y unos Juegos en 2016 que nadie se ha equivocado. Para ello, los responsables
60 no han querido perder tiempo y ya el sábado tendrá lugar en Río la primera reunión de trabajo para poner en marcha la poderosa máquina olímpica, bajo la presidencia de Carlos Arthur Nuzman, presidente del comité nacional, a quien todos reconocen una parte no pequeña del
65 mérito de haber logrado que el sueño acariciado desde 1995 se hiciera realidad.

Disponible en: <http://www.elpais.com/articulo/ deportes/Adios/ complejo/perros/callejeros/ elpepidep/20091004elpepidep_3/Tes>.

(Técnico – BNDES – 2010 – CESGRANRIO) Tras la lectura atenta del Texto I se advierte que

(A) nadie creía en el éxito final de la ciudad de Río de Janeiro.
(B) no hay brasileño que no padezca del complejo de perro callejero.
(C) el reto con el que soñaban los cariocas se ha cumplido.
(D) los demás concurrentes no se han conformado con la elección de Río.
(E) los brasileños ya sabían de antemano de la victoria de Río.

(Interpretación) Tras la lectura atenta del texto I, se deduce que el reto, o el desafío, con el que contaban los cariocas, es decir, hacer de su ciudad la sede de los Juegos Olímpicos de 2016, se ha cumplido. Rio de Janeiro fue electa la próxima ciudad olímpica.
Gabarito "C".

(Técnico – BNDES – 2010 – CESGRANRIO) El texto cita por cuatro veces hechos ocurridos "ayer".

El adverbio de tiempo destacado se refiere

(A) al día 04, la fecha de publicación del periódico.
(B) al día de la llegada a Dinamarca del equipo representante de Río.
(C) a la forma metafórica presente en el vocablo.
(D) a la víspera de la publicación del artículo.
(E) a un tiempo no declarado.

(Interpretación) Conforme se lee en la línea 3, el adverbio de tiempo "ayer" se refiere a la víspera de la publicación del artículo.
Gabarito "D".

(Técnico – BNDES – 2010 – CESGRANRIO) En el título del artículo, el sustantivo "perros" y su atributo "callejeros" reflejan

(A) el punto de vista personal de Merval Pereira.
(B) la manera por la cual nos ven los demás pueblos.
(C) que se trata de una paradoja.
(D) que el periodista J. Arias comparte la opinión del político brasileño.
(E) que al carioca le gusta callejear.

(Interpretación) En las líneas 7, 8 y 9, se explica que la expresión "perros callejeros" esgrime un punto de vista personal de Merval Pereira, "unos de los más importantes analistas políticos".
Gabarito "A".

(Técnico – BNDES – 2010 – CESGRANRIO) El conector "sino", que aparece tres veces en el texto (líneas 12, 31, 52), aunque tiene sentido de adversidad, manifiesta a la par, sentido de

(A) afirmación.
(B) inclusión.
(C) negación.
(D) exclusión.
(E) conclusión.

(Gramática) El conector "sino", en las líneas 12, 31 y 52, expresa no solamente sentido de adversidad, pero también de inclusión. En la líneas 12, por ejemplo, se comenta que Brasil cuenta no únicamente para la región latinoamericana, sino también para el planeta.
Gabarito "B".

(Técnico – BNDES – 2010 – CESGRANRIO) Entre las opciones abajo, la única que remite al pasado es

(A) "... los Juegos Olímpicos son más que un momento de fiesta deportiva," (líneas 15 y 16)
(B) "... representan la ocasión 'para que se amalgamen deportes, economía, educación, política, cultura y cuestiones sociales.' " (líneas 16 a 18)
(C) "... los Juegos podrán hacer en la transformación de Río, clave económica, cultural y emblemática de Brasil," (líneas 19 a 21)
(D) "Lula – contó (...) que Barack Obama (...) le telefoneó (...) y le demostró su agrado..." (líneas 23 a 25)
(E) "el gran reto es demostrar a los que han confiado en que Brasil es capaz de llevar a cabo una Copa del Mundo de fútbol en 2014..." (líneas 56 a 58)

(Gramática) El empleo del verbo "contar" en el tiempo verbal pretérito perfecto simple, es decir, conjugado como "contó", remite al pasado.
Gabarito "D".

(Técnico – BNDES – 2010 – CESGRANRIO) En el tercer párrafo, el pronombre "ello" tiene como referente

(A) el periodo anterior.
(B) el periodo posterior.
(C) Lula.
(D) Barack Obama.
(E) Brasil.

(Gramática) En el tercer párrafo, el pronombre "ello" tiene como referente el período pasado. Se refiere a "demostrar que nadie se ha equivocado [en el pasado]".
Gabarito "A".

(Técnico – BNDES – 2010 – CESGRANRIO) Hay en el penúltimo párrafo del texto una referencia a los 16 años a través de los cuales el país viene progresando.

Entre las causas a seguir, señale la que **NO** se incluye en ese proceso de desarrollo.

(A) El éxito del Plan Real con Itamar Franco.
(B) El término de la inflación de tres dígitos.
(C) El control de la economía con Lula.
(D) La política del socialdemócrata F. H. Cardoso.
(E) La dictadura militar.

(Interpretación) En la línea 43, se lee que el progreso brasileño ha comenzado tras la dictadura, con lo cual, el periodo militar es visto como una barrera al proceso de desarrollo.
Gabarito "E".

Texto II

GALLARDON PRESENTA EL LOGOTIPO PARA LA CANDIDATURA OLÍMPICA DE MADRID 20

Disponible en:< http://comicaire.blogspot.com/2007_10_01_archive.html >.

(Técnico – BNDES – 2010 – CESGRANRIO) La lectura del Texto II nos permite afirmar que

(A) todos los españoles estaban involucrados con la candidatura madrileña.
(B) hubo mucha oposición popular relación a la candidatura de Madrid a las olimpiadas.
(C) aunque el gobierno quisiera la candidatura, la población no estaba de acuerdo.
(D) no es la primera vez que Madrid pierde como candidata a recibir las olimpiadas
(E) es la segunda vez que Gallardón anuncia el rechazo de Madrid como ciudad candidata.

(**Interpretación**) El texto de la historieta nos permite afirmar que no es la primera vez que Madrid pierde como ciudad candidata a los Juegos Olímpicos. Se entiende que la ciudad fue rechazada en 2012, por lo cual se hicieron cambios en la candidatura para presentarla nuevamente para los Juegos de 2016.
Gabarito "D".

UNA CUESTIÓN DE PIEL

Por Carla Maldonado

Los defensores de los animales en la capital de la moda aseguran que detrás de cada abrigo hay una historia de sufrimiento y muerte. El tema enfrenta a ecologistas con productores de cuero, mientras los diseñadores parecen ajenos al debate.

MILÁN – Unos seis millones y medio de mujeres italianas tiene uno o más abrigos de piel. Y hay otros 4,3 millones que sueñan con comprar al menos uno por primera vez. La obsesión por esta prenda sigue condimentando el
5 debate ambiental: en un estado de ánimo dramáticamente opuesto al de las consumidoras, los defensores de los animales insisten en que detrás de cada uno de estos abrigos hay una historia de sufrimiento y muerte.
Italia es el primer fabricante de abrigos y accesorios
10 de piel en Europa: posee cuatro mil empresas pequeñas y medianas, 55 mil 964 empleados y factura dos mil 229 millones de dólares anuales (venta local y en Europa, Asia y Norteamérica).
"La confección en piel es una parte importante de la moda
15 'made in Italy' y está en crecimiento. Hay muchos controles, se respetan las leyes y la prohibición de utilizar especies en peligro de extinción. En Italia sólo se usan animales de criaderos para elaborar los abrigos", dijo a Tierramérica Alexandra Dagnino, portavoz de la Asociación
20 Italiana de Peletería.
El visón es una de las principales materias primas para abrigos en Italia. Es la única especie que nace, crece y muere en este país. La nutria, la marmota, el armiño y el zorro son otras valiosas especies, que se importan
25 de los países nórdicos y de Argentina, por un valor de 254 millones de dólares.
"Cada año, en Italia se matan 230 mil animales. Estos viven encerrados en jaulas y enloquecen. Están expuestos al frío, porque así el pelo endurece y el precio aumenta",
30 aseguró a Tierramérica Simona Cariat, responsable de pieles de la Liga Antidisección-Lav, la principal asociación en defensa de los animales en Italia.
La activista sostiene que los métodos para exterminar los animales que se usan en la fabricación de abrigos,
35 "son terroríficos, se parecen a los que usaban los nazis con los judíos. Les introducen en cámaras de gas, les electrocutan, les matan a bastonazos o les ahorcan, y después les botan fuera como si fueran basura".
Pero los fabricantes rechazan las acusaciones y aseguran
40 que siguen las normas europeas al pie de la letra (decreto 98/58 sobre el bienestar de los animales y el decreto 93/119 sobre el sacrificio de animales).
"No es verdad lo que dicen. En los criaderos los animales viven bajo cobertizos. No pueden mojarse con la lluvia o
45 asolearse, porque eso cambiaría el color de su pelo. Están encerrados en jaulas que tienen las medidas reglamentarias y están bien alimentados, comen alas y cuellos de pollo. Usamos el óxido de carbón que les hace morir en un minuto sin sufrir", dijo a Tierramérica Augusto
50 De Nardo, presidente de la Asociación de Criaderos de Animales.
Aún así, en julio de 2001, murieron 20 mil visones en los criaderos italianos. La causa fue el exceso de calor y la deshidratación, según grupos no gubernamentales.
55 Muchos consumidores ignoran que para confeccionar un solo abrigo, trabajado a mano durante tres días, se matan 54 visones. Si se desea una prenda hecha de piel de marmota, como las que usa el símbolo de la belleza francesa Catherine Deneuve, se requiere sacrificar
60 200 ejemplares.
Los ambientalistas más pragmáticos promueven un nuevo tipo de pieles: las ecológicas.
A simple vista los abrigos fabricados con estas fibras sintéticas parecen de visón o de marta. Dan la misma
65 sensación de calor que los auténticos y no necesitan someter a suplicios a ningún animal. Su material es lavable a mano, resistente, liviano y menos costoso (desde 170 dólares hasta 900 dólares).
Por todas estas cualidades, los defensores de los
70 animales consideran que la "piel ecológica' representa una alternativa. Para los fabricantes de piel, sin embargo, es una tomadura de pelo.
"La ley de 1966 prohíbe utilizar esa denominación a algo que no es piel. Es una mentira para el consumidor, el
76 material es de plástico, por lo tanto no es biodegradable", sostuvo Dagnino de la Asociación Italiana de Peletería.
"Es decir, no es piel, ni es ecológica".
La industria de la moda, entretanto, sigue ajena al debate ambiental. Unos 170 "stilistas" (diseñadores), la mayoría
80 italianos y los más importantes del mundo, como Armani, Fendi, Versacce, Valentino, Gian Franco Ferre, Trussardi y Dolce & Gabana, crean cada año una colección de abrigos de piel, que incluye chaquetas, chalecos, faldas y carteras.
85 Sus abrigos recuperan la tradición y el estilo clásico: prefieren el color natural, el largo hasta las rodillas y el corte menos amplio.
Las pieles también se combinan con otros materiales: tela de mezclilla o plumas en el cuello o mangas. El último
90 grito de la moda es el abrigo reversible. Los precios varían, entre 4 mil y 40 mil dólares.

Disponible en:< http//www.tierramérica.net/2003/01/12/articulo. Shtm>. Consulta del 26 mar. 2008.

(Técnico – BNDES – 2008 – CESGRANRIO) En "El tema **enfrenta** a ecologistas con productores de cuero," la palabra en negrito significa lo mismo que

(A) se rinde
(B) somete
(C) arregla
(D) opone
(E) olvida

(Vocabulario) El verbo enfrentar es sinónimo de confrontar, de encarar, de contraponer y de oponer.
Gabarito "D".

(Técnico – BNDES – 2008 – CESGRANRIO) "Están expuestos al frío, **porque** así el pelo endurece y El precio aumenta" (líneas 28 y 29). La palabra en negrito en el fragmento tiene sentido de

(A) consecuencia
(B) finalidad
(C) concesión
(D) simultaneidad
(E) causa

(Gramática) En este caso, la conjunción "porque" tiene sentido de finalidad, y no de causa. En otras palabras, y refiriéndonos al texto, se exponen los animal al frio con la finalidad de endurecerles el pelo y, así, de aumentar los precios de venta.
Gabarito "B".

(Técnico – BNDES – 2008 – CESGRANRIO) "…después les botan fuera como si fueran basura." (línea 38) Se puede sustituir **basura** por

(A) cerdo
(B) limosna
(C) resto inservible
(D) reciclaje de peluche
(E) peso de adobe

(Vocabulario) Basura quiere decir desecho o resto inservible.
Gabarito "C".

(Técnico – BNDES – 2008 – CESGRANRIO) "…tomadura de pelo." (línea 72) Se puede inferir por el contexto que dicha expresión significa lo mismo que

(A) sometimiento
(B) burla
(C) despiste
(D) aburrimiento
(E) esquileo

(Vocabulario) La expresión "tomadura de pelo" quiere decir burlarse de alguien o engañar. Otras expresiones con la palabra "pelo" son: "estar al pelo", que quiere decir en perfecto estado; "no tener pelos en la lengua", que quiere decir no temer a decir la verdad"; "montar al pelo", que es cabalgar sin montadura.
Gabarito "B".

(Técnico – BNDES – 2008 – CESGRANRIO) "La ley de 1966 prohíbe utilizar **esa denominación** a algo que no es piel." (líneas 73 y 74) Las palabras en negrito se refieren a

(A) abrigo
(B) pelo
(C) visón
(D) fibra
(E) piel

(Gramática) "Esa denominación" se refiere a "pelo ecológico", que figura en la línea 70.
Gabarito "E".

(Técnico – BNDES – 2008 – CESGRANRIO) En "…una colección de abrigos de piel, **que** incluye chaquetas, chalecos," (líneas 82 y 83). La partícula **que** equivale a

(A) la cual
(B) los cuales
(C) adónde
(D) quien
(E) cuyo

(Gramática) La partícula "que", cuya referencia es "una colección", equivale, en este caso, a "la cual".
Gabarito "A".

(Técnico – BNDES – 2008 – CESGRANRIO) La frase que sintetiza el argumento de la Asociación Italiana de Peletería en contra del material sintético es

(A) "Es decir, no es piel, ni es ecológica." (línea 77)
(B) "… están bien alimentados, comen alas y cuellos de pollo." (líneas 47 y 48)
(C) " No es verdad lo que dicen." (línea 43)
(D) "… así el pelo endurece y el precio aumenta" (línea 29)
(E) "… sólo se usan animales de criaderos…" (líneas 17 y 18)

(Interpretación) El argumento de la Asociación Italiana de Peletería está reflejado en la frase "es decir, no es piel, ni es ecológica". La Asociación se opone al discurso ambiental, que defiende el uso de pieles ecológicas, porque no son verdaderas pieles, lo que podría confundir el consumidor, ni productos biodegradables, lo que impide clasificarlas como ecológicas.
Gabarito "A".

(Técnico – BNDES – 2008 – CESGRANRIO) Teniendo en cuenta lo leído en "Una Cuestión de Piel", sea la piel ecológica o auténtica, sólo **NO** se puede afirmar que

(A) Italia es el más antiguo fabricante de artículos de piel en Europa.
(B) Catherine Deneuve suele llevar abrigos de piel auténticos.
(C) los abrigos sintéticos calientan y valen menos de 1000 dólares.
(D) algunas pieles parecen una mezcla de pinturas.
(E) muchos "stilistas" siguen creando colecciones de abrigos de piel.

(Interpretación) Todas las opciones figuran en el texto, excepto la D, según la cual se afirma que algunas pieles parecen una mezcla de pinturas. No hay referencia a la palabra "pintura" en el texto.
Gabarito "D".

Texto para los siguientes ítems.

Operadoras de telecomunicaciones invertirán 4.000 millones en Madrid

1   Las operadoras de telecomunicaciones invertirán 4.000 millones de euros en Madrid entre 2009 y 2016 para cambiar las viejas redes de cobre por fibra óptica y extender
4   la banda ancha en la telefonía móvil, con el objetivo de conseguir velocidades de transmisión de entre 30 y 100 megas.
7   Las empresas ejecutarán esta inversión en el marco de un Plan Director de Infraestructuras de Telecomunicación que el Ayuntamiento de Madrid ha redactado en
10 colaboración con ellas para conseguir que los beneficios de la sociedad de la información lleguen por igual a toda la ciudad y con criterios estéticos y de respeto al medio
13 ambiente.
    El Plan ha sido presentado hoy por el alcalde, Alberto Ruiz-Gallardón, ante numerosos representantes del
16 sector, que ha expresado su voluntad de colocar a Madrid en este ámbito en "una situación de liderazgo en la Unión Europea" que le permita, además, competir con
19 ciudades como Nueva York, Londres, Pekín o Singapur.
    El Ayuntamiento de Madrid ha querido con este plan hacer compatible su derecho a velar por un desarrollo
22 equilibrado y sostenible de la ciudad con el derecho de las operadoras a ocupar el dominio público para extender sus redes.
25 Las condiciones en que equilibrará ambos derechos se plasmarán en una Ordenanza para la Implantación de las Nuevas Tecnologías que actualizará la vigente desde 1999 y
28 que ha comenzado su tramitación hoy mismo.
    Esta Ordenanza reconocerá el "derecho" de los madrileños a acceder a la sociedad de la información y
31 facilitará el despliegue de las redes necesarias "desde el máximo respeto a los criterios de integración urbanística y respeto medioambiental", según el alcalde.
34 Ruiz-Gallardón ha relacionado el desarrollo de esta tecnología con la aspiración de Madrid a organizar los Juegos Olímpicos de 2016 al decir que sólo una ciudad
37 dotada de las más modernas tecnologías de telecomunicaciones puede convencer al COI de que merece acoger un acontecimiento de esa magnitud.

Internet: <www.finanzas.com> (con adaptaciones).

(Analista – ANATEL – 2009 – CESPE) De acuerdo con las ideas del texto, juzgue los ítems siguientes.

(1) La sociedad de la información en el Madrid de hoy se caracteriza por la carencia de desigualdades.

(2) Las inversiones previstas en el Plan Director de Infraestructuras de Telecomunicación comenzarán a ser aplicadas en 2009.

(3) En el ámbito de las telecomunicaciones Madrid compite con Londres y Singapur.

(Interpretación) 1: incorrecto. En las líneas 7 a 13, el autor explica que el Plan Director de Infraestructura de Telecomunicación ha sido redactado con el fin de extender por igual los beneficios de la sociedad de la información a toda la ciudad, con lo cual se entiende que existen carencia de igualdad, y no de desigualdad; 2: correcto. En la línea, se explica que las operadoras de telecomunicación invertirán 4.000 millones de euros en Madrid entre 2009 y 2016. En la línea 7, se comenta que esas empresas, es decir, las operadoras de telecomunicación, ejecutarán esa inversión en el marco del Plan Director; 3: incorrecto. Según se lee en las líneas 14 a 19, el alcalde de Madrid ha expresado su voluntad de colocar la ciudad en situación de liderazgo ante Nuevo York, Londres, Pekín y Singapur. En otros términos, se busca competir con esas ciudades, y no hacer que participen en el ámbito de las telecomunicaciones de Madrid; Gabarito 1E, 2C, 3E

(Analista – ANATEL – 2009 – CESPE) juzgue los ítems siguientes.

(1) Las operadoras de telecomunicación ocupan generalmente el espacio público de una forma desordenada y no respetan las condiciones medioambientales de la ciudad de Madrid.

(2) Se puede inferir que el alcalde de Madrid considera que El COI lleva en consideración el estado de las telecomunicaciones a la hora de decidir qué ciudad será sede de los Juegos Olímpicos.

(Interpretación) 1: incorrecto. En la línea 31, se explica que las condiciones de implantación de las nuevas tecnologías deberán respetar los criterios de integración urbanística y de respeto al medio ambiente; 2: correcto. En las líneas 34 a 37, se comenta que Ruiz-Gallardón, el alcalde de Madrid, ha relacionado el desarrollo de la tecnología con la aspiración de Madrid a organizar los Juegos Olímpicos de 2016, con lo cual se deduce que el COI reconoce la importancia de la implementación de modernas tecnologías de telecomunicación. Gabarito 1E, 2C

(Analista – ANATEL – 2009 – CESPE) Con respecto a las estructuras lingüísticas del texto, juzgue los siguientes ítems.

(1) La forma verbal "ha redactado" (ℓ.9) puede ser reemplazada por redactó sin producir alteraciones semánticas o gramaticales en el texto.

(2) El uso del modo subjuntivo en la forma verbal "lleguen" (ℓ.11) es debido al hecho de que es el núcleo verbal de una oración subordinada final.

(Gramática) 1: incorrecto. La substitución de la forma gramatical "ha redactado", en el pretérito perfecto compuesto, por "redactó", en el pretérito perfecto simple (o pretérito indefinido), implica un cambio de tiempo verbal; con lo cual, ocurre un cambio semántico, más allá del simple cambio gramatical; 2: incorrecto. La forma verbal "lleguen" constituye ejemplo de uso del modo substantivo, pero no está inserida en una oración subordinada final; Gabarito 1E, 2E

(Analista – ANATEL – 2009 – CESPE) juzgue los siguientes ítems.

(1) El elemento "a" en la estructura "a los que" (ℓ.16) introduce un complemento indirecto.

(2) El elemento "le" (ℓ.18) tiene como antecedente "Alberto Ruíz-Gallardón" (ℓ.15).

(3) En varios trechos del texto se utiliza el pretérito indefinido.

(Gramática) 1: correcto. La partícula "a" introduce, en este caso, un complemento indirecto; 2: incorrecto. El elemento "le", en la línea 18, tiene como antecedente "Madrid", en la línea 17; 3: incorrecto. El texto se caracteriza por utilizar el pretérito perfecto compuesto, y no el pretérito indefinido (o pretérito perfecto simple). Gabarito 1C, 2E, 3E

Texto para los siguientes ítems.

La OCU reclama un mayor controlde los alimentos funcionales

1   La Organización de Consumidores y Usuarios (OCU) ha planteado abiertamente la necesidad de un mayor control y regulación legal de los alimentos funcionales. En boga desde hace dos décadas, centran su peculiaridad en propiedades supuestamente beneficiosas para la salud a través del enriquecimiento con determinados micronutrientes. Pese a ello, las etiquetas
4   de muchos de ellos continúan siendo poco claras, lo que puede causar confusión entre los consumidores, por lo que se hace cada vez más necesario establecer algún tipo de control que garantice una información veraz. En opinión de José María Múgica, director de la OCU, muchos de los productos de esta categoría que actualmente pueden adquirirse en el mercado español utilizan
7   fórmulas que permiten escapar a cualquier normativa. "Lo que pedimos es que se controlen las menciones que se pueden incluir en este tipo de productos y que pueden inducir a la confusión entre los consumidores".
    Por ejemplo, cuando se habla de que un determinado producto adelgaza, se establece una relación de causa-efecto,
10   mientras que si se especifica que el producto concreto ayuda a adelgazar, "se está jugando con las palabras", de modo que se traslada al consumidor el mensaje que espera, cuando en realidad "todo puede ayudar a adelgazar", dice Múgica.
    Desde la organización consumerista se exige la regulación de los alimentos funcionales. En caso contrario, explica
13   Múgica, en pocos años entraríamos en el mundo de los *alicamentos*, alimentos que pretenden tener cualidades terapéuticas y preventivas como algunos medicamentos, pero que deberán ser demostradas a través de análisis científicos.
    La OCU lamenta, además, que muchas de las indicaciones contenidas en las etiquetas de los alimentos funcionales no
16   son demostrables científicamente. Por otra parte, al igual que en los productos destinados al público infantil, recuerdan la obligatoriedad de mencionar los beneficios de la lactancia materna, en los funcionales debería incluirse un mensaje que recordara que la salud depende de una dieta variada y equilibrada. El objetivo es que no se traslade al consumidor la idea de que un alimento
19   tiene un "efecto beneficioso y directo" sobre la salud, y evitar así que términos como salud o saludable no se empleen "con tanta alegría".
    Los alimentos funcionales son "producto del márqueting". "En muchos momentos se hace pensar a los consumidores que
22   unos productos son superiores a otros", señala el director de la OCU. Pero detrás de expresiones más o menos afortunadas, añade, la realidad acaba demostrando que en muchos casos se trata de simples "juegos de palabras". Por ejemplo, "con más sabor, ¿pero a qué?, o producto más rico, ¿en qué?".
25   Lo que sí ha conseguido la tecnología alimentaria es alcanzar estándares de calidad más homogéneos. Desde la OCU, explica Múgica, cuando se realizan análisis comparativos de productos en alimentación, con mucha frecuencia se observa una homogeneidad en los parámetros de calidad. Desde hace unos años han observado que las diferencias no se encuentran en el
28   producto propiamente dicho, aspecto que ha propiciado la aparición en el mercado de una batería de productos enriquecidos con micronutrientes como elemento diferencial, fundamentalmente en los lácteos, zumos y cereales. "Y cada vez van a aparecer más", predice.

Internet: <http://www.madrimasd.org> (adaptado).

(Analista – ANVISA – 2004 – CESPE) Según el texto, juzgue los siguientes ítems.

(1) Los alimentos funcionales son esenciales para la salud.
(2) En las etiquetas de un número significativo de productos funcionales, la información que se ofrece no está controlada por la OCU.
(3) Hay una base científicamente demostrada a la hora del márqueting de los productos funcionales.
(4) En términos de la condición y naturaleza de los productos funcionales, la tecnología alimentaria ha alcanzado una uniformidad.

(Interpretación) 1: incorrecto. En las líneas 1 a 4, se aclara que los alimentos deberían ser controlados y regulados debido a sus propiedades supuestamente beneficiosas para la salud. Además de esa suposición, se especifica que las etiquetas de los productos son poco claras y causan confusión; 2: correcto. Si la OCU ha planteado abiertamente la necesidad de un mayor control y regulación legal de los alimentos funcionales, se supone que la información que se ofrece en las etiquetas no está controlada por la OCU. Además, en la línea 7, se comenta que los productos pueden adquirirse en el mercado español sin control de cualquier normativa; 3: incorrecto. Por lo que se entiende en las líneas 21 a 23, el márqueting se vale de juegos de palabras, con los cuales se hace pensar que unos productos son superiores a otros. En ese sentido, no hay comprobación científica del contenido de dichos productos; 4: incorrecto. En la línea 25, se aclara que la tecnología alimentaria ha conseguido alcanzar estándares de calidad más homogéneos, pero no una homogeneidad total. Más adelante, en la línea 26, se comenta que la homogeneidad se refiere a los parámetros de calidad, y no en la tecnología alimentaria (alterado/atualizado).
Gabarito 1E, 2C, 3E, 4E

(Analista – ANVISA – 2004 – CESPE) En cuanto a su clasificación, uso y significado en el texto,

(1) El verbo "garantice" (ℓ.5) está en modo indicativo.
(2) La partícula "se", en las expresiones "se habla" (ℓ.9), "se establece" (ℓ.9) y "se especifica" (ℓ.10), le da un carácter impersonal al verbo.
(3) Las palabras "los" (ℓ.13) y "unos" (ℓ.22) son ambas artículos en el plural.
(4) La expresión "con tanta alegría" (ℓ.19-20) se refiere a entusiasmo, júbilo y alborozo.
(5) la partícula subrayada en "van a aparecer" (ℓ.29) es una preposición que pertenece al segundo verbo.

(Gramática) 1: incorrecto. El verbo "garantice" está en el modo subjuntivo; 2: correcto. La partícula "se", en esas situaciones, le agrega un carácter impersonal al verbo; 3: correcto. Los artículos "los" (ℓ. 13) y "unos" (ℓ.22) se refieren, respectivamente, a "alicamentos" y a "productos"; por lo tanto, están en el plural; 4: incorrecto. Aunque "entusiasmo", "júbilo" y "alborozo" sean sinónimos de "alegría", en este caso, la expresión "con tanta alegría" se refiere "efecto beneficioso y directo" (ℓ.19); 5: incorrecto. La partícula "a" no pertenece al segundo verbo, sino que introduce un verbo en el modo infinitivo.
Gabarito 1E, 2C, 3C, 4E, 5E

Texto I

Economía incomprensible

Por CLAUDIO SILVA / Ingeniero Agrónomo Cesante, U. de Chile.

Hijo y poblador de La Pintana

Mientras discuten acerca de los atributos masculinos del ministro Velasco (titular el día lunes), algunos nos hemos hecho muchas preguntas acerca del panorama económico del país, y de la labor de los economistas,
5 ampliamente laureados, que manejan la macroeconomía nacional e internacional. Cuando me enseñaron economía, me mostraron una amplia jerga financiera, además de varias formas matemáticas y gráficas de complejo entendimiento. No obstante la alta
10 matemática usada, vemos sendas diferencias en las proyecciones económicas entre varios actores de la economía (economistas, empresas y consultoras), en donde las palabras "incertidumbre" y "volatilidad" se repiten con inquietante frecuencia.
15 El primer objetivo de IPoM (Informe de Política Monetaria) es "informar y explicar al Senado, al Gobierno y al público general la visión del Consejo del Banco Central sobre la evolución reciente y esperada de la inflación y sus consecuencias para la conducción de la
20 política monetaria". Sin embargo, es olvidado el público en general, el cual, de ver estos informes, queda intimidado con toda la jerga bancaria y la espectacular gráfica. En la presentación del IPoM al senado, al presidente del Banco Central se le preguntó: "¿qué le diría Ud. a la dueña
25 de casa o a la gente común?". Por supuesto la pregunta fue eludida con una elegante verborrea financiera y proyectista.
En lo personal, esto me lleva a pensar que la economía y la política monetaria, en todo el mundo, se
30 manejan a punta de corazonadas y de completar las líneas de los gráficos siguiendo tendencias y correlaciones, condimentadas con "noticias no previstas", algo poco esperado para gente con Ph.D. de la casas de estudio con mayor prestigio del mundo.
35 Situaciones como ésta hacen que la gente común no se interese en temas económicos, y se mantenga el "status quo" –y la casta dominante– en la economía y en la política.

Disponible en: <http://www.theclinic.cl/2009/05/27/economiaincomprensible/>.

(Analista – BNDES – 2010 – CESGRANRIO) Marque la opción que representa un punto de vista **divergente** de la opinión del autor.

(A) A menudo, los del área económica emplean términos como incertidumbre y volatilidad de manera inquietante.
(B) A las tendencias del mercado y sus correlaciones se suman las noticias no previstas.
(C) Muchos de los economistas que manejan la macroeconomía han recibido sus certificados de PhD en instituciones de alto prestigio.
(D) La gente en general no alcanza el sentido de la jerga bancaria y la gráfica utilizadas.
(E) El IPoM suele informar con exactitud al público general, acerca de la política monetaria.

(Interpretación) Según el informe, se entiende que el IPoM no informa con exactitud al público general sobre la conducción de la política monetaria. En la línea 20, se comenta que la jerga bancaria olvida el público en general, el cual queda intimidado con la poca claridad de los informes.
Gabarito "E".

(Analista – BNDES – 2010 – CESGRANRIO) En los renglones 9 y 20 los periodos empiezan por dos conectores lingüísticos respectivamente "no obstante" y "sin embargo", que introducen a seguir una idea de

(A) aclaración.
(B) adversidad.
(C) finalidad.
(D) causa.
(E) suposición.

(Gramática) Los conectores lingüísticos "no obstante" y "sin embargo" introducen ideas de adversidad.
Gabarito "B".

(Analista – BNDES – 2010 – CESGRANRIO) Claudio Silva a veces se vale de la ironía de forma explícita, tal como en la opción que se presenta abajo, al referirse a

(A) la discusión acerca de los atributos físicos del ministro Velasco.
(B) la utilización excesiva de los términos incertidumbre y volatilidad.
(C) la elegante verborrea financiera y proyectista.
(D) el mantenimiento de la casta dominante en la economía y en la política.
(E) los economistas laureados que manejan la macroeconomía nacional e internacional.

(Interpretación) La ironía caracteriza una situación en la cual se dice lo contrario de lo que se piensa, dejando entender lo contrario de lo que se dice. La ironía, en este caso, está ejemplificada en la línea 1, por la cual se deja entender que los informes del IPoM son más importantes para el país que las discusiones acerca de los atributos masculinos del ministro Velasco.
Gabarito "A".

(Analista – BNDES – 2010 – CESGRANRIO) En las opciones abajo la única en que el articulista **NO** se incluye en el cuerpo del texto es

(A) "Claudio Silva/Ingeniero Agrónomo Cesante,"
(B) "algunos nos hemos hecho muchas preguntas..." (líneas 2 y 3)
(C) "Cuando me enseñaron economía," (líneas 6 y 7)
(D) "me mostraron una amplia jerga financiera," (líneas 7 y 8)
(E) "En lo personal, esto me lleva a pensar. ..." (línea 28)

(Gramática) La alternativa correcta es la letra A. En esta opción no constan las partículas "me" o "nos", que indican inclusión del articulista.
Gabarito "A".

(Analista – BNDES – 2010 – CESGRANRIO) "… la economía y la política monetaria, en todo el mundo, se manejan **a punta de corazonadas**..." (líneas 28 a 30)

Tomándose el texto como base, en el trozo anterior la expresión subrayada se acerca semánticamente al sentido presente en

(A) certidumbres.
(B) deseos inconfesables.
(C) impulsos espontáneos.
(D) noticias previsibles.
(E) estudios económicos.

(Vocabulario) La expresión "a punta de corazonadas" se refiere a impulsos espontáneos, con lo cual no puede ser una certidumbre, un deseo inconfesable, una noticia previsible o estudios económicos.
Gabarito "C".

Texto II

Del consumismo a la "economía de guerra" familiar

Los expertos creen que los hogares elevarán su tasa de ahorro durante años. El miedo al paro y el peso de la deuda condicionan las decisiones de gasto.

En apenas dos años, los hogares españoles han pasado del consumismo voraz y el endeudamiento sin complejos a una *economía de guerra*. Cada casa es un mundo y esta conclusión tendrá miles de excepciones,
5 pero es lo que cuenta la lectura simplificadora de las estadísticas. Las familias ahorran ya, en conjunto, un 17,5% de su renta disponible, una cifra inédita desde hace más de 40 años. Los expertos señalan que este drástico cambio de prioridades tendrá consecuencias en la
10 demanda y retrasará la recuperación. Pero, también, que era inevitable y que ha llegado para quedarse.
La facilidad para acceder al crédito, las buenas cifras de empleo y la percepción de que cada vez eran más ricos (al menos para los que eran propietarios de
15 viviendas o acciones), incentivaron a los hogares a consumir más y pedir más préstamos hasta hace bien poco. El súbito endeudamiento de las familias españolas fue una de las señales más nítidas de que la burbuja se hinchaba. Como lo fue que la tasa de ahorro cayera hasta
20 niveles mínimos en la historia moderna, cerca del 10%. La economía española se situó más cerca que nunca del modelo imperante en EE UU y Reino Unido, los paraísos del consumismo: mínimo ahorro familiar y deuda masiva.
Josep Oliver, catedrático de Economía de la
25 Universidad Autónoma de Barcelona, recalca el peso de los factores psicológicos en la economía, mayor aún si cabe en las decisiones domésticas. "Hay una enorme inquietud, muy marcada por lo que ocurre en el mercado de trabajo y por el elevado grado de endeudamiento",
30 explica.
Con la tasa de paro apuntando al 20%, impera el miedo a perder el puesto de trabajo y, con ello, la principal fuente de ingresos. La losa de afrontar el pago de una cuota hipotecaria cada mes, es otro incentivo a
35 reservar cada euro. Es lo que los economistas han bautizado como el ahorro por motivo de precaución. ¿Está siendo demasiado rápido el ajuste? Laborda y Oliver, dos de los principales estudiosos del tema en España, coinciden en que el repunte ha superado sus
40 expectativas. Pero no creen que sea negativo. "Quizá el consumo tarde algo más en volver a crecer, pero es un proceso inevitable, los mercados internacionales no nos van a permitir el grado de endeudamiento de esta última década prodigiosa", señala Oliver, que anticipa una tasa
45 de ahorro alta durante varios años más, más cercana a lo que es habitual en Alemania, Francia o Italia. "La destrucción de empleo empieza a ser menor, los hogares pueden volver a consumir pronto, es una cuestión de confianza", opina Laborda, quien cree que la forma en la
50 que el Gobierno ha comunicado la subida de impuestos no ayuda.
"Los ajustes que serán necesarios para devolver al sector privado a niveles de endeudamiento razonables son todavía enormes", avisa Giada Giani, analista de Citigroup,
55 en un reciente informe sobre la evolución del ahorro familiar español. La deuda acumulada por los hogares apenas acaba de empezar a caer (ver gráfico recién publicado). Y, dada su naturaleza (en su mayoría
60 préstamos hipotecarios a largo plazo), el descenso será muy gradual. Con el crédito escaso en todo el mundo, eso se traducirá en más ahorro, aumentos del consumo muy tibios y un crecimiento con el freno de mano echado.

Disponible en: <http://www.elpais.com/articulo/ economia/consumismo/economia/guerra/familiar/ elpepueco/20091011elpepieco_2/Tes>.

(Analista – BNDES – 2010 – CESGRANRIO) Señale la asertiva correcta según el texto.

(A) Josep Oliver atribuye a los factores psicológicos domésticos el origen de la crisis en España.
(B) La gente no se asusta con el paro, ya que consigue mantener más de una fuente de ingreso.
(C) La burbuja se hinchó exclusivamente en España con la subida de la tasa de ahorro a los más altos niveles.
(D) Las facilidades encontradas por los ricos propietarios estimularon los hogares al consumo y a las deudas excesivas.
(E) No se puede afirmar que la crisis tuvo como modelo los países anglófonos – EEUU y Reino Unido.

(Interpretación) En las líneas 12, 13, 14, 15 y 16, se lee que las facilidades al crédito y la percepción de propietarios de viviendas o acciones sobre un supuesto enriquecimiento estimularan los hogares al consumo y a las deudas excesivas.
Gabarito "D".

(Analista – BNDES – 2010 – CESGRANRIO) Las opiniones de los economistas que se vuelcan hacia el endeudamiento y el ahorro se apoyan a menudo en argumentos distintos. Marque la alternativa en la cual **NO** se presenta un aspecto dubitativo.

(A) "¿Está siendo demasiado rápido el ajuste?" (línea 37)
(B) "… no creen que sea negativo." (línea 40)
(C) " 'Quizá el consumo tarde algo más en volver a crecer,' " (líneas 40 y 41)
(D) " 'los hogares pueden volver a consumir pronto, es una cuestión de confianza,' " (líneas 47 a 49)
(E) "La deuda acumulada por los hogares apenas acaba de empezar a caer (ver gráfico recién publicado)." (líneas 56 y 58)

(Interpretación) En las líneas 56 y 58, la afirmación al respecto de la diminución de la deuda acumulada no expresa un aspecto dubitativo.
Gabarito "E".

(Analista – BNDES – 2010 – CESGRANRIO) En el 4º párrafo el pronombre **ello** se refiere a

(A) la afirmación precedente
(B) los vocablos siguientes
(C) el paro
(D) el miedo
(E) el puesto de trabajo

(Gramática) El pronombre "ello", en el cuarto párrafo, se refiere a la afirmación precedente, es decir, al miedo a perder puestos de trabajo.
Gabarito "A".

(Analista – BNDES – 2010 – CESGRANRIO)

I. El súbito endeudamiento de las familias españolas fue una de las señales más nítidas de que la burbuja se hinchaba.
II. Como lo fue que la tasa de ahorro cayera hasta niveles mínimos en la historia moderna, cerca del 10%.
III. La economía española se situó más cerca que nunca del modelo imperante en EE UU y Reino Unido, los paraísos del consumismo: mínimo ahorro familiar y deuda masiva.

El fragmento anterior está formado por tres partes, acerca de las cuales se puede decir que

(A) aunque los tres fragmentos formen parte del mismo párrafo, se tratan de informaciones contradictorias.
(B) la primera y tercera hablan específicamente de la economía española, al paso que la segunda no.
(C) la primera y la segunda son ejemplos de una determinada situación y la tercera una comparación.
(D) la segunda es a la vez consecuencia de la primera y causa de la tercera.
(E) las dos primeras se oponen y la tercera se presenta como posible alternativa de solución.

(Interpretación) Los dos primeros segmentos son ejemplos de una afirmación al respecto del endeudamiento y de la tasa de ahorro; el tercer, en cambio, es una comparación con los modelos de los Estados Unidos y del Reino Unido.
Gabarito "C".

Texto III

Disponible en: <http://elequilibrioperfecto.files.wordpress.com/2009/03/080124pobrescrisis.jpg>.

(Analista – BNDES – 2010 – CESGRANRIO) Enlazando los tres textos se puede llegar a la conclusión que

(A) el primero y el último tienen marcas de una visión crítica bastante explícita respecto a la economía.
(B) el primero se refiere a los expertos de la economía mientras los dos últimos están en contra las personas comunes.
(C) los dos primeros se dirigen hacia personas preocupadas con la economía, mientras el tercero tiene como único objetivo entretener al lector.
(D) solo el primero presenta un posicionamiento explícito por parte del autor relación al tema de la economía.
(E) una vez que los dos primeros textos son noticias, las informaciones se presentan de forma neutral.

(Interpretación) El primer y último texto presenta visiones críticas al respecto de la economía española. El argumento personal de los autores está reflejado en las palabras empleadas. Se proponen alternativas y críticas a las políticas llevadas a cabo por el gobierno.
Gabarito "A".

LA OCDE CUESTIONA LA ESCASA EFICIENCIA Y RENTABILIDAD DE LOS BIOCARBURANTES

La Unión Europea se ha comprometido a que el 10% de sus combustibles serán biológicos para 2020

Laura Villena. Servicio Especial
Bruselas. La contribución de los biocarburantes a la mitigación del cambio climático es cada vez más cuestionada. Ayer, la Organización para Cooperación y
5 el Desarrollo Económico (OCDE) revivió el debate con la publicación del informe "Biocombustibles:¿es el remedio peor que la enfermedad?", en el que se ponen en duda la rentabilidad y el beneficio medioambiental del uso de combustibles biológicos.
10 El informe denuncia que la creciente demanda de biocombustibles para sustituir a los carburantes fósiles *carbón, petróleo o gas natural* tendrá consecuencias económicas a nivel mundial. Pone el ejemplo del conflicto "comida contra combustibles", que obligará a los
15 agricultores a decantarse por destinar sus campos de cultivo a la alimentación o a la elaboración de biocombustibles, producidos sobre todo de maíz, caña de azúcar o cereal.
La consecuencia de cualquier desvío de la
20 producción hacia la generación de energía biológica encarecerá el precio de la comida, según el informe, que augura ya una subida para la próxima década. Y es que, a pesar de que son las regiones tropicales las más adecuadas para dedicarse a estos cultivos, el hecho de
25 que los productos medioambientales estén subvencionados y cuenten con incentivos en la UE provocará, según el texto, una destrucción de los ecosistemas naturales, como bosques, humedales y pastos, en favor de las cosechas para energía biológica.
30 **Amenaza al medio ambiente**
La obsesión por los biocarburantes puede suponer una amenaza para el medio ambiente y la biodiversidad. El informe alerta de que se tienen en cuenta la acidificación de la tierra, el uso de fertilizantes, la pérdida de
35 biodiversidad y la toxicidad del uso de pesticidas agrícolas durante el proceso de producción de bioetanol o biodiesel, su impacto medioambiental "puede superar fácilmente el de la gasolina o el diesel mineral".
El progresivo uso de biocarburantes creará
40 problemas que, según la OCDE, no aportarán a cambio ningún beneficio medioambiental, puesto que la reducción de las emisiones de CO2 no superará el 3%.
El empeño por preservar su liderazgo y la lucha global contra el cambio climático han empujado a la UE a
45 imponer medidas y firmar compromisos de manera desenfrenada durante los últimos años. Pero lo que un día se firmó con el convencimiento de que era el camino más corto hacia la reducción de emisiones, despierta hoy más de una incógnita.
50 El primer ejemplo de que la UE no acaba de dar con la fórmula para frenar el cambio climático fue el sistema de comercio de emisiones (ETS, en sus siglas en inglés), cuya primera fase está a punto de concluir con un fracaso a la espalda y la esperanza de la Comisión Europea de
55 que la segunda fase traiga consigo resultados.
Si los pronósticos de la FAO y la OCDE se cumplen, al chasco del ETS podría sumarse en de unos años el de los biocombustibles. La UE apostó por ellos el pasado marzo, cuando se comprometió a que al menos el 10%
60 de los combustibles consumidos por los automóviles europeos sean de origen biológico para 2020. Este compromiso supone la importación del 20% del biocombustible necesario y el uso de 59 millones de toneladas de cereales –el 18% de la producción
65 Interna–.

Segunda generación

Ante esta apuesta y los riesgos presentados en su informe, la OCDE invita a la UE y a sus Gobiernos a interesarse por los biocarburantes de segunda generación –que pueden
70 producirse a partir de fuentes no alimentarias como residuos agrícolas (paja) y desechos de madera– y les insta imponer políticas "más eficientes", como los impuestos sobre el carbón. Por último, llama la atención de "sostenible" para los biocarburantes.
75 La OCDE también llama a los países en vías de desarrollo, como Brasil, de donde proceden en muchos casos el bioetanol y otros combustibles biológicos, a utilizar sus fuentes energéticas no sólo desde el "cómodo" punto de vista de la exportación, sino como la vía para
80 identificar nuevas formas de progreso económico, como la investigación en bioenergía.

Más información en: <http://www.oecd.org>.
ABC Miércoles, 12-09-2007.

(Analista – BNDES – 2008 – CESGRANRIO) "... **mitigación** del cambio climático..." (línea 3) Se puede inferir por el contexto (1er párrafo) que la palabra en negrito significa:

(A) aislamiento.
(B) exacerbación.
(C) enfurecimiento.
(D) atenuación.
(E) preocupación.

(Vocabulario) El substantivo "mitigación" tiene como sinónimos moderación, atenuación y aplacamiento.
Gabarito "D".

(Analista – BNDES – 2008 – CESGRANRIO) Según el texto la publicación del informe "Biocombustibles: ¿es el remedio peor que la enfermedad?" (líneas 6-7) ocurrió el día:

(A) jueves 10/09/2007.
(B) martes 11/09/2007.
(C) miércoles 12/09/2007.
(D) viernes 13/09/2007.
(E) lunes 14/09/2007.

(Interpretación) Según se lee en la nota al pie del texto, la publicación ocurrió el miércoles 12/09/2007.
Gabarito "B".

(Analista – BNDES – 2008 – CESGRANRIO) La creciente demanda de biocombustibles biológicos llevará los agricultores a vivir bajo el conflicto "comida o combustible" lo que, de acuerdo con el texto, exigiría por parte de estos una actitud de:

(A) indiferencia.
(B) enfrentamiento.
(C) ponderación.
(D) encantamiento.
(E) desprecio.

(Interpretación) Según se lee en las líneas 15, 16 y 17, la creciente demanda por biocombustibles llevará los agricultores a "decantarse por destinar sus campos de cultivo a la alimentación **0** a la elaboración de biocombustibles"; por consiguiente, se infiere que se trata de una ponderación entre esto y aquello.
Gabarito "C".

(Analista – BNDES – 2008 – CESGRANRIO) Según el texto, el informe de la OCDE apunta desventajas en el uso de los biocarburantes, relacionadas en las opciones abajo, EXCEPTO en la/el:

(A) baja significativa en el porcentaje de las emisiones de CO_2.
(B) amenaza para el medioambiente y la biodiversidad.
(C) destrucción de los ecosistemas naturales.
(D) conflicto comida contra combustible.
(E) encarecimiento del precio de la comida.

(Interpretación) Todos las opciones constan en el informe de la OCDE, salvo la opción A. Precisamente, los informes de la OCDE apuntan para un elevado porcentaje de emisiones de CO_2 derivadas del uso de biocarburantes.
Gabarito "A".

(Analista – BNDES – 2008 – CESGRANRIO) "no aportarán a cambio ningún benificio medioambiental, puesto que la reducción de las emisiones de CO_2 no superará el 3%." (líneas 40-42)

El conector **puesto que** establece en la frase una relación de:

(A) temporalidad.
(B) adversidad.
(C) finalidad.
(D) causalidad.
(E) simultaneidad.

(Gramática) A diferencia del portugués, "puesto que" no esgrime una concesión, sino una causalidad. En este caso, no habrá cambio, porque la reducción de las emisiones de CO_2 no superarán el 3%.
Gabarito "D".

(Analista – BNDES – 2008 – CESGRANRIO) "...UE no **acaba de dar** con la fórmula para frenar el cambio climático..." (líneas 50-51) Se comprende el sentido de la expresión en negrito como:

(A) acertar.
(B) quitar.
(C) ahorrar.
(D) plantear.
(E) rechazar.

(Vocabulario) La expresión no "acabo de dar", en este caso, significa no "acaba de acertar" al respeto de cual fórmula adoptar para frenar el cambio climático.
Gabarito "A".

(Analista – BNDES – 2008 – CESGRANRIO) De las siglas del texto las que se refieren a organismos que coinciden en sus expectativas sobre la apuesta por los biocombustibles son:

(A) OCDE – UE – ETS
(B) OCDE – FAO
(C) FAO – UE
(D) FAO – UE – OCDE
(E) UE – ETS

(Interpretación) En la línea 56, se lee que los pronósticos de la OCDE y de la FAO apuntan para el mismo sentido.
Gabarito "B".

(Analista – BNDES – 2008 – CESGRANRIO) "La UE apostó por **ellos** el pasado marzo," (líneas 58-59). El pronombre em negrito se refiere a:

(A) cambios climáticos.
(B) productos agrícolas.
(C) alimentos.
(D) emisiones.
(E) biocombustibles.

(Gramática) El pronombre "ellos", en este caso, se refiere a la palabra "biocombustiles", destacada en la línea 58.
Gabarito "E".

(Analista – BNDES – 2008 – CESGRANRIO) En la frase "y les insta imponer políticas 'más eficientes'," (líneas 71-72-), el pronombre **les** sustituye a:

(A) biocarburantes de segunda generación.
(B) fuentes alimentarias como residuos agrícolas.
(C) UE y sus gobiernos.
(D) desechos de madera.
(E) impuestos sobre carbón.

(Gramática) En este caso, el pronombre "les" se refiere a la UE y sus gobiernos, destacados en la línea 68.
Gabarito "C".

(Analista – BNDES – 2008 – CESGRANRIO) Para alcanzar su objetivo "... 10% de los combustibles consumidos por los automóviles europeos sean de origen biológico para 2020." (líneas 59-61). UE tendrá que:

(A) subir los precios de sus productos.
(B) aprovechar 40% de sus tierras cultivadas.
(C) disminuir el consumo de biocarburantes.
(D) importar parte del biocombustible necesario.
(E) importar cereales para su consumo.

(Interpretación) Según se lee en las líneas 62, 63 y 64, para alcanzar su objetivo, la UE tendrá que importar parte del biocombustible necesario.
Gabarito "D".

Instruções: Para responder às quatro questões seguintes, utilize o texto abaixo.

El primer concepto de Constitución tuvo lugar en Europa. Allí, pese a darse la primera Constitución en Francia en 1791, como consecuencia directa de la Revolución Francesa, razones políticas de peso llevaron a restarle fuerza jurídica, pues no se la concebía como obligatoria para los órganos del Estado. Por parte de los gobernantes, en general formas de gobierno monárquicas, su violación no se calificaba como antijurídica. Inglaterra, cuna del constitucionalismo, nunca tuvo Constitución escrita y su legitimación se apoya sobre la soberanía del Parlamento y no en la sumisión de éste a normas jurídicas explicitadas en un texto constitucional. A pesar de fallidos intentos de controlar el Parlamento, debemos conceder que éste se autorregula con estricto respeto por el contenido de las leyes que dicta.

(...) Esta concepción se debilita después de la Primera Guerra Mundial. Tras la Segunda Guerra los Estados Europeos adoptaron, en general, una jurisdicción constitucional que centraliza el control de constitucionalidad de las leyes mediante las Cortes o Consejos constitucionales.

(...) El otro concepto de Constitución nació en los Estados Unidos de Norteamérica. Allí, desde el dictado de la Constitución de 1787, puesta en vigor en 1789, se considera a la Constitución como derecho supremo. Las normas que la integran obligan a los gobernantes a sujetarse a ellas, y son las que les otorgan competencias y a la vez las limitan. Ese concepto de Constitución está sintetizado en lo dicho por el Juez Marshall: "Los poderes del legislativo son definitivos y limitados y para que tales límites no se confundan u olviden se ha escrito la Constitución".

(...) Este concepto de Constitución es el que logro aceptación general; la norma constitucional devino norma jurídica obligatoria para garantizar los derechos, deberes y poderes que mediante ella se aseguran y organizan.

Adaptado de Leonardi de Herbón, H. (2004). "Introducción". In: Constitución de la Nación Argentina. Buenos Aires, Eudeba, pp. 20-23.

(Analista Legislativo – Câmara dos Deputados – 2007 – FCC) Marque a alternativa em que o fragmento "tras la Segunda Guerra", sublinhado na segunda linha do segundo parágrafo, está corretamente traduzido ao português.

(A) Apesar da Segunda Guerra
(B) Por trás da Segunda Guerra
(C) Durante a Segunda Guerra
(D) Atrás da Segunda Guerra
(E) Depois da Segunda Guerra

(Vocabulario) La expresión "tras la Segunda Guerra" significa depués de la Segunda Guerra.
Gabarito "E".

(Analista Legislativo – Câmara dos Deputados – 2007 – FCC) Marque a alternativa que contém uma correta interpretação para algo que se diz no primeiro parágrafo do texto.

(A) A Inglaterra se apóia na soberania do parlamento para escrever sua Constituição.
(B) As normas jurídicas de seu texto constitucional prejudicam a soberania do parlamento inglês.
(C) A submissão do texto constitucional às normas jurídicas legitima a Constituição da Inglaterra.
(D) O parlamento inglês não se submete às normas jurídicas explicitadas em um texto constitucional.
(E) A Inglaterra é o único país do planeta que não possui uma Constituição escrita.

(Interpretación) En el primer párrafo, se informa que Inglaterra nunca tuvo una Constitución escrita y su legitimación se apoya sobre la soberanía del Parlamento.
Gabarito "D".

(Analista Legislativo – Câmara dos Deputados – 2007 – FCC) Marque a alternativa que interpreta corretamente o fragmento sublinhado no terceiro parágrafo.

(A) Os governantes dos Estados Unidos são obrigados, de acordo com a Constituição, a outorgarem e limitarem a competência de suas normas.

(B) A Constituição dos Estados Unidos obriga seus governantes a sujeitarem-se a suas competências e limitações.
(C) As normas que integram a Constituição norte-americana sujeitam os governantes, outorgam-lhes competências e, ao mesmo tempo, limitam-nas.
(D) As competências e limitações da Constituição dos Estados Unidos integram as obrigações de seus governantes.
(E) Os governantes norte-americanos submetem as normas que integram a Constituição de seu país a suas competências e limitações.

(Interpretación) Según se lee en el tercer párrafo, las normas que integran la Constitución de los Estados Unidos obligan a los gobernantes a sujetarse a ellas, y son las que les otorgan competencias y a la vez las limitan.
Gabarito "C".

(Analista Legislativo – Câmara dos Deputados – 2007 – FCC)
Marque a alternativa que contém um possível título, escrito em espanhol, para o texto:

(A) Francia, Inglaterra y Estados Unidos: tres diferentes modelos de Constitución.
(B) Ascensión y caída de los conceptos de Constitución.
(C) Modelos constitucionales de Europa y América después de la Segunda Guerra.
(D) Revolución Francesa y Segunda Guerra: marcos para los modelos de las Constituciones de Francia, Inglaterra y Estados Unidos.
(E) Dos conceptos de Constitución: el francés y el estadounidense.

(Interpretación) El título que mejor explica el articula es "Dos conceptos de Constitución: el francés y el estadounidense", puesto que se presentan dos paradigmas constitucionales, y no tres, con lo cual no podemos decir que el modelo británico este desarrollado en el texto.
Gabarito "E".

ING no cree que España logre sus objetivos de déficit ni en 2012 ni en 2013

El banco holandés ING cree que España no logrará sus objetivos de déficit fiscal ni en 2012 ni en 2013, cuando calcula que el desfase entre ingresos y gastos de las cuentas públicas roce el 5% del PIB, casi dos puntos más de lo previsto (6,1% del PIB, por encima del 5,3% previsto por el Gobierno este año y 4,9% en 2013, un desfase de casi 21.000 millones en comparación con el objetivo de España). Con estas previsiones, los expertos de ING no descartan que el país vaya a necesitar un rescate que pasaría por pedir ayuda del Fondo Europeo de Estabilidad Financiera para sanear el sistema financiero.

"Con la sombría perspectiva económica y la crisis del sector inmobiliario, los bancos españoles podrían necesitar más capital que el previsto actualmente. El sistema bancario también sigue siendo vulnerable a las presiones de financiación", añade ING. Para el banco holandés, el desequilibrio de las cuentas españolas se deberá principalmente a que los gobiernos autónomos no cumplirán los objetivos de déficit fijados, del 1,5% del PIB, mientras que los ingresos del Estado serán menores de lo previsto por la recesión de la economía española, que persistirá al menos hasta finales de 2013, en términos interanuales.

Texto adaptado de CincoDías.com – Madrid – 24/04/2012.
Disponible en: <http://www.cincodias.com/articulofinanzas-
-personales/ing-cree-espanalogre- objetivos-deficit-2012
2013/20120424cdscdsfpe_1/>.

(Analista – CGU – 2012 – ESAF) De acuerdo con los expertos del banco holandés ING, el déficit fiscal previsto por las autoridades españolas:

(A) llegará a 21 mil millones de euros en 2012 y 2013.
(B) se logrará a duras penas.
(C) supondrá ayudas externas superiores al 5% del PIB.
(D) no se alcanzará.
(E) contribuirá al saneamiento del sistema financiero.

(Interpretación) Según se lee en el título del artículo, el ING no cree que España logre sus objetivos de déficit ni en 2012 ni en 2013. Dicho de otra manera, el déficit fiscal previsto por las autoridades españolas no se alcanzará. La primera línea del artículo justifica esta posición. La respuesta A es incorrecta, dado que la cifra de 21 millones representa un desfase en comparación con el objetivo de España, y no el monto total del déficit. La respuesta B está incorrecta, teniéndose en cuenta que el texto dispone sobre la incapacidad de alcanzar el déficit previsto. La respuesta C está incorrecta, dado que el texto no estipula una cifra porcentual específica para las ayudas exteriores. Por fin, la respuesta E está incorrecta, ya que el déficit fiscal bajo ninguna perspectiva puede contribuir para subsanar el sistema financiero.
Gabarito "D".

(Analista – CGU – 2012 – ESAF) Según las previsiones del ING, el desfase entre ingresos y gastos de las cuentas públicas españolas en 2012 y 2013:

(A) exigirá financiación externa dentro del sistema europeo.
(B) será consecuencia de la recesión y de incumplimientos en las autonomías.
(C) superará en 5,3% lo previsto por el gobierno.
(D) se deberá a la crisis del sector inmobiliario.
(E) estará por debajo del 5% del PIB.

(Interpretación) Según se lee en la primera línea, el banco holandés ING cree que España no logrará sus objetivos de déficit fiscal. Según se lee en el segundo párrafo, el desequilibrio fiscal de las cuentas españolas, es decir, el desfase entre ingresos y gastos, será consecuencia principalmente del hecho que los gobiernos autónomos no cumplirán los objetivos de déficit fijados. Al mismo tiempo, los ingresos del Estado español serán menores de lo previsto por la recesión.
Gabarito "B".

Europa ha fracasado en la política de empleo: OIT

Los gobiernos europeos han fracasado en la política de empleo, según reporta la Organización Internacional del Trabajo (OIT) en su nuevo informe "Mundo del trabajo", donde señala que con SUS programas de ahorro, los países europeos, sobre todo los del sur, no se han centrado en crear puestos de trabajo, sino en recortar el déficit. El autor principal del informe, Raymond Torres, apela en su análisis a los países a que emprendan "un cambio dramático" en el rumbo político. Agrega que la estrategia de los países europeos de reducir el déficit apuntaba a allanar el camino a una mayor inversión y crecimiento; "pero esas expectativas no se han cumplido", por su incapacidad de estimular la inversión privada.

El director de la investigación señala que "la intensa concentración de muchos países de la eurozona en la política de ahorro ha profundizado la crisis de empleo y podría conducir a más recesión en Europa". Por el contrario, aquellos países que apuestan por una política de fomentar el empleo arrojan mejores datos económicos. "Tenemos que observar bien esa experiencia y sacar conclusión de ello", añadió. Desde 2011 el desempleo vuelve a crecer. Y especialmente problemático considera esta agencia de la ONU el desempleo juvenil y de larga duración. Para los países industrializados, la OIT no espera una recuperación en las cifras del desempleo hasta 2016, cuando habrá cifras como las de antes de la crisis de 2008.

La Jornada, en línea, 30.04.12. Disponible en: <http://www.jornada.unam.mx/ultimas/2012/04/30/103310864-acusa-oit-a-europa-de-fracasar-en-lapolitica-de-empleo>.

(Analista – CGU – 2012 – ESAF) Según el texto, la política europea de empleo ha fracasado porque:

(A) ha faltado incentivo a la inversión.
(B) se han incumplido los programas de austeridad.
(C) ha habido un cambio de modelo productivo.
(D) ha continuado alto el déficit fiscal.
(E) ha aumentado el desempleo juvenil.

(Interpretación) Según se lee en el primer párrafo, la estrategia de los países europeos de reducir el déficit apuntaba a allanar el camino a una mayor inversión. En otros términos, la política europea ha optado por reducir el déficit en vez de combatirlo con mayor inversión y crecimiento.
Gabarito "A".

(Analista – CGU – 2012 – ESAF) En las líneas 5 y 6 del texto (… no se han centrado en crear puestos de trabajo, sino en recortar el déficit), la palabra "sino" denota:

(A) idea de excepción.
(B) solamente.
(C) contraposición de ideas.
(D) adición de otro elemento.
(E) afrenta.

(Gramática) En este caso, el conector "sino" denota contraposición de ideas. En otras palabras, y refiriéndonos al texto, se ha optado por combatir el déficit en lugar de crear puestos de trabajo.
Gabarito "C".

CGR imputó Responsabilidad Fiscal al Ex Gobernador Luis Alfredo Ramos y dos de sus ex secretarios

La Contraloría General de la República (CGR) imputó cargos de responsabilidad fiscal, por un presunto detrimento patrimonial superior a $18 mil millones de pesos, contra el ex Gobernador de Antioquia, Luis Alfredo Ramos Botero, los ex secretarios de Infraestructura Física, Mauricio Restrepo Gutiérrez y María Cristina Mesa Zapata, 10 consorcios y uniones temporales que abarcan 20 empresas de obras civiles y la Fundación para el Buen Gobierno (hoy Fundación Cubo). La decisión se origina al verificar, en más de 22 indagaciones preliminares y procesos fiscales, que hubo deficiencias en la planeación contractual, demoras injustificadas en la ejecución de las obras contratadas y adiciones no justificadas, entre otras irregularidades.

De otra parte, es importante señalar que en desarrollo de las indagaciones preliminares y procesos de responsabilidad fiscal que se adelantaron en su momento sobre estos hechos, en las vigencias 2008 a 2010, se presentaron situaciones irregulares en la actuación de funcionarios de la CGR de la gerencia departamental de Antioquia de esa época, que fueron puestos en conocimiento de la Fiscalía General de la Nación, Regional Medellín.

Adaptado de Contraloría General de la República de Colombia, 16.04.12.

(Analista – CGU – 2012 – ESAF) En el texto se dice que la Contraloría General de Colombia:

(A) acusó al ex Gobernador y descubrió irregularidades en la actuación de funcionarios de la CGR.
(B) calculó pérdidas patrimoniales de $18 mil millones de pesos, imputables al ex Gobernador de Antioquia.
(C) abrió 22 procesos contra el ex Gobernador de Antioquia y funcionarios de su gobierno.
(D) reconoció la implicación de funcionarios suyos en el desvío de recursos públicos.
(E) informó a la Fiscalía sobre la participación de funcionarios de la CGR en actos de cohecho.

(Interpretación) Según se lee en las dos primeras líneas del primer párrafo y en la tercera del segundo, la Contraloría General de la República (CGR) acusó el ex Gobernador de Antioquia, Luis Alfredo Ramos Botero, y descubrió irregularidades en la actuación de funcionarios de la CGR. Se deduce de la nota al pie del texto que se trata de la CGR de Colombia.
Gabarito "A".

EL IPC DE ESPAÑA

Para el Cuerpo de Técnicos de Gestión de la Hacienda Pública (Gestha), el repunte de la inflación armonizada (4,3% en tasa interanual) y el consecuente diferencial de la economía española respecto a la media de la zona euro (1,2 puntos) no se deben a la dependencia energética de ese país y al encarecimiento de los alimentos, sino al mayor porcentaje de economía sumergida (estimada en el 23% del PIB, frente a la media europea de 10%) y al exceso de dinero negro en circulación existente en España (56.438 millones de euros). Desde la entrada en funcionamiento del euro, el volumen de crédito bancario en España dobla ya al del resto de los países con la misma moneda.

Gestha opina que este nivel de economía sumergida agrava el diferencial de precios con respecto al de la zona euro, lo cual merma el poder adquisitivo –unos diez puntos por encima de otros países europeos– y la competitividad del comercio exterior, que sitúa a España a la cabeza del déficit del PIB exterior mundial. Los Técnicos de Hacienda proponen un aumento de los ingresos, una reducción del fraude fiscal y la economía sumergida, a lo que hay que sumar una rebaja específica del IRPF.

El Mundo. España, 16.01.08.

(Analista – CGU – 2008 – ESAF) En el texto se dice que la tasa inflacionaria española:

(A) rebasa la media europea.
(B) es menor que la media de la zona euro.
(C) ha aumentado.
(D) presiona el volumen de crédito bancario.
(E) está bajo el influjo de los precios energéticos y alimenticios.

(Interpretación) En la primera línea, se lee que el repunte de la inflación ha alcanzado 4,3% en tasas interanuales, con lo cual, se trata de un aumento del nivel de precios.
Gabarito "C".

(Analista – CGU – 2008 – ESAF) De acuerdo con el texto, para los técnicos de Gestha, el diferencial de precios español con respecto al de la zona euro:

(A) afecta la capacidad económica para adquirir bienes y servicios.
(B) se estima en un 23% del PIB español.
(C) eleva la capacidad exportadora del país.
(D) ha estimulado la circulación de dinero ilegal.
(E) supone un aumento de los ingresos.

(Interpretación) Según se deduce de las líneas 2, 3 y 4 del segundo párrafo, el Gestha estima que el diferencial de precios con respecto al de la zona euro, merma, o disminuye, el poder adquisitivo y la competitividad del comercio exterior español. Afecta, por lo tanto, la capacidad económica española de adquirir bienes y servicios.
Gabarito "A".

Vigilancia del erario cuesta

La Secretaría de la Función Pública (SFP) prevé un gasto de 122 millones 66 mil pesos para sus labores de auditoría del erario público federal. Eso representa 8% de sus recursos, pues el presupuesto global de la dependencia, a cargo de Salvador Vega Casillas, es de mil 520 millones 601 mil 500 pesos para 2008. El gobierno federal destina más de 3 mil millones de pesos anuales a fiscalización y cada oficina gubernamental con un órgano interno de control (OIC) debe pagar su operación de su presupuesto, aunque su autoridad máxima es la SFP.

En la administración pública federal encabezada por la Presidencia de la República existen 212 OIC, es decir, uno por cada dependencia federal. De enero a junio de 2006, el costo de esos órganos fue de mil 811.7 millones de pesos; para el mismo periodo de 2007 pasó a mil 796 millones de pesos, según información de la SFP.

Para 2008 aún no hay datos sobre el gasto de los 212 OIC; sin embargo, a partir de datos de los dos años previos se infiere un gasto anual de alrededor de 3 mil millones de pesos, integrando el presupuesto de la SFP y el costo de los OIC. Según la SFP "una de las funciones centrales de la Secretaría es reforzar los mecanismos de fiscalización para mejorar la gestión pública".

(El Universal, México, 11.01.08.

(Analista – CGU – 2008 – ESAF) De acuerdo con el texto, la Secretaría de la Función Pública (SFP) de México prevé:

(A) gastos menores en 2008.
(B) menos del 10% de sus recursos para fiscalizar el tesoro público.
(C) recursos adicionales para fiscalizar el erario.
(D) más de tres billones de pesos para auditoría.
(E) un aumento de sus dependencias.

(Interpretación) Según se deduce de las líneas 1 y 2, la Secretaria de la Función Pública de México prevé un gasto de 122 millones 66 mil pesos para sus labores de auditoría del erario público federal, lo que representa 8% de sus recursos, es decir, menos de 10%.
Gabarito "B".

(Analista – CGU – 2008 – ESAF) En el contexto del texto y sin ninguna alteración de significado o estructura, la palabra "aunque" puede ser sustituida por:

(A) mientras.
(B) pese a.
(C) pero.
(D) entretanto.
(E) más.

(Gramática) En este caso, "aunque" equivale a "pero". Expresa adversidad, por lo tanto.
Gabarito "C".

(Analista – CGU – 2008 – ESAF) En el texto se dice que los órganos internos de control mexicanos:

(A) generan recursos propios.
(B) dependen del presupuesto de la SFP.
(C) costarán 3 mil millones de pesos en 2008.
(D) funcionan en cada oficina federal.
(E) están desvinculados de la SFP.

(Interpretación) En la línea 5 se explica que los órganos internos de control mexicanos funcionan en cada oficina gubernamental.
Gabarito "D".

Sin embargo, la hipotética integración de los diversos bancos confederados no es ni mucho menos fácil. Un ejemplo: la remuneración media en el Banco Exterior es la más alta de la banca, un 30% superior a la media. En este contexto, si se propusiera la fusión sin más del Exterior y Caja Postal, lo lógico es que los empleados de esta última entidad quisieran igualarse, y no precisamente por debajo, con los de la primera.

REAL ACADEMIA ESPAÑOLA: Banco de datos (CORDE) [en línea]. Corpus diacrónico del español. Disponible en: <http://www.rae.es> [Consulta del 20.01.08].

(Analista – CGU – 2008 – ESAF) En el contexto del texto la palabra "propusiera" significa que la fusión:

(A) se había propuesto.
(B) no se habría propuesto.
(C) se propuso.
(D) se propondrá.
(E) no se ha propuesto.

(Gramática) Conjugado en el subjuntivo imperfecto, el verbo proponer expresa posibilidad aún no concretada. Por lo tanto, todavía "no se ha propuesto".
Gabarito "E".

CPC espera conocer propuesta de reforma tributaria antes que sea enviada al Congreso

Su deseo de conocer el proyecto de reforma tributaria que prepara el gobierno antes de que sea enviado al Parlamento manifestó el timonel de la Confederación de la Producción y del Comercio (CPC), Lorenzo Constans, quien dijo que, de todas formas, esa es una decisión que debe tomar el presidente chileno, Sebastián Piñera.

Asimismo, planteó que no opinará sobre los cambios tributarios hasta que no se conozcan en detalle, pero aprovechó para enviar un consejo al presidente Piñera en momentos previos a la reunión que sostendría con el primer ministro japonés, teniendo en cuenta que también se está discutiendo una reforma de este tipo en este país. "Esperemos que se reúnan, que tenga una información que sirva para comparar, porque también, a lo mejor, hay que alivianar la carga", dijo Constans.

Texto adaptado de Diario Financiero, 31. 03.2012.

(Analista – MDICE – 2012 – ESAF) En el texto se dice que el presidente de la CPC solo emitirá su opinión sobre los cambios tributarios cuando estos se conozcan:

(A) de oficio.
(B) bajo mano.
(C) al detalle.
(D) sin dilación.
(E) de público.

(Interpretación) En la primera línea del segundo párrafo, se dice que Lorenzo Constant, presidente, o timonel, en sentido figurado, de la CPC, no opinará sobre los cambios tributarios hasta que no se conozcan en detalle.
Gabarito "C".

(Analista – MDICE – 2012 – ESAF) De acuerdo con el texto, el Sr. Constans espera que de la reunión con el primer ministro de Japón surjan datos a partir de los cuales:

(A) habrá que equilibrar los impuestos.
(B) se redefina la estructura tributaria.
(C) tal vez sea necesario elevar gravámenes.
(D) será preferible aliviar la carga.
(E) quizá se tenga que aligerar la tributación.

(Interpretación) En las propias palabras de Constans, se espera que el encuentro con el primer ministro japonés resulte en, a lo mejor, perspectivas para aliviar, o aligerar, la carga tributaria.
Gabarito "E".

Amparos contra aranceles a importaciones de EU

Diversas empresas mexicanas han promovido al menos 45 demandas de amparo en siete estados Del país para impugnar la constitucionalidad del decreto que impuso aranceles de entre 10 y 20 por ciento a diversos productos estadounidenses en represalia por no permitir el acceso a transportistas mexicanos. La mayoría de las compañías inconformes han argumentado la inequidad, porque el castigo sólo se aplicó a ciertos productos dentro de las mismas fracciones arancelarias.

El impacto de los aranceles ya se refleja en diversos productos, ya que, por ejemplo, las manzanas y las fresas han subido 20 por ciento para los importadores, quienes transmiten el costo a las ventas por menudeo.

Fragmento de La Jornada, 04.04.12

(Analista – MDICE – 2012 – ESAF) Según el texto, las demandas presentadas por diversas compañías mexicanas:

(A) buscan equilibrar el comercio bilateral.
(B) persiguen elevar los precios al por menor.
(C) rechazan la aplicación equitativa de gravámenes a las importaciones.
(D) refutan las tarifas a productos estadounidenses.
(E) reivindican el acceso de los transportistas locales al mercado de Estados Unidos.

(Interpretación) En línea 2, se deduce que las demandas de amparo presentadas por compañías mexicanas buscaron contrarrestar la constitucionalidad del decreto que impuso aranceles a diversos productos estadounidenses, es decir, que colocaran barreras aduaneras.
Gabarito "D".

La crisis no da tregua en Portugal

Portugal cumple ahora un año intervenida sin que el rescate financiero haya mejorado sus cifras macroeconómicas, lo que se refleja en la "vida real" en forma de aumento de parados y emigrantes, así como en la profundización de las brechas sociales. Los 78.000 millones de euros concedidos por la Unión Europea y el Fondo Monetario Internacional han servido para garantizar que el país cumpla con sus compromisos y evite el riesgo de impago, aunque no para revitalizar de momento su economía ni reducir la presión de los mercados. En ese lapso han perdido el trabajo más de 100.000 portugueses y se prevé que este año sigan sus pasos otros 40.000 más; su PIB se ha contraído un 1,6% y caerá el doble en 2012; mientras el gasto y la inversión pública se han desplomado.

La recesión ha contribuido a que la deuda pública del país supere ya incluso el valor total de su economía, sobrepasando así los 180.000 millones de euros. El préstamo de la troika llevaba, como contrapartida, la adopción de un vasto programa de ajustes que el Gobierno luso ha aplicado con firmeza. Entre ellos destaca el incremento de la carga fiscal, a través de un aumento del IVA que ha encarecido para todos los portugueses por igual desde la luz, el gas y el combustible hasta la compra de alimentos, lo que ha penalizado el consumo privado, considerado fundamental para regresar a la senda del crecimiento.

Texto adaptado de Elmundo.es, 07.04.12

(Analista – MDICE – 2012 – ESAF) El sentido del primer párrafo del texto se mantendría inalterado si la palabra "aunque" se sustituyera por:

(A) más
(B) pero
(C) igual
(D) aún
(E) todavía

(Gramática) En este caso, la palabra "aunque" tiene sentido de adversidad, por lo tanto, podría ser substituida por la conjunción "pero". Gabarito "B".

(Analista – MDICE – 2012 – ESAF) A juzgar por la información contenida en el texto, el préstamo concedido a Portugal por la Unión Europea y el Fondo Monetario Internacional ha:

(A) supuesto un mínimo de control y fiscalización externa.
(B) aumentado el desempleo y la inmigración.
(C) asegurado la capacidad estatal de honrar obligaciones financieras.
(D) de garantizar el regreso de Portugal a la senda del crecimiento este año.
(E) de disminuir la deuda pública del país.

(Interpretación) Según se lee en la línea 5, el préstamo concedido a Portugal por la Unión Europea y el Fondo Monetario Internacional ha servido para garantizar que el país cumpla con sus compromisos, es decir, para asegurar la capacidad estatal de honrar obligaciones fiscales. Gabarito "C".

El Gobierno propondrá retrasar la edad de jubilación a los 67 años

1   El Gobierno presentó su propuesta de reforma de las pensiones, que contempla el retraso en la edad de jubilación entre las medidas para garantizar el mantenimiento del sistema
4   a medio y largo plazo. Según fuentes del Ejecutivo, la edad laboral se ampliará de los 65 años actuales hasta los 67.
La medida, de salir adelante — tiene que ser debatida
7   con patronal y sindicatos en la Comisión del Pacto de Toledo —, se aplicará de forma progresiva a partir de 2013, año en el que los que cumplan 65 deberán trabajar dos meses más, y en
10 2025 quedará totalmente implantada. Así, en 2025 habrá que seguir trabajando durante dos años más para poder percibir el 100% de la prestación. De cumplirse los planes del Ejecutivo,
13 en 2025 España será el primer país de la Unión Europea donde todos los trabajadores se jubilarán a los 67 años.
La reforma, que el Gobierno espera aprobar en un
16 plazo no demasiado largo, supone que han triunfado las tesis de la vicepresidenta y ministra de Economía, Elena Salgado, que en varias ocasiones se ha mostrado a favor de medidas que
19 permitan aumentar la llamada edad efectiva de jubilación — que establece la media a la que la gente se jubila y que está en 63,5 años en España — o bien mojarse y poner sobre la mesa
22 una edad exacta de jubilación.

Internet: <www.elpaís.com> (con adaptaciones).

(Analista – PREVIC – 2011 – CESPE) Juzgue los ítems siguientes de acuerdo con el texto de arriba.

(1) Del texto es correcto inferir que muchos españoles se jubilan antes de completar la edad establecida para percibir el 100% de la prestación por jubilación.
(2) El vocablo "*mojarse*" (ℓ.21) es utilizado en el texto en el sentido literal de derramar agua sobre sí mismo.
(3) Es correcto inferir del texto que, antes de la reforma propuesta por el Gobierno, para percibir el 100% de la prestación por jubilación hay que trabajar hasta los 65 años.
(4) La expresión "de salir adelante" (ℓ.6) tiene sentido condicional.
(5) La Comisión del Pacto de Toledo está constituida exclusivamente por representantes de la patronal y de los sindicatos.
(6) Quien se jubile en 2013, si quiere percibir el 100% de la prestación por jubilación, deberá haber trabajado 65 años y dos meses.

1: correcta. **(Interpretación)** En las líneas 7, 8, 9, 10, 11, 12, se lee que los españoles tendrán que trabajar más para alcanzar el 100% de la prestación por jubilación. En la línea 21, se dice que la media de edad de jubilación en España es de 63,5 años. En la línea 4, se afirma que la edad actual de jubilación es de 65 años. De esas tres premisas se puede inferir que muchos españoles se jubilan antes de completar la edad establecida para percibir el 100% de la prestación por jubilación; 2: incorrecta. **(Vocabulario)** El vocablo "mojarse", en la línea 21, está empleado en sentido figurado o quiere decir arriesgarse. 3: correcta. **(Interpretación)** En la línea 5, se afirma que, por el presente sistema de jubilación, la población tiene que alcanzar la edad de 65 para percibir el 100% de las prestaciones. 4: correcta. **(Vocabulario)** La expresión "de salir adelante", en la línea 6, significa "con la condición de que realmente se aplique". 5: incorrecta. **(Interpretación)** En la línea 8, se afirma que la propuesta tiene que ser debatida con el patronal y los sindicatos en la Comisión del Pacto de Toledo, lo que no quiere decir que esa Comisión este constituida exclusivamente por representantes patronales y por sindicatos. 6: incorrecta. **(Interpretación)** Según se lee en las líneas 5 y 14, los empleados que quieran percibir el 100% de las prestaciones de jubilación tendrán alcanzar la edad de 67 años trabajados. Gabarito 1C, 2E, 3C, 4C, 5E, 6E.

Texto

Telecomunicaciones en Brasil

1   La historia de las telecomunicaciones en Brasil se remonta al siglo XIX y hasta el año de 1962 nada se había hecho para regularlas globalmente en el país. Ese año, con
4   unas 1.200 compañías diferentes ofreciendo servicio telefónico, el Congreso brasileño promulgó el Código Brasileño de Telecomunicaciones que, entre otras cosas, creó
7   el primer regulador nacional (CONTEL). También fue establecido un fondo para financiar infraestructuras, y se establecieron las bases para la formación de una compañía
10 nacional que se hiciera cargo de las redes troncales. De esta forma nació EMBRATEL que, con la ayuda del fondo nacional, se embarcó en la interconexión de las redes
13 existentes y la creación de otras nuevas.
En 1967 se estableció el Ministerio de Comunicaciones. El mismo reclamó para sí las contiendas
16 reguladoras, hasta entonces dispersas en la estructura gubernamental brasileña, y se hizo cargo tanto de CONTEL como de EMBRATEL. En 1972 se concibió TELEBRÁS, una
19 nueva compañía nacional que se hizo cargo de parte de los activos de EMBRATEL. El objetivo era mejorar la calidad del

servicio local, aún muy deficiente. Mientras tanto otras
22 compañías quedaban bajo régimen mixto, con participación
privada.
TELEBRÁS rápidamente comenzó a comprar
25 compañías (con ayuda del fondo gubernamental), y alrededor
de los años 90 controlaba al menos el 90% de los teléfonos de
Brasil, estando el resto repartidos entre cuatro compañías: tres
28 bajo gobiernos locales y una privada. En 1995 se inició el
proceso de modificar la constitución para abrir el marco
legislativo, con el objetivo de liberalizar el mercado. En 1997
31 se instaura el nuevo regulador, ANATEL. En 1998 se produce
la partición de TELEBRÁS y la creación de las llamadas Baby
Bras que son privatizadas. La entrada de la competencia ha
34 hecho posible que los cargos de acceso a la Red estén entre los
más bajos de la región.

Internet: <www.baquia.com/com/legacy/8630.htmL>
(con adaptaciones).

(Analista – ANATEL – 2006 – CESPE) Con relación a las ideas del texto, juzgue los siguientes ítems.

(1) A partir de la década de los 90 empieza una interligación entre las redes de telecomunicación.
(2) Hasta 1967 era poca la centralización gubernamental que existía de las compañías en las telecomunicaciones.
(3) CONTEL y ANATEL tenían las mismas funciones.
(4) El fondo nacional fue de poca ayuda para la compra de otras compañías.
(5) En cuanto a su empleo en el texto, es correcto afirmar que el presente de "creó" (ℓ.6) es criar.

1: correcto. **(Interpretación)** Según se lee entre las líneas 28 a 30, a partir de 1990, específicamente en 1995, se estableció un marco legal para liberalizar el mercado de las telecomunicaciones. Bajo esa lógica administrativa, se establecieron, en la década siguiente, las bases para la formación de una compañía nacional que se hiciera cargo de las redes troncales, con lo cual, profundó la inter ligación entre redes de telecomunicación, según se lee en el primer párrafo; 2: correcto. **(Interpretación)** Se deduce de la línea 14 que, luego del establecimiento del Ministerio de Comunicaciones, se centralizaron las contiendas reguladoras, lo que significa que, antes, había dispersión en la estructura brasileña de telecomunicación; 3: correcto. **(Interpretación)** En la línea 31, se lee que ANATEL estableció el nuevo marco regulador y, en la línea 7, que CONTEL fue creada como entidad nacional reguladora de las telecomunicaciones. Se infiere, por lo tanto, que hay identidad funcional entre esos dos organismos; 4: incorrecto. **(Interpretación)** En la línea 10, se advierte que EMBRATEL fue creada gracias al fondo nacional. Con ese nuevo organismo, se embarcó en la interconexión de las redes existentes y en la creación de otras nuevas; 5: incorrecto. **(Gramática)** El presente de "creó" es crear;
Gabarito 1C, 2C, 3C, 4E, 5E

(Analista – ANATEL – 2006 – CESPE) juzgue los siguientes ítems.

(1) el vocablo "primer" (ℓ.7) se puede intercambiar por primero sin alterar su significado.
(2) la palabra "aún" (ℓ.21) equivale a todavía.
(3) la palabra "alrededor" (ℓ.25) tiene el significado de contorno.
(4) el vocablo "bajo" (ℓ.28) significa bajar.

1: incorrecto. **(Gramática)** El vocablo "primer", cuando empleado como adjetivo masculino, no puede ser reemplazado por "primero"; 2: correcto. **(Vocabulario)** "Aún" y "todavía" son sinónimos en castellano; 3: incorrecto. **(Vocabulario)** La palabra "alrededor" significa en torno a una persona o cosa, rodeándola completamente; 4: incorrecto. **(Vocabulario)** En este caso, el vocablo "bajo" no deriva del verbo bajar, conjugado en el presente del indicativo. Se trata de la preposición "bajo", que indica, en la línea 28, situación de dependencia por subordinación.
Gabarito 1E, 2C, 3E, 4E

"La calle" está tranquila

Zapatero ha declarado a Newsweek que para comprobar que España no se hunde "sólo hay que salir a la calle". Subraya así la paradoja de que no exista conflictividad social con cuatro millones de parados. Tiene razón en parte, aunque quizá debería preguntarse por qué La calle está tranquila y entonces su análisis no podría ser tan complaciente. Según publicamos hoy, la economía sumergida ha aumentado el 30% en el verano que ahora finaliza. Es el cálculo de los inspectores de Trabajo, que han estimado en 320 millones de euros la recaudación en multas para 2009, una cifra récord. Así pues, en el auge de la economía sumergida –de la que un país no puede sentirse orgulloso, sino todo lo contrario– está la explicación de la calma de la calle, puesto que los parados optan por las "chapuzas" para ir tirando. Aquí estaría la explicación de otro dato que Zapatero comentó, asombrado, ante el Comité Federal: sólo 28.000 parados sin ingresos han solicitado los 420 euros, cuando los posibles beneficiarios de esta medida son en torno a un millón. Como el subsidio lleva aparejada la obligación de asistir a cursos de formación, tal vez la mayoría de estos desempleados sin ingresos en realidad sí cobran por algún trabajo, aunque no declaran, ni cotizan. Ello quiere decir que la política social de Zapatero se vuelve contra él y contra los que él dice proteger. El empleo que se crea es clandestino por las rigideces del mercado laboral y al subir los impuestos aumentará la economía del dinero negro.

(El mundo, 22/09/09)

(Auditor Fiscal da Receita Federal – 2010 – ESAF) En el texto se dice que en España no hay conflictividad social:

(A) por la solidez institucional.
(B) gracias a las prestaciones públicas asistenciales.
(C) a pesar del desempleo.
(D) debido a la eficacia de la política laboral del gobierno.
(E) pese al aumento de la recaudación por multas.

(Interpretación) La única alternativa correcta es la letra C. El texto indica que a pesar del desempleo, no hay conflictividad social. La frase que nos permite así concluir es la primera del texto: "Zapatero ha declarado a Newsweek que para comprobar que España no se hunde 'sólo hay que salir a la calle'. Subraya así la paradoja de que no exista conflictividad social con cuatro millones de parados".
Gabarito "C"

(Auditor Fiscal da Receita Federal – 2010 – ESAF) De acuerdo con el texto, las actividades económicas marginales en España:

(A) disminuirán si suben los impuestos.
(B) han aumentado.
(C) elevarán las cotizaciones al tesoro.
(D) garantizan un aumento de los ingresos públicos.
(E) ocupan a cerca de un millón de parados.

(Interpretación) La única alternativa correcta es la letra B. Léase el fragmento siguiente: "Como el subsidio lleva aparejada la obligación de asistir a cursos de formación, tal vez la mayoría de estos desempleados sin ingresos en realidad sí cobran por algún trabajo, aunque no declaran, ni cotizan. Ello quiere decir que la política social de Zapatero se vuelve contra él y contra los que él dice proteger. El empleo que se crea es clandestino por las rigideces del mercado laboral y al subir los impuestos aumentará la economía del dinero negro".
Gabarito "B".

(Auditor Fiscal da Receita Federal – 2010 – ESAF) Dentro del texto, la palabra "chapuzas" significa:

(A) pequeñas contravenciones.
(B) obras sin arte ni esmero.
(C) contratos temporales.
(D) cursos de reciclaje profesional.
(E) subsidios fraudulentos.

(Vocabulario) La única alternativa correcta es la letra B. "Chapuzas" equivale a "obras sin arte ni esmero".
Gabarito "B".

Periodo recesivo hasta 2010: UNAM

José Luis Calva Téllez, académico del Instituto de Investigaciones Económicas de la Universidad Nacional Autónoma de México (UNAM), dijo que de aprobarse el paquete económico del presidente Felipe Calderón, habría una pérdida en 2010 de 200 mil empleos y una contracción del Producto Interno Bruto (PIB) de 1.8 por ciento. Para ese especialista, la inflación alcanzaría 6.1 por ciento anual a causa de las alzas de impuestos; y el déficit de la cuenta corriente se situaría en 12 mil millones de dólares.

Destacó que esos resultados negativos estarán influenciados aún por la recesión económica del país, por la carga fiscal que se enfrentaría con la aprobación Del presupuesto económico como lo presentó el Ejecutivo federal ante el Congreso; y por la baja inversión que habrá por parte del sector privado. "La Secretaría de Hacienda y Crédito Público está esperando que la economía de Estados Unidos levante a México, pero en aquel país la recuperación se está enfocando a amortizar deudas y por consecuencia el consumo seguirá deprimido", indicó.

Excélsior, 22/09/09.

(Auditor Fiscal da Receita Federal – 2010 – ESAF) En el texto, la locución "de aprobarse" tiene valor:

(A) condicional.
(B) concesivo.
(C) temporal.
(D) causal.
(E) imperativo.

(Gramática) La única alternativa correcta es la letra A. La locución "de aprobarse" tiene valor condicional. Podría ser substituida por "si es que se aprobase".
Gabarito "A".

(Auditor Fiscal da Receita Federal – 2010 – ESAF) De acuerdo con las declaraciones del académico de la UNAM, recogidas en el texto, en 2010:

(A) la inflación anual se elevará al 6,1%.
(B) igual el sector privado invierte menos.
(C) a lo mejor se expande el PIB.
(D) se enfocará la amortización de deudas.
(E) puede que desaparezcan empleos en México.

(Interpretación) La única alternativa que tiene respaldo en el texto es la letra E. Lo que nos permite así afirmar es la línea siguiente: "José Luis Calva Téllez, académico del Instituto de Investigaciones Económicas de la Universidad Nacional Autónoma de México (UNAM), dijo que de aprobarse el paquete económico del presidente Felipe Calderón, habría una pérdida en 2010 de 200 mil empleos y una contracción del Producto Interno Bruto (PIB) de 1.8 por ciento". En otras palabras, si el proyecto llegara a ser aprobado, habría (posiblemente y según las estimativas) una pérdida en 210 de 200 mil empleos.
Gabarito "E".

Los 17 mil chilenos con mayores ingresos entregan el 35% del impuesto a la renta.

En Chile, 1.329.297 personas pagan impuestos a la renta, ya sea bajo la modalidad de segunda categoría o de global complementario. A estas se suman otras 6.346.693 que si bien son formalmente contribuyentes para los registros del Servicio de Impuestos Internos (SII), en la práctica están en el primer tramo impositivo, que es cero. De este 1,32 millón de chilenos, el 1,27% está en el tramo más alto de impuestos –con una tasa marginal del 40%–, que es para quienes tienen ingresos de cerca de $5,5 millones de pesos mensuales o más. En conjunto, pagan más tributos al año que los bancos o todo el sector comercio. De acuerdo con los datos del SII, este grupo es el responsable del 35,1% de la recaudación por impuesto a la renta; es decir, US$ 908 millones del total de US$ 2.589 millones que los contribuyentes chilenos aportan por este concepto.

Para el socio principal de Ernst & Young, Cristián Levefre, la cifra demuestra que el grueso del aporte de impuestos lo entregan quienes más dinero reciben. Según él, existe una discriminación entre los contribuyentes de los tramos altos. Los independientes – muchos de ellos empresarios – tienen opciones de desarrollar una planificación tributaria para reducir el pago y los dependientes no las tienen. A su juicio, Chile debería impulsar beneficios para este segmento, como los que hay en economías más desarrolladas, como EE.UU., Inglaterra y España, donde se deduce por pago de colegios e intereses de créditos hipotecarios.

El Mercurio, 25/09/09.

(Auditor Fiscal da Receita Federal – 2010 – ESAF) Según el texto, el cobro del impuesto sobre la renta en Chile:

(A) se concentra en los mayores ingresos.
(B) incluye a la mayoría de la población.
(C) alcanza al 35% de los trabajadores.

(D) castiga a los autónomos.
(E) es menor entre los empleados bancarios.

(Interpretación) La única alternativa que tiene respaldo en el texto es la letra A. Lo que nos permite así afirmar es el fragmento siguiente: "En Chile, 1.329.297 personas pagan impuestos a la renta, ya sea bajo la modalidad de segunda categoría o de global complementario. A estas se suman otras 6.346.693 que si bien son formalmente contribuyentes para los registros del Servicio de Impuestos Internos (SII), en la práctica están en el primer tramo impositivo, que es cero. De este 1,32 millón de chilenos, el 1,27% está en el tramo más alto de impuestos –con una tasa marginal del 40%–, que es para quienes tienen ingresos de cerca de $5,5 millones de pesos mensuales o más. En conjunto, pagan más tributos al año que los bancos o todo el sector comercio. De acuerdo con los datos del SII, este grupo es el responsable del 35,1% de la recaudación por impuesto a la renta; es decir, US$ 908 millones del total de US$ 2.589 millones que los contribuyentes chilenos aportan por este concepto".
Gabarito "A".

(Auditor Fiscal da Receita Federal – 2010 – ESAF) En el texto se aconseja:

(A) aumentar los tributos al sector bancario.
(B) disminuir los intervalos impositivos.
(C) introducir deducciones por determinados pagos.
(D) reducir la tasa marginal de los tramos de impuestos.
(E) gravar más a los independientes.

(Interpretación) La única alternativa que tiene respaldo en el texto es la letra C. Lo que nos permite así afirmar es el fragmento siguiente: "A su juicio, Chile debería impulsar beneficios para este segmento, como los que hay en economías más desarrolladas, como EE.UU., Inglaterra y España, donde se deduce por pago de colegios e intereses de créditos hipotecarios" (segundo párrafo).
Gabarito "C".

(Auditor Fiscal da Receita Federal – 2010 – ESAF) En el contexto del texto, "a su juicio" conserva su sentido al sustituirse por:

(A) a su aire.
(B) en su prejuicio.
(C) a lo suyo.
(D) en su opinión.
(E) a regañadientes.

(Interpretación) La única alternativa correcta es la letra D. La expresión "a su juicio" tiene el mismo valor semántico que "en su opinión".
Gabarito "D".

(Auditor Fiscal da Receita Federal – 2010 – ESAF) De acuerdo con el texto, los contribuyentes dependientes chilenos:

(A) se benefician con desgravaciones.
(B) están concentrados en los tramos impositivos intermedios.
(C) cotizan más que los bancos.
(D) planifican el pago de sus tributos.
(E) sufren discriminación.

(Interpretación) La única alternativa correcta es la letra E. Se indica en el primer párrafo que los autónomos tienen opciones para reducir su pagamiento, con lo cual podemos concluir que los contribuyentes chilenos sufren discriminación.
Gabarito "E".

Necesidad de préstamos

Los gobiernos latinoamericanos necesitarán entre 350 y 400 billones de dólares en préstamos en 2010 para reactivar sus economías tras la crisis financiera global, según la vicepresidenta del Banco Mundial para América Latina y el Caribe, Pamela Fox. La obtención de préstamos no será fácil, incluso para proyectos de inversión, advirtió la funcionaria, debido a las dificultades para conseguir fondos que están restringidos por la enorme demanda internacional de las naciones desarrolladas para sus paquetes de estímulo.

"A raíz de la crisis el papel del Estado ha crecido a niveles que eran inimaginables años atrás", dijo Fox, pero el Estado dispone de menos recursos, de forma tal que "este momento exige más de los ciudadanos que pagan impuestos, especialmente de aquéllos con más ingresos, que deberían tener que afrontar una mayor carga tributaria", indicó. La funcionaria destacó que según la Organización de Cooperación Económica y Desarrollo menos de un 4% de los ingresos públicos en América Latina provienen de pagos de impuestos personales, comparado con un 27% en las naciones industrializadas.

(El Nacional, 29/09/09)

(Auditor Fiscal da Receita Federal – 2010 – ESAF) Según el texto, la reactivación económica de América Latina tras la crisis financiera global:

(A) supondrá una mayor regulación de la intervención estatal.
(B) demandará entre 350 y 400 mil millones de dólares.
(C) recabará más de toda la ciudadanía.
(D) exigirá entre 350 y 400 millones de millones de dólares.
(E) incidirá en los paquetes de estímulo de los países desarrollados.

(Interpretación) La única alternativa correcta es la letra D. El fragmento en el texto que nos permite así afirmar es el siguiente: "Los gobiernos latinoamericanos necesitarán entre 350 y 400 billones de dólares en préstamos en 2010 para reactivar sus economías tras la crisis financiera global, según la vicepresidenta del Banco Mundial para América Latina y el Caribe, Pamela Fox" (línea 1). Nótese que el numeral millones de millones equivale a billones.
Gabarito "D".

Detener la crisis: los líderes mundiales forjan un "Pacto Mundial por el Empleo"

El Pacto Mundial para el Empleo constituye la respuesta mundial de más amplio alcance a la crisis económica, adoptado en un año en el que la OIT celebra su 90º aniversario. En él se insta a gobiernos y organizaciones representantes de trabajadores y de empleadores para que colaboren a abordar colectivamente la crisis mundial del empleo mediante políticas en línea con el Programa de Trabajo Decente de la Organización.

El Pacto se aprobó en el contexto creado por un reciente informe de la OIT en el que se pone de relieve el aumento sin precedentes del desempleo en todo el mundo, así como la persistencia de niveles de pobreza muy elevados. El director General de la OIT, Juan Somavia, señaló que, aun cuando la recuperación económica comience a asentarse este año o el próximo, la crisis mundial del empleo podría persistir durante seis a ocho años. Añadió que, con 45 millones de trabajadores de nuevo acceso al mercado mundial del empleo cada año (en su mayoría, hombres y mujeres jóvenes), la economía mundial tendría que generar unos 300 millones de nuevos puestos de trabajo en los próximos cinco años sólo para regresar a los niveles de desempleo anteriores a la crisis.

Fragmento adaptado del reportaje de igual título, disponible en: <http://www.ilo.org/wow/Articles/lang--es/WCMS_115506/index.htm>.

(Auditor Fiscal do Trabalho – 2010 – ESAF) De acuerdo con el texto, la respuesta mundial a la crisis económica:

(A) exhorta a una colaboración tripartita.
(B) es el programa de mayor alcance en 90 años.
(C) generará 300 millones de empleos en 5 años.
(D) ha sido el Programa de Trabajo Decente de la OIT.
(E) sacará del paro a 45 millones de trabajadores.

(Interpretación) La única alternativa correcta es la letra A. El fragmento en el texto que nos permite así afirmar es el siguiente: "El Pacto Mundial para el Empleo constituye la respuesta mundial de más amplio alcance a la crisis económica, adoptado en un año en el que la OIT celebra su 90º aniversario. En él se insta a gobiernos y organizaciones representantes de trabajadores y de empleadores para que colaboren a abordar colectivamente la crisis mundial del empleo mediante políticas en línea con el Programa de Trabajo Decente de la Organización" (líneas 1 y 2).
Gabarito "A".

(Auditor Fiscal do Trabalho – 2010 – ESAF) El significado del enunciado "El director...o el próximo" (. 15 y 17) se mantiene si "aún cuando" se sustituye por:

(A) conque.
(B) en cuanto.
(C) aunque.
(D) desde que.
(E) mientras.

(Gramática) La única alternativa correcta es la letra C. La expresión "aún cuando" puede substituirse, sin pérdida de valor semántico, por "aunque"; ambos tienen valor concesivo.
Gabarito "C".

Fallo de la Suprema sobre IPC negativo

El fallo de la Tercera Sala de la Corte Suprema que prohibió bajar los salarios ante un escenario de inflación negativa tuvo un coletazo inesperado: los jubilados comenzaron a preguntarse si la definición de reajuste que usó el máximo tribunal también serviría para defender sus pensiones.

El debate comenzó a fraguarse en agosto de 2009, cuando los trabajadores de la compañía Metalúrgica Sorena Norte (MSN) recurrieron a la Dirección del Trabajo (DT) para denunciar a su empleador por haber corregido los salarios a la baja, basándose en las cifras de inflación negativa que se registraron ese año. El organismo fiscalizador aplico una multa y, como respuesta, la compañía recurrió a los tribunales cuestionando las atribuciones de la DT para interpretar la aplicación de un contrato entre privados.

Lo que precipitó un debate mayor es que la Corte Suprema no se limitó a revisar el proceder de la DT, sino que fue al fondo del asunto y determinó que la expresión reajuste entraña la noción de aumentar la cuantía. A ojos del diputado Pablo Lorenzini, el fallo de la Corte lleva a una discusión de fondo y fija una línea que debe aplicarse más allá de un escenario que se presenta cada 15 años. Agregó que lo importante es la injerencia que deben tener las agencias del Estado respecto a cláusulas abusivas.

El Mercurio, 6.02.2010.

(Auditor Fiscal do Trabalho – 2010 – ESAF) Según el texto, los empleados de la MSN acudieron a la DT

(A) para garantizar derechos de jubilación.
(B) en defensa del aumento de las pensiones.
(C) a favor de un cambio de modelo productivo.
(D) porque habían sido perjudicados.
(E) a causa de los bajos sueldos.

(Interpretación) La única alternativa que tiene respaldo en el texto es la letra D. Según el texto, "el debate comenzó a fraguarse en agosto de 2009, cuando los trabajadores de la compañía Metalúrgica Sorena Norte (MSN) recurrieron a la Dirección del Trabajo (DT) para denunciar a su empleador por haber corregido los salarios a la baja, basándose en las cifras de inflación negativa que se registraron ese año" (segundo párrafo), con lo cual podemos deducir que los empleados de la MSN acudieron a la DT porque habían sido perjudicados.
Gabarito "D".

(Auditor Fiscal do Trabalho – 2010 – ESAF) De acuerdo con el texto, el fallo de la Corte Suprema:

(A) podría favorecer a los retirados.
(B) es positivo para algunos pensionados.
(C) frena la intromisión estatal en asuntos laborales.
(D) es el primero de su tipo en 15 años.
(E) absolvió a la MSN.

(Interpretación) La única alternativa que tiene respaldo en el texto es la letra A. Según el texto, "el fallo de la Tercera Sala de la Corte Suprema que prohibió bajar los salarios ante un escenario de inflación negativa tuvo un coletazo inesperado: los jubilados comenzaron a preguntarse si la definición de reajuste que usó el máximo tribunal también serviría para defender sus pensiones" (línea 1), con lo cual podemos concluir que el fallo de la Corte Suprema podría favorecer a los retirados.
Gabarito "A".

(Auditor Fiscal do Trabalho – 2010 – ESAF) En el texto se dice que la MSN recibió una multa:

(A) de la Tercera Sala de la Corte Suprema.
(B) pero no la pagó.

(C) y preguntó a los tribunales sobre las atribuciones de la DT.
(D) por corregir salarios con base en la deflación.
(E) por la injerencia de un diputado.

(Interpretación) La única alternativa que tiene respaldo en el texto es la letra D. Lo que nos permite así concluir es la oración siguiente del segundo párrafo: "el organismo fiscalizador aplico una multa y, como respuesta, la compañía recurrió a los tribunales cuestionando las atribuciones de la DT para interpretar la aplicación de un contrato entre privados".
Gabarito "D".

Todos los caminos llevan a Suecia

En el sistema de seguridad social español, los trabajadores en activo son los que pagan las pensiones de los jubilados y, aunque ese modelo desafía a la demografía, apenas ha sido modificado. Existe cierto consenso en Europa sobre las soluciones más apropiadas. Buena parte de los analistas descartan la instauración de un modelo totalmente privado, pero aceptan reforzar el componente de capitalización del sistema, que puede ser privado o público, algo que se ha hecho en países con sistemas de bienestar tan acreditados como el sueco. El país nórdico introdujo entre 1994 y 1998 una reforma profunda en su modelo de seguridad social, en el que las pensiones están correlacionadas con las contribuciones, la redistribución es pequeña y el sistema se estabiliza, algo fundamental.

Las proyecciones de la Comisión Europea (CE) indican que en 2050 España prácticamente habrá duplicado el coste que suponen las pensiones para el PIB, pasando del 8,6% en 2004 hasta el 15,7% a mediados de siglo. Un incremento insostenible, salvo que el PIB español se doble en el mismo periodo, para lo que haría falta un crecimiento anual algo por debajo del 2% durante cuatro décadas. Los especialistas consultados coinciden en la necesidad de una reforma urgente y, en general, están a favor de las propuestas del Gobierno (retrasar la jubilación hasta los 67 años y aumentar la base de cotización), e incluso de que se compute, como ocurre en Francia, prácticamente toda la vida laboral de los trabajadores. Ésa es la esencia del modelo sueco, donde los trabajadores tienen cuentas propias que registran sus aportaciones a lo largo del tiempo para, posteriormente, hacer las devoluciones. Allí, además, el trabajador puede administrar parte del importe eligiendo fondos de capitalización privados o públicos.

Texto adaptado de El mundo, 07.02.2010.

(Auditor Fiscal do Trabalho – 2010 – ESAF) De acuerdo con el texto, el sistema de seguridad social español:

(A) se parece al sueco.
(B) casi no ha sido transformado.
(C) duplicará los beneficios de los pensionados hasta 2050.
(D) reducirá las contribuciones de los trabajadores en activo.
(E) va a aumentar su base de cotización.

(Interpretación) La única alternativa que tiene respaldo en el texto es la letra B. En la primera línea del texto, se afirma que "En el sistema de seguridad social español, los trabajadores en activo son los que pagan las pensiones de los jubilados y, aunque ese modelo desafía a la demografía, apenas ha sido modificado", con lo cual podemos decir que el sistema de seguridad social casi no ha sido modificado.
Gabarito "B".

(Auditor Fiscal do Trabalho – 2010 – ESAF) En el texto se favorece la adopción de un sistema de pensiones:

(A) privado.
(B) totalmente estatal.
(C) mixto.
(D) con contribuciones de los jubilados.
(E) desvinculado del comportamiento del PIB.

(Interpretación) La única alternativa que tiene respaldo en el texto es la letra C. Según el texto, "existe cierto consenso en Europa sobre las soluciones más apropiadas. Buena parte de los analistas descartan la instauración de un modelo totalmente privado, pero aceptan reforzar el componente de capitalización del sistema, que puede ser privado o público, algo que se ha hecho en países con sistemas de bienestar tan acreditados como el sueco" (primer párrafo). Además, "ésa es la esencia del modelo sueco, donde los trabajadores tienen cuentas propias que registran sus aportaciones a lo largo del tiempo para, posteriormente, hacer las devoluciones. Allí, además, el trabajador puede administrar parte del importe eligiendo fondos de capitalización privados o públicos" (segundo párrafo). Los dos fragmentos nos permiten afirmar que el texto favorece la adopción de un sistema de pensiones mixto.
Gabarito "C".

Las políticas de exclusión

Muchas industrias han adoptado algún tipo de medida para proteger a los trabajadores. A menudo, se trata de negarles trabajo o trasladar a los que consideran más susceptibles a los riesgos para la reproducción, que suelen ser las mujeres en edad de procrear. Se ha afirmado, sin embargo, que esas políticas no tienen por objeto proteger a los trabajadores, sino al empleador de cualquier litigio futuro. Por lo general no se aplican con coherencia ni uniformemente las políticas que excluyen a las mujeres de determinados puestos laborales. Por ejemplo, se ponen en práctica en aquellos que tradicionalmente han estado fuera del alcance de las mujeres, al tiempo que excluir a las mujeres de determinados puestos laborales no es una política seguida en industrias en las que ellas han sido y siguen siendo un porcentaje considerable de la mano de obra. En esas industrias, a menudo se las emplea a pesar de las posibilidades de que estén expuestas a riesgos para su función reproductora. Es, por ejemplo, el caso de los ayudantes de rayos X, los esteticistas, los limpiadores en seco y lavanderos, así como el personal de los quirófanos.

Uno de los problemas mayores que plantean las políticas de exclusión de las mujeres es que, al tiempo que discriminan a las fértiles denegándoles la asunción de determinados puestos de trabajo, o apartándolas de ellos, los hombres fértiles están expuestos en los mismos. Es esencial que se preste atención también a los problemas de reproducción de los hombres. Lamentablemente, a la fecha no se han estudiado bien las consecuencias de los riesgos en La función reproductora de los varones.

Adaptado de OIT, La Salud y la Seguridad en el Trabajo, disponible en: <http://training.itcilo.it/ actrav_cdrom2/es/osh/>.

(Auditor Fiscal do Trabalho – 2010 – ESAF) En el texto se dice que las medidas de protección a los trabajadores, adoptadas por muchas industrias:

(A) se aplican de manera coherente y uniforme.
(B) rebasan las expectativas de los trabajadores.
(C) benefician a ambos sexos.
(D) buscan proteger a los empleadores.
(E) dan prioridad a los traslados.

(Interpretación) La única alternativa que tiene respaldo en el texto es la letra D. Según el texto, "muchas industrias han adoptado algún tipo de medida para proteger a los trabajadores" (línea 1).
Gabarito "D".

(Auditor Fiscal do Trabalho – 2010 – ESAF) De acuerdo con el texto, pese a la exposición a los riesgos para la reproducción, las industrias donde las mujeres han representado un importante porcentaje de mano de obra las contratan:

(A) esporádicamente.
(B) para funciones muy específicas.
(C) de cuando en cuando.
(D) en casos excepcionales.
(E) frecuentemente.

(Interpretación) La única alternativa que tiene respaldo en el texto es la letra E. Según el texto, "por ejemplo, se ponen en práctica en aquellos que tradicionalmente han estado fuera del alcance de las mujeres, al tiempo que excluir a las mujeres de determinados puestos laborales no es una política seguida en industrias en las que ellas han sido y siguen siendo un porcentaje considerable de la mano de obra. En esas industrias, a menudo se las emplea a pesar de las posibilidades de que estén expuestas a riesgos para su función reproductora. Es, por ejemplo, el caso de los ayudantes de rayos X, los esteticistas, los limpiadores en seco y lavanderos, así como el personal de los quirófanos" (primer párrafo). Nótese que la expresión "a menudo" equivale a "frecuentemente".
Gabarito "E".

(Auditor Fiscal do Trabalho – 2010 – ESAF) De acuerdo con el texto, las políticas de exclusión de muchas industrias:

(A) contemplan a los varones fértiles.
(B) incluyen la no contratación de mujeres fértiles.
(C) prevén los riesgos a la función reproductora.
(D) se basan en estudios sobre salud reproductiva.
(E) son justas y eficaces.

(Interpretación) La única alternativa que tiene respaldo en el texto es la letra B. Según el texto, "Por ejemplo, se ponen en práctica en aquellos que tradicionalmente han estado fuera del alcance de las mujeres, al tiempo que excluir a las mujeres de determinados puestos laborales no es una política seguida en industrias en las que ellas han sido y siguen siendo un porcentaje considerable de la mano de obra. En esas industrias, a menudo se las emplea a pesar de las posibilidades de que estén expuestas a riesgos para su función reproductora. Es, por ejemplo, el caso de los ayudantes de rayos X, los esteticistas, los limpiadores en seco y lavanderos, así como el personal de los quirófanos" (primer párrafo). El fragmento "riesgos para su función reproductora" es un equivalente semántico de fertilidad en este caso.
Gabarito "B".